Housing Law

an adviser's handbook

Diane Astin is a solicitor specialising in housing law, with many years experience in private practice and in the voluntary sector. She regularly trains and lectures in housing law, community care and asylum support for organisations including Legal Action Group, Shelter, Carers UK and the Refugee Council. Diane was previously a part time visiting lecturer at London Metropolitan University and was a member of the Law Society Housing Law Committee from 1997 to 2006.

Housing Law
an adviser's handbook

FIRST EDITION

Diane Astin

 Legal Action Group
2008

This edition published in Great Britain 2008
by LAG Education and Service Trust Limited
242 Pentonville Road, London N1 9UN
www.lag.org.uk

British Library Cataloguing in Publication Data
a CIP catalogue record for this book is available from the British Library.

ISBN 978 1 903307 43 4

Typeset by The Charlesworth Group, West Yorkshire
Printed in Great Britain by Hobbs the Printers Ltd, Totton, Hampshire.

Note on developments since August 2008

Since this first edition of *Housing Law: an adviser's handbook* was published, the following important legislative and case-law developments have taken place. Please note that this is not a comprehensive list of statutory or other changes since then.

The references below denote the principal paragraphs or chapters in this book which should be read in the light of these changes.

Family intervention tenancies

Chapter 2

In January 2009 a new type of tenancy was introduced by section 297 of the Housing and Regeneration Act 2008: the Family Intervention Tenancy. Family Intervention Tenancies may be offered as an alternative to evicting tenants on the grounds of anti-social behaviour and must involve a package of support for the tenant and family. See the *Guidance on the use of Family Intervention Tenancies* published by the Department for Communities and Local Government, available at: www.communities.gov.uk/documents/housing/pdf/familyinterventiontenancies.pdf.

Article 8 and possession claims

Paragraphs 6.129–6.134 (*Kay, McCann, Doherty*); paragraph 5.81 (demoted tenancies)

In *Manchester City Council v Pinnock* [2009] EWCA Civ 852, 31 July 2009, the Court of Appeal held that when considering a claim for possession against a demoted tenant the role of the county court was limited to matters of procedure. It could not review the substance or rationality of the decision to evict or consider whether the decision was consistent with the tenant's Convention rights.

Permission has been granted for an appeal to the Supreme Court and is expected to be heard in mid-2010 before all nine Supreme Court judges.

Tolerated trespass

Paragraphs 5.126–5.143

Most of the provisions of Schedule 11 of the Housing and Regeneration Act 2008 came into force on 20 May 2009, effectively abolishing tolerated trespass. In relation to assured tenancies, the House of Lords had already held that the doctrine of tolerated trespass did not apply: *Knowsley Housing Trust v White* [2008] UKHL 70, 10 December 2008.

Setting aside possession orders

Paragraphs 5.152–5.157

In *Forcelux Ltd v Binnie* [2009] EWCA Civ 854, 21 October 2009, the Court of Appeal held that a possession order made in the undefended list was not an order made at a 'trial'. It followed that if a tenant who was absent when the order was made applied to set the possession order aside, it was not necessary to satisfy the requirements of CPR 39.3. The court had the power to set aside the order under CPR 3.1. It is not therefore a *strict* requirement that the tenant acted promptly in making the application although it is one of several factors the court will take into account when deciding whether or not to set aside a possession order.

Disability discrimination

Paragraphs 6.105–6.116

The Equality Bill will reverse the effect of *Lewisham v Malcolm* by prohibiting indirect discrimination but introducing a more general form of justification. Clause 14 provides that it is discrimination if a person treats a disabled person in a particular way which, because of the disability, amounts to a detriment where it cannot be shown that the treatment is a proportionate means of achieving a legitimate aim. However, this does not apply if the person did not know, and could not reasonably have been expected to know, that the person had the disability. It does not matter if the person discriminating has complied with a duty to make reasonable adjustments.

Mortgage possession claims

The mortgage arrears protocol was introduced on 16 November 2008 (see CPR 48th update).

Homelessness eligibility – EEA nationals

Paragraph 13.120

The European Court of Justice gave judgment in the cases of *Ibrahim v Harrow* and *Teixeira v Lambeth LBC* on 23 February 2010. The children of an EEA national who works, or has worked, in another member state and the parent who is their primary carer have a right of residence by virtue of article 12 of Directive 1612/68 and that right is not conditional on their having sufficient resources and comprehensive sickness insurance in that member state.

Paragraph 13.84–13.85

The interpretation of the requirement of having 'resided legally for a continuous period of five years' in order to establish a permanent right to reside in the UK, was referred to the European Court of Justice by the Court of Appeal in two cases: *Secretary of State for Work and Pensions v Lassal* [2009] EWCA Civ 157, 10 March 2009 and *Secretary of State for Work and Pensions v Dias* [2009] EWCA Civ 807, 31 July 2009.

Ineligible household members – restricted cases

Paragraphs 13.130–13.132

The government has acted to rectify the incompatibility of section 185(4) of the Housing Act 1996 with the ECHR by creating a new class of eligible person: a 'restricted person' (see section 314 and Schedule 15 of the Housing and Regeneration Act 2008). This amendment only assists applicants who are British nationals or EEA nationals with a right to reside. Where such an applicant is homeless or has priority need by virtue of a person who is ineligible, such a person is a 'restricted person' and the case is a 'restricted case': the local authority's housing duty is limited to providing a suitable private sector assured shorthold tenancy for a period of 12 months. However, the provision does not help applicants who are themselves Persons Subject to Immigration Control; the authority may still ignore the existence of the ineligible person when deciding on homelessness and priority need.

Priority need: dependent children

Paragraphs 13.197, 13.208

In *Holmes-Moorhouse v London Borough of Richmond upon Thames* [2009] UKHL 7, 4 February 2009, the House of Lords reversed the decision of the Court of Appeal. The House of Lords held:

(1) a joint residence order made by the family court does not determine the issue of whether it is reasonable for the children to live with both parents, in separate accommodation;

(2) it was not unlawful for the housing authority to consider the scarcity of accommodation when deciding whether it would be reasonable for the children to live with the both parents;

(3) the family courts should not make joint residence orders unless it appears reasonably likely that both parties will have accommodation in which the children can reside and should not make such orders to place pressure on the housing authority to allocate accommodation in a particular way.

Further, it was held, in relation to the decision letter that the court should not subject the decisions of housing officers to the same sort of analysis as may be applied to contracts drafted by solicitors, Acts of Parliament or court judgments. Rather, a benevolent approach should be adopted and the court should not take too technical a view of the language used or search for inconsistencies, although they should not approve incomprehensible or misguided reasoning.

Intentional homelessness and discharge of the full housing duty

Paragraph 13.253 (note 141) and paragraphs 15.22–15.24

The Supreme Court gave a single judgment in the two cases of *Birmingham CC v Ali; Moran v Manchester CC* [2009] UKHL 36, 1 July 2009. The *Birmingham* case was previously reported as *Aweys v Birmingham* (see paragraph 15.24). In the *Birmingham* case the Supreme Court held that when considering homelessness under section 175(3) and intentional homelessness under section 191(1) it was necessary to look to the future as well as to the present: it may not be reasonable for a person to occupy accommodation indefinitely but it may be reasonable for them to continue to do so in the short term. Thus it was not unlawful for Birmingham to accept that a family was homeless because it was not reasonable for them to occupy severely overcrowded accommodation yet at the same time discharge their duty to provide accommodation under section 193(2) by virtue of the family remaining in the same accommodation in the short term. The accommodation could be suitable for the purposes of the section 193(2) duty. However, it would not be lawful for an authority to leave a family in the accommodation indefinitely and there would be bound to come a time when the accommodation could no longer be described as suitable. What was not made clear is whether a homeless applicant who contended that that time had come, should challenge the authority by requesting a review of suitability or by judicial review.

In the *Manchester* case, the court held that it would not be reasonable for a woman to continue to occupy a women's refuge place indefinitely therefore a women in a refuge is homeless while in the refuge. Further, if she loses her place there, even because of her own conduct, she does not become homeless intentionally.

This decision means that accommodation that is suitable initially may become unsuitable if the homeless applicant is left in that accommodation for an extended period. See, also the case of *Muse v Brent LBC* [2008] EWCA Civ 1447, 19 December 2008: the Court of Appeal held that the section 193 duty came to an end where a homeless applicant refused an offer of alternative temporary accommodation made by the authority where the initial temporary accommodation had become unsuitable by virtue of the growth of the applicant's family.

Allocation of social housing

Paragraphs 16.78–16.81

In *R (Ahmad) v Newham LBC* [2009] UKHL 14, 4 March 2009 the Supreme Court upheld the local authority's appeal: the allocation policy was not unlawful by virtue of failing to give priority to applicants in greater housing need than others placed within the same band. The stipulation in the Code of Guidance that allocations schemes must give the highest priority to those in the most need does not require an authority to assess relative priority within a band. All of the case law on assessing 'cumulative need' is overruled. It is not unlawful to give priority to applicants within the same band by reference to waiting time. Nor is it unlawful for an authority to allocate a proportion of accommodation to transfer applicants who are not in any of the reasonable preference categories.

In response, on 4 December 2009, the government issued a new Code of Guidance: *Fair and Flexible: statutory guidance on social housing allocations for local authorities in England.* This replaces certain parts of the Allocations Guidance issued in November 2002 and in August 2008 (see paragraph 16.8).

Accommodation duty for homeless children – Children Act 1989 s20

Paragraph 18.18

In *R (G) v Southwark LBC* [2009] UKHL 26, 26 May 2009, the House of Lords upheld G's appeal, approving the dissenting judgment of Rix LJ. Where the conditions under section 20 of the Children Act 1989 are met, the social services authority is under a duty to provide accommodation under that section and the child will become a 'looked after child'. The social services authority cannot discharge its duty by referring the child to the housing authority to be housed as a homeless applicant in priority need.

Social services complaints procedures

Paragraphs 17.68–17.71

The procedure in relation to adult social services has changed. The Local Authority Social Services and National Health Service Complaints (England) Regulations 2009 (SI No 3090) revoked the Local Authority Social Services Complaints (England) Regulations 2006 so that the time scales set out in the chart no longer apply to complaints about adult services. Instead of a three stage internal complaints procedure with statutory time limits, local authorities (and other bodies providing adult social care, such as voluntary organisations and private companies) must: acknowledge the complaint within three working days, discuss with the complainant how the complaint is to be investigated; keep the complainant informed of progress and should notify the complainant of the outcome of the investigation within six months. If the complainant is not satisfied with the response he or she can complain directly to the Ombudsman.

Housing and human rights

Paragraphs 6.39, 21.49, 21.88

In *R (Weaver) v London & Quadrant Housing Trust* [2009] EWCA Civ 587, 18 June 2009, the Court of Appeal dismissed the landlord's appeal: the Trust was a public body for the purposes of the Human Rights Act 1998. The management of social housing, both its allocation and its termination, was a public and not a private function for the purposes of section 6(5).

Paragraphs 21.20–21.22

In *Tomlinson v Birmingham CC* [2010] UKSC 8, 17 February 2010, the Supreme Court held that a local authority's decision that it's housing duty under HA 1996 s193 had ended was not a determination of a 'civil right' for the purposes of article 6.

Diane Astin
February 2010

Preface

What do housing advisers do? They help people to get, improve and keep homes. When 'housing law' became a recognised specialism in the 1970s much of the work of the housing adviser was about enforcing private tenant's rights: resisting claims for possession, suing landlords who unlawfully evicted or harassed their tenants and getting repairs done. In addition, following the first Act dealing specifically with homelessness in 1977, it was about helping homeless people to obtain accommodation from local authorities. As local authorities were also large scale landlords, council tenants formed a large proportion of the client group. The main areas of housing law could be summarised as: possession proceedings, disrepair, unlawful eviction and harassment and homelessness.

When advising private tenants facing eviction, it was always enjoyable to explain just how the Rent Act operated. Not only could they stay in their homes even though their landlord wanted them out but they were entitled to have repairs carried out and to have a 'fair' rent registered to replace the contractual rent. Under the Rent Acts private tenants had rights that were worth enforcing. The private sector , however, was changed dramatically by the introduction of the Housing Act 1988. Rent control and long term security for private tenants was abandoned. Landlords could grant short term lettings by way of the assured shorthold tenancy. Since 1997 this has become the 'default' tenancy in the private sector which means that many of the rights of private tenants are in practice unenforceable: the landlord's response to a complaint about disrepair will usually be the service of a possession notice to which the tenant has no defence.

At the same time the sale of council houses, which began in 1980, has significantly reduced the role of local authorities as landlords. Large scale stock transfer of dwellings to other social landlords has increased the role of Registered Social Landlords who now equal local authorities as the providers of social housing.

The lack of security and the abandonment of rent control in the private sector means that, for those on a low income, only a social tenancy offers any hope of a long-term, affordable home. Not surprisingly, housing waiting lists are at an all time high and the allocation of social housing has also become a significant part of housing law. The promotion of choice based lettings schemes has resulted in a flurry of legal challenges to local authority policies.

The last 10 years has seen other important developments affecting housing law. The policy of excluding migrants from housing and social welfare provision, which started in 1996, has created a large population of destitute people. Housing advisers now regularly use 'community care' law to assist those who are destitute to obtain 'safety net' services, including accommodation. The development of complex eligibility rules governing access to housing and benefits also means that housing advisers must navigate their way around immigration law and European law.

The government's drive to address 'anti-social behaviour' has also had a major impact on housing law. Many local authorities now use 'probationary' tenancies, giving tenants limited rights for the first 12 months, and all social landlords have the option of 'demoting' tenancies because of anti-social behaviour. Anti social behaviour injunctions and anti social behaviour orders are now also available to social landlords.

One of the few positive developments from the point of view of the housing adviser was the introduction of the Human Rights Act. However, this has introduced a level of complexity to such 'bread and butter' housing advice work as possession proceedings, as recent decisions by the European Court of Human Rights and the House of Lords has demonstrated.

The result of all of this is that housing law has become more complex and wide-ranging. So, although it is still about helping people to get, improve and keep accommodation, the breadth of knowledge required to do this is much more extensive. Not only must advisers be able to identify different types of occupation rights, understand the different kinds of tenancies and the many statutory rights enjoyed by tenants, but must also use community care law for the benefit of their clients, must have a grasp of immigration law, in particular the rights of European nationals, and understand the application of human rights to housing law.

All of the above may be a lame excuse for my inability to produce a comprehensive handbook for housing advisers that is nevertheless concise. This book is much longer than intended but I have endeavoured to give sufficient attention to those areas of housing law which, in my experience, the housing adviser will regularly encounter. I have endeavoured to state the law as at 1st August 2008.

I have had invaluable help from those who read and commented on various chapters and I thank Tony Benjamin, Tor Brandon, Andrew Brookes, John Gallagher, Sonal Ghelani, Mary McDowall, Chris Morris, Sally Morshead, Nigel Parkinson, Georgina Tully and Sue Willman. I know this was an onerous task and am amazed that some even managed to read several chapters. I am truly grateful.

When I worked at North Islington Law Centre we were once informed that we had to devise a mission statement. The best one we came up with, sadly not the one finally approved, was 'We don't guess the law. We look it up'. I still think that this should be the motto of every adviser and I hope that this book assists.

Diane Astin
September 2008

This book is dedicated to my mother, who taught me to type, as well as many other even more valuable things.

Contents

Table of cases

L

lorem

Table of statutes

References in the right-hand column are to paragraph numbers.

li

Table of statutory instruments

References to the right hand column are to paragraph numbers.

Civil Procedure Rules 1998 (SI 1998/3132) *continued*

Table of European Legislation

Treaties

Table of Circulars

Table of abbreviations

AIA 1999	Asylum and Immigration Act 1999
AJA 1970	Administration of Justice Act 1970
AJA 1973	Administration of Justice Act 1973
ALMO	Arms-length Management Organization
AOG	Adjudication Officers' Guide
ASBA 2003	Anti Social Behaviour Act 2003
ASBI	anti-social behaviour injunction
ASBO	anti-social behaviour order
CA 1989	Children Act 1989
CCA 1974	Consumer Credit Act 1974
CDA 1998	Crime and Disorder Act 1998
CFA	Conditional Fee Agreement
CLA 1977	Criminal Law Act 1977
CLRA 2002	Commonhold and Leasehold Reform Act 2002
CPA 2004	Civil Partnership Act 2004
CPR 1999	Civil Procedure Rules 1999
CSDPA 1970	Chronically Sick and Disabled Persons Act 1970
CTA	Common Travel Area
DCLG	Department of Communities and Local Government
DDA 1995	Disability Discrimination Act 1995
DFG	disabled facilities grants
DHP	discretionary housing payment
DoH	Department of Health
DPA 1972	Defective Premises Act 1972
DPA 1998	Data Protection Act 1998
DPS	Deposit Protection Services
DRO	displaced residential occupiers
DWP	Department of Work and Pensions
ECHR	European Convention on Human Rights
ECtHR	European Court of Human Rights
EEA	European Economic Area
EFTA	European Free Trade Association
EHO	environmental health officer
ELR	exceptional leave to remain
EPA 1990	Environmental Protection Act 1990
FACS	Fair Access to Care Services
FIA 2000	Freedom of Information Act 2000

FLA 1996	Family Law Act 1996
FOS	Financial Ombudsman Service
FSA	Financial Services Authority
HA 1980	Housing Act 1980
HA 1985	Housing Act 1985
HA 1988	Housing Act 1988
HA 1996	Housing Act 1996
HA 2004	Housing Act 2004
HAT	housing action trust
HBRB	Housing Benefit Review Board
HGCRA 1996	Housing Grants, Construction and Regeneration Act 1996
HHSRS	Housing Health and Safety Rating System
HIA	Home Improvement Agency
HMO	house in multiple occupation
HOS	Housing Ombudsman Service
HRA 1998	Human Rights Act 1998
HRT	habitual residence test
HSE	Health and Safety Executive
HSPHA 1968	Health Services and Public Health Act 1968
IA 1971	Immigration Act 1971
IA 1988	Immigration Act 1988
IAA 1999	Immigration and Asylum Act 1999
ILR	indefinite leave to remain
IPO	interim possession order
IS	Income Support
JSA	Jobseekers' Allowance
LASSA 1970	Local Authority Social Services Act 1970
LGA 2000	Local Government Act 2000
LGO	Local Government Ombudsman
LHA	local housing allowance
LPA 1925	Law of Property Act 1925
LRA 1967	Leasehold Reform Act 1967
LRA 2002	Land Registration Act 2002
LRHUDA 1999	Leasehold Reform, Housing and Urban Development Act 1993
LSC	Legal Services Commission
LSCT	large scale voluntary transfer
LTA 1954	Landlord and Tenant Act 1954
LTA 1985	Landlord and Tenant Act 1985
LTA 1987	Landlord and Tenant Act 1987
LVT	Leasehold Valuation Tribunal
MCA 1973	Matrimonial Causes Act 1973
MCA 2005	Mental Capacity Act 2005
MCOB	Mortgage Conduct of Business rules
MHA 1983	Mental Health Act 1983
NAA 1948	National Assistance Act 1948
NASS	National Asylum Support Service
NHSA 1977	National Health Service Act 1977

NHSCCA 1990	NHS & Community Care Act 1990
NIA 2002	Nationality, Immigration and Asylum Act 2002
NOSP	Notice of Seeking Possession
NSP	Notice Seeking Possession
ODPM	Office of the Deputy Prime Minister
OFT	Office of Fair Trading
PEA 1977	Prevention from Eviction Act 1977
PFI	Private Finance Initiatives
PHA 1997	Protection from Harassment Act 1997
PIO	protected intending occupiers
PPO	postponed possession order
PSL	private sector leasing
PST	protected shorthold tenancy
RA 1977	Rent Act 1977
RMO	responsible medical officer
RSL	Registered Social Landlord
SJE	Single Joint Expert
SSCBA 1992	Social Security Contributions and Benefits Act 1992
SSCSA	Social Security and Child Support Appeal
TLATA 1996	Trusts of Land and Appointment of Trustees Act 1996
UKBA	UK Border Agency
UTCCR 1999	Unfair Terms in Consumer Contracts Regulations 1999
YOI	Youth Offenders Institution

Occupiers' rights: basic principles

continued

Key points

- In English law land is not 'owned'. Rather a person may have an estate or interest in land.
- A tenancy is an interest in land.
- A tenancy is distinct from a licence which is a personal right.
- A tenancy may be created without a written agreement.
- The 'hallmarks of a tenancy' are: the grant of exclusive possession of premises; for a period of time; in return for the payment of rent.
- If these features are present an agreement will be a tenancy unless it falls into a specific category of recognised exceptions.
- A tenancy can be for a fixed term or periodic. A periodic tenancy runs automatically from one period to the next.
- Security of tenure is about the restriction on a landlord's right to evict. It may be 'procedural' (the landlord must follow a certain procedure to evict) or 'substantive' (the landlord cannot evict unless there are grounds).
- In the private sector, only tenants can enjoy substantive security of tenure.
- Licensees will enjoy procedural security of tenure unless they are 'excluded occupiers' as listed in the Protection from Eviction Act 1977.
- Excluded occupiers can be evicted without a court order.
- A tenant can end a tenancy by either serving notice to quit or by surrender. Notice to quit only operates to end a periodic tenancy. Surrender brings any sort of tenancy to an end but all parties must agree to a surrender.
- A notice to quit served by one joint tenant ends the tenancy.
- A person who does not have a legal interest in land may nevertheless have an equitable interest.

Introduction

1.1   Most of this book deals with the rights of those who occupy accommodation as a home. This is largely governed by statute. In some cases the statutory rights are in addition to rights set out in the agreement to occupy, in other cases the statutory rights override the agreement. The statutory intervention largely protects occupiers and restricts the rights of landlords. However, some occupiers fall outside statutory schemes of protection which means that the panties' rights, such as the right to end an occupation agreement, are not restricted by statute. A significant part of the relationship between an occupier and a landlord is therefore governed by the occupation agreement or the general legal principles applying to rights over land.

1.2   This chapter examines some of these basic legal principles. The nature of a tenancy is examined and the different levels of security enjoyed by occupiers are explained, with particular reference to occupiers who are excluded from any protection. In addition, some difficult situations are explored, for example hotel and bed and breakfast accommodation and premises that are let for both business and residential use. Finally, the relevance of the law of trusts and equity to occupiers' rights is briefly explained.

Security of tenure

1.3   When giving housing advice to any occupier it will be necessary to identify the nature of the person's right to remain in occupation, in other words whether the person has 'security of tenure'. There are two levels of security of tenure. At the higher level a tenant may have the right not to be evicted unless the landlord can prove a statutory ground for possession and at the lower level an occupier may have the right not to be evicted unless the landlord follows a certain procedure (serving notice and obtaining a possession order).[1] These will be referred to as 'substantive security of tenure' and 'procedural security of tenure' respectively.

1.4   Whether an occupier has any security of tenure and, if so, whether this is procedural or substantive, depends on the status of the occupier. This involves an understanding of both:

- the common law principles concerning rights over land; and
- the statutory rights enjoyed by occupiers.

Common law

1.5   The 'common law' refers to previous decisions of the courts which have established certain legal principles and rules. These govern relationships, such as that between a landlord and tenant, or between

---

1 The lower level of security of tenure is often referred to as 'basic protection' or 'protection from eviction'. However, such occupiers are sometimes also referred to as having 'unprotected tenancies' which causes confusion.

neighbouring occupiers. The system of law in England and Wales is a 'common law' system. The law is interpreted by judges and the decisions of the higher courts are binding on the lower courts.

1.6 Until the beginning of the twentieth century the relationship of landlord and tenant was almost entirely governed by the common law. It was determined by the principles of 'land law' and 'contract law' as they had developed through decided cases. Land law is the law relating to the creation and transfer of legal interests in land. A tenancy is a legal interest in land. Contract law refers to the principles governing legally binding contracts, which can be enforced through the civil courts. A tenancy agreement is both an agreement creating an interest in land and a contract and an understanding of some of the principles of both land law and contract law is necessary before giving housing advice.

Statutory law

1.7 Statutory law refers to legislation made by Parliament. It includes 'primary legislation' which means statutes or Acts of Parliament and 'secondary legislation' (also called delegated or subordinate legislation). Secondary legislation is authorised to be made by primary legislation (known as enabling legislation). Most secondary legislation is made by way of a statutory instrument. In some cases secondary legislation merely sets out the detail of a requirement contained in primary legislation. In other cases the secondary legislation sets out the substance of a provision. An example of the former would be the requirements for a notice seeking possession. The primary legislation provides that notice must be in 'prescribed form' and contain certain information but the detail of the prescribed form is set out in a statutory instrument: see paragraph 5.28 below. An example of the latter would be the provisions about eligibility for homeless assistance, the substance of which is predominantly found in the relevant statutory instruments: see paragraph 13.3 below.

1.8 Statutory law takes precedence over the common law but statutory rights are enforced through the courts so judges must interpret the statutes. A court's decision about the interpretation of a statute will be binding on lower courts.

1.9 Since 1915 there has been extensive statutory interference in the relationship of landlord and tenant. Mostly, statutes protect the rights of tenants.

1.10 Occupiers who are not tenants may also enjoy some statutory rights. For example, the eviction of many residential occupiers can only be carried out by using the civil courts.

1.11   The particular rights enjoyed by tenants depend on which statute applies to the agreement. The main statutes governing different types of tenancies are: the Rent Act (RA) 1977, the Housing Act (HA) 1985 and the Housing Act (HA) 1988. These are dealt with in chapter 2. This chapter describes some of the important legal principles that apply generally in relation to occupier's rights and to the relationship of landlord and tenant.

Interests in land

1.12   Although land and premises are 'bought' and 'sold', technically English law does not recognise the 'ownership' of land. It is said that the only true owner of land is the Crown. Rather, a person may have an 'interest' or 'estate' in land and the nature of the interest will determine how much control the person has over the land. Different 'interests' may exist in relation to the same land. This may sound artificial but it is important to understand the nature of an 'interest' in land. The chart below sets out the recognised legal interests and the rights that flow from the interest.

Interest	Rights
Freehold	This is the nearest thing to outright ownership – it is an interest or estate for unlimited duration. A freeholder may sell the freehold or may grant lesser interests to others, such as a lease or tenancy.
Legal charge/ mortgage	A person who lends money to another may secure the loan by taking a charge on property owned by the borrower. This entitles the lender to take possession if the borrower defaults.
Leasehold	A lease is a 'term of years', ie the grant of exclusive possession for a limited period of time. A person with a long lease may grant a shorter lease or may assign the remaining period of the lease to another person.
Tenancy	The term tenancy and lease mean the same but the term tenancy is commonly used to refer to a lease granted for a short period only.
Commonhold	Commonhold is a new kind of interest created by statute: it enables those 'owning' parts of a building or estate to 'own' the common parts through a commonhold association. It is an alternative to a lease being held by one party and the freehold by another.

1.13   All of the above are 'legal interests' in land. This means that they can be transferred to another person.

1.14   The same land may be subject to a number of different interests at the same time. For example, a house 'owner' may have a mortgage and may grant a long lease to another person who in turn may grant a tenancy to another person. In such a case there will exist a freehold, a legal charge, a long lease and a short-term lease all in respect of the same land.

1.15   A person may occupy premises without any legal interest but because they are permitted to do so, ie they have a 'licence' to occupy. They are known as 'licensees'. A licence is a personal interest and cannot be transferred to another person. Sometimes it can be difficult to ascertain whether a person occupies as a tenant or a licensee.

What is a tenancy?

1.16   A tenancy or lease is the granting of an interest in land for a period of time. The term tenancy and lease mean the same but 'tenancy' is usually used to refer to short-term tenancies whereas the term 'lease' is commonly used to describe a tenancy granted for a longer period of time.

1.17   The period of time for which a tenancy may be granted is either:

- fixed; or
- periodic.

1.18   A fixed term tenancy is created where, for example, the tenancy is granted for a period of six or 12 months. A periodic tenancy is created where no fixed period is identified or the tenancy is expressed to run from week to week or month to month, or to be a 'weekly tenancy' or a 'monthly tenancy'.

1.19   At common law a tenancy for a fixed period ends at the end of the period or 'term'. A periodic tenancy continues from one period to the next until one party serves notice that he or she does not want the tenancy to continue beyond the end of the next complete period. However, if the tenant enjoys statutory rights this will mean that either the tenancy continues or that the landlord cannot evict the tenant without following a certain procedure.

1.20   A person may occupy accommodation under a tenancy or simply with the permission of the owner. An occupier who does not have an interest as a tenant but is permitted to occupy is a 'licensee', ie he or

she has a 'licence' to occupy. The person who grants the permission
is a 'licensor'.

1.21   The statutory protection, first introduced in 1915 and continuing
throughout the twentieth century, was enjoyed only by tenants. To
avoid an occupier having statutory protection many landlords sought
to create licences instead of tenancies. This practice led to a number
of cases in which the courts considered the difference between a
tenancy and a licence, the most important of which are discussed
below at paragraphs 1.23 and 1.57.

1.22   Much of this case law is still important in understanding the
nature of a tenancy. However, because most tenancies in the private
sector now offer very limited rights to tenants, there is little incentive
for landlords to try to avoid creating a tenancy. Since 1997 almost all
new private tenancies are assured shorthold tenancies and it is less
common for advisers to come across 'sham licences'. Nevertheless,
the difference between licences and tenancies still has some practical
importance.

The difference between a tenancy and a licence

1.23   If a tenancy is created, regardless of the provisions of the tenancy
agreement, additional statutory rights may be enjoyed by the tenant.
Examples of these rights are:

- the right not to be evicted unless there are grounds (the grounds
  being set out in the statute);
- the right to have repairs carried out by a landlord;
- the right to pass on the tenancy to a family member on death.

1.24   These rights are not given to licensees. Usually the most a licensee
will enjoy will be some protection against summary eviction.[2] A
licence is a personal permission to occupy. It may be withdrawn by
the licensor and cannot be transferred to another person.

1.25   Landlords seeking to avoid the statutory protection given to
tenants would either simply describe the agreement as a licence
agreement or include terms in the agreement that suggested it was
a licence rather than a tenancy. Prior to the House of Lords decision
in the case of *Street v Mountford*[3] in 1985 the courts' approach had

---

2   One exception to this is the 'secure licence' which is discussed below. However,
such licences are very rare.
3   (1985) 17 HLR 402, HL.

been to examine the terms of a disputed agreement and if, on balance, they suggested a licence rather than a tenancy the agreement was construed as a licence. However, in *Street v Mountford* the House of Lords rejected this approach.

In *Street v Mountford* a house was divided into furnished rooms. Mrs Mountford signed an agreement entitled a 'licence agreement' to occupy the top floor. The landlord conceded that she had exclusive possession of this part of the house. However, the agreement she signed included rules limiting the way the accommodation was to be used. The agreement referred to a licence fee and included a statement signed by Mrs Mountford stating: 'I understand and accept that a licence in the above form does not and is not intended to give me a tenancy protected under the Rent Acts'.

The owner sought a declaration that Mrs Mountford did not have a tenancy. The county court held that she did and the owner appealed. The Court of Appeal allowed the landlords appeal; it examined all of the express terms and decided that many were inconsistent with the grant of a tenancy. Further, it held that the statement signed by Mrs Mountford was a clear indication of the parties' intentions. In the absence of misrepresentation, undue influence or mistake the burden was on the occupant to displace the express statement of intention by showing that it was either a deliberate sham or at least an inaccurate summary of the true substance of the real agreement.

The House of Lords allowed Mrs Mountford's appeal: it is the substance of the agreement and not the label attached to it that matters. In the words of Lord Templeman: 'The manufacture of a five pronged implement for manual digging results in a fork even if the manufacturer, unfamiliar with the English language, insists that he intended to make and has made a spade'.[4] To examine the terms to see which suggested a tenancy and which a licence was not the correct approach. Rather, if the 'hallmarks of a tenancy' were present, the agreement would be a tenancy agreement unless it fell within a class of recognised exceptions.

The hallmarks of a tenancy are:

(1) the grant of exclusive possession;

4   (1985) 17 HLR 402 at 411.

(2) for a period of time;
(3) in return for the payment of rent.

If these features are present the agreement will be a tenancy unless it is of a type previously recognised by the courts as being exceptional. These exceptional kinds of agreements are:

(1) tied accommodation – accommodation occupied by employees;
(2) acts of charity and family arrangements – where there was no intention to enter into legally binding relations; and
(3) cases in which there is a legal relationship, but not that of landlord and tenant.

What is a lodger?

1.26   A lodger is someone who occupies part of a house but whose occupation is under the control of a landlord or his or her representative who resides in or retains possession or control over the house.[5]

1.27   In most cases a hotel occupier will also be a lodger or licensee.[6] However, exceptionally, it is possible for a person to occupy a 'dwelling' within a 'hotel' as a tenant, see below paragraphs 1.28 and 2.14.

1.28   A lodger is a licensee and will not enjoy long-term rights. Further, if accommodation is shared with a landlord, he or she may be subject to eviction without a court order, see para 1.101 below.

The hallmarks of a tenancy

Exclusive possession

1.29   The grant of 'exclusive possession' is essential to a tenancy. If an occupier does not have exclusive possession he or she cannot be a tenant.

1.30   Exclusive possession means more than being the only occupier. Exclusive 'possession' means being the person in control of the premises. A tenant can exclude the whole world, including the landlord. In contrast someone in exclusive 'occupation' can exclude the whole world, except the landlord. 'Possession' is distinct from 'occupation': a hotel guest may have exclusive occupation of a room

5   *Thompson v Ward* [1906] 1 KB 60.
6   *Luganda v Service Hotels* [1969] 2 Ch 209.

but does not have exclusive possession because the hotel management retains control of the room.

1.31   Landlords sometimes include in a tenancy agreement terms that suggest that the occupier does not have exclusive possession. Examples include terms reserving a right of unlimited access and terms stating that the landlord has the right to move other occupiers into the premises or to move into the premises him or herself. Such terms may be 'pretences' or 'shams'. This is explained at paragraphs 1.46–1.48 below.

1.32   It should be noted that a landlord's right of access for the purpose of inspection and repair does not mean that the tenant does not have exclusive possession. In fact the inclusion of a term reserving such a right suggests that it is the tenant not the landlord who has control of the premises.

For a period of time

1.33   This may be expressly indicated in the tenancy agreement. In most fixed term tenancies the period will be expressly stated in a written agreement, although it is possible to create a fixed-term tenancy orally. If there is no such agreed term, or perhaps no written agreement at all, the tenancy will be a periodic tenancy. The period will be implied by reference to the 'rental period'. If it is stated that 'the weekly rent is £x' or that the rent is '£x per week' the tenancy will be a weekly periodic tenancy. This is different from an agreement about the way in which rent is paid. For example, if a tenancy agreement states that 'the rent is £x per week, payable four weekly in advance', the period of the agreement is weekly, not four weekly.[7]

At a rent

1.34   In *Street v Mountford* the House of Lords suggested that the payment of rent was essential to a tenancy agreement. However, it is theoretically possible to create a tenancy without the payment of rent.[8] In fact where no rent is payable this will often suggest that a legally binding tenancy has not been created. Further, such agreements have always been outside statutory protection[9] and, since 1989, occupiers who pay no rent have been excluded from any sort of security and can be evicted without a court order (see paragraph 1.112).

7   *Ladies Hosiery and Underwear v Packer* [1930] Ch 304, CA.
8   *Ashburn Anstalt v Arnold* [1988] 2 WLR 706, CA.
9   Tenancies for no rent, or at a low rent, are excluded from the Rent Act 1977 and the Housing Act 1988.

The exceptions

1.35   If there is no exclusive possession there can be no tenancy. However, there are some situations in which an occupier may apparently enjoy exclusive possession but not be a tenant. These situations can be summarised as follows.

Service occupiers

1.36   This is also known as 'tied accommodation'. Service occupation arises where:

- accommodation is provided by the occupant's employer; and
- it is a term of the employment contract that the employee occupies the accommodation in order to carry out the employment duties, or to better perform those duties.

1.37   Although an employee may enjoy exclusive occupation under such an agreement this is deemed to be on behalf of the employer and the occupier is a licensee rather than a tenant.[10]

1.38   If there is a term in the employment contract stating that the employee is required to live in the premises, it is sufficient that this is for the better performance of the employment duties. If a requirement to occupy is not an express term of the contract the court may imply such a term but will only do so if it is necessary, ie the job cannot be performed without the employee living in the premises.[11]

1.39   Service occupiers have procedural security of tenure, (unless they are also 'excluded occupiers', as listed at paragraph 1.101. This means that a court order must be obtained by the landlord before the occupier can be evicted.

No intention to enter into a legal relationship

1.40   In a number of cases where the agreement was between family members or where the agreement was considered to be an 'act of charity' the courts have held no tenancy was created. In *Street v Mountford* the House of Lords held that these cases had been decided on the basis that there had been no intention between the parties to enter into a legally binding agreement.

---

10 *Mayhew v Suttle* (1845) 4 El & Bl 347: the possession and occupation of the 'servant' is treated as being that of the 'master'.
11 *Glasgow Corporation v Johnstone* [1965] AC 609, HL.

Family arrangements

1.41 It is presumed that when an agreement is between family members there is no intention to create legal obligations. This presumption can however be overturned if there is sufficient evidence of an intention to be legally bound by the agreement, for example the drawing up of a formal tenancy agreement at a market rent.

1.42 The fact that the landlord and the occupier are related does not automatically prevent a tenancy arising.[12] However, the closer the relationship is the stronger will be the presumption that the parties do not intend to be legally bound.

Acts of charity

1.43 Similarly, where the agreement has come about through an act of charity or generosity there is a presumption that no legal relationship was intended. It is not always easy to identify such situations. A person may offer to allow a friend to live in a property 'as a favour'. The surrounding circumstances will be relevant to decide whether a tenancy is created or the agreement is, exceptionally, an act of charity. Relevant factors will be the amount of 'rent' agreed and whether any kind of agreement is drawn up. The fact that a landlord may wish to gain possession at will does not mean that a tenancy has not been created. When deciding whether parties intend to be legally bound the question is not whether the parties intended to create a tenancy but whether they thought they were bound by the arrangement, ie that one party was obliged to pay rent in return for which he or she had the right to live in the property. Cases in which the courts found that no tenancy was created include the following:

Booker v Palmer,[13] in which an owner of a cottage agreed to allow a friend to place an evacuee in a cottage for the duration of the war.

Marcroft Wagons Ltd v Smith[14] where the tenant died and her daughter claimed to be entitled to succeed to the tenancy. The landlords expressly denied that she was so entitled but while they

12 *Nunn v Dalrymple* (1989) 21 HLR 569, CA.
13 [1942] 2 All ER 674, CA.
14 [1951] 2 KB 496.

considered their position allowed her to remain in occupation paying rent. The landlords indicated that if they decided to take possession the monies paid would be treated as 'mesne profits' (a form of damages for unlawful occupation) and, if they accepted her claim, as rent. When they did claim possession the Court of Appeal held that there had been no intention to enter into contractual relations during that period.

Heslop v Burns,[15] in which an owner allowed friends to stay in a property rent free.

Legal relationship but no tenancy

1.44   In some cases the parties do intend to be legally bound by the agreement but the relationship is not that of landlord and tenant. An example is *Sopwich v Stuchbury*[16] in which a man selling a property let the prospective purchaser into occupation prior to the sale. This was held not to amount to the creation of a tenancy.

1.45   Also included in this category would be a person who occupies as a 'tolerated trespasser'. While the hallmarks of a tenancy appear to be present, there is a different legal relationship: the occupier's tenancy has been ended by a court order but the landlord must apply to the court for a warrant to evict and the court retains a discretion to restrict the right to evict. In light of this, the landlord 'tolerates' the continued occupation of the former tenant. See chapter 6 for a discussion of tolerated trespass.

Shams and pretences

1.46   *Street v Mounford* re-asserted three principles:[17]

- parties to an agreement cannot contract out of statutory protection;
- in the absence of special circumstances, the enjoyment of exclusive possession for a term in return for periodical payment, creates a tenancy; and

15   [1974] 1 WLR 1241.
16   (1984) 17 HLR 50, CA.
17   See *AG Securities v Vaughan, Antoniades v Villiers* (1988) 21 HLR 79, Lord Templeman at 91.

- where the language of the agreement suggests a licence rather than a tenancy, the facts prevail.

1.47   A court may decide that a term or a whole agreement is a 'sham' or 'pretence'. A sham is a term included in a contract which does not reflect the true agreement and which is intended to mislead a third party.[18] Where both parties do not intend to deceive another, the term will not be a sham but, if it does not reflect the true agreement, may be a pretence.

1.48   It is usually the case that the landlord draws up the occupation agreement and those seeking accommodation will rarely be in a position to negotiate. The occupiers may not read or understand the terms. If, however, a term is included that neither party ever intended would really apply, the term may be held to be a 'pretence'. It is sufficient that, if the parties had been asked at the time whether a particular term would apply they would indicate that it would not. In deciding the issue, it is the intention of the parties *at the time the agreement was made* that is relevant. However, in deciding what that intention was, account may be taken of the way the parties have subsequently behaved. An example would be a term that permitted the landlord to move an occupier from one room to another. The fact that the landlord has never exercised the right does not, of itself, mean that the term is not genuine but may be relevant when deciding what the parties intended when they made the agreement. In such a case, the nature of the accommodation will also be relevant. A social landlord running a special needs hostel is more likely to need such control than a private landlord letting rooms in an ordinary house in multiple occupation (HMO).

Shared accommodation

1.49   In cases where accommodation is shared it can be difficult to decide whether the occupiers are tenants or licensees. In such a case the legal arrangement may be:

- a joint tenancy of the whole of the premises;
- individual tenancies of rooms with shared use of common parts, such as living room, kitchen and bathroom;
- a tenancy granted to one or more occupants, with others occupying as sub-tenants or lodgers of the tenant/s; or
- individual licensees.

18 *Snook v London and West Riding Investments Ltd* [1967] 2 QB 786.

Joint tenancies

1.50   For a joint tenancy to be created the 'four unities' must be present:

- unity of title;
- unity of time;
- unity of interest; and
- unity of possession.

1.51   This means that each tenant claims his or her right to occupy under the same act or document (unity of title); that the interest of each tenant commences at the same time (unity of time); that the interest of each tenant is the same in extent, nature and duration (unity of interest); and, each tenant is as much entitled to possession of the premises as any of the others (unity of possession).

1.52   Joint tenants jointly occupy the whole of the premises. One tenant cannot exclude another tenant from part of the premises.[19] Joint tenants are 'jointly and severally' liable for the rent and other obligations under the agreement. This means that a landlord is entitled to sue one or all of the joint tenants for the whole of the rent.

1.53   A joint tenancy will be created when more than one occupier signs the same tenancy agreement at the same time and together they occupy the whole of the premises. The fact that the joint tenants may choose to occupy different parts of the premises and agree individual contributions to the rent will not alter the nature of the agreement between the landlord and the tenants.

Individual tenancies of parts of the premises

1.54   In this case each tenant must have an agreement with the landlord under which he or she has exclusive possession of part of the premises, eg a particular room. In the private sector there is specific provision for such a tenant to have security of tenure even where other accommodation is shared with other tenants.[20]

A tenancy with sub-letting

1.55   Where a tenancy of the whole of the premises is granted by the landlord to one or more tenants, the tenant/s may then sub-let parts

---

19   This can only be done by virtue of a court order made under the Family Law Act 1996 because of domestic violence or relationship breakdown, see chapter 11.
20   Rent Act 1977 s22 and Housing Act 1988 s3. See chapter 2, Part 1.

of the premises to others. This would be the case, for example, where two joint tenants of a four-bedroom house sub-let the unoccupied bedrooms to two others. In such a case there will be no legal relationship between the two sub-tenants and the landlord. In fact the 'sub-tenants' are more likely to be licensees (lodgers) if living as part of the same household as the tenants. In any event if there is sharing of accommodation the sub-tenants/lodgers will have little protection as against the tenants, who may evict them without a court order (see at below). Sub-tenancies are referred to paragraph 1.101 and in more detail in chapter 3.

Individual licensees

1.56   While it is possible to have a tenancy of a room, with shared use of other parts of the premises, sometimes the arrangement is so fluid that this cannot be established. Unless there is a joint tenancy, it will be necessary for each occupier to have an agreement with the landlord for the letting of a specific room. In the absence of such an agreement there can be no tenancy.

1.57   The following cases, heard together by the House of Lords, illustrate the correct approach to shared accommodation and the identification of genuine or sham terms.

In *AG Securities v Vaughan*[21] four men occupied a four-bedroom property with two living rooms, kitchen and bathroom. Each had signed separate agreements with the landlord at different times and at different rents. When a room became vacant the remaining occupiers would move so that the best rooms were occupied and the least attractive offered to the newest occupier. The House of Lords rejected the occupiers' argument that they had a joint tenancy as the four unities essential to a joint tenancy were not present. Further, none of the occupiers had an agreement with the landlord identifying a specific room therefore they could not be tenants of individual rooms. The occupiers were therefore licensees.

21 [1988] WLR 1205.

The House of Lords considered at the same time, in *Antoniades v Villiers*, the case of a co-habiting couple who occupied a small furnished flat comprising a bedroom, sitting room, kitchen and bathroom. When they moved in, each signed a separate 'licence agreement' which stated that neither enjoyed exclusive possession and that the landlord had the right to take up occupation or to nominate other occupiers to share with them. The identical agreements were signed on the same day at the same time. The occupiers also indicated that they would like a double bed to be provided rather than two single beds. The House of Lords held that there had been no genuine intention that the occupiers would be required to share with anyone else: the term was included by the landlord solely to avoid the protection of the Rent Act 1977 and the reality of the agreement was that the couple together enjoyed exclusive possession and were therefore joint tenants.

The termination of a tenancy

1.58   For tenants with security of tenure there will be statutory limits on the landlord's right to end the tenancy and take possession: see chapters 2, 5 and 6. However, some tenancies fall outside the statutory provisions and termination is governed solely by the common law.

1.59   Under the common law a tenancy may be brought to an end in the following ways:

- Periodic tenancies may be ended by either the landlord or the tenant serving notice to quit.
- Fixed-term tenancies end automatically at the end of the agreed period (by 'effluxion of time').
- A periodic or a fixed-term tenancy may be ended by an agreement between the landlord and the tenant that the tenancy is surrendered.
- A landlord may 'forfeit' (end) a fixed term tenancy if the tenant breaches the agreement, provided the agreement permits this. This is usually drafted as a clause that allows the landlord to 're-enter' the premises.

1.60   The fact that legislation intervenes to protect residential tenants means that in most cases there are restrictions on the landlord's right to serve notice to quit and to forfeit a tenancy. Also, at the end of a fixed-term a tenant who remains in occupation may automatically become a 'statutory periodic tenant'. This is because it is provided by statute that a periodic tenancy arises in such a situation. These restrictions, however, only apply to a landlord's right to terminate a tenancy.

1.61   There is no restriction on the termination of a tenancy by way of:

- tenant's notice to quit; or
- surrender.

Termination by the tenant

Tenant's notice to quit

1.62   A periodic tenancy can be ended by the tenant by service of notice to quit on the landlord. A notice to quit is a notice indicating that the tenant intends to quit and give up possession to the landlord. At common law the minimum period of a notice to quit is a complete period of the tenancy. The notice can expire on either the last or the first day of the period. However, section 5 of the Protection from Eviction Act (PEA) 1977 provides that a valid notice to quit, including one served by a tenant, must be at least 28 days long. Shorter notice may be accepted by the landlord but this will take effect as a 'surrender' – the ending of the tenancy by agreement between the landlord and the tenant.

1.63   A tenant's notice to quit unilaterally ends the tenancy. The landlord need not agree and is bound to accept the tenant's notice. A fixed-term tenancy cannot be ended by notice to quit. However, the agreement may contain a 'break clause' allowing either party to serve notice to end the tenancy within the fixed period, see paragraph 1.81 below.

1.64   A precedent for a tenant's notice to quit is included at the appendix to this chapter.

Notices to quit and joint tenancies

1.65   Where there is a joint periodic tenancy one tenant can end the tenancy by serving notice to quit.[22] This is the case even if the other joint tenant does not want the tenancy to end, and even if he or she is unaware of the notice; the notice to quit must be served on the landlord not the

---

22 *Hammersmith and Fulham LBC v Monk* (1991) 24 HLR 206, HL.

other tenant/s.[23] The failure of one joint tenant to consult the other/s before serving notice is not a breach of trust.[24]

1.66   After expiry of the notice any person remaining in occupation is technically a trespasser although in most cases the landlord cannot take possession without obtaining a possession order.[25] If the landlord is a public authority consideration must be given to the right of the remaining occupier to respect for his or her home under the European Convention on Human Rights (see paragraph 21.41 below).

1.67   If a sole tenant serves notice that is technically deficient, for example, not being for the required period, a landlord may nevertheless accept and act upon the notice and the tenancy will end. However, this is not the case if the notice is served by one joint tenant. To terminate a joint tenancy, the notice must strictly comply with the legal requirements and, in particular, must be for the correct period, ie 28 days or a complete period of the tenancy, whichever is longer.[26]

Surrender

1.68   A surrender is an agreement between the landlord and the tenant that the tenancy shall come to an end. It can either be express or implied 'by operation of law'. Surrender is effective to end a periodic or a fixed-term agreement.

1.69   Because surrender is an agreement between the parties, all the joint tenants must agree to the surrender if the tenancy is a joint tenancy.[27]

Express surrender

1.70   Express surrender must be by deed.[28] A deed is an agreement in writing, clearly expressed to be a deed and which is properly executed, ie signed by all parties who intend to be bound by the provisions of the deed and whose signatures are witnessed.[29]

---

23   Clearly, however, it would be good practice to send a copy of the notice to all affected parties.

24   See *Crawley Borough Council v Ure* (1996) 1 All ER 724, CA and *Frank Brackley v Notting Hill Housing Trust and Julie Brackley* [2001] EWCA Civ 601, the latter case being decided after the Trusts of Land and Appointment of Trustees Act 1996 came into force.

25   See PEA s3 1977.

26   *Hounslow LBC v Pilling* (1993) 25 HLR 305, CA; PEA 1977 s5.

27   *Leek and Moorlands Building Society v Clarke* [1952] 2 All ER 492, CA.

28   Law of Property Act 1925 ss52–53.

29   Law of Property (Miscellaneous Provisions) Act 1989 s1.

Implied surrender

1.71   In certain circumstances surrender may take effect by operation of law. This is also known as 'implied surrender'.

1.72   For surrender to be implied it is necessary that there is conduct by both parties that unequivocally amounts to an acceptance that the tenancy has ended. This may be either:

- relinquishment of possession and its acceptance by the landlord; or
- other conduct consistent only with the ending of the tenancy, where the circumstances are such as to make it inequitable for either the tenant or the landlord to dispute that the tenancy has ended.[30]

1.73   In each case, it is a question of fact for the court to decide whether these conditions are met.

Giving and acceptance of possession

1.74   If keys are returned and accepted by the landlord as ending the tenancy with immediate effect this will be an implied surrender. However, a tenant may give keys to the landlord for a reason other than wishing to surrender and a landlord is not bound to accept that the return of keys ends the tenancy immediately.

In *Laine v Cadwallader*[31] the tenants put the keys through the landlord's letter box. The landlord later made a claim against the tenant for four weeks' rent on the basis that the tenants had been required to give notice to terminate the agreement. The Court of Appeal held that the dropping in of keys cannot constitute more than an offer to surrender which a landlord is free to accept or reject. The landlord was entitled to treat the act as the giving of informal notice to quit or terminate the tenancy and the tenants were liable for the four weeks' rent following the delivery of the keys.

---

30 This is the formulation contained in *Woodfall on Landlord and Tenant* (Sweet & Maxwell, looseleaf) as approved by the Court of Appeal, with a small addition, in the cases of *Proudcreed Ltd v Microgen Holdings plc* (1995) 72 P&CR 388 and *Bellcourt Estates Ltd v Adesina*, see para 1.75 below.

31 (2000) 33 HLR 397, CA.

It should be noted that in *Laine v Cadwallader* the landlord would have been entitled to treat the tenancy as continuing indefinitely, in which case, the tenant would have had a continuing obligation for rent. If a tenant wishes to terminate a periodic tenancy he or she must serve a formal notice to quit that complies with the common law and statutory requirements (see paragraph 1.62 above). Such a notice operates unilaterally and does not depend on the landlord's agreement.

Tenant abandoning premises

In *Bellcourt Estates Ltd v Victoria Adesina*[32] a tenancy agreement was entered into for premises that comprised both residential and business units. The tenant paid part of the agreed deposit but no rent and subsequently complained about the state of the premises. She ceased to occupy the premises about three months after the start of the tenancy and asked the landlord to return the money she had paid. The landlord was aware that she had ceased to occupy and did not make any demand for the next rent payment. However, the landlord did inform the local authority's business rates department that Ms Adesina was the tenant and liable for the rates.

The county court judge held that the landlord's awareness that the tenant had left the premises, together with the failure to demand rent, amounted to surrender. However, the Court of Appeal upheld the landlord's appeal holding that the landlord's conduct could not be held to be unequivocal conduct inconsistent with the continuation of the tenancy. All that the landlord had done was to omit to demand rent, service charges or arrears and to have failed to continue the correspondence with the tenant. This was not sufficient to establish surrender.

1.76   Many social landlords have procedures to take possession of dwellings they believe have been 'abandoned' by the tenants. However, the term 'abandonment' has no specific legal meaning and, even if a property has apparently been abandoned by the tenant and the landlord wishes to take possession, this is not enough to establish that the tenancy has ended.

32 [2005] EWCA Civ 208, 18 February 2005.

In *Preston v Fairclough*[33] the tenants of a local authority house invited another person to live in the house and then moved out, leaving arrears of rent. When the local authority became aware of this a claim for possession was made against the occupier. The Court of Appeal held that the authority was not entitled to possession. It had taken no steps to end the tenancy and the abandonment by the tenants plus the arrears of rent were insufficient to establish surrender.

1.77 If there is an unequivocal act indicating a wish to surrender, the acceptance of the surrender by the landlord may be established by the landlord's conduct over a period of time rather than by a single act.

In *Brent LBC v Sharma and Vyas*[34] the sole tenant had lived in her home with her partner. She moved out and was granted a council tenancy elsewhere following which she wrote to her landlords stating that she was no longer sharing the flat with her partner and would not object to a transfer of the tenancy into his name. At this stage there were rent arrears of £4,000. On receipt of the letter the landlords closed the rent account and served notice to quit requiring the tenant's partner to leave. It was later held that the notice was ineffective. Several months later a claim for possession was made. A possession order was made on the basis that the tenant's letter was an unequivocal act showing that she wished to surrender and that this had been accepted by the landlords. The tenant and her partner appealed, arguing that there was no evidence of unequivocal conduct by the landlord to treat the tenancy as at an end and that the service of the notice to quit was only consistent with the continued existence of a tenancy. The Court of Appeal dismissed their appeal holding that the court was entitled to look at the whole of the landlord's conduct before the claim for possession was made. The combination of no longer charging rent to the tenant and the service of the notice (a 'belt and braces effort by the council') clearly showed that from the

33 (1982) 8 HLR 70.
34 (1992) 25 HLR 257.

expiry of the notice the landlords were treating the tenancy as at an end. By the time the proceedings were issued the landlords had unequivocally shown that the tenancy no longer existed.

1.78   A landlord who believes that premises have been abandoned by a tenant is not entitled to possession until the tenancy has ended. If surrender can be established this ends the tenancy. If not, but the tenant is no longer residing in the premises, a landlord may be able to end the tenancy by serving notice to quit. However, it should be noted that a tenant may be considered still to be resident even during an extended absence (see paragraph 3.5).

Liability for rent

Fixed-term agreements

1.79   Where a tenant enters into a tenancy agreement for a fixed period, he or she is liable for the rent for the whole period, unless the agreement contains a 'break clause', (see para 1.81 below). Where a tenant wants to leave and end the tenancy early the landlord has no obligation to accept a surrender. Further, if the tenant quits the premises and stops paying the rent, the landlord has no duty to treat the tenancy as at an end or to find another tenant in order to 'mitigate loss'. The landlord can sue the tenant for the whole of the rent for the remainder of the term.[35]

1.80   A tenant who wants to end a fixed-term tenancy early would be well advised to find someone who wishes to take on the tenancy. The landlord may then be more likely to agree to a surrender.

Break clauses

1.81   A break clause is a term that gives either party the right to end a fixed-term agreement early. The break clause will specify the length of notice that must be given and may be conditional on the tenant having complied with the obligations of the tenancy. This would mean that a tenant in rent arrears would be unable to trigger the

35   *Reichman & Dunn v Beveridge & Gauntlett* [2006] EWCA Civ 1659, 13 December 2006. A person claiming damages for breach of contract has a duty to mitigate (minimise) his or her losses, see chapter 7. However, where a fixed-term tenancy is concerned the landlord has no obligation to terminate the tenancy because if the tenancy was terminated the landlord would lose the right to seek rent for the remaining term or damages for loss of future rent.

break clause. If there is more than one tenant all must agree to serve notice under a break clause unless the agreement specifics otherwise.

Periodic agreements

1.82 If a tenant serves notice to quit the tenant's rent liability ends when the notice expires. If the tenant simply leaves the premises without serving an effective notice to quit liability for rent continues. This is the case even if the landlord is informed that the tenant wants to end the tenancy or is moving out. The landlord is not obliged to treat the tenancy as at an end and may sue the tenant for unpaid rent until the date the tenancy is formally ended, see *Laine v Cadwallader* at paragraph 1.74 above. If, however, the landlord takes possession or lets the premises to someone else this would be taken as an acceptance of the tenant's surrender and the tenancy and rent liability would come to an end.

Sub-tenancies

1.83 Many tenants rent accommodation from landlords who are themselves tenants of higher landlords. For example, a long-leaseholder may let a flat to a tenant or a local authority may let a house to a tenant who then sublets a room to a sub-tenant. In such cases the middle tenant is known as the 'mesne tenant'; he or she is both a tenant and a landlord. A mesne tenant cannot grant a sub-tenancy for a period that is longer than the tenancy he or she has. There may be more than one sub-tenancy in relation to the same premises.

1.84 The issues that arise when sub-tenancies are created are explained at para 3.90.

Statutory intervention

1.85 The way legislation governs residential tenancies is that a tenancy created at a certain date by a certain kind of landlord will be a certain type of tenancy, governed by a particular statute. The parties cannot contract out of the statutory protection given to tenants. So, regardless of the express terms of the tenancy agreement, certain statutory provisions will apply. For example, the tenancy agreement may state that a landlord can forfeit (end) the lease and take possession if the tenant is in arrears of rent. However, if the tenant has statutory protection, a landlord cannot enforce this right and take possession.

The only way to take possession is to follow the procedure set out in the relevant statute. In relation to rents, under the Rent Act 1977 the parties could agree a certain contractual rent but the tenant could immediately apply for a fair rent to be registered which would then become the maximum rent that could be charged.

The private sector

1.86   Since the Increase of Rent and Mortgage Interest (War Restrictions) Act 1915 there has been extensive statutory intervention restricting the right of landlords to evict residential tenants.

1.87   The 1915 Act was introduced as an emergency wartime measure to prevent private landlords from exploiting the shortage of rented accommodation in certain areas of the UK. The Act introduced for the first time security of tenure and rent control: tenants could not be evicted unless they failed to pay their rent or otherwise breached the tenancy agreement and landlords' right to increase rents was restricted.

1.88   Clearly, security of tenure and rent control operate in tandem. Unless there is a restriction on a landlord's right to evict a tenant there is no point in restricting the right to increase the rent. Otherwise, the landlord would be able to evict the tenant and enter into a contract with a new tenant at a higher rent.

1.89   The controls were intended only to last during the war. However, the scarcity of rented accommodation continued and successive governments found it impossible to remove the restrictions entirely. Various Rent Acts and Housing Acts were passed between 1914 and 1977 all providing for differing levels of security of tenure and rent control. The Rent Act 1977 still governs tenancies granted in the private sector before 15 January 1989. Under the Rent Act 1977 tenants have a high level of security of tenure and rent is controlled by being limited to a 'fair rent' set by an independent rent officer (see paragraph 3.173).

1.90   The Housing Act 1988 made it possible for landlords to grant short-term tenancies by way of the assured shorthold tenancy. The assured shorthold tenancy is now the main form of tenure for private tenants. It gives only limited security and a landlord may obtain a possession order as of right, following service of two months' written notice. However, the courts will not make a possession order to take effect before the end of six months from the start of the tenancy or before any fixed period has ended, whichever is longer. The Housing Act 1988 also effectively abandoned rent control for private tenants.

While there are some limited rights to challenge very high rents and rent increases, the presumption is that rents should be 'market rents' as opposed to 'fair rents' as under the Rent Act 1977. Fair rents are set by deducting from the market rent any element deemed to be attributable to the scarcity of accommodation. Market rents are, by definition, set by the market, taking full account of the scarcity of accommodation. Rent control for different kinds of tenants is explained chapter 3.

Social housing

1.91   Social housing refers to accommodation provided by local authorities and Registered Social Landlords (RSLs). RSLs are not-for-profit housing providers, principally housing associations. At the time of writing RSLs are registered and monitored by the Housing Corporation. The Housing and Regeneration Bill, expected to come into force late in 2008, will create a new regulatory system for RSLs. The Housing Corporation will be dissolved and replaced by the Regulator of Social Housing. The new regulatory regime will apply to the 'providers of social housing' which will include not only landlords providing low cost rented accommodation but also bodies providing low cost home ownership schemes.

1.92   Before 1980 the tenants of local authorities and housing associations did not enjoy statutory security of tenure. The tenants' rights were governed by the tenancy agreement which would usually provide that the landlord would not take possession save in certain circumstances. This would include failure to pay rent and other breaches of the tenancy agreement. Housing association tenants did have rent control through the fair rent mechanism of the Rent Acts.

1.93   The Housing Act 1980 provided that the tenants of local authorities and housing associations would be 'secure tenants' with similar security of tenure to that of most private tenants. Secure tenants could only be evicted if one of the grounds for possession was proved. Additional statutory rights, including succession on the death of the tenant and the right to mutual exchange, were also granted to secure tenants. The secure tenants of local authorities also had a right to buy their home from the authority. The rights of secure tenants are now set out in the Housing Act 1985.

1.94   The Housing Act 1988 took new housing association tenancies outside the provisions of the Housing Act 1985. From 15 January 1989 they would be under the same regime as the tenancies created by private landlord.

Chapter 2 provides for a summary of the different kinds of tenancy and the relevant statutes.

Security of tenure: levels of protection

1.96   As indicated above, there are two levels of security of tenure: substantive security of tenure and procedural security of tenure. Some residential occupiers have no security of tenure at all and can be evicted without a court order being obtained, although not forcibly.

1.97   The main statutes applying to residential tenancies are: the Rent Act 1977, the Housing Act 1985 and the Housing Act 1988. These Acts and the types of tenancies they govern are discussed in detail in chapter 2. Each Act sets out the conditions for a tenancy under which the tenant enjoys substantive security of tenure. In each Act the tenancy has a different name: under the Rent Act 1977, a 'protected' or 'statutory' tenancy (also known as a 'regulated' tenancy); under the Housing Act 1985, a 'secure' tenancy; and under the Housing Act 1988, an 'assured' tenancy (as distinct from an assured shorthold tenancy).

1.98   In addition, there are tenancies under which a tenant has more limited rights such as the 'restricted contract' under the Rent Act 1977 and the assured shorthold tenancy under the Housing Act 1988, see paragraphs 2.90 and 2.55. More recently, under anti-social behaviour provisions, the 'introductory' tenancy and the 'demoted' tenancy give tenants no substantive security of tenure but nevertheless impose some limits on the landlords' right to evict. These types of tenancy are explained in detail in chapter 2.

1.99   In addition to specific tenancies giving limited rights, some agreements simply fall outside the scope of statutory protection and the tenancy is referred to as, for example, a 'non-secure' tenancy or a 'contractual' tenancy.

1.100   A tenant who does not have substantive security of tenure may nevertheless have procedural security of tenure. The right to procedural security of tenure originates in the Protection from Eviction Act (PEA) 1977.[36] PEA 1977 s3 provides that certain occupiers can only be evicted by bringing possession proceedings in the county court. The occupiers protected by section 3 are those who, when a tenancy or licence comes to an end, are lawfully residing in premises, where the letting was neither 'statutorily protected' nor

---

36 The provisions of PEA 1977 are described in detail in chapter 7.

'excluded'. This means that a tenant who does not have substantive security of tenure but who is not an 'excluded occupier' will have the right to a court order before being evicted. PEA 1977 s3A lists the agreements that are excluded from the requirement to obtain a possession order. These are set out below.

Excluded occupiers

1.101 Excluded occupiers can be lawfully evicted without the landlord obtaining a possession order. The list of excluded occupiers is as follows:

Resident landlords with shared accommodation

Sharing accommodation with the landlord

1.102 A tenancy or licence is excluded if the following conditions are met:

- under the terms of the agreement the occupier shares any accommodation[37] with the landlord; and
- immediately before it was granted, and at the time when it comes to an end, the landlord was a resident landlord (ie he or she occupied the premises, of which the shared accommodation forms part, as his or her only, or principal, home).

Sharing accommodation with a resident landlord's family

1.103 A tenancy or licence is also excluded if the following conditions are met:

- under the terms of the agreement the occupier shares any accommodation with a member of the family of the landlord; and
- immediately before it was granted, and at the time when it comes to an end, the landlord was a resident landlord and the family member also occupied the premises as his or her only or principal home.

1.104 'Member of the family' is defined in section 113 of the Housing Act 1985. It includes the following: spouse, civil partner, co-habitees (those living together as if spouse or civil partner), parent, grandparent, child, grand-child, brother, sister, uncle, aunt, nephew or niece. Relationships of marriage are treated as relationships of blood, half-blood relationships are treated as whole blood

---

37 'Accommodation' means any accommodation other than storage areas or means of access: PEA 1977 s3A(5).

relationships, stepchildren are treated as children and illegitimate children are treated as the legitimate children of the mother and reputed father.

.05   The latter situation will be rare. It will arise only where there is a resident landlord in a different part of the building and a sharing of accommodation with a member of his or her family.

1.106   It should be noted that it is necessary for the landlord (and family member, if relevant) to occupy the premises at the beginning and at the end of the letting. It is not necessary that the landlord intends the occupation to be permanent or long term and where a landlord does not intend to continue to occupy after evicting the occupier this does not change the status of the occupier.[38]

1.107   Before 1989 those who were lodging as part of the household of another were termed 'bare licensees' with no security of tenure. Since 1989 anyone sharing a person's home will necessarily be sharing accommodation with the landlord (or licensor) and will be an excluded occupier.

1.108   Advisers should always be aware of the possibility of agreements that are 'pretences', ie they do not reflect the reality of the situation. An agreement that states that the landlord resides in the premises and shares accommodation with the tenant will not make the occupier an excluded occupier if this is a pretence (see paragraphs 1.47–1.48 above).

Licences granted to trespassers

1.109   A tenancy or licence granted as a temporary expedient to someone who entered the premises as a trespasser is excluded.

1.110   This would be the case where a landlord discovers that an empty property is occupied by trespassers and agrees to allow the trespassers to stay on a temporary basis, paying a weekly fee, or rent, until possession is taken.

Holiday lets

1.111   Where a tenancy or licence gives to a person the right to occupy premises for a holiday only it is excluded. Again, advisers should be alert to the possibility that the agreement may be labelled a holiday let but that this may be a pretence (see paras 1.47–1.48).

Rent-free accommodation

1.112   A tenancy or licence granted otherwise than for money or money's worth is excluded.

38 *Sumeghova v McMahon* [2002] EWCA Civ 1581, 24 October 2002.

1.113   The term 'money's worth' includes anything of value given or performed in return for the right or permission to occupy. A person who agrees to perform services, eg cleaning, in return for 'rent-free' occupation would not be excluded, regardless of the value of the services.

Licensees of hostel accommodation

1.114 A licence is excluded if it grants the right of occupation in a public sector hostel.[39]

1.115 A 'hostel' is defined as

> . . . a building in which is provided, for persons generally or for a class of persons:
>
> (a) residential accommodation otherwise than in separate and self-contained sets of premises, and
> (b) either board or facilities for the preparation of food adequate to the needs of those persons, or both.[40]

1.116   It should be noted that to be excluded therefore the following conditions must be met:

- the landlord must be of a specified type;
- the agreement must be a licence agreement; and
- the premises must be a 'hostel' as defined above.

1.117 The mere fact that an accommodation provider describes the building as a 'hostel' or the agreement as a 'licence' does not determine of the issue. An occupier may be able to establish that he or she is in reality a tenant, having been granted exclusive possession of a room. If this is the case, he or she will not be excluded. The key issue is whether the occupier or the landlord retains control of the room, (see paragraphs 1.29–1.32 above). Many public sector hostels are for those with special needs and additional support may be provided. This does not of itself mean that the occupier will be excluded but makes it more likely that the landlord will genuinely retain overall control of an occupier's room.

39 The public bodies that can grant excluded agreements are local authorities, development corporations, New Town Commissions, urban development corporations, housing action trusts, the Housing Corporation, the Secretary of State under section 89 of the Housing Associations Act 1985 and a housing trust which is a charity or a registered social landlord. Other bodies can be specified by order made by the Secretary of State. To date orders have been made in favour of the London Hostels Association Ltd (SI 1991 No 1943), The Shaftesbury Society (SI 1999 No 1758) and Royal British Legion Industries Ltd (SI 2003 No 2436).

40 Housing Act 1985 s622.

Accommodation provided to asylum-seekers

18   In April 2000 a new system was introduced whereby support and accommodation for asylum-seekers was to be provided by a branch of the Home Office, now the UK Border Agency (UKBA). This is known as 'NASS support'.[41] Such accommodation is provided under Part VI of the Immigration and Asylum Act (IAA) 1999 and any tenancy or licence granted under these provisions will be excluded.

1.119   In fact the providers of the accommodation are mostly private individuals and voluntary sector agencies under contracts with UKBA. Regardless of the identity of the provider, occupiers will be excluded if the arrangements are made under Part VI of IAA 1999.

1.120   Some asylum-seekers are accommodated by local authority social services departments because they have community care needs or are children and such arrangements are not governed by Part VI of IAA 1999.

1.121   Asylum-seekers who are granted leave to remain in the UK cease to be asylum-seekers and become eligible for homeless assistance and social housing. Former asylum-seekers who are accommodated as homeless or allocated social housing have the same rights as others with the same type of tenancy or licence.

Evicting excluded occupiers

1.122   Excluded occupiers can be evicted without a court order. The tenancy or licence must first be brought to an end by giving either the notice specified in any agreement or, if there is no such agreement, reasonable notice.[42] After the notice has expired the occupier may be peaceably excluded from the premises, ie the locks may be changed. However, it is a criminal offence to use or threaten violence to gain entry to premises when there is someone inside who is opposed to entry.[43] This includes violence to property so could cover breaking a window or door. See paragraph 7.41.

Reasonable notice

1.123   What is considered reasonable is to be determined according to the circumstances. Because the minimum period of a notice to quit is

---

41   NASS stands for the National Asylum Support Service, a department within the Home Office which no longer exists. However, the term NASS is still widely used to refer to the support system for asylum-seekers under the IAA 1999.

42   *Smith v Northside Developments Ltd* (1988) 55 P&CR 164.

43   Criminal Law Act 1977 s6.

28 days, this is usually deemed to be sufficient notice. However, shorter notice may be reasonable if, for example, the occupier has not been in occupation for long or if he or she has behaved violently. Conversely, a longer period of notice may be appropriate in certain circumstances.

> In *Mehta v Royal Bank of Scotland*[44] it was held that an occupier of a room in a hotel was a contractual licensee and that the agreement between the parties was that the licence could be determined on 'reasonable notice'. Mr Mehta was bringing a claim for unlawful eviction and it was necessary for the court to decide what reasonable notice would have been. Taking into account the references by the hotel owners to Mr Mehta being a 'long term occupier' the court held that a period of four months would have constituted reasonable notice.

1.124   Where a person is excluded because he or she is sharing another person's home, enforcing a right to 'reasonable notice' may be impossible: a court will be reluctant to order someone to allow another person to occupy his or her home for a further period of time when the relationship has clearly broken down.

Trespassers

1.125   The term 'trespasser' means any person in occupation of land unlawfully. It includes a person who was at one time lawfully occupying but whose right to occupy has ended. This would include a sub-tenant when his or her landlord's (the mesne tenant) interest is brought to an end or a joint tenant when the tenancy is ended by a tenant's notice to quit.

1.126   Those who were occupying lawfully when a tenancy or licence is brought to an end usually have procedural security of tenure (unless they are excluded occupiers). However, trespassers who entered as trespassers have no security of tenure. They can be evicted without a court order, but not forcibly. Special provision is made for the eviction of trespassers who are preventing a person from residing in the accommodation. This is described in chapter 7. Such trespassers are often referred to as 'squatters' but the term squatter has no specific legal meaning.

44   (2000) 32 HLR 45, QBD.

Difficult situations

Hotels

127   A hotel is, according to the *Oxford English Dictionary*, 'an establishment providing accommodation and meals for travellers and tourists'.

1.128   Some people 'live' in hotels. It is possible that accommodation occupied within a hotel can constitute a letting of a 'dwelling' and attract security of tenure.[45] More likely a hotel occupier will be a licensee with no more than procedural security of tenure, as in the case of *Mehta v Royal Bank of Scotland* (at paragraph 1.123 above). If the letting is for the purpose of a holiday only, the occupier will be excluded from any sort of protection (see paragraph 1.111 above). So, depending on the circumstances surrounding the 'letting' an occupier of hotel accommodation could be a tenant with long-term rights, a licensee with procedural rights only or an excluded occupier.

'Bed and breakfast' establishments

1.129   Many hotels provide accommodation on a 'bed and breakfast' basis. Those occupying such accommodation for a holiday are excluded occupiers. Some owners of bed and breakfast establishments have arrangements with local authorities to provide emergency accommodation for those to whom the authority has a statutory accommodation duty. Such a duty may be owed by the homeless persons department or the social services department. Where the accommodation is provided on an emergency basis the occupier will not gain any security of tenure, whether substantive or procedural.[46]

---

45 See *Uratemps Ventures Ltd v Collins* [2001] UKHL 43, 11 October 2001, discussed in chapter 2.

46 In the case of *Mohammed v Manek and RLBC Kensington & Chelsea* (1995) 27 HLR 439, the Court of Appeal decided that those occupying bed and breakfast accommodation while awaiting a decision on a homeless decision did not enjoy any procedural security of tenure. The case of *Roma Desnousse v (1) Newham LBC, (2) Paddington Churches HA, (3) Veni Properties Ltd* [2006] EWCA Civ 547, 17 May 2006, went further. The court held that any licensee awaiting a homeless decision was in the same position – he or she could be evicted without a court order. See paragraph 7.19. Although both of these cases concerned a duty owed by the housing authority, it is likely to follow that those placed in similar accommodation by social services would similarly have no procedural security of tenure.

1.130   Because it is possible to evict a person placed in bed and breakfast accommodation by a local authority, without a court order, some accommodation providers designate all accommodation, including self-contained dwellings, 'bed and breakfast'. However, as is the case when identifying tenancies and licences, what determines the nature of a letting is the factual situation, not the label applied. Advisers should be alert to the possibility that the describing accommodation as 'bed and breakfast' may be a pretence, and that occupiers may have a tenancy. While the tenancy is unlikely to attract substantive security of tenure, the occupier may have the right not to be evicted without a court order.

Hostels

1.131   Licensees in hostels run by specified public bodies are excluded occupiers. However, this only applies to licensees and not tenants. A person who has exclusive possession of a room in a hostel will usually be a tenant. If the hostel is run by an RSL he or she will be an assured shorthold tenant (see paragraph 2.55). If the hostel is run by a local authority he or she will be a secure tenant only if the premises let are self-contained, ie include cooking facilities, (see paragraph 2.100).

1.132   If the hostel is not run by one of the specified bodies or does not satisfy the definition of 'hostel', as explained above, a licensee will have procedural security of tenure.

Mixed business and residential use

1.133   The Landlord and Tenant Act (LTA) 1954 Part II applies to 'any tenancy where the property comprised in the tenancy is or includes premises which are occupied by the tenant and are so occupied for the purposes of a business carried on by him or for those and other purposes'.[47]

1.134   If LTA 1954 Part II applies to a tenancy the tenant cannot be a protected or statutory tenant under the Rent Act 1977 and cannot be secure or assured. This is the case even if the premises include residential accommodation. However, the business use must be significant; if it is incidental to the use of the premises as a home the tenant will not be excluded from residential security.

47   LTA 1954 s23(1).

Is business use significant or incidental?

1.135   This is a question of fact to be determined by a court if at issue. The following two cases were heard at the same time by the Court of Appeal:[48]

> In *Cheryl Investments Ltd v Saldanha* a businessman rented residential premises but almost immediately began to use them for the purposes of his business. The business had no other premises, stationery was printed and a business telephone and other office equipment were installed at the premises. The court held that the tenancy was governed by the LTA 1954 Part II and not the Rent Act 1977.
>
> A different conclusion was reached in *Royal Life Saving Society v Page* in which a doctor took a lease of residential premises and, with the consent of the landlord, installed a consulting room where he occasionally saw patients. His principal practice and consulting rooms were elsewhere. The court held that the degree of business user was insufficient for the LTA 1954 to apply as the letting was residential.

1.136   Although a change of use may bring the tenancy within the LTA 1954, spare time activities, even for financial reward, do not necessarily change the character of the user from residential to business.

> In *Gurton v Parrot*[49] the main purpose of the tenant's occupation was to reside in the premises as his home and it was found that the running of a kennel business from the premises was incidental to that purpose.

Occupying for the purpose of a business

1.137   The above cases concerned residential premises also used for business purposes. The courts examined whether the business use was significant or incidental to the residential use. Where the stated

48   [1978] 1 WLR 1329, CA.
49   (1990) 23 HLR 418, CA.

purpose of a lease is for business use, the LTA 1954 will apply, even if the premises also includes residential accommodation.

> In *Broadway Investments Hackney Ltd v Grant*[50] the lease stated that the permitted use for the ground floor was for sale and catering for fish and the upper part was for residential purposes only. The tenant was obliged to keep the premises open as a shop throughout the year during business hours. Initially it had not been possible to conduct business because of the need for substantial works to the shop premises. In a claim for possession the tenant argued therefore that the purpose of the letting had been residential. The Court of Appeal held that even if that had been the case initially by the time the issue came to be determined the tenant was using the premises for the purpose of a business in accordance with the terms of the lease. The tenancy was governed by the LTA 1954.

1.138   However, the fact that tenants of mixed business and residential premises may not enjoy long-term security does not mean that they can be evicted without a court order.

> In *Patel v Pirabakaran*[51] the Court of Appeal held that premises, including both business and residential premises, were 'let as a dwelling' for the purpose of the Protection from Eviction Act 1977. The landlord was required to obtain a possession order to lawfully evict the tenants.

Trusts and the law of equity

Trusts

1.139   A trust exists where one person holds property for the benefit of another person. The person who holds the property is the trustee and the person for whom the property is held is the beneficiary. Trusts are used for a variety of purposes, for example when a person wants to leave or transfer property for the benefit of a child or wishes to control the way property is used by another person. In such a case

50   [2006] EWCA Civ 1709, 20 December 2006.
51   [2006] EWCA Civ 685, 26 May 2006.

an express trust may be created, the terms of the trust and the powers of the trustees being set out in a deed of trust.

1.140   In addition to express trusts, certain circumstances result in the creation of a trust by implication of law. For example, where two people purchase property in the sole name of one but contribute equally to the purchase price, intending both parties to benefit equally, a trust is created, despite the absence of an express deed of trust. While the 'legal' ownership of the property is in the name of one party, the law implies a trust whereby the legal owner holds the property on trust for the benefit of both parties. The parties are joint 'equitable' owners, see paragraphs 11.96–11.104.

1.141   Further, under English law, jointly owned property is always owned under a 'trust of land'. The joint owners own the legal interest for the benefit of themselves. Such trusts are now governed by the Trusts of Land and Appointment of Trustees Act (TLATA) 1996. The fact that jointly held property is held by way of a trust enables one party to apply to a court for an order for sale. The presumption is that, if one trustee no longer wants the property to remain in joint ownership, the property should be sold and the 'equity' divided between the parties.

1.142   The matters that must be considered by the court when considering an application for sale are set out in TLATA 1996 s15 and are:

- the intentions of those who created the trust;
- the purposes for which the property is held;
- the welfare of any child who lives in the property or might reasonably be expected to;
- the interests of any secured creditor; and
- the circumstances and wishes of each of the beneficiaries who are entitled to occupy the property.

The law of equity

1.143   Trusts are a creation of the 'law of equity'. The law of equity is a system of rules and principles that developed alongside the common law. It evolved through the decisions of the Court of Chancery (originally a court of equity) to remedy some of the defects of the common law.

1.144   Other equitable principles have been developed so as to achieve fairness between parties. Where parties intend to create a certain legal relationship, but fail to take the correct legal steps or there is some obstacle to the legal relationship intended, the law of equity may intervene to ensure a fair (equitable) outcome. An example is where a tenancy is granted to a minor. A minor cannot hold a legal tenancy but if a person purports to grant a tenancy to a minor the result will be an equitable tenancy, held on trust for the minor until he or she becomes an adult. This is based on the doctrine of 'estoppel': a party is prevented ('estopped') from denying his or her acts or representations where this would be unfair to the other party.

Estoppel

1.145 The following are examples of the operation of estoppel in landlord and tenant law:

- *estoppel by conduct* (known as '*estoppel in pais*') means that a tenant who has accepted a lease cannot dispute the landlord's title;
- *promissory estoppel* refers to a situation in which a person makes unequivocal representations to another (whether by words or conduct), on which the other person relies to his or her detriment. The 'promissor' may be estopped from denying the representations. A tenant may raise such an argument against a landlord who represents that he or she will accept less than the full contractual rent but subsequently seeks possession on the ground of rent arrears;
- *proprietary estoppel* means that a person is prevented from denying another person's rights in property. An example would be where a person relies on another person's representations (whether by words or conduct) that he or she will have some interest in property. Where that person, relying on the representations, has spent money on the property he or she may gain an equitable interest in it, see chapter 11.

The court's discretion

1.146 One central feature of the law of equity is that remedies granted by the courts are discretionary. A person who relies on equity must come to the court with 'clean hands' which means that a person who has not behaved well or honestly in the transaction may be refused relief.

1.147 At one time claims based on the law of equity had to be brought in the Court of Chancery but an equitable claim can now be brought in any civil court.

Tenant's Notice to Quit

NOTICE TO QUIT

To: [LANDLORD'S NAME AND ADDRESS]
I, [TENANT'S NAME], of [TENANT'S ADDRESS]

Give you Notice that I intend to quit and to deliver possession of the premises at [ADDRESS OF THE PREMISES]

On [INSERT DATE – must be the last or the first day of a period of the tenancy] or on the day on which a complete period of my tenancy expires next after the end of four weeks from the service of this notice.

Date: ....

Signed: ....[by tenant]

Different kinds of tenancies

continued

Key points

- The type of tenancy a person has will be determined by the identity of the landlord and the date the tenancy started.
- Each of the main schemes operate in a similar way. For a tenant to have long-term rights he or she must live in the premises as a home.
- In each scheme certain kinds of tenancies cannot be protected. These include tenancies for a very high or very low rent, licensed premises and tenancies where there is a resident landlord. For local authorities this also includes tenancies granted to homeless applicants.
- A tenant who has long-term rights ('substantive security of tenure') cannot be evicted unless there is a reason (ground for possession). The landlord must apply to the court for a possession order.
- The majority of private lettings are now assured shorthold tenancies where the tenant has no long-term rights. In most cases the tenant can be evicted after the first six months. The landlord must obtain a possession order but does not need a reason to evict.
- The legislation introduced to address anti-social behaviour created two types of tenancy under which the tenant does not have long-term rights: the introductory tenancy and the demoted tenancy. In both cases the tenant is 'on probation' for a period of 12 months, which may be extended. If not evicted during this period the tenant reverts to having long-term rights.

Introduction

2.1 Different schemes of statutory protection apply to residential tenancies depending on whether the landlord is a private or social landlord and the date the tenancy commenced. In each scheme certain conditions must be met for the tenant to enjoy substantive security of tenure and there is a list of tenancies that fall outside statutory protection. The main Acts and types of tenancies granted under each are summarised below.

The Act	Type of tenancy	Type of landlord and date of grant
Rent Act 1977	Protected tenancy and statutory tenancy – both also known as regulated tenancies	Tenancies granted by private landlords before 15 January 1989.
Housing Act 1985	Secure tenancy	Tenancies granted by local authorities whenever granted; and tenancies granted by housing associations before 15 January 1989.
Housing Act 1988	Assured tenancy and assured shorthold tenancy	Tenancies granted by private landlords and housing associations on or after 15 January 1989.
Housing Act 1996	Introductory tenancy	Probationary tenancies granted by local authorities.
Anti Social Behaviour Act 2003	Demoted tenancy	Previously secure tenancies granted by local authorities but demoted by the court.

Housing Act 1988: assured and assured shorthold tenancies

2.2   The Housing Act (HA) 1988 introduced a new regime in the private sector. Most tenancies granted by private landlords on or after 15 January 1989 will be either:

- an assured tenancy; or
- an assured shorthold tenancy.

2.3   The HA 1988 also brought non-local authority social housing within the private sector regime. The tenancies granted by Registered Social Landlords (RSLs), principally housing associations, will also be assured and assured shorthold tenancies if granted on or after 15 January 1989. Before that date housing associations could grant secure tenancies and housing association tenancies granted before that date remain secure tenancies.

2.4   An assured tenant enjoys substantive security of tenure whereas an assured shorthold tenant has security only for an initial period of six months. For both types of tenancy there is very limited rent control. In practice, there are few assured tenancies in the private sector; most are granted by RSLs to tenants who have been nominated for an allocation of social housing (see chapter 16). However, RSLs also use assured shorthold tenancies, mainly when operating a 'probationary tenancy' schemes, or when accommodating homeless applicants by arrangement with a local authority.

2.5 Initially there were certain formal requirements for the creation of an assured shorthold tenancy. If a landlord failed to comply with these formalities an assured tenancy would be created by default. The Housing Act 1996 changed this: from 28 February 1997 any new tenancy created by a private landlord or an RSL will be an assured shorthold tenancy unless it is expressly stated that it is not an assured shorthold tenancy.

2.6 An assured shorthold tenancy is a type of assured tenancy. If a tenancy cannot be an assured tenancy it cannot be an assured shorthold tenancy. This section is therefore in three parts:

1) the necessary conditions for the creation of any assured tenancy, including an assured shorthold;
2) the specific characteristics of assured tenancies (as distinct from assured shorthold tenancies);
3) the specific characteristics of assured shorthold tenancies.

Conditions for all assured tenancies

2.7 To create an assured tenancy the following conditions must be satisfied:[1]

- the tenancy must be of a dwelling-house 'let as a separate dwelling';
- the tenant must be an individual, or if there are joint tenants all must be individuals;
- the tenant must occupy as his or her only or principal home. If there are joint tenants at least one must occupy as his or her only or principal home;
- the tenancy must not be one excluded by Schedule 1 of the Housing Act 1988.

2.8 In all cases there must be a tenancy.[2] An occupier who does not have exclusive possession of at least some part of the premises cannot be a tenant, see chapter 1.

---

1   HA 1988 s1.
2   See chapter 1 for an explanation of the characteristics of a tenancy.

'Dwelling house let as a separate dwelling'

2.9   Section 1(1) of the HA 1988 provides that there must be as follows. '*A tenancy under which a dwelling-house is let as a separate dwelling*'.

2.10   This condition contains two separate elements.

A 'dwelling-house'

2.11   This includes part of a dwelling-house.[3] Whether a particular letting is of a 'dwelling-house' depends on the facts of the case. A caravan was held to be a dwelling-house where the wheels had been raised and it had been connected to mains services.[4] However, if a caravan is let as moveable property it cannot be a dwelling-house.[5] A houseboat does not have sufficient degree of attachment and annexation to the land to become part of it and cannot be a dwelling-house.[6] In any particular case, the relative degrees of permanence and mobility will be relevant.

'Let as a separate dwelling'

2.12   The main purpose of the letting must be to provide a home for the tenant.

2.13   It has long been a condition for a tenant to have substantive security of tenure that the premises are let as a separate dwelling. This was principally to prevent a tenant who shared accommodation with his or her landlord from having long-term security. However, express provision is now made for the following situations:

- a tenant sharing accommodation with a landlord, see para 1.101;
- a tenant sharing accommodation with other tenants, see paras 2.51 and 2.81.

2.14   The early case law is therefore of limited relevance and the issue of whether a tenant occupies 'a dwelling house let as a separate dwelling' mainly arises in relation to occupiers of accommodation in hotels and hostels. The phrase 'let as a separate dwelling' had been interpreted by the courts as meaning that the premises let had to be capable of being lived in and that the absence of a kitchen meant that

---

3   HA 1988 s45.

4   *R v Guildford Area Rent Tribunal ex p Grubey* (1951) (unreported), DC.

5   *R v Rent Officer of Nottingham Registration Area ex p Allen* (1985) 17 HLR 481, QBD.

6   *Chelsea Yacht and Boat Co Ltd v Pope* [2001] 2 All ER 409.

premises were not let as a separate dwelling.[7] However, in the case of *Uratemps Ventures Ltd v Collins*[8] this approach was rejected.

In *Uratemps Ventures Ltd v Collins* Mr Collins occupied a hotel room which was basically furnished and did not include any cooking facilities, although there was a power point. Breakfast had initially been available in the restaurant and included in the rent. Mr Collins brought in a pizza warmer, a toasted sandwich maker, a kettle and a warming plate. The landlords sought possession arguing that that Mr Collins could not be an assured tenant under the Housing Act 1988 as there was no 'letting of a dwelling-house as a separate dwelling'.

The House of Lords held that the word 'dwelling' is not a term of art with a specialised legal meaning. It is 'the place where [an occupier] lives and to which he returns and which forms the centre of his existence ... No doubt he will sleep there and usually eat there; he will often prepare at least some of his meals there.'[9] However, there is no legislative requirement that cooking facilities must be available for premises to qualify as a dwelling. In deciding whether an occupant has security of tenure:

> The first step is to identify the subject-matter of the tenancy agreement. If this is a house or part of a house of which the tenant has exclusive possession with no element of sharing, the only question is whether, at the date when proceedings were brought, it was the tenant's home. If so, it was his dwelling ... The presence or absence of cooking facilities in the part of the premises of which the tenant has exclusive occupation is not relevant.[10]

The House of Lords held that Mr Collins was an assured tenant.

Tenant/s must be individual/s

2.15   A letting to a company cannot be an assured tenancy.

---

7   This is in contrast to the sharing of facilities such as bathroom and toilet which did not prevent there being a letting of a separate dwelling.

8   [2001] UKHL 43, 11 October 2001.

9   Millet LJ at [31].

10   Millet LJ at [58].

Tenant/s must occupy as only or principal home

2.16 It should be noted that this condition is stricter than under the Rent Act where the equivalent requirement is that the tenant occupies the premises as a residence. For an assured tenancy to exist the premise must be the tenant's only or main home. Under the Rent Act it was possible for a person to reside in more than one place and to be a statutory tenant of two homes at the same time.

2.17 The residence condition may still be met even during the tenant's absence provided that there remains:

- an intention by the tenant to return; and
- some physical sign of that intention.[11]

2.18 This issue is discussed in detail at paragraphs 3.2–3.8.

Agreements that cannot be assured

2.19 Schedule 1 of HA 1988 sets out those agreements that cannot be assured tenancies. They are:

Tenancies entered into before HA 1988: para 1

2.20 A tenancy entered into before 15 January 1989, or pursuant to a contract made before that date.

High value tenancies: para 2

2.21 Any tenancy entered into on or after 1 April 1990 for which the rent 'for the time being' is more than £25,000 a year.[12] 'Rent' does not include any sum expressed to be payable in respect of rates, council tax, services, management, repairs, maintenance or insurance.

2.22 A rent increase that takes the rent above the limit will take the tenancy out of the scope of the HA 1988; the tenant will lose substantive security of tenure and will simply be a contractual tenant. However, the courts have held that a rent increase clause designed deliberately to take the tenancy outside the HA 1988 at a future date, so that possession could be obtained by the landlord, was unenforceable.[13]

---

11 *Brown v Brash* [1948] 2 KB 247.
12 For tenancies entered into between 15 January 1989 and 31 March 1990 the test is set by the rateable value. If the rateable value was in excess of £1,500 in greater London or £750 elsewhere, the tenancy cannot be an assured tenancy.
13 *Bankway Properties v Dunsford* [2001] 26 EG 164.

Tenancies at a low rent or no rent: para 3

2.23 This means either:

(1) A tenancy under which, for the time being, no rent is payable; or

(2) A tenancy entered into on or after 1 April 1990 under which the rent for the time being payable is £1,000 or less if the premises are in Greater London, and £250 or less elsewhere.[14]

Where services are provided in return for the accommodation, the tenancy will not be a 'no rent' tenancy provided the value of the services is capable of quantification. If capable of quantification, the value of the services must exceed £1,000 per year for the tenancy to be an assured tenancy. If the nature of the services means that the value cannot be quantified, this will mean that the tenancy cannot be assured.

If no rent is paid or services provided, the tenancy will also be an 'excluded tenancy' which means that the tenant can be evicted without a court order.[15]

Business tenancies: para 4

2.24 A tenancy of premises occupied primarily for business purposes will be governed by the Landlord and Tenant Act 1954 and not the HA 1988. See paras 1.133–1.136 regarding premises occupied for mixed business and residential use.

Licences premises: para 5

2.25 A tenancy of premises or part of premises licensed for the sale of intoxicating liquor for consumption on the premises.

Tenancies of agricultural land: para 6

2.26 A tenancy under which agricultural land, exceeding two acres, is let together with the dwelling house.

Agricultural holdings: para 7

2.27 A tenancy under which the dwelling-house is comprised in:

- an agricultural holding occupied by the person responsible for the control of the farming of the holding; or

14 For tenancies entered into between 15 January 1989 and 31 March 1990, the tenancy is a low rent tenancy if the rent for the time being payable is less than two-thirds of the rateable value on 31 March 1990.

15 PEA 1977 s3A and para 1.112.

- a holding held under a farm business tenancy occupied by the person responsible for the control of the management of the holding.[16]

Specified student lettings: para 8

2.28   A tenancy granted to a student pursuing or intending to pursue a course of study, provided by a specified educational institution, and which is granted either by that institution or by another specified institution or body of persons.

'Specified' means specified by regulations.[17]

Holiday lettings: para 9

2.29   A tenancy the purpose of which is to give the tenant the right to occupy for a holiday. Such tenancies are also 'excluded tenancies' and a landlord need not obtain a court order to evict.

Resident landlords: para 10

2.30   Tenants with a resident landlord. See paragraphs 3.13–3.27 below for the definition of resident landlord and the conditions that must be satisfied.

Crown tenancies: para 11

2.31   A tenancy under which the landlord is Her Majesty or a government department or where the premises are held in trust for Her Majesty for the purpose of a government department.

Local authority and other tenancies: para 12

2.32   A tenancy in which the landlord is one of the following bodies:
- a local authority;[18]
- the Commission for the New Towns;
- an urban development corporation established by an order under section 135 of the Local Government, Planning and Land Act 1980;

16 The term 'agricultural holding' is defined in the Agricultural Holdings Act 1986 and the terms 'farm business tenancy', and 'holding' are defined in the Agricultural Tenancies Act 1995.

17 The current regulations are the Assured and Protected Tenancies (Lettings to Students) Regulations 1998 (SI No 1967).

18 Local authorities include the London Fire and Emergency Planning Authority and a police authority.

- a development corporation within the meaning of the New Towns Act 1981;
- a 'waste disposal authority' established under section 10 of the Local Government Act 1985;
- a residuary body, within the meaning of the Local Government Act 1985;
- the Residuary Body for Wales;
- a fully mutual housing association; or
- a housing action trust established under Part III of the HA 1988.

Accommodation for asylum-seekers: para 12A

2.33   A tenancy granted by a private landlord under arrangements made for the provision of support for asylum-seekers and their dependents under Part VI of the Immigration and Asylum Act 1999. Such tenancies are also excluded tenancies and the occupiers can be evicted without a court order.

Accommodation for people with temporary protection: para 12B

2.34   A tenancy granted by a private landlord under arrangements for the provision of accommodation for people with temporary protection made under the Displaced Persons (Temporary Protection) Regulations 2005.[19]

Transitional cases: para 13

2.35   The following tenancies are not assured because they are governed by different statutes, all of which are explained below:

(1) a protected tenancy, within the meaning of the Rent Act 1977;
(2) a housing association tenancy granted before 15 January 1989;
(3) a secure tenancy;
(4) a protected occupier under the Rent (Agriculture) Act 1976.

The features of an assured tenancy

Security of tenure

2.36   An assured tenant (in contrast to an assured shorthold tenant) has substantive security of tenure: he or she can only be evicted if the

---

19   These regulations bring into force a European Directive (2001/55/EC) that requires member states to apply minimum standards for giving temporary protection to persons in the event of a mass influx of displaced persons. In the event that such persons had to be accommodated, any tenancy granted by a private landlord would not be capable of being an assured tenancy.

landlord obtains a possession order and an order will only be made if one of the grounds for possession is proved. Under the HA 1988 a landlord cannot end an assured tenancy other than by obtaining a possession order; it is the possession order that brings the tenancy to an end.

2.37   HA 1988 s5(1) provides:

- An assured tenancy cannot be brought to an end by the landlord except by obtaining an order of the court; and that
- the service by the landlord of a notice to quit shall be of no effect in relation to a periodic assured tenancy.[20]

2.38   In the case of a fixed term tenancy containing a power for the landlord to determine the tenancy,[21] the landlord can bring the tenancy to an end by exercising that power. However, HA 1988 s5(2) provides that where a fixed term tenancy comes to an end, other than by an order of the court or the tenant's surrender, the tenant is entitled to remain in possession as a 'statutory periodic tenant'.

2.39   This means that when an assured fixed term tenancy ends, either by the landlord exercising a right to end the tenancy, or by 'effluxion of time' (ie, the fixed period expires) a tenant who remains in occupation automatically becomes a statutory periodic tenant.

2.40   The only way a landlord can end a periodic assured tenancy (including a statutory periodic tenancy) is by obtaining a possession order, and HA 1988 s7 provides:

> ... the court shall not make an order for possession of a dwelling-house let on an assured tenancy except on one or more of the grounds set out in Schedule 2 to this Act.

2.41   So, although a landlord may end a fixed term assured tenancy under the agreement, the statutory periodic tenancy that then arises can only be brought to an end by obtaining a possession order.

2.42   The grounds for possession are explained in detail in chapter 6.

Periodic assured tenancies

2.43   An assured tenancy may be a periodic tenancy from the outset. This will be the case if it is expressed to be a weekly or monthly tenancy. If no term is specifically agreed, the period will be implied from the

---

20 Note however that this does not prevent a tenant, including a joint tenant ending a tenancy by serving notice to quit.

21 This does not include a power of re-entry or forfeiture: s45(4). Re-entry and forfeiture are explained at para 4.18.

'rental period'. The rental period is not the same as the way rent is paid. The rental period refers to the way rent is calculated, not the way rent is actually paid, although in most cases these will be the same.[22] So, if the tenancy agreement states that the rent is a certain amount per month the tenancy will be a monthly periodic tenancy. This is regardless of the fact that the rent may actually be paid, for example, four weekly in arrears (as is usual when a tenant relies on housing benefit).

2.44   If the tenancy was originally a fixed term tenancy it becomes a statutory periodic tenancy on the expiry of the fixed term. It is deemed granted by the same landlord to the same tenant in relation to the same dwelling-house as under the fixed term agreement.[23]

2.45   RSLs usually grant periodic assured tenancies. Fixed term agreements are more common in the private sector.

The terms of a statutory periodic assured tenancy

2.46   HA 1988 s5(3) provides:

- the statutory periodic tenancy takes effect immediately on the coming to an end of the fixed term tenancy;
- the periods of the tenancy are the same as those for which rent was last payable under the fixed term tenancy; and
- the other terms are the same as under the fixed term tenancy. However, any term that makes provision for the landlord or tenant to end the agreement is of no effect while the tenancy remains assured.

2.47   A statutory periodic tenancy does not arise if a new tenancy of the same or substantially the same dwelling-house is granted on the end of the fixed term tenancy.

2.48   Ascertaining the correct period of the statutory tenancy may be crucial when considering the validity of a possession notice served by a landlord.

In *Church Commissioners for England v Gisele Meya*[24] the fixed term agreement, prior to the statutory periodic tenancy arising, had been for a term of one year less a day. Rent had been expressed to be a certain amount per annum, payable by equal quarterly payments in advance on the usual quarter days.

22 See para 1.33.
23 HA 1988 s5(3)(a)–(c).
24 [2006] EWCA Civ 821, 21 June 2006.

At common law a periodic tenancy arising by implication would be an annual tenancy. However, the Court of Appeal held that section 5(3)(d) meant that in respect of a statutory periodic assured tenancy, the period was to be calculated by reference to the way rent was *payable*, not to the way rent was calculated.

The statutory tenancy which arose at the end of the fixed term was therefore a quarterly periodic tenancy and not, as the tenant contended, an annual tenancy.

2.49 Possession notices are discussed in more detail in chapter 5.

Tenant sharing accommodation with others

2.50 Even if a tenant shares accommodation with others, he or she may still be an assured tenant. However, there must be some accommodation of which the tenant has exclusive possession.

2.51 HA 1988 s3(1) provides that a person may have an assured tenancy of 'the separate accommodation' (ie, the room/s of which exclusive possession is granted) despite the fact that the agreement provides for the sharing of other accommodation with other people, not including the landlord.[25]

2.52 Further, as long as the tenant remains in possession of the separate accommodation, any term of the tenancy modifying or terminating the right to use the shared accommodation will be of no effect.[26] However, a term permitting variation or increase in the number of people with whom the tenant shares accommodation is enforceable.[27]

Tenant sub-letting part of the accommodation

2.53 Where a tenant has sub-let part of his or her premises to another person this will not prevent the tenancy from remaining an assured tenancy even though the tenant now shares accommodation with others.[28]

2.54 However, sub-letting is prohibited in most assured tenancy agreements. Sub-letting could therefore lead to the landlord claiming

25 For the position of tenants who share accommodation with their landlords see para 1.101.
26 HA 1988 s3(3).
27 HA 1988 s3(4).
28 HA 1988 s4.

possession on the grounds that the tenant has breached the tenancy agreement. See paras 3.108–3.114.

The features of an assured shorthold tenancy

Security of tenure

2.55   Unless the tenant is granted a fixed term tenancy of longer than six months, after the first six months the assured shorthold tenant has no substantive security of tenure: the landlord is entitled to a possession order but must serve notice and obtain a possession order. No ground or reason for requiring possession is needed. The procedure for obtaining possession of premises let on an assured shorthold tenancy is described in chapter 5.

Formalities prior to 28 February 1997

2.56   On or after 28 February 1997 all new assured tenancies will be assured shorthold tenancies unless it is expressly provided that the tenancy is not an assured shorthold tenancy. In contrast, to create an assured shorthold tenancy before 28 February 1997 the following conditions had to be satisfied:[29]

- the tenancy had to be for a fixed term of not less than six months with no provision for the landlord to end the tenancy within the first six months;[30] and
- notice in a prescribed form must have been served by the landlord on the tenant before the tenancy was entered into.

2.57   If these conditions were not met, the tenancy was an assured tenancy and the tenant had substantive security of tenure.

2.58   In most cases where it was argued that there had been a failure to comply with the formalities, the issue was the validity of the prescribed notice, known as the 'section 20 notice'.

HA 1988 'section 20 notice'

In prescribed form

2.59   'Prescribed' means prescribed by regulations. The current prescribed form is set out in the Assured Tenancies and Agricultural Occupancies (Forms) Regulations 1988.[31]

---

29 HA 1988 s20.
30 This does not include a term for re-entry or forfeiture, see below.
31 SI No 2203.

2.60   It is sufficient that the notice is in 'a form substantially to the same effect' as the prescribed form.[32] This means that if there is an error or omission on the form itself, or it is completed incorrectly, it may nevertheless be valid provided it is 'substantially to the same effect' as a properly completed prescribed form.

2.61   In some of the early cases where the courts considered the validity of section 20 notices, the test applied was whether the error was obvious to the tenant so that he or she did not suffer detriment as a result of the error. It was held that such an error did not invalidate the notice.[33]

2.62   However, where important information for the tenant was omitted it was held that the notice was invalid.

In the case of *Manel v Memon*[34] the notice had omitted bullet points with instructions and advice to the tenant. The Court of Appeal held that the bullet points, in particular the exhortation to take legal advice and the statement that the giving of the notice did not commit the tenant to take the tenancy, were part of the substance of the notice. Without them the notice was not 'substantially to the same effect' as the prescribed form. The notice was defective and a possession order made by the district judge was set aside.

2.63   More recently the Court of Appeal have rejected the approach to errors that focuses on whether the error is obvious and whether it has caused detriment to the tenant. Rather, it has been held that there is only one question: whether the notice accomplishes the statutory purpose of warning the tenant of the special nature of an assured shorthold tenancy.[35]

In *Osborne & Co Ltd v Dior and Marito Holdings SA v Deneche and Lundborg*[36] the Court of Appeal considered two notices challenged by the tenants.

---

32 Regulation 2.
33 *Brewer v Andrews* and *York v Ross & Casey* (1999) 31 HLR 209, CA.
34 (2001) 33 HLR 24, CA.
35 *Ravenseft Properties Ltd v Hall* [2001] EWCA Civ 2034, 19 December 2001.
36 [2003] EWCA Civ 281, 22 January 2003.

In the first case the notice was signed by an employee of the managing agents and the space for the landlord's details left blank. In the second case the notice was also signed by the agent. In the box for the landlord's details the name of a company was entered but the company was not, in fact, the landlord.

The Court of Appeal held, following *Ravenseft*, the test which the court must apply is whether, notwithstanding any errors or omissions that have been demonstrated, the notice is 'substantially to the same effect' as a notice in the proper form which has been duly completed. In reaching its conclusion, the court must bear in mind the statutory purpose of the notice, namely that of telling the proposed tenant of the special nature of an assured shorthold tenancy.[37]

Both notices were held to be valid and the tenancies were assured shorthold tenancies.

Must be served by the landlord on the tenant

Joint landlords and tenants

2.64   The section 20 notice must have been served by one of two or more joint landlords.[38] The notice must have been served on all the joint tenants.[39]

Agency

2.65   It is common for landlords to instruct agents to manage properties. A section 20 notice may be signed and served by a landlord's agent. Even where an agent fails to indicate the identity of the landlord, or gives incorrect details for the landlord, this will not necessarily invalidate the notice (see *Osborne & Co Ltd v Dior* at paragraph 2.63 above). This, however, is a different issue from the tenant's right to be informed of the identity of the landlord which is dealt with at paragraphs 3.127–3.131.

2.66   A section 20 notice can be served on an agent acting for the tenant.[40] However, this will only be in circumstances where the tenant has instructed an agent to act on his or her behalf in relation to the tenancy, which is unusual *service*.

37 Arden LJ at [37].
38 HA 1988 s20(6).
39 HA 1988 s45(3).
40 *Yenula Properties Ltd v Naidu* [2002] EWCA Civ 719, 23 May 2002.

2.67   It must be served before the tenancy is entered into. This is a question of fact in each case.[41] A landlord who has failed to serve notice at the appropriate time may seek to remedy this by delivering a backdated notice to the tenant. The fact that there may be no documentary evidence to prove the date when notice was served does not prevent a tenant from defending a claim for possession on the grounds that the tenancy is not an assured shorthold tenancy. The tenant can give oral evidence to a court about the circumstances in which the notice was served. If the evidence is disputed the court must decide who is more likely to be telling the truth. In a possession claim the burden is on the landlord to satisfy the court 'on balance of probabilities'; if the court cannot decide who is telling the truth, the claim should be dismissed.

Understanding the notice

2.68   It is not necessary that the notice is understood by the tenant; serving a notice simply means delivering it to the tenant.[42]

New tenancies granted to existing tenants

Existing assured tenants

2.69   Where a tenant is already an assured tenant the drawing up of a new assured shorthold tenancy and service of a section 20 notice is of no effect. This is the case even if the landlord grants the tenant a tenancy of different premises.

2.70   Section 20(3) of HA 1988 provides that if:

> immediately before a [new] tenancy is granted, the persons to whom it is granted or, as the case may be, at least one of [them], was a tenant under an assured tenancy which was not a shorthold tenancy, and the new tenancy is granted by the person who, immediately before the beginning of the tenancy, was the landlord under the assured tenancy ... the new tenancy cannot be an assured shorthold tenancy.

2.71   A landlord cannot therefore remedy a failure to follow the proper procedure after the start of the tenancy. Simply getting the tenant to sign a new tenancy agreement that is a shorthold agreement will not 'convert' an assured tenancy into an assured shorthold tenancy. However, the circumstances may be such that the old tenancy is deemed to have ended before the commencement of the new tenancy.

---

41   *Bedding v McCarthy* (1993) 27 HLR 103.
42   *Tadema Holdings v Ferguson* (2000) 32 HLR 866.

In *Dibbs v Cambell*[43] it was held that tenants who signed a deed of surrender one day and entered into a new tenancy agreement the following day, were not tenants immediately before the grant of the new agreement. This was the case even though the tenants had not vacated the premises.

Existing assured shorthold tenants

2.72   Where an assured shorthold tenant simply remains in occupation after the end of the fixed term he or she becomes a statutory periodic assured shorthold tenant. It is not necessary for the parties to enter into a new agreement. However, it is common for an assured shorthold tenant to be given a succession of fixed term agreements by a landlord.[44] Section 20(4) of the HA 1988 provides that in such a case it is not necessary for the landlord to comply with the formalities of section 20 each time a new tenancy is granted; any new tenancy will be an assured shorthold tenancy.[45]

Existing 'Rent Act' tenants: HA 1988 s34

2.73   As described below, tenants under the Rent Act 1977 have the strongest rights: the grounds for possession are the most restrictive and rents are controlled by the fair rent system. A landlord would have a strong incentive for wishing to 'convert' a Rent Act tenancy into an assured or assured shorthold tenancy. There is no express protection in terms similar to section 20(3) above. Rather, the position is governed by HA 1988 s34(1) which provides that tenancies entered into on or after 15 January 1989 cannot be protected (under the Rent Act 1977) except in certain circumstances. These circumstances include a tenancy which 'is granted to a person (alone or jointly with others) who, immediately before the tenancy was granted, was a protected or statutory tenant and is so granted by the

---

43 (1988) 20 HLR 372, CA. This case was about similar anti-avoidance provisions to prevent a landlord converting a protected tenancy into a protected shorthold tenancy. Protected shorthold tenancies are described below at para 2.179.

44 Many local authorities insist, incorrectly, that housing benefit is not payable unless a new tenancy agreement is drawn up.

45 The landlord may, however, serve notice that the new tenancy is not to be an assured shorthold tenancy: s20(5).

person who at that time was the landlord (or one of the joint landlords) under the protected or statutory tenancy'.[46]

2.74   Although the terms of section 34 suggest only that it is *possible* to create a new protected tenancy in such a situation, the courts have held that any new tenancy *will* be a protected tenancy, provided the landlord and tenant are the same, even if the tenancy is of different premises.[47]

> In *Rajah v Arogol Co Ltd*[48] the defendant had been a Rent Act tenant of a room on the ground floor of a property since 1982. In 1990 he moved to the entire floor. In possession proceedings the landlord argued that he was no longer a protected tenant. The county court made an order for possession, holding that there had been a surrender of the protected tenancy when the parties entered into a tenancy for the whole floor. The Court of Appeal upheld the tenant's appeal: the protection of section 34(1)(b) of HA 1988 was not limited to the same or substantially the same premises. The move did not constitute a surrender and the defendant retained the protection of the Rent Act.

2.75   It is, however, always necessary that the tenant is a protected or statutory tenancy 'immediately before the [new] tenancy was granted'.

> In *The Governing Body of Rugby School v Edwards*[49] the defendant had been a protected tenant of the claimants. Possession proceedings were brought on the grounds of substantial rent arrears. The proceedings were compromised by a Consent Order which provided that the defendant give up possession in consideration for the claimants agreeing not to enforce payment of the agreed rent arrears of £7,885. It was also agreed, although not part of the consent order, that the claimants would grant to the defendant a three-year assured tenancy of a smaller property. Rent arrears accrued in the new property and a claim for possession

---

46   Section 34(1)(b).
47   *Laimond Properties Ltd v Al Skarcharchi* (1998) 30 HLR 1099.
48   [2001] EWCA Civ 454.
49   Mayors & City County Court, July 2004 *Legal Action* 17.

made. The defendant argued that he was a protected tenant as section 34(1) applied; as such, his case was that rather than being in arrears of £4,500 he had overpaid rent of about £15,000. The district judge, however, found that he had surrendered his previous tenancy as part of the agreement *before* being granted a new tenancy of the smaller property. He was not therefore a protected or statutory tenancy immediately before the grant of the new tenancy and section 34 did not apply. The decision was upheld by a circuit judge.

2.76   Section 34 also enables new protected tenancies to be granted when a possession order is made on the grounds that suitable alternative accommodation is available to the tenant. However, such a tenancy is not automatically protected; rather, section 34(1)(c) permits the court to order that a new tenancy be protected if that is necessary for it to constitute a suitable alternative to the existing accommodation. This is dealt with in chapter 6.

Rent Act 1977: protected and statutory tenancies

2.77   The Rent Act (RA) 1977 governs tenancies granted by private landlords before 15 January 1989. A contractual tenancy which gives a tenant substantive security of tenure under RA 1977 is known as a 'protected tenancy'.

2.78   The Rent Act 1977 has a similar structure to the HA 1988: the Act sets out the conditions for a protected tenancy and a schedule lists the types of tenancy that cannot be protected. However, the way in which security of tenure operates is different. Under the HA 1988 a landlord cannot bring an assured tenancy to an end except by a court order. Under RA 1977 there is no restriction on the landlord's right to bring the tenancy to an end but, when the protected tenancy ends, a 'statutory tenancy' comes into existence, provided the tenant is residing in the premises. This is why, under RA 1977 the tenancy is known as 'protected' during the contractual term and 'statutory' after the contractual term has ended. Both kinds of tenancy are called 'regulated tenancies'.[50]

---

50 Section 18(1). Under section 18A and Schedule 17 of RA 1977 tenancies governed by previous Rent Acts, known as 'controlled tenancies' were converted into regulated tenancies.

Conditions for protected tenancies

2.79   The tenancy must be one 'under which a dwelling-house (which may be a house or part of a house) is let as a separate dwelling'.[51] See paragraphs 2.10–2.14 above for a discussion of the case law on this condition which also applies under HA 1988.

Sharing with other tenants

2.80   As for assured tenancies, there is specific provision that the sharing of accommodation with other tenants does not prevent the tenancy being protected. The Rent Act 1977 s22 provides that where a tenant has exclusive occupation of separate accommodation but the terms of the agreement include the use of other accommodation in common with others, not being the landlord, the separate accommodation shall be deemed a dwelling-house let on a protected or statutory tenancy. Any term terminating or modifying the right to use the shared living accommodation shall be of no effect but the terms may provide for a variation and/or increase in the number of persons with whom the tenant must share.

Ending the protected tenancy

2.81   As the RA 1977 places no restriction on a landlord's right to end a tenancy, the service of a notice to quit ends a periodic protected tenancy.

2.82   A fixed term protected tenancy ends when the fixed term expires ('by effluxion of time').

2.83   Whether the tenancy ends by notice to quit or at the end of a fixed period, a tenant who remains in residence becomes a statutory tenant and can only be evicted if a possession order is obtained. A possession order will only be made if one of the statutory grounds is proved.

2.84   Further, a notice of rent increase operates to convert a periodic protected tenancy into a statutory tenancy.[52]

2.85   Even where a tenant serves notice to quit on a landlord this only ends the protected tenancy; the tenant who remains in residence becomes a statutory tenant. There is, however, a ground for possession where the landlord has relied on the notice and contracted to sell or let the premises or is otherwise prejudiced.[53]

51   RA 1977 s1(1).
52   RA 1977 s49(4).
53   RA 1977 Sch 15, Case 5, see appendix to chapter 6.

The statutory tenancy

2.86 RA 1977 s2(1)(a) provides that:

> after the termination of a protected tenancy of a dwelling-house the person who, immediately before that termination, was the protected tenant of the dwelling-house shall, if and so long as he occupies the dwelling-house as his residence, be the statutory tenant of it.

Security of tenure

2.87 A protected or statutory tenant cannot be evicted by a landlord unless either:[54]

- one of the grounds for possession is proved to a court; or
- suitable alternative accommodation is available to the tenant.

2.88 As is the case under the Housing Acts 1985 and 1988 security of tenure is only enjoyed if a person is occupying the premises as a home. Under RA 1977 the statutory tenant must be occupying premises as his or her residence[55] and under the Housing Acts he or she must occupy premises as his or her only or principal home. The residence condition is discussed in detail below at paragraphs 3.2–3.12.

Exceptions to Rent Act protection

2.89 The RA 1977 lists those tenancies that cannot be protected:

- tenancies with a high rateable value (section 4);[56]
- tenancies under which no rent or a low rent is paid. A low rent is a rent of less than two thirds of the rateable value (section 5);[57]
- dwelling houses let with more than two acres of agricultural land (sections 6 and 26);

---

54 RA 1977 ss98 and 99.
55 It is not necessary that a protected tenant resides in the premises. It is unlikely that many RA tenancies are still protected. This will only be the case if the original contract is still in existence and no notice to quit or notice of rent increase has been served since the tenancy started.
56 What constitutes a high rateable value depends on when the tenancy was granted and whether the property is in Greater London or elsewhere. See RA 1977 s25. Rates on domestic premises were abolished in 1990. Few local authorities keep old ratings lists but archived lists may be held by local libraries.
57 Again, the relevant rateable value depends on when and where the tenancy was granted and it may be necessary to consulted archived ratings lists.

- tenancies which include payments for board or attendance provided the payment forms a substantial part of the rent: section 7. Board means the provision of food (as in 'board and lodgings'). Attendances means the provision of services personal to the tenancy, such as room cleaning and the supply of clean linen;
- certain tenancies granted to students by specified educational institutions: section 8. The conditions are the same as under the HA 1988, see para 2.28 above;
- holiday lets: section 9;
- tenancies of agricultural holdings and farm business lets: section 10, see para 2.185 below;
- tenancies of licensed premises: section 11;
- tenancies where there is a resident landlord: section 12. This is discussed in detail at paras 3.14–3.27;
- crown tenancies: section 13;
- business tenancies: section 24. Mixed business and residential tenancies are discussed at paras 1.133–1.136;
- tenancies granted by exempt landlords such as local authorities, housing associations and housing co-operatives (sections 14, 15 and 16).

In most cases, even if a tenancy cannot be protected for one of the above reasons, it will be a contractual tenancy and the tenant's rights will depend on the agreed terms. In most cases the tenant will be protected from eviction without a court order, see chapter 7.

Restricted contracts

2.90   Under RA 1977 some tenancies were 'restricted contracts' under which tenants had limited rights: the possible postponement of a notice to quit and some rent control. A restricted contract was created in two situations:

- where there was a resident landlord; and
- where the tenant made payments for board but where the payments were not substantial.

The majority of restricted contracts were granted by resident landlords. No new restricted contracts can be granted after 15 January 1989 and any change in the terms of the agreement, including a rent increase, after that date will mean that the tenancy is no longer a restricted contract but is governed by the HA 1988 (or, more correctly falls outside the HA 1988 and is simply a contractual tenancy).

Fair rents

2.91   Under the RA 1977 all protected and statutory tenants have the right to have a 'fair rent' registered. This will be the maximum rent that can be charged. The fair rent system is explained below at paragraphs 3.173–3.174.

'Sitting tenants' and being 'bought out'

2.92   The term 'sitting tenant' refers to a tenant who is entitled to remain in occupation of premises so that if ownership of the premises changes the new owner takes the premises subject to the tenant's interest. Tenancies, being interests in land, bind a purchaser.[58] A landlord cannot evict a tenant simply because he or she wishes to sell, or because he or she has just purchased the premises and wishes to obtain vacant possession.

2.93   Clearly, some tenancies can be ended more easily than others; an owner with an assured shorthold tenant in occupation can evict the tenant by serving two months notice and obtaining a possession order through the accelerated procedure (see chapter 5) before selling with vacant possession. Alternatively, a purchaser can obtain possession in the same way following completion of the purchase. Because a statutory tenant under RA 1977 has the strongest rights possible, the term 'sitting tenant' is usually used to refer to such tenants. An owner of premises subject to a statutory tenancy may wish to pay the tenant a sum of money to give up his or her tenancy. The question arises: how is such an interest valued?

2.94   There is no statutory formula for determining the value of a tenant's interest. Any agreement will depend on how much the landlord is prepared to pay and how much the tenant is prepared to accept. A tenant who wishes to move in with family members may accept less than someone who needs to secure alternative accommodation. If the tenant is elderly the landlord may prefer to keep the property until the tenant dies rather than pay a substantial sum to gain vacant possession.

2.95   If negotiating such an agreement, the tenant may wish to obtain expert valuation evidence as the increased value of the property with vacant possession is often underestimated. However, agreement

58   Land Registration Act 2002 Sch 1 and 3.

always depends on reaching a compromise and if a landlord is unwilling to pay the amount asked by the tenant, the tenant will remain in occupation as a statutory tenancy. Advisers should be aware, however, that a possession order may be made by a court if suitable alternative accommodation is available to the tenant. A landlord may choose to offer alternative accommodation to obtain vacant possession rather than pay the tenant to leave. Suitable alternative accommodation as a ground for possession is discussed at paragraphs 6.81–6.90.

Local authority tenancies

2.96   Tenancies under which the landlord is a local authority will be one of the following:

- a secure tenancy – a long term tenancy with security of tenure;
- an introductory tenancy – granted initially for a probationary period before becoming secure;
- a demoted tenancy; or
- a non-secure tenancy – a tenancy which is excluded from being secure.

Housing association secure tenancies

2.97   Before 15 January 1989 housing associations also granted secure tenancies, governed by HA 1985. Tenants of housing associations whose tenancy started before that date will remain secure tenants, while tenants whose tenancy was granted on or after that date will be assured tenants.

2.98   The secure tenants of housing associations have the same rights as the secure tenants of local authorities with two main differences: (1) secure tenants of housing associations do not have the 'right to buy' and (2) secure tenancies of housing associations are subject to the fair rent scheme under Rent Act 1977, this is described at paragraph 3.173.

Secure tenancies

Conditions for secure tenancies

2.99   The Housing Act 1985 Part IV sets out the conditions for creating secure tenancies and the rights of secure tenants.

The conditions for the creation of a secure tenancy are that:

- the premises are 'let as a separate dwelling';
- the landlord condition is satisfied;
- the tenant condition is satisfied; and
- the tenancy is not excluded by Schedule 1.

Separate dwelling

2.100   Section 79(1) provides that the tenancy must be one 'under which a dwelling-house is let as a separate dwelling'.

2.101   As in all of the statutes that provide for security of tenure this is a condition that must be met for a secure tenancy to exist, see paragraphs 2.9–2.14 above.

2.102   Unlike tenancies in the private sector there is no provision for a secure tenancy where a tenant has possession of a room only, with shared use of other accommodation. Such a letting cannot be a secure tenancy because there is no letting of a separate dwelling.

Secure licences

2.103   Section 79(3) provides that the rights of secure tenants, not including the right to buy, apply also to licensees of dwelling houses (except those granted to trespassers as a temporary measure, see paragraph 2.106 below). So, under the HA 1985 there is the possibility of a 'secure licence'.

2.104   One situation in which a secure licence may be granted is when a right to occupy is granted to a person under the age of 18 years. A minor cannot legally hold a tenancy but there are two possible ways of granting a right to occupy to a child. Either a secure licence can be granted until the child reaches the age of 18 when it will become a tenancy, or a secure tenancy can be granted, to be held on trust by some other person for the benefit of the child, until he or she reaches the age of 18, see paragraph 1.139 for an explanation of such trusts.

2.105   Additionally, an occupier of a single room who shares facilities with others may have a secure licence provided he or she has exclusive possession of the room.[59]

2.106   A licence may also be granted to a trespasser as a 'temporary expedient' pending the recovery of possession. Such a licence will not be secure and the trespasser/licensee is an excluded occupier,

---

59 *Westminster CC v Clarke* (1992) 24 HLR 360, HL.

who can be evicted without a court order after the licence is ended.[60]

Landlord and tenant conditions

2.107   In addition, a tenancy will only be secure if the landlord and the tenant conditions are satisfied. Section 79 provides that the tenancy will be secure 'at any time when' those conditions are satisfied. The same tenancy may therefore be at one time secure and at another time not secure if the conditions are not met, eg there is a change of landlord or the tenant ceases to live in the premises.

Landlord condition

2.108   Section 80 provides that the landlord must be one of the following specified authorities or bodies:

- a local authority;
- a new town corporation;
- a housing action trust;
- an urban development corporation; or
- a certain kind of housing co-operative (see paragraph 2.110 below).

2.109   However, before 15 January 1989 most housing trusts and housing associations could grant secure tenancies. A secure tenancy granted by such a body before that date will remain secure and the following notes therefore apply also to the secure tenants of housing trusts and housing associations.

Housing co-operatives

2.110   Most housing co-operatives are 'fully mutual' associations registered under the Industrial and Provident Societies Act 1965.[61] Such organisations cannot grant secure tenancies and the tenants of such co-ops do not enjoy any substantive security of tenure. They are non-profit making organisations run by the members who are also the tenants of the co-op. The tenants' rights will be set out in the tenancy agreement and the rules of the association.

---

60   HA 1985 s79(4) and PEA 1977 s3A.

61   The registering authority for such societies is currently the Financial Services Authority (FSA) whose website, www.fsa.gov.uk, gives information about the registration requirements.

2.111   Housing co-operatives are sometimes employed as agents by local authorities to manage their accommodation.[62] In such a case the tenancies can be secure as the landlord is the local authority and not the co-op. The tenancy agreement should make this clear but, in cases of doubt, a tenant is entitled to be informed of the identity of his or her landlord, see paragraphs 3.127–3.137 below.

The tenant condition

2.112   Section 81 provides that the tenant must be an individual who occupies the dwelling house as his or her only or principal home. If there are joint tenants each must be an individual and at least one of them must occupy the premises as his or her only or principal home.

2.113   If at any time the tenant condition is not met, i.e. the tenant is not occupying the premises as his or her only or principal home, the tenant stops being a secure tenant. He or she enjoys only a non-secure contractual tenancy at this time. However, the secure status can be regained if the tenant resumes occupation as his or her only or principal home, provided there has not been a sub-letting or parting with possession of the whole of the premise, see paragraph 3.11.

Exceptions

2.114   Certain tenancies cannot be secure. These are set out in Schedule 1 of HA 1985 and are:

Long leases: para 1

2.115   A 'long tenancy' is defined in section 115 and includes a lease granted for a fixed period of more than 21 years and any lease granted under the right to buy or right to acquire provisions.[63]

Introductory tenancies: para 1A

2.116   Introductory tenancies are governed by Part V of the HA 1996, see paragraphs 2.144–2.162 below. Also excluded are tenancies that have ceased to be introductory following the death of the tenant or where the tenant is not occupying as his or her only or principal home.

---

62 See HA 1985 s27.
63 The 'right to buy' enjoyed by secure tenants is set out in Part V of the HA 1985. The 'right to acquire' for assured tenants of RSLs is set out in sections 16–17 Housing Act 1996. Both schemes are outside the scope of this book.

Tenancies granted to employees: para 2

2.117   Tenancies granted to employees of the landlord or certain specified bodies where it is a condition of the employment contract that the employee occupies the dwelling house for the better performance of his or her duties.[64]

2.118   Those who are required to occupy accommodation owned by an employer for the better performance of the employment duties will, under the common law, be licensees and not tenants (see chapter 1). However, this exception to secure status extends to those who are employed by one specified body and accommodated by another. The specified bodies are:

- local authorities;
- new town corporations;
- housing actions trusts;
- urban development corporations; and
- the governors of an aided school.

2.119   In all cases the employment contract must specify that the employee must live in the particular accommodation.

2.120   This exclusion also deals specifically with rent-free accommodation provided to the police and fire authority employees.

2.121   Where the landlord is a local housing authority the tenancy does not become secure unless the authority notifies the tenant that it is secure.

2.122   Where the authority is not a local housing authority the tenancy will become secure automatically if the conditions are not met for a period of three years in aggregate.

Short-life tenancies on land acquired for development: para 3

2.123   Tenancies granted to provide temporary accommodation on land acquired for development, pending the development. Development is defined by section 55 of the Town and Country Planning Act 1990: 'the carrying out of building, engineering, mining or other operations in, on, and over or under land, or the making of any material change in the use of buildings or other land.'

---

64 Schedule 1 provides that the employment contract may be express or implied and an express contract may be an oral contract. However, a term requiring occupation will only be implied into the employment contract if occupation is necessary in order for the employee to do the job: *Hughes & Hughes v Greenwich LBC* (1993) 26 HLR 99.

2.124   Although the provision is for 'temporary' accommodation the occupiers may be in occupation for long periods, and even under long fixed term lettings, provided development is pending. The exception applies even if the identity of the landlord changes. However, if the development plans are rejected or abandoned and no alternative development plan is pending the exception will cease to apply and any tenants will become secure.[65]

Homeless accommodation: para 4

2.125   Tenancies granted to homeless applicants under HA 1996 Part VII. This includes accommodation pending inquiries and accommodation provided under section 193 following acceptance of a housing duty.

Asylum-seekers: para 4A

2.126   Accommodation provided to asylum-seekers under Part VI of the Immigration and Asylum Act 1999 (ie, by arrangement with the UK Border Agency. However, the landlord may notify the tenant that the tenancy is to become secure. This will only happen if the asylum seeker is granted some form of leave and becomes entitled to an allocation under Part VI HA 1996 (see chapter 16).

Temporary accommodation to people taking up employment: para 5

2.127   This exception applies to schemes under which an authority offers temporary accommodation to those taking up employment in the district or surrounding area. The tenant must be informed in writing, before the grant of the tenancy, that the exception applies. Unless the authority is a local housing authority the tenancy will automatically become secure one year after the start of the tenancy. In the case of a local housing authority the tenancy will only become secure if the authority notifies the tenant. In practice, such schemes are now rare.

Short term sub-leasing schemes: para 6

2.128   Where the accommodation has been leased to the landlord for use as temporary housing accommodation, with a provision that vacant possession will be given back by the landlord after a certain period. This exception covers 'private sector leasing' (PSL) arrangements

---

65 *Lillieshall Road Housing Co-operative Ltd v Brennan & Brennan* (1991) 24 HLR 195, CA.

in which private landlords let vacant property to a local authority or housing association who then sublet the accommodation on a temporary basis to homeless applicants.

Temporary accommodation during works: para 7

2.129   Where a tenancy is offered to a person on a temporary basis to enable works to be carried out to the tenant's home. The exception does not apply if the tenant was already a secure tenant of the home being repaired. In such a case the tenant will become a secure tenant of the temporary accommodation but there is a discretionary ground for possession available to the landlord to compel the tenant to return to the repaired property.

2.130   This provision enables an authority to offer to a private or RSL tenant temporary accommodation to facilitate the landlord carrying out major works. In the past some authorities had a policy of doing this when serving repair or improvement notices on private landlords where vacant possession was needed to complete the major works. However, given the shortage of local authority accommodation such policies are now rare.

Agricultural holdings: para 8

2.131   Tenancies granted to tenants who are also engaged in farming land where the accommodation is part of an agricultural land. Such tenancies are governed by the Agricultural Holdings Act 1986 and the Agricultural Tenancies Act 1995 (see para 2.185 below).

Licences premises: para 9

2.132   A tenancy of premises or part of premises licensed for the sale of intoxicating liquor for consumption on the premises.

Specified student lettings: para 10

2.133   A tenancy granted to a student to enable the tenant to attend a designated course at a university or further education establishment is not a secure tenancy. In this case a written notice must be served on the tenant before the tenancy is granted, stating that the tenancy falls within this exception and specifying the proposed educational establishment.

2.134   Unless the landlord is a local authority the tenancy will automatically become secure six months after the tenant ceases to attend the designated course (or, if the tenant fails to take up the course, six months from the date of grant). If the landlord is a local authority the tenancy will only become secure if the landlord notifies the tenant.

Business tenancies: para 11

2.135 A tenancy of premises occupied primarily for business purposes is governed by the Landlord and Tenant Act 1954. See chapter 1 for the issues arising when there is mixed business and residential use.

Almshouses: para 12

2.136 A licence to occupy an almshouse dwelling will not be a secure tenancy. Almshouse occupiers are licensees and not tenants because the grant of the right of occupation is a charitable act.[66] The licence must have been granted by or on behalf of a charity which is authorised to maintain the dwelling house as an almshouse and which has no power to grant a tenancy of the dwelling house.

Becoming a secure tenant of a local authority

2.137 It should be noted that where there is provision for tenancies to become secure by default, after a certain period (paras 2, 4A, 5 and 10), if the landlord is a local authority the tenancy will only become secure if the authority notifies the tenant. This is to ensure that only those who qualify for an allocation of accommodation under Part VI of the HA 1996 become local authority tenants.

The features of a secure tenancy

Security of tenure

2.138 HA 1985 s82 provides that a secure tenancy can only be ended by a landlord by obtaining a possession order. The tenancy ends on the date on which the tenant is to give up possession in pursuance of the order.

2.139 Section 84 provides that a possession order will only be made on one of more of the possession grounds set out in Schedule 2 to HA 1985.

2.140 The grounds for possession are set out in the appendix to chapter 6. They include grounds in which it is alleged the tenant is at fault,

---

66 *Gray v Taylor* [1998] 1 WLR 1093 CA.

which are all discretionary. In addition, there are grounds which depend on the landlord making available suitable alternative accommodation for the tenant. Some of these grounds are discretionary and some mandatory. These grounds enable public sector landlords to exercise control over the occupancy of accommodation designed for those with special needs and to forcibly re-house tenants to facilitate development.

Other statutory rights

2.141   Secure tenants also have the following additional statutory rights:

- succession – the right to pass the tenancy to a partner or family member after death;
- transfer of the tenancy – in limited circumstances;
- mutual exchange – the right to 'swap' the tenancy with an other tenant of a social landlords;
- the right to take in lodgers;
- the right to make improvements;
- the right to buy the property.

HA 1985 s110 provides that the county court has the power to deal with all disputes regarding the rights of secure tenants.

Variation of secure tenancies

2.142   A feature peculiar to the secure tenancy regime is that the landlord has the right to vary the terms of a periodic secure tenancy. The general rule is that once a contract has been entered into, both parties are bound by the agreed terms and can only vary the terms by agreement. However, HA 1985 provides that a landlord can unilaterally vary the terms of the tenancy agreement by following the procedure set out in section 103. This requires the landlord to serve notice of variation on the tenant in advance and to invite comment. The variation cannot take effect sooner than four weeks from the date of the notice.

2.143   The right to buy is outside the scope of this book. The other rights are discussed in chapter 3.

Introductory tenancies

2.144   The 'introductory tenancy' was created by the Housing Act (HA) 1996.[67] Local authorities and housing action trusts (HATs) may adopt

---

67 The introductory tenancy scheme is set out in Part V of HA 1996 and came into force on 12 February 1997.

a scheme whereby all new tenancies, which would otherwise be secure, are 'probationary' tenancies for an initial period of one year. If an authority operates an introductory tenancy scheme it must grant introductory tenancies to *all* new tenants.[68] An authority cannot offer introductory tenancies to particular tenants or types of tenants and unless a scheme has been adopted it has no power to grant any form of introductory or probationary tenancy.

2.145   An exception is where a new tenancy is granted to someone who was already a secure tenant or an assured tenant of an RSL of the same or another dwelling.[69] In such a case he or she will not become an introductory tenant.

Conditions of an introductory tenancy

2.146   If a housing authority or HAT has elected to operate a regime of introductory tenancies, every periodic tenancy entered into shall, if it would otherwise be secure, be an introductory tenancy.[70] So, if a tenancy could not be a secure tenancy, because the necessary conditions are not met, it cannot be an introductory tenancy. The conditions for a secure tenancy are described at paras 2.99–2.114 above.

The features of an introductory tenancy

2.147   An introductory tenant has limited security of tenure; the landlord may serve notice that it has been decided to apply to the court for a possession order. The notice must give reasons and advise the tenant of the right to request a review of the decision by the authority (see para 5.65). The conduct of the review is governed by regulations (see 5.78).

2.148   If no review is requested or the decision is confirmed on review, an application may be made for a possession order. It has been held in a number of cases that the court cannot entertain a defence to a claim for possession based on an allegation that the review process was not conducted fairly. However, recent cases in the House of Lords and the European Court of Human Rights suggest otherwise (see para 5.81 and chapter 6).

---

68   HA 1996 s124(2).
69   HA 1996 s124(2)(a) and (b).
70   HA 1996 s124(2).

2.149   Introductory tenancies were introduced as part of a raft of measures to tackle anti-social behaviour. However, most introductory tenancies are terminated because of rent arrears.

Licences[71]

2.150   Where an authority or HAT has made an election to use introductory tenancies any licences granted will be subject to the same rules.

2.151   An exception is a licence granted to trespassers as a temporary expedient. Such licensees remain excluded occupiers.

The 'trial' period

2.152   The tenancy will remain an introductory tenancy until one year has passed unless:[72]

- the circumstances are such that the tenancy would no longer be secure, eg the tenant no longer lives in the dwelling house as his or her only or principal home;
- a person or body other than the authority or HAT becomes the landlord;
- the election (to operate a scheme of introductory tenancies) is revoked;
- the tenant dies and there is no one entitled to succeed:
- the period of the introductory tenancy is extended by the authority (see para 2.157 below);
- the landlord starts a claim for possession (see chapter 5).

2.153   At the end of the one-year period, if none of the above has happened, the tenancy automatically becomes secure.

2.154   The one-year period is calculated from:

- the date the tenancy is entered into; or
- if later, the date on which the tenant becomes entitled to possession; or,
- if the tenancy is adopted by the authority or HAT, from the date of the adoption.[73]

---

71 HA 1996 s126.

72 HA 1996 s125(5).

73 A tenancy is adopted if the landlord changes because of a disposal or surrender and the new landlord is a local authority or HAT that operates an introductory tenancy scheme. Such a tenancy will only become an introductory tenancy if it was not a secure or assured tenancy granted by an RSL. See HA 1996 s124(2) and (4).

Previous probationary tenancies

2.155 Any time immediately prior to a new tenancy during which the tenant was an introductory tenant of another landlord or another property, or an assured shorthold tenant of a registered social landlord,[74] will count towards the trial period, provided there is no interruption in the cumulative period.[75]

2.156   Where the introductory tenants are joint tenants the trial period starts at the earliest date when any of the joint tenants was a probationary tenant under a previous tenancy agreement.[76]

Extending the trial period

2.157 A landlord may extend the introductory tenancy for six months. Notice must be served on the tenant giving reasons and the tenant has the right to seek a review of the decision.[77]

The statutory rights of introductory tenants

2.158 Introductory tenants have rights similar to those of secure tenants in relation to succession but more limited rights of assignment. These are described at paras 3.31–3.82. No specific provision is made regarding lodgers and sub-letting. Introductory tenants also have the same rights to have repairs carried out as all other short-term tenants. These are dealt with in chapter 9.

Information about introductory tenancies

2.159 Authorities or HATs operating introductory tenancies must from time to time publish information about such tenancies, in whatever form it considers most suitable, and 'so far as it considers it appropriate' to explain in simple terms:[78]

- the express terms of its introductory tenancies;

---

74 RSLs cannot grant introductory tenancies. However, if they wish to operate 'probationary' or 'starter' tenancies they may do so by granting assured shorthold tenancies for an initial period. However, such tenancies do not automatically become assured after the initial period: the landlord must serve a notice indicating that the tenancy is no longer an assured shorthold tenancy or a new assured tenancy agreement must be entered into.

75 HA 1996 s125(3).

76 HA 1996 s125(4).

77 See section 179 of the Housing Act 2004; see sections 125A and 125B of HA 1996.

78 HA 1996 s136.

- the law relating to introductory tenancies;
- the implied repairing obligations.

2.160   This information should be supplied to a tenant who is granted an introductory tenancy together with a written statement of the terms of the tenancy. This should be given to the tenant on the grant of the tenancy, 'or as soon as practicable afterwards'.

Consultation

2.161   An authority or HAT that lets dwelling houses on introductory tenancies must maintain arrangements to consult introductory tenants regarding matters of housing management likely to substantially affect such tenants.[79]

Powers of the county court

2.162   As is the case for secure tenancies, a county court has the power to determine questions arising under the provisions of Part V of the HA 1996.

Demoted tenancies

2.163   A demoted tenancy is one that was previously secure but that has been 'demoted' by the court, on the landlord's application. Demotion is often sought as an alternative to possession, see chapter 5. A demotion order has the effect of bringing to an end a secure tenancy and replacing it with a demoted tenancy.

2.164   The nature of a demoted tenancy is similar to an introductory tenancy.

The features of a demoted tenancy

2.165   A demoted tenancy remains demoted for 12 months before becoming secure again, unless during the 12 months the landlord applies for possession.[80]

---

79 HA 1996 s137.
80 HA 1996 s143B(1). The tenancy also ceases to be a demoted tenancy if the landlord or tenant conditions are not met, if the demotion order is quashed, or if the tenant dies and there is no one to succeed to the tenancy: HA 1996 s143B(2).

2.166   There is a right to succeed to a demoted tenancy if the tenant dies, but the conditions are slightly different to those applying to secure or introductory tenancies,[81] see para 3.33. A demoted tenant may only assign the tenancy pursuant to a court order made in the event of relationship breakdown or for the benefit of children.[82]

2.167   A demoted tenant does not have substantive security of tenure: a landlord need not prove a statutory ground for possession in order to obtain a possession order.

2.168   A landlord may decide to seek a possession order against a demoted tenant for any reason. A notice of intention to seek possession must be served setting out the reasons and informing the tenant of the right to request an internal review of the decision. The review procedure is governed by regulation.[83]

2.169   If the review confirms the decision, or the tenant fails to request a review, the court must make a possession order against a demoted tenant unless the proper procedure has not been followed by the landlord. However, see para 5.81.

2.170   The procedure for seeking possession of a demoted tenancy is discussed at paras 5.70–5.78.

Non-secure tenancies

2.171   A tenancy that is 'non-secure' is nevertheless still a contractually binding tenancy. Non-secure tenants enjoy the rights that are implied into all tenancy agreements such as the right to have repairs carried out by the landlord and the right to peaceful enjoyment of the premises. Non-secure tenants do not have substantive security of tenure. However, unless the letting is 'excluded' from the Protection from Eviction Act 1977, see para 1.101, a landlord who wishes to evict must serve notice to quit to end the tenancy and obtain a possession order.

2.172   A non-secure tenancy must be ended by service of a notice to quit before a claim for possession can be made. Once the tenancy has come to an end the landlord has a right of possession and need not prove any grounds, see para 5.

---

81   HA 1996 s143H–J.

82   HA 1996 s143K.

83   The Demoted Tenancies (Review of Decisions)(England) Regulations 2004 (SI No 1679) and the Demoted Tenancies (Review of Decisions)(Wales) Regulations 2005 (SI No 1228, W86).

Other types of tenancy

2.173 Most residential tenancies fall into one of the categories described above. However, advisers may also come across the following types of tenancy:

- assured tenancies created under the Housing Act 1980; and
- protected shorthold tenancies.

2.174 'Old style' assured tenancies created under HA 1980 will have automatically become 'new style' assured tenancies under HA 1988.[84]

2.175 Protected shorthold tenancies are described briefly below.

2.176 In addition there are different statutory schemes that govern tenancies of agricultural land and agricultural holdings. These are also described briefly below.

'Unprotected tenancies'

2.177 Many tenancies cannot be any of main types of tenancy as they fall outside the provisions of the RA 1977 and the HAs 1985 and 1988. The most common reasons for this are:

- the tenant does not reside in the premises (see paras 3.2–3.4);
- the tenant has a resident landlord (see paras 3.13–3.27);
- the tenant has been granted a 'non-secure' tenancy by a local authority following a homeless application;
- the tenancy is excluded for some other reason, such as, for example, a very low or very high rent, or because the premises are licensed for the sale of alcohol.[85]

2.178 Such tenancies are sometimes referred to as 'unprotected tenancies' or 'contractual tenancies'. The tenant has only the rights under the tenancy agreement. He or she does not enjoy substantive security of tenure: the landlord can end the tenancy and is entitled to possession when the tenancy ends. However, it will be necessary to bring a claim for possession in order to evict the tenant unless the tenancy is an excluded letting (see para 1.101).

---

84 These tenancies were introduced to encourage the expansion of private sector lettings. They were modelled on the business code and a market rent was payable. Sections 1(3) and 37 of HA 1988 provides that such tenancies were converted into 'new style' assured tenancies when HA 1988 came into force.

85 All of the exceptions under the various statutes are listed above.

Protected shorthold tenancies

2.179 The protected shorthold tenancy (PST) was an early attempt to enable private landlords to grant short-term tenancies. They are now very rare. Under the Housing Act (HA) 1980 the following conditions must have been met in order to create a PST:[86]

- the tenancy was for a fixed term of not less than one year and not more than five years;
- there was no provision for the landlord to end the tenancy before the expiry of the fixed term;[87]
- before the grant of the tenancy, the landlord must have given to the tenant a notice in prescribed form, stating the tenancy was to be a protected shorthold. However, on a claim for possession the court has the power to waive this requirement if it is just and equitable to make a possession order;[88]
- if there was not already a registered rent, the landlord must apply for rent to be registered no later than 28 days after the beginning of the period of the tenancy;

If those conditions were not met the tenancy created will have been a protected tenancy, provided the relevant conditions were satisfied. Such a tenancy is likely now to have become a statutory tenancy. Under section 55(2) of HA 1980 the court has a discretion to waive those requirement if it is 'just and equitable' to do so.

2.180 A landlord cannot grant a PST to a tenant who, immediately before the grant, was a protected or statutory tenant.[89] So, a tenancy cannot be 'converted' into a PST if the initial requirements were not met.

A PST becoming an assured shorthold tenancy

2.181 The Housing Act 1988 provides that no new PST can be created on or after 15 January 1989.[90] Further, if a tenancy is entered into after that date by the same landlord and tenant as at the coming to an end of the PST, the new agreement will be an assured shorthold tenancy regardless of whether the conditions under HA 1988 s20 were not met.[91]

---

86 HA 1980 s52(1).
87 Excepting a right of forfeiture or re-entry.
88 See appendix to chapter 6.
89 HA 1980 s52(2).
90 HA 1988 s34(1).
91 HA 1988 s34(3).

Claiming possession of a PST

2.182   If a tenancy is still a PST there is a mandatory ground for possession but the landlord must serve notice on the tenant before bringing a claim for possession. The notice must be served within three months of the anniversary of the end of the PST.[92]

Occupiers of agricultural land

2.183   A distinction is made between those who occupy agricultural land by virtue of their employment in agriculture (farm workers) and those who occupy agricultural land as farmers or farm managers. The occupation rights of farm workers are governed by statutory schemes similar to RA 1977 and HA 1988 while the rights of farmers and farm managers are similar to those of business tenants.

Farm workers and former farm workers

2.184   The key features of the statutory schemes are as follows:

- Special protection is given to tenants and licensees who work in agriculture and forestry. Such occupiers are referred to as 'agricultural occupiers'.
- An agricultural occupier may be protected even though he or she pays a low rent, or no rent at all.
- The rights of most agricultural occupiers whose agreement began before 15 January 1989 are governed by the Rent (Agriculture) Act 1976 which is similar to Rent Act 1977. Protected agreements are called 'protected occupancies' and 'statutory tenancies'.
- For those whose agreement began on or after 15 January 1989, chapter III of Part I of HA 1988 applies. Sections 24–26 provide that an assured tenancy, other than an assured shorthold tenancy, will be an 'assured agricultural occupancy'.
- Many agricultural occupiers are required to live in the premises as a condition of their employment for the better performance of their employment duties. Under the common law such an occupier cannot be a tenant, see paras 1.36–1.39. Under both the 1976 Act and HA 1988 protection extends to agricultural licensees (ie service occupiers), provided they have exclusive possession.

92   RA 1977 Sch 15, Case 19.

- Under both Acts certain conditions must be met regarding the employment of the occupier in agriculture or forestry for a minimum period.[93]
- Protection may continue even after the agricultural occupier has retired. However, to facilitate efficient management of agricultural land, the landlord will have a right to possession if suitable alternative accommodation is available, provided either by the landlord or the local authority.
- Special provision is made for unprotected agricultural occupiers in section 4 of the Protection from Eviction Act 1977: a court may suspend the execution of a possession order for up to six months.

Farmers and farm managers

2.185   Protection under the 1976 Act and under sections 24–26 of HA 1988 is given to a person who is employed in agriculture. The tenants of agricultural holdings, who are in control of the holding, do not enjoy this protection. They are excluded from RA 1977, HA 1985 and HA 1988.

Such agreements will usually be governed by the Agricultural Holdings Act 1986 or the Agricultural Tenancies Act 1995, which operate on a similar basis to the Landlord and Tenant Act 1954 which applies to business tenancies.

In addition, under RA 1977 and HA 1988 a tenancy cannot be protected or assured if it includes more than two acres of agricultural land, even if the main purpose of the letting is to provide a home.

93 See Rent (Agriculture) Act 1976 s1(1) and HA 1988 Sch 3.

Common issues for tenants

continued

continued

Key points

- To enjoy substantive security of tenure a tenant must satisfy a residence condition: he or she must live in a dwelling as his or her home. During an extended absence a person may continue to satisfy the residence condition provided there is an intention to return and physical evidence of this.
- Tenants with resident landlords do not enjoy substantive security of tenure but the landlord must be resident when the tenancy starts and continuously throughout.
- If a tenant dies the tenancy may be passed to a family member who lives with the tenant by succession. Each scheme of protection has different conditions for succession.
- Assignment of a tenancy means transferring it to someone else. Mostly this is prohibited except in specific circumstances.
- Sub-letting is when the tenant grants a tenancy to someone else but retains his or her tenancy. Sub-letting is mostly prohibited in short-term residential tenancies.
- There is statutory provision for a tenant to obtain information about the identity of his or her landlord. Failure to provide information may be a criminal offence.
- Since 6 April 2007 there has been a mandatory scheme for the protection of rent deposits paid in respect of assured shorthold tenancies. A landlord who fails to protect the deposit in one of the prescribed schemes cannot serve a possession notice until the deposit is protected. Further the court can award the tenant a sum equivalent to three times the deposit.
- Terms in tenancy agreements that are unfair may be unenforceable. Only a court can declare a term to be unenforceable.
- Tenants under assured tenancies have little rent control: rents are set at market levels. Tenants under the Rent Act and housing association secure tenants have strong rent control: fair rents are set by the rent officer. For local authority tenants the authority must set a 'reasonable rent'. These tend to be much lower than market rents.

3.1   This chapter examines issues that commonly arise in relation to residential tenancies and explains how the rules apply to each type of tenancy. The following issues are considered:

- the tenancy condition – residing in the premises;
- resident landlords;
- succession (the tenancy passing to another on the death of the tenant);
- assignment (transfer of the tenancy);
- sub-letting;
- obtaining information about a landlord;
- rent deposits;
- unfair contract terms;
- rent control.

The tenancy condition – residing in the premises

3.2 At common law a tenant is not required to live in the premises let. However, statutory security of tenure is to protect a tenant's home; only a tenant who resides in premises can enjoy security of tenure.

3.3 Under the RA 1977 it is provided that after the (contractual) tenancy ends the tenant remains a statutory tenancy if and so long as he or she occupies the premises as a residence. A statutory tenant can only be evicted if a possession order is made and an order will only be made if a statutory ground for possession is proved. The Housing Acts 1985 and 1988 provide that a tenancy is only secure or assured when the tenant is occupying the premises as his or her only or principal home; the only way a landlord can end a secure or assured tenancy is by obtaining a possession order; and, an order will only be made if a statutory ground for possession is proved.

3.4 It should be noted that the condition under the RA 1977 is not so strict as under the Housing Acts: occupation as *a residence* is required as opposed to occupation as the tenant's *only or principal home*. In several cases concerning Rent Act tenants it was held that a person can occupy more than one dwelling as a residence. Under the Housing Acts the dwelling must be the person's only or principal home to enjoy security of tenure.

Absence of the tenant

3.5 Clearly, a tenant need not be physically present at all times to be residing in premises. It is recognised that a tenant may continue to be resident in premises even during an extended absence. In such a case the tenant may continue to reside in or occupy premises as a home provided that:

- the tenant intends to return; and
- there is some physical evidence of that intention.[1]

In the case of *Amoah v Barking and Dagenham*[2] a secure tenant was sentenced to 12 years imprisonment. He left items of furniture in his flat and appointed a relative to act as a 'caretaker' in his absence. The council served notice to quit and obtained a possession order on the basis that he had lost his secure status.

On appeal it was held that he had retained his secure status. The correct approach was that a prolonged absence raised a presumption that a tenant no longer occupied. That presumption must be rebutted by the tenant who must establish:

(1) an intention to return;
(2) a practical or real possibility of fulfilment of the intention within a reasonable time; and
(3) some outward and visible sign of the intention.

In this case, in spite of the length of the expected absence, the tenant had continued to reside in the premises as his only or principal home and could only be evicted if a ground for possession could be proved.

3.6   It is common for those who are imprisoned to lose their tenancies but this is usually because the tenant cannot ensure that rent is paid during the absence: housing benefit can only be paid for a limited period during a tenant's absence (see paras 8.42–8.49). Sub-letting the whole will result in the loss of security (see para 3.105 below) and an arrangement between family members would only be possible if the family member looking after the premises for the tenant was able to pay the rent without reliance on housing benefit.[3]

3.7   Another common situation is when an elderly tenant becomes unwell and is absent in hospital or a residential home for respite care. Provided the tenant intends to return home he or she should

---

1   *Brown v Brash* [1948] 2 KB 247.
2   [2001] 82 P&CR DG6, CA.
3   This is because housing benefit will not normally be paid where the occupier is a family member of the 'landlord': see para 8.30 below.

be considered to be continuing to reside there.[4] However, a problem may arise when the tenant's physical or mental health deteriorates so that return becomes unlikely or impossible. When the intention to return ends the tenant can no longer be said to reside in the premises. However, care must be taken to ascertain the tenant's enduring intention.

Hammersmith & Fulham LBC v Clarke[5] concerned a frail, elderly tenant who since 1981 had lived in council accommodation that was been adapted for her needs. In 1997 her grandson and wife moved in to look after her and in 1998 a joint right to buy application was submitted. The tenant was subsequently admitted to a nursing home suffering from depression and physical disabilities. While at the nursing home she signed a note prepared by a council social worker stating that she had decided to become a permanent resident of the nursing home and that she no longer intended to return home. The next month the authority served notice to quit and sought possession. The tenant returned home before the trial. Her evidence was that she had gone to the nursing home intending to return home and had signed the note at a time when she was depressed and when her medication had just been sorted out. The claim for possession was dismissed.

The authority appealed arguing that the tenant's earlier intention was irrelevant, that the material date was the date of the expiry of the notice to quit and that the social worker's note was the best evidence of this. The Court of Appeal accepted that the relevant time for determining the tenant's intention was the date of the expiry of the notice but held that the court should focus on 'the enduring intention of that person' and not 'fleeting changes of mind'. This was particularly true of an elderly tenant in poor health whose intentions may have fluctuated from day to day. The judge was entitled to find that the note did not represent the tenant's more general and enduring intention which was borne out by her evidence, the continuing presence of her family and furniture and all the other circumstances.

---

4   See para 8.48 for an explanation of housing benefit entitlement during such an absence.

5   (2002) HLR 37, CA.

3.8   Secure tenants can assign a tenancy to a person who would be entitled to succeed to the tenancy in the event of the tenant's death (see below at para 3.76). However, such an assignment will only be effective to transfer a secure tenancy if, at the date of the assignment, the tenant is still secure, ie still occupying the premises as his or her only or principal home. If assignment is only considered after the tenant has been absent for some time and no longer intends to return home the tenancy will no longer be secure.

Statutory tenancies

3.9   A statutory tenancy arises when a protected tenancy ends provided the tenant is in occupation. Such a tenant 'shall, if and so long as he occupies the dwelling-house as his residence, be the statutory tenant of it'.[6]

Assured tenancies

3.10   The same wording is used in HA 1988: a tenancy is only assured 'if and so long as' the conditions, including occupation as only or principal home, are met.[7]

Secure tenancies

3.11   A secure tenant is secure 'at any time when' the conditions are met, including the condition that the tenant occupies the dwelling as his or her only or principal home.[8] This means that a tenant who has lost secure status by moving out may regain the status of a secure tenant by resuming occupation. A tenancy that is no longer secure can be ended by a landlord's notice to quit but if a tenant resumes occupation before a notice to quit expires, it will have no effect; the tenant will have again become a secure tenant and a secure tenancy can only be ended by a court order.[9] However, if a secure tenant sub-lets the whole of the premises the tenancy ceases to be secure and cannot subsequently become a secure tenancy.[10]

---

6 RA 1977 s2(1)(a).
7 HA 1988 s1(1).
8 HA 1985 ss79(1) and 81.
9 *Hussey v Camden LBC* (1995) 27 HLR 5, CA.
10 HA 1985 s93(2), see para 3.105 below.

Occupation by spouse/civil partner

3.12   The occupation of the spouse or civil partner of the tenant is sufficient to satisfy the tenant condition. This is the case whether the tenancy is assured, statutory or secure. However, this ceases to be the case after the termination of the marriage or civil partnership. If the tenant is out of occupation, it is therefore essential that any transfer of the tenancy takes place before the decree absolute or dissolution of the civil partnership (see chapter 11).

Resident landlords

3.13   Under both RA 1977 and HA 1988 tenants who have a resident landlord, as defined below, do not have substantive security of tenure: they cannot be protected or assured. Under RA 1977 such a tenant had a 'restricted contract', see below, which gave the tenant very limited rights. Under HA 1988 there is no specific provision; the tenancy cannot be assured and is therefore an unprotected or basic contractual tenancy. In both cases although the tenant does not have substantive security of tenure he or she cannot be evicted without a court order, unless the agreement was made on or after 15 January 1989 *and* the landlord and tenant share accommodation (see para 1.101).

Meaning of 'resident landlord'[11]

3.14   A tenant has a resident landlord where:
- the premises let form part of a building, and that building is not a purpose built block of flats;
- the landlord lives in other premises in the same building; and
- has done so since the tenancy began and continuously throughout the tenancy.

The premises

3.15   A landlord may be a resident landlord even if the premises he or she occupies are completely separate from those occupied by the tenant, if they are in the same building. Only purpose built flats are excluded so that a landlord residing in a converted house may be a resident landlord, regardless of when the conversion was completed and even if the premises have separate entrances.

11 The conditions are set out in RA 1977 s12 and HA 1988 Sch 1 para 10.

Landlord's residence

3.16   The landlord must be a resident landlord when the tenancy commences; a landlord who begins to reside in the building after the tenancy started does not become a resident landlord for these purposes. The occupation by any one of joint landlords is sufficient to retain the resident landlord status.[12]

3.17   A tenant who is already protected, statutory or assured, who is granted a new tenancy by the same landlord (whether of the same or different premises in the building) will remain a protected, statutory or assured tenant.[13]

3.18   The residence condition is different under RA 1977 and the HA 1988: under RA 1977 the landlord must 'occupy the premises as a residence'; under HA 1988 the landlord must 'occupy the premises as his or her "only or principal home"'. A landlord who has more than one home may qualify as a resident landlord under RA 1977 whereas under HA 1988 he or she will not unless the premises in the shared building in the only or main home of the landlord.

3.19   If a landlord ceases to satisfy the residence condition, the tenancy will no longer be excluded from the provisions of RA 1977 or HA 1988, see below.

3.20   However, as for tenants, physical absence alone does not mean that a landlord no longer resides in premises. A landlord may continue to satisfy the residence condition provided he or she intends to resume occupation and there is physical evidence of the intention (see para 3.5 above).

Transfer of ownership

3.21   If ownership of the premises changes certain periods of time are disregarded for the purposes of determining continuous residence. These are known as 'periods of disregard'.[14]

Lifetime transfer

3.22   Where ownership of the premises changes during the resident landlord's life, the new owner has 28 days in which to take up occupation. This can be extended to six months if the new landlord gives notice in writing that he or she intends to reside in the premises. This notice must be given within the 28-day period.

---

12 *Cooper v Tait* (1984) 15 HLR 98, CA, and HA 1988 Sch 1, para 10(2).
13 RA 1977 s12(2) and HA 1988 Sch 1 para 10(3).
14 See RA 1977 Sch 2 and HA 1988 Sch I, Part III.

3.23   A new landlord cannot serve a notice to quit during this period unless he or she takes up residence. If he or she fails to take up residence within the 28 days, or six months if extended, the tenancy ceases to be excluded from the protection of either RA 1977 or HA 1988.

Death of resident landlord

3.24   Where the landlord dies and the property passes to personal representatives[15] the residence requirement is deemed to be satisfied for a period of up to two years, commencing with the death of the landlord.

3.25   The difference between a lifetime transfer and a transfer on death should be noted: the PRs of a deceased resident landlord may serve notice to quit to end the tenancy within the two-year period of disregard.[16] If there is a lifetime transfer, the new landlord must actually take up occupation to retain the resident landlord status. Notice to quit cannot be served by a non-resident landlord during the period of disregard: during this period the tenant may only be evicted on a statutory ground, as if he or she were a statutory or assured tenant.

Restricted contracts

3.26   No new restricted contracts may be granted after 15 January 1989. Most will now have ceased to be restricted contracts and become unprotected tenancies, outside the scope of HA 1988. Section 36(2)(a) of HA 1988 provides that if there has been an increase of rent (other than by reference to the rent tribunal), the agreement is treated as though made at the date of the increase and therefore ceases to be a restricted contract. Similarly, a fundamental variation of other terms would mean that a new agreement was entered into at the date of the variation.

---

15 Personal representatives means executors named in the will or, where there is no will, anyone who applies, as next of kin, for authority to deal with the estate (known as 'letters of administration').

16 The situation is more complicated under RA 1977 in that if the landlord's interest is vested in trustees (including the trustee in bankruptcy) or the Public Trustee (as happens if the landlord dies without a will) up to two years is disregarded, during which no notice to quit can be served. If the premises then pass to PRs, appointed to deal with the estate, there is a further period of up to two years during which the resident landlord condition is deemed to be satisfied so that notice to quit can be served.

Landlord ceasing to be resident

3.27   If the resident landlord condition ceases to be met, the tenant is no longer excluded from the provisions of the relevant Act. However, one issue remains unclear: whether the type of tenancy is determined by the date of the commencement of the original tenancy or the date it ceases to be excluded. This will be significant if the tenancy commenced between 15 January 1989 and 28 February 1997 and the landlord ceases to be resident after 28 February 1997. If the date of commencement of the tenancy is decisive it will be an assured tenancy unless the landlord complied with the relevant formalities to create an assured shorthold tenancy when the tenancy was granted. However, it is unlikely that a landlord would have done so as, at the date of the grant, the tenancy would have been excluded from the HA 1988 and therefore could not have been an assured shorthold tenancy.

Succession

3.28   Succession means one person becoming entitled to something after another person's entitlement ends, for example inheriting the property of someone who dies. A tenancy, being an interest in land, is property that can be inherited. However, each statutory scheme provides that a person can succeed to a tenancy with security of tenure only if certain conditions are satisfied.

3.29   Under RA 1977 more than one succession was permitted and currently it is still possible for there to be two successions although the second can only be to an assured and not a statutory tenancy. Under HA 1985 and HA 1988 there can be only one succession. Under the HA 1988 only the spouse, civil partner or co-habitee can succeed whereas under RA 1977 and HA 1985 other family members may also succeed. In all cases the person succeeding to the tenancy must be residing in the premises at the date of death.

3.30   Succession happens by 'operation of law' and is not something that is 'granted' by a landlord. However, it is often the case that there is a dispute between a landlord and a tenant about whether the necessary conditions are satisfied. Unless agreement can be reached any dispute must be resolved by a court. This may happen when the landlord claims possession against the occupiers. Alternatively, an occupier may seek a declaration from the county court to confirm that he or she is a tenant by succession.

Summary of succession rights

3.31   The following chart sets out the different rules relating to succession for different kinds of tenancy.

	Rent Act 1977[17]	Housing Act 1985[18]	Housing Act 1988[19]
Type of Tenancy	Protected and statutory tenancies.	Secure and introductory tenancies.	Assured tenancies, including assured shorthold tenancies.
Who can succeed?	Spouse Civil Partner Co-habitee Member of family (not defined).	Spouse Civil Partner Member of family (defined, and includes co-habitee).	Spouse Civil Partner Co-habitee.
Conditions	Spouse/Civil Partner/co-habitee must be residing in premises immediately before death. Family member must be residing in premises for two years before death.	Spouse/Civil Partner must be occupying as only or principal home at the time of death. Co-habitee/ family member must have been residing with the deceased for 12 months before death and be occupying premises as only or principal home at time of death.[20]	Must be occupying as only or principal home immediately before death.

17 RA 1977 Sch 1 Pt 1.
18 HA 1985 ss 87–89.
19 HA 1988 s17.
20 It is not necessary that the 12 months' residence is premises occupied at the time of death. This means that there can be succession to a tenancy granted less than 12 months before the death of the tenant providing the successor was living with the deceased tenant for at least 12 months before the death: *Waltham Forest v Thomas* [1992] 24 HLR 622.

What kind of tenancy does successor get?	Spouse/Civil Partner/ Co-habitee gets statutory tenancy. Family member gets assured tenancy.	The tenancy of the deceased: secure or introductory tenancy.	The tenancy of the deceased: assured or assured shorthold tenancy.
Number of successions	Two are possible only if first succession (to a statutory tenancy) is by Spouse/Civil partner/Co-habitee and second succession (to an assured tenancy) is by a person who is a family member of both original and the successor tenant.	One only. Joint tenancy becomes sole tenancy = one succession. If there has been an assignment to a potential successor no 'further' successions possible.	One only. Only a sole assured tenancy carries a right of succession.

3.32   In the above chart the term 'co-habitee' refers to a person who is living with the tenant as the tenant's husband or wife or as if they were civil partners.

Demoted tenants and succession

3.33   There is a right of succession to a demoted tenancy. However, the conditions are different to the conditions for succession to a secure or introductory tenancy. Any family member (including spouse or civil partner) who occupies the premises as his or her only or principal home at the time of death, may succeed to the tenancy but must have resided with the tenant for a period of 12 months ending with the tenant's death.[21] If there is more than one potential successor, the spouse or civil partner is preferred; if there is no spouse or civil partner, a cohabitee (defined as one who lived with the deceased as a couple in an enduring family relationship, whether of the opposite or same sex) is preferred. Family members are defined in the same way as for secure tenants (see paras 3.38–3.39 below).[22] If the potential successors cannot agree who shall succeed the landlord will select the successor.[23]

21 HA 1996 s143H(1).
22 HA 1996 s143P.
23 HA 1996 s143H(5)(b).

Joint tenancies

3.34   Under HA 1985 and HA 1988 it is specifically provided that where a joint tenant has become a sole tenant he or she is treated as a successor and no further succession is possible. When a joint tenant dies the other tenant becomes the sole tenant not by succession but by 'survivorship' (ie he or she was already a joint tenant and becomes a sole tenant simply by having survived the other joint tenant). This is not a succession but the surviving sole tenant is treated as a successor.[24] However, this is not the case for a secure tenancy where the tenancy became a sole tenancy before the Housing Act 1980 came into force.[25] This means that whenever there is a joint tenancy there is no possibility of a statutory succession. However, some local authorities and RSLs operate policies whereby, in certain circumstances, they will grant a 'non-statutory succession' to another family member. In reality this takes effect as the grant of a new tenancy to the family member (see below at paras 3.47–3.50).

3.35   Under RA 1977 there is nothing to prevent a succession to a sole statutory tenancy where the deceased tenant had previously been a joint statutory or protected tenant with another person.

Common problems

Dispute about whether conditions are satisfied

3.36   When a tenant dies the potential successor should notify the landlord and will be asked for evidence of residence. For family members, a specific period of residence with the tenancy is necessary: for secure and introductory tenancies this is 12 months and for statutory tenancies it is two years. Landlords sometimes indicate that only certain kinds of documentary evidence will be accepted. However, the issue is a factual one and any evidence confirming a person's residence should be obtained and submitted. Letters and witness statements from neighbours and friends may be obtained although evidence from more neutral and/or official sources, such as doctors or teachers, the benefits agency or inland revenue, are likely to be more persuasive.

3.37   Occupiers in receipt of housing benefit are required to declare who is in occupation of the premises. Because this usually results in a reduction of benefit some occupiers falsely declare that they live

---

24   HA 1985 s88(1)(b); HA 1988 s17(2)(b).
25   *Birmingham City Council v Walker* [2007] UKHL 22, 16 May 2007.

alone. Local authority landlords with access to this information may suggest that this is decisive and proves that the potential successor was not living in the property. Obviously, such evidence does suggest that the potential successor does not satisfy the conditions. However, other evidence may be strong enough to persuade an authority (or a court) that the declaration was untrue and that the succession conditions are satisfied.

Relationship between successor and deceased tenant

3.38   Where the relationship is that of spouse or civil partner documentary evidence of identity and marriage or civil partnership will be required. In relation to secure and introductory tenancies the family members are defined in HA 1985 s113 (see para 1.104). They are: a person living with the tenant as husband and wife or as civil partner; parents, grandparents, children and grandchildren; brothers and sisters; uncles, aunts, nephews and nieces.

3.39   Relationships of marriage or civil partnership are treated as relationships of blood. This means that the relative of a person's spouse or civil partner is treated as a relative of that person. Half (blood) relatives are included, step-children are treated as children of the step parent and illegitimate children are treated as the legitimate children of the mother and the reputed father.

3.40   Disputes may arise with regard to 'co-habitees'. It is not enough to be residing in the premises and to be in an intimate relationship with the deceased tenant; the quality of the relationship must be similar to that of marriage or civil partnership.

In *Nutting v Southern Housing Group*[26] the gay partner of a deceased assured tenant claimed he was entitled to succeed to the tenancy. The case was heard before the Civil Partnership Act 2004 but it had been established that gay couples could live together as if they were husband and wife and thereby qualify for succession.[27] However, the court rejected the claim on the basis that the relationship did not have the necessary characteristics such that it could be said that they were living together as if they were husband and wife. The two men had lived together for just over two years before the tenant's death. The relationship was characterised by alcohol abuse and the tenant had obtained a non-molestation order at one point against the appellant. However,

26   [2004] EWHC 2982 (Ch).
27   *Mendoza v Ghaidon* [2004] UKHL 30, 21 June 2004.

it was accepted that the appellant was living with the tenant immediately before his death. On appeal by the tenant the court upheld the decision. The tests applied by the judge, and approved by the appeal court, included: whether the relationship one of mutual lifetime commitment rather than simply one of convenience, friendship, companionship or the living together as lovers; and whether the relationship was one that had been presented to the outside world openly and unequivocally so that society considers it to be of permanent intent.

The appeal was dismissed, the judge had been entitled to find that the appellant had failed to demonstrate that the relationship displayed a sufficient commitment to permanence to meet the test.

More than one potential successor

3.41 When the tenant dies it is possible that more than one person qualifies to succeed to the tenancy. The way the successor is selected is different in each Act.

HA 1985: secure and introductory tenancies[28]

3.42 The tenant's spouse or civil partner is preferred over other members of the family. If there is no spouse or civil partner the family members should agree who will be the successor and, if no agreement is possible, the landlord may select the successor.

HA 1988: assured and assured shorthold tenancies[29]

3.43 The issue is determined by agreement between the potential successors and, in the absence of agreement, by the county court. The problem is less likely to arise under the HA 1988 as it would require there to be a spouse or civil partner *and* a co-habitee both of whom were living with the deceased at the time of death.

RA 1977: statutory tenancies[30]

3.44 The tenant's spouse or civil partner is preferred over other members of the family. If there is more than one person entitled to succeed, the potential successors should agree who will be the successor and,

28 HA 1985 s89(2).
29 HA 1988 s17(5).
30 RA 1977 Sch 1, Pt 1, para 2.

if no agreement is possible, the issue will be determined by the county court.

Succession by children

3.45   A child can succeed to a tenancy provided the relevant conditions are satisfied. If the deceased tenant leaves a will appointing a personal representative or trustee, the tenancy is held on trust by that person until the child becomes an adult. The child holds an equitable tenancy that automatically becomes a legal tenancy when he or she reaches the age of 18. Where no person is expressly appointed as trustee the tenancy will usually be held on trust by the landlord until the child reaches the age of 18. See paragraph 1.139 for an explanation of trusts and legal and equitable interests.

In *Royal Borough of Kingston upon Thames v Prince*[31] the tenant of a three-bedroom house died, leaving in occupation his adult daughter who had lived with him for six months and his 13-year-old granddaughter who had lived with him for three years. The local authority served notice on the daughter requiring her to vacate. Possession proceedings were issued against the daughter and a possession order made. An application was made to join the granddaughter and to set aside the possession order. The application was granted and the Circuit Judge dismissed the authority's appeal, making a declaration that the tenancy was held by the daughter on trust for the granddaughter until she reached the age of majority; further, the tenancy had been so held since the death of the tenant. The authority appealed, arguing that a minor could not hold a legal estate and there was no provision in the 1985 Act for the creation of secure equitable tenancies.

The Court of Appeal held that a minor can hold an equitable tenancy of any property, including a council house. Property law provided that where a legal estate in land was granted to or devolved to a child it operated as a trust, with the legal estate held by a trustee for the benefit of the child and that there was nothing to stop a local authority granting to a child a tenancy effective in equity.[32] The authority's appeal was dismissed.

31   (1999) 31 HLR 794.
32   The tenant had died before the Trusts of Land and Appointment of Trustees Act 1996 which now governs such trusts. However, the Court of Appeal held that this did not change the previous position.

Succession and housing benefit

3.46   Even where there is a dispute about whether the conditions for succession are satisfied, as a matter of law, if the conditions are satisfied, the tenancy vests in the successor automatically on the death of the tenant. Those claiming a right to succeed who qualify for housing benefit should ensure that an application is submitted as soon as possible. Where the succession is disputed the application may be suspended but, if the right to succession is subsequently established, benefit will be payable from the date of the application.[33]

'Non-statutory' succession

3.47   Some social landlords operate what are usually called 'non-statutory' succession schemes. This means an agreement or policy that 'succession' will be allowed in certain circumstances even where the 'successor' does not qualify under the relevant statute. Some local authorities operate such policies in relation to the children of deceased tenants who would be entitled to succeed if the original tenancy had not been a joint tenancy.

3.48   Further, under large scale voluntary transfers (LSVT) of local authority properties to RSLs, tenants who were originally secure become assured with less generous succession rights. Most RSLs offer to such tenants enhanced rights by way of 'non-statutory' succession to those family members who would have been entitled to succeed to the secure tenancy.

3.49   Despite the name a tenancy granted to such a person is not 'succession' at all; it is the grant of a new tenancy.

3.50   Where local authorities operate such policies they must be reflected in the allocation policy since the grant of a new tenancy is an allocation governed by Part VI of the Housing Act 1996 (see chapter 16).

Disputes about non-statutory succession

3.51   To benefit from a non-statutory succession scheme a person will have to satisfy the conditions of the particular scheme. As is the case for statutory succession, a dispute may arise as to whether the conditions are met. The way such disputes are resolved will depend

33 Housing benefit should be paid regardless of whether the succession is established, where the 'successor' occupies the premises as a home. Such an occupier has a liability to make payments equivalent to rent even if in unlawful occupation, see paras 8.9–8.11.

on whether the right to non-statutory succession is reflected in a policy or is a term of the tenancy agreement.

3.52   Where the concession is operated as a policy by a local authority, and is part of the general allocation scheme, a refusal to grant a tenancy could be challenged by way of judicial review.[34] However, the issue may arise in possession proceedings and the occupier may be able to argue the entitlement to non-statutory succession as a defence to the claim. Alternatively, an occupier may be able to obtain an adjournment of a possession claim pending a judicial review.

3.53   If the scheme is part of an RSL policy judicial review will only be possible if the RSL is deemed to be a public authority (see para 21.50).

3.54   Whether the landlord is a local authority or an RSL, an alternative remedy would be to make a formal complaint followed by an Ombudsman complaint.

3.55   If, instead of a policy, the provision for non-statutory succession is contained in the tenancy agreement, a problem may arise as to whether the agreement can be enforced by a person who was not party to the agreement. If the tenancy agreement was entered into on or after 11 November 1999 this should not be a problem; the person claiming the tenancy can rely on the Contracts (Rights of Third Parties) Act 1999 which provides that a person may enforce a contract if the contract 'purports to confer a benefit' on him or her.

Assignment

3.56   An assignment is the transfer of the tenancy during the life of the tenant. The person who transfers the tenancy is the 'assignor' and the person to whom the tenancy is transferred is the 'assignee'. The effect of an assignment is that the assignee becomes the tenant of the landlord under the same tenancy agreement. For this reason, in most properly drafted leases assignment is permitted only with the landlord's consent.

3.57   An assignment is the transfer of a legal interest in land and to be valid must be done by deed.[35] An attempt to assign by deed that does not comply with the relevant formalities may however still be effective between the parties to the assignment although it will not

---

34   See *R v Lambeth LBC ex p Trabi* (1997) 30 HLR 975, QBD.
35   Law of Property Act 1925 s52.

bind the landlord.[36] References in this section to assignor and assignee refer to the parties to a valid assignment by deed.

3.58 The general rule is that tenancies, as legal interests in land, are capable of being assigned. However, that does not necessarily mean that the statutory security of tenure enjoyed by the tenant can also be assigned. Each Act specifies the limited situations in which a tenancy can be transferred to someone else so that that 'statutory security' is also transferred.

Rent Act 1977

3.59 A protected tenancy is capable of assignment but if assignment is prohibited under the terms of the tenancy, the landlord may have a ground for possession against the assignee.

3.60 A statutory tenancy, being personal to the statutory tenant, is not capable of assignment, other than in matrimonial proceedings, see chapter 11.[37]

Housing Act 1985

3.61 The HA 1985 provides that a secure tenancy is not capable of assignment save in three situations.[38] These are set out in section 91(3):

- assignment by way of mutual exchange;
- assignment made pursuant to a court order in certain matrimonial, civil partnership or Children Act proceedings;
- assignment to a potential successor.

3.62 Any assignment in circumstances other than those expressly permitted under section 91(3) will be ineffective to transfer the secure tenancy; the assignee will become the tenant but the tenancy will no longer be secure. The assignee will have a contractual tenancy only which the landlord can terminate by service of notice to quit. Further, as the original secure tenant will have parted with possession of the whole of the premises he or she cannot regain secure status by taking back possession of the premises assigned (see para 3.105).

36 Law of Property (Miscellaneous Provisions) Act 1989 s2: if evidenced in writing it may take effect as an enforceable contract for the assignment.
37 RA 1977 makes provision for the transfer of a statutory tenancy by written agreement with the landlord: Sch 1, para 13. However, it is impossible to imagine why a landlord would now enter into such an agreement.
38 HA 1985 s91(1).

Mutual exchange

3.63   It is a term of every secure tenancy that the tenant has the right to exchange his or her tenancy with another secure or assured tenant of a social landlord provided both parties have the written consent of their respective landlords.

Consent

3.64   The landlord can only withhold consent to a secure tenant on certain grounds which are set out in HA 1985, Sch 3. If the landlord withholds consent for reasons not set out in Schedule 3, consent is deemed to be given.[39] The grounds upon which consent can be refused are:

1) either tenant is obliged to give up possession under a court order;
2) proceedings have been commenced under Grounds 1 to 6, or notice of seeking possession under one or more of those grounds has been served (Grounds 1 to 6 are the 'tenant's fault' grounds);
3) the accommodation is substantially more extensive than is reasonably required by the assignee;
4) the extent of the accommodation is not reasonably suitable to the needs of the assignee and family;
5) the accommodation was let to the tenant in consequence of employment, relating to non-housing purposes;
6) the assignment would conflict with the purposes of a landlord who is a charity;
7) the premises are adapted for a disabled person;
8) the assignment would conflict with the purposes of a landlord who is a specialist housing association or trust;
9) the accommodation is sheltered accommodation;
10) the property is managed by a housing association and the assignee refuses to become a member of the housing association.

3.65   If consent is sought and the landlord wishes to withhold consent the landlord must give notice to the tenant stating the ground upon which consent is withheld and giving particulars. This notice must be served within 42 days of the tenant's application. If no notice is served within the 42 days the landlord loses the right to withhold consent on

---

39   HA 1985 s92(3).

any of the specified grounds. However, in the absence of any response, consent is not deemed to have been given. The tenant must therefore persuade the landlord to give consent, on the basis that the landlord has lost the right to refuse consent, or apply to the court for an order that the landlord must give consent. The tenant cannot simply proceed as if consent had been given.

3.66   The county court has jurisdiction to resolve issues regarding secure tenancies, including issues about the giving or withholding of consent under Schedule 3.[40]

3.67   Where the tenant is in arrears of rent or is otherwise in breach of the tenancy agreement the landlord can give conditional consent, requiring the tenant to pay the outstanding rent or remedy the breach: section 93(5). A landlord can give such conditional consent even after the 42-day period has expired: section 93(6). Otherwise, the landlord is not entitled to impose a condition on the giving of consent and any condition imposed can be disregarded by the tenant.

3.68   So a tenant can proceed if:

- the landlord gives written consent;
- consent is withheld for reasons other than those specified in Schedule 3;
- consent is given subject to conditions other than relating to arrears of rent or the remedying of a breach of the tenancy agreement;
- conditions attached relating to rent arrears or other breach are met.

3.69   In all cases the other tenant must also have the written consent of his or her landlord also.

3.70   The tenant cannot proceed if the landlord has failed to respond to the request for consent.

Rent arrears

3.71   Landlords will always insist that rent arrears are cleared before an exchange can proceed. It is sometimes the case that the exchanging tenant is so keen to move that he or she will offer money so that the other tenant can clear his or her arrears. Advisers should be aware that if payment is made by either tenant as part of the agreement to exchange this provides the landlord with a ground for possession. The ground is a discretionary one and where a landlord has been aware of the transaction made to clear arrears the court is unlikely to grant a possession order.

---

40 HA 1985 s110.

Matrimonial or Children Act assignment

3.72   In divorce or judicial separation proceedings the court can, under the Matrimonial Causes Act (MCA) 1973, order one party to assign a tenancy to the other party, see chapter 11. It is more usual now for a transfer of tenancy to be ordered under the Family Law Act (FLA) 1996. Under FLA 1996 it is the court order that actually transfers the tenancy. Under MCA 1973 the transfer happens when the parties enter into a deed of assignment and if they fail to do this the tenancy is not transferred.[41]

3.73   The Matrimonial and Family Proceedings Act 1984 also gives the court the power to order assignments where divorce proceedings take place abroad.

3.74   Under Schedule 1 of the Children Act 1989 a court can make orders for the assignment of tenancies for the benefit of children (see chapter 11).

3.75   Assignments pursuant to court orders made under these Acts are effective to transfer the secure tenancy into the name of the assignee.

Assignments to potential successors

3.76   It is possible to assign a secure tenancy to a person who would, if the tenant died, be qualified to succeed (see para 3.31 above). This enables a tenant who wishes to move out of the premises to transfer the tenancy to a family member before doing so. It is important that the assignment is done before the person moves out. The tenancy must be secure at the date of the assignment. If the tenant has ceased to occupy the premises as his or her only or principal home the tenancy will no longer be secure and this right will have been lost (see para 2.112 above).[42]

3.77   If an assignment to a potential successor is made there can be no succession when the assignee tenant dies.[43]

---

41 *Crago v Julian* (1991) 24 HLR 306, CA.

42 HA 1985 s95 specifically provides that the restrictions on assignment under section 91 apply also to a tenancy that ceases to be secure because the tenant condition is not satisfied.

43 HA 1985 s88(1)(d).

Landlord's consent

3.78 Other than in relation to mutual exchange, there is no requirement under HA 1985 that the tenant must obtain the landlord's consent to an assignment. However, the tenancy agreement itself may require that the landlord's consent be obtained. If so, an assignment without the landlord's consent will be effective to transfer the secure tenancy but will be a breach of the tenancy agreement. This will give the landlord the right to seek possession against the assignee. The ground is discretionary so the court would have to be satisfied not only that the assignment was in breach of the agreement but also that making a possession order was reasonable.

3.79 Where a tenancy agreement provides that consent must be sought, the landlord must not withhold consent unreasonably.[44]

3.80 If a secure tenancy has been assigned without the landlord's consent a request for consent can be made retrospectively. The landlord must still consider the request and, if reasonable, give consent. If a landlord refuses to respond to a request and seeks possession against the assignee, the court would take this into account when considering whether it was reasonable to make a possession order. The likely outcome is that the court would refuse to make an order if it found that the landlord would not have had any reasonable grounds on which to refuse consent.[45]

3.81 Even if the tenancy agreement prohibits assignment absolutely, if the necessary conditions are satisfied, the assignment will be effective to transfer the secure tenancy to the assignee. However, the assignment will be in breach of the tenancy agreement so that the landlord could make a claim for possession against the assignee tenant.[46] Again, an order would only be made if the court considered it reasonable to make a possession order.

Introductory tenancies

3.82 Introductory tenancies cannot be assigned except in the following circumstances:[47]

- an assignment on relationship breakdown or for the benefit of children, as for secure tenancies;
- an assignment to a potential successor.

---

44 Landlord and Tenant Act 1927 s19(1).
45 *Leeward Securities Ltd v Lilyheath Properties Ltd* (1983) 17 HLR 35, CA.
46 See *Peabody Donation Fund v Higgins* [1983] 10 HLR 82, CA.
47 HA 1996 s134.

3.83   An introductory tenant does not have the right to mutual exchange.

Demoted tenancies

3.84   A demoted tenancy cannot be assigned except on relationship breakdown or for the benefit of children.[48]

3.85   A demoted tenant does not have the right to mutual exchange or to assign to a potential successor.

Housing Act 1988

3.86   In advising an assured tenant about assignment the starting point is the tenancy agreement. Most written agreements will either prohibit assignment absolutely or permit assignment only with the landlord's consent. If the agreement is silent, or there is no written agreement, HA 1988 may imply a term prohibiting assignment.

3.87   Under section 15(2) of HA 1988 where the agreement is silent unless the tenant has paid a premium[49] it is an implied term of a periodic assured tenancy that the tenant cannot assign the tenancy without the consent of the landlord. Further, in such a case the landlord can refuse consent for any reason.[50]

3.88   So the situation for assured and assured shorthold tenancies will be as follows:

Agreement prohibits assignment	Assignment not possible.
Agreement permits assignment with the consent of the landlord	Consent required and must not be unreasonably withheld.
Agreement is silent	Periodic tenancy (no premium paid): assignment not possible without landlord's consent and landlord may withhold consent for any reason. Fixed term tenancy/periodic tenancy where premium paid: assignment is possible and the landlord's consent is not required.

---

48 HA 1996 s143K.

49 A premium is a sum of money paid by the tenant for the grant of the tenancy. It is distinct from advance rent or a deposit.

50 Under section 19 of the Landlord and Tenant Act 1927 where the landlord's consent is required it is an implied term that such consent shall not be unreasonably withheld. However, this is specifically excluded by section 15(2) of the HA 1988.

3.89   Even where assignment is absolutely prohibited a landlord may agree to an assignment. However, the landlord is entitled to refuse and need not have any reason.

Sub-letting

What is sub-letting?

3.90   Sub-letting is when a tenant creates a tenancy out of his or her interest, but remains in the position of tenant against a higher landlord. This is distinct from an assignment where the tenant transfers the whole of his or her interest to someone else. In an assignment the assignee becomes the tenant of the landlord. The relationship between the parties is shown below:

Sub-letting	Assignment	
[Head] Landlord	Landlord	
↑↓	↑↖	Assignee becomes direct tenant of landlord
[Mesne] Tenant		
↑↓	↓ ↘	
Sub-tenant	Tenant 1 ⟷	Tenant 2
	(assignor)	(assignee)

3.91   There is no limit to the number of sub-tenancies of the same premises so long as each sub-tenancy is shorter than the tenancy out of which it is created. There may also be several joint tenants or joint landlords at each level.

3.92   Sub-letting must be distinguished from lodging (which creates a licence). For sub-letting the hallmarks of a tenancy must be present: the grant of exclusive possession, for a period of time, in return for rent (see paras 1.29–1.34). In situations where the tenant shares the accommodation with another person it is more likely to be an arrangement of 'lodging' than sub-letting (see para 1.26).

3.93   For the purpose of this section it is assumed that there are three parties only: the 'head landlord'; the 'mesne tenant'[51]; and the sub-tenant.

---

51 'Mesne' means 'intermediate'. It is pronounced 'mean'.

The issues

3.94   The questions that arise are:

- Is a tenant allowed to sub-let?
- What happens if a tenant who isn't allowed to sub-let does so?
- What happens to a sub-tenant when the mesne tenancy ends?

3.95   The answers to these questions depend on the terms of the tenancy agreement and the statutory provisions that apply to the tenancy. There is a distinction between sub-letting part of the premises and sub-letting the whole of the premises.

Is the tenant allowed to sub-let?

3.96   Save for secure tenants where the position is governed by statute, the starting point is the tenancy agreement:

- if the tenancy agreement permits sub-letting, it is allowed;
- if the tenancy agreement permits sub-letting only with the landlord's consent, consent must be sought but the landlord must not unreasonably withhold consent;
- if the tenancy agreement prohibits sub-letting, it is not allowed;
- if the tenancy agreement is silent (or there is no tenancy agreement) the answer depends on the type of the tenancy.

3.97   It should be noted that where a tenant sub-lets in breach of the tenancy agreement the landlord may 'waive' the breach if he or she, with knowledge of the breach, confirms the existence of the tenancy. This may make an unlawful sub-letting lawful. Waiver is generally only established by positive, intentional acts and not by a failure to act.

Rent Act tenancies

Sub-letting part

3.98   A protected or statutory tenant may sub-let part of the premises. However, if sub-letting is prohibited or subject to the landlord's consent and consent is not obtained, it will be a breach of a term of the tenancy agreement. This gives the landlord a ground for possession but the ground is discretionary so the court would have to be satisfied that it is reasonable to make a possession order.

Sub-letting the whole

3.99   Sub-letting of the whole of the dwelling is only possible if the tenancy is protected, ie still within the contractual period. However, there is a ground for possession where a tenant has sub-let the whole without the landlord's consent. This applies even if the tenancy agreement does not prohibit sub-letting, see appendix to chapter 6.

3.100   If the tenancy has become statutory, sub-letting the whole will result in the loss of the tenancy: a statutory tenancy lasts only if and so long as the tenant resides in the premises.

Secure tenancies

3.101   The right of a secure tenant to sub-let is entirely governed by statute.

Sub-letting part

3.102   A secure tenant may take in lodgers without the consent of the landlord[52] and has a right to sub-let part of the premises with the written consent of the landlord.[53]

3.103   HA 1985 s94 sets out detailed provisions regarding consent and provides:

- consent cannot be unreasonably withheld: section 94(2);
- consent cannot be given subject to conditions: section 94(5);
- if the tenant applies in writing for consent and the landlord refuses consent, a written statement of reasons must be given: section 94(6)(a);
- in deciding whether to give consent, relevant issues include whether the sub-letting would lead to overcrowding and any proposed works that would affect the sub-tenant's accommodation: section 94(3);
- if the landlord neither gives nor refuses consent, or fails to reply within a reasonably time, consent is treated as being withheld: section 94(6)(b);
- in contrast, if a landlord refuses consent unreasonably, or gives consent subject to a condition, consent is treated as being given unconditionally: section 94(2) and (5).

3.104   Any issue regarding consent may be dealt with by a county court.[54] A tenant may apply for an injunction or declaration or the issue may arise in possession proceedings. If there is an issue as to whether

---

52 HA 1985 s93(1)(a).
53 HA 1985 s93(1)(b).
54 HA 1985 s110.

consent was withheld unreasonably, it is for the landlord to show that it was not: section 94(2).

Sub-letting the whole

3.105   Section 93(2) provides that a secure tenant who sub-lets or parts with possession of the whole premises ceases to be secure and cannot subsequently become secure.[55]

Introductory tenancies

Sub-letting part

3.106   Whether an introductory tenant can sub-let part of the premises will depend on the terms of the tenancy agreement. In most cases it will be prohibited or subject to the landlord's consent.

Sub-letting the whole

3.107   Although there is no specific prohibition on sub-letting for introductory tenancies section 124(5) of the HA 1996 provides that an introductory tenancy ceases to be an introductory tenancy if the circumstances are such that a secure tenant would no longer be secure. Sub-letting of the whole would therefore mean that the tenancy ceased to be introductory.

Assured tenancies and assured shorthold tenancies

3.108   Whether or not sub-letting is allowed depends on the terms of the tenancy agreement. If the agreement is silent in most cases the HA 1988 implies a term prohibiting sub-letting. The term is not implied into fixed term tenancies or to tenancies where the tenant has paid a premium to the landlord for the grant of the tenancy.[56] In most of those cases the tenancy agreement will make specific provision about sub-letting.

3.109   So for a periodic tenancy where there is no written agreement or no specific provision sub-letting is prohibited and a landlord may refuse consent to sub-letting for any reason.[57]

---

55   This is in contrast to a tenant who ceases to be secure because of not occupying the premises as only or principal home. Such a tenant can become a secure tenant again by re-occupying but a tenant who sub-lets the whole cannot regain secure status.

56   HA 1988 s15(3).

57   HA 1988 s15(1)(b) and (2).

3.110   For most assured and assured shorthold tenants, therefore, sub-letting, whether of part or the whole, will be prohibited, either expressly in the tenancy agreement or by implication, under HA 1988 s15.

What happens if a tenant who isn't allowed to sub-let does so?

3.111   If a tenant is prohibited from sub-letting this does not mean that a sub-tenancy created by the tenant is invalid or void. The sub-tenancy will create the relationship of landlord and tenant between the mesne tenant and the sub-tenant. However, if it is in breach of the mesne tenancy agreement this will usually give the head landlord the right to end the mesne tenancy and take possession. In most cases the sub-tenant will have no right to remain in possession against the head landlord.

3.112   The position of the tenant and the sub-tenant must be considered separately.

The tenant

3.113   A sub-letting in breach of the tenancy agreement gives the landlord a ground for possession: breach of a term of the tenancy agreement. Further, for secure and assured tenants a sub-letting of the whole will mean that the mesne tenant no longer occupies the premises and thereby loses the secure or assured status. A landlord may therefore serve notice to quit on the mesne tenant and claim possession on the basis that the tenancy has ended.

The sub-tenant

3.114   The fact that the sub-letting is in breach of the mesne tenancy agreement does not give the head landlord a right to possession against the sub-tenant without first ending the mesne tenancy. Landlords who discover that their tenant is no longer in occupation sometimes serve notice on the occupiers/sub-tenants indicating that they are in unlawful occupation and must leave. This is not the case; the sub-tenant is lawfully occupying under the sub-tenancy until the point at which the mesne tenancy is brought to an end. A landlord cannot take any action, whether through the courts or otherwise, to take possession against a sub-tenant until the mesne tenancy is terminated.

3.115   Moreover, the fact that the sub-tenancy is in breach of the mesne tenancy agreement does not give the mesne tenant the right to possession against the sub-tenant. The mesne tenant has created a binding sub tenancy agreement. Unless the sub-tenant agrees to give up possession the mesne tenant can only obtain possession by serving notice and obtaining a possession order against the sub-tenant.[58] An attempt to gain possession forcibly will be unlawful under the Protection from Eviction Act 1977, see chapter 7.

What happens to a sub-tenant when the mesne tenancy ends?

The general rule

3.116   The general rule is that when a mesne tenancy ends, any sub-tenancies or licences also come to an end and the head landlord is entitled to possession of the premises.

3.117   However, there are two common law exceptions to this and specific provision is made in the RA 1977 and the HA 1988.

The common law exceptions

3.118   Under the common law, a sub-tenant may become the direct tenant of the head landlord in the following situations.

- where the mesne tenancy is ended by surrender;[59]
- where the mesne tenancy is ended by forfeiture.

Surrender

3.119   Surrender is an agreement between a tenant and a landlord that the tenancy is given up, see paras 1.68–1.78. The landlord must agree to the surrender and, in doing so, takes back the premises subject to any rights and interests created by the tenant. For this reason when a mesne tenant surrenders the tenancy, the sub-tenant becomes the direct tenant of the head landlord. This applies whether or not the sub-tenancy is in breach of the tenancy agreement.

The unusual case of *Basingstoke and Deane BC v Paice*[60] illustrates how this doctrine operates. The tenancy was of commercial

---

58 A sub-tenancy granted by a private individual to another private individual after 28 February 1997 will usually be an assured shorthold tenancy. See chapter 6 for information about possession claims against assured shorthold tenants.

59 *Parker v Jones* [1910] 2 KB 32.

60 (1995) 27 HLR 433, CA.

premises owned by the local authority. The tenant of the commercial premises carried out works to create a dwelling within the premises which he then sub-let. The authority subsequently accepted the surrender of the tenancy of the commercial premises, at which point the sub-tenant became the direct tenant of the authority. As the landlord and tenant conditions were satisfied the tenancy was a secure tenancy.

Forfeiture

3.120   Forfeiture is described in more detail at paras 4.7–4.23. It is a common law remedy giving the landlord the right to end a fixed term tenancy if the tenant breaches the terms of the agreement. If the tenant is able to remedy the breach he or she may apply to a court for 'relief against forfeiture' which restores the lease. Sub-tenants may also apply for relief against forfeiture and the court may make an order effectively transferring the tenancy to the sub-tenant.

3.121   However, relief against forfeiture depends on the tenant or sub-tenant being able to remedy any breach. If the breach complained of is the unlawful sub-letting, relief will not be granted to the sub-tenant because the breach cannot be remedied by the sub-tenant.

Statutory provision

3.122   The Rent Act 1977 and the Housing Act 1988 make specific provision for sub-tenancies and set out circumstance in which a sub-tenant may become a direct tenant, with statutory protection, against a head landlord.

Rent Act Tenancies

3.123   Section 137 of the RA 1977 provides that if certain conditions are met a sub-tenant may become the protected or statutory tenant of the head landlord when the mesne tenancy ends. The conditions are that:

• the tenancy (ie, the agreement between the head landlord and the mesne tenant) must be a 'statutory protected tenancy';
• the sub-tenancy (ie, the agreement between the mesne tenant and the sub-tenant) must be a protected or statutory tenancy; and
• the sub-tenancy must be lawful.

3.124   These conditions will rarely be satisfied for the following reasons:

- if the head tenancy is a statutory tenancy under RA 1977 this will end if the statutory tenant no longer resides in the premises;
- if the statutory tenant shares the premises with the sub-tenant he or she will be a resident landlord which means that the sub-tenancy cannot be protected or statutory;
- most written tenancy agreements prohibit sub-letting so that the sub-tenancy will not be lawful.

The Housing Act 1988

3.125   If there is a lawful sub-letting to an assured sub-tenant he or she becomes the assured tenant of the head landlord when the mesne tenancy ends.[61] If the sub-tenancy is an assured shorthold tenancy the sub-tenant will become the assured shorthold tenant of the head landlord.

3.126   It should be noted that the sub-tenancy must be a lawful assured sub-tenancy, ie one which is permitted under the mesne tenancy agreement.

Obtaining information about the landlord

3.127   Tenancies may be created with little formality; no documentation is necessary and negotiations are often conducted by agents. A tenant may therefore be in a legally binding relationship but have little information about the identity of his or her landlord.

3.128   The following provisions assist a tenant who wishes to know the name and address of his or her landlord.

Requesting information

3.129   The Landlord and Tenant Act (LTA) 1985 s1 provides that a tenant of a dwelling can make a written request for the landlord's name and address to any person demanding rent or who last received rent, or to anyone acting as the landlord's agent. The person receiving the request must supply to the tenant a written statement of the landlord's name and address within 21 days.

---

61   HA 1988 s18. This is not possible, however, if the tenancy is excluded by Schedule 1 of the Act.

3.130   If the landlord is a company the tenant may make a further written request to the landlord for the name and address of every director and the secretary of the company: LTA 1985 s2. The request may be made to the agent or the person who demands rent and must be forwarded to the landlord 'as soon as may be'. The landlord must provide this information within 21 days of receiving the request.

Change of landlord

3.131   If the landlord sells or otherwise transfers his or her interest the new landlord must inform the tenant of his or her name and address no later than two months after the transfer, or if rent is not payable within that two month period, no later than the next day on which rent is payable: LTA 1985 s3.[62]

3.132   If the tenant is not informed of the new landlord's name and address the previous landlord remains liable for any breach of the tenancy agreement (eg, disrepair) up to the date when notice is given.[63]

Criminal penalties

3.133   The sanction for failure, without reasonable excuse, to give information to tenants about the identity of the landlord is that the landlord, or rent collector or agent, can be prosecuted. The penalty for offences under sections 1, 2 and 3 of LTA 1985 is the same: a fine, not exceeding level four, currently £2,500. Such cases are not prosecuted by the police but by local authorities.

3.134   It is often the case that a tenant is seeking information about the landlord because of complaints about disrepair and local authorities' Environmental Health or Housing Standards departments may assist the tenant but prosecutions are rare. The withholding of rent will often be sufficient to force a landlord to provide the information required but tenants must be advised clearly that any rent withheld becomes payable as soon as the landlord gives the information, see below.

---

62 Some tenants have the 'right of first refusal' and must, under LTA 1985 s3A, be served with notice to that effect.
63 LTA 1985 s3(3A).

Withholding rent

3.135   Under section 48 of the Landlord and Tenant Act 1987 a landlord must provide a tenant with an address in England and Wales at which notices may be served on the landlord by the tenant. If the landlord fails to do so any rent or service charge otherwise due to the landlord shall be treated as not being due 'at any time before' the landlord complies. Advisers should note that the tenant's liability for the rent is not extinguished by the landlord's failure to give this information: the moment the landlord gives the information the whole of any unpaid rent or service charge becomes payable.

3.136   The information need not be given in a specific notice; it is sufficient if the information is stated in the tenancy agreement or in a possession notice.[64]

3.137   In addition to these specific statutory rights, other ways of obtaining information are summarised below.

The Land Registry

3.138   Most land in England and Wales is registered at the Land Registry. The Land Registry records the name and address of the registered proprietor and any registered charges (mortgages). It should be noted that the registered proprietor may not be the landlord. Any member of the public can request this information for any address by completing a form (Form 313: Who Owns That Property?) available to download from the Land Registry website at www.landreg.gov.uk. The current fee payable is £4.00.

Other rights to information

The Data Protection Act 1998

3.139   For tenants of public bodies useful information may be obtained under the Data Protection Act 1998. However, the Act covers information held on the 'data subject' rather than on the landlord.

Housing Act 1985 – housing applications

3.140   Under section 106(5) of the Housing Act 1985 a person may obtain information held by a housing authority in relation to an application for housing.

---

64   *Rogan v Woodfield Building Services Ltd* (1994) 27 HLR 78; *Drew-Morgan v Hamid-Zadeh* (2000) 32 HLR 316.

Deposits

3.141 In the private sector most landlords insist that the tenant pays a returnable deposit as well as rent in advance at the start of the tenancy. Because of the difficulty faced by many tenants in recovering the deposit at the end of the tenancy, the Housing Act 2004 introduced a compulsory scheme under which private landlords granting assured shorthold tenancies must deal with deposits in a certain way. The provisions are set out in sections 212–215 of HA 2004 and apply to any deposit received on or after 6 April 2007.

Tenancy deposit schemes

3.142 The scheme provides that:
- the landlord must protect any deposit in a certain way; and
- the landlord must, within 14 days of receiving the deposit, give to the tenant prescribed information and must comply with the requirements of the particular deposit scheme being used.

3.143 A landlord's failure to comply means that:
- an application may be made to a county court and the landlord may be ordered to pay a sum equivalent to three times the amount of the deposit; and
- the landlord may not claim possession (unless there are grounds) until the requirements have been complied with.

Deposit paid by third party

3.144 The rights of tenants in relation to deposits are also given to 'any relevant person'. This is defined as 'any person who, in accordance with arrangements made with the tenant, paid the deposit on behalf of the tenant'.[65] This may include a local authority operating a tenancy deposit scheme whereby deposits are paid to landlords to facilitate the granting of an assured shorthold tenancy. Prescribed information must be given to such a person and an application to the county court may be made by such a person, even if the tenant does not wish to take action.

---

65 HA 2004 s213(10).

Protecting the deposit

3.145   'Tenancy deposit' is defined as 'money intended to be held ... as security for – (a) the performance of any obligations of the tenant, or (b) the discharge of any liability of his, arising in connection with the tenancy.'[66]

3.146   Any tenancy deposit paid to a person in connection with a shorthold tenancy must, as from the time when it is received, be dealt with in accordance with an authorised scheme.[67] Further, the landlord must comply with the 'initial requirements' of the authorised scheme within 14 days from the date of receipt.[68] There are two types of authorised scheme:

- *Custodial schemes*: the landlord pays the deposit into a deposit protection scheme. There is presently one such scheme – the Deposit Protection Services (DPS). The DPS is a government-authorised scheme that is free to use. Transactions can be made on-line.
- *Insurance based schemes*: the landlord keeps the deposit but pays a premium for an insurance policy against which the tenant can claim if the landlord fails to return the deposit. Currently there are two insurance-based schemes available to landlords: Tenancy Deposit Solutions Ltd and The Tenancy Deposit Scheme. In both schemes fees are payable by the landlord or agent.

3.147   Information about the options for landlords is available on the government website: www.directgov.uk.

Dispute resolution

3.148   The tenancy deposit schemes are intended to ensure that the tenant is able to recover the deposit at the end of the tenancy. Disputes may arise about whether the landlord is entitled to withhold the deposit or part of it because of damage caused by the tenant or unpaid bills. The authorised schemes also provide a dispute resolution mechanism to resolve such issues as between the landlord and the tenant.

Prescribed information

3.149   Within 14 days of receiving the deposit the landlord or agent must give certain prescribed information to the tenant and to any relevant

66   HA 2004 s212(8).
67   HA 2004 s213(1).
68   HA 2004 s213(3).

person (ie, the person who actually paid the deposit, see para 3.144 above).[69] The prescribed information is:

- contact details of the scheme administrator where the deposit is held;
- information provided by the scheme administrator to the landlord explaining the requirements of HA 2004 in relation to deposits;
- the procedures for recovering the deposit at the end of the tenancy, including the procedures applying if either the landlord or tenant cannot be contacted;
- the procedures applying where there are disputes about the amount to be returned and the facilities available for resolving disputes;
- information about the tenancy and the deposit: the amount paid; the address of the property; and, the contact details of the landlord and the tenant which will be used by the administrator of the scheme at the end of the tenancy;
- the circumstances in which all or part of the deposit may be retained by the landlord;
- confirmation by the landlord that the information given is accurate to the best of his or her knowledge or belief and that he or she has given the tenant the opportunity to sign to confirm that the information is accurate to the best of the tenant's knowledge and belief.

Sanctions for non-compliance

County court action

3.150 Where a deposit has been paid and any of the above requirements have not been met, or the scheme administrator has not confirmed that the deposit is being held in accordance with the scheme, an application may be made to the county court.[70] The application may be made either by the tenant or the person who paid the deposit.

3.151 If the court is satisfied that:

- the initial requirements of the particular scheme have not been complied with;
- the prescribed information has not be provided; or

---

69 HA 2004 s213(5) and (6); The Housing (Tenancy Deposits)(Prescribed Information) Order 2007 (SI No 797). In addition the HA 2004 states that the landlord must comply with the initial requirement of the particular scheme being used, within 14 days. A particular scheme may require other information to be given to the tenant.

70 HA 2004 s214.

- the deposit is not being held in accordance with an authorised scheme.

The court *must* make an order that:

- the person who appears to be holding the deposit either repay it to the applicant, or pay it into the designated account of an authorised custodial scheme; and
- that the landlord pays to the applicant a sum equal to three times the amount of the deposit within 14 days.

3.152   Although the provisions are unclear, it is likely that, where a landlord complies with the requirements, albeit outside the 14-day period but before any hearing, a court will find that it no longer has the power to apply the sanctions set out in section 214. The position will be different where the issue is the validity of a section 21 notice. See below.

Non-monetary deposits

3.153   It is unlawful for a person to require a deposit that consists of property other than money in connection with an assured shorthold tenancy.[71] However, if such a deposit is taken it is provided that the property is 'recoverable' from the person holding it.[72] There is no specific provision for a county court claim but a person seeking the return of such a deposit may bring an ordinary action in the county court. It is unclear whether a claim for three times the value of the non-monetary deposit may also be made.

Restriction on possession proceedings

3.154   No notice requiring possession, under section 21 of the HA 1988 (see chapter 5), may be given by a landlord 'at any time when':[73]

- the deposit is not being held in accordance with an authorised scheme;
- the initial requirements of the particular scheme being used have not been complied with;
- the prescribed information has not been given to the tenant; or
- a non-monetary deposit has been taken and not returned to the tenant.

---

71   HA 2004 s213(7).
72   HA 2004 s214(5).
73   HA 2004 s215.

3.155 If the landlord complies with the relevant requirements, a section 21 notice may be served notwithstanding that he or she failed to comply at the appropriate time or unlawfully demanded a non-monetary deposit. Further, a landlord is not preventing from serving a Notice Seeking Possession where there are grounds for a possession order to be made (eg, rent arrears or nuisance).

3.156 The claim form used under the accelerated procedure (form N5B) requires a landlord to provide evidence that the deposit is safeguarded with an authorised tenancy deposit scheme. The tenant has the opportunity to dispute the landlord's statement in the defence form (form N11B).

3.157 If proceedings are brought under the accelerated procedure the court should refuse an order if satisfied that the landlord has not complied with the relevant requirements. If there is a dispute between the landlord and the tenant regarding compliance a hearing should be listed for the dispute to be resolved. A tenant may wish to apply for an order under section 214 (see paras 3.150–3.152 above) at the same time as disputing the claim for possession. Under the accelerated procedure the landlord cannot make a money claim so, arguably, the tenant's application cannot be brought as a 'counterclaim'. A tenant may indicate on the defence form that he or she wishes to apply for an order under section 214. However, given the consequences for the landlord (being ordered to pay three times the deposit) and the fact that the court has no discretion, the court may be unwilling to deal with a tenant's application in this way. A safer course of action would be to issue a separate claim against the landlord[74] and request that the court list the claim for consideration at the same time as hearing the claim for possession.

Unfair contract terms in tenancy agreements

3.158 The Unfair Terms in Consumer Contracts Regulations (UTCCR 1999)[75] apply to contracts between 'suppliers' and 'consumers', including tenancy agreements. To apply the following conditions must be met:

74 A claim could be brought under Part 8 of the Civil Procedure Rules. See chapter 22.

75 SI No 2089. UTCCR 1999 came into force on 1 October 1999. They replaced the 1994 Regulations that applied to all contracts entered into on or after 1 July 1995. The purpose of the 1994 Regulations was to give effect to a European Community Directive, effective from 1 January 1995. There is therefore an argument that the 1994 Regulations (and the 1999 Regulations) apply to contracts entered into by emanations of the state, including Local Authorities, as from 1 January 1995.

- the tenant must be an individual not acting in the course of a trade, business or profession;
- the landlord may be an individual or a company, but must be acting for purposes relating to his or her trade, business or profession, whether publicly or privately owned;
- the agreement or particular term must not have been individually negotiated. Where an agreement is in a pre-formulated standard contract the terms will always be regarded as not having been individually negotiated. However, if a particular term has been agreed expressly between the parties that term will not be subject to the Regulations. If it is argued that a term was individually negotiated the burden is on the landlord to show that it was.

3.159   UTCCR 1999 apply to tenancies granted by RSLs and local authorities as well as private landlords.[76]

When is a term unfair?

3.160   A contractual term ... shall be regarded as unfair if, contrary to the requirements of good faith, it causes a significant imbalance in the parties' rights and obligations arising under the contract to the detriment of the consumer.[77]

3.161   The assessment of fairness does not apply to:[78]

- the definition of the main subject matter of the contract (eg the extent of the letting); or
- the 'adequacy of the price or remuneration, as against the goods or services supplied' – in the context of tenancy agreements this would exclude an argument that the rent is excessive. Other provisions may be used to challenge excessive rents, see below.

Plain language

3.162   The landlord must ensure that any written tenancy agreement is expressed in plain, intelligible language. If there is any doubt about the meaning of a written term, the interpretation most favourable to the consumer shall prevail.[79]

---

76 *London Borough of Newham v Khatun, Zeb, Iqbal & OFT,* [2004] EWCA Civ 55.
77 Reg 5(1).
78 Reg 6(2), although such terms must be in 'plain intelligible language' and could be challenged under the regulations if not.
79 Reg 7.

Effect of unfair terms

3.163 An unfair term is not binding on the tenant. However, the remainder of the tenancy agreement continues to be binding provided it can operate in the absence of the unfair term.

Enforcing the regulations

3.164 The Office of Fair Trading (OFT) can take legal action to prevent the use of unfair terms. In September 2005 the OFT produced guidance on terms considered potentially unfair in assured and assured shorthold tenancies. The guidance can be downloaded from the OFT website at: www.oft.gov.uk. Complaint may be made to the OFT about particular agreements but the OFT cannot become involved in individual disputes.

3.165 For tenants it is more likely that the issue will arise in court proceedings when a landlord is seeking to rely on the disputed term. The tenant must indicate in the defence that the particular term is alleged to be unfair. If the court finds that the term is an unfair term under the Regulations, it is unenforceable.

3.166 In the following cases the courts have considered the application of the Regulations to tenancy agreements.

In *Camden LBC v McBride*,[80] Central London County court considered the application of the previous regulations to a 'nuisance' clause in a local authority tenancy agreement. The clause prohibited the tenant from doing anything which in the landlord's opinion might be or become a nuisance. The court held that the term was unenforceable and unfair because the question of its breach was to be determined subjectively by the landlord.

In *Cody v Philps*[81] the tenancy agreement contained a clause that prevented the tenant from making any 'set-off' or deduction whatsoever against rent. The tenant had a claim for damages for disrepair and wished to set off the damages awarded against the agreed rent arrears. West London County Court found that the clause was contrary to good faith and caused significant imbalance between the parties. It was therefore unfair and unenforceable; the tenant was entitled to set off the damages against the arrears of rent.

---

80 1999 1 CL 284.
81 January 2005 *Legal Action* 28.

Examples of unfair terms in tenancy agreements

3.167 Schedule 2 of the Regulations set out a non-exhaustive list of terms that may be regarded as unfair. Further, the OFT guidance suggests a number of terms in tenancy agreements that would be considered unfair. These include:

- clauses that allow the landlord to determine whether the tenant is in breach of contract;
- clauses that give the landlord the final decision as to whether repairs have been properly done, or whether work is rechargeable to the tenant;
- clauses that require the tenant to go through an arbitration process before he or she can go to court;
- clauses that give the landlord an excessive right of access to the property;
- clauses that require a tenant to pay a 'penalty' charge for breach that is in excess of the landlord's loss. This would include excessive interest charged on late rent;
- excessive restrictions on day-to-day use of the property.

3.168 However, the OFT cannot determine whether a term is or is not unfair. Only the courts can decide whether a term is unfair and therefore whether it is enforceable.

Rents

3.169 Under a tenancy agreement the amount of rent payable is agreed between the parties and, if there is a written agreement, this will be stated in the agreement. Provision may be made for rent to be increased in the future. This may be expressed to be by a fixed amount or to be calculated by a specified formula. Alternatively, the agreement may simply give the landlord the right to increase rent on a periodic basis, the amount to be determined by the landlord.

3.170 If the agreement provides that no rent is payable it is unlikely to be a tenancy. If a rent free tenancy *is* created the tenant will have few rights (see para 1.12).

3.171 In all cases where a tenant has substantive security of tenure it is a ground for possession that the tenant has failed to pay rent 'lawfully due'. It is therefore crucial to understand how rents are set and increased.

Rents in the private sector

3.172   Rent control was effectively abandoned by the HA 1988: the rents for assured and assured shorthold tenancies are expected to be market rents. Although assured shorthold tenants have the right to challenge a rent that is significantly higher than the market rent, the fact that such a tenant has no long-term security means that such challenges are rare. Assured tenants may challenge rent increases only if the tenancy agreement makes no provision for rent increases, and any challenge will be on the basis that the proposed increase is in excess of a market rent.

RA 1977: fair rents

3.173   Prior to 15 January 1989 private and housing association tenants enjoyed a high level of rent control. Under RA 1977, regardless of what was agreed between the parties, either the tenant or the landlord could apply for the rent to be 'registered' by a Rent Officer. The rent registered would be a 'fair rent', assessed by discounting from the appropriate market rent any sum deemed attributable to the scarcity of accommodation. The registered rent became the maximum rent a landlord could charge. Further, the only way a landlord could increase the rent was by applying for a registered rent, or for an increase in the registered rent. Most remaining statutory tenants will already have a registered rent. If not, a statutory tenant can apply for a fair rent to be registered for the first time.

3.174   Both private tenants (protected or statutory) and housing association (secure) tenants whose tenancy began before 15 January 1989 have the right to fair rents under Parts III and IV of RA 1977. The features of fair rents are as follows:

- If there is a registered rent for a particular property, that is the maximum rent that the landlord can recover.[82] A rent registered in respect of a previous tenancy was binding even if the parties to a later tenancy were completely different.
- If there is no registered rent, the maximum rent the landlord can recover is the original contractual rent. The only way this can be increased is by an agreement complying with RA 1977 s51: see below, or by applying to the Rent Officer for a new (fair) rent to be registered.

82   RA 1977 s44(1).

- An agreement to increase the rent is only valid if it is in writing and complies with RA 1977 s51: it must include a statement that the tenant's security of tenure will not be affected by a refusal to sign and that the agreement does not prevent a future application for a registered rent.[83]
- If a landlord purports to increase the rent, otherwise than under section 51 or by applying for a new rent to be registered, the tenant may recover from the landlord any rent overpaid over the previous two years.[84] Recovery may be made by deductions from future rent or by bringing a claim in the county court. Because of the limit on the period for which recovery can be made a claim should be made without delay.
- Where there is a registered rent the landlord can apply for an increase in the registered rent two years after it was last registered, unless there are other reasons justifying an increase, such as improvement works, or an increase in rates or service charges payable by the tenant. In such a case the landlord must apply for a new rent to be registered and the decision as to the new rent will be made by a Rent Officer.
- Rent Officers are employed by the Rent Service, a government department that is part of the DWP. They value property both for the purposes of the registration of rents and for the setting of housing benefit levels. Usually a Rent Officer will inspect a property for the purpose of setting a fair rent or when asked to increase a fair rent. The website of the Rent Service is: www.therentservice.gov.uk. All leaflets and relevant forms can be downloaded from the site.
- Since 1999 there has been a cap on the level of increases to fair rents.[85] An increase cannot exceed a sum calculated as follows: the difference in the Retail Price Index at the date of last registration and the date of the current registration plus 7.5 per cent on the first increase after February 1999 and 5 per cent on any subsequent increase. However, this does not apply if repairs or improvements carried out by the landlord justify an increase in the rent.[86]

---

83 Further, this information must be set out in 'characters not less conspicuous than those used in any other part of the agreement'.
84 RA 1977 s57. Where the overpayment of rent was because of a failure to comply with the technical requirement of section 51 the recovery period is one year: section 54.
85 Rent Acts (Maximum Fair Rent) Order 1999 (SI No 6).
86 Article 2(7).

- If rent is increased following an application to a Rent Officer, the increased rent does not become payable until the landlord has served a valid notice of increase on the tenant in prescribed form.[87]

3.175 The rents for tenancies granted by housing associations, housing trusts and the Housing Corporation that would have been protected tenancies, if it were not for the identity of the landlord, are subject to the fair rent scheme.[88] Such tenancies must have been created before 15 January 1989.

HA 1988: assured and assured shorthold tenancies

Challenging the agreed rent

3.176 An assured shorthold tenant can apply to a rent assessment committee for a determination of the rent.[89] An application can only be made in the first six months of the tenancy and must be made in prescribed form. If successive agreements are entered into by the same parties this does not revive the right to apply to the committee.

3.177 The assessment committee will only make a determination if:

- there are a sufficient number of similar dwellings let on similar tenancies in the locality; and
- the rent payable is 'significantly higher' than the market rent, having regard to the rents for those other dwellings.

3.178 If the assessment committee makes a determination, that becomes the maximum rent the landlord can recover.

3.179 Given that a landlord can evict an assured shorthold tenant as of right after six months, this right is seldom enforced.

3.180 An assured tenant has no right to challenge the agreed rent.

Rent increases

3.181 Section 13 of the HA 1988 gives to some assured or assured shorthold tenants the right to refer proposed rent increases to a rent committee. It applies to:

- a statutory periodic assured tenancy; and

---

87 RA 1977 s45(2)(b) and (3).
88 RA 1977 s86.
89 HA 1988 s22.

- any other periodic tenancy which is an assured tenancy, other than one in relation to which there is a provision, for the time being binding on the tenant, under which the rent for a particular period of the tenancy will or may be greater than the rent for an earlier period.[90]

3.182   So, section 13 applies to a periodic tenancy that comes into being at the end of a fixed term. Where the tenancy has always been a periodic tenancy section 13 applies only if there is no term in the agreement that provides for future rent increases.

3.183   It had often been argued that section 13 was only excluded if there was a term that made provision for a specified increase at a future date. However, the Court of Appeal has held that this is not the case.

> In *Contour Homes Ltd v Rowen*[91] the agreement was a periodic tenancy that included a term stating: 'The rent will be reviewed by the Association in April of each year. The Association shall give to the tenant no less than four weeks notice of the revised amount payable. The revised Net Rent shall be the amount specified in the notice of increase.' On receiving a notice of increase the tenant referred the notice to the Rent Committee under section 13 but the Committee decided that the notice was not in prescribed form, as required by section 13, and refused to deal with the referral. The landlords appealed against the decision to the High Court. Their appeal was dismissed, the court holding that section 13 applied. Section 13 was only excluded in relation to tenancies with a fixed agreed uplift and not to tenancies that simply reserved to the landlord the right to increase rent by serving notice.
>
> The Court of Appeal upheld the landlords' further appeal: section 13 did not apply if there was *any* provision in the tenancy agreement for the rent to be increased if certain events occur, in this case the service by the landlord of a notice.

3.184   So, if the tenancy agreement makes some provision for the landlord to increase the rent a tenant will have no right to challenge the increase on the basis that it exceeds a market rent. However, where rent increases are imposed for the purpose of removing a tenant's

90   HA 1988 s13(1)(b).
91   [2007] EWCA Civ 842, 26 June 2007.

security by taking the tenancy outside the provisions of the HA 1988 they may be held to be unenforceable.[92]

3.185   Section 13 will still apply to statutory periodic tenancies that arise at the end of a fixed term tenancy. However, most of these will be assured shorthold tenancies and a tenant who challenges a proposed rent increase is likely to face eviction.

Section 13 procedure

3.186   If section 13 does apply a landlord must serve a prescribed notice on the tenant stating the proposed new rent. The increased rent cannot take effect before a certain date, being no earlier than one year since the last increase. Further a certain period must elapse between service of the notice and the increase taking effect.[93] If the tenant wishes to object, he or she can refer the notice to a rent assessment committee. The referral must be made (ie, received by the committee[94]) before the increase takes effect. The committee will determine an open market rent which will be the maximum rent the landlord can charge. This may be done at a hearing. If a tenant wishes to challenge the rent as being in excess of a market rent he or she will need to provide evidence of market rents for similar properties in the locality.

3.187   Legal aid is not available for representation at committee hearings.

Varying the rent by agreement

3.188   A landlord and tenant under an assured tenancy agreement may agree a rent increase or any other variation of terms.[95]

Rents set by social landlords

Local authorities

Setting 'reasonable rents'

3.189   Local authorities may make such reasonable charges for the occupation of their dwellings as they determine and must from time

---

92 *Bankway Properties Ltd v Pensfold Dunsford* [2001] EWCA Civ 528.
93 This varies, depending on the period of the tenancy, see section 13(2)–(3).
94 *R on the application of Lester v London RAC* [2003] EWCA Civ 319, 12 March 2003.
95 HA 1988 s13(5).

to time review their rents: HA 1985 s24. Authorities therefore have a wide discretion as to how much rent to charge for their properties. However, the discretion is not absolute and the authority must act reasonably and take into account relevant considerations when deciding on rent levels. The 'relevant considerations' would include the relevant legislation, the duty to balance the 'Housing Revenue Account' and the subsidies received. Section 24 also provides that an authority must have regard to the principle that rents of houses of any class or description should bear broadly the same proportion to private sector rents as the rents of houses of any other class or description. This does not mean that local authority rents should be similar to private sector rents but that the difference in market rents, say, for high rise flats, as compared to converted flats or houses, should also be reflected in local authority rents. In other words, the local authority rent for a desirable property should be more than for a less desirable property.

3.190   In practice local authority rents remain substantially lower than private sector rents and are usually also lower than the rents charged by RSLs.[96] However, in 2002 the ODPM implemented a ten year 'rent restructuring' programme which aims to ensure that at the end of the programme the rent levels of both local authority and RSL dwellings are equivalent.

Increasing rents

3.191   Most local authorities increase rents on an annual basis. For secure and introductory tenancies rent can be increased by agreement between the parties or under the terms of the tenancy agreement. Further, in respect of all periodic tenancies (which means almost all secure and introductory tenancies) a notice of variation may be served on the tenant to increase the rent. The increased rent cannot take effect before the end of a complete period of the tenancy, or four weeks, whichever is the longer period. A tenant who does not wish to pay the increased rent can serve notice to quit on the landlord to bring the tenancy to an end. However, the tenant would then lose his or her tenancy. Unlike other variations of terms the authority is not required to consult before increasing the rent (see para 2.142).

---

96 Statistical information comparing averages rents is available on the website of the Government's Communities and Local Governments Department on www. communities.gov.uk.

Challenging rent increases

3.192 If the authority has acted unlawfully in setting the rent levels an application for judicial review may be made. A tenant has 'sufficient interest' to bring such an action. The decision must be shown to be unlawful under the usual principles of public law (see chapter 21). Alternatively, the validity of a rent increase may be raised as a defence to possession proceedings.

In *Wandsworth LBC v Winder (No 1)*[97] the House of Lords held that a tenant could defend a claim for possession on the grounds that a rent increase was unlawful on public law grounds. Although such a challenge could be brought by way of judicial review it was not an abuse of process to raise the arguments in a defence in the county court. However, this merely indicated the process by which an increase could be challenged. In *Wandsworth LBC v Winder (No 2)*[98] the Court of Appeal held that the increase was lawful. Mr Winder's arguments that it was unreasonable and flawed because of a failure to take into account the means of ratepayers in the district were rejected.

Registered social landlords

Setting rents

3.193 Housing association secure tenants have access to the fair rent regime under the RA 1977, see above. For the assured and assured shorthold tenants of RSLs the mechanism for challenging rents and rent increases is the same as for private tenants. However, RSLs are regulated by the Housing Corporation and are non-profit making organisations whose purpose is the provision of affordable accommodation. RSLs must take account of Housing Corporation guidance when setting and increasing rents. Housing Corporation circulars are regularly issued on issues of housing management including the setting and increasing of rents.

3.194 The current guidance urges RSLs to maximise rental income but at the same time to keep rents 'affordable' for people in low paid employment. RSLs are also expected to act in accordance with the

97 [1984] UKHL 2, 29 November 1984.
98 (1988) 20 HLR 400.

'rent restructuring' programme announced by the government in 2002, referred to above para 3.190. The programme is designed to ensure that rents for larger or more desirable properties are higher than for smaller and less desirable properties. However, because of the danger of the rents on larger properties becoming unaffordable, there is a cap on total that can be charged. Also, there are limits to the level or rent *increases* to ensure that the rents do not increase so steeply as to become unaffordable. Details of the guidance and restrictions on RSLs can be found on the website of the Housing Corporation at: www.housingcorp.gov.uk.[99]

Rent increases

3.195　RSLs usually grant periodic assured and assured shorthold tenancies and most agreements will include a term providing for annual rent increases. In light of the Court of Appeal decision in *Contour Homes Ltd v Rowen* (at para 3.183 above), it is not necessary for a landlord to serve a prescribed notice of increase under HA 1988 s13 and a tenant will have no right to challange an increase by applying to the rent assessment committee.

3.196　If the agreement contains no provision for the increase of the rent, the RSL must follow the procedure set out in HA 1988 s13 and the tenant can challenge the proposed increase (see above para 3.186). However, it is unlikely that a rent assessment committee will uphold a challenge as the committee's remit is to set a market rent and RSL rents tend to be much lower than market rents.

3.197　Chapter 21 describes the ways in which decisions by local authorities and RSLs may be challenged.

99 Advisers should note that the Housing Corporation will be replaced by the 'Regulator of Social Housing' when the relevant provisions of the Housing Regeneration Act 2008 come into force.

CHAPTER 4

Leaseholders' rights

continued

Key points

- A 'long lease' for most purposes is a lease granted for a term of at least 21 years.
- A long lease may be ended (forfeited) by a landlord if the lease-holder breaches the lease. If the premises are residential the right of forfeiture can only be enforced by obtaining a possession order.
- A landlord's right to forfeit the lease is restricted by statute: formal notice must be served and a lease cannot be forfeited for small amounts of arrears unless they have been outstanding for more than three years. Other breaches must be agreed or determined by a court or tribunal before the landlord can start the forfeiture procedure.
- In all cases a leaseholder can apply to a court for relief against forfeiture.
- Long leases will set out the landlord's obligation to insure, repair and maintain the premises and the right to recover the cost of doing so from the leaseholder by way of service charges and administration charges.
- Leaseholders can challenge demands for service charges and administration charges. Only charges that are reasonable can be recovered.
- At the end of the lease a leaseholder may be able to remain in occupation as a statutory tenant.
- A leaseholder may also be able to extend the lease or force the landlord to sell the freehold.

Introduction

4.1   A 'lease' is an interest in land granted for a fixed period. The term 'lease' and the term 'tenancy' have the same meaning. The person who grants a lease may be referred to as the lessor or landlord and the person to whom the lease is granted, the lessee, leaseholder or tenant. In this chapter the terms 'landlord' and 'leaseholder' will be used.

---

1   Such tenancies are excluded from the Rent Act 1977 and the Housing Act 1988 because they are at a low rent. They are expressly excluded from the Housing Act 1985.

4.2   A long lease is the same as any tenancy for a fixed period: the grant of exclusive possession for a specified period of time. However, many of the statutory rights of periodic tenants or tenants with short fixed term agreements (described in chapters 2 and 3) are not enjoyed by those whose tenancy or lease is for a long period of time.[1] Most of the rights and obligations of the landlord and the leaseholder are set out in the lease. However, long leaseholders have some statutory rights over and above those contained in the lease. In most of the statutes that deal with these rights a long lease is defined as a lease for a fixed period of at least 21 years.

4.3   The rights of long-leaseholders are complex and contained in a number of different statutes. This chapter contains only an overview. Advice and information on leaseholders' rights may be obtained from LEASE, the leasehold advisory service. LEASE is funded by the Department of Communities and Local Government (DCLG), the Court Service and the Welsh Assembly Government. Their website is at www.lease-advice.org and useful leaflets on different aspects of leaseholder's rights can be downloaded. In addition the website contains a list of solicitors and surveyors who claim expertise in leaseholders' rights.

4.4   This chapter examines briefly the following issues:

- forfeiture;
- service charges;
- security of tenure at the end of the lease; and
- enfranchisement – the right to purchase the freehold or to extend the lease.

Key features of long leases

4.5   Some of the key features of a 'long lease', as distinct from a short-term, tenancy are summarised below:

A fixed term tenancy or lease for a period of three years or more must be created by deed.[2] See paragraph 1.70 for the requirements of a deed.

A long lease has a value and can be transferred (assigned) to another person (the assignee) in return for a sum of money (a premium).

2   Law of Property Act ss52 and 54.

The 'rent' payable under a long lease is usually a nominal sum, often as little as £10 per year, referred to as 'ground rent'.

Most long leases will permit the assignment of the lease during the fixed term with the consent of the landlord. The landlord's consent must not be unreasonably withheld.

Most long leases will also permit the leaseholder to sub-let, again with the landlord's consent which must not be unreasonably withheld.

The respective repairing obligations of the landlord and the leaseholder are set out in the lease. Section 11 of the Landlord and Tenant Act 1985 (the landlords' implied repairing obligation (described in chapter 9)) does not apply to leases for a fixed period of seven years or more.

A long lease will provide that the landlord carries out certain works of repair and maintenance and will also provide that the leaseholder must reimburse the landlord's costs by way of a service charge. Unreasonable service charges can be challenged by application to the Leasehold Valuation Tribunal (LVT).

The main cost of a long lease is the purchase price or premium which will usually be funded by a mortgage and the lender will have the right to take possession if the terms of the mortgage are breached, see chapter 6.

Leaseholders do not have statutory security of tenure during the term of the lease; their right to possession is by virtue the lease. However, at the end of the lease a statutory tenancy may come into being if the leaseholder is residing in the premises.

Most long leases include a 'forfeiture' clause which entitles the landlord to end the lease and/or re-enter the premises if the leaseholder breaches the terms of the lease. The leaseholder has the right to apply to a court for 'relief against forfeiture' to have the lease re-instated.

Many disputes between a landlord and a leaseholder can be determined by the LVT. However, claims for possession and relief against forfeiture are dealt with in the county court or the High Court.

Right to information

4.6 A leaseholder has the right to obtain information about the landlord in the same way as any other tenants. These rights include the right to be notified of the landlords name and address and to be informed of a change of landlord. They are described in chapter 3.

Forfeiture

4.7   A landlord only has a right to forfeit a lease if this is expressly provided in the lease. Most long leases contain a forfeiture clause. The clause will usually state that if the tenant commits a breach of covenant or fails to pay rent the landlord may re-enter the premises and the lease will come to an end. Alternatively, a lease may provide that it is granted 'on condition that' or 'provided that' the tenant fulfils certain obligations. This also gives the landlord a right of forfeiture.

4.8   At common law, the power of forfeiture was enforced by the landlord 're-entering' the land and taking possession. However, if there is a residential occupier in the premises it is unlawful for a landlord to re-enter without obtaining a possession order.[3] Further, there are now statutory restrictions on the right of forfeiture, described below.

4.9   A landlord may claim the right of forfeiture for the non-payment of rent or for other breaches of the lease. The procedure for each differs.

Forfeiture for rent arrears

Formal demand

4.10 The common law position was that a landlord who wished to forfeit for the non-payment of rent must have made a formal demand for payment. However, a lease could, and usually would, provide that the landlord was exempt from this requirement. This loophole was closed by the Commonhold and Leasehold Reform Act (CLRA) 2002 which provides that a long leaseholder is not liable to pay rent unless the landlord has served notice demanding payment.[4] The notice must be in prescribed form and must state:

- the amount of the payment and the date by which it is payable;[5]
- the name of the leaseholder to whom notice is given;

---

3   Protection from Eviction Act 1977 s2. If there is a residential occupier taking possession without obtaining a court order is both a civil wrong and a criminal offence. A further criminal offence would be committed under section 6 of the Criminal Law Act if a landlord forcibly takes possession while a person is in the premises. These offences are described in chapter 7.

4   CLRA 2002 s166(1).

5   The date payment is due must be no sooner than 30 days or later than 60 days after the notice is served and cannot be earlier than payment is required under the lease: s166(3).

- the period to which the rent demanded is attributable;
- the name of the person to whom payment is to be made and the address for payment;
- the name of the landlord by whom notice is given and the landlord's address;
- the information for landlords and tenants contained in the prescribed form.[6]

Restriction on forfeiture for small arrears

4.11 CLRA 2002 also provides that a landlord cannot forfeit a lease for unpaid rent, service charges or administration charges unless the total amount exceeds a prescribed sum, currently £350[7] or unless the total amount includes a sum that has been outstanding for more than a prescribed period, currently three years.[8]

Unpaid service charges and administration charges

4.12 Further protection is given by the Housing Act 1996 s81 which prevents a landlord from exercising a right of re-entry or forfeiture of premises let as a dwelling for the non payment of services charge demands unless the amount claimed is either agreed or determined by a court or tribunal.[9]

Forfeiture for unpaid rent – tenant's rights

4.13 Where the landlord is applying to the court to enforce a right of re-entry or forfeiture for non-payment of rent, section 138 of the County Courts Act 1984 provides that the tenant has the following rights:

- the tenant can pay all of the rent arrears and costs into court at least five days before the first hearing date. If this is done the lease continues as if proceedings had not been issued;

6   See CLRA 2002 s166 and the Landlord and Tenant (Notice of Rent)(England) Regulations 2004 (SI No 3096) and the Landlord and Tenant (Notice of Rent) (Wales) Regulations 2005 (SI No 1355).

7   This sum excludes any 'default' charge imposed for a failure to pay on time: section 167(3).

8   CLRA 2002 s167(1) and the Rights of Re-entry and Forfeiture (Prescribed Sum and Period)(England) Regulations 2004 (SI No 3086) and the Rights of Re-entry and Forfeiture (Prescribed Sum and Period)(Wales) Regulations 2005 (SI No 1352).

9   The provision applies to all proceedings started on or after 24 September 1996.

- at the hearing the court must delay possession for at least four weeks during which the tenant has the opportunity to pay the arrears and costs. If the tenant pays in full, there is 'relief against forfeiture' and the lease continues;
- within six months of the landlord actually taking possession, the tenant can apply to the court for relief against forfeiture.

Forfeiture for other breach

4.14   The Law of Property Act (LPA) 1925 s146 provides that before exercising a power of forfeiture for breaches other than the non-payment of rent a landlord must serve notice on the tenant, known as a 'section 146 notice'.

4.15   Under the CLRA 2002 s168 a landlord under a long lease cannot serve a section 146 notice unless:

- it has been finally determined on an application by the landlord to the LVT that the alleged breach has occurred; or
- the tenant has admitted the breach; or
- a court or tribunal has finally determined that the breach has occurred.

Section 146 notice

4.16   Where a landlord is claiming forfeiture for breaches other than the non-payment of rent the section 146 notice must:

- specify the breach complained of;
- if the breach is capable of remedy, require the leaseholder to remedy the breach;
- require the tenant to pay compensation to the landlord if required; and
- give the tenant a reasonable time to comply with the notice.[10]

Tenant's response

4.17   If the tenant remedies the breach within the specified period the landlord will be unable to exercise the power of forfeiture. Even if the tenant cannot remedy the breach or pay any compensation within the period, the tenant may still apply to the local county court for relief against forfeiture. However, if there is a residential occupier a claim for possession must be made in the county court so it is more common for the leaseholder to make the claim for relief against forfeiture in response to the possession claim.

10 LPA 1925 s146(1).

4.18   The section 146 notice must be served on any sub-tenant who also has the right to seek relief against forfeiture.[11]

Relief against forfeiture

4.19   The right to relief generally depends on the leaseholder paying the arrears and the landlord's costs or otherwise remedying any breach.

4.20   The court's discretion when considering an application for relief against forfeiture is very wide and relief may be granted on terms. LPA 1925 s146(2) provides that:

> the court may grant or refuse relief, as the court, having regard to the proceedings and conduct of the parties ... and to all other circumstances, thinks fit; and ... may grant [relief] ... on such terms, if any, as to costs, expenses, damages, compensation, penalty, or otherwise, including the granting of an injunction to restrain any like breach in the future, as the court, in the circumstances of each case, thinks fit.

4.21   The courts have been generally reluctant to lay down principles to be applied in the exercise of the discretion.[12]

4.22   The court can order relief on terms that the lease be sold so that the leaseholder can benefit from the value of the lease and the landlord recover any monies outstanding.[13]

Waiver

4.23   A landlord may 'waive' the right to forfeit the lease by taking positive steps to confirm the existence of the lease while aware of the breach. However, this does not prevent a landlord from taking other action to enforce a covenant.

Service charges and administration charges

4.24   In addition to the payment of ground rent the lease will specify that the leaseholder must pay other sums as 'service charges' and 'administration charges'. Such charges are a common source of

---

11 LPA 1925 s146(5).
12 See *Greenwood Reversions Limited v World Environment Foundation Limited and Madhav Mehra* [2008] EWCA Civ 47, in which the Court of Appeal dismissed the leaseholder's appeal against the refusal of relief.
13 *Khar v Delbounty Ltd* [1996] NPC 163, CA.

conflict between landlords and leaseholders. Service charges and administration charges are only recoverable to the extent that they are reasonable and this may be determined by the LVT.

4.25 A landlord may only charge the leaseholder for costs incurred if the lease expressly provides this. A lease will usually set out a landlord's obligation for maintenance, repairs and other services and the right to be reimbursed by the leaseholder for the costs incurred. It will also set out how the charges are apportioned between different leaseholders in the same building or estate.

Service charges

4.26 A service charge is 'an amount payable by a tenant of a dwelling as part of or in addition to the rent ... for services, repairs maintenance, improvements or insurance or the landlord's costs of management, ... the whole or part of which varies or may vary according to the relevant costs'.[14]

Administration charges

4.27 An administration charge is an amount payable by a leaseholder as part of or in addition to rent that is payable, directly or indirectly for costs relating to:[15]

- the consideration of and grant of approvals under the lease, eg consent to alterations or sub-letting;
- the provision of information or documents by or on behalf of the landlord or a person who is party to the lease, other than between the landlord and leaseholder, (eg in connection with the sale of the leasehold);
- a failure by the leaseholder to make payments due under the lease;
- a breach or alleged breach of covenant or condition in the lease.

Demand for payment

4.28 Service charges and administration charges are not payable until a demand has been served on the leaseholder accompanied by a summary of the rights and obligations of the leaseholder.[16] The

14 LTA 1985 s18(1).
15 CLRA 2002 Sch 11 para 1.
16 LTA 1985 s21B and CLRA 2002 Sch 11 para 4. The prescribed information is set out in the Service Charges (Summary of Rights and Obligations, and Transitional Provisions)(England) Regulations 2007 (SI No 1257). The Welsh regulations are contained in SI No 3160.

demand must contain the name and address of the landlord. If the address is not in England or Wales an address in England or Wales must be given at which notices may be served on the landlord.[17]

Reasonableness of service charges

4.29 The Landlord and Tenant Act (LTA) 1985 s19(1) provides that service charges can be recovered from the tenant:

(a) 'only to the extent that they are reasonably incurred; and

(b) where they are incurred on the provision of services or the carrying out of works, only if the services or works are of a reasonable standard;

and the amount payable shall be limited accordingly.'

4.30 Further, where a landlord can charge in advance of the costs being incurred, only a reasonable amount is payable and the landlord must make an adjustment after the costs have been incurred, including repayment where appropriate.[18]

4.31 In relation to a service charge demand the leaseholder may apply to an LVT for a determination as to:[19]

• whether costs incurred for services, repairs, maintenance, insurance or management were reasonably incurred;

• whether services or works for which costs were incurred are of a reasonable standard; or

• whether an amount payable before costs are incurred is reasonable.

4.32 In addition, either a landlord or a leaseholder may apply in advance to an LVT for a determination as to whether:

• costs for services, repairs, maintenance, insurance, or management of a specified description would be reasonable;

• services provided or works carried out to a particular specification would be of a reasonable standard; or

• what amount payable before costs are incurred would be reasonable.

4.33 However, no application to the LVT can be made in respect of a matter that has been agreed or admitted by the tenant, which is

17 LTA 1987 s47.
18 LTA 1985 s19(2).
19 LTA 1985 s19(2A).

subject to resolution by arbitration or where a court or tribunal has already made a determination.[20]

Information about service charges

4.34   Landlords must supply to leaseholders a statement of account for the charges made, no later than six months after the end of the accounting period.[21] This must be accompanied by an accountant's certificate and a summary of the leaseholder's rights and obligations (see para 4.28 above). Leaseholders may request facilities to inspect documents supporting the statement of account, such as receipts and estimates.

What is reasonable?

4.35   There is no definition of what is reasonable in the relevant legislation. Where the dispute is about whether works were necessary or about the standard of work carried out, expert evidence will usually be needed.

4.36   Costs are not necessarily unreasonable because it may have been possible to do works or provide services more cheaply. The question is whether the costs would have been incurred if the landlord had been responsible for bearing the cost. The issue of whether costs are reasonable is therefore decided from the landlord's perspective.

4.37   It should be noted that even if it is decided that charges are unreasonable or the works not done to a reasonable standard this does not mean that nothing is payable. The LVT will assess what is a reasonable amount.

Right to buy leases

4.38   There are additional restrictions on service charge demands for 'right to buy' leaseholders. During the right to buy process a landlord must provide information to the leaseholder about service charges including an estimate of the cost of repairs or improvements over the next five years.[22] For the five-year period the leaseholder cannot be required to pay service charges in excess of the estimated costs. Right to buy leaseholders may also be entitled to a loan from the landlord if the service charges exceed a certain amount.[23]

20   LTA 1985 s19(2C).
21   LTA 1985 s21.
22   HA 1985 s125.
23   HA 1985 s450A.

Reasonableness of administration charges

4.39 CLRA 2002 introduced similar controls in relation to administration charges. It provides that a variable administration charge is payable only to the extent that the amount of the charge is reasonable.[24]

4.40 A leaseholder can also apply to the LVT to vary the lease on the grounds that any administration charge specified in the lease is unreasonable or that any formula in the lease for calculating the administration charge is unreasonable.[25]

Consultation

4.41 Landlords must consult leaseholders before carrying out works above a certain value or entering into a long-term agreement for the provision of services.[26] If a landlord fails to consult the leaseholders the services charges recoverable may be capped.

4.42 The consultation provisions are complex and different rules and costs thresholds apply depending on when the works were carried out. The requirements changed on 31 October 2003 in England and on 31 March 2004 in Wales.

Unfair Contract Terms

4.43 Further protection for leaseholders may be found in the Unfair Terms in Consumer Contracts Regulations 1999. The regulations are described at paragraph 3.158 above.

Leasehold Valuation Tribunals

4.44 Disputes about the amount of service charges are mostly dealt with by the LVT. The LVT is part of the Residential Property Tribunal Service whose website is: www.rpts.gov.uk. The forms used to make applications to the LVT are available on-line. Most cases are resolved at a hearing but the parties can agree to a determination without a hearing. The hearing will be before a three-person panel, and one of the panel will be a lawyer or a person experienced in land valuation. Hearings in London usually take place at the panel offices in central London. Outside London hearings are arranged near the location of

---

24 CLRA 2002 Sch 11 para 2.
25 CLRA 2002 Sch 11 para 3.
26 LTA 1985 s20.

the property in public buildings such as church halls and town halls.

4.45   Public funding is not available for legal representation at an LVT hearing but assistance to prepare for a hearing may be funded under the Legal Help scheme, see chapter 22. As a general rule the LVT will not order a party to pay the legal costs of the other party but can order a party to reimburse other fees incurred. It can also make an order to prevent a landlord from enforcing a term in the lease to recover legal costs incurred in taking or defending a claim in the LVT.[27]

4.46   An appeal from an LVT decision is made to the Lands Tribunal. Permission to appeal must be sought from the LVT within 14 days of the reasons for the decision being sent. If permission is refused an application may be made directly to the Lands Tribunal for permission. The Lands Tribunal is a court of law and its decisions are appealed to the Court of Appeal.

Security of tenure at the end of the lease

4.47   Subject to the landlord's right of forfeiture a leaseholder has exclusive possession and therefore a right of occupation during the term of the lease. When the lease expires the leaseholder may continue to occupy under a statutory tenancy provided certain conditions are met. The main condition is that the leaseholder is occupying the premises as a 'home'. Whether the statutory tenancy is governed by RA 1977 or HA 1988 depends on when the lease commenced or expired. In each case the kinds of agreement that are excluded from the Act apply (see paras 2.19 and 2.89) save for the provision that excludes tenancies at a low rent.

4.48   If the lease expired before 15 January 1999 the tenant will be a statutory tenant under RA 1977.[28]

4.49   If the lease commenced after 1 January 1990 or expires after 15 January 1999 the statutory tenancy will be an assured tenancy under HA 1988.[29]

4.50   There are complex provisions regarding the service of notices by the landlord and the leaseholder. A landlord may serve notice either proposing the terms of a new assured tenancy or indicating an intention to seek possession. The leaseholder should respond by

---

27 LTA 1987 s20C.
28 LTA 1954 Part X.
29 Local Government and Housing Act 1989 Sch 10.

serving a counter notice. The leaseholder may wish to exercise the right to a lease extension or to purchase the freehold, see para 4.68 below. If so, it is essential that the relevant notices are served within the time limits otherwise the rights may be lost. Further, if the landlord is proposing a new assured tenancy and the leaseholder fails to serve a counter notice, the leaseholder will be bound by the terms proposed by the landlord.

4.51   If no notice is served the lease continues on the same terms until the landlords does serve notice.

4.52   If the parties wish to enter into a new assured tenancy agreement but cannot agree on a new rent, an application can be made to the Rent Assessment Committee.

4.53   If the landlord wishes to obtain possession an application must be made to the court and grounds must be proved before a possession order will be made.

Enfranchisement

4.54   Enfranchisement refers to the right of a leaseholder to force a freeholder to extend the lease or to grant a new one, or to sell the freehold. Rights of enfranchisement have developed and expanded over the last 40 years and a number of different statutes apply. The qualifying conditions and procedures are extremely complex and outside the scope of this book. A leaseholder who wishes to exercise the right will need help from a specialist solicitor or surveyor. This section contains only a brief summary.

Leaseholds of houses

4.55   Most long leases are of flats. However, it is also possible to hold a long lease of a house and leasehold houses are common in some parts of the UK. The rights of leaseholders of houses are set out in the Leasehold Reform Act (LRA) 1967. It gives leaseholders of houses the following rights:

- the right to an extension of the lease for 50 years at no cost; or
- the right to purchase the freehold at an agreed price or a price fixed by the LVT.

4.56   LRA 1967 applies to leases of 21 years or more (when originally granted) and to some right to buy leases for a shorter term.[30]

---

30 CLRA 2002 s76(2).

Leaseholds of flats

4.57   Most flats are held on long leases because they form part only of a building. The Leasehold Reform, Housing and Urban Development Act (LRHUDA) 1993 gives to the leaseholders of flats:

- the right to a new lease of 90 years for an agreed price or a price set by the LVT; and
- the collective right of a group of leaseholders to purchase the freehold of the building – collective enfranchisement.

Collective enfranchisement

4.58   Where there are a number of leaseholders in a building the right to purchase the freehold depends on there being a minimum number of 'qualifying tenants' a minimum proportion of whom must want to exercise the right. The purchase will usually be made by a company formed by the leaseholders for this purpose.

4.59   Long leaseholders may also rely on the rights in Part I of LTA 1987. This gives to qualifying leaseholders the right of first refusal if the landlord proposes to dispose of the freehold. In addition, under Part III of the Act there is a right to apply to a court for a compulsory 'acquisition order' if the following conditions are met:

- the freeholder is in breach of the obligations under the lease; or
- the freeholder cannot be found.

Commonhold

4.60   CLRA 2002 created a new type of property ownership: commonhold. This allows for the ownership of individual commonhold units within a building or estate, the common parts being owned and managed jointly by the unit-holders through a commonhold association.

Right to manage

4.61   CLRA 2002 also provides for a right to manage by way of a 'Right to Manage Company' set up by leaseholders of flats. The leaseholders can force a transfer of the landlord's management functions to the company. The right is not dependent on the landlord being in default of the obligations under the lease.

CHAPTER 5

Possession claims – procedure

continued

Key points

- Most residential occupiers cannot be evicted without a court order. Exceptions are 'excluded occupiers' and trespassers who entered as trespassers.
- In most cases formal notice must be given to the occupier before the claim can be issued. Some notices must be in prescribed form.
- Failure to serve valid notice may mean that the possession claim is struck out or dismissed.
- Where the landlord is relying on a discretionary ground for possession the court may only make a possession order if it is satisfied it is reasonable to do so.
- If the court makes an order on a discretionary ground it may also adjourn the claim, postpone possession or suspend enforcement.
- The court may exercise these powers up to the date of eviction.
- The possession order must be enforced by application for a warrant. The warrant authorises court bailiffs to evict the occupiers.
- Even after eviction a warrant may be set aside on the grounds of fraud, abuse of process or oppression.
- A possession order may be outright or conditional. An occupier who breaches a conditional order or remains in occupation after an outright order is a tolerated trespasser. The status of tolerated trespasser will be abolished by the Housing and Regeneration Act 2008.

Introduction

5.1   Chapters 1 and 2 explain which tenants have substantive security of tenure, which occupiers have procedural security of tenure and which occupiers can be evicted without a possession order. Even occupiers who have no substantive defence to a claim may nevertheless avoid eviction if the correct procedure has not been followed by the landlord. This chapter examines each stage of the procedure in a claim for possession:

- steps before serving notice;
- notices;
- issuing the claim;
- the hearing;

- the possession order;
- enforcing the order;
- possible action after eviction.

Steps before serving notice

5.2   A landlord who intends to take action against a tenant because of a failure to pay rent or because of complaints of nuisance or who simply wants a tenant to leave premises will usually contact the tenant before serving formal notice. There is no requirement that a private landlord contacts a tenant before serving formal notice but a failure to do so will be relevant if the court is considering whether it is reasonable to make a possession order. For social landlords, however, there are certain requirements in relation to managing both rent arrears and complaints of nuisance.

Nuisance and anti-social behaviour

5.3   Social landlords usually have policies and procedures setting out the steps that will be taken prior to deciding to seek possession. Under the Anti Social Behaviour Act (ASBA) 2003 social landlords must have a published policy stating how complaints of nuisance will be dealt with.[1] Usually a certain level of investigation must be undertaken before serving notice. However, in cases where serious anti-social behaviour is alleged a claim for possession may be commenced at the same time as serving notice of seeking possession.

Rent arrears

Pre-Action Protocol

5.4   On 4 October 2006 a Pre-Action Protocol was introduced for possession proceedings brought by public sector landlords claiming possession on the grounds of rent arrears. The Protocol can be downloaded from: www.justice.gov.uk/civil/procrules. The Protocol sets out steps that should be taken before serving notice and after serving notice but before the hearing.

5.5   The Protocol applies to all claims for possession of residential premises brought by social landlords (local authorities, RSLs and Housing Action Trusts) solely on the grounds of rent arrears. It does

---

1   ASBA 2003 s 12.

not apply to claims in respect of long leases or where the occupier has no security of tenure (this would include assured shorthold tenants and non-secure tenants even if the reason for taking action is the existence of rent arrears). The Protocol has four sections, summarised below.

(1) Initial contact

5.6 The landlord should contact the tenant when the tenant falls into arrears. The landlord and tenant should try to agreed affordable sums for the tenant to pay towards the arrears. The landlord should provide quarterly rent statements and, if aware of difficulties in reading or understanding information, should take reasonable steps to ensure the tenant understands any information given.

Tenants who are under 18 or vulnerable

5.7 If the landlord is aware that a tenant is under 18 or particularly vulnerable, the landlord should consider at an early stage:
- whether the tenant has capacity and, if not, to apply for a litigation friend to be appointed;
- whether any issue arises under the Disability Discrimination Act 1995; and
- if the landlord is a local authority, whether there is a need for a community care assessment.

Housing benefit

5.8 The landlord should offer to assist the tenant in any claim the tenant may have for housing benefit. The landlord should not start possession proceedings against a tenant who can demonstrate that s/he has provided the authority with all evidence required to process the claim, s/he has a reasonable expectation of eligibility and has paid other sums due not covered by housing benefit.

5.9 The landlord should make every effort to establish effective ongoing liaison with housing benefit departments, and should, with the tenant's consent, make direct contact with the housing benefit department prior to taking enforcement action.

5.10 The landlord and tenant should work together to resolve any housing benefit problems.

5.11 The landlord should arrange for arrears to be paid by the DWP if the criteria are met.

(2) After service of statutory notices

5.12   After service of notice but before issue of proceedings the landlord should make reasonable attempts to contact the tenant, to discuss the amount of arrears, the cause of the arrears, repayment of the arrears and the housing benefit position.

5.13   If the tenant complies with an agreement the landlord should agree to postpone court proceedings as long as the tenant keeps to the agreement.

5.14   If the tenant fails to comply with the agreement the landlord should warn the tenant of the intention to bring proceedings and give the tenant clear time limits within which to comply.

(3) Alternative dispute resolution

5.15   The parties should consider whether it is possible to resolve the issues by discussion and negotiation without recourse to litigation. The parties may be required by the court to provide evidence that alternative means of resolving the dispute were considered. Courts take the view that litigation should be a last resort, and that claims should not be issued prematurely when a settlement is still actively being explored.

(4) Court proceedings

5.16   No later than 10 days before the hearing, the landlord should:
- provide to the tenant up to date rent statements;
- disclose what the landlord knows about the tenant's housing benefit.

5.17   The landlord should inform the tenant of the date and time of any court hearing and the order applied for. The landlord should advise the tenant to attend the hearing and should record such advice.

5.18   If the tenant complies with an agreement made after the issue of proceedings the landlord should agree to postpone court proceedings so long as the tenant keeps to the agreement.

5.19   If the tenant ceases to comply with the agreement, the landlord should warn the tenant of the intention to restore the proceedings and give clear time limits within which to comply.

Sanctions for non-compliance

5.20   If the landlord unreasonably fails to comply with the terms of the protocol, the court may:
- make an order for costs;
- adjourn, strike out or dismiss claims (except where the claim is brought solely on a mandatory ground).

5.21   If the tenant unreasonably fails to comply with the terms of the protocol, the court may take such failure into account when considering whether it is reasonable to make a possession order.

Possession notices

5.22   When a landlord or owner is required to obtain a possession order to evict an occupier, there is usually some form of notice that must be given to the occupier before the claim can be issued. The type of notice depends on the type of tenancy or agreement. The Housing Acts 1985 and 1988 provide that a landlord can only terminate certain kinds of tenancy by obtaining a possession order. For such tenancies the relevant statute sets out the kind of notice that must be served before applying for a court order. For tenancies that fall outside the Housing Acts, and for Rent Act tenancies, the common law applies: a periodic tenancy must be ended by service of a notice to quit. A 'notice to quit' is a common law instrument that ends a contractual periodic tenancy so as to give the landlord the right to possession. However, there are some statutory requirements as to the content and length of a notice to quit. A notice to quit that does not comply with these requirements will not be effective to end the tenancy.

Summary of possession notices

5.23   The chart below summarises the notices applicable to each type of tenancy or agreement.

Type of occupier	Notice	Authority	Requirements	Length of notice
Assured tenancy	Notice seeking possession	HA 1988 s8	Prescribed form or form substantially to the same effect.	Depends on grounds: if nuisance ground proceedings can start immediately. Otherwise, either two weeks or two months.

Type of occupier	Notice	Authority	Requirements	Length of notice
Assured shorthold tenancy	Notice requiring possession	HA 1988 s21	Must be in writing. Not a prescribed form. If tenancy is periodic must require possession after last day of a period of the tenancy.	At least two months.
Secure tenancy	Notice of Seeking Possession	HA 1985 s83	Prescribed form or form substantially to the same effect	Depends on grounds: if nuisance ground proceedings can start immediately. Otherwise, at least 28 days
Introductory tenancy	Notice of proceedings	HA 1996 s128	Notice not in prescribed form but must contain certain information	At least 28 days. Notice gives tenant right to seek a review and review must be completed before claim started
Demoted tenancy	Notice of proceedings	HA 1996 s143E	Notice not in prescribed form but must contain certain information	At least 28 days. Notice gives tenant right to seek a review and review must be completed before claim started

Type of occupier	Notice	Authority	Requirements	Length of notice
Rent Act periodic tenancy (protected or statutory)[2] or other contractual tenancy not governed by HA 1985 or HA 1988 and not excluded letting	Notice to quit	Common law and PEA 1977 s5	Notice not in prescribed form but must be in writing and contain prescribed information	A complete period of the tenancy or 28 days, whichever is longer
Contractual licensee (not 'excluded occupier')	Notice to quit	Common law and PEA 1977 s5	Notice not in prescribed form but must be in writing and contain prescribed information	What the contract provides or 28 days, whichever is longer.

5.24   In the case of notices to quit and notices served on assured shorthold tenants, a failure to serve valid notice means the claim must be dismissed. For statutory notices seeking possession served on assured and secure tenants the court has the power to hear a claim for possession even where no notice has been served and can permit the landlord to amend the notice (see below at paragraphs 5.35–5.38).

5.25   The detailed requirements for each kind of notice are set out below.

Secure and assured tenants – notices seeking possession

5.26   Secure and assured tenants have substantive security. This operates in the same way for both types of tenant: a landlord can only bring the tenancy to an end by obtaining a possession order. Before a claim for possession can be brought a statutory notice must be served. The notice must:

2   A periodic protected tenancy is ended by a notice to quit but a tenant who remains in occupation becomes a statutory tenant.

- be in prescribed form, or form substantially to the same effect;
- must state the ground/s on which the court will be asked to make a possession order;
- give particulars of the ground/s (ie, an explanation of why each ground is being is relied on); and
- state the earliest date on which the claim can be commenced.

5.27   The prescribed forms give information about the procedure to be followed, the requirements of particular grounds and the tenant's rights. The particular prescribed form is different for each type of tenancy and there are some differences in the time limits. In both cases the court has the power to waive the notice requirement if it is 'just and equitable' and can permit the landlord to amend the notice.

Secure tenants

5.28   The prescribed form for a secure tenant is a Notice of Seeking Possession[3] (referred to as a NSP or NOSP). The general rule is that the earliest date the proceedings can commence is no earlier than the tenancy could be ended by a notice to quit, ie a complete period of the tenancy, or four weeks, whichever is longer. However, if the landlord is relying on the nuisance ground (Ground 2) proceedings can be started immediately although the tenant cannot be required to give up possession earlier than the tenancy could be ended by a notice to quit. The notice expires 12 months after the date specified as the earliest date on which proceedings can commence. After that date the notice lapses.

Assured tenants

5.29   The prescribed form for an assured tenant is a Notice Seeking Possession[4] (NSP). The earliest date on which proceedings can commence depends on which grounds are relied on. If the nuisance ground (Ground 14) is relied on proceedings may be commenced immediately. Otherwise, the proceedings may be commenced two weeks or two months after service of the notice. For all of the grounds relying on rent arrears or some other breach of the tenancy agreement two weeks notice must be given. The notice expires 12 months after the date it is served, after which it lapses.

---

3   See Secure Tenancies (Notices) Regulations 1987 (SI No 755) and Secure Tenancies (Notices)(Amendment) Regulations (SI No 71).

4   See Assured Tenancies and Agricultural Occupancies (Forms) Regulations 1997 (SI No 194).

Challenging notices seeking possession

Errors in the notice

5.30   The notice must be in prescribed form or in a form substantially to the same effect. An NSP that is incorrectly completed may nevertheless be held by a court to be 'substantially to the same effect' as a properly completed notice. The cases in which the courts have examined the same provision in relation to section 20 notices (see paragraph 2.62), suggest that where the prescribed information for tenants is omitted the notice may be held to be invalid. Whether a notice is 'substantially to the same effect' as a properly completed notice will depend on the nature of any error or omission. While the court has an overriding discretion to waive the requirement to serve notice or to permit amendments, a district judge may be persuaded that a notice that is not properly completed or is not in the prescribed form is invalid and that the proceedings should be struck out. Much will depend on the merits of the claim. Where there is evidence of serious and continuing nuisance a court will be more likely to exercise its discretion than in a claim involving less serious allegations or alleging a low level of rent arrears.[5]

5.31   If the grounds relied on are summarised incorrectly this may invalidate the notice.

> In *Mountain v Hastings*[6] a private landlord was seeking possession on Ground 8. Ground 8 required there were arrears of rent of at least three months at the date of the notice and at the date of the hearing.[7] However, in the notice the ground was summarised in the following terms: 'at least three months rent is unpaid.' Although other grounds were also specified, because Ground 8 is mandatory the court made an order for possession at the first hearing on the tenant admitting the level of arrears. The tenant appealed. The Court of Appeal held that the notice was invalid as the purpose of the notice 'is to give to the tenant the information ... to enable the tenant to consider what she should do and, with or without advice, to do that which is in her power and which will

---

5   See *Kelsey Housing Association v King* (1995) 28 HLR 270, CA, see para 5.35 below.
6   (1993) 25 HLR 427.
7   The requirement is now only two months rent arrears.

best protect her against the loss of her home'.[8] The failure of the notice to specify that the ground requires the level of arrears to exist at the date of the hearing meant that it was not substantially to the same effect as a notice that correctly set out Ground 8. The possession order was set aside and the case remitted to the county court.

5.32   Similarly, if insufficient particulars of the allegations against the tenant are given the notice may be held to be invalid:

In *Torridge District Council v Jones*[9] the rent arrears ground was correctly set out. However, the only particulars given were: 'the reasons for taking this action are non-payment of rent.' A possession order was made, the judge holding that the tenant had suffered no injustice or embarrassment because of the failure to set out the amount of the arrears. The Court of Appeal upheld the tenant's appeal: 'nothing short of a specification of the amount which is claimed as being in arrear could ... amount to a proper particular of the ground upon which possession was sought.' What is required is 'a specification sufficient to tell the tenant what it is he has to do to put matters right before the proceedings are commenced'.[10]

5.33   However, this does not mean that if the figure given is incorrect, the notice will necessarily be invalid.

The notice in *Dudley Metropolitan Borough Council v Bailey*[11] stated that the tenant was in arrears of a certain amount as at the date of the notice. Subsequently, the local authority accepted that the figure stated included arrears of rates and water rates as well as rent. The Court of Appeal held that an error in the particulars made in good faith would not invalidate the notice providing there is a statement in summary form of the facts which the landlord intends to prove to support the claim for possession.

8 Ralph Gibson LJ at 433.
9 (1985) 18 HLR, 107.
10 Oliver LJ at 114.
11 (1990) 22 HLR 424.

5.34 Further, it has been held that even if a figure is not given in the notice, the notice will be valid if the figure can easily be ascertained by the tenant.

> In *Marath v MacGillivray*[12] the particulars stated only that 'at a meeting between the landlord and tenant on 24 July 1994 the arrears were agreed at £103.29 ... Since that date no payments of rent have been made.' The total arrears at the date of the notice were not stated. The Court of Appeal held that the notice was valid and that s8 was satisfied provided 'it is made clear ... that more than three months' rent is at the date of that notice unpaid and due and provided also that in some way or other that notice makes it clear either how much, or how the tenant can ascertain how much, is alleged to be due'.

Courts' power to waive notice

5.35 For both secure and assured tenants it is provided that 'the court shall not entertain proceedings' for possession unless notice has been served on the tenant, or 'the court considers it just and equitable to dispense with the requirement of such a notice'.[13]

> In *Kelsey Housing Association v King*[14] the defendants were alleged to have been violent, abusive and threatening towards neighbours and there had been a conviction for actual bodily harm. The Housing Association served a Notice to Quit in February 1994 when they should have served a notice seeking possession. The case was commenced in May 1994 and possession was claimed on Grounds 12 and 14. The allegations were detailed in an appendix to the summons. A defence was served denying the allegations. In November 1994 the defendants applied for the summons to be dismissed because of the failure to serve notice seeking possession. The court refused, holding that it was just and equitable to waive the requirement. The defendants appealed.

12 (1996) 28 HLR 484, CA.
13 HA 1985 s83 and HA 1988 s8. For assured tenants it is also stated that the proceedings must be begun within the time limits stated in the notice.
14 (1995) 28 HLR 270.

The Court of Appeal dismissed the appeal holding that: 'in deciding whether the requirement should be waived the court should weigh all of the factors, taking into account the view of the landlord and the tenant.' Even if the failure to give notice created prejudice to the tenant that was not itself decisive; the court was entitled to take account of things which occurred after the proceedings had commenced; the court was right to conclude that the defendants had suffered no prejudice; by the time of the hearing the defendants had had time to put things right. Further, an application to dismiss a claim for possession should be made promptly, at about the same time as serving the defence or even before.

Assured tenants: Ground 8

5.36   It should be noted that the court does not have the power to waive the notice requirement when possession is sought against an assured tenant on ground 8.[15] The ground is only made out if the arrears of rent exist at the date of the notice and at the date of the hearing, see para 6.30 below.

Courts' power to allow amendments

5.37   The court cannot make an order for possession on any ground unless that ground and particulars of it are specified in the notice. However, the court may give permission for the specified grounds to be altered or added to.[16] This includes a power to add or amend the particulars of the ground.[17]

5.38   Whether a court will exercise its discretion will depend on the nature and extent of the proposed amendment or addition. Moreover, the time at which the application is made will be relevant. A court may permit a minor amendment at a late stage but is less likely to do so if the amendment significantly changes what is at issue between the parties. An application for permission to amend at an early stage, before the defence has been filed, is more likely to succeed.

---

15   HA 1988 s8(5).
16   HA 1985 s84(3); HA 1988 s8(2).
17   *Camden LBC v Oppong* (1996) 28 HLR 701, CA.

Service of the notice

5.39 No special method of service is required but the burden is on the claimant to satisfy the court, on balance of probabilities, that the notice was received by the tenant.

5.40 The requirement is simply that the notice must be delivered to the tenant. It is not necessary that the notice is understood by the recipient.[18] However, the Rent Arrears Protocol provides that a landlord who is aware that a tenant may be vulnerable must consider whether a litigation friend should be appointed, see para 5.7. Moreover, the tenant's understanding of a notice will be relevant if the court is considering whether it is reasonable to make a possession order.

Assured shorthold tenants – notice requiring possession

5.41 The possession notice for an assured shorthold tenant is not a prescribed notice. The requirements are set out in HA 1988 s21 and the notice is commonly referred to as a 'section 21 notice' or 'notice requiring possession'.

5.42 An assured shorthold tenancy is a form of assured tenancy and, as such, cannot be ended by a landlord other than by obtaining a court order (see para 2.55). Section 21 of HA 1988 sets out the conditions that must be satisfied for the court to make a possession order, including that the landlord must have given notice to the tenant. The requirements are different for a notice given within a fixed term and for a notice given in respect of a periodic tenancy.

5.43 A possession order will not be made against an assured shorthold tenant under section 21 to take effect earlier than six months after the start of the tenancy, or within a fixed term agreement.[19]

Notice within fixed term

5.44 If notice is served before the end of the fixed term, including the last day of the fixed term, the requirement is that the landlord, or at least one joint landlord, 'has given to the tenant not less than two months' notice in writing stating that he requires possession of the dwelling house'.[20]

---

18 *Tadema Holdings v Ferguson* (2000) 32 HLR 866.
19 Section 21(1) and (5).
20 HA 1988 s21(1)(b).

Notice in respect of a periodic tenancy

5.45 At the end of a fixed term tenancy agreement, a tenant who remains in occupation becomes a statutory periodic tenant. For such a tenant, or for an assured shorthold tenant who has always been a periodic tenant, the requirement is different. The notice must:

- be in writing;
- state that possession is required by virtue of section 21;
- after a date specified in the notice, being:
  the last day of a period of the tenancy;
  not earlier than two months from the date the notice was given; and
  not earlier than the date on which the tenancy could be brought to an end by service of a notice to quit.

5.46 The court cannot waive the requirement to serve a section 21 notice or permit amendment to the notice. A notice that does not comply with the requirements of section 21 will not be a valid notice.

In *McDonald v Fernandez*[21] the period of the tenancy was monthly, from the fourth day of each month to the third day of the following month. A section 21 notice was served stating that possession was required 'on 4 January 2003'. The Court of Appeal upheld the tenant's appeal against the making of a possession order: while a notice to quit would be valid if it expired on the last or first day of a period of the tenancy this did not apply to a section 21 notice. Section 21(4)(a) provides that the notice must require possession 'after a date specified in the notice, being the last day of a period of the tenancy'. The notice should have stated that possession was required *after* 3 January 2003.

5.47 If there is uncertainty about the precise period of the tenancy it is generally sufficient if the notice contains a 'saving phrase' such as:

Possession is required after [date] or after the last day of a period of your tenancy which will end next after expiration of two months from the service upon you of this notice.

21 [2003] EWCA Civ 1219.

In *Notting Hill Housing Trust v Roomus*[22] the landlords served notice relying on a saving phrase in the following terms:

> possession is required (by virtue of section 21(4) of the Housing Act 1988) ... of the [property] ... which you hold as tenant at the end of the period of your tenancy which will end after expiry of two months from the service upon you of this notice.

The tenant argued that the notice was invalid because it contained the phrase '*at the end of* the period of your tenancy' rather than '*after the end of* the period of your tenancy'. The Court of Appeal rejected the tenant's appeal holding that the phrase 'at the end of the period of your tenancy' means the same as 'after the end of the period of your tenancy'.

5.48   No higher court cases have examined the requirement in section 21 that the notice should state that possession 'is required by virtue of this section' but in the county court case of *Adamson v Mather*[23] a notice that made no reference to section 21 was held to be defective and the possession claim dismissed.

Grounds for possession

5.49   The section 21 notice does not require a landlord to give reasons for seeking possession: the landlord is entitled to possession as of right. However, an assured shorthold tenancy is a form of assured tenancy and all of the statutory grounds relevant to assured tenancies are available. A landlord may seek an order for possession within the first six months if he or she can prove a ground is made out. To do so the landlord must serve a notice seeking possession under section 8 of HA 1988, see above.

Section 21 notices and rent deposits

5.50   Since 6 April 2007 landlords who receive deposits are required to deal with them in a certain way. Within 14 days of receiving the deposit prescribed information must be given to the tenant and the deposit protected either by being paid into an authorised custodial scheme or protected by an authorised insurance scheme.[24]

---

22 [2006] EWCA Civ 407.
23 24 September 2004, Harrogate County Court, November 2004 *Legal Action* 25.
24 See para 3.142.

5.51   The sanctions for non-compliance include a provision that no section 21 notice may be given by a landlord at any time when:[25]

- the deposit is not being held in accordance with an authorised scheme;
- the initial requirements required by the particular scheme being used have not been complied with;
- the prescribed information has not been given to the tenant; or
- a non-monetary deposit has been taken and not returned to the tenant.

Notices to quit

5.52   A notice to quit is a notice given by either landlord or tenant, stating that the tenant should or intends to 'quit' the premises. A periodic tenancy continues automatically from one period to the next unless one party indicates that he or she wants the tenancy to end. A notice to quit is an indication that, at the end of the next complete period of the tenancy, the tenancy will end. Landlords' notices to quit do not have any effect in respect of secure and assured tenancies; the only way a landlord can determine a secure or assured tenancy is by obtaining a possession order.[26] However, any contractual periodic tenancy that is not secure or assured must still be ended by notice to quit before a landlord can make a claim for possession. All periodic tenancies can be ended by a tenant's notice to quit (see para 1.62).

5.53   A notice to quit must therefore be served to end the following types of tenancy:

- tenancies that have ceased to be secure or assured because the tenant no longer resides in the premises;
- tenancies that are excluded from the secure a assured schemes, eg tenancies with a resident landlord, tenancies of licensed premises, nonsecure tenancies offered to homeless applicants;[27]
- protected and statutory tenancies under RA 1977.

5.54   Further, a contractual licensee is entitled to a notice to quit before a claim for possession can be brought, provided the licence is not an excluded letting (see para 1.101).[28]

---

25 Housing Act 2004 s215.
26 See chapter 2.
27 See paras 2.19 and 2.14.
28 PEA 1977 s3(2B).

Form of notice to quit

5.55   There is no prescribed form for a notice to quit but PEA 1977 requires that the notice is in writing and includes prescribed information about the tenant's rights.[29]

Time limits

5.56   A notice to quit must give a minimum of 28 days notice or a complete period of the tenancy, whichever is longer.

5.57   The notice must expire either on the last or first day of a period of the tenancy. Again, a notice may include a saving phrase such as: 'I require you to quit and deliver up possession on [date] or the day on which a complete period of your tenancy expires next after the end of four weeks from the service of this notice'.

5.58   There is no statutory time limit on how long a notice to quit can be relied upon following service. However, it is for the landlord to prove that the contractual tenancy has been ended and usually a notice to quit is served shortly before the claim is issued.

5.59   A claim for possession cannot be commenced before a notice to quit has expired.[30]

Errors in a notice to quit

5.60   Minor errors relating to the description of the premises or the name of the tenant will not invalidate the notice provided the tenant is not prejudiced by the error. An error in the date for the giving up of possession will invalidate the notice.

5.61   If the court holds that the notice is not valid any claim for possession must fail since the contractual tenancy or licence must have been ended before a possession order can be made. The court cannot waive the requirement to serve notice to quit.

Service

5.62   The notice may be served by posting it, hand delivering it to the address of the tenant or by personally serving it on the tenant. The burden is on the landlord to prove that the notice was received by the tenant so most landlords will deliver or personally serve the notice.

29 PEA 1977 s5.
30 *Plaschkes v Jones* (1982) 9 HLR 110.

5.63   Problems may arise when a tenant has vacated premises and the landlord wishes to end the tenancy before taking possession. A notice to quit left at premises when the tenant is absent will not be effective unless the tenancy agreement specifically refers to the requirement to serve notice to quit. If so, the notice can be served by leaving it at the last known place of abode or business.[31]

Introductory and demoted tenancies

5.64   An introductory tenancy is a local authority 'probationary' tenancy. A demoted tenancy is a tenancy that was once secure but has been demoted by a court. Both are described at paras 2.144–2.170. A landlord must obtain a possession order before such a tenant can be evicted and notice must be served before the claim can be issued:

Introductory tenancies

Notice of proceedings

5.65   The notice is not a prescribed form but must:[32]

- state that the court will be asked to make an order for possession;
- set out the reasons for the landlord's decision to apply for the order;
- specify the date after which proceedings for possession may be begun;
- inform the tenant of the right to request a review of the decision;
- inform the tenant of the time within which such a request must be made (14 days); and
- inform the tenant that if he or she needs help or advice about the notice, he or she should take it immediately to a citizens' advice bureau, housing aid centre or a solicitor.

5.66   The date after which proceedings may be begun cannot be earlier than the date a tenancy could be ended by notice to quit, which means at least 28 days or a complete period of the tenancy if longer.

5.67   The court has no power to waive the notice requirement or to permit amendment.

---

31 *Wandsworth LBC v Atwell* (1995) 27 HLR 536; Law of Property Act 1925 s196(5).
32 HA 1996 s128(1).

Demoted tenancies

5.68 A demoted tenancy is one that was secure or assured but has been demoted by the court. Therefore two kinds of notices must be considered:

- the notice served prior to a demotion application; and
- the notice served prior to an application for possession of a demoted tenancy.

Notice of intention to apply for a demotion order

5.69 Before applying for a demotion order the landlord must serve notice of intention to apply to demote the tenancy. As for notices seeking possession, the court may dispense with the requirement if it is just and equitable to do so.[33] This applies whether the tenant is secure or assured.

5.70 A landlord may make an application solely for a demotion order but most applications will be in conjunction with an application for possession; the demotion being sought as an alternative to a possession order. In such a case two notices must be served: notice of seeking possession and notice of intention to apply for a demotion order.

Secure tenants

5.71 For secure tenants the notice must be in prescribed form.[34] It is similar to a notice of seeking possession, requiring the following information be given:[35]

- particulars of the conduct that has caused the landlord to seek a demotion order;
- the earliest date upon which the proceedings may be begun, being no earlier than the date the tenancy could be ended by notice to quit (at least 28 days or a complete period of the tenancy, whichever is longer, ending on the first or last day of a period).

5.72 The notice lapses 12 months after the date specified.

Assured tenants

5.73 A landlord must serve a notice of intention to apply for a demotion of the tenancy before commencing proceedings, but there is no

33 HA 1985 s83(1)(b); HA 1988 s6A(5)(b).
34 HA 1985 s83(2) and the Secure Tenancies (Notices)(Amendment)(England) Regulations 2004 (SI No 1627).
35 HA 1985 s83(4A)(a).

prescribed form of notice. However, HA 1988 s6A(6) provides that the notice must:

- give particulars of the conduct complained of;
- state that proceedings will not begin before the date specified in the notice, being at least two weeks from the date of the notice; and
- state that proceedings will not begin later than 12 months after the notice was served.

5.74   If the tenancy is demoted a former secure tenant of a local authority will become a demoted tenant. A former assured tenant and a former secure tenant with an RSL landlord will become a demoted assured shorthold tenant.

Notice before applying for possession

5.75   Demoted and assured shorthold tenants have limited security of tenure. However, if the landlord wishes to evict a demoted tenant, a possession order must be obtained and before the claim is made further notice must be given to the demoted tenant.

Demoted tenancies

5.76   For demoted tenancies the requirements of the notice are the same as the notice served on an introductory tenant. There is no prescribed form of notice but the notice must:[36]

- state that the court will be asked to make an order for possession;
- set out the reasons for the landlord's decision to apply for the order;
- specify the date after which proceedings for possession may be begun, being no earlier than the date the tenancy could be terminated by notice to quit;
- inform the tenant of the right to request a review of the decision and the time within which the request must be made (14 days); and
- inform the tenant that if he or she needs help or advice about the notice, he or she should take it immediately to a citizens' advice bureau, housing aid centre or a solicitor.

36 ASBA 2003 s143E.

Reviews: Introductory and demoted tenants

5.77 The decision to seek possession against an introductory or a demoted tenancy is subject to the tenant's right to seek a review within 14 days of receiving notice. If a review is requested the authority must conduct the review before issuing the claim for possession.

5.78 The review process for both is governed by regulation and provides:[37]

- the review must be carried out by someone not involved in the decision to apply for a possession order;
- if the review is carried out by an officer, he or she must be senior to the officer who made the decision;
- the tenant may request an oral hearing but must do so within the 14 day period;
- if there is a hearing the tenant may attend and may be accompanied by another person or representative and may call evidence, put questions to other people giving evidence and make written representations;
- the tenant must be given notice of the hearing not less than five days after the request for a hearing is received;
- a hearing may be postponed or adjourned or may proceed in the tenant's absence.

Demoted assured shorthold tenancies

5.79 A demoted assured shorthold tenancy is similar to an ordinary assured shorthold tenancy and a landlord must serve a notice complying with HA 1988 s21.

5.80 An RSL is not required to offer to a tenant a review of the decision although many RSLs may have a policy of doing so.

Challenging the review process

5.81 In relation to both introductory and demoted tenancies it has been held by the Court of Appeal that the county court has no discretion regarding the making of a possession order once it is satisfied that the authority has followed the statutory notice and review procedure, and that the only way to challenge the decision is by way of judicial

---

37 See Introductory Tenants (Review) Regulations 1997 (SI No 72) and Demoted Tenancies (Review of Decisions)(England) Regulations 2004 (SI No 1679).

review.[38] However, in the case of *Sandwell LBC v Constantinou*[39] in Walsall County Court an appeal brought by an introductory tenant against the making of a possession order was allowed. The Circuit Judge held that at the time the order was made there had been no affidavit or witness statement from the council explaining how the procedure had operated. Further, Mr Constantinou's application for permission to bring a judicial review claim was refused on the basis that the public law challenge to the lawfulness of the decision to claim possession should be decided by the county court. In light of the European Court of Human Rights decision *McCann v UK* (see paras 6.131 and 21.41), and the decision of the House of Lords in *Doherty v Birmingham CC* (see para 6.132), it may be that such issues may in the future be raised by way of a defence to the claim for possession.

Issuing a possession claim

5.82   The procedure for issuing possession claims is set out in Part 55 of the Civil Procedure Rules (CPR). A failure to comply with the requirements of Part 55 may be grounds for a claim to be struck out or adjourned. Part 55 and the practice direction to Part 55 can be downloaded from the website of the Ministry of Justice www.justice.gov.uk.

5.83   See chapter 22 for a general explanation of civil claims in the county court.

5.84   Claims for possession will usually be issued in the county court.[40] Each county court covers a certain geographical area and the claim must be issued in the county court that has jurisdiction for the area in which the premises are situated. To find out which court has jurisdiction for a particular address, the court service website has a search facility which can be found at: www.hmcourts-service.gov.uk/HMCSCourtFinder.

5.85   Under CPR Part 55 there are three types of possession claim:

- ordinary claims against tenants, licensees and trespassers and mortgage possession claims, when the claim is dealt with at a hearing (CPR 55 Part I);

---

38 *Manchester CC v Cochrane* (1999) 1 WLR 809, CA; *R(Gilboy) v Liverpool CCC and SSCLG* [2008] EWCA Civ 751, 2 July 2008.

39 16 November 2007, March 2008 *Legal Action* 18.

40 Only in exceptional circumstances can a possession claim be brought in the High Court, see CPR 55 PD 1.1 and 1.3.

- claims under the accelerated procedure when a possession order may be made without a hearing. This procedure is only available against assured shorthold tenants (CPR 55 Part II);
- claims for interim possession orders against trespassers when the claim is dealt with at a hearing but with very short notice to the occupiers (CPR 55 Part III).

Ordinary possession claims – CPR 55 Part I

5.86 This Part will be used where the claim for possession is against:

- a tenant with substantive security of tenure;
- an occupier with procedural security of tenure;
- an assured shorthold tenant where the landlord also wishes to claim a money judgment for unpaid rent or where there is no written tenancy agreement;
- a borrower (mortgagor) by a lender (mortgagee).

5.87 The claim is commenced by the landlord (claimant) sending to the court the following:

- claim form (N5) and copies (one for each defendant);
- particulars of claim and copies;[41]
- written evidence relied on or required by CPR; and
- court fee.

5.88 On receipt the court will:

- give the case a reference number – prefaced with the initials of the court;
- set a date for the first hearing;
- post to the defendant copies of the following:
  - the Claim form, endorsed with the hearing date,
  - Particulars of Claim,
  - a Form of Reply[42] with guidance notes;
- post to the claimant notice confirming issue and giving notice of the hearing date.

5.89 In some county courts some possession claims can be issued online.[43]

---

41 The Particulars of Claim is on form N119 if based on rent arrears and N120 if the claim is a mortgage possession claim.

42 Form N11R if rent arrears and N11M if mortgage possession claim.

43 See Practice Direction: Possession Claims Online.

Particulars of claim

5.90   In any civil claim the particulars of claim set out 'a concise statement of the facts on which the claimant relies'.[44] For particular kinds of claim Practice Directions (PDs) specify certain information that must be included in the particulars of claim. The PD to CPR 55 provides that the particulars of claim must:[45]

- identify the land to which the claim relates;
- state whether the claim relates to residential property;
- state the ground on which possession is claimed;
- give full details about any mortgage or tenancy agreement; and
- give details of every person who, to the best of the claimant's knowledge, is in possession of the property.

5.91   If the claim relies on a statutory ground or grounds the particulars of claim must specify the ground or grounds relied on.[46]

Rent arrears cases

5.92   If the claim includes a claim for non-payment of rent the particulars of claim must also set out specific information about the arrears. In particular, a schedule of arrears must be provided. This must cover the two-year period immediately before issue, or, if the first date of default occurred less than two years before the date of issue, from the first date of default. The schedule must give a running total of the arrears.

5.93   If the claimant wishes to rely on a history of arrears that is longer than two years, this should be stated in the particulars and a full or longer schedule attached to a witness statement.[47]

5.94   The following information must also be given:

- information about the defendant's circumstances, if known, including whether he or she is in receipt of social security benefits and whether any direct payments are made to the claimants from benefit;
- details of any previous steps taken to recover the arrears, including previous proceedings;

---

44 CPR 16.4(a).
45 PD 55.4, para 2.1.
46 PD 55.4, para 2.4B.
47 PD 55.4, para 2.3A.

Nuisance and anti social behaviour cases

5.95   If the claim for possession relates to the conduct of the tenant, details of the conduct alleged must be included in the particulars of claim.[48]

Mortgage arrears cases

5.96   If the claim for possession is brought by a mortgagee (lender of a secured loan) the particulars of claim must state whether certain notices and charges have been registered under the Matrimonial Homes Act 1967, the Matrimonial Homes Act 1983 or the Family Law Act 1996.[49]

5.97   Full details about the state of the mortgage account must be given, including the amount of the advance; any periodic payments; any interest payments required; the amount needed to redeem the mortgage at a stated date not more than 14 days after issue, including any adjustment for early settlement and specifying the amount of solicitors' costs and administration charges that would be payable. If the claim is brought because of failure to pay the periodic payments when due, detailed information must be given about the arrears, as for rented properties, in schedule form.

5.98   If the claimant wishes to rely on a history of arrears that is longer than two years, this should be stated in the particulars and a full or longer schedule attached to a witness statement.[50]

5.99   If the loan is a regulated consumer credit agreement (see para 6.155), this must be stated.

5.100   The following information must also be given:

- Information about the defendant's circumstances, if known, including whether he or she is in receipt of social security benefits and whether any direct payments are made to the claimants from benefit;
- Details of any previous steps taken to recover the arrears, including previous proceedings are given below.

Statements of truth

5.101   The claim form, the particulars of claim and defences are 'statements of claim' and must be endorsed with a statement of truth. This

---

48   PD 55.4, para 2.4A.
49   PD 55.4, para 2.5. These refer to the occupation rights of spouses and civil partners, see chapter 11.
50   PD 55.4, para 2.5A.

should be signed by a person able to verify the truth of the facts stated in the document.[51]

Service of the claim by the court

5.102   The claim form and particulars of claim are served on the defendant by the court usually by first class post. The papers are deemed to be received by the defendant on the second day after posting. At least 21 days' notice of the hearing must be given and the hearing should be within eight weeks of issue.[52] However, the court has the power to shorten the time before the hearing of the claim.[53]

Defendant's response to the claim

5.103   Form N5 states that the defendant must complete the form of reply and return it to the court within 14 days. However, the rules do not require the defendant to do so.

5.104   Failure to file a form of reply or a defence will not prevent the defendant from attending the hearing and defending the claim; there is no provision for default judgement under CPR 55.[54] However, the court can order the defendant to pay any legal costs that would not have been incurred had the defence or form of reply been filed on time.[55]

5.105   If the defendant intends to defend a claim but cannot file a full defence before the hearing, the claimant should be informed of the defendant's position before the hearing.

5.106   Where a defence is to be filed it may be possible for the parties to agree what case management directions the court should make (see para 5.111 below). Agreed case management may be submitted to the court in advance and the parties may avoid having to attend the first hearing. Even if agreement is not possible, it is important to inform the claimant that the claim is defended so that the claimant does not attend court expecting the claim to be disposed of.

---

51   CPR 22.
52   CPR 55.5(3).
53   CPR 3.1(2)(a) and (b). PD 55.5, para 3.2 refers specifically to situations in which the defendant has committed or threatened to commit assault or damage to property but the power is not limited to such situations.
54   Unlike most other civil claims, see chapter 22.
55   CPR 55.7.

The first hearing

5.107   Most courts list a large number of possession claims for hearing during a morning or afternoon session. This means that each claim will be allocated very little court time (sometimes as little as five or ten minutes). This usually means that only simple cases, or undefended claims will be disposed of at the first hearing.

5.108   Possession claims concerning rent arrears, mortgage arrears and applications to suspend possession warrants are held in private, ie members of the public cannot sit in court. Nevertheless, rent arrears cases are in theory heard in 'open court' rather than 'in chambers', as is the case for mortgage cases and warrants. Rights of audience differ according to whether a case is in open court or in chambers. See para 22.95 below.

Evidence

5.109   Unless the claimant knows that the claim is defended and therefore cannot be finally decided at the first hearing, the claimant should attend court with the necessary evidence to prove the case. This means sufficient evidence to prove any ground for possession and, if necessary, that it is reasonable to make possession order.

5.110   In most cases the claimant will arrange for an appropriate witness to attend court to give evidence orally. A private landlord may present his or her own case *and* give evidence. However, it is possible to rely on written evidence such as the particulars of claim and any witness statements provided these have been served in advance.[56] Nevertheless, if the defendant challenges the truth of a written statement the hearing will usually be adjourned for the maker of the statement to attend court.[57]

Possible outcome of first hearing

5.111   At the first hearing the possible outcomes are:
- that a possession order is made;
- the claim is dismissed or struck out;
- the claim is adjourned generally, or to a date in the future; or
- case management directions are given, setting out the steps the parties must take before the claim comes back before the court.

56   See CPR 55.8(4).
57   PD 55.8, para 5.1–5.4.

The accelerated possession procedure – CPR 55 Part II

5.112   The accelerated possession procedure is available only in relation to assured shorthold tenancies. The procedure can only be used where:

- the original tenancy agreement is a written agreement;
- the only remedy sought is a possession order – rent arrears or any other form of relief cannot be claimed under the accelerated procedure.

Procedure

5.113   The landlord completes the claim form (form N5B) which must be endorsed with a statement of truth. Copies of the documents relied on (ie, the tenancy agreement, the notice requiring possession and any documents confirming compliance with the tenancy deposit scheme) must also be attached. These documents are sent to the court with a court fee. The court then sends to the tenant a copy of the form N5B and the copy documents together with a form of reply (form N11B). The tenant's reply indicates what is agreed and what is contested. The tenant has 14 days to complete and return the form N11B. Even if a tenant agrees with the contents of the form N5B he or she may use the form of reply to ask the court to postpone the effect of any possession order for up to 42 days on the grounds of 'exceptional hardship'. The tenant may also ask for time to pay the court costs (the court fee and the fixed costs which may be claimed if a solicitor is instructed to complete the form N5B).

5.114   If the tenant files a reply this is sent to the landlord and the papers referred to a judge. If the tenant does not file a reply within 14 days the landlord should file a request for a possession order to be made and this will be referred to a judge.

5.115   If the judge is satisfied that the landlord is entitled to possession a possession order will be made. If not, the judge may fix a hearing for the parties to attend, or dismiss the application. If a hearing is fixed the parties should be given at least 14 days notice and the judge may give directions as to what steps the parties should take before the hearing.

Interim possession orders – CPR 55 Part III

5.116   A quicker procedure for obtaining an interim possession order against trespassers is available under CPR 55 Part III. It does not apply to all claims against trespassers. An application for an interim possession order (IPO) may only be made if:[58]

- the only claim is a possession claim against trespassers;
- the claimant has an immediate right to possession and has had such a right throughout the period of unlawful occupation;
- the occupiers entered the land as trespassers; and
- the claim is made within 28 days of the date the claimant became aware of the defendants' occupation, or the date the claimant ought reasonably to have known of the occupation.

5.117 An application for an IPO cannot be made against someone who entered or remained on premises with the consent of the person who, at the time, had an immediate right to possession. This would include a person allowed into occupation by a tenant where the tenancy is subsequently ended so that the occupier becomes a trespasser.

5.118 Strict time limits apply. The papers must be served on the defendants within 24 hours of issue and a hearing may be listed on as little as three clear days notice to the defendants. A final hearing should be listed no sooner than seven days after an IPO is made.

5.119 It is a criminal offence to be on premises as a trespasser while the IPO is in force. However, no offence is committed if the trespasser leaves the premises within 24 hours and does not return.

5.120 An IPO will lapse on the date of the final hearing. Either a final possession order will be made, the court will dismiss the claim or give directions for a future hearing.

Possession orders

The extended discretion

5.121 When considering a claim for possession on a discretionary ground[59] the court has an 'extended discretion'[60] under which it may:

- adjourn the proceedings for such period or periods as it thinks fit; and

on making an order for possession or at any time before the order is executed the court may;

---

58 CPR 55.21.
59 See appendix to chapter 6 for a full list of all of the discretionary grounds for possession.
60 RA 1977 s100, HA 1985 s85, HA 1988 s9.

- stay or suspend the execution of the order;
- postpone the date of possession;

for such period or periods as it thinks fit.

5.122   On any such adjournment, stay, suspension or postponement the court must impose conditions regarding the payment of rent arrears and rent (or payments in respect of occupation after the termination of the tenancy) and may impose such other conditions as it thinks fit.

5.123   If the conditions are complied with, the court may discharge or rescind the order for possession.

5.124   The court then may adjourn possession proceedings either generally or on terms. In addition it may make orders under which the right to possession is postponed or the enforcement of the right to possession suspended. However, these powers are only available if the claim for possession is made on a discretionary ground.

5.125   If the claim for possession is established on a mandatory ground, or where no grounds are required, eg claims against assured shorthold tenants or against non-secure tenants, the court must make an 'outright' order fixing the date for possession. In such a case the court may postpone the effect of the possession order only for a maximum of six weeks if the tenant can show exceptional hardship if an earlier order were made.[61]

Tolerated trespass

5.126   The widespread use of conditional – 'postponed' or 'suspended' – orders for possession created a new class of occupier: the 'tolerated trespasser'. Initially, it was understood that an order for possession suspended on terms meant that if those terms were breached the tenancy ended and the occupier became a tolerated trespasser.[62] This was the case for both secure and assured tenancies.[63] To evict a tolerated trespasser the landlord had to apply for a warrant of eviction

---

61   HA 1980 s89.
62   *Thompson v Elmbridge BC* [1987] 1 WLR 1425; *Burrows v Brent LBC* [1996] 4 All ER 577.
63   *Knowsley Housing Trust v White* [2007] EWCA Civ 404. Tolerated trespass does not arise in relation to Rent Act tenancies. Under the Housing Acts the possession order determines the tenancy whereas under the Rent Act 1977 the statutory tenancy under which the tenant occupies continues until a possession order is executed: *Payne v Cooper* [1958] 1 QB 174. The Housing and Regeneration Act 2008 will amend the Housing Acts to create the same effect for secure and assured tenants.

and the occupier could prevent the eviction by applying for a suspension of the warrant on terms or by applying to further postpone the date for possession. A tolerated trespasser could not rely on the terms of the tenancy agreement such as the right to have repairs carried out. Futher, if the tolerated trespasser died there was no right of succession. However, if the court varied the order so as to further postpone the date for the giving of possession this would have the effect of reviving the tenancy retrospectively.[64] A court could only vary an order in this way if the order had been made on a discretionary ground for possession.

5.127 However, the concept of the tolerated trespasser has been the subject of much scrutiny by the courts in recent years and it is clear that different forms of 'suspended' orders have different effects. The Housing and Regeneration Act 2008 will effectively abolish tolerated trespass.[65] However, until the provision comes into force advisers should be aware of the effect of different types of conditional orders for possession.

Different types of conditional possession order

5.128 There are broadly four types of possession order under which the right of possession is suspended or postponed so long as the tenant complies with conditions set by the court. These are set out below with a summary of the effect of each type of order.

(1) Possession postponed until breach of terms

5.129 An order may provide that the claimant 'do recover possession' or that the defendant 'must give the claimant possession' but that the order may not be enforced for 28 days in any event, and for so long thereafter as the defendant pays the current rent plus arrears by instalments and costs.

5.130 Such an order means that the tenancy ends if the tenant misses a payment. He or she is then a tolerated trespasser but can apply to vary the order so as to further postpone the right of possession and thereby revive the tenancy.[66]

---

64 *Rogers v Lambeth LBC* (2000) HLR 32.
65 The Act received Royal Assent on 22 July 2008 but at the time of writing it is not known when the provision will come into force.
66 The order reviving the tenancy must first impose a further condition and when the tenant has complied with that condition the order can be discharged.

(2) Enforcement suspended

5.131   An order may provide that the claimant will have possession of the premises on a specified date, but that the order may not be enforced so long as the tenant complies with terms regarding the payment of current rent plus instalments of arrears and costs.

5.132   This kind of order means that the tenancy ends on the date specified even if the tenant strictly complies with the order.[67] An application can, however, be made to vary the order so as to postpone the right of possession (as opposed to enforcement). This will have the effect of reviving the tenancy.

(3) 'Swindon v Aston' orders

5.133   In the case of *Swindon DC v Aston*[68] the Court of Appeal considered an order that provided that 'the judgment shall cease to be enforceable when the arrears of rent and costs referred to above are satisfied'. While intended to protect an occupier from being evicted after the original arrears had been cleared, the court held that the term also meant that the order could not be varied after the tenant had repaid all of the arrears and costs. The effect therefore is to create an 'entrenched' tolerated trespasser who may remain in occupation but is unable to revive the tenancy.

5.134   In the cases of *London & Quadrant Housing Trust v Ansell*[69] and *Porter v Shepherds Bush Housing Association*[70] the order contained a term that stated: 'When you have paid the total amount mentioned, the claimant will not be able to take any steps to evict you as a result of this order'. The Court of Appeal confirmed that the effect of such a term was the same: the court could not vary the order if the total amount had been paid.

5.135   Such a term may be included in either of the orders described above (possession postponed or enforcement suspended). In either case an occupier who wishes to apply for the tenancy to be revived must make the application *before* clearing the arrears and costs.

(4) Two-stage postponed possession orders

5.136   Since July 2006 the two-stage postponed possession order (PPO) has been widely used by the courts (although some judges and courts do

---

67 *Harlow v Hall* [2006] EWCA Civ 156, 28 February 2006.
68 [2002] EWCA Civ 1850, 19 December 2002.
69 [2007] EWCA Civ 326, 19 April 2007.
70 [2008] EWCA Civ 196, 19 March 2008.

still make orders in which possession is given but enforcement suspended). Under a PPO no date is fixed for the giving of possession. Rather, the landlord must make a further application for a date to be fixed and the landlord's right to do so is postponed on terms. The tenant must be notified by the landlord of the intention to apply, with details of the alleged breach. The tenant has a right to reply and both the notice and reply must be sent by the landlord to the court when applying to fix a date for possession. Most applications are dealt with without a further hearing. If a date is fixed the landlord may proceed to obtain a warrant of eviction. If a warrant is not requested, or if the warrant is suspended, the occupier will become a tolerated trespasser after the date fixed for possession. As with other conditional possession orders made on discretionary grounds, the court retains a discretion to vary the order up to the date of eviction.

Housing and Regeneration Act 2008 solution

5.137 The Housing and Regeneration Act 2008 will amend the law relating to tolerated trespass. It will apply to secure, assured, assured short-hold, introductory and demoted tenancies.[71]

5.138 Where a possession order is made, whether outright or conditional, the tenancy will not come to an end until the execution of the order for possession ie the eviction of the tenant.

5.139 The court's power to discharge or rescind an order for possession will not depend on the conditions of any order having been complied with. Instead the court will have a general power to discharge or rescind the order if it thinks it appropriate to do so having regard to any conditions imposed by the court and the conduct of the tenant in connection with those conditions.

5.140 Not only will the Act propose to resolve the problem for future tenants against whom possession orders are made, but for existing tolerated trespassers a 'new tenancy' will automatically arise on the date the relevant provision comes into force. The new tenancy will be the same type of tenancy as the original tenancy (ie an ex-secure tenant will get a new secure tenancy, an ex-demoted tenant will get a new demoted tenancy etc). The possession order made in respect of the original tenancy will still apply to the new tenancy but the new tenancy will not come to an end until the tenant is actually evicted, or gives up possession voluntarily.

---

71 The relevant provisions are set out in Schedule 11 of the Act.

5.141   The new tenancy and the original tenancy will be treated as the same tenancy continuing uninterrupted for the following purposes:

- in deciding whether the ex-tenant is a successor in relation to the new tenancy;
- for calculating the qualifying period and discount for the purpose of a right to buy application; and
- in deciding whether Ground 8 of HA 1985 is made out.[72]

5.142   In addition, in certain proceedings the court may order that the new tenancy and the original tenancy are to be treated for the purpose of the claim as the same tenancy continuing uninterrupted. This includes a claim by either the tenant or the landlord for a breach of the original tenancy.[73]

5.143   This provision will be relevant to claims for disrepair. A tenant who was for a period a tolerated trespasser but gained a new tenancy by virtue of the Housing and Regeneration Act would ordinarily not be able to claim damages for any period during which he or she was a tolerated trespasser. However, the court can order that the new tenancy and the original tenancy should be treated as the same uninterrupted tenancy so that damages can be awarded for the whole of the period of disrepair.

Enforcing possession orders

5.144   Possession orders of residential premises must be enforced by application for a warrant from the court.[74] The warrant is executed by court bailiffs. There is often a delay of several weeks from the date of the application for a warrant to the date of eviction.

5.145   The landlord may apply for a warrant after the date for the giving of possession (ie after the date fixed by the order or, if enforcement is suspended on terms, after the terms have been breached). Applying for a warrant is an administrative act. No further hearing will take place; the completion of a form requesting that a warrant be issued is sufficient. The court will send notice to the occupier that a

---

72 Ground 8 applies when a tenancy is accepted as temporary accommodation pending works, see appendix to chapter 6.

73 The court will have the power where the claim commences after the new tenancy arises or in an existing claim that has not been finally resolved when the new tenancy arises. The court will also have the power where the claim is for breach of statutory duty brought by the tenant against the landlord.

74 *Haniff & Robinson* (1994) 26 HLR 386, CA.

warrant has been issued, indicating the date and time of the eviction. If the order for possession was made on a discretionary ground the occupier may apply for the warrant to be suspended or stayed. If no such application is made the court bailiffs will attend the premises and can use reasonable force to secure entry.

Challenging the possession order

5.146   Where a possession order is made a defendant may:

- appeal against the order;
- apply to set the order aside; or
- apply to vary the order.

Appeals

5.147   A defendant can appeal against the making of a possession order but will be successful only it can be established that the decision was:

- wrong; or
- unjust because of a serious procedural or other irregularity in the proceedings in the lower court.[75]

5.148   In all cases the permission of the court is required. Permission may be obtained from the judge who made the order or from the judge or court to which the appeal is made.[76] An appeal against a district judge's order is heard by a circuit judge and an appeal against a circuit judge's order by the Court of Appeal.

5.149   The Civil Procedure Rules (CPR) Part 52 set out the procedure for bringing appeals. The deadline for commencing the appeal is 21 days from the date of the order.

5.150   It should be noted that lodging an appeal does not mean that the order cannot be enforced.[77] Unless the landlord agrees not to enforce the order until the appeal is heard, a separate application must be made for a stay of execution.

---

75 CPR 52.11(3).

76 Where a party wishes to appeal, permission should be sought orally from the judge immediately after the judge has made his or her order. However, it is often the case that the party is un-represented or it may not be clear that there are grounds to appeal until after the hearing. If permission is not requested or is refused by the judge who made the order, permission must be sought on the 'Appellant's Notice' (Form N161) which is submitted to the appeal court.

77 CPR 52.7.

5.151   A party who is unsuccessful in an appeal will usually be ordered to pay any legal costs incurred by the other party, see chapter 22. A landlord who has not instructed solicitors to obtain the possession order may do so if an appeal is lodged. A tenant considering an appeal should be advised of the increased liability for costs and, if possible, public funding should be obtained so that he or she has some protection against being ordered to pay further costs, see para 22.153.

Setting aside an order

5.152   An order may be set aside if the tenant or the tenant's legal representatives were not in court when the order was made.

5.153   Civil Procedure Rule 39.3 provides that the court will only set aside an order made in a party's absence if satisfied that the party:

- acted promptly when he or she found out that the court had made the order;
- had a good reason for not attending the hearing; and
- had a reasonable prospect of success at the trial.

5.154   In practice, the courts will usually accept genuine reasons for not attending, including, for example, attending the wrong court, oversleeping and arriving at the court after the hearing had taken place. The courts will generally not accept as 'good reason' a deliberate decision not to attend unless this was because of advice from a landlord that it was not necessary to attend.

5.155   Reasonable prospects of success would include the likelihood of obtaining an adjournment of a suspended or postponed possession order being made instead of an outright order.

5.156   All applications must be supported by evidence addressing these three criteria. This may be in the form of a witness statement prepared separately or endorsed on the application form (N244). Any supporting evidence, eg medical reports, should be attached to the witness statement.

5.157   A possession order may be set aside even after it has been executed, ie after eviction,[78] see below.

Variation, stay or suspension

5.158   Where an order has been made on a discretionary ground for possession, the court retains the 'extended discretion' (see para 5.121

---

78   *Peabody Donation Fund Governors v Hay* [1986] 19 HLR, CA.

above) up to the date of eviction. Under the extended discretion the possession order may be varied if the court thinks it reasonable to do so. In addition the enforcement of the order may be suspended or stayed.

5.159　Where an outright order has been made in the tenant's absence an application may be made to set aside the order and, as an alternative within the same application, to postpone the date of possession or to suspend enforcement on terms.

After eviction

5.160　After eviction the court no longer has a discretion to stay or suspend execution or to vary the possession order. There are, however, two possible ways for the tenant to regain occupation:

- setting aside the order under CPR 39, see paras 5.152–5.157 above; or
- setting aside the warrant.

5.161　If the possession order is set aside, the warrant itself 'falls away' and the tenant is entitled to re-occupy. However, because of the need to act promptly on finding out about the order it may be difficult to satisfy the requirements of CPR 39.

5.162　In any case, when a person has been evicted it is essential to act quickly in applying to the court. Where there is an inevitable delay in applying to the court the landlord should be contacted and quickly of the intended application and requested not to re-let the premises until it has been dealt with. If premises are let to someone else before the court considers the application it will be too late to obtain an order allowing the occupier to return.

Setting aside a warrant

5.163　A court may set aside a warrant of possession after eviction if satisfied that:

- the warrant was defective;
- the warrant was obtained by fraud; or
- there has been an abuse of process or oppression in the execution of the warrant.[79]

---

79 *Hammersmith & Fulham LBC v Hill* (1994) 27 HLR 368, CA.

Abuse of process

In *Hackney LBC v White*[80] the local authority had obtained a possession order in 1986. Subsequently several warrants had been issued and suspended on the tenant's application. In 1995 a further warrant was issued and the tenant evicted. The tenant sought to set aside the warrant because the court rules required that permission to issue was required in relation to an order made more than six years before. The Court of Appeal upheld the tenant's appeal holding that the warrant had been improperly issued and was an abuse of process.

Oppression

5.164   A warrant can be set aside if there has been oppression in the execution of the warrant. Misleading information given by a landlord to a tenant may constitute oppression.

In *Lambeth LBC v Hughes*[81] a warrant was issued, following which the council wrote to the tenant giving the date for eviction and stating that the only way to stop the eviction was to pay all the arrears in full. The tenant then saw his housing officer who said the same thing but said he could take legal advice. The tenant tried but failed to get advice. He went to the court office but his file could not be found. The court told him to await receipt of a letter from the court bailiff which would contain the eviction date and details of how to stop the eviction. The bailiff's letter was sent on 22 October by 2nd class post. It arrived on 28 October as the eviction was taking place.

The Court of Appeal held that:

(1) the council's message that only payment in full could prevent eviction was misleading and oppressive, in the absence of any reference to an application to the court;
(2) the oppression was not cured by the reference to taking legal advice without indicating what he could seek advice about;
(3) the failure of the court office to advise of the procedure was also oppressive; and
(4) the failure to post the bailiff's letter in sufficient time for it to be acted upon also made the execution oppressive.

---

80 (1995) 28 HLR 219, CA.
81 (2001) 33 HLR 33, CA.

5.165 It is not necessary that the 'oppression' is deliberate and may not be caused by the landlord.

> In *Hammersmith & Fulham LBC v Lemeh*[82] the occupier was aware of the impending eviction and attended court the day before it was scheduled. He was told by the court, mistakenly, that no warrant had been issued and advised to contact the council. The following day he was evicted and applied to have the warrant set aside on the grounds of oppression. The Court of Appeal held that there is no reason why misleading information given by the court cannot amount to oppression. It is a question of fact and it was clear that if the court had not given the wrong information to Mr Lemeh he would have been able to make his application to stay or suspend execution and have it heard before the eviction took place.

5.166 Occupiers often contact their landlord on receiving notice of an eviction to reach agreement. While a landlord is not bound to accept the tenant's proposals the landlord may be guilty of oppression if it is suggested that the only way to stop the eviction is to pay the whole of the arrears. Instead, the landlord may indicate that it is not willing to withdraw the warrant but should make clear that the tenant may apply to the court and that it is for the court to decide whether the eviction can go ahead.

5.167 To establish oppression it is necessary, for the tenant to be misled so that an application is not made to the court before the eviction takes place.

> In *Jephson Homes Housing Association v Moisejevs*[83] the occupier took advice from a Citizens Advice Bureau following receipt of a notice of eviction. The Bureau drafted an application to suspend the warrant for the occupier to take to court. However, instead of lodging the application she decided instead to pay to the landlord an amount equal to the shortfall under the terms of the order,

---

82 (2001) 33 HLR 23, CA.

83 (2001) 2 All ER 901, CA. See also *Circle 33 Housing Trust Ltd v Ellis* (2006) HLR, CA. See however *Southwark LBC v Augustus*, Lambeth County Court, 24 November 2006, February 2007 *Legal Action* 29, in which a warrant was set aside on the basis of oppression where the landlord had failed to follow its stated rent arrears policy requiring it to use eviction only as a last resort.

plus the costs of obtaining the warrant. Despite this, the landlord proceeded with the eviction. The occupier applied to set aside the warrant but her application was dismissed and permission to appeal refused. The court accepted that she was under a genuine misapprehension about what she needed to do to prevent the eviction but held that the court did not have a free-standing power to remedy the unfairness of the eviction. The Court of Appeal held that if the court process has been properly used without fault on the part of the landlord or the court, a warrant will not be set aside.

5.168   The court's powers to set aside warrants will remain under the provisions of the Housing and Regeneration Act 2008 but the effect of setting aside a warrant will be to automatically restore the tenancy.

CHAPTER 6

Defending possession claims

continued

Key points

- There are three types of possession claims: claims based on discretionary grounds, claims based on mandatory grounds, and claims for which no ground is needed.
- The most commonly used grounds are those relying on rent arrears and nuisance or anti-social behaviour.
- Most rent arrears grounds are discretionary grounds: it must be reasonable to make a possession order.
- For assured tenants only there is a mandatory rent arrears ground where more than eight weeks rent is in arrears.
- The nuisance ground for possession is discretionary but outright orders will usually be made for serious breaches of the tenancy or serious anti-social behaviour unless there are exceptional circumstances.
- Social landlords have other powers to deal with anti-social behaviour: they can apply for demotion of tenancies and for anti-social behaviour injunctions to exclude people from their homes or the neighbourhood. Powers of arrest may be attached to such injunctions.
- The county court can also now make ASBOs.
- Even where tenants have no legal right to resist a claim for possession a defence may exceptionally arise under the Human Rights Act 1998 or under the Disability Discrimination Act 1995.
- A mortgage usually gives the lender the right of possession so in mortgage possession proceedings have a true 'defence' to the claim is rare.
- In mortgage possession claims the court has the power to postpone or suspend possession only if the borrower can repay mortgage arrears within a reasonable period of time.

6.1   Chapter 5 deals with the procedural requirements of possession claims, including notice requirements. This chapter examines the most commonly used grounds for possession. Also considered are possible defences under the Disability Discrimination Act (DDA) 1995 and the Human Rights Act (HRA) 1998. Claims for possession of mortgaged property are briefly described. The appendix contains a list of all of the statutory possession grounds.

Possession claims against assured shorthold tenants

6.2   Since 28 February 1997 almost all tenancies granted by private landlords will be assured shorthold tenancies, see paragraph 2.58. An assured shorthold tenant has very limited security of tenure; he or she may be evicted after the first six months unless a longer fixed period is granted. The possible defences to a claim for possession against an assured shorthold tenant are:

- the tenancy is not an assured shorthold tenancy;[1]
- the notice requiring possession is not valid (see para 5.41);
- the landlord cannot rely on the notice because of a failure to comply with the mandatory tenancy deposit requirements, see paragraphs 3.150 and 5.50;
- the requirements of the Civil Procedure Rules have not been met.[2]

6.3   Additionally, recent case law suggests that in exceptional cases it may be possible for an assured shorthold tenant to defend a claim on the basis that the eviction is unlawful under the DDA 1995 (see para 6.105 below).

Rent arrears grounds

6.4   The majority of claims for possession are brought because a tenant is in arrears of rent. It should be noted that public sector landlords, including RSLs, must follow the rent arrears protocol before claiming possession on the grounds of rent arrears. See paragraph 5.4.[3]

Discretionary rent arrears grounds

6.5   For regulated, secure and assured tenants there is a discretionary ground for possession where 'rent lawfully due from the tenant' has not been paid.[4]

---

1   This may be because the tenancy was granted before 28 February 1997 and the necessary formalities were not complied with or because the tenant is claiming the protection of the anti-avoidance provisions of section 20(3), see para 2.69.
2   An example would be where a landlord brings a claim under the accelerated procedure but fails to produce a written tenancy agreement. See para 5.112 and chapter 22.
3   Unless the tenant has no security of tenure.
4   RA 1977, Case 1; HA 1985, Ground 1; HA 1988, Ground 10. Under RA 1977 and HA 1985 the full ground is that rent is in arrears or that the tenant is in breach of some other obligation under the tenancy. Under HA 1988 a separate ground exists for other breach: Ground 12.

6.6   In addition, for assured tenants only, there is a further discretionary ground (Ground 11) where the tenant has persistently delayed in paying rent.

The mandatory rent arrears ground

6.7   For assured tenants only, there is a mandatory rent arrears ground. Where at least eight weeks rent (or, if rent is paid monthly, two months rent) is in arrears both when the notice seeking possession is served and at the date of the hearing the mandatory ground is made out.

6.8   All of the rent arrears grounds are set out in full in the appendix to this chapter.

Rent arrears – defending claims for possession

6.9   In all cases the landlord must establish that each of the following elements is considered:

- rent;
- lawfully due;
- has not been paid (or there has been persistent delay in payment).

Rent

6.10   Many social landlords collect other charges as part of the rent, including water rates, heating and hot water charges and insurance contributions. Whether such charges can properly be treated as rent for the purpose of a claim for possession is undecided.

> In the case of *Lambeth LBC v Thomas*[5] the Court of Appeal considered a claim for possession brought because of arrears of water rates collected by the council. The court held that it was not necessary to decide whether such sums constituted rent because Ground 1 included other breaches of the tenancy agreement so the ground was made out in any event. However, the court indicated that there was force in the argument that the term rent should be given the meaning adopted in earlier Rent Act cases: all sums payable to the landlord.[6]

5   (1998) 30 HLR 89, CA.
6   This was the view taken in the county court case of *Lewisham LBC v Simba-Tola*, June 1993 *Legal Action* 14, Bromley County Court in which a possession order was made based on arrears entirely attributed to general rates, water rates and other charges, full housing benefit having been paid throughout the tenancy.

6.11   If the tenancy agreement makes provision for the payment of the other charges, failure to pay will constitute a breach of the tenancy agreement and therefore a ground for possession in any event. However, the amount of the total debt made up of non-rent charges will be relevant and advisers should, where possible, ensure that these are distinguished from the arrears of net rent.

6.12   Certainly, in the case of a Ground 8 claim, where the court *must* make an outright order if a certain level of arrears is proved, the narrow definition of rent should be applied and the court should exclude from the arrears figure any sums due to charges other than the net rent.

Lawfully due

6.13   In all cases the landlord must prove that the unpaid rent is 'lawfully due'.

Rent increases

6.14   The ways landlords can lawfully increase rents is described at paragraphs 3.172–3.197. If the landlord has not followed the correct procedure, the tenant may have a defence that the rent claimed was not 'lawfully due'. Advisers must ascertain the correct rent (ie the rent payable before any unlawful increase) and calculate whether there would be arrears in any event. Even if this is the case the court may nevertheless be prepared to dismiss the claim, depending on the true level of arrears, or, at the very least, adjourn the claim while the landlord prepares an amended rent schedule.

Landlord and Tenant Act 1987 s48

6.15   Under LTA 1987 s48 rent is not treated as due where a landlord has not given to the tenant an address in England and Wales at which notices may be served. However, it should be noted that as soon as the landlord gives the information, the whole of any rent due becomes payable (see paragraph 3.135).

Has not been paid

6.16   Where the landlord relies on one of the discretionary grounds that some rent is unpaid, the ground is made out if there were arrears both when notice was served and at the date of issue. Clearing the arrears before the date of the hearing does not mean that the ground is not made out. However, it is unlikely that a judge will find it reasonable to make a possession order in such a case. It is, however, likely that the tenant will be ordered to pay the landlord's legal costs.

6.17 If Ground 11 is used against an assured tenant the allegation is of 'persistent delay'. It is not necessary that there are arrears at the date of the notice or the date of issue, only that there is a history of late payment or the repeated accrual of arrears before payment is made, and that it is reasonable to make an order.

Rent schedules

6.18 The landlord must prove that the rent is unpaid and CPR Part 55 requires that a schedule must be attached to the Particulars of Claim (see para 5.92). The requirement is mandatory and a failure to comply may lead to a claim being struck out or, at least adjourned. An adjournment can be crucial to enable a tenant to resolve outstanding benefit issues and to begin making regular payments before the possession claim is considered by the court.

6.19 The rent schedules must be examined carefully with any evidence the tenant has of payment. Recent payments may not appear on the schedule and it is common for large public sector landlords to operate alternative accounts to recover arrears for previous tenancies and payments may be wrongly credited to those accounts.

Offers of rent

6.20 Where rent has been offered and refused by the landlord, this provides the defence of 'tender'. Private landlords sometimes refuse to accept payments of rent, or fail to bank cheques, with the aim of establishing a ground for possession. Although having offered payment gives the tenant a defence, the liability for rent is not extinguished even if the offer of payment has been refused. Tenants must therefore ensure that the rent is set aside so that it is available at the date of any hearing.

6.21 Where a cheque is accepted by the landlord the rent is treated as being paid on the date the cheque is delivered provided the cheque is subsequently honoured (see below at para 6.37).

Housing benefit problems

6.22 Chapter 8 summarises the housing benefit system. Many claims for possession are triggered by problems faced by tenants in relation to housing benefit, particularly in the social rented sector.[7]

7 For the last ten years the proportion of heads of households not in paid work in the social rented sector has remained steady at two-thirds (Source: Labour Force Survey, Office for National Statistics) and this is reflected in the proportion of households in the social rented sector relying on housing benefit which is also currently two-thirds (Source: DWP 'Housing operational database' available on the DWP website).

6.23   Arrears may accrue entirely as a result of an authority's inefficiency in administering housing benefit claims. However, more often there is a combination of maladministration and some failure on the part of the tenant, eg failing to comply with requests for information or evidence or to submit claims in time.

6.24   It is important to obtain as much information as possible before a possession hearing about any housing benefit problems. The court will expect detailed information about the outstanding issues, in particular what action is needed to resolve the issues, how long it is likely to take and how much housing benefit is likely to be paid.

6.25   The following housing benefit issues commonly cause or contribute to the accrual of rent arrears.

Issue	Suggested action
Tenant delays or fails to make or renew claim	Consider request to backdate. See paras 8.106–8.110.
Local authority delays processing claim for private tenant	Consider legal action to compel payment on account. See paras 8.104–8.105.
Overpayment recovery	Consider whether decision on recoverability can be challenged; request reduction of rate of recovery. See paras 8.115–8.116.
Non-dependent deductions	Check deduction correctly applied and at correct rate; advise tenant of need to claim contribution from non-dependent/to obtain information on non-dependent's income; advise tenant on right to evict non-dependent who refuses to contribute. See paras 8.93–8.96.
Local authority claim tenant's failure to provide evidence	Obtain information from authority as to what is required/request copy letters sent to tenant;[8] advise tenant on what to provide and to obtain receipts; consider backdating request if claim closed.
Unexplained delay in processing claim/ backlog in HB department	Consider issuing witness summons requiring housing benefit manager to attend court.[9]

---

8   Local authority landlords sometimes refer to these letters in the Particulars of Claim as part of the information about previous steps taken to recover the arrears. A party may make a written request for a copy of any document referred to in a statement of case and, provided an undertaking to pay reasonable costs is given, copies must be provided within seven days of the request: see CPR 31.14–15.

9   The procedure is set out in CPR 34.

Eligible rent or Local Housing Allowance is less than current rent	Consider application for Discretionary Housing Payment. See para 8.97.
For some other reason housing benefit does not meet the full rent	Ascertain reason and consider appeal against assessment of entitlement or advise tenant of amount he or she must pay each week for non-eligible charges and/or because income is too high to receive full housing benefit.

6.26   Where rent arrears have accrued as a result of local authority inefficiency or error, an application may be made for the authority to be joined to the proceedings and ordered to pay the costs.[10] Where the landlord *is* the local authority an application for costs can be made against the authority as claimant.

The relevance of housing benefit problems

6.27   In most cases housing benefit problems are relevant to the issue of whether it is reasonable to make a possession order rather than whether rent lawfully due is unpaid. There is an argument that rent is not 'unpaid' in the case of a local authority tenant who receives a rent rebate which the authority subsequently decide he or she was not entitled to.[11] However, it is rare for the whole of a tenant's arrears to be caused by the recovery of an overpayment. Further, this will not assist a tenant of a non-local authority landlord.[12]

6.28   A tenant awaiting a decision on a housing benefit claim should always be advised to pay the non-rebated charges. If the likely entitlement can be assessed, he or she should also be advised to pay any anticipated shortfall. Where there are bound to be arrears, even after housing benefit has been paid, instalments towards the arrears should also be paid. A failure to do this may mean that there are significant arrears when the housing benefit issues are resolved and a possession order may be made. If adjournments are granted to resolve housing benefit problems, the court may make it a condition of the adjournment that the tenant pays the non-rebated charge plus a sum towards the arrears.

6.29   It should be noted that in Ground 8 claims it will not assist a tenant that the arrears have accrued as a result of housing benefit

10 *Asra v Coke*, June 2001, *Legal Action*, 31. See para 22.167 below.
11 See Social Security Administration Act 1992 s134(2).
12 See HB Regs 2006 reg 95(2).

problems.[13] Advisers must try to ensure that all outstanding issues are resolved before the hearing of the possession claim and that the arrears are below the mandatory level of eight weeks.

The mandatory rent arrears ground: assured tenants only

6.30   Under HA 1988, Ground 8, a mandatory ground for possession is available where at least eight weeks' rent (for a weekly or fortnightly tenancy) or two months' rent (for a monthly tenancy) is in arrears both at the date the notice seeking possession was served and at the date of the hearing.[14]

6.31   If Ground 8 is proved the court has no discretion: an outright possession order must be made. This will usually be a 14-day order but if it appears to the court that this would cause exceptional hardship this may be extended to a maximum of six weeks.[15]

6.32   Rent means rent lawfully due from the tenant so advisers should consider the issues referred to above at paragraphs 6.10–6.15. Landlords usually rely on Grounds 8, 10 and 11 at the same time so that if Ground 8 is not made out, the court can still make an order under one of the discretionary grounds. However, under Grounds 10 and 11 the court may make a conditional order instead of an outright order (see para 5.121).

6.33   The court does not have an 'extended discretion' when Ground 8 is made out. Possession orders cannot be postponed or suspended. A possession order should clearly state whether it has been made on Ground 8. If it does not, the court can, at a later date, exercise its discretion.[16]

Adjournments

6.34   Whether a court could adjourn the hearing of a Ground 8 claim to enable a tenant to resolve housing benefit problems was considered by various county court with different outcomes. The issue came before the Court of Appeal in 2004.

---

13 See *North British v Mathews* [2004] EWCA Civ 1736 at para 6.34 below.
14 For yearly or quarterly tenancies, the figure is at least three months' rent or one quarters' rent, in arrears for at least three months. The ground is set out in full in the appendix to this chapter.
15 HA 1980 s89.
16 *Diab v Countrywide Rentals 1 plc*, ChD, (2001), *Independent*, 5 November.

North British Housing Association Ltd v Matthews & Others, London & Quadrant Housing Limited v Morgan[17] concerned four tenants of RSLs against whom possession was claimed on Ground 8. All had at least eight weeks arrears of rent at the date of service of the NSP and at the date of the hearing. In each case the tenants submitted that the arrears were caused by the failure of their local authorities to pay housing benefit and that the arrears would be cleared when the outstanding housing benefit claims or appeals were dealt with. In each case the judge refused adjournments on the day of the hearing and possession orders were made. The tenants appealed.

The Court of Appeal held that the power to adjourn a hearing to enable a tenant to reduce the arrears to below the Ground 8 threshold may only be exercised in exceptional circumstances and the fact that the arrears are attributable to maladministration on the part of the housing benefit authority is not an exceptional circumstance.

However, the court did refer to examples of cases where the court may properly exercise its discretion to adjourn. One of which was 'where the landlord is a public body, and the tenant may have an arguable defence based on abuse of power: the landlord is said to be acting unfairly and therefore unlawfully in pursuing a claim for possession. Where the court is satisfied that there is a real chance that the tenant would be given permission to apply for judicial review of the landlord's decisions to claim possession, the court may grant an adjournment of the possession proceedings to allow the tenant to take that course ... A yet further example is where, before or at the hearing date, the landlord accepts a cheque from the tenant for a sufficient sum to bring the arrears below the Ground 8 threshold, but the cheque is conditional payment, it may be a proper exercise of discretion to adjourn the claim for possession to see whether the cheque will be honoured'.[18]

6.35 This does not, however, mean that in the absence of such exceptional circumstances a court can never adjourn such a hearing. The court has an inherent power to control its own procedure. If a tenant raises a defence or procedural argument that the court does not have time to resolve, an adjournment may be granted for the case to be listed

---

17 [2004] EWCA Civ 1736.

18 Dyson LJ at [12]. Further examples given were of a tenant being robbed on the way to court and a computer failure leading to a payment not being credited by the local authority.

for a longer hearing. Or, where a tenant intends to bring a counterclaim for damages for disrepair, the court may give case management directions. What the court cannot do is adjourn for the express purpose of giving the tenant an opportunity to reduce the arrears below the minimum level.

6.36   When seeking an adjournment in such a case it is essential to make the application before the court has heard evidence. Otherwise, it may be argued that, the court being satisfied that the ground is made out, an order for possession must be made.

Payment by cheque

6.37   If, before the hearing, the tenant makes a payment to reduce the arrears to less than eight weeks the ground will not be made out.

> In *Coltrane v Day*[19] a cheque for the full amount of the arrears was sent by the tenant's solicitors to the claimant's solicitors five days before the hearing. Had it been paid into the landlady's account on the day of receipt it would not have cleared before the hearing. In fact, the cheque was given to the claimant by her solicitors on the day of the hearing and subsequently paid into her account. The district judge adjourned the hearing for 56 days. The circuit judge upheld the landlady's appeal holding that at the date of the hearing the rent was unpaid. An order for possession was made.
>
> The Court of Appeal allowed the tenant's appeal. It is an established principle of contract law that if a cheque is delivered and is not returned by the creditor the debt is discharged as at the date of delivery, provided the cheque is met on first presentation. In this case rent had always been paid by cheque, the landlady had accepted the cheque and paid it into her account where it was met on first presentation. However, if in such a case the cheque does not clear on first presentation an order for possession must be made; the date of the hearing being, for the purposes of Ground 8, the earlier and not the adjourned hearing. Further, in the absence of express or implied agreement regarding the payment of rent by cheque a landlord is not bound to accept a last minute cheque from the tenant.

19 [2003] EWCA Civ 342, 14 March 2003.

> The district judge had been right to adjourn the hearing but the appropriate adjournment would have been 7 or 14 days: 56 days was excessive.

6.38   So, unless there is an agreement that rent is paid by cheque, a tenant who wishes to make payment shortly before or at the hearing must do so by paying cash.

Ground 8 and Registered Social Landlords

6.39   In *R on the application of Weaver v London & Quadrant Housing Trust*[20] the tenant sought to judicially review the Trust's use of Ground 8 arguing that she had a 'legitimate expectation' that the Trust would follow Housing Corporation guidance. The Guidance suggested that RSLs should use all reasonable alternatives to recover rent arrears before using Ground 8. The court dismissed the claim, holding that the tenant could not establish legitimate expectation having been unaware of the guidance. Further, on the facts, the Trust could not be said to have failed to use reasonable alternatives before pursuing the claim for possession under Ground 8. See paragraph 21.49 for a full summary of the case.

Counterclaims

6.40   The defence of 'set-off' may be available to a claim for possession based on rent arrears. Set off means that the defendant acknowledges monies owed but claims the right to set off against the debt an amount due from the claimant to the defendant. Commonly the defendant will seek to set off damages for the claimant's breach of the repairing obligation. Even where damages are yet to be assessed the defendant has a right to equitable set-off.[21] However, the defendant's right of action must exist at the date the claim was issued. Chapter 9 describes in detail the repairing obligations of landlords and the way compensation is assessed. Advisers must be aware that a disrepair counterclaim will only exist where:

- there is 'disrepair' as opposed to poor conditions caused eg by poor design or overcrowding;

---

20 [2008] EWHC 1377 (Admin), 24 June 2008.
21 *British Anzani (Felixstowe) Ltd v International Marine Management (UK) Ltd* (1979) 2 All ER 1063.

- the repairs are the landlord's responsibility;
- the landlord has had notice of the need for repairs;
- the landlord has failed to carry out the repairs within a reasonable period; and
- the tenant has suffered loss and inconvenience.

6.41   If the assessed damages do not extinguish the arrears the court may make a possession order.[22] A tenant should therefore be advised to pay current rent plus a sum towards the arrears until the proceedings are disposed of.

6.42   The court has the power to order that a counterclaim be heard separately. Provided the court is satisfied that the defendant has a genuine claim this is unlikely but a court may exercise this power if the issue is raised at the first hearing without any evidence of the disrepair (such as photographs or a report) or where the counterclaim is unlikely to result in more than minimal damages and the arrears are substantial.

Nuisance

6.43   Part V of HA 1996 introduced several measures to address 'anti-social behaviour' in social housing. These included:

- amending the nuisance ground for secure and assured tenants;
- creating a type of probationary tenancy for local authorities – the 'introductory tenancy'; and
- giving local authorities the power to apply for anti-social behaviour injunctions (ASBIs) against persons who were not tenants of the authority and to which power of arrest could be attached.

6.44   The Anti-Social Behaviour Act (ASBA) 2003 strengthened these provisions by making anti-social behaviour injunctions available to other social landlords and by widening the scope of an injunction to include a power to exclude the person from his or her home and from the neighbourhood. ASBA 2003 also gave county courts the power to make anti-social behaviour orders (ASBOs) within existing proceedings.

The nuisance ground for possession

6.45   For secure and assured tenants the possession ground was amended to provide that the ground is made out where: [23]

22 See *Haringey v Stewart* (1991) 23 HLR 557.
23 HA 1985, Schedule 2, Ground 2; HA 1988, Schedule 2, Ground 14.

The tenant or a person residing in *or visiting* the dwelling-house – has been guilty of conduct causing *or likely to cause* a nuisance or annoyance to a person residing, *visiting or otherwise engaging in a lawful activity in the locality*, or has been convicted of using the dwelling-house or allowing it to be used for immoral or illegal purposes, or *an indictable offence*[24] committed in, or in the locality of, the dwelling-house.

6.46 The following should be noted:

- it is not necessary to prove that nuisance or annoyance has been caused to another person, only conduct *likely* to cause nuisance or annoyance. This means that it is not necessary for a 'victim' of the behaviour to give evidence;
- the conduct may be that of a visitor to the premises;
- the likely nuisance and annoyance need not be to neighbouring occupiers but may be to someone visiting or engaged in a lawful activity in the locality;
- any indictable offence committed in the premises or in the locality of the premises is sufficient. The offence need not be such as to be likely to cause nuisance;
- there must be a conviction for such an offence, not merely an allegation or charge.

6.47 However, the nuisance ground is discretionary and such issues as whether the conduct is that of the tenant or a visitor and the seriousness of any offence will be relevant to the reasonableness of making an order.

6.48 The case law since the ground was amended shows that the courts are now more likely to make outright orders against tenants where there has been serious anti-social behaviour and/or convictions for drug offences.

Bristol CC v Mousah[25] concerned a possession claim against a sole tenant who had recently been granted the tenancy. It was an

24 An indictable offence means any offence other than one that can only be tried in the magistrates court (known as a summary offence). It includes theft, assault (other then common assault) and all offences relating to the possession of controlled drugs.
25 (1998) 30 HLR 32, CA. In several cases the Court of Appeal have upheld a landlord's appeal against the refusal of a county court judge to make a possession order: *Darlington BC v Sterling* (1997) 29 HLR 309, CA; *West Kent Housing Association Ltd v Davies* (1999) 31 HLR 415, CA; *Newcastle upon Tyne CC v Morrison* (2000) 32 HLR 891, CA.

express term of his tenancy agreement that the tenant must not supply from or in the neighbourhood controlled drugs. Within the first nine months of the tenancy the premises were raided by police several times and it was clear that drugs were being sold from the premises. The tenant's evidence was that he had not been present at the time of the raids and had not been aware of what had been going on. He also gave evidence that he had previously received psychiatric treatment. The county court judge found that the tenant had been aware of the drug dealing but declined to make a possession taking into account the tenant's medical circumstances and that he would be unlikely to be housed as a homeless person if evicted.

The Court of Appeal allowed the council's appeal. The proper approach was that where there was a very serious breach of the tenancy agreement, it was reasonable to make possession order unless there were exceptional circumstances.

6.49   However, even where there is a serious breach of the tenancy agreement, the circumstances may be such that the court may decline to make an order or may postponed or suspend the order.

In the county court case of *Tai Cymdogaeth Cyfngedig v Griffiths*[26] the defendant was an assured tenant. Her partner was convicted of possession of Class B drugs on four occasions between July 2000 and May 2001, and in November 2000 of possession with intent to supply. In June 2002 an outright possession order was made on Grounds 12 and 14. The tenant appealed to the Circuit Judge. The judge held that the court must first consider whether it was reasonable for an order for possession to be made at all and, then, whether it was reasonable to suspend the order. The judge rejected the council's argument that the Court of Appeal's judgment in *Bristol CC v Mousah* meant that where a serious crime was committed, in the absence of exceptional circumstances, a possession order must be made. While it will be rare for the court to avoid a possession order in such a case, the suggestion that the burden moves to the tenant to establish exceptional circumstances was wrong. Most of the convictions were for possession only, the drugs were restricted to Class B, and there

26 Swansea County Court, February 2003 *Legal Action* 36.

was no evidence of users coming to the premises or causing nuisance; there had been no breach of any terms of the tenancy agreement in the 12 months before the hearing. Further, the following factors were relevant: the tenant herself was not involved save to the extent of allowing the premises to be used; she had not breached any other term and had always paid the rent; she was suffering from depression and had a nine year old granddaughter living with her. Also, her partner had left the premises although it was possible that he might return. The order was varied to an order suspended for 12 months on condition that the tenant complied with the terms of the tenancy agreement. The Court of Appeal refused the landlords permission to appeal the order.

The court's discretion

6.50   The Anti-Social Behaviour Act 2003 imposed on judges a duty to focus on the effect of the nuisance on others when considering whether to make a possession order.[27] This is referred to as the 'structured discretion' under which:

> The court must consider, in particular – the effect that the nuisance or annoyance has had on persons other than the person against whom the order is sought; any continuing effect the nuisance or annoyance is likely to have on such persons; the effect that the nuisance or annoyance would be likely to have on such persons if the conduct is repeated.

Suspending orders

6.51   As the nuisance ground is a discretionary ground, the court may suspend enforcement or postpone a possession order on terms. However, there must be some evidence that the tenant will comply with the terms.

In *Manchester CC v Higgins*[28] a suspended possession order was made against a tenant whose 12-year-old son had been guilty of

---

27   ASBA 2003 s16(1): the effect was to insert section 85A into HA 1985 and section 9A into HA 1988.
28   [2005] EWCA Civ 1423, 21 November 2005.

'appalling misbehaviour'. The behaviour included abusing and assaulting a neighbour's disabled sons, and smashing the windows of the neighbour's house and car. An injunction was obtained against the tenant with little effect and an ASBO was obtained against her son. His abusive behaviour continued and he was arrested and placed in a bail hostel. By the time of the trial he was subject to a 12-month secure accommodation order. The tenant also had a two-year old child with serious health problems. The judge found the tenant's evidence was 'inadequate' and that her approach was that if her son told her he had not done something then he had not done it. Nevertheless, the judge indicated that the family needed support and that it would be wrong to give up on any chance that the tenant's son could make some sort of improvement in his behaviour.

The Court of Appeal upheld the council's appeal against the decision to suspend the order. While the discretion in whether to make an order and whether to suspend it was wide, the judge had failed to take sufficient account of the effect of the behaviour on the neighbours and there was no evidence to support the view that the nuisance may cease. 'Previous unheeded warnings point one way: genuine remorse the other. The level of support available to a parent who is making proper efforts to control an errant child will be relevant. There must, however, always be a sound basis for the hope that the anti-social behaviour will cease.'[29]

Other measures

6.52   It may be argued that the availability of other measures to control anti-social behaviour, such as injunctions and ASBOs, means that an outright possession order is not necessary. On the other hand the fact that the behaviour warrants such measures may support the argument that the conduct is so serious that a possession order must be made.

6.53   As was pointed out in *Manchester CC v Higgins*:

> In one case the facts giving rise to the making of an ASBO may be so serious that both the making a possession order and the refusal to suspend it will be self evident. In another case the making of the ASBO may have served its purpose of restraining future misbehaviour

29 Ward LJ at 37.

so that although past conduct might make it reasonable to order possession yet suspension might be possible.[30]

6.54   In summary, where there is evidence of conduct causing, or likely to cause, significant nuisance or a conviction for a serious criminal offence, the kinds of exceptional factors that may help avoid an outright order are:

- the person causing the nuisance has left the premises;
- the tenant has shown genuine remorse and a willingness to modify his or her behaviour;
- other measure, such as injunctions or ASBOs, have proved effective.

In *Greenwich v Grogan*[31] it was a term of the defendant's tenancy that he must not 'use the property for any illegal purposes'. At the age of 17 he was convicted of handling stolen goods and sentenced to six months in a young offenders' institution. The offence consisted of receiving boilers stolen from council flats in the same block. Possession was sought under Grounds 1 and 2(b). An outright possession order was made. The tenant appealed. In the Court of Appeal it was conceded that the ground for possession was made out and that it was reasonable to make a possession order. However, the appeal was allowed on the ground that the judge had given insufficient consideration to the power to suspend the order on terms. The court referred to the possibility the tenant may be attempting to live a life free of crime and that that this was more likely if he was given the opportunity to continue living in the flat. The court suspended the order for 12 months on the condition that there be no further breach of the tenancy agreement.

6.55   It is important that tenants accused of nuisance are advised realistically. If a tenant's defence is that all of the allegations are unfounded it will be very difficult, if the nuisance, is proved to persuade a court that the tenant is willing to change his or her behaviour and that a possession order should be suspended or postponed.

---

30 Ward LJ at 35. See para 6.51 above.
31 (2001) 33 HLR 140, CA.

In the case of *Canterbury CC v Lowe*[32] the court heard evidence of serious harassment of neighbours, including threats to kill. The judge suspended an order for possession, taking into account the fact that there had been no incidents since injunctions had been granted eight days before the hearing and that the tenant's partner had belatedly indicated that 'common sense should prevail'. The council appealed seeking an outright order.

The Court of Appeal allowed the appeal. The judge had treated the compliance with the injunction as decisive rather than one of a number of relevant facts. Given that it had only been in force for eight days, its importance had been overestimated. Also, the statement attributed to the partner had been made in a closing speech by his barrister at a time when he was still denying the harassment. On the evidence of the serious harassment and its impact on the neighbour's family, the only proper conclusion was an outright possession order.

6.56   See, however, the case of *Moat Housing Group South Ltd v Harris and Hartless* at paragraph 6.72 below, which concerned an appeal against the making of an anti-social behaviour injunction, an anti social behaviour order and an outright possession order. The Court of Appeal replaced the outright order with a suspended order and set aside the ASBO.

Tenants with mental health problems

6.57   Complaints of nuisance may be made against a tenant with mental health problems. In such a case there may be a defence under the DDA 1995 (see para 6.107 below). However, if the landlord can 'justify' the eviction on the grounds that it is necessary to protect the health and safety of the tenant or others the eviction will not be unlawful. In all cases it will be relevant to consider the steps a social landlord has taken to offer support to the tenant and to consider, where appropriate, whether the tenant can be offered alternative accommodation.

6.58   The rent arrears protocol requires social landlords to consider in relation to tenants known to be is vulnerable whether a community care assessment is needed before issuing possession proceedings. Where a landlord fails to take similar steps in a nuisance case, the failure will be relevant to the reasonableness of a possession order.

32 (2001) 33 HLR 53, CA.

6.59   Moreover, the fact that a tenant's behaviour may be caused or exacerbated by mental health problems will always be relevant to the reasonableness of making a possession order.[33]

Other anti-social behaviour provisions

6.60   In addition to, or as an alternative to, claiming possession social landlords have other powers to deal with anti-social behaviour.

Anti-social behaviour injunctions (ASBIs)

6.61   Any landlord can apply for an injunction within possession proceedings to restrain a tenant from breaching the tenancy agreement until the final hearing. However, HA 1996, as amended by ASBA 2003 gives social landlords the power to apply for much more wide-ranging injunctions: ASBIs. These are not restricted to tenants of the landlord and the scope of the injunction is wide.

6.62   An ASBI may be obtained by a 'relevant landlord' which means: a housing action trust, a local authority and an RSL.[34] The following conditions must be satisfied.[35]

6.63   The person against whom the injunction is sought is engaging, has engaged or threatens to engage in conduct capable of causing nuisance or annoyance to:

- a person with a right to reside in or occupy housing accommodation owned or managed by the relevant landlord or in other housing accommodation in the neighbourhood; or
- a person engaged in lawful activity in the neighbourhood; or
- a person employed in connection with the landlord's housing management functions.

6.64   It does not matter where the conduct occurs.[36]

Ouster/exclusion and power of arrest

6.65   Further powers are given to the court where:[37]

- the conduct consists of or includes the use or threatened use of violence; or

---

33 See *Croydon LBC v Moody* (1999) 31 HLR 738.
34 HA 1996 s153E(7).
35 HA 1996 s153A.
36 HA 1996 s153A(5).
37 HA 1996 s153C.

- there is a significant risk of harm to the person the order seeks to protect.

6.66   If the court is satisfied that *either* of these conditions are met, the ASBI may include a provision prohibiting the person from entering or being in any premises specified (including premises occupied under a tenancy) or from any area specified in the injunction. Further, a power of arrest may be attached to the ASBI. However, if an ASBI is made without notice to the occupier *both* the conditions must be met before the court can exercise the power to make an ouster or exclusion order or to attach a power of arrest.[38]

Anti-social behaviour orders

6.67   The criminal courts have been able to make ASBOs since April 1999.[39] The power is contained in section 1 of the Crime and Disorder Act (CDA) 1998. ASBA 2003 amended CDA 1998 to permit applications to be made in the county court by a 'relevant authority'. Relevant authorities are: local authorities, police forces, RSLs and HATs.[40] Before making the application the applicant must consult with at least one other relevant authority.[41]

6.68   An application may only be made within existing proceedings. A freestanding application for an ASBO cannot be made in the county court. A relevant authority may make an application in proceedings in which it is already a party or may apply to be joined in proceedings for the purpose of applying for an ASBO, eg possession proceedings brought by a private landlord or family proceedings. The application will usually be against a person who is already a party to proceedings. However, an application may be made to join someone not already a party to proceedings in order to be made the subject of an ASBO, eg a family member of the tenant in a possession claim.

6.69   The procedure for county court ASBOs is set out in Part 65 of the Civil Procedure Rules.

6.70   To obtain an order it must be proved that:

- the person has acted in an antisocial manner, ie a manner that caused or was likely to cause harassment, alarm or distress to one or more persons not of the same household; and

38 See *Moat Housing Group South Ltd v Harris and Hartless* at para 6.72 below.
39 Up to December 2006 12,675 ASBOs had been made.
40 CDA 1998 s1(1A).
41 CDA 1998 s1E.

- the order is necessary to protect other people from further anti-social acts by the person.

6.71 The following features of county court ASBOs should be noted:

- the order may prohibit the person from 'doing anything described in the order'. It cannot compel a person to perform an act;[42]
- there is no limit to the duration of an ASBO but it must last a minimum of two years.[43] It can only be discharged within two years of being served if the parties agree.
- An ASBO cannot be made by consent.[44]
- A relevant authority must make an application for an ASBO; the court cannot make an order of its own motion.
- The standard of proof in relation to the antisocial behaviour is the criminal standard: beyond reasonable doubt.[45]
- The penalty for breach is not committal but prosecution for the criminal offence of breaching an ASBO without reasonable excuse.[46]

Challenging county court ASBOs

6.72 The decision to apply for an ASBO is the exercise of a discretion and may be challenged by way of judicial review. However, it will usually be more appropriate to challenge the application within the county court proceedings, either by applying to strike out the application or simply defending the application and arguing that the conditions are not made out.

> In the case of *Moat Housing Group-South Ltd v Harris and Hartless*[47] the Court of Appeal considered the making of an ASBI, an ASBO and an outright possession order.
>
> An ASBI with power of arrest had been granted without notice against a tenant with four dependent children. The ASBI required her to vacate her home and excluded her from the neighbourhood. The order was served at 9.00 pm on a Friday evening, three hours

---

42 *Lonergan v Brighton & Hove CC* [2005] EWHC 457 (Admin) 23 March 2005.
43 CDA 1998 s1(7).
44 *R on the application of T v Manchester Crown Court* [2005] EWHC 1396 (Admin) 7 June 2005.
45 *R on the application of McCann v Manchester Crown Court* [2002] UKHL 39 17 October 2002.
46 CDA 1998 s1(10).
47 [2005] EWCA Civ 287, 16 March 2005.

after the time specified for compliance with the order. The tenant was able to obtain a stay on the order from the High Court until the matters could be considered at a hearing the following week in the county court.

No previous warnings had been given to the tenant by the landlord about the allegations of antisocial behaviour by herself and two of her children. Most of the evidence of antisocial behaviour in the neighbourhood concerned a different family. Notice of Seeking Possession was subsequently served and at the possession hearing, which took place four weeks after the ASBI had been served, an outright possession order was made together with an ASBO for a period of four years. Much of the evidence presented to the court was hearsay, some from anonymous witnesses.

Considering the granting of the ASBI without notice the Court of Appeal reiterated the long standing principle that 'to grant an injunction without notice is to grant an exceptional remedy' and that 'As a matter of principle no order should be made in civil or family proceedings without notice to the other side unless there is a very good reason for departing from the general rule that notice must be given. Needless to say, the more intrusive the order, the stronger must be the reasons for the departure.'[48]

Making an ouster order or an exclusion order without notice was neither proportionate nor necessary to the harm sought to be avoided. The without notice ASBI should have been limited only to that which was necessary, ie an injunction against approaching witnesses. Further, it should not have been made for a period of six months but only until the further hearing. There was no justification for an ASBO for a four-year period and the judge had failed to consider the alternative of an ordinary injunction or undertakings that could be enforced by committal proceedings. In making the outright possession order the judge had failed to have regard to the needs of the tenant and her family.

The Court of Appeal set aside the ASBO ordering that an injunction or undertakings should be substituted. Further the outright possession order was set aside and replaced by an order suspended on terms.

48 Brooke LJ at [71] and [63].

Demotion orders

6.73   The nature of the demoted tenancy is dealt with at paragraphs 2.163–2.170 above.

6.74   The court must not make a demotion order unless it is satisfied that the tenant or a person residing in or visiting the dwelling has engaged or threatened to engage in:

- conduct which is capable of causing nuisance or annoyance to any person and which directly or indirectly relates to or affects the housing management functions of the relevant landlord; or
- conduct which consists of or involves using or threatening to use housing accommodation for an unlawful purpose.[49]

The court must also be satisfied that it is reasonable to make the order.

6.75   In most cases a landlord will apply for a demotion order at the same time as claiming possession on the nuisance ground. A demotion order may be made as an alternative to making a possession order that is postponed on terms.

Suitable alternative accommodation

6.76   For protected, statutory and assured tenants the availability of suitable alternative accommodation provides a discretionary ground for possession.[50] For secure tenants there are two classes of grounds under which, in addition to other matters being proved, suitable alternative accommodation must be available to the tenant.

6.77   In all cases where the landlord relies on a suitable alternative accommodation ground the accommodation must be available at the date the order is made or takes effect. The previous refusal of an offer of suitable accommodation does not give the landlord a ground for possession. So, where a tenant does refuse a suitable offer he or she will not be rendered homeless if a possession order is made; rather there will be the option of taking up the alternative accommodation. This may be the same accommodation previously offered or different accommodation. However, where a tenant has unsuccessfully challenged the decision that the accommodation offered is suitable he or she is likely to be ordered to pay the costs of the landlord.

---

49 See HA 1985 s82A, HA 1988 and HA 1996 ss 153A and 153B.
50 RA 1977 s98(1)(a); HA 1988, Ground 9.

6.78   In most cases the accommodation will be offered by the existing landlord or by arrangement with the existing landlord.

How is suitability assessed?

6.79   Each statute sets out the necessary conditions and relevant matters are set.[51]

Private tenants

6.80   A local authority certificate showing that it will provide suitable alternative accommodation on a specified date is conclusive evidence that suitable alternative accommodation will be available by that date. Such certificates are increasingly rare.

Level of security

6.81   In all cases the alternative accommodation must be let as a separate dwelling. The kind of tenancy offered must be the same kind of tenancy or one with 'equivalent security'.

6.82   For an existing protected or statutory tenant a new protected tenancy may be granted.[52] However, an assured tenancy is capable of offering 'equivalent security' to a protected or statutory tenancy.[53]

6.83   The new protected or assured tenancy cannot be one which would be subject to a mandatory notice ground, see appendix or an assured shorthold tenancy.

Other factors

6.84   The accommodation must be reasonably suitable to the needs of the tenant and the tenant's family in relation to proximity to a work place.

6.85   The accommodation must also be either:

- similar to accommodation let by the local authority to those with similar needs, in terms of the rent and the size of the accommodation; or
- reasonably suitable to the means and needs of the tenant and the tenant's family in terms of the extent and character of the accommodation.

---

51   RA 1977 Sch 15 Part IV; HA 1985 Sch 2 Part IV; HA 1988 Sch 2 Part III.
52   HA 1988 s34(1)(c).
53   *Laimond Properties Ltd v Al-Sharkarchi* (1998) 30 HLR 1099.

6.86   Accommodation cannot be suitable if it would be statutorily overcrowded.

Secure tenants

6.87   It should be noted that the availability of suitable alternative accommodation is not a 'free standing' ground for possession for secure tenants. It is one element of other grounds, some of which are discretionary. Most of the grounds are to facilitate development or to ensure that special needs or adapted accommodation is occupied by those who need such accommodation. Ground 16, however, provides that where a tenancy is obtained by succession, possession may be obtained on the ground of 'under-occupation'. Apart from Ground 16, which is only available for a limited period after the succession, under-occupation is not a ground for possession.

6.88   In all cases the following are factors the court must have regard to:

- the nature of the accommodation which it is the practice of the landlord to allocate to persons with similar needs;
- the distance from the places of work or education of the tenant and the tenant's family;
- the distance from the home of any other family members if proximity is 'essential' to the well-being of the tenant or other family member;
- the needs (as regards the extent of accommodation) and means of the tenant and the tenant's family;
- the terms on which the accommodation is available and the terms of the secure tenancy.

Level of security

6.89   In most cases the authority will offer to the tenant another secure tenancy. However, it is possible for a protected or assured tenancy to be deemed suitable alternative accommodation (not including those subject to mandatory notice grounds or assured shorthold tenancies).

Ground 16

6.90   Where the landlord is relying on Ground 16 certain additional matters must be taken into account in deciding whether it is reasonable to make an order. These are:

- the age of the tenant;
- the period during which the tenant has occupied the dwelling-house as his or her only or principal home; and
- any financial or other support given by the tenant to the previous tenant.

6.91   To rely on Ground 16 the authority must serve notice of seeking possession between 6 and 12 months after the previous tenant's death.

6.92   It should be noted that the ground is not available against a successor who was the spouse or civil partner of the deceased tenant.

6.93   If the tenant accepts suitable alternative accommodation he or she will be treated as a successor in that accommodation, unless the landlord agrees otherwise.

6.94   The date for assessing whether the accommodation is under-occupied is the date of the hearing, not the date of the succession.[54]

Discretionary grounds – reasonableness

6.95   When the landlord is relying on a discretionary ground the burden is on the landlord to prove that:

- the ground is made out; and
- it is reasonable to grant possession.

6.96   The court must always consider whether it is reasonable to grant possession in the particular circumstances. It is for the judge to decide which are the most significant factors:

> The duty of the judge is to take into account all relevant circumstances as they exist at the date of the hearing. That he must do in what I venture to call a broad common-sense way giving weight as he thinks right to the various factors in the situation. Some factors may have little or no weight others may be decisive.[55]

6.97   Because of this requirement, a possession order cannot be made by consent.[56] If the tenant does not oppose an order he or she must specifically admit all the necessary facts for the court to be satisfied that it is reasonable to grant possession.

---

54 *Wandsworth LBC v Randall* [2007] EWCA Civ 1126, 7 November 2007.

55 Lord Greene MR in *Cumming v Danson* [1942] 2 All ER 653 at 655.

56 See *Plaschkes v Jones* (1983) 9 HLR 110, *R v Bloomsbury & Marylebone County Court ex p Blackburne* (1985) 14 HLR 56 and *Wandsworth LBC v Fadayomi* (1987) 19 HLR 512.

6.98   Consideration of an occupier's right to respect for the home under article 8 of the European Convention on Human Rights (ECHR) should be part of the overall consideration of the question of whether it is reasonable to make an order (see para 6.130 below).

6.99   Note that when the court is exercising its discretion in relation to the nuisance ground it must take certain specific factors into account (see para 6.50 above).

Claims where no defence in domestic law

6.100   Before 1997 claims for possession could be described as falling into three fairly distinct categories:

(1) claims based on discretionary grounds where a possession order would be made only if it was reasonable to do so;

(2) claims based on mandatory grounds in which a possession order must be made if the ground was made out; and

(3) claims in which the landlord had an incontestable right of possession but was obliged to obtain an order to enforce that right.

6.101   Only in relations to claims in the first category did the court have any discretion as to the making of a possession order. The position is now less clear as a result of the following developments:

• legislation to combat anti-social behaviour;

• the incorporation of the European Convention on Human Rights by the Human Rights Act 1998; and

• legislation to protect the rights of the disabled, including tenants.

6.102   The anti-social behaviour provisions created two new types of tenancy: the introductory and the demoted tenancy (see chapter 2). Such tenants do not have substantive security of tenure and the local authority landlord need not prove a ground for possession. Nevertheless, before commencing a possession claim the landlord must inform the tenant of the reasons for the decision to seek possession and the tenant has the right to seek a review. As a public body, the authority must act lawfully both in making the decision and in the way the review is conducted. Further, as a public authority, it is bound to act in a way that is compatible with the ECHR.

6.103   The Human Rights Act 1998 raised the possibility of an occupier arguing in the county court that an order for possession would breach his or her rights under article 8 (the right to respect for the home).

6.104   The Disability Discrimination Act (DDA) 1995 applies to the management of premises, including evictions. To evict a person for a reason related to his or her disability is unlawful unless it can be justified. DDA 1995 applies whether or not the landlord is a public body.

Disability Discrimination Act 1995

6.105   DDA 1995 makes it unlawful to discriminate against disabled persons in relation to:

- employment;
- education;
- access to goods, facilities and services; and
- renting and buying land or property.

Meaning of disability

6.106   In all cases it is necessary that the person alleging discrimination is a disabled person. Disability is defined in DDA 1995[57] and the Disability Discrimination (Meaning of Disability) Regulations 1996.[58]

DDA 1995 and possession claims

6.107   The relevant provisions are found in DDA 1995 ss22–24:

6.108   Section 22(3)(c) provides that:

> It is unlawful for a person managing any premises to discriminate against a disabled person occupying those premises ... by evicting the disabled person or subjecting him to any other detriment.

6.109   Section 24(1) provides that:

> For this purpose a person ('A') discriminates against a disabled person if:
>
> (a) for a reason which relates to the disabled person's disability, he treats him less favourably than he treats or would treat others to whom that reason does or would not apply; and
> (b) he cannot show that the treatment in question is justified.

---

57   See DDA 1995 s1(1) and Sch 1.
58   SI No 1455.

Section 24(2) provides:

... treatment is justified only if:

(a) in A's opinion ... [the treatment is necessary in order not to endanger the health or safety of any person (which may include that of the disabled person)]; and

(b) it is reasonable, in all the circumstances of the case, for [A] to hold that opinion.

6.110   The difficulty in applying the provisions lies in section 24(1)(a). The questions which arise are: how does one assess what the 'reason' for the treatment is; what does it mean for the reason to 'relate to' the disability; and, is it necessary for the alleged discriminator to know of the disability for the action to be unlawful.

6.111   To decide whether a person has been treated less favourably for a reason relating to that person's disability it is necessary to compare his or her treatment with the treatment of a non-disabled person. Until the House of Lords decision in *Lewisham LBC v Malcolm*, below, the authority on the issue of 'comparators' was the Court of Appeal's decision in the employment case of *Clark v Novacold*.[59] The case concerned a dismissal on the grounds of absenteeism and the employers argued that they were not discriminating as they would have dismissed a non-disabled person who was so frequently absent from work. However, the Court of Appeal held that where an employee is absent from work for a disability-related reason, the correct comparator is someone without the disability and therefore without the absence, and not someone who is absent for a non-disability reason.

In *North Devon Homes Limited v Christine Brazier*[60] the landlords claimed possession on the grounds of nuisance. The tenant had been diagnosed as suffering from paranoid psychosis and had a long history of being in conflict with her neighbours. Having been moved once, she had continued to behave in an aggressive way towards her neighbours. At the hearing the tenant had argued that the landlord's claim for possession was in breach of DDA 1995 and that a possession order should not be made. The judge found that the landlord's conduct was unlawful by virtue of DDA 1995 but that nonetheless it was reasonable to make a possession order on the grounds that:

59 [1999] 1 CR 95.
60 [2003] EWHC 574 (QB), 28 March 2003.

(1) it was not reasonable for the other tenants to put up with the admitted conduct of the tenant;

(2) the tenant had been re-housed once already by the landlords;

(3) there was little chance of improvement in the tenant's condition; and

(4) it was not appropriate to allow DDA 1995 to override the court's discretion given by HA 1988.

The tenant appealed. The landlords argued that they were not treating the tenant less favourably than other people because they would have evicted any tenant behaving in the same way. However, following *Clark v Novacold*, see above, the Court of Appeal rejected this and held that, as there was no evidence that the eviction was 'justified' under DDA 1995, the eviction was therefore unlawful under DDA 1995 and the possession order was set aside.

6.112   This approach to the issue of the appropriate comparator is, however, wrong in light of the House of Lords decision in *Malcolm v Lewisham LBC* (see para 6.115 below).

Causation and justification

In *Manchester CC v Romano* and *Manchester CC v Samari*[61] the Court of Appeal considered appeals by two tenants against possession orders made on the grounds of nuisance.

In *Romano* there was evidence that the tenant suffered from depression but the judge had found that this was not sufficiently severe that she was a disabled person under DDA 1995. The complaints included complaints about loud music played by her son and DIY activities. One of her neighbours gave evidence that he was stressed and tired because of the noise caused by the defendant. The tenant's appeal was on the basis that the eviction was discriminatory and had not been justified. The Court of Appeal held that the neighbour's evidence had been sufficient to lead to a conclusion that his health was endangered by frequent loss of sleep. In any event, it was difficult to relate some of the nuisance (loud hammering and music) to the tenant's mental

61 [2004] EWCA Civ 834, 29 June 2004.

impairment. It was therefore not necessary to decide whether the judge was correct to find that she was not a disabled person.

In the *Samari* case, the tenant was diagnosed as suffering from a personality disorder. She was alleged to have behaved in an aggressive and abusive way towards her neighbour. The neighbour's evidence that she was at the end of her tether and felt she could no longer cope with the behaviour of the defendant and her family. The Court of Appeal held that this was sufficient for the council to conclude that the eviction was justified in order not to endanger the neighbour's health. It was also reasonable, in all the circumstances, for the council to hold that opinion.

The appeals were dismissed.

Cases where the court has no discretion

6.113 *Brazier* and *Romano*, above, concerned claims for possession brought on the grounds of nuisance where the court has a discretion regarding the making of the order and where a landlord may be able to justify the eviction as necessary to avoid endangering health or safety. However, DDA 1995 raises more difficult issues in cases where the court has no discretion and where issues of health and safety are unlikely to arise.

6.114 In a case brought by a private landlord on the mandatory rent arrears ground the Court of Appeal decided that there was no breach of DDA 1995.

In *S v Floyd and Equality and Human Rights Commission*[62] a possession order had been made against the tenant on Ground 8. The tenant, who suffered from Obsessive Compulsive Disorder, admitted withholding rent and that there were arrears of more than £7,000. An outright possession order was made, the judge holding that there could be no defence to the claim given that the tenant admitted the arrears. The tenant appealed but the Court of Appeal dismissed the appeal holding that there was no reason to treat the case other than as one in which the reason for the landlord's claim for possession was the non-payment of rent and that no question of unlawful discrimination could arise so as to require the landlord to justify her claim or to disentitle her to a possession order.

62 [2008] EWCA Civ 201, 18 March 2008.

6.115   Although the outcome of the *Floyd* case was approved by the House of Lords in *Malcolm v Lewisham LBC* the House of Lords held that *Floyd* had been wrong to suggest that DDA 1995 could not apply in a case in which the landlord had an entitlement to possession and where the court had no discretion.

> In *Malcolm v Lewisham LBC*[63] the tenant had lost his secure tenancy by sub-letting his flat. The authority served notice to quit to determine the contractual tenancy and sought a possession order. The tenant argued that DDA 1995 applied as he suffered from schizophrenia which affected his judgment. At the hearing the court had held that DDA 1995 did not apply because the secure tenancy had been lost and therefore the court had no discretion to withhold a possession order. It was also stated that the tenant was not a disabled person because his condition was controlled by medication, that his actions had not been caused by his disability and that the authority would only be discriminating if it was aware of the tenant's disability.
>
> The Court of Appeal upheld the tenant's appeal finding that his mental impairment did have a substantial effect on his ability to carry out normal day-to-day activities and that he was therefore disabled. It was not necessary for the tenant to establish that the disability was the direct cause of the sub-letting. What was necessary was that there was a causal link with the disability.
>
> The House of Lords upheld the landlord's appeal. *Clarke v Novacold* had been wrongly decided: the true comparator was not a non-disabled person who had not sub-let his flat but with a non-disabled person who had sub-let his flat. Mr Malcolm was not being treated less favourably as the authority would terminate the tenancy and seek a possession order against any person sub-letting a flat held on a secure tenancy.

6.116   Further, the House held that a landlord must be aware of the disability to be guilty of discrimination under DDA 1995.

Disabled tenants: other relevant provisions

Rent arrears protocol

6.117   Where a claim is brought by a social landlord on the grounds of rent arrears the pre-action protocol expressly refers to the landlords

---

63 [2008] UKHL 43, 25 July 2007.

obligation to consider DDA 1995 and the possible need for community care assessment (see para 5.7 in relation to a tenant known to be vulnerable).

Litigation friends

6.118 Under the Civil Procedure Rules a 'protected party' must have a litigation friend appointed to conduct proceedings on his or her behalf.[64] A protected party means 'a party, or an intended party, who lacks capacity to conduct the proceedings'.[65]

6.119 If proceedings are issued against a protected party, a person may not take any steps in the proceedings until the party has a litigation friend.

6.120 A person appointed by the Court of Protection (see below) may conduct proceedings on behalf of the protected party. Otherwise, a person may put him or herself forward as a litigation friend by filing and serving on all parties a 'certificate of suitability' (form N235) stating that the necessary conditions are met. The conditions are that the person must be able to fairly and competently conduct proceedings on behalf of the party and must have no interest adverse to that of the party.[66] The certificate of suitability must also state the grounds of the person's belief that the party lacks capacity and, if based on a medical or other expert opinion, must attach relevant documents.[67]

6.121 An application for the appointment of a litigation friend may be made to the court by the person who wishes to be the litigation friend or by one of the parties to the proceedings.

6.122 If a claim is made against a protected party without a litigation friend the claimant *must* apply for an order appointing a litigation friend.

Capacity

6.123 The Mental Capacity Act (MCA) 2005 set out a new framework for assessing capacity and for dealing with the affairs of those who lack capacity. The detailed provisions of the Act are outside the scope of this book. The following, however, are some of the central principles of which advisers should be aware:[68]

---

64 CPR 21.

65 CPR 21.1(2).

66 CPR 21.4–21.5. If a claim is brought by a litigation friend (as opposed to being defended) the person must also undertake to pay any costs the protected party may be ordered to pay, subject to any right to be repaid from the party's assets.

67 CPR 21, PD para 2.2(c).

68 These are set out in MCA 2005 s1.

- a person is assumed to have capacity unless it is established that he or she lacks capacity;
- a person is not to be treated as unable to make a decision unless all practicable steps to help him to do so have been taken without success;
- a person is not to be treated as unable to make a decision merely because he makes an unwise decision.

Inability to make decisions

6.124   Capacity is to be assessed not in general terms but in relation to particular decisions and MCA 2005 s3 provides that a person is unable to make a decision for him or herself if unable:

- to understand the information relevant to the decision,
- to retain that information,
- to use or weigh that information as part of the process of making the decision, or
- to communicate his or her decision (whether by talking, using sign language or any other means).

6.125   A person is not to be regarded as unable to understand relevant information if he or she can understand an explanation given in an appropriate way, using, for example, simple language, visual aids or other means.

6.126   The fact that a person is able to retain relevant information only for a short period does not prevent a person being regarded as able to make a decision.

6.127   In most cases medical evidence will be needed to establish a lack of capacity so as to require a litigation friend. However, CPR Part 21 does not require this and the opinion of a friend or family member who offers to act as a litigation friend may be sufficient. However, it should be noted that MCA 2005 specifically provides that:

> A lack of capacity cannot be established merely by reference to a person's age or appearance, or a ... condition or an aspect of [the person's] behaviour, which might lead others to make unjustified assumptions about his [or her] capacity.[69]

The Court of Protection

6.128   The Mental Capacity Act 2005 provided for a new Court of Protection to make decisions regarding the property and affairs, healthcare and

---

69   MCA 2005 s2(3).

personal welfare of those who lack capacity. The Court of Protection has powers equivalent to the High Court and can make decisions about whether someone has the capacity to make a particular decision.

Human Rights Act 1998: article 8 defences

6.129 The substantive application of article 8 to claims for possession is examined in chapter 21. This section considers the issue of how article 8 arguments should be raised: whether they provide a defence to a claim for possession or can be raised only in ancillary proceedings by way of judicial review.

6.130 In possession claims brought on discretionary grounds the court must consider whether it is reasonable to make a possession order. The Court of Appeal has held that in such cases this involves a consideration of the defendant's rights under article 8. Article 8 merely reinforces the importance of only making an order that deprives a person of his or her home where a clear cause for doing so has been made out.[70] However, this does not apply where the court is not required to consider the reasonableness of making an order. Where the court has, under domestic law, no discretion as to the making of a possession order, how should an occupier raise an argument that an eviction would be in breach of his or her rights under article 8? It has long been held that an argument that an eviction would be unlawful on public law grounds could be raised in an application for judicial review and that a claim for possession should be adjourned pending the outcome of such an application. However, it has also been recognised that in some circumstances such an argument may be raised as a defence to a claim for possession.[71] HRA 1998 has led to a number of recent cases in which the courts have considered when an argument based on Article 8 may found a defence to a claim for possession in the county court.

> In *Kay v Lambeth LBC, Leeds CC v Price*,[72] the House of Lords considered appeals brought by the occupiers of 'short-life' accommodation and by travellers being evicted from a local authority site. It was held, by a majority of 4:3, that where a public authority has an unqualified right to possession there were only

70 *Gallagher v Castle Vale Action Trust Limited* (2001) 33 HLR 810, CA.
71 *Wandsworth v Winder (No 1)* [1984] UKHL 2, 29 November 1984.
72 [2006] UKHL 10, 8 March 2006.

two situations in which it would be open to the court to refrain from proceeding to summary judgment and making a possession order. Firstly '(a) if a seriously arguable point is raised that the law which enables the court to make the possession order is incompatible with article 8' and, secondly '(b) if the defendant wishes to challenge the decision of a public authority to recover possession as an improper exercise of its powers at common law on the ground that it was a decision that no reasonable person would consider justifiable, he should be permitted to do this provided again that the point is seriously arguable.'[73]

6.131   So, the two possible defences would be either that the law the claimant relies on is incompatible with the ECHR or that the decision to recover possession is one that no reasonable person could consider justified.

In the case of *McCann v UK*[74] the ECtHR considered a claim by a man evicted by the local authority following the ending of the tenancy by the service of a notice to quit by his joint tenant. The court held that the eviction had been in breach of the occupier's article 8 rights since the local authority landlord had not considered at all the potential interference with article 8 and the occupier had been denied the opportunity to raise the issue in the domestic proceedings. Further, the Court commented that judicial review was not appropriate for resolving sensitive factual questions which should be considered by the county court responsible for ordering possession.

6.132   Following *McCann*, the House of Lords considered again the issue of article 8 in relation to the eviction of travellers from a gypsy site.

Doherty v Birmingham CC[75] concerned the eviction of a family who had lived on a local authority gypsy site for 17 years. The authority sought to evict the family using a summary procedure. The Court of Appeal had held that there was no arguable basis to challenge the local authority's decision. The House of Lords upheld Mr Doherty's appeal confirming the earlier decision in *Kay* regarding the two possible challenges to a claim for possession, referring to

73 Hope LJ at [110].
74 Application 19009/04, 13 May 2008.
75 [2008] UKHL 57, 30 July 2008.

challenge to the law itself, and 'gateway (b)' – a challenge to the decision to evict. The case was remitted to the county court to consider the lawfulness of the decision to evict. In relation to the way in which a county court should consider such defences it was held that 'If the defence is focused not on the legislation but on the housing authority's decision-making process the judge will in effect be hearing an application for judicial review on traditional review grounds. It is clear that any defence on these lines may now be raised and decided on oral evidence given in the County Court. It will no longer be necessary to have an adjournment to enable the defendant to make a separate application for judicial review (in which oral evidence would probably not be permitted).'[76]

6.133 It remains to be seen how the county court will deal with such defences and how an occupier will be able to establish 'a seriously arguable case' such that the court should not proceed to summary judgment and a possession order. In the dissenting judgment of Bingham LJ in Kay the following principles were set out which may assist the county courts in dealing with such issues:

- Courts should proceed on the assumption that domestic law strikes a fair balance and is compatible with article 8 – an authority need not plead or prove in every case that the law is compatible.
- If the court is satisfied that the domestic law requirements for making a possession order have been met it should make an order unless the occupier can show that there is a seriously arguable case under ECHR. This will be highly exceptional.
- Deciding whether the defendant has a seriously arguable case will not call for a full-blown trial. It should be decided summarily on the basis of an affidavit or the defence. The aim of the court should be to decide the question as quickly as is consistent with giving the defendant a fair opportunity to present his or her case on this issue.
- If the court decides the defendant does not have a seriously arguable case it should proceed to make a possession order.
- If a seriously arguable case is raised the court should decide the issue unless the issue is one of alleged compatibility of legislation in which case consideration should be given to referring the proceedings to the High Court.[77]

76 Walker LJ, at [123].
77 These principles were set out in the dissenting judgment of Bingham LJ in *Kay* at [39].

6.134   What is not clear is whether this affects the position regarding claims for possession against introductory and demoted tenants (see para 5.81).

Mortgage possession claims

6.135   A mortgage operates as the grant of an interest in land giving the right of possession to the lender. It is important to note that, unlike the position regarding claims for possession against tenants, a lender already has a right of possession and is not dependent on the court to grant the right. Rather, the lender applies to the court for an order to enforce the right of possession and, in relation to residential premises, the court has statutory powers to postpone the exercise of the right of possession.

6.136   The mortgage agreement will usually provide that the lender's right of possession cannot be enforced unless the borrower breaches the terms of the mortgage so the lender will have to prove the breach. The Civil Procedure Rules require very specific information to be provided by the lender in the court documents (see para 5.96).

6.137   This section examines briefly the court's powers to restrict a lender's right of possession and some situations in which a person may apply to set aside a mortgage so as to defeat the claim for possession.

Regulation of mortgages

6.138   Since October 2004, the Financial Services Authority (FSA) has been responsible for regulating the sale of mortgages. The Mortgage Conduct of Business Rules (MCOB) came into effect on 31 October 2004. They replace the Voluntary Mortgage Code which had been in effect since 1997. The MCOB applies to 'regulated mortgage contracts' entered into on or after 31 October 2004.

6.139   The MCOB includes rules for:

- responsible lending, ie giving proper consideration to a borrower's ability to pay;
- the giving of information in prescribed format throughout the life of the loan;
- the giving of prescribed information, including an official FSA leaflet, to borrowers who fall into arrears; and
- the way firms deal with arrears and possession cases.

6.140 The MCOB rules can be downloaded from the FSA website www.fsahandbook.info/FSA/html/handbook/MCOB.

6.141 The FSA operates a dispute resolution procedure through the Financial Ombudsman Service (FOS) and awards of compensation can be made.

6.142 A lender's failure to follow the MCOB does not prevent a claim for possession being made but may be taken into account by the court when considering whether to exercise its discretion.

Claims for possession

6.143 There are two separate regimes governing the courts' powers in relation to possession claims of residential property subject to a mortgage:

6.144 The Consumer Credit Act (CCA) 1974[78] governs 'regulated agreements'. Previously, the CCA 1974 only applied to agreements where the credit did not exceed £25,000. However, this limit has been removed by the CCA 2006. Agreements that are exempt from the CCA 1974 are those entered into with banks and building societies and all loans which are regulated mortgage contracts.

6.145 The Administration of Justice Acts 1970 and 1973 govern other mortgages of residential premises that are not regulated under the CCA 1974.

The Administration of Justice Acts

6.146 Where a lender (mortgagee) seeks a possession order of residential premises against a borrower (mortgagor) the court has similar powers to adjourn, postpone or suspend an order as under the extended discretion in relation to tenants (see para 5.121). However, the power is dependent on the borrower being able to pay 'the sums due' or remedy the default within a reasonable period. The courts powers are contained in the Administration of Justice Act (AJA) 1970 and the Administration of Justice Act 1973. Section 36 of AJA 1970 provides that where a mortgagee makes a claim for possession of a dwelling house:

> (1) ... the court may exercise any of the powers conferred on it by subsection (2) below if it appears to the court that in the event of its exercising the power the mortgagor is likely to be able within a reasonable period to pay any sums due under the mortgage or to

---

78 As amended by CCA 2006.

remedy a default consisting of a breach of any other obligation arising under or by virtue of the mortgage.

(2) The court–

    (a) may adjourn the proceedings, or

    (b) on giving judgment, or making an order, for delivery of possession of the mortgaged property, or at any time before the execution of such judgment or order, may–

        (i) stay or suspend execution of the judgment or order, or

        (ii) postpone the date for delivery of possession, for such period or periods as the court thinks reasonable.

(3) Any such adjournment, stay, suspension or postponement as is referred to in subsection (2) above may be made subject to such conditions with regard to payment by the mortgagor of any sum secured by the mortgage or the remedying of any default as the court thinks fit.

(4) The court may from time to time vary or revoke any condition imposed by virtue of this section.

6.147   This power does not apply where the agreement is regulated under the Consumer Credit Act 1974.[79]

6.148   AJA 1973 s8(2) makes clear that the borrower must be able to pay not only the amount in arrears but the further amounts due, including interest, during the life of the agreement. Effectively, the borrower must be able to show that he or she can resume payment of the current instalments plus regular payment towards the arrears (or a lump sum payment of the arrears) so that at the end of the reasonable period the arrears will have been paid.

6.149   It should be noted therefore that in all cases the court may adjourn, stay or suspend execution or postpone the giving of possession only if it appears to the court that the borrower is likely to be able to repay the arrears within a reasonable period.

What is a reasonable period?

6.150   This is to be decided having regard to the rights and obligations of both the lender and the borrower. The Court of Appeal considered the issue in the case of *Cheltenham & Gloucester Building Society v Norgan*.[80] The court held that in determining the 'reasonable period' the court 'should take as its starting point the full term of the mortgage and pose at the outset the question: would it be possible

79 AJA 1970 s38A.
80 [1996] 1 All ER 449.

for the mortgagor to maintain payment-off of the arrears by instalments over that period?'.[81] The relevant factors in determining the reasonable period were summarised as follows:[82]

- how much the borrower can reasonably afford to pay currently and in the future;
- if the borrower is in temporary difficulty, how long the difficulty is likely to last;
- the reason for the arrears;
- the period of the remaining term;
- the contractual terms, ie the type of mortgage and when the principal sum is due to be repaid;
- whether it is appropriate to disregard any provision in the agreement for the lender to demand early repayment;
- whether it is reasonable to expect the lender to recoup the arrears of interest over the whole term, within a shorter period or even within a longer period;
- whether it is reasonable to expect the lender to capitalise the interest or not;
- any reasons affecting the security which should influence the length of the period for repayment.

6.151   Much will depend on the amount of equity in the property. Where there is substantial equity the court is more likely to be willing to permit a longer period for the borrower to repay the arrears.

6.152   Clearly, where a borrower wants the court to exercises its powers under AJA 1970 it will be necessary to produce evidence of the borrower's ability to pay the amounts due within a reasonable period. Evidence of the value of the property, and therefore the amount of equity, should also be obtained.

Adjourning or suspending to permit a sale by the borrower

6.153   The court can grant an adjournment or suspension to allow the borrower time to sell the property. To do so the court must be satisfied that the proceeds of sale will be sufficient to discharge the whole of the mortgage debt, including the arrears, within a reasonable period. If the borrower is in negative equity the court cannot suspend possession to permit the borrower to sell unless he or she has other funds to make up the shortfall.[83]

---

81   Waite LJ at 458J.
82   Evans LJ at 463A.
83   *Cheltenham and Gloucester plc v Krauz* [1997] 1 All ER 21, CA.

6.154   Where a borrower wants the property to be sold but the lender does not (which may happen where the amount owed exceeds the value of the property and the lender wishes to wait until the value increases) an application can be made by the borrower under section 91(2) of the Law of Property Act 1925. Under section 91 the court has a wide discretion as to whether to order a sale and, if so, on what terms. However, the court is unlikely to order a sale where the proceeds of sale are likely to be substantially less than the amount owed.

Regulated agreements under the Consumer Credit Act 1974

6.155   The Consumer Credit Act (CCA) 1974 deals with a large range of credit agreements and prescribes the way in which regulated agreements are entered into. Under CCA 1974 the court has more extensive powers than under the AJAs. In particular, a borrower can apply for a 'time order' under which the court can extend the time for repayment of the loan and can reduce the contractual interest rate.

6.156   CCA 1974 also contains provision for a court to 'reopen the credit agreement so as to do justice between the parties' in relation to an 'extortionate credit bargain'. The Consumer Credit Act 2006 replaces these provisions with similar powers based on an 'unfair relationship'.

6.157   Some types of loans are specifically exempt from the Consumer Credit Act. Because of the strict procedural requirements regarding regulated agreements it will be clear from the court documents whether or not an agreement is regulated.

Substantive defences to mortgage possession claims

6.158   A lender has the right to possession by virtue of the mortgage. An application to the court to exercise its discretion is not a 'defence' a claim for possession. The substantive defences that may be raised are summarised.

Spouse or civil partner in occupation who did not consent to the mortgage

6.159   Where a mortgage is entered into by a sole owner of premises, a spouse or civil partner who is in occupation of the premises has an 'overriding interest' under the Land Registration Act (LRA) 2002.[84] This means that the lender's interest is subject to the right of

84 See Sch 3 para 2.

occupation. Unless the person consented to the mortgage, it will not be binding on him or her.[85] Most lenders will make specific enquiry of such a person and obtain consent before entering into a mortgage.

Forgery

6.160 Where one spouse or civil partner forges the signature of the other the mortgage is ineffective. However, an equitable charge is granted to the lender in relation to the share of the premises owned by the party who entered into the mortgage agreement. In such a case the lender can apply for a money judgment against the borrower and can then apply for a charging order and subsequently an order for sale under section 13 of the Trusts of Land and Appointment of Trustees Act 1996. Section 15 sets out the relevant factors to be considered when the court is considering an order for sale (see para 1.141).

Misrepresentation/undue influence

6.161 It is unusual for a borrower to establish that a lender has misrepresented the effect of the mortgage or placed undue pressure on the borrower to enter into the mortgage. Where a borrower can establish that the lender has been negligent in representing the terms of the mortgage (negligent misstatement) this may give rise to a claim for damages but does not usually mean that the mortgage will be set aside, unless it can be shown that the lender has taken unfair advantage of the borrower.[86]

6.162 Defences based on undue influence are usually raised where a party has acted as surety. The allegation is that the principal debtor has placed undue influence on the person who agreed to act as surety. Most of the cases have involved a husband who has persuaded a wife to enter into an agreement to secure a business debt on the shared home. To establish undue influence it is necessary to prove not only that there has been misrepresentation, undue influence or other wrong but also that the lender should be affected by the wrong. For this it must be proved that the lender had actual or constructive notice of the wrong.[87]

---

85 Unless inquiry was made and the interest not disclosed.
86 *Cornish v Midland Bank plc* [1985] 3 All ER 513.
87 Or, unusually, that the wrongdoer was acting as the lender's agent.

6.163   The House of Lords considered the issue in the cases of *Barclays Bank v O'Brien*[88] and *Royal Bank of Scotland v Etridge (No 2)*[89] and gave guidance as to the steps that a lender should take to satisfy itself that a wife's agreement has been properly obtained. In *O'Brien* the House indicated that a lender should:

- take steps to ensure the wife is aware of the risks she is running; and
- advise her to take independent advice.

6.164   In *Etridge* the court elaborated on the duty to communicate with the wife directly or with her solicitor and on the duty of the solicitor who is advising the wife.

6.165   Although these cases concerned husbands and wives, the same principles apply wherever there is an emotional relationship between the parties, including a same sex partnership.

Unfair terms

6.166   The Unfair Terms in Consumer Contracts Regulations 1999 apply to mortgage agreements (see para 3.158). If a term is deemed unfair by the court it is unenforceable.

Tenants of borrowers

6.167   Where a landlord borrows money on a mortgage, the power to grant a tenancy can only be exercised where no contrary intention is expressed in the mortgage deed.[90] Most mortgage deeds contain a term preventing the borrower from granting a tenancy.

6.168   The position of the tenant of a borrower depends on two factors:

- whether the tenancy commenced before or after the property was mortgaged; and
- whether the lender gave consent.

Tenancy granted before the mortgage

6.169   A tenancy granted by the landlord/borrower before the mortgage was created is valid as against the lender.

6.170   Where the mortgage deed prohibits the creation of a tenancy, this does not prevent an existing tenancy from binding the lender: if the

---

88 [1994] 1 AC 180, HL.
89 [2001] 4 All ER 449, HL.
90 Law of Property Act 1925 s99.

lender obtains possession against the landlord/borrower, the tenant becomes the direct tenant of the lender.

6.171   A lender may take advantage of certain of the possession grounds available to landlords.[91] Further, if the tenancy is an assured shorthold tenancy the lender will be able to obtain possession by serving two months' notice and obtaining a possession order against the tenant, provided any fixed term has ended.

Tenancy granted after the mortgage

6.172   If the tenancy is granted with the lender's consent it is binding on the lender.

6.173   If the tenancy is granted without the lenders consent it will not be binding on the lender and when the lender obtains a possession order the tenants can be evicted.[92]

Notifying occupiers

6.174   Clearly any tenants in occupation will need to be aware of the proceedings in order to assert their interest. CPR 55.10 requires that the claimant must send notice addressed to 'the occupiers' at least 14 days before the hearing. The notice must state that a possession claim has started, give the name and address of the claimant, the defendant and the court, and give details of the hearing. At the hearing the claimant must produce a copy of the notice and evidence of service.

---

91 Under RA 1977 if the tenancy is subject to possession under Case 11, Case 12 or Case 20 and under HA 1988, if the tenancy is subject to possession under Ground 1, a lender may obtain possession under Ground 2. See appendix to this chapter below.

92 *Dudley and District Building Society v Emerson* [1949] 2 All ER 252, CA.

APPENDIX

Housing Act 1985 Sch 2

STATUTORY GROUNDS FOR POSSESSION

Part I: discretionary grounds – grounds on which the court may order possession if it considers it reasonable

Ground 1 – rent arrears or breach of tenancy agreement

Rent lawfully due from the tenant has not been paid or an obligation of the tenancy has been broken or not performed.

Ground 2 – nuisance and annoyance

The tenant or a person residing in or visiting the dwelling-house–

- (a) has been guilty of conduct causing or likely to cause a nuisance or annoyance to a person residing, visiting or otherwise engaging in a lawful activity in the locality, or
- (b) has been convicted of–
  - (i) using the dwelling-house or allowing it to be used for immoral or illegal purposes, or
  - (ii) an indictable offence committed in, or in the locality of, the dwelling-house.

Ground 2A – domestic violence

The dwelling-house was occupied (whether alone or with others) by a married couple or a couple living together as husband and wife and–

- (a) one or both of the partners is a tenant of the dwelling-house,
- (b) one partner has left because of violence or threats of violence by the other towards–
  - (i) that partner, or

(ii) a member of the family of that partner who was residing with that partner immediately before the partner left, and

(c) the court is satisfied that the partner who has left is unlikely to return.

Ground 3 – damage to property

The condition of the dwelling-house or common parts has deteriorated due to acts of waste, neglect or default of the tenant or a person residing in the dwelling-house. If the acts are those of a sub-tenant or lodger, the tenant has not taken such steps as he or she ought reasonably to have taken to remove that person.

Ground 4 – damage to furniture

The condition of furniture provided by the landlord has deteriorated due to acts of waste, neglect or default of the tenant or a person residing in the dwelling-house. If the acts are those of a sub-tenant or lodger, the tenant has not taken such steps as he or she ought reasonably to have taken to remove that person.

Ground 5 – tenancy granted because of false statement

The tenant is the person, or one of the persons, to whom the tenancy was granted and the landlord was induced to grant the tenancy by a false statement made knowingly or recklessly by–

(a) the tenant, or
(b) a person acting at the tenant's instigation.

Ground 6 – mutual exchange for payment

The tenancy was assigned to the tenant by way of mutual exchange and a premium was paid in connection with the assignment.

The ground also available if the assignment (for which payment was made) was to a member of the tenant's family, who lives with the tenant, and who passed the tenancy to the current tenant.

Ground 7 – employment related accommodation and inappropriate conduct

The dwelling-house is part of or within the grounds of a building held by the landlord mainly for non-housing purposes and consists mainly of accommodation other than housing accommodation, and

- was let to the tenant in consequence of the tenant being employed by the landlord, or a local authority, a new town corporation, a housing action trust, an urban development corporation or the governors of an aided school, and
- the tenant or another person living in the dwelling-house has been guilty of conduct such that, having regard to the purpose for which the building is used, it would not be right for the tenant to continue in occupation.

The ground also applies if a previous tenant, who passed the tenancy to the current tenant was the person to whom the tenancy was granted in consequence of employment.

Ground 8 – *temporary accommodation pending works*

The tenancy was granted as temporary accommodation pending works to the tenant's home and the works have been completed and the other dwelling-house is available for occupation.

Part II: grounds on which the court may order possession if suitable alternative accommodation is available

Ground 9 – *statutory overcrowding*

The dwelling house is statutorily overcrowded, as defined in HA 1985 (see para 10.78).

Ground 10 – *demolition or reconstruction*

The landlord intends, within a reasonable time, to demolish or reconstruct the building or part of the building comprising the dwelling-house, or to carry out works and cannot do so without obtaining possession.

Ground 10A – *redevelopment schemes*

The dwelling-house or part of it is in an area which is the subject of a redevelopment scheme and the landlord intends within a reasonable time to dispose of the dwelling-house in accordance with the scheme and for that purpose reasonably requires possession.

Ground 11 – *charities*

The landlord is a charity and the tenant's continued occupation of the dwelling-house would conflict with the objects of the charity.

Part III: grounds on which the court may order possession if it is reasonable to make a possession order *and* suitable alternative accommodation is available

Ground 12 – non-housing employment related accommodation

The dwelling-house forms part of, or is within the grounds of, a building held mainly for non-housing purposes and consists mainly of non-housing accommodation, or is in a cemetery, and:

- it was let to the tenant in consequence of employment by the landlord or a local authority, a new town corporation, a housing action trust, an urban development corporation, or the governors of an aided school; and
- that employment has ceased; and
- the landlord reasonably requires the dwelling-house for occupation by a new employee.

The ground also applies if a previous tenant, who passed the tenancy to the current tenant was the person to whom the tenancy was granted in consequence of employment.

Ground 13 – disabled adapted accommodation

The dwelling-house has features which are substantially different from those of ordinary dwelling-houses and which are designed to make it suitable for occupation by a physically disabled person who needs such accommodation and–

- there is no longer such a person residing in the dwelling-house; and
- the landlord needs it for occupation by such a person.

Ground 14 – special needs accommodation – housing associations and trusts

The landlord is a housing association or housing trust which lets dwelling-houses only for occupation by persons whose circumstances make it especially difficult to obtain housing, and:

- either there is no longer such a person residing in the dwelling-house or the tenant has received an offer of a secure tenancy of a separate dwelling; and
- the landlord needs the dwelling-house for another person with such needs.

Ground 15 – special needs accommodation – close to special facilities

The dwelling-house is one of a group of dwelling-houses which it is the practice of the landlord to let for occupation by persons with special needs and–

- a social service or special facility is provided near to the group of dwelling-houses to assist persons with those special needs; and
- there is no longer a person with those special needs residing in the dwelling-house; and
- the landlord needs the dwelling-house for occupation by a person who has those special needs.

Ground 16 – succession and under-occupation

The tenant became the tenant by succession under section 87(b) (ie not as spouse or civil partner but as family member) and

- the accommodation is more extensive than is reasonably required by the tenant; and
- notice of proceedings was served (or if no notice was served, the proceedings were begun) more than six months but less than twelve months after the date of the previous tenant's death.

The matters to be taken into account by the court in deciding whether it is reasonable to make a possession order include:

- the age of the tenant;
- the period during which the tenant has occupied the dwelling-house as his or her only or principal home; and
- any financial or other support given by the tenant to the previous tenant.

Housing Act 1988 Sch 2

MANDATORY GROUNDS

Notice Grounds 1–5

Ground 1 – landlord is previous owner occupier or needs premises as home

The landlord who is seeking possession, or if there are joint landlords, at least one of them, either:

- occupied the dwelling-house as his or her only or principal home at some time before the beginning of the tenancy; or

- requires the dwelling-house as only or principle home for him or herself or spouse or civil partner and the landlord did not (or if there are joint landlords none of them) purchase the property after the tenancy commenced.

The landlord must have given notice in writing to the tenant, before the beginning of the tenancy, that possession might be recovered under this ground unless the court is satisfied that it is just and equitable to dispense with the notice requirement.

Ground 2 – tenancy subject to Ground 1 and lender taking possession

The dwelling-house is subject to a mortgage granted before the beginning of the tenancy and the lender is entitled to exercise a power of sale under the mortgage and needs possession to dispose of it with vacant possession.

The notice requirement is that the landlord gave notice that possession may be required under Ground 1 unless the court is satisfied that it is just and equitable to dispense with the notice requirement.

Ground 3 – out of season holiday let

The tenancy is a fixed term tenancy for no longer than eight months and within the 12 months preceding the start of the tenancy it was occupied as a holiday let.

The landlord must have given notice in writing to the tenant, before the beginning of the tenancy, that possession might be recovered under this ground.

Ground 4 – student accommodation let to non-students

The tenancy is a fixed term tenancy for no longer than 12 months and within the 12 months preceding the start of the tenancy it was occupied as student accommodation under HA 1988 Sch 1 para 8.

The landlord must have given notice in writing to the tenant, before the beginning of the tenancy, that possession might be recovered under this ground.

Ground 5 – minister of religion

The dwelling-house is held for the purpose of being available for occupation by a minister of religion from which to perform the duties of that office and it is required for occupation by a minister of religion as such a residence.

The landlord must have given notice in writing to the tenant, before the beginning of the tenancy, that possession might be recovered under this ground.

Mandatory grounds not requiring advance notice

Ground 6 – demolition or reconstruction

The landlord intends to demolish or reconstruct the whole or a substantial part of the dwelling-house or to carry out substantial works on it or any part of it or the building of which it is a part.

The following conditions must be met:

The intended work cannot reasonably be carried out without the tenant giving up possession because:

- the tenant is not willing to agree to a variation of the tenancy as would enable the work to be carried out, or
- the nature of the work is such that no such variation is practicable, or
- the tenant is not willing to accept an assured tenancy of a 'reduced part' of the dwelling-house to enable the works to be carried out, or
- the nature of the work is such that such a tenancy is not practicable.

The ground is not available if:

- the landlord acquired the interest after the grant of the tenancy; or
- the assured tenancy came into being on succession to a previous Rent Act tenancy.

Where the immediate landlord is an RSL or a charitable housing trust the ground is made out if the demolition or reconstruction is intended by the superior landlord.

Ground 7 – tenant dies and no right of succession

Where a periodic tenancy devolves under the will or intestacy of the previous tenant, provided possession proceedings are commenced no later than 12 months after the death of the former tenant, or, if the court so directs, after the date on which, in the opinion of the court, the landlord became aware of the former tenant's death. Note that the ground will not apply if a spouse, civil partner or co-habitee is entitled to succeed to the tenancy (see para 3.31).

For the purpose of Ground 7, the acceptance of rent from the new tenant will not be regarded as creating a new tenancy unless the landlord agrees in writing to a change in the amount of the rent, the period of the tenancy, the premises that are let or any other term of the tenancy.

Ground 8 – mandatory rent arrears ground

Both at the date of the service of the notice under section 8 of this Act relating to the proceedings for possession and at the date of the hearing:

(a) if rent is payable weekly or fortnightly, at least eight weeks rent is unpaid;

(b) if rent is payable monthly, at least two months rent is unpaid;

(c) if rent is payable quarterly, at least one quarter's rent is more than three months in arrears; and

(d) if rent is payable yearly, at least three months' rent is more than three months in arrears;

and for the purpose of this ground 'rent' means rent lawfully due from the tenant.

Discretionary grounds – grounds on which the court may order possession if it considers it reasonable

Ground 9 – suitable alternative accommodation

Suitable alternative accommodation is available for the tenant or will be available for him when the possession order takes effect.

Ground 10 – rent arrears or breach of tenancy agreement

Some rent lawfully due from the tenant–

is unpaid on the date on which the proceedings for possession are begun; and

except where [the court considers it just and equitable to dispense with the requirement to serve notice] was in arrears at the date of the service of the notice [seeking possession].'

Ground 11 – persistent delay in paying rent

Whether or not any rent is in arrears on the date on which proceedings for possession are begun, the tenant has persistently delayed paying rent which has become lawfully due.

Ground 12 – other breach

Any obligation of the tenancy (other than one related to the payment of rent) has been broken or not performed.

Ground 13 – damage to premises

The condition of the dwelling house or any of the common parts has deteriorated due to acts of waste, neglect or default of the tenant or a person residing in the dwelling. If the acts are those of a sub-tenant or lodger, the tenant has not taken such steps as he or she ought reasonably to have taken to remove that person.

Ground 14 – nuisance and annoyance

The tenant or a person residing in or visiting the dwelling-house–

(a) has been guilty of conduct causing or likely to cause a nuisance or annoyance to a person residing, visiting or otherwise engaging in a lawful activity in the locality, or

(b) has been convicted of–

(i) using the dwelling-house or allowing it to be used for immoral or illegal purposes, or

(ii) an indictable offence committed in, or in the locality of, the dwelling-house.

Ground 14A – domestic violence

The dwelling-house was occupied (whether alone or with others) by a married couple or a couple living together as husband and wife and–

(a) one or both of the partners is a tenant of the dwelling-house,

(b) the landlord who is seeking possession is a registered social landlord or a charitable housing trust,

(c) one partner has left because of violence or threats of violence by the other towards–

(i) that partner, or

(ii) a member of the family of that partner who was residing with that partner immediately before the partner left, and

(d) the court is satisfied that the partner who has left is unlikely to return.

Ground 15 – deterioration of furniture

The condition of furniture provided under the tenancy has deteriorated due to ill-treatment by the tenant or other person living in the dwelling-house and, if the ill-treatment is by a lodger or sub-tenant, the tenant has not taken reasonable steps to remove that person.

Ground 16 – employment related accommodation

The dwelling-house was let to the tenant in consequence of employment by the landlord, or a previous landlord, and the tenant has ceased to be in that employment.

Ground 17 – tenancy granted because of false statement

The tenant is the person, or one of the persons, to whom the tenancy was granted and the landlord was induced to grant the tenancy by a false statement made knowingly or recklessly by–

the tenant, or

a person acting at the tenant's instigation.

Rent Act 1977: Sch 15

Suitable alternative accommodation

In addition to the 'cases' set out in Schedule 15, section 98(1)(a) provides that a possession order may be made if suitable alternative accommodation is available to the tenant.

Part I: discretionary grounds – cases in which the court *may* order possession

Case 1 – rent arrears or breach of tenancy agreement

Where any rent lawfully due from the tenant has not been paid, or any obligation of the protected or statutory tenancy ... has been broken or not performed.

Case 2 – nuisance and annoyance

Where the tenant or any person residing or lodging with him or any sub-tenant of his has been guilty of conduct which is a nuisance or annoyance to adjoining occupiers, or has been convicted of using the dwelling-house or allowing the dwelling-house to be used for immoral or illegal purposes.

Case 3 – damage to the premises

Where the condition of the dwelling-house has ... deteriorated owing to acts of waste by, or the neglect or default of, the tenant or any person residing or lodging with him or any sub-tenant of his and, in the case of any act of waste by, or the neglect or default of, a person lodging with the tenant or a sub-tenant of his, where the court is satisfied that the tenant has not, before the making of the order in question, taken such steps as he ought reasonably have taken for the removal of the lodger or sub-tenant, as the case may be.

Case 4 – damage to furniture

Where the condition of any furniture provided for use under the tenancy has ... deteriorated owing to ill-treatment by the tenant or any person residing or lodging with him or any sub-tenant of his and, in the case of any ill-treatment by a person lodging with the tenant or a sub-tenant of his, where the court is satisfied that the tenant has not, before the making of the order in question, taken such steps as he ought reasonably to have taken for the removal of the lodger or sub-tenant, as the case may be.

Case 5 – tenant's notice to quit

Where the tenant has given notice to quit and, in consequence of that notice, the landlord has contracted to sell or let the dwelling-house or has taken any other steps as the result of which he would, in the opinion of the court, be seriously prejudiced if he could not obtain possession.

Case 6 – sub-letting or assignment without consent

Where, without the consent of the landlord, the tenant has ... assigned or sublet the whole of the dwelling-house or sublet part of the dwelling-house, the remainder already being sublet.[93]

---

93 For certain kinds of tenancies the sub-letting or assignment must have taken place after a certain date, the latest of which is 14 August 1974.

Case 7 [repealed]

Case 8 – employment related accommodation, needed for new employee

Where the dwelling-house is reasonably required by the landlord for occupation as a residence for some person engaged in his whole-time employment, or in the whole-time employment of some tenant from him or with whom, conditional on housing being provided, a contract for such employment has been entered into, and the tenant was in the employment of the landlord or a former landlord, and the dwelling-house was let to him in consequence of that employment and he has ceased to be in that employment.[94]

Case 9 – accommodation needed as residence for landlord or family

There are three specific conditions that must be met under Case 9:

(1) The dwelling-house must be reasonably required by the landlord for occupation as a residence for:

- the landlord;
- any adult son or daughter of the landlord;
- the landlord's father or mother; or
- the father or mother of the landlord's wife, husband or civil partner.

(2) The landlord did not become landlord by purchasing the dwelling-house.[95]

(3) An order may not be made if the court is satisfied that greater hardship would be caused by making the order than by refusing it. The court must have regard to all the circumstances, including the availability of other accommodation to the landlord and to the tenant.

Further, as the ground is discretionary the court must also be satisfied that it is reasonable to make an order.

---

94 Note that if an employee is *required* to live in premises for the better performance of the job there will be no tenancy: see para 1.36.

95 This condition applies to purchases after a certain date, the latest of which is 24 May 1974, depending on the particular type of tenancy and how it came to be governed by RA 1977.

Case 10 – tenant sub-letting for excessive rent

Where the tenant is sub-letting part of the premises and is charging a rent in excess of a registered fair rent.

Part II: mandatory grounds – cases in which the court *must* order possession

Under RA 1977 for all mandatory cases, other than those relating to farm tenancies (cases 16 to 18), the landlord must have served prior notice on the tenant unless the court dispenses with the requirement. The detailed grounds are complex with different requirements depending on the date the tenancy commenced. These grounds are only briefly summarised here.

Notice grounds – Cases 11 to 16, 19 and 20

In all cases depending on notice the following conditions must be satisfied:

- the landlord gave notice in writing to the tenant that possession might be recovered under the particular ground; or
- the court is satisfied that it is just and equitable to dispense with the notice requirement.

Case 11 – returning owner occupier + notice

The landlord must have previously occupied the premises as a residence and it must be required as a residence or for sale with vacant possession to enable the landlord to purchase a residence. Alternatively, the owner has died and the person who has inherited wants to sell with vacant possession or a mortgagee is entitled to possession.

Case 12 – accommodation purchased for retirement + notice

The landlord must have intended to occupy the dwelling-house as a residence on retirement and it must be required as a residence or for sale with vacant possession to enable the landlord to purchase a residence. Alternatively, the owner has died and the person who has inherited wants to sell with vacant possession or a mortgagee is entitled to possession.

Case 13 – out of season holiday let + notice

The dwelling-house is let on a fixed term tenancy not exceeding eight months and have previously been occupied as a holiday let.

Case 14 – out of term student accommodation + notice

The dwelling-house is let on a fixed term tenancy not exceeding 12 months and have been previously occupied as student accommodation.

Case 15 – letting to minister of religion + notice

The dwelling-house is let to a minister of religion as a residence from which to perform the duties of the office; and is required for occupation by a minister of religion as such a residence.

Case 16 – accommodation used for agricultural employees + notice

The dwelling-house was at any time occupied by a person as an agricultural employee; and the tenant is not so employed, nor ever was and is not the widow of someone who was so employed; and it is required for occupation by an agricultural employee.

Cases 17 and 18

Further grounds applying where the dwelling-house is needed for an agricultural occupier.

Case 19 – protected shorthold tenancy

This ground applies only to protected shorthold tenancies.

In addition to the notice requirements when the tenancy was created, the landlord must have served a possession notice which:

- is in writing and states that proceedings may be commenced under Case 19 after the notice expires;
- must expire no earlier than three months after service; and
- must be served in the three months immediately preceding the anniversary of the last day of the tenancy.

The court can waive the requirements for the creation of the protected shorthold tenancy where it is 'just and equitable' to do so, see para 2.179.

Case 20 – landlord was in armed forces and needs accommodation + notice

The dwelling house was let after 28 November 1980 by someone who, at the time of acquisition and at the time of the letting, was a member of the regular armed forces; and it must be required as a residence or for sale with vacant possession to enable the landlord to purchase a residence. Alternatively, the owner has died and the person who has inherited wants to sell with vacant possession or a mortgagee is entitled to possession.

Unlawful eviction and harassment by landlords

continued

Key points

- An unlawful eviction means excluding an occupier from his or her home without following the proper procedure. In most cases the proper procedure includes the service of notice, the obtaining of a possession order and the enforcement of the order by the court bailiffs.

- Some occupiers can be evicted without following this procedure but violent eviction is always a criminal offence.

- Harassment means acts likely to interfere with the occupiers' peace and comfort or withdrawing essential services. The acts must be done knowing they are likely to make the occupier leave, or deter the occupier from asserting his or her legal rights.

- Unlawful eviction and harassment are criminal offences. They are usually prosecuted by local authorities. Because of limited resources, prosecutions are rare but the threat of prosecution may be used to persuade a landlord to resolve a dispute, eg let a tenant back into occupation.

- Unlawful eviction and harassment by a landlord also gives a tenant the right to take civil action – to seek damages and/or an injunction.

- Substantial damages may be awarded if an unlawfully evicted tenant had security of tenure. These damages are calculated on the basis of the difference in value of the premises with the tenant in occupation and with vacant possession.

- In any case significant damages may be awarded to tenants who have been harassed and unlawfully evicted. Further, the court can order the landlord to let the occupier back into the premises. In an emergency an order may be obtained very quickly, sometimes on the day of the eviction.

Criminal offences

The offences of harassment and unlawful eviction

7.1   The criminal offences of unlawful eviction and harassment were introduced in 1964 and 1965 respectively and are now contained in the Protection from Eviction Act (PEA) 1977, as amended by the Housing Act 1988.

7.2   Under PEA 1977 there are two offences:

- unlawful eviction of a residential occupier.
- harassment of a 'residential occupier'; and

7.3   The first issue then is the definition of a 'residential occupier'.

Residential occupier

7.4   A residential occupier means:

> in relation to any premises ... a person occupying the premises as a residence, whether under a contract or by virtue of any enactment or rule of law giving him the right to remain in occupation or restricting the right of any other person to recover possession of the premises.[1]

7.5   There are two aspects to the definition: first, the factual issue of whether the person is occupying as a residence; and, second, whether the person has a right to occupy or there is some restriction on the right of another person to recover possession.

Occupying premises as a residence

7.6   This is always a question of fact. To be a residential occupier there must be a substantial degree of regular personal occupation.[2] However, it is possible to reside in more than one place.[3]

7.7   A person may be physically absent from premises yet retain the status of residential occupier. In the case of an extended absence it will be necessary for the occupier to prove that he or she had an intention to return to the premises and that there was physical evidence of the continued occupation (eg belongings, furnishings or friends or family 'looking after' the premises).[4] See paras 3.5–3.8 for a summary of the cases concerning the extended absence of an occupier.

7.8   As will be seen, however, a landlord has a defence both in criminal and civil proceedings if he or she reasonably believed that the residential occupier had ceased to occupy

---

1   PEA 1977 s1(1).
2   *Herbert v Byrne* [1964] 1 All ER 882 CA.
3   *Langford Property Co v Athanassoglou* [1948] 2 All ER 722, CA. Note that it is not necessary to occupy as only or principal home to be a residential occupier, as is the case to retain secure or assured status.
4   *Brown v Brash* [1948] 1 All ER 922, CA.

The 'right to occupy'

7.9   In addition to the fact of occupation, the residential occupier must occupy:

- under a contract; or
- by virtue of some enactment or rule of law that either gives the occupier the right to remain in occupation or restricts the right of any other person to recover possession.

7.10   Clearly, tenants are residential occupiers as they occupy under a contract. In addition, for those tenants with 'security of tenure' there is a restriction on the landlord's right to recover possession after the tenancy comes to an end. Those who are married or in a civil partnership have a statutory right to occupy accommodation even if the agreement is in the name of their spouse/civil partner provided the premises have been their shared home.[5] All of these occupiers then are 'residential occupiers'. In addition, the PEA 1977 itself provides that for other occupiers, except those who are specifically 'excluded', when an agreement to occupy has been ended an eviction may only be carried out by taking court proceedings. This is a restriction on the right to recover possession and means that the person is a residential occupier.

Restriction on eviction other than by court proceedings: PEA 1977 s3

7.11   PEA 1977 s3 applies where 'premises have been let as a dwelling under a tenancy which is neither a statutorily protected tenancy nor an excluded tenancy'. It also applies to licences provided they are not excluded licences. It provides that where the tenancy or licence has come to an end but the occupier continues to reside in the premises, or a part of them, it is not lawful for the owner to enforce the right of possession otherwise than by possession proceedings in the court.

'Statutorily protected' tenancies

7.12   The term 'statutorily protected tenancy' is defined in PEA 1977 s8 and means the following kinds of tenancies:

- protected and statutory tenancies under the Rent Act 1977 and the Rent (Agriculture) Act 1976;

---

5   See chapter 11.

- statutory tenancies arising at the end of a long lease;[6]
- tenancies which include premises occupied for business purposes, to which Part II of the Landlord and Tenant Act 1954 applies;
- agricultural tenancies;[7] and
- assured and assured shorthold tenancies.

'Excluded occupiers'

7.13   The following are excluded occupiers:[8]

- occupiers who have a resident landlord and who share accommodation with the resident landlord, or with a member of the family of the resident landlord;
- former trespassers granted a temporary licence;
- occupiers granted the right to occupy for a holiday only;
- occupiers granted the right to occupy other than 'for money or money's worth';
- asylum-seekers accommodated under the Immigration and Asylum Act 1999;
- occupiers of hostel accommodation where the landlord is a public sector body and the occupation is under a licence and not a tenancy.

7.14   Excluded occupiers, are described in detail at para 1.101.

7.15   What section 3 therefore provides is that, with very limited exceptions described below, on the termination of a right to occupy under a licence or tenancy the landlord must use court proceedings to evict the occupier, unless he or she is an excluded occupier. This then is an enactment that restricts the right of another person to recover possession: a person protected by PEA 1977 s3 is a 'residential occupier'.

---

6   These are governed by Part I of the Landlord and Tenant Act 1954 and Schedule 10 of the Local Government Act 1989, see chapter 3.

7   Including tenancies of agricultural holdings under the Agricultural Holdings Act 1986, assured agricultural occupancy agreements under the Housing Act 1988 and farm business tenancies within the meaning of the Agricultural Tenancies Act 1995.

8   PEA 1977 s3A.

7.16   It must be noted that section 3 applies only to occupiers who are 'lawfully residing in the premises or part of them at the termination of the former tenancy or licence'.[9]

Evicting an excluded occupier

7.17   Before the occupier can be evicted the occupation agreement must be brought to an end. If the occupation agreement is a tenancy, a notice to quit must be served. If the occupation agreement is a licence, the contractual period of notice must be given. For excluded tenants the usual requirement that a notice to quit be at least 28 days long does not apply;[10] the only requirement is the common law rule that the notice must be for at least a period of the tenancy (eg one week or one month, usually depending on the rental period). If there is no tenancy and no express provision about notice, 'reasonable notice' must be given to end the agreement[11] (see para 1.123 for consideration of what constitutes reasonable notice).

7.18   After notice has expired the occupier may be excluded by the owner without obtaining a court order. However, an occupier may not be forcibly evicted as this may constitute a criminal offence under the Criminal Law Act 1977 (see para 7.40 below).

Homeless applicants awaiting a decision

7.19   In the case of *Roma Desnousse v Newham LBC, Paddington Churches HA, Veni Properties Ltd*[12] the Court of Appeal considered the position of a person occupying accommodation provided by a local authority, pending a decision on a homeless application.

Ms Desnousse made a homeless application to the local authority. She and her two children were placed by the local authority in a self-contained flat while her homeless application was investigated. After five months the authority decided that she was intentionally homeless and that no long term housing duty was owed. Subsequently she was informed that the accommodation booking

9   PEA 1977 s3(2) and (2B). The fact that the protection is given to those lawfully residing in the premises means that the unlawful tenants of a borrower have no protection against a lender entitled to possession: *Bolton Building Society v Cobb & Others* [1965] 3 All ER 814. The position of unlawful sub-tenants as against the 'head landlord' is more complex and is dealt with at paras 3.111–3.126.

10   PEA 1977s 5.

11   *Smith v Northside Developments Ltd* (1988) 55 P&CR 164.

12   [2006] EWCA Civ 547.

would be cancelled. She applied to the court for an injunction to prevent the authority or the accommodation providers from evicting her without obtaining a possession order.

The Court of Appeal held that Ms Desnousse was not protected by the PEA 1977 because of the transient nature of her occupation. It was not necessary for court proceedings to be brought by either the authority or the owners of the premises in order for her to be lawfully evicted.[13]

7.20   It is not therefore necessary to obtain a possession order to evict a licensee occupying accommodation pending a homeless decision. However, the situation will be different if the person remains in the same accommodation after a housing duty has been accepted even though the nature of the occupation agreement and the parties may remain the same.

7.21   So, the following occupiers of residential accommodation may be evicted by a landlord without a court order:

- excluded occupiers listed in PEA 1977 s3A;
- homeless applicants granted a licence pending a homeless decision;
- trespassers who entered as trespassers.

7.22   For all other 'residential occupiers' an eviction without a court order will be unlawful, giving rise to a civil claim for damages and an injunction. It may also be a criminal offence. The criminal offences are summarised below.

Unlawful eviction

7.23   The offence is committed if:

> Any person unlawfully deprives the residential occupier of any premises of his or her occupation of the premises or any part of the premises, or attempts to do so [PEA 1977 s1(2)].

7.24   However, no offence is committed if the person proves that he or she believed, and had reasonable cause to believe, that the residential occupier had ceased to reside in the premises.

---

13 The case was argued on the grounds that Ms Desnousse was a licensee not a tenant and the court left open the question of whether PEA 1977 would apply if the occupier was granted a tenancy pending decision.

Harassment by landlord or agent

7.25   There are two different offences under PEA 1977: one committed by a landlord or agent and one committed by any person. The offence by a landlord or agent is described below.

7.26   The offence is committed if:

- a landlord or landlord's agent does acts likely to interfere with the peace or comfort of the residential occupier or members of the household, or persistently withdraws or withholds services reasonably required for the occupation of the premises as a residence; and
- he or she knows, or has reasonable cause to believe, that the conduct is likely to cause the residential occupiers to give up occupation of the whole or part of the premises or to refrain from exercising any right or pursuing any remedy in respect of the whole or part of the premises.[14]

7.27   The first part of the definition of the offence describes the two kinds of act that make out the offence. It should be noted that a single act likely to interfere with peace or comfort of the occupier is sufficient; if the complaint is about the withdrawal or witholding of services this must be 'persistent', meaning that there must be more than a single act or there must be 'deliberate continuity' (eg a refusal to reconnect a service).[15]

7.28   In either case there must also be the necessary intention; the act or acts must be done by someone who knows that the likely outcome is that the occupier will leave or refrain from exercising rights in relation to the premises.[16]

7.29   It should be noted that to commit the offence of harassment it is not necessary that the likely outcome is that the occupier leaves the premises; for example it is sufficient that it is likely to deter an occupier from pursuing a complaint to the council or from taking legal action about disrepair. An intention to force an occupier to give up occupation temporarily whilst building works are carried out is not sufficient.[17]

---

14   PEA 1977 s1(3A).
15   *R v Varol* [1972] Crim LR 318, CA.
16   *R v Burke* (1990) 22 HLR 433 (HL) & *R v Yuthiwattana* (1984) 16 HLR 49, CA.
17   *Schon v L. B Camden* (1986) 18 HLR 341, QBD.

Definition of 'landlord' and 'agent'[18]

7.30   The 'landlord' means the 'immediate' landlord and any 'superior' landlord (ie a landlord who granted to the immediate landlord his or her interest). The immediate landlord is the person who would be entitled to possession but for the occupier's right to remain in occupation. This includes a person to whom the original landlord sold or transferred ownership.

7.31   An 'agent of the landlord' is not defined in PEA 1977. An agent is any person who acts on behalf of the landlord. It includes someone who has an express agreement to act on the landlord's behalf, whether written or oral. This would include a lettings agent or rent collector. It can also include any person who implicitly acts on behalf of the landlord. This can be difficult to prove but in many cases the evidence makes it clear that the acts have been carried out on behalf of the landlord. However, even if it is the case that the acts are done on behalf of the landlord it is the agent who commits the offence.

7.32   It is a defence to the offence of harassment if the landlord or agent can prove that he or she had reasonable grounds for doing the acts or withdrawing or withholding the services in question.

Offence committed by 'any person'

7.33   An offence of harassment under PEA 1977 may also be committed by any person, not necessarily the landlord or agent. In this case the person must 'intend' to cause the occupier to give up occupation of the whole or part or to refrain from exercising any right or remedy in respect of the premises: PEA 1977 s1(3).

Local Authority Powers

Prosecutions

7.34   Local authorities have the power to prosecute offences committed under the PEA 1977. However, prosecutions are rare.[19] This is partly because of the limited resources of local authorities who must carry

---

18   PEA 1977 s1(3)(c).

19   The number of prosecutions has declined since the early 1990s. In the majority of cases if the prosecution is successful the penalty will be a fine and it is rare that an immediate prison sentence is imposed.

out all of the investigations and evidence gathering and, to succeed, must prove the case 'beyond reasonable doubt'. Even if a prosecution is successful, the penalties imposed by the courts are usually insufficient to operate as a deterrent. Few local authorities now employ specialist officers (usually known as 'Tenancy Relations Officers') to deal with such cases. Although the police may prosecute such offences they rarely do so, leaving enforcement of PEA 1977 to local authorities.

7.35   Nevertheless, local authorities may use the threat of an eviction to persuade a landlord to resolve a dispute, eg to allow a tenant back into occupation, to re-connect services or stop committing acts of harassment.

Criminal penalties

7.36   The offences under PEA 1977 may be tried in a magistrates' court or the Crown Court. If tried in a magistrates' court the maximum penalty is six months in prison and/or a fine of up to £5,000. In the Crown Court the maximum term of imprisonment is two years and/or an unlimited fine. The court also has the usual range of sentencing powers and may grant an absolute or conditional discharge, make a probation or community service order, or make a suspended sentence of imprisonment.

7.37   In addition, the court can order that compensation be paid to the victim 'for personal injury, loss or damage' resulting from the offence.[20] However, awards of compensation by the criminal courts are confined to simple and straightforward cases.[21] Where an offence under PEA 1977 has been committed the victim will almost certainly have the right to claim damages in the county court (see paras 7.117–7.123 below).

7.38   Under the PEA 1977 the criminal courts cannot order that a victim of unlawful eviction be re-instated or restrain future unlawful behaviour by the landlord. In most cases where a landlord is prosecuted, a civil action will be also be brought by the victim to claim damages and an injunction. There is no bar on the two sets of legal proceedings being pursued at the same time.

---

20 Powers of the Criminal Courts (Sentencing) Act 2000 s130.
21 *Herbert v Lambeth LBC* (1991) 24 HLR 299, QBD.

Re-connecting services

7.39   Local authorities also have the power to make arrangements to secure the restoration or continuance of gas, water or electricity supplies where the supplies have been or are likely to be cut off because of failure by the owner to pay for the services.[22] Many authorities are reluctant to use these powers as it involves expenditure which it may be difficult or impossible to recover from the landlord. Some authorities only use the powers as a last resort if the occupiers include young children or the elderly. Nevertheless, local authorities should be asked to exercise their powers. An authority's unwillingness to do so may assist a person applying as homeless to the same authority as he or she may argue that it is not reasonable to continue to occupy accommodation without necessary services.

Offences under the Criminal Law Act 1977

7.40   The offences under PEA 1977 are committed against 'residential occupiers' which means those who have a right to occupy or where there is a legal requirement that the landlord use the civil courts to enforce the right of possession. Even where there is no such right or requirement, it is a criminal offence to use violence in order to secure entry to premises.

7.41   Section 6(1) of the Criminal Law Act (CLA) 1977 provides that it is an offence if:

> any person who, without lawful authority, uses or threatens violence for the purpose of securing entry into any premises for himself or for any other person ... provided that:
>
> (a) there is someone present on those premises at the time who is opposed to the entry which the violence is intended to secure; and
>
> (b) the person using or threatening the violence knows that is the case.

7.42   The violence may be directed against the person or against property.[23] Forcing open a door or window is therefore an offence, provided there is someone in the premises who is opposed to the entry and this is known to the perpetrator.

---

22 Local Government (Miscellaneous Provisions) Act 1976 s33.
23 CLA 1977 s6(4)(a).

7.43   The offence is committed when violence is used to 'secure entry' into the premises. It is immaterial whether it is intended to secure 'possession' or for some other purpose.[24]

Lawful authority

7.44   'Lawful authority' means the authority to use reasonable force to secure entry, not having the legal right to possession.

7.45   The Act specifies situations in which no offence is committed by the use of force to secure entry to premises, ie the situations in which a person does have 'lawful authority' to use reasonable force:

Displaced residential occupiers (DROs)

7.46   Any person who was occupying premises as a residence immediately before being excluded by someone who entered those premises as a trespasser is a DRO. This does not include a person who was occupying as a trespasser or who was let into occupation by a trespasser.[25]

7.47   A person continues to be a DRO so long as he or she continues to be excluded from occupation by the original trespasser or any subsequent trespasser.[26]

7.48   The use of reasonable force by a DRO to gain access is not an offence under the CLA 1977.[27]

Protected intending occupiers (PIOs)

7.49   PIOs are individuals, who require the premises as a residence, and are excluded from occupation by trespassers.

7.50   There are three kinds of PIOs:

- freeholders and long-leaseholders;
- private tenants and licensees;
- tenants and licensees of social landlords, including local authorities.

7.51   In all cases the PIO must require the property for his or her own occupation as a residence. The interest of the PIO must be established by documentary evidence in prescribed form. For freeholders,

---

24 CLA 1977 s6(4)(b).
25 CLA 1977 s12(4) and (6)
26 CLA 1977 s12(3).
27 CLA 1977 s 6(1A).

leaseholders and their tenants or licensees, this means a statement witnessed by a Justice of the Peace. For the tenants and licensees of social landlords a certificate issued by the landlord is sufficient.

7.52　The use of reasonable force by a PIO to gain access is not an offence under CLA 1977.

7.53　As is indicated below, it is a criminal offence for a trespasser not to leave premises when required to do so by a DRO or PIO. The most common practice will be for the DRO or PIO to attend the premises with police officers. If the person requested to leave refuses to do so he or she can be arrested and removed forcibly by the police thereby enabling the DRO or PIO to take possession.

7.54　The following persons also have 'lawful authority' to use reasonable force to secure entry into residential premises:

Court bailiffs

7.55　A court bailiff executing a possession order may use reasonable force to secure entry.

Police officers

7.56　A police officer exercising a power of arrest or search under the criminal law may use reasonable force to secure entry.

7.57　There are certain specific criminal offences relating to trespass for which an officer may use these powers thereby effectively removing the trespasser. These include:

- a person on premises as a trespasser, having entered as a trespasser, who fails to leave premises on being required to do so by a DRO or PIO following the above procedure;[28]
- a person who is on premises as a trespasser, having entered as a trespasser, who has with him or her on the premises an offensive weapon;[29]
- a person who is evicted following the making of an Interim Possession Order who re-enters the premises.[30] The procedure for obtaining an Interim Possession Order is described in chapter 5.

---

28 CLA 1977 s7.
29 CLA 1977 s8.
30 Criminal Justice and Public Order Act 1994 s76.

Prosecutions

7.58 Unlike PEA 1977, local authorities have no power to prosecute offences under CLA 1977. Such offences are investigated by the police and prosecuted by the Crown Prosecution Service. The maximum penalties are the same as for PEA 1977 offences described above.

Civil proceedings

Causes of action

7.59 When a landlord has harassed or unlawfully evicted an occupier there will usually be a number of potential causes of action, based in contract and in tort.

Contract

7.60 A tenancy agreement is a legally binding contract. If one party breaches the contract the other party can bring an action for damages (compensation) and ask the court to grant an injunction to restrain future breaches of the contract. Cases of unlawful eviction and/or harassment usually require urgent action to obtain an injunction. This may be to force the landlord to allow a tenant back into occupation, to re-instate services or stop doing things that interfere with the tenant's peaceful enjoyment of the tenancy.

Relevant terms of the tenancy agreement

7.61 There are two terms implied into all tenancy agreements that are relevant in claims based on harassment or unlawful eviction by landlords:

- the covenant of quiet enjoyment; and
- the covenant not to 'derogate from grant'.

Quiet enjoyment

7.62 Some tenancy agreements expressly state that the landlord 'covenants' (promises) to give the tenant quiet enjoyment. In any event, it is an implied term of all tenancy agreements that the landlord is bound by this covenant. However, the term is not implied into licence agreements. This term will always be relied on in a civil claim for unlawful eviction or harassment brought by a tenant.

7.63   Conduct by a landlord that interferes with the right to occupy undisturbed will usually be a breach of the covenant of quiet enjoyment.[31] This can range from minor interference to an actual eviction.

Derogation from grant

7.64   It is also implied into all tenancy agreements that the landlord covenants not to 'derogate' from the grant of the tenancy. This covenant may be relevant if the landlord retains possession of part of the premises, such as the common parts, or of neighbouring premises. A landlord will breach the covenant if he or she does anything in relation to the premises he or she controls that makes the tenant's premises materially less fit for the purpose of the letting. This could include letting the other premises for a purpose that interferes with peaceful residential use of the tenant's home.

Tort

7.65   A tort is a recognised civil wrong. Some torts exist because of recognition by the courts ('common law torts') and others are created by statute ('statutory torts'). The following torts will often be relied on by tenants in civil actions for unlawful eviction and harassment:

- nuisance;
- trespass;
- assault and battery; and
- intimidation,

Nuisance

7.66   Nuisance is based on interference with the use and enjoyment of land. It may be a state of affairs, condition or activity that interferes with the use of neighbouring land. It includes causing physical damage to premises as well as interference with the use or enjoyment of premises, such as loud noise or obnoxious smells.

7.67   Whether acts complained of amount to a nuisance must be judged according to the standard of a reasonable person[32] and what is judged to be a nuisance depends on the circumstances. Noise caused by home improvements may not constitute a nuisance if

---

31 There may, however, be instances where the landlord's conduct does disturb the tenant's quiet enjoyment but is not a breach of the covenant, eg carrying out necessary repairs provided reasonable steps are taken to minimize the disturbance, see para 9.70.

32 *Robinson v Kilvert* (1889) 41 ChD 88, CA.

carried on for a limited period at a reasonable time. The same level of noise may constitute a nuisance if caused intentionally in order to annoy or if the activities are conducted at unsocial times such as early in the morning or late at night.[33]

7.68 Traditionally, an action in nuisance could be brought only by a person entitled to possession of land or premises. However, the Court of Appeal held in 1993 that an action in nuisance could be brought by a young woman to restrain harassment, 'pestering' and communications by a former friend.[34] The introduction of the Protection from Harassment Act 1997 (see below) now provides a statutory tort to restrain harassment.

Trespass

7.69 There are three kinds of trespass: trespass to land; trespass to goods; and trespass to the person.

Trespass to land

7.70 Trespass means entering premises without the permission of the person entitled to possession, or remaining on premises after permission has been withdrawn.

7.71 Only a person entitled to possession can sue in trespass. A tenant can make a claim in trespass but a licensee cannot since a licensee does not have a legal right to possession.

Trespass to goods

7.72 This means the unlawful interference with goods belonging to another. If the goods are taken and used without permission this is known as 'conversion'.

7.73 Action can be taken by the person who owns the goods and does not depend on rights in relation to the premises.

7.74 A landlord who simply disposes of an occupier's belongings or removes them and leaves them outside the premises may face an action for damages, even if the eviction itself was not unlawful.[35] The

---

33 *Christie v Davey* [1893] 1 ChD 316.

34 *Khorasandjian v Bush* (1993) 25 HLR 392, CA.

35 Under the law of bailment a person who comes into possession of another person's belongings has a duty to take reasonable care of the property for a reasonable period and to give the person a reasonable opportunity to collect them. For local authorities there is statutory provision regarding tenant's belongings, under the Local Government (Miscellaneous Provisions) Act 1982 s41.

occupier can claim damages sufficient to replace the items lost. Whether or not the occupier can prove the existence of the items and their value depends on the available evidence. However, it is not necessary to be able to produce receipts or proof of purchase of each and every item. The oral evidence of the occupier and anyone else with knowledge of what was in the premises may be sufficient. However, much will depend on how realistic the extent and estimated value of the belongings appears.

Trespass to the person

7.75   This is also known as 'assault and battery'. As well as being a criminal offence, an assault is a tort.

7.76   An assault is an act that puts the victim in immediate and reasonable fear of being physically attacked. Battery is the actual application of physical force to another person.

7.77   Action can be taken by the victim regardless of their rights in relation to the premises.

Intimidation

7.78   The tort of intimidation is committed when a person makes a demand accompanied by an unlawful threat which results in damage to the person threatened or to some other person. The threat may be made verbally or by acts but must be contrary to the criminal or civil law. An example would be a threat to unlawfully evict or assault a person if rent was not paid by a certain date or time.

Statutory torts

7.79   There are two statutory torts relevant to claims for unlawful eviction and harassment against landlords:

- unlawful eviction under the Housing Act 1988;
- harassment under the Protection from the Harassment Act 1997.

7.80   In both cases the relevant Act also sets out a particular remedy that is available if the tort is proved.

Housing Act 1988: unlawful eviction

7.81   Section 27 of the Housing Act (HA) 1988 created a specific tort of unlawful eviction. The definition of the tort is based on the criminal offences under PEA 1977. There are two ways in which the tort can be committed.

Unlawful eviction

7.82   Under HA 1988 s27(1) the tort of unlawful eviction is committed when a landlord or any person acting on behalf of the landlord unlawfully deprives a residential occupier of any premises of his or her occupation of the whole or part of the premises.

Attempted eviction/harassment

7.83   The tort under HA 1988 s27(2) is committed where a landlord or any person acting on behalf of the landlord either:

- attempts to unlawfully evict a residential occupier; or
- harasses a residential occupier;
- with the result that the occupier gives up occupation.[36]

7.84   An example of the tort under section 27(2) would be where a landlord attempts to exclude the tenant by changing the locks but the tenant is able to gain entry. If the tenant subsequently gives up occupation because of the landlord's conduct, the tort under section 27(2) would be committed. If the landlord had successfully excluded the tenant the tort under section 27(1) would have been committed.

7.85   Harassment is defined in the same terms as for the criminal offence. The tort is committed where the landlord or any person acting on behalf of the landlord does acts likely to interfere with the peace or comfort of the residential occupier or members of his or her household, or persistently withdraws or withholds services reasonably required for the occupation of the premises as a residence. Further, he or she must know or have reasonable cause to believe that the conduct is likely to cause the residential occupier to give up occupation of the premises or any part, or to refrain from exercising any right or pursuing any remedy in respect of the premises or any part. However, if the harassment does not result in the occupier giving up occupation, the statutory tort is not committed; the tenant can still bring a civil claim relying on the torts described above, as well as breach of contract.

7.86   As indicated above, in relation to the criminal offence of harassment, it is not necessary that the behaviour is intended or likely to make the occupier leave the premises. It is sufficient that

36 HA 1988 s27(2).

the perpetrator knows it is likely to dissuade an occupier from exercising rights, such as taking action about disrepair or complaining to the local authority about the premises or the landlord.

Who to sue

7.87 Although the tort may be committed by someone acting on the landlord's behalf, it is the landlord who is liable to pay damages.[37] This is in contrast to a prosecution of a criminal offence under PEA 1977 which is brought against the person committing the acts, eg the landlord's agent.

Defences

7.88 The defences available to a landlord are also the same as for the criminal offences.[38] It is a defence if the landlord can prove the following:

- that he or she believed and had reasonable cause to believe that the person had ceased to reside in the premises; or
- if harassment is alleged, that he or she had reasonable grounds for doing the acts complained of or withdrawing or withholding the services.

7.89 'Reasonable grounds' would include disconnecting services because they were dangerous or where necessary works of repair interfered with the occupier's peace or comfort. It would not extend to harassment by a landlord who had a legitimate claim for possession or rent arrears against an occupier.

7.90 If the tort under HA 1988 s27 is proved the damages will be calculated according to a formula set out in section 28.

'Section 28 damages'

7.91 HA 1988 s28 damages are assessed on the basis of the difference between:

- the landlord's interest valued on the basis that the residential occupier continues to have the same right to occupy the premises as before giving up occupation or being evicted; and
- the interest valued on the basis that the residential occupier has ceased to have that right.

37 HA 1988 s27(3).
38 HA 1988 s27(8).

7.92 To determine the relevant values expert evidence will be needed.[39]

Reduction of section 28 damages

7.93 The amount of damages may be reduced by the court in the following circumstances:[40]

- where, prior to the acts complained of, the victim was guilty of conduct which makes it reasonable to reduce the amount of damages; or
- where, before the start of the proceedings the landlord offered to reinstate the victim who unreasonably refused the offer.[41]

7.94 In both cases the court may reduce the damages 'as it thinks appropriate'.

7.95 The offer of re-instatement must be genuine: handing the tenant a key to a lock which did not work and where the room formerly occupied had been wrecked was held not to be an offer of re-instatement for these purposes.[42]

Re-instatement of occupier

7.96 No damages can be awarded under section 28 if, before court proceedings are finally disposed of, the victim is re-instated so as to become a residential occupier again. This may be by agreement or by order of the court.[43]

7.97 So, a tenant who is granted an injunction for re-instatement and re-occupies cannot be awarded section 28 damages.

Offers to re-instate

7.98 The significance of offers to re-instate can be summarised as follows:

---

39 The relevant values are assessed as at the time immediately before the person ceased to occupy. Certain assumptions are made for the purposes of the valuation, namely that the landlord is selling on the open market to a willing buyer; that neither the residential occupier nor a member of his or her family wish to buy; and, is disregarded the potential development value of the land: s28(3).

40 HA 1988 s27(7).

41 Further, damages may be reduced even if the victim has obtained alternative accommodation before the offer was made, if the court considers that it would have been unreasonable to refuse the offer had he or she not obtained alternative accommodation: s27(7)(b).

42 *Tagro v Cafane and Patel* (1991) 23 HLR 250, CA.

43 Section 27(6).

- if an offer to re-instate is made *before* the claim for unlawful eviction is *commenced*, an unreasonable refusal may result in a reduction of damages;
- if the offer is made *after* the claim for unlawful eviction is *commenced* the offer may be refused without any consequence in relation to the award of section 28 damages;
- a tenant who *accepts* an offer of re-instatement, before the proceedings are *concluded*, cannot be awarded section 28 damages. Damages for other causes of action, such as breach of contract, nuisance, trespass etc may still be awarded.

Valuing the tenant's interest

7.99   The valuation must be carried out on the basis of the tenant's actual interest and not on a notional basis. This means that the level of section 28 damages in relation to tenants with no long-term security will be limited.

> In *King v Jackson*[44] an assured shorthold tenant was unlawfully evicted. In the county court she was awarded £11,000 under section 28. The Court of Appeal upheld the landlord's appeal: where a property was let to a tenant with little security at a market rent the difference in the value of the premises with the tenant in occupation and with vacant possession would be minimal, if anything. An award of £1,500 was substituted.

7.100   In *Wandworth LBC v Osei-Bonsu*[45] the Court of Appeal considered both the way in which damages should be assessed and the power to reduce damages where the victim is guilty of conduct that justifies a reduction.

> Mr Osei-Bonsu was a joint secure tenant with his wife, who had left the premises as a result of his violence. The authority evicted him following the service by his wife of a defective notice to quit. He succeeded in his claim for unlawful eviction under section 27 and was awarded £30,000 on the basis of agreed valuation evidence.

44   (1997) 30 HLR 541, CA.
45   (1998) 31 HLR 515, CA.

The Court of Appeal reduced this by two-thirds to £10,000 on the basis of the husband's violence towards his wife. It was also held that the valuers had failed to have regard to the actual circumstances existing at the time of the eviction, namely that the tenancy was precarious and could be ended by a correct notice to quit. Appropriate damages would have been £2,000. However, the court did not interfere with the valuation evidence as this had been agreed by the parties.

Protection from Harassment Act 1997

7.101   The Protection from Harassment Act (PHA) 1997 provides that harassment is both a criminal offence and a tort. PHA 1997 was introduced to address the problem of 'stalking', where one person's behaviour towards another may not be explicitly threatening or intended to cause fear but nevertheless does cause 'alarm or distress'.

What is 'harassment'?

7.102   The term 'harassment' is not defined in the Act but section 1(1) provides that a person must not pursue a course of conduct which amounts to harassment of another, and which he or she knows or ought to know amounts to harassment of the other.[46] Section 7 offers the following definitions:

- a 'course of conduct' must involve conduct on at least two occasions;
- references to harassing a person include alarming the person or causing the person distress;
- 'conduct' includes speech; and
- aiding, abetting, counselling or procuring harassment by another person is also prohibited.

7.103   It is a defence to show that:[47]

---

46   Section 1(1). A person 'ought to know that it amounts to harassment of another if a reasonable person in possession of the same information would think the course of conduct amounted to harassment of the other': s1(2).

47   PHA 1997 s1(3). In additions to these defences, certain acts, certified by the Home Secretary, and done on behalf of the Crown relating to national security, the economic well-being of the UK or to prevent or detect serious crime are excluded from the PHA 1997: s12.

- the conduct was pursued to prevent or detect crime. This would include the actions of not only police officers but also tenancy relations officers and private individuals;
- the conduct was pursued under any statute or rule of law or to comply with a statutory condition or requirement. This could include sending a statutory demand for a debt or a notice to quit; or
- the pursuit of the conduct was reasonable in the circumstances.

Enforcement

7.104 As the behaviour prohibited under PHA 1997 is both a tort and a criminal offence, the victim has two options: bringing a civil claim against the perpetrator for damages and an injunction; or, reporting the behaviour to the police to investigate and prosecute the perpetrator.

7.105 Unusually, the civil and criminal remedies overlap in that a breach of a civil injunction is a criminal offence and the criminal courts can make a 'restraining order' to prevent future harassment.

Criminal offences under PHA 1997

Harassment

7.106 Harassment, as defined above, is a criminal offence punishable by a fine of up to £5,000 and/or up to six months imprisonment.[48] However, if the offence was 'racially or religiously aggravated' the maximum penalty is two years imprisonment.[49]

Violent harassment

7.107 The offence of 'violent harassment' is committed where a person pursues a course of conduct which 'causes another to fear, on at least two occasions, that violence will be used against him ... if he know or ought to know that the course of conduct will cause the other so to fear on each of those occasions.'[50]

---

48 PHA 1997 s2.
49 Crime and Disorder Act 1998 s32. A crime is racially or religiously aggravated if, at the time the offence is committed, there is evidence of a hostility based on the victim's membership or presumed membership of a racial or religious group, or the offence is motivated by such hostility: s28.
50 PHA 1997 s4(1).

7.108   The offence is punishable by a fine of up to £5,000 and/or imprisonment for up to six months in the magistrates' court, and, in the Crown Court by an unlimited fine and/or imprisonment for up to five years. If the offence was 'racially or religiously aggravated' the maximum penalty is seven years imprisonment.

7.109   The defences available to a charge of violent harassment are the same as the defences to an allegation of harassment (listed above) save that if the person is accused of violent harassment there is no general defence that the conduct was reasonable; the defendant must show that the conduct was reasonable 'for the protection of himself or another or for the protection of his or another's property'.[51]

Breach of a restraining order

7.110   Following a conviction for either offence the criminal courts can impose restraining orders to protect the victim from further harassment or conduct causing a fear of violence.[52]

7.111   Breach of a restraining order without reasonable excuse is also a criminal offence. The maximum penalty is a fine of up to £5,000 and/or imprisonment of up to six months in the magistrates' court, and, in the Crown Court by an unlimited fine and/or imprisonment of up to five years.

Breach of a civil injunction

7.112   Where a civil injunction has been granted to restrain the defendant from pursuing a course of conduct that amounts to harassment, it is a criminal offence to do anything prohibited by the injunction without reasonable excuse.[53]

7.113   The offence is punishable by a fine of up to £5,000 and/or imprisonment for up to six months in the magistrates' court, and, in the Crown Court by an unlimited fine and/or imprisonment for up to five years.[54]

7.114   Civil injunctions are enforceable in the civil courts by an application for committal to prison for contempt of court. The PHA 1997 provides that the civil courts may issue a warrant for the arrest

---

51 PHA 1997 s4(3).
52 PHA 1997 s5.
53 PHA 1997 s3(6).
54 PHA 1997 s3(9).

of a person if there is evidence of breach of the injunction[55] and contempt of court may be punished by up to two years imprisonment. However, a person convicted of the offence of breaching a civil injunction cannot also be punished for contempt of court. Similarly, a person punished for contempt of court cannot also be convicted of the offence.[56]

Remedies in the civil courts

7.115   The above notes describe the particular remedies available to a claimant who proves the statutory torts of unlawful eviction under HA 1988 or harassment under PHA 1997. However, even if such claims are not made, the usual civil remedies are available to a claimant alleging harassment or unlawful eviction by a landlord.

7.116   A claim may be made for:

- damages; and
- an injunction – to prevent future harassment and/or to force a landlord to re-admit.

Damages

7.117   A claimant may claim the following types of damages:

Special damages

7.118   Special damages are for quantifiable loss or expenditure incurred as a result of the landlord's unlawful actions. They may include amounts for the value of damaged goods, the cost of temporary accommodation and any other loss that can be quantified.

General damages

7.119   General damages are assessed by the court to compensate the claimant for unquantifiable loss or inconvenience.

7.120   General damages may include amounts to compensate a claimant for the anxiety, distress and inconvenience suffered as a result of the landlord's unlawful behaviour, as well as any personal injury suffered. Examples of damages awards are set out below:

---

55   PHA 1997 s3(3)–(5).
56   PHA 1997 s3(7) and (8).

In *Addison v Croft*[57] the claimant was an assured shorthold tenant whose landlady was selling the property. When the landlady entered the premises without warning, accompanied by an estate agent and prospective purchaser, there was an argument between the landlady and the tenant's girlfriend. Later the landlady came to the premises and insisted that the girlfriend leave. Two weeks later the front door was kicked in and four men threw the tenant and his girlfriend out onto the street. One of the men was the landlady's former boyfriend. The tenant suffered bruises and scratches. The landlady refused to re-admit the tenant until after he obtained an injunction. He slept in his van for 20 nights. The tenant was awarded general damages of £3,000 for the actual eviction and the fact that the tenant was deprived of his home and belongings for 20 days. He was also awarded aggravated damages of £1,000 and exemplary damages of £1,000.

7.121   It is common in claims for unlawful eviction and harassment for additional damages to be claimed under the following heads:

Aggravated damages

7.122   These may be awarded if the defendant has behaved in a particularly unpleasant or violent way or where he or she has ignored the orders of the court.

In *Youziel v Andrews*[58] the claimant was an assured shorthold tenant of a one bedroom flat. The defendant was initially his landlord but then transferred his interest to a third party. Notice of this was not given to the tenant and the defendant continued to manage the property. Rent arrears accrued because the defendant was an asylum-seeker not eligible for benefits. Over a six-week period the defendant subjected the claimant to a campaign of harassment. On ten occasions he threatened the claimant, by entering the flat, telephoning and shouting threats, including that the claimant 'would pay with his life'. He and two friends also

57   Preston County Court, 17 April 2008, June 2008 *Legal Action* 31.
58   Lambeth County Court, 23 January 2003, March 2003 *Legal Action* 30.

assaulted the claimant, slapping and kicking him and throwing him to the ground. He sustained an injury to his knee and suffered stress and anxiety and weight loss.

At Lambeth County Court he was awarded general damages of £13,000 for the personal injuries sustained, £4,300 in aggravated damages for the tort of assault, and £2,700 in respect of breach of covenant of quiet enjoyment. The total award was £20,000 plus interest of £200.

Exemplary damages

7.123   Exemplary damages may be awarded if the defendant intended to profit from the unlawful act. Such damages are in addition to compensatory damages and are intended to punish or set an example in order to deter unlawful behaviour.[59] They are calculated to ensure that any financial gain resulting from the unlawful action is paid in damages to the victim.

In *Drane v Evangelou*[60] the tenant's rent was reduced following an application to the rent officer. In response, the landlord moved other people into the premises, changed the locks and moved the tenant's belongings into the back yard. An injunction was granted but the tenant was not able to return to the premises for ten weeks. Exemplary damages of £1,000 were awarded for what was described as the landlord's 'monstrous behaviour'. The Court of Appeal dismissed the landlord's appeal: it was appropriate to award exemplary damages where the defendant's conduct had been calculated to make a profit and those damages may exceed the compensation ordinarily payable. It was said: 'To deprive a man of a roof over his head in my judgment is one of the worst torts which can be committed. It causes stress, worry and anxiety.'[61]

59   *Rookes v Barnard* [1964] 1 All ER 367, HL.
60   [1978] 2 All ER 437.
61   Lawton LJ at 461.

7.124   Aggravated and exemplary damages can only be awarded in respect of a tort and not breach of contract[62]

7.125   The statutory damages awarded under section 28 of the HA 1988 are calculated in a similar way and exemplary damages will not be awarded in addition to section 28 damages.[63]

7.126   Although many of the reported cases were concern tenants with long-term rights, damages may be substantial even where the occupier occupies under a short-term agreement.

> In *Ahmed v Bains*[64] the claimant was an assured shorthold tenant of a room in a shared house. The landlords were a married couple who lived elsewhere. The husband moved into the living room at the premises, was noisy and prevented the tenants from using the room. When the claimant complained he was threatened with violence and then served with notice of seeking possession. On the day the notice expired the husband and another man assaulted the claimant. His possessions were disposed of and his room re-let the same day. He stayed with friends for about three months before finding alternative accommodation. At Brentford County Court he was awarded general damages of £1,000 for the harassment prior to the eviction; £7,800 for the unlawful eviction and homelessness; £1,500 aggravated damages; £1,500 exemplary damages; and £1,695 special damages for loss of his belongings. The total award was £13,495.

Injunctions

7.127   An injunction is a court order compelling a person to do something or to stop doing something. The terms of an injunction must be clear so that the respondent knows exactly what he or she must do and any time limit. If a person does not comply with an injunction an application may be made to the court for the person to be committed to prison for contempt of court (see para 7.138 below).

7.128   An injunction is a discretionary remedy. This means that the court may refuse to grant the injunction even if satisfied that the defendant has behaved unlawfully. The court can take account of

---

62   *Kralj v McGrath* [1986] 1 All ER 54; *Addis v Gramaphone Co Ltd* [1909] AC 488.
63   Section 27(5).
64   September 2001 *Legal Action* 25.

the claimant's behaviour in deciding whether to grant an injunction.

Interim injunctions

7.129   In cases of unlawful eviction and harassment it is common to seek an interim injunction to ensure that the occupier is re-instated and/ or to restrain further acts of harassment until the claim can be tried by the court. In fact, in cases of unlawful eviction, if an occupier is re-instated in compliance with an injunction, there may be no further hearings; the claim for damages may be settled by agreement between the parties.

7.130   To obtain an interim injunction the applicant must show that:[65]

- damages are not a sufficient remedy;
- there is a serious issue to be tried; and
- the 'balance of convenience' favours the making of an injunction.

7.131   In most cases of unlawful eviction it is clear that the action is unlawful and the court will make an order that the landlord allows the occupier back into the premises. However, this may not be possible if the premises have been re-let (see below).

Cases of urgency

7.132   Normally at least three days notice must be given of an application for an interim injunction.[66] However, in some circumstances it is possible to obtain an injunction without giving notice to the defendant. A 'without notice' injunction may be applied for where there is 'exceptional urgency'.[67] If the case is too urgent to give three days notice the landlord should nevertheless be informed of the application by telephone or fax if possible.

7.133   Additionally, if there is a risk of violence to the claimant from the defendant, a without notice application may be made to ensure that the defendant is protected by an injunction before the defendant is given notice of the proceedings.

7.134   Where a without notice order is obtained, the defendant must be served with the order, the application notice, evidence, and notice of

---

65   *American Cynamid Co v Ethicon* [1975] AC 396, HL.

66   Civil Procedure Rules (CPR) Part 23, Practice Direction para 4.1.

67   See CPR Part 3.1(2) and Part 23.4(2).

any further hearing as soon as possible. Injunctions should always be personally served on the defendant.

7.135 An order made on a 'without notice' application will usually be for a very limited period. The court may list a further 'on notice' hearing within a few days and the injunction will last until that hearing. Alternatively, the defendant may be given the opportunity to apply to discharge the injunction at short notice. In any event the injunction will be reconsidered at any final hearing.

Homeless applications

7.136 A person with a right to occupy but who cannot secure entry to premises is homeless.[68] A person who has been unlawfully evicted should be given emergency accommodation by a local authority provided he or she appears to be eligible and in priority need. Usually an authority will provide emergency accommodation only until an injunction can be obtained and enforced. However, if the landlord's conduct is such that it would be unreasonable to continue to occupy the premises, a long-term housing duty may be owed, see para 13.157.

Injunctions where premises have been re-let

7.137 Where premises have already been let to innocent third parties the court will not make an injunction against the landlord: for the landlord to comply he or she would have to unlawfully evict the new tenants. Rather, if the unlawfully evicted tenants wish to regain possession they can take possession proceedings against the new 'tenants' on the basis that they are in fact trespassers, the landlord having no lawful authority to let the premises.

In *Love v Herrity*[69] a landlord changed the locks to premises and re-let them following service of 'notice to quit' because of arrears of rent. A without notice injunction was obtained for re-entry but later discharged on the basis that the balance of convenience favoured waiting until final trial to decide the issues. The Court of Appeal held that the court had been wrong to find that there was any serious issue to be tried as it was admitted that there was an

68 HA 1996 s175(2)(a).
69 (1991) 23 HLR 217.

assured tenancy that could only be determined by a court order; the tenants had clearly been unlawfully evicted. However, as the premises had been re-let it would be pointless to grant an injunction. A declaration was granted that, as against the landlord, the tenants were entitled to possession and the tenants were given permission to join the new tenant as a defendant to enable them to claim possession against her. It would have been possible for the tenants to apply for a possession order against the new tenant directly using the summary procedure, on the basis that she was a trespasser.

Final injunctions

7.138 An injunction can also be part of the final order made by the court after trial.

In *Saxby v McKinley*[70] a landlord unlawfully evicted tenants by changing the locks. The tenants' solicitors informed the landlord that he was not entitled to evict the tenants in this way and that he had committed a criminal offence. This was confirmed in writing. The landlord did not re-admit the tenants. The tenants then obtained an injunction without notice. The injunction required the landlord to provide keys and permit them to re-enter. The landlord failed to comply. At a further hearing, of which the landlord was given notice, the landlord did not appear and the injunction was continued. It was not until 21 days later that the landlord allowed the tenants back into the premises. The tenants applied to commit the landlord to prison for contempt of court. The judge held there had been a serious contempt and ordered an immediate sentence of imprisonment of 28 days. The landlord appealed but his appeal was dismissed. It was held that there had been a serious contempt of court and the consequence for the tenants was potentially, if not actually, disastrous. The landlord had shown cynical disregard for the order over a substantial period of time.

70 (1996) 29 HLR 569, CA.

Public funding

7.139   Subject to the means test, public funding will usually be granted to pursue cases of unlawful eviction and harassment. However, if an occupier is re-admitted and the only claim before the court is for damages it may be difficult to satisfy the 'costs-benefit' test (i.e. that the potential benefit to the occupier justifies the likely legal cost of pursuing the claim).

7.140   The Civil Procedure Rules provide that cases of unlawful eviction and harassment should not be referred to the small claims track whatever the value.[71] This does not necessarily mean that public funding will be granted where the likely damages are not substantial. The parties may, however, agree that the claim should be dealt with as a small claim.

7.141   See chapter 22 for a fuller explanation of public funding and civil proceedings.

71 CPR 26.7(4).

CHAPTER 8

Housing benefit

continued

Key points

- Housing benefit is paid to help meet rent payments for people on low incomes. It does not cover mortgage payments. It can only be paid for accommodation occupied as a home.
- Not all people are eligible for housing benefit, including some people from abroad and some full time students.
- Some kinds of agreements are excluded from the housing benefit scheme, eg some agreements between relatives and other agreements considered not to be commercial.
- For private tenants housing benefit may be less than the contractual rent a person pays: for most private tenants the 'maximum housing benefit' is set by a rent officer. For claims made after 7 April 2008, the maximum housing benefit will be limited to the Local Housing Allowance – a set amount depending on the size and location of the property.
- Housing benefit does not cover certain charges such as water rates and heating and hot water charges.
- Claimants on Income Support, income based Job Seekers' Allowance and Pension Guarantee Credit are entitled to the maximum housing benefit. For other claimants income and capital are assessed to decide how much, if any, housing benefit can be paid.
- For tenants of landlords other than the local authority, payment should be made within 14 days of a claim that is supported by all relevant information and evidence. If entitlement cannot be assessed within this time a payment on account must be made.
- A particular claimant's housing benefit may be reduced because of other adults living in the home. These are known as 'non-dependent deductions'.
- Overpayment of housing benefit may be recovered by deduction from future housing benefit so that the claimant has to pay the shortfall to avoid falling into rent arrears.
- Most decisions can be appealed. Local authorities may also revise a decision.
- Housing benefit claims can be backdated for up to 12 months if there is continuous good cause.[1]

---

1   At the time of writing it is proposed to reduce this to three months.

Introduction

8.1   Housing benefit is a means tested benefit available to assist those on a low income to pay for a dwelling occupied as a home. It is administered by local housing authorities. The rules regarding entitlement and the assessment of claims are complex. This chapter contains an overview of the housing benefit system with a focus on the problems commonly experienced by claimants. However, housing benefit problems often lead to rent arrears and possession claims and a basic understanding of the housing benefit system is essential for housing advisers.

8.2   The Social Security Contributions and Benefits Act (SSCBA) 1992 provides for the payment of housing benefit. The details of the housing benefit scheme are found in regulations, principally the Housing Benefit Regulations (HB Regs) 2006[2]. For those over the retirement age the relevant regulations are the Housing Benefit (Persons who have attained the qualifying age for state pension credit) Regulations (HB(PC) Regs) 2006[3] which mirror the provisions of the HB Regs 2006. These notes mostly give references only to the HB Regs 2006.

8.3   Although administered by local authorities, the scheme is a national scheme set out in regulations. The Department of Work and Pensions (DWP) Housing Benefit Guidance Manual, though not law, provides a comprehensive summary of the regulations and the way they should be applied by local authorities. The manual can be downloaded from the DWP website at: www.dwp.gov.uk/housingbenefit/manuals.

8.4   Housing benefit cannot be paid to cover mortgage payments[4] or other housing costs paid by owner occupiers, such as service charges and insurance payments.

8.5   Owner occupiers who receive income support or pension credit may receive, as part of their benefit, sums in respect of these housing costs. Such housing costs can include interest on home loans (but not capital repayments), service charges and insurance. Again, the rules are complex and are outside the scope of this book.

---

2   SI No 213.
3   SI No 214.
4   SSCBA 1992 s130(2).

Entitlement to housing benefit

8.6   Entitlement to housing benefit depends on the following conditions:[5]

* the claimant must be liable to make payments in respect of a dwelling in Great Britain;
* the dwelling must be occupied as a home;
* there is a maximum amount of housing benefit that will be paid;
* the claimant's income and savings must be below a certain level.

8.7   However, some people cannot claim housing benefit because of their immigration status or because they are full time students. Each of these conditions is dealt with below.

Liability to make payments

8.8   Mostly housing benefit is paid in respect of a person's liability for rent. However, a liability other than rent may qualify for housing benefit and a person other than the tenant (or person legally liable to make the payment) can be treated as liable.

8.9   Housing benefit can be paid in respect of:[6]

* rent;
* licence payments;
* mesne profits;
* use and occupation charges;
* service charges, payment of which is a condition on which the right to occupy depends;[7]
* mooring charges for a houseboat;
* site payments for a caravan or mobile home;
* certain costs charged by housing associations and charities for the maintenance of almshouses and essential services;[8]
* payments under a rental purchase agreement.

---

5   SSCBA 1992 s130(1).
6   HB Regs 2006 reg 12(1).
7   See 8.14 below.
8   Because the provision of almshouses is charitable, the occupiers cannot be tenants, see para 1.43. However, the providers may make charges to the occupiers, for which housing benefit is payable.

Mesne profits and charges for use and occupation

8.10   'Mesne profits' are damages for which a trespasser is liable. They are usually assessed on the basis of rent as this represents the income lost by the landlord/owner as a result of the unlawful occupation. 'Use and occupation' charges are charges made or agreed when an occupier has no legal right to occupy land. The terms 'mesne profits' and 'use and occupation charges' are often used interchangeably. Landlords who are denying that a person has any legal right to occupy may indicate that payments made will be accepted as mesne profits or use and occupation charges only. This is to guard against the occupier arguing that the acceptance of 'rent' is evidence that a tenancy exists. This is common after the expiry of a notice to quit served by a private landlord or when a landlord is disputing a person's right to succeed to a tenancy, see para 3.36.

8.11   In some cases the landlord may refuse to accept any payment, either as rent or use and occupation charges, while pursuing a claim for possession. However, the person in occupation remains liable and an application for housing benefit should be made. The authority may suspend actual payment but, provided a timely application has been made, housing benefit may be paid when the dispute has been resolved, either as rent (if the occupier succeeds in establishing a right to occupy) or mesne profits (if the landlord succeeds in establishing unlawful occupation).

8.12   Housing benefit is not paid in respect of:[9]

- payments under a long tenancy[10] except a shared ownership tenancy granted by a housing association or housing authority;
- payments under a co-ownership scheme;
- payments by an owner;
- payments under a hire purchase, credit sale or conditional sale agreement, except to the extent that the agreement is in respect of land;
- payments by a Crown tenant;[11] and
- payments in respect of a dwelling owned by the claimant's partner.

---

9   HB Regs 2006 reg 12(2).
10 A long tenancy is defined as a tenancy for a fixed period of 21 years or more: HB Regs 2006 reg 2.
11 See para 2.31 for the definition of a Crown tenant. Crown tenants on income support or pension credit can claim housing costs. Crown tenants may also claim a rent rebate from the landlord under a voluntary scheme. Inquiries should be made to the landlord.

Non-eligible charges

8.13   Where the weekly amount paid as 'rent' includes sums that are for charges other than the right to occupy the accommodation, the other charges will usually be 'non-eligible charges' and housing benefit will not cover those charges.

8.14   Non-eligible charges include water rates, heating and hot water charges for the premises (as opposed to the common parts) and some service charges. However, service charges that must be paid as a condition of occupation are 'eligible charges' for which housing benefit can be paid. These include charges for such services as general management costs, lifts, entry phones and rubbish removal. Services charges that are not eligible will include services that are personal to the occupier. Some service charges in supported accommodation may be paid for by the local authority's social services department, depending on the occupier's means.

Who can claim housing benefit

8.15   Housing benefit will normally be paid to the person who is liable to make the payments, eg the tenant or licensee.[12] However, the following may be treated as being liable so as to be eligible to receive housing benefit:[13]

- a partner of the person who is liable;
- a person who has to make the payments in order to continue to live in the home because the person liable to make them is not doing so. The person must be a former partner of the liable person or it must be reasonable to treat that person as liable to make the payments;
- a person whose rent liability has been waived by the landlord as compensation for works of repair carried out by the tenant, for which the landlord is responsible, for a maximum period of eight weeks;
- a partner of a student who cannot claim housing benefit (see para 8.29).

---

12 HB Regs 2006 reg 8(1)(a).
13 HB Regs 2006, reg 8(1)(b)–(e).

Persons ineligible for housing benefit

Persons from abroad

8.16   Housing benefit cannot be paid to certain people because of their immigration status or because they are not habitually resident in the UK.

8.17   Broadly there are three categories under which a person may be ineligible for housing benefit:

- those subject to immigration control;
- EEA nationals with no right to reside;[14] and
- persons who are not habitually resident.

8.18   The Immigration and Asylum Act 1999 (IAA 1999) sets out a definition of persons 'subject to immigration control' who are not entitled to claim any social security benefits, including housing benefit.[15]

8.19   In addition the HB Regs 2006 makes certain people ineligible for housing benefit by providing that such people shall not be treated as liable to make payments. Regulation 10 provides that:

- a 'person from abroad' who is liable to make payments in respect of a dwelling shall be treated as if he or she were not liable;
- 'person from abroad' means a person who is not habitually resident in the UK, the Channel Islands or the Isle of Man or the Republic of Ireland (the Common Travel Area: CTA). This can include a British national who has lived abroad;
- no person shall be treated as habitually resident in the CTA unless he or she has a right to reside in the CTA other than one of the limited rights to reside enjoyed for the purpose of free movement and work-seeking.
- most EEA nationals who are exercising EU rights are not required to be habitually resident.

8.20   The combined effect of IAA 1999 s115 and regulation 10 of the HB Regs 2006 is that the following people are not entitled to housing benefit:

---

14   EEA refers to the European Economic Area. For an explanation of the rights of EEA nationals, in particular the 'right to reside' see para 13.38.

15   AIA 1999 s115, see para 19.6.

Persons subject to immigration control

- a person who needs leave to enter or remain in the UK and does not have it;
- a person who has leave to enter or remain in the UK that is subject to a condition that he or she does not have recourse to public funds;
- a person who has leave to enter or remain in the UK given as a result of a maintenance undertaking;
- a person who continues to have leave to enter or remain in the United Kingdom only as a result of an appeal against a decision to vary, or to refuse to vary any limited leave.

EEA nationals

- an EEA national who does not have a right to reside, or whose only right to reside is as a job seeker or for an initial period of three months.

Habitual residence

- a person who is not habitually resident in the CTA, subject to those listed below who are not required to be habitually resident.

Those exempt from the habitual residence test

8.21 The following people do not have to satisfy the habitual residence test[16] because they are relying on European Union rights:

- an EEA worker;
- a self-employed EEA national;
- EEA nationals who are, for a temporary period, no longer working or self-employed because of illness or accident, involuntary unemployment or vocational training;[17]
- family members of the above, as defined in the EEA Regulations 2006;
- a person with a right to reside permanently in the UK;
- a registered accession state worker;

---

16 Under reg 10(2) they are not defined as 'persons from abroad'.
17 These rights are set out in Article 7.3 of the EU Directive 2004/38. Certain conditions are attached to those who are involuntarily unemployed or engaged in training. See para 13.54.

8.22   Others exempt from the habitual residence include the following:

- a refugee;
- a person with exceptional leave to enter or remain in the UK, granted outside the immigration rules;
- a person with humanitarian protection granted under the immigration rules;
- a person who is not subject to immigration control and who is in the UK as a result of deportation, expulsion or other compulsory removal from another country to the UK;
- a person who left Monserrat after 1 November 1995 as a result of volcanic eruption;
- a person who left Lebanon on or after 12 July 2006 because of the armed conflict there;
- a person in receipt of income support or income-based jobseekers' allowance.

8.23   It should be noted that persons who are exempt from the habitual residence test must still have a right to reside in the UK to be eligible for housing benefit. Those who are exempt because they are relying on EU rights have a right to reside under EU law. Those who are exempt because of having fled Monserrat or Lebanon in the circumstances specified are only eligible if they have a right to reside.

The application of the habitual residence test

8.24   The habitual residence test is therefore of most relevance to:

- persons with indefinite leave to remain, other than refugees; and
- British nationals.

8.25   See paras 13.127–13.128 for an explanation of the application of the habitual residence test.

The right to reside

8.26   The EEA Regulations 2006, which are intended to set out the rights contained in the EU Directive 2004/38, describe the circumstances in which EEA nationals and their families have the right to reside. This is explained in more detail at paras 13.38–13.113. However, there remains an issue as to whether a right to reside can exist only in the circumstances set out in the regulations and the directive or whether such a right may be established by reliance on other treaty rights.

8.27   In the case of *Harrow LBC v Ibrahim & Secretary of State for the Home Department*[18] the Court of Appeal considered the issue and referred it to the ECJ for a determination (see para 13.120).

8.28   To date the Social Security and Child Support Commissioners, who deal with housing benefit appeals, have rejected the argument that rights to reside can be established outside the terms of the EEA Regulations 2006. Until the ECJ make its decision in *Ibrahim* it is likely that housing benefit will continue to be refused to EEA nationals who cannot establish a right to reside under the EEA Regulations 2006.

Students

8.29   The general rule is that full-time students[19] are ineligible for housing benefit.[20] However, the following full time students are eligible for housing benefit:[21]

- a person on income support or income-based jobseeker's allowance;
- a lone parent;
- those who would qualify for the following premiums paid to housing benefit claimants: pensioner premium, higher pensioner premium, disability premium or severe disability premium;
- those who are incapable of work or treated as being incapable of work for a continuous period of not less than 196 days;
- a person who has a partner who is also a full-time student, if either is responsible for a child or young person;
- a single claimant who is fostering a child placed by the local authority or a voluntary organisation;
- a person aged under 19 whose course of study is not a course of higher education;
- a person who has been awarded a certain kind of educational grant or allowance because of disability by reason of deafness.

---

18 [2008] EWCA Civ 386, 21 April 2008.

19 'Full-time student' is defined as a person attending a full-time course of study including a sandwich course. See HB Regs 2006 reg 53 which provides extensive definition of all terms relevant to students.

20 HB Regs 2006 reg 56(1). As for persons from abroad, they are treated as not being liable to make payments.

21 HB Regs 2006 reg 56(2).

Agreements that are excluded from housing benefit

8.30   In addition to individuals being ineligible, certain kinds of agreements are also excluded. A person who is liable to make payment is treated as not being liable where:[22]

Non-commercial agreements

- the tenancy or other occupation agreement is not on a commercial basis.

Liability to family members/partners

- the liability under the agreement is to a person also living in the dwelling who is a close relative[23] of the claimant or his or her partner;
- the liability under the agreement is:
  - to the claimant's former partner in respect of a dwelling the couple previously occupied together, or
  - to the claimant's partner's former partner in respect of a dwelling the couple (the partner and his or her former partner) previously occupied together;
- the claimant or his or her partner is responsible for a child of the person to whom the claimant is liable under the agreement;
- under the agreement the liability is to a trust of which a child of the claimant or the claimant's partner is a beneficiary.

Accommodation previously owned by claimant or partner

- the claimant or the claimant's partner previously owned the dwelling, within the last five years (or were tenants under a long lease). However, this will not apply if the claimant satisfies the authority that it was necessary to relinquish ownership of the lease in order to continue in occupation.

Employment-related accommodation

- the occupation of the claimant or the claimant's partner is a condition of employment.

22   HB Regs 2006 reg 9.
23   As defined in HB Regs 2006 reg 2(1).

Religious orders

- the claimant is a member of a religious order and is wholly maintained by the order.

Care homes

- the claimant is in a care home or independent hospital.

Agreements created to take advantage of the housing benefit scheme

8.31 In addition to the specific exclusions above, an agreement will be excluded if the liability was created to take advantage of the housing benefit scheme.

8.32 The following are excluded unless the claimant can satisfy the authority that the liability was not intended to be a way of taking advantage of the housing benefit scheme:

- an agreement under which the liability is to a company or trust, under which any of the following are directors or employees, or trustees or beneficiaries: the claimant; his or her partner; a close relative (of the claimant or his or her partner) who resides with the claimant; or a former partner (of the claimant or the claimant's partner);
- where, before the liability was created, the claimant was a non-dependant of someone who resided and continues to reside in the dwelling (see paras 8.93–8.96 below for an explanation of non-dependants).

8.33 It should be noted that a liability to a close relative is only automatically excluded where he or she shares the dwelling. However, a tenancy agreement between close relatives may be considered not to be on a commercial basis even where the accommodation is not shared. If the claim does not fall within one of the specific situations listed above, the question of whether an agreement is a commercial agreement is a question of fact in each case.

Non-commercial agreements

8.34 When deciding whether an agreement is on a commercial basis the authority must have regard to whether the agreed terms are legally enforceable.[24]

24 HB Regs 2006 reg 9(2).

8.35   Authorities may allege that an agreement is not commercial because the landlord has not taken action to enforce the payment of the full rent where there is a shortfall between the rent and the maximum housing benefit. This issue was considered in the Commissioner's case CH 1076/2002. The Commissioner overturned the tribunal decision that the agreement was not commercial, holding that the tribunal had failed to give sufficient weight to the evidence that it was common practice for landlords to accept the amount of rent paid by housing benefit. The Commissioner found that there was nothing to suggest that this was not a sensible commercial decision for the landlord to make. Further, the tribunal had attached too much weight to the parties' failure to formally vary the tenancy agreement so as to lower the rent to the amount housing benefit was paying. The issue should have been assessed in the context of parties who knew and could trust each other.

8.36   The DWP Guidance also refers to the following criteria as being relevant to the issue:

- the relationship between the parties – it is important to remember that there is nothing inherently non-commercial about letting to a close friend or relative, but the nature of any personal ties should be considered;
- the living arrangements – where the landlord is resident it is worth considering whether the tenant has exclusive use of any part of the property and how chores and food storage are arranged etc;
- amount of rent payable – a low rent is not in itself indicative of a non-commercial agreement. Many landlords do not seek to profit from renting out property;
- evidence of payments made – evidence of non-payment may suggest non-commerciality.

8.37   It should be noted that a tenancy and a liability to pay rent does not depend on there being a written agreement. An authority should not refuse to pay housing benefit because there is no written agreement provided there is other evidence of the tenancy, eg letter from the landlord, rent book or other proof of the amount of rent payable. Further, it is not necessary to draw up a new tenancy agreement when a fixed term agreement expires: a legally binding statutory tenancy automatically comes into existence. See paras 2.44–2.46 above.

Occupying the dwelling as a home

8.38 The general rule is that a person is entitled to housing benefit in respect of a liability to make payments for a dwelling occupied as his or her home.[25] However, this is subject to express provision for temporary absences and for the payment of housing benefit on two properties.

8.39 As is explained in chapter 3, an occupier who is temporarily absent does not necessarily cease to occupy premises as his or her home. Even during an extended absence a person may continue to occupy a dwelling provided:[26]

- he or she intends to return; and
- there is some physical evidence of that intention.

8.40 However, this does not necessarily mean that a person who is absent for an extended period will continue to be entitled to receive housing benefit.

8.41 Specific provision is made in the Regulations for:

- periods of absence when housing benefit will continue to be paid; and
- circumstances in which housing benefit will be paid in respect of two dwellings.

Temporary absence

Up to 13 weeks' absence

8.42 Any claimant temporarily absent from home for any reason, eg holiday, visiting friends and family, may continue to receive housing benefit for a period of up to 13 weeks provided the following conditions are met:[27]

- the claimant intends to return to occupy the dwelling as his or her home;
- it has not been let or sublet during the claimant's absence; and
- the period of absence is unlikely to exceed 13 weeks.

8.43 It should be noted that this does not mean that housing benefit can be paid for the first 13 weeks of an absence which is likely to exceed 13 weeks. If the absence is likely to exceed 13 weeks no housing

---

25 SSCBA 1992 s130(1).
26 See para 3.5.
27 HB Regs 2006 reg 7(13).

benefit is payable. Further, if, during the absence, there is a change of circumstance and it becomes likely that the absence will extend beyond 13 weeks, entitlement ends at that point.

Prisoners

8.44   This rule applies to an absence caused by being imprisoned *after* conviction and sentence for a criminal offence. Again, it should be noted that benefit is only payable if the likely absence will not exceed 13 weeks. This means that an assessment must be made of the likely release date. Most prisoners on short term sentences serve only half the term of imprisonment and may be released earlier under the discretionary Home Detention Curfew schemes ('tagging').

8.45   In contrast, prisoners who are detained on remand pending trial or sentence are entitled to receive housing benefit for up to 52 weeks, see below para 8.48.

Trial period of residential care

8.46   There is specific provision that housing benefit can be paid for up to 13 weeks in respect of a claimant who goes into residential accommodation on a trial basis.[28]

8.47   In such a case the claimant must intend to return to occupy the dwelling as his or her home only in the event that the residential accommodation proves not to be suitable. As in all cases of housing benefit paid during a temporary absence the home must not be let or sub-let during the absence.

Up to 52 weeks' absence

8.48   Housing benefit may be paid during an absence of up to 52 weeks to the following claimants:[29]

- a prisoner on remand pending trial or sentence;[30]
- a person on bail who is required to live in an approved bail hostel or an address other than the person's usual home;
- a person who is in a hospital or similar institution as a patient;

---

28   HB Regs 2006 reg 7(11) and (12).
29   HB Regs 2006 reg 7(16) and (17).
30   If the prisoner is convicted and sentenced to a term of imprisonment his or her entitlement is then dealt with under the 13-week rule, see para 8.44 above. A prisoner who has already received housing benefit for a period of 13 weeks on remand, will be entitled to no further housing benefit.

- a person who is, or whose partner or child is, undergoing medical treatment or medically-approved[31] convalescence in the UK or abroad, other than in residential accommodation;[32]
- a person who is receiving medically approved care in the UK or abroad, other than in residential accommodation;
- a person who is providing medically approved care to someone else residing in the UK or elsewhere;
- a person who is caring for a child whose parent or guardian is away from home receiving medically approved care or medical treatment;
- a person undertaking an 'approved training course' in the UK or abroad;[33]
- a person who is a student who would be entitled to housing benefit if not absent from home;
- a person in 'residential accommodation' for respite care. This is different from a person in residential accommodation for a trial period when the maximum period for which housing benefit can be paid is 13 weeks;
- a person who is away from home because of fear of violence in the home or from a former family member.

8.49 In all cases it is necessary that the following conditions are met:
- the claimant intends to return to occupy the dwelling as his or her home;
- it has not been let or sublet during the claimant's absence;
- the period of absence is unlikely to exceed 52 weeks or, in exceptional circumstances, is unlikely to substantially exceed that period.

8.50 It should be noted that although there is provision for benefit to be paid even where the absence is likely to exceed 52 weeks (in exceptional circumstances) the total period for which benefit cannot exceed 52 weeks.

---

31 'Medically approved' means certified by a medical practitioner: reg 7(18).
32 Residential accommodation means a care home, an independent hospital or an Abbeyfield Home: reg 7(18).
33 See HB Regs 2006 reg 7(18). An approved training course means a course provided by, or on behalf of, or approved by a government department or the Secretary of State, Scottish Enterprise or Highlands and Islands Enterprise. They include courses under various EU initiatives which involve periods abroad and courses for occupational, vocational or social rehabilitation skills offered to disabled persons by the Department for Innovation, Universities and Skills and the Department of Health.

Housing benefit for two homes

8.51   The general rule is that housing benefit can only be paid in respect of one home. However, in certain circumstances housing benefit may be paid on two dwellings.[34]

Unavoidable liability for previous home: up to four weeks

8.52   When a person moves into a new home but remains liable to make payment on his or her previous home, housing benefit can be paid on both homes for up to four weeks, where the dual liability could not reasonably have been avoided.[35] This commonly occurs when a person is allocated a social tenancy under the local authority's allocations scheme (see chapter 16) and the new tenancy is to start before old tenancy can be terminated. See paras 1.62–1.69 regarding the termination of tenancies by tenants.

Delay in moving into new home: up to four weeks

8.53   As housing benefit may only be paid in respect of a home actually occupied, if a person takes on a liability but delays actually moving into a dwelling, housing benefit cannot usually be paid. However, provision is made for a person to be treated as occupying a new home for up to four weeks if the delay is caused by any of the following:[36]

- the delay was necessary to carry out disabled adaptations to the new home;
- the move was delayed pending the outcome of an application for a social fund payment necessary to meet needs arising out of the move or in setting up the home. This applies only if:
  - a member of the claimant's family is aged five or under,
  - the claimant is receiving a disability premium, or
  - the claimant is over 60 and neither the claimant nor his or her partner is getting IS or JSA, or
- the claimant became liable to make payments in respect of the new dwelling while he or she was a patient or in residential accommodation.

8.54   In all cases the claim for housing benefit must be made before the person moves into the new home. If refused, a new claim must be

---

34   HB Regs 2006 reg 7(6).
35   HB Regs 2006 reg 7(6)(d) and (7).
36   HB Regs 2006 reg 7(6)(e) and (8).

made within four weeks of moving to qualify. Payment will not actually be made until the claimant moves into the new home.

Fleeing violence: up to 52 weeks

8.55 Where a person remains absent because of a fear of violence in the home or from a former family member housing benefit may be paid on two homes for up to 52 weeks where it is considered reasonable to do so.[37] This entitlement depends on the victim having a continuing intention to return to occupy the home.

Fleeing violence: up to four weeks

8.56 In addition, benefit may be paid on two homes for up to four weeks even where the victim does not have an intention to return to the home he or she has left.[38]

Accommodation in two dwellings: indefinitely

8.57 Where, because of the number of people in the household, a housing authority has accommodated the household in two separate dwellings, housing benefit will be paid on both dwellings.[39]

Couple including an eligible student: indefinitely

8.58 Where a student who is eligible for housing benefit (see above at para 8.29) is part of a couple benefit may be paid on two homes if it is unavoidable that they should occupy two separate dwellings and it is reasonable to pay housing benefit on both.[40] The same rule applies if he or she is on an approved training course (see above para 8.48).

The maximum housing benefit

8.59 Even where a claimant is entitled to 'full housing benefit', this may not cover the whole of the net rent. The amount of housing benefit paid cannot exceed the 'maximum' housing benefit.[41] For

---

37 HB Regs 2006 reg 7(6)(a).
38 HB Regs 2006 reg 7(10).
39 HB Regs 2006 reg 7(6)(c).
40 HB Regs 2006 reg 7(6)(b).
41 SSCBA 1992 s130(4) and HB Regs 2006 reg 12(3)(a) and reg 13.

local authority tenants and Rent Act tenants the maximum housing benefit is the contractual rent. For tenants in the unregulated private sector the maximum housing benefit may be less than the contractual rent.

The old system: eligible rents

8.60   On 2 January 1996 a system was introduced whereby rent officers would decide on the eligible rent for tenants of private landlords.[42] The eligible rent was the amount the rent officer considered to be a reasonable rent taking into account local rent levels for accommodation of a suitable size for the household.[43] This was calculated on the basis of what was considered to be:

- a reasonable rent for the actual property; or
- (if the actual property was deemed too large) a reasonable rent for a property of a suitable size, in the immediate area (the 'claim related rent'); and
- a reasonable rent for a property of a suitable size in the broader locality (the 'local reference rent').

8.61   The lowest of these was the 'maximum housing benefit' (the 'eligible rent') that could be paid. The assessment was carried out following a claim for housing benefit being made in respect of a particular agreement for particular premises.

8.62   For most applicants under the age of 25 the maximum rent was calculated on the basis of a reasonable rent for a single room in a shared house: the 'single room rent'.

8.63   The system of assessing maximum housing benefit changed on 7 April 2008. For claimants who remain in the same accommodation and whose claim continues after that date housing benefit will still be limited by reference to the eligible rent. However, a claimant may withdraw his or her claim and submit a new claim for a Local Housing Allowance (see para 8.86 below).

8.64   One problem with 'eligible rents' as a method of assessing the maximum amount of housing benefit is that claimants often had to sign a tenancy agreement before knowing how much housing

---

42 The previous scheme is known as 'the Old Scheme' and some claims are still governed by the Old Scheme.

43 See the Rent Officers (Housing Benefit Functions) Order 1997 ('Rent Officers Order') (SI No 1984).

benefit would be paid.[44] Many tenants are therefore contractually obliged to pay a rent that is not met in full by housing benefit. Some tenants pay the shortfall from their limited income. In some cases the landlord does not insist on payment of the shortfall but may, after arrears have built up, use the failure to pay as a ground for possession or may seek a money judgment against the tenant.

8.65   Another problem was that referring claims to the rent officer added to the delay in assessing and paying housing benefit at the start of the tenancy.

8.66   Local authority rents were not subject to rent officer assessment. For RSL tenancies referrals to the rent officer were possible but only made if the rent seemed unreasonably high or the premises were larger than required. Also, private tenancies that started prior to 15 January 1989 (regulated tenancies) were not subject to the scheme; such tenants have the right to a 'fair rent' (see para 3.173).

The new system: Local Housing Allowances

8.67   As from 7 April 2008 a new system of 'local housing allowances' (LHAs) is in force nationally, following a pilot in 18 areas. The key principle of the LHA is that the maximum rent is based on a flat rate allowance rather than a rent officer assessment for an individual claimant. LHAs are set and published locally so that the LHA in a particular area for a certain size of property will be known by tenants and landlords in advance. Also, if the actual rent paid is less than the LHA, a tenant can keep the excess, subject to a maximum of £15 per week.

8.68   LHAs apply to claims made on or after 7 April 2008 and will apply to existing claimants who move to a new property on or after 7 April 2008.

8.69   The LHA scheme also applies only to private sector tenancies. It does not apply to:[45]

- tenancies where the landlord is a local authority;[46]
- tenancies where the landlord is an RSL;

---

44 It was possible to obtain a 'pre-tenancy determination' but often, to secure the property, the claimant would have to sign a tenancy agreement before this could be done.

45 HB Regs 2006 reg 13C.

46 The scheme applies only to cases in which a rent allowance may be awarded. Local authority tenants receive a rebate and not a rent allowance.

- exempt accommodation (shelters and supported accommodation);
- excluded tenancies, which includes regulated tenancies (to which the fair rent scheme applies);
- houseboats, caravans, mobile homes, hostels and tenancies where a substantial amount of the rent is attributable to board and attendance.

8.70   LHAs are based on the area in which the claimant lives and the size of the property. The number of people in the claimant's household determines the size of the property to which the claimant is entitled.

The area

8.71   The areas for which rents are calculated are based on Broad Market Rental Areas and the amount of housing benefit payable is based on the median rents (ie the middle of the range of rents, not the average).

8.72   The area for which the LHA can be claimed must be an area in which the claimant could reasonably be expected to live, having regard to facilities and for health, education, recreation, banking and shopping, and taking account of public and private transport to and facilities and services.[47]

Size of accommodation

8.73   The size of accommodation deemed appropriate for a particular household is set out in the Rent Officers Order.[48]

8.74   A household is entitled to one bedroom for:

- every adult couple, whether married or unmarried;
- each other adult aged 16 or over;
- any two children of the same sex aged under 16;
- any two children aged under 10;
- any other child.

Shared accommodation

8.75   For single applicants under the age of 25 the LHA is based on the cost of a shared room.

---

47 See *R on the application of Heffernan & Rent Service* [2008] UKHL 58, 30 July 2008.

48 See note 43 above. The Order has been amended by the Rent Officers (Housing Benefit Functions) Amendment Order 2007.

8.76   For single applicants over 25 and couples with no dependents who live in shared accommodation with exclusive use of only one room the LHA shared room rate will apply. However, if the claimant or couple occupies more than one room exclusively or has self-contained accommodation the full LHA for a one bedroom self-contained property will apply.

Exceptions

8.77   Care leavers under the age of 22 years are entitled to the LHA for a self-contained one-bedroom property. See chapter 18 for the definition of 'care leaver'.

8.78   Claimants who are severely disabled are also entitled to the LHA for a self-contained one-bedroom property.

Payment of the Local Housing Allowance

8.79   Under the previous scheme a claimant could elect for housing benefit to be paid direct to the landlord. Also, payment was made direct to the landlord automatically if the tenant had arrears of rent of at least eight weeks or payment of rent arrears was being made direct from benefits. Under the LHA scheme payment will be made to the claimant unless one of the following applies:

- the authority considers that the claimant is likely to have difficulty in managing his or her financial affairs;
- the authority considers that it is improbable that the claimant will pay his or her rent;
- payment was previously made directly to the landlord because of rent arrears, see above.

8.80   While considering whether to make payment direct to the landlord an authority may pay direct to the landlord for up to eight weeks.

8.81   There is a right of appeal, by either the tenant or the landlord, about a decision on whether to make payments to the landlord.

8.82   If the local authority has exercised its powers to pay direct to the landlord, it may also pay an amount exceeding the rent as payment towards any arrears.[49] So, an excess of LHA over the actual rent, up to a maximum of £15 per week could be paid to clear arrears.

49 HB Regs 2006 reg 95(2A).

Information about Local Housing Allowances

8.83   LHAs will be published at the end of each month to apply the following month. They can be checked on-line through each local authorities' website or through 'LHA-direct' which is part of the Rent Service website: www.therentservice.gov.uk.

8.84   Although LHAs are reviewed each month the LHA payable to a particular claimant will not be reviewed until 12 months after the claim is made.

Transitional arrangements

8.85   When the rules changed in 1996 those claimants who were already receiving housing benefit on 1 January 1996 continued to have their claims assessed under the 'Old Scheme'. Those who have been in receipt of housing benefit continually since 1 January 1996 continue to be dealt with under the Old Scheme. Those whose claims were made on or after 1 January 1996 but before 7 April 2008 will continue to have the maximum rent assessed on the basis of the reference rent as determined by the Rent Service.

8.86   For some claimants the LHA will be higher than the current rent officer assessment. A claimant may withdraw his or her claim and to make a new claim for the same property which will be determined in accordance with the LHA.[50]

Assessment of income and capital

8.87   Subject to the rules regarding the maximum amount of housing benefit described above, the amount of housing benefit a claimant receives depends on an assessment of his or her income and capital.

8.88   Claimants who receive Income Support, Income-based Job Seekers' Allowance or the guarantee credit of Pension Credit are entitled to maximum housing benefit. This may however be less than the rent payable if the maximum housing benefit is less than the contractual rent (see para 8.59 above), or the benefit is subject to 'non-dependent deductions' (see para 8.93 below).

---

50 See the DWP Guidance: HB/CTB G10/2008, dated 21 May 2008 which can be obtained from the DWP website: www.dwp.gov.uk/housingbenefit. The Guidance indicates that there must be a gap of at least one week between the withdrawal and the new claim.

8.89   For other claimants an assessment is made which depends on the claimant's 'applicable amount'. The applicable amount for a claimant depends on the age of the claimant, the number and age of any dependents and whether the claimant or a member of the household has any special needs. The claimant's weekly income, less the applicable amount equals 'excess income'. If this is zero or less than zero the person is entitled to full housing benefit (ie the maximum amount). If it is greater than zero, the amount of housing benefit payable will be the maximum housing benefit less 65 per cent of the weekly excess income. Obviously, if the excess income is above a certain level no housing benefit will be payable. Certain income is disregarded: Disability Living Allowance, Attendance Allowance, Mobility Allowance, War Widows' Pension and a proportion of War Disablement Pension.

8.90   If a person has savings (including investments) of £16,000 or more, no housing benefit is payable. Savings below this level may mean that the claimant does not receive full housing benefit, different rules applying for those over the age of 60.

8.91   Many local authorities include on their websites a self-assessment service so that a potential claimant can assess if housing benefit will be payable and at what level.

Shared accommodation

8.92   Where accommodation is shared, eg by joint tenants (other than couples), the liability is apportioned between the occupiers.[51] This is the case even though legally each tenant is liable for the whole of the rent (see para 1.52). If only one person is the tenant and liable for the rent, a deduction may be made for other occupiers as 'non-dependent deductions', see below.

Non-dependent deductions

8.93   'Non-dependants' are people who normally reside with a claimant, other than dependent children and partners. Because such people are expected to contribute to the rent, a deduction is made from the claimant's housing benefit for each non-dependant in the household. The amount of the deduction depends on the income of the non-dependant. The definition is set out in the HB Regs 2006 reg 3, and includes:

---

51 This is not the case if the LHA scheme applies, see para 8.76 above.

316 Housing Law: an adviser's handbook / chapter 8

- any member of the claimant's family (apart from one who is part of the claimant's family for benefit purposes);
- a lodger;
- a carer.

8.94 For certain non-dependants no deduction is made. The most common examples are:

- those under the age of 25 who are in receipt of income support or income based job-seeker's allowance;[52]
- those in receipt of pension credit;[53]
- full time students;[54]
- any person who resides with a claimant where the claimant's blind, or in receipt of attendance allowance or the care component of disability living allowance.[55]

8.95 Where a non-dependant deduction is made, if the non-dependant is in 'remunerative work' this is based on the person's weekly income and is applied on a sliding scale, ranging from £7.40 per week to £47.75 per week, at the time of writing. If the non-dependant is not in full time paid work the deduction is £7.40 per week regardless of income. Remunerative work means paid employment for not less than 16 hours a week.[56]

8.96 It is the claimant's responsibility to submit evidence of the income of a non-dependant. Where no such evidence is submitted the DWP guidance previously indicated that the authority should make the maximum deduction. However, this approach was successfully challenged in a Commissioner's appeal when it was held that the authority should have made an assessment based on the evidence it did have (ie, the likely income of a 19-year-old shop worker).[57] The guidance now provides that if no, or inadequate, information about the non-dependant's gross income is provided, the highest deduction should only be made after considering all the relevant facts.

---

52 HB Regs 2006 reg 74(8).
53 HB Regs 2006 reg 74(1).
54 HB Regs 2006 reg 74(7)(c).
55 HB Regs 2006 reg 74(6).
56 HB Regs 2006 reg 6.
57 See CH/48/2006 available on the Commissioners' website at: www.osscsc.gov. uk.

Discretionary housing payments

8.97   Discretionary housing payments (DHPs) are not strictly housing benefit.[58] They are, as indicated, discretionary and can be awarded to a person who receives housing benefit where the authority are satisfied that the person needs additional help with housing costs. The budget for DHPs is cash limited. DHPs can be paid to enable a person to meet a shortfall between the contractual rent and housing benefit but can only be paid for a period when the person is in receipt of housing benefit. Generally, they may be used to cover a shortfall arising because of the difference between the contractual rent and the 'maximum housing benefit'. However, DHPs cannot be awarded to cover any of the following:[59]

- ineligible services charges;
- water rates;
- reductions in social security benefits;
- repayment of rent arrears;
- shortfalls arising because of the recovery of previous overpayments.

8.98   The DWP publish useful guidance on DHPs which is also available on the DWP website: Guidance for Local Authorities on the Operation of Discretionary Housing Payments.

Housing benefit applications

8.99   Although the housing benefit scheme is a national scheme each local authority has its own application forms on which housing benefit is claimed. An application form should be completed and given to the local authority as soon as possible so no benefit is lost. Claims may also be made at the same time as a claim is made for Income Support, Jobseekers' Allowance or Pension Credit.

8.100   In addition to completing an application form, the claimant must also provide further information and evidence as indicated by the form or as the authority subsequently decide is reasonably required to determine entitlement. This will usually include, as a minimum,

---

58 See Discretionary Financial Assistance Regulations 2001(SI No 1167), as amended by the Discretionary Financial Assistance (Amendment) Regulations 2008 (SI No 637).

59 Regulation 3 sets out the full list of excluded payments.

318 Housing Law: an adviser's handbook / chapter 8

proof of identity, rental liability, residence and income and any documents necessary to establish immigration status, if relevant.

8.101   The authority are only obliged to process the claim when all this information and evidence has been submitted.

8.102   Authorities often request further information and evidence following receipt of a claim and the general rule is that this must be provided within one month of the request, or a longer period if the authority considers this reasonable. If the information is not provided within the specified time period the claim may be assessed as being made at a date later than the date the application form was delivered to the authority. This will mean a loss of benefit and the accrual of rent arrears. In such a case a person may make an application for backdated housing benefit (see para 8.106 below).

8.103   Disputes as to whether information and evidence has been provided are common and claimants should always obtain and keep receipts for information delivered to local authority offices.

Delays

8.104 Following receipt of the written application form together with all supporting evidence the local authority must make a decision within 14 days or as soon as reasonably practicable thereafter.[60] The authority should notify the claimant of its determination within 14 days or as soon as reasonably practicable.

Payments on account

8.105 Where the landlord is not the local authority, if it is impracticable for a decision to be made within 14 days, the authority *must* make a payment on account of entitlement.[61] This duty arises only if the delay in making a decision is not caused by the claimant's failure, without reasonable excuse, to provide information or evidence. The amount of the payment will be the amount the authority considers reasonable having regard to the information that is available. Usually, authorities will pay a percentage of the anticipated entitlement. Authorities routinely ignore this provision often resulting in substantial arrears of rent arising at the start of the tenancy. Legal action may be taken in the county court to enforce the duty to make interim payments on account. In practice, the threat

60 HB Regs 2006 reg 89(2).
61 HB Regs 2006 reg 93(1).

of a claim based breach of the statutory duty often results either in a payment on account being made or the claimant's entitlement being assessed.

Backdating housing benefit

8.106   Claims for housing benefit can be backdated for up to 52 weeks.[62]

8.107   If a claimant is aged 60 or over and is not (and his or her partner is not) on Income Support or income based Jobeseekers' Allowance it is necessary only to prove entitlement to housing benefit during the relevant period.[63]

8.108   For other claimants there must be continuous 'good cause' for the failure to claim.[64]

8.109   In deciding whether a claimant has shown good cause for not claiming earlier the authority must be satisfied that the reason for not claiming earlier is such that any reasonable person of that age, health and experience would probably not have claimed earlier in the same way as the claimant. The burden of proving good cause rests on the claimant but the authority must examine all the relevant facts in each case.

8.110   Annex A to the Adjudication Officers' Guide (AOG) contains a useful summary of the situations in which good cause should be accepted, based on Commissioners decisions. Although the AOG is no longer current the Annex is still referred to in the DWP Guidance Manual (see para 8.3 above).

Overpayments of housing benefit

8.111   Where a person receives housing benefit that he or she was not entitled to, this is an overpayment and will be recoverable unless:

- it was the result of an official error; and
- the claimant did not materially contribute to the error; and
- he or she could not reasonably have realised that he or she was being overpaid.

8.112   This definition of a recoverable overpayment means that most overpayments are recoverable. However, decisions regarding

---

62 At the time of writing the DWP has indicated an intention to reduce the period to three months.

63 HB(PC) Regs 2006 reg 64(1).

64 HB Regs 2006 reg 83(12).

overpayment of housing benefit are contentious and the DWP website contains guidance (HB/CTB Overpayments Guide) which runs to 277 pages.

Notification

8.113   The authority must notify a claimant that he or she has been overpaid and that the overpayment is recoverable. The notification should also inform the claimant of the right of appeal and must:[65]

- state that there is a recoverable overpayment;
- give the reason why there is a recoverable overpayment;
- state the amount of the recoverable overpayment;
- explain how the amount has been calculated;
- indicate the benefit weeks to which the recoverable overpayment relates; and
- if recovery is to be made by deduction from future housing benefit this must be stated and, if so, the amount of the deduction;
- if recovery is to be made from the landlord, the notice must identify the person on whose behalf the recoverable overpayment was made and the person (ie another tenant) from whose benefit deduction will be made.

Underlying entitlement

8.114   An overpayment may occur when a person's situation changes, for example, when he or she moves from one type of benefit to another, or commences employment. If the authority are not notified at the time, an overpayment will occur. However, it may be the case that the claimant would have continued to be entitled to housing benefit. In all such cases the local authority should calculate the claimant's 'underlying entitlement' and deduct from the overpayment any housing benefit that he or she was entitled to.[66] If the authority needs more information or evidence to calculate the underlying entitlement it must request this of the claimant. The claimant need not make an application for underlying entitlement to be assessed. However, if the claimant fails to respond to a request for information within one month, the full amount of the overpayment will be recoverable and the claimant should receive notification of this.

---

65 HB Regs 2006 Sch 9 para 15.
66 HB Regs 2006 reg 104.

Recovery of overpayments

By deduction from future benefit

8.115   An authority can recover a previous overpayment by making deductions from a claimant's future benefit.[67] The maximum deduction, calculated as a percentage of a claimant's personal allowance, is £9.00 per week plus 50 per cent of any income disregarded for benefit purposes, (£12.00, at time of writing, per week where the overpayment is the result of fraud). However, authorities may reduce the weekly deductions where this is causing hardship.

8.116   Advisers should always request a deduction in the rate of recovery when a claimant on means tested benefit is in arrears of rent. If the maximum deduction continues, the claimant will be expected (by the landlord or by the court) to pay at least £3.00 per week towards the arrears as well as to make up the shortfall of housing benefit, resulting in a weekly payment of more than £12.00 plus water rates and any service charges. Most claimants will be unable to maintain the payments resulting in breaches of any agreement or conditions imposed by the court.

As a 'lump sum' from the tenant

8.117   An authority cannot suspend the payment of housing benefit until the whole overpayment is recovered. Nor can a housing authority that is also the tenant's landlord recover an overpayment by entering the sum as arrears on the rent account. However, where there is a delay in assessing a claim, an authority may recover any outstanding overpayment from a lump sum that is due to a claimant for a past period. This will place a claimant in arrears. For example, a claimant may have an outstanding overpayment in the sum of £2,000. Following a delay in assessing a renewed claim, the authority may decide that a credit of £1,000 is due in respect of the period between the making of the claim and the assessment. The authority may set off the £1,000 against the amount outstanding so that although weekly housing benefit payments commence, the lump sum of £1,000 is not paid. The result is that the tenant is in rent arrears of £1,000 and the balance of the outstanding overpayment is reduced to £1,000.

---

67   HB Regs 2006 reg 102.

8.118   The authority can make a claim to a county court for a money judgment, see chapter 22.

From the landlord

8.119   Where payment was made to the landlord the authority may recover the overpayment from the landlord.[68] If the authority does this the landlord is entitled to treat the rent as 'unpaid'.[69]

Challenging decisions

Decisions

8.120   A claimant is entitled to notification of a decision in writing[70] and the notification must include certain information, including:[71]

- the right to request a written statement of reasons; and
- the right to apply for a revision and the right to appeal against the decision, and the time limits and way to do so.

8.121   Particular kinds of decision require particular information to be given. For example, where a decision is made that a recoverable overpayment has been made (see para 8.113 above).

Time Limits

8.122   The time limit for appealing against a decision is one calendar month. However, if a claimant requests written reasons for a decision the time stops running until the reasons are given. This means that if a request for reasons is made 10 days before the deadline for appealing, on receipt of the reasons, the claimant still has 10 days in which to bring an appeal.

Revisions

8.123   In response to a request for reasons or an indication that the claimant wishes to appeal, an authority may reconsider its decision.

---

68   HB Regs 2006 reg 101.
69   HB Regs reg 95(2), see para 6.27 above.
70   HB Regs 2006 reg 90.
71   HB Regs 2006 Sch 9.

If the authority accepts that the decision was wrong it can 'revise' the decision. A revised decision takes effect from the date the decision was first made. An example would be an error in the calculation of the claimant's income.

8.124   A claimant who believes the authority have made an error may request a reconsideration. However, a claimant should also indicate an intention to appeal as a request a reconsideration does not extend or suspend the time limit for appealing.

Supersession

8.125 Where the claimant's representations indicate a change of circumstances, a decision may be superseded. An example would be a change in income or a change or the make up of the household. Supersession takes effect from the date of the change of circumstance (or, in fact, the first Monday following notification of the change of circumstance).

8.126   If an authority supersedes a decision the claimant can still appeal against the original decision on the basis that it was wrong at the time.

Appeals

8.127 Some decisions may not be appealed. These include decisions by the rent officer about the eligible rent or the level of the Local Housing Allowance and decisions to suspend the payment of housing benefit.

8.128   Where there is a right of appearl, any person affected by the decision may appeal, including the landlord.

8.129   If the authority are not willing to revise the decision the appeal will be referred to the Social Security and Child Support Appeal (SSCSA) Tribunal.

8.130   Appeals are usually dealt with at a hearing but may be determined without a hearing if both parties agree.

8.131   Public funding is not available for representation at an appeal but assistance may be given to prepare for a hearing under the Legal Help scheme, see chapter 22.

8.132   An appeal against a decision of the SSCSA Tribunal is made to the Social Security Commissioners. An appeal against the Commissioners is made to the Court of Appeal. Public funding is available for appeals to the Commissioners on points of law and for appeals to the Court of Appeal.

Disrepair and housing conditions – action by occupiers

continued

Key points

- An occupier can take two sorts of legal action to address disrepair and poor housing conditions: a civil action in the county court and a criminal action in the magistrates' court. Legal aid is available for representation in civil actions but not for criminal actions.
- Most civil actions rely on contractual rights under a tenancy agreement.
- In all short-term tenancies a landlord has a legal obligation to keep in repair the structure and exterior and the installations for gas, electricity, sanitation and heating. This applies whether or not the tenancy agreement is in writing. The landlord cannot avoid this obligation.
- Usually a landlord will not be in breach of the obligation until the tenant has given notice of the necessary repairs and a 'reasonable time' has elapsed.
- If a landlord is in breach of the repairing obligation a county court can award compensation and order the landlord to carry out the necessary works of repair.
- In addition, in a civil action, the law of tort may be used by a tenant. Some legal duties relating to injury or loss caused by disrepair are set out in statute. The law of nuisance and negligence may also be relevant.
- In most tenancies there is no legal requirement on a landlord that premises let as dwellings are fit for human habitation. A tenant cannot therefore take civil legal action against a landlord because premises are unfit unless this is caused by disrepair.
- The general rule is that a tenant can only take civil action against a landlord if there is 'disrepair' as opposed to poor housing conditions caused by bad design or insufficient amenities.
- Where poor housing conditions are caused by bad design and/ or lack of amenities, an occupier can bring a criminal prosecution. Legal aid is not available for prosecutions but some solicitors will act under conditional fee agreements.
- An occupier with a social landlord may also make a formal complaint about a landlord's failure to carry out repairs and an Ombudsman complaint if the landlord does not resolve the problem.

- It is generally inadvisable for a tenant to withhold rent because of disrepair. However, damages for disrepair may be set off against arrears of rent and may provide a defence to a claim for possession.

Introduction

9.1   Many people who live in rented accommodation are unhappy about their living conditions. They may wish to obtain more suitable and healthy accommodation from a social landlord. Unfortunately, the shortage of affordable accommodation is such that even those in great need may wait for many years to be offered more appropriate accommodation.[1] Advisers will need to be familiar with the transfer and allocation policies of local authorities and other social landlords to be able to advise realistically about the prospects of obtaining better accommodation. Chapter 16 explains the law relating to local authorities' duties to operate fair allocations and transfer systems. This chapter examines the action occupiers may take to obtain repairs or improvements to their homes.

9.2   This chapter considers the following options available to an occupier:

- a civil claim in the county court for compensation and an order for works of repair;
- a criminal action in the magistrates' court for an abatement order and compensation;
- a formal complaint to a social landlord;
- using the rent to pay for repairs.

Occupier's status

9.3   Before advising anyone about the best course of action consideration must be given to the occupier's status. Most private tenants are assured shorthold tenants with no more than six months' security. A private landlord may respond to a complaint or threat of legal action by serving notice requiring possession and applying to the court for a possession order to which there is no defence.

---

1   1.6 million households are currently on council waiting lists: *Councils and the Housing Crisis*, LGA, May 2008.

9.4   Further, many 'tenants' of social landlords will have lost their tenancies as a result of suspended possession orders made previously. Such occupiers became tolerated trespassers when the tenancy ended. The Housing and Regeneration Act 2008 will abolish tolerated trespass and existing tolerated trespassers will automatically become new tenants when the provision comes into force. However, the new tenancy is deemed to start on the date the provision comes into force. To claim damages for historic disrepair an application must be made to the court for an order treating the tenancy as a tenancy continuing uninterrupted. In the absence of such an order no damages will be payable for the period between the end of the previous tenancy and the new tenancy arising (see paras 9.93 and 9.94 below).

Action in the county court

9.5   A county court claim will usually be based on two 'causes of action':[2]

- breach of contract; and
- tort.

Breach of contract

The 'repairing covenant'

9.6   A claim for breach of contract relies on the landlord's repairing 'covenant'. This means the landlord's legal obligation to repair the premises set out in the tenancy agreement, or implied by statute or by common law.

The express terms of the tenancy agreement

9.7   A tenancy agreement is a legal contract and the obligations on the landlord and tenant are legally binding. A written tenancy agreement may contain express terms setting out the landlord's and the tenant's respective obligations for repairs. There is a minimum obligation on the landlord that cannot be overridden by the express terms (see below). However, the tenancy agreement may set out more extensive obligations on the landlords and advisers should always obtain a

---

2   See para 22.10.

copy of the tenancy agreement. Tenancy agreements issued by private landlords often say little or nothing about the landlord's repairing obligations. Tenancy agreements issued by social landlords usually set out the landlord's obligations. In more recent standard tenancy agreements the express repairing obligation tends to mirror the minimum legal standard but older tenancy agreements, particularly local authority agreements, often contain more generous repairing covenants.

In the case of *Welsh v Greenwich LBC*[3] the landlord's obligation was to keep the premises 'in good condition and repair' which was held to include liability for severe condensation. This would not normally fall within the landlord's repairing obligations.

In *Long v Southwark LBC*[4] the landlords covenanted 'to take reasonable steps to keep the estate and common parts clean and tidy'. The tenant brought a claim against the landlords because of inadequate arrangements for collecting rubbish on the estate. The Court of Appeal held that a failure to supervise the performance of outside contractors engaged to collect rubbish amounted to a failure to take reasonable steps and the landlords were in breach of the tenancy agreement.

Variation of tenancy agreement

9.8   Local authorities are able to vary the terms of a tenancy agreement provided they follow the proper procedure (see para 2.142). Advisers should therefore check to see whether the original tenancy agreement has been varied.

Section 11: The landlord's implied repairing obligation

9.9   Under section 11 of the Landlord and Tenant Act 1985 implied into every tenancy agreement granted for a period of seven years or less is an obligation on the landlord to carry out certain repairs. In this chapter this is referred to as 'section 11'. Disrepair claims in the county court are often referred to as 'section 11 claims'.

---

3   (2001) 33 HLR 438, CA.
4   [2002] EWCA Civ 403.

Section 11 – the dwelling-house

9.10 In relation to the premises let to the tenant, section 11 provides that there is an implied covenant on the landlord:

(a) to keep in repair the structure and exterior of the dwelling-house (including drains, gutters and external pipes);

(b) to keep in repair and proper working order the installations in the dwelling-house for the supply of water, gas and electricity and for sanitation (including basins, sinks, baths and sanitary conveniences but not other fixtures, fittings and appliances for making use of the supply of water, gas or electricity); and

(c) to keep in repair and proper working order the installations in the dwelling house for space heating and heating water.

Section 11 – the building

9.11 For tenancies that began on or after 15 January 1989 the covenant extends to other parts of the building in which the dwelling-house is situated, provided that the building is also owned by the landlord. In such a case section 11(1A) provides that the landlord must also keep in repair the structure and exterior of the building. Further, he or she must keep in repair and proper working order any installation that serves the dwelling, directly or indirectly, provided that it is part of the building that the landlord owns or it is in the landlord's control.

9.12 The wider duty applies only if the disrepair affects the tenant's enjoyment of his or her own dwelling or of the common parts.[5]

The limits of section 11

9.13 Section 11 is implied into almost all tenancy agreements.[6] It is implied into a weekly or monthly periodic agreement, even if the tenant has lived in the accommodation for seven years or more.

9.14 Section 11 is not implied if:[7]

- the tenancy began before 24 October 1961; or
- the tenancy is for a fixed term of seven years or more.

Section 11 is unavoidable

9.15 Landlords cannot avoid section 11 by providing in the tenancy agreement that the repairing obligations fall on the tenant or by

5 LTA 1985 s11(1B).
6 This includes tenancy agreements that are not in writing.
7 LTA 1985 s13(1).

seeking to exclude section 11. Any attempt to contract out of the section 11 duty is void.[8] A term in the tenancy agreement that limits or restricts the landlord's obligation under section 11 is only valid if authorised by a county court. The court can only do this if the parties agree and the court considers that it is reasonable.[9]

9.16   Further, terms that seek to make the landlord's repairing obligation dependant on the tenant complying with the tenancy agreement or to prevent a tenant from setting off damages for disrepair against rent arrears may be held to be unfair and unenforceable.[10]

What does section 11 cover?

'Keep in repair the structure and exterior'

9.17   'Keep in repair' has been interpreted by the courts to mean 'put and keep in repair'.[11] It is no defence for a landlord to argue that the item was in disrepair when the tenancy started.

9.18   The 'structure and exterior of the dwelling house' does not mean 'the entire dwelling-house, or the entire constructed building' but 'consists of those elements of the overall dwelling-house which give it its essential appearance, stability and shape'. This is to be contrasted with 'the many and various ways in which the dwelling-house will be fitted out, equipped, decorated and generally made to be habitable'. It is not limited to 'those aspects of the dwelling-house which are load bearing ... but ... to be part of the structure of the dwelling-house a particular element must be a material or significant element in the overall construction'.[12]

9.19   It includes:

- drains, gutters and external pipes (section 11 expressly states this);
- all outside parts of the dwelling;[13]
- the external walls;[14]

---

8 LTA 1985 s12(1).

9 LTA 1985 s12(1)(b).

10 See para 3.158, the Unfair Terms in Consumer Contracts Regulations 1999; *Cody v Philps*, 4 November 2004, January 2005 *Legal Action* 28.

11 *Saner v Bilton* [1876] 7 Ch D 815.

12 *Irvine v Moran* (1990) 24 HLR 1, QB.

13 *Campden Hill Towers Ltd v Gardner* (1976) 13 HLR 64, CA.

14 *Campden Hill Towers Ltd v Gardner* (1976) 13 HLR 64, CA.

- partition walls between the dwelling and another house or flat;[15]
- partition walls within the flat;[16]
- the roof (including skylights). However, if the dwelling is a flat, only if it is a top floor flat and the ceiling and roof are part of the same unit;[17]
- external joinery;
- external doors;
- windows including glass, sashes and necessary window furniture;[18]
- paths and steps that are part of the immediate access to the dwelling.[19]

9.20   The following are not part of the structure and exterior:

- internal doors;
- internal glazing;
- internal joinery such as skirting boards and architraves;[20]
- floor coverings;
- internal plaster. The only decided case on this issue held that internal plaster was more in the nature of a decorative finish and is not part of the structure of the dwelling house.[21] However, most social landlords accept a responsibility for internal plaster.[22]

The installations

9.21   The landlord's obligation is to keep the installations 'in repair and proper working order'. If there is a defective installation in the dwelling

---

15   *Green v Eales* (1841) 2 QB 225.
16   *Campden Hill Towers Ltd v Gardner* (1976) 13 HLR 64, CA.
17   *Douglas-Scott v Scorgie* (1984) 13 HLR 97, CA. If disrepair to the roof of a building is causing damage to a flat within the building the tenant could rely on section 11(1A) which places on the landlord an obligation to keep in repair the structure and exterior of the building. This is only possible if the landlord owns the building and the tenancy started on or after 15 January 1989. If the tenancy commenced before this date an action in nuisance may be possible, see below.
18   *Irvine v Moran* (1990) 24 HLR 1.
19   *Brown v Liverpool Corporation* [1969] 3 All ER 1345, CA.
20   *Irvine v Moran* (1990) 24 HLR 1.
21   However in *Hussein v Mehlman* [1992] 2 EGLR 87 missing ceiling plaster was held to be a breach of s11.
22   In the following reported cases landlords have conceded liability for damage to internal plaster: *Quick v Taff-Ely BC* [1986] QB 809; *Staves v Leeds CC* (1991) 23 HLR 107; *Palmer v Sandwell MBC* (1978) 20 HLR 74.

when the tenancy commences the landlord must put it in a state of repair and proper working order. Further, it is no defence if an installation is not in working order because of a design defect.[23]

9.22   'Installations' include:

- basins, sinks, baths and toilets;
- radiators;
- gas fires;
- fitted electric fires or heaters (including storage heaters) but not moveable plug-in electric heaters;
- boilers within the premises;
- water tanks within the premises;
- water and gas pipes and electrical wiring;
- under-floor heating vents.

9.23   It does not include fixtures and fittings for sanitation apart from basins, sinks, baths and toilets. This means that installations such as showers or bidets will not be the landlord's obligation unless specified in the tenancy agreement.

9.24   However, if there is no installation (eg, no central heating system or hot water boiler) there is no obligation on the landlord to provide one. Tenants may be able to persuade the local authority to take action against a landlord to improve the premises by installing some facility if it is necessary to make the accommodation free from 'hazards' (see chapter 10).

9.25   In addition a landlord must comply with the Gas Safety (Installation and Use) Regulations 1998 (see para 10.87).

Landlord's right of access

9.26   Section 11(6) provides that there is an implied covenant on a tenant to allow the landlord (or someone authorised in writing by the landlord) to enter to inspect the premises. The right is to enter at reasonable times of the day and on giving 24 hours notice in writing.

9.27   In addition to section 11 the landlord can rely on the following provisions to gain access:

- at common law a landlord who has a duty to keep premises in repair has a right to enter premises to carry out the works;[24]

---

23 *Liverpool City Council v Irwin* (1976) 13 HLR 38, HL.
24 *Saner v Bilton.*

- sections 3(2) and 148 of the Rent Act 1977 places a duty on statutory tenants and protected tenants to give access to a landlord to carry out repairs;
- under section 16 of the Housing Act 1988 it is an implied term of every assured tenancy that the tenant shall give access to a landlord to carry out repairs.

9.28   Almost all written tenancy agreements also contain an express obligation on the tenant to given access to the landlord to inspect or carry out works.

When is the landlord in breach of section 11?

9.29   Before action can be taken in the county court the landlord must be in breach of his or her contractual repairing obligations. The tenant must therefore prove:

- that there is disrepair that falls within the landlord's repairing covenant;
- that the landlord knows about the disrepair (the position is different if the disrepair is outside the dwelling, see below);
- that the landlord has failed to carry out repairs within a reasonable time;
- if damages are claimed, that the tenant has suffered some inconvenience or loss.

9.30   Each of these aspects of a claim are considered below.

Disrepair

9.31   There must be 'disrepair'. This means that part of the dwelling is in a worse condition than it was at some earlier time as opposed to lacking some amenity or being of defective design.[25]

9.32   The disrepair must be because of a failure by the landlord to carry out repairs for which he or she is responsible under the tenancy agreement.

Defective installations or absent installations

9.33   As indicated above, the fact that the accommodation is in poor condition because of the absence of an installation does not mean

---

25 *Post Office v Aquarius Properties* [1987] 1 ALL ER 1055; *Quick v Taff Ely BC* [1986] QB 809.

that the property is in disrepair. Under the terms of the tenancy agreement a landlord can be forced to repair a defective installation but not to install something that is not present in the dwelling when the tenancy started.

Disrepair or design defect?

9.34   Poor housing conditions such as damp and cold may be caused by disrepair or by the design of the dwelling, or sometimes a combination of both. In some local authority accommodation condensation dampness is common. This is frequently caused by poor design: inadequate insulation, poor ventilation and insufficient heating. This is not disrepair.

> In the case of *Quick v Taff Ely Borough Council*[26] the tenant occupied a house on an estate constructed in the 1970s. It was agreed that there was severe condensation such that the house was virtually unfit for habitation in winter. The cause of the condensation was a combination of the following factors: cold bridging due to lack of insulation, sweating from the windows and inadequate heating. The condensation had caused extensive damage to the tenant's belongings. The county court judge awarded damages and, in accordance with the tenant's expert evidence, ordered the landlords to replace the windows and install insulation to alleviate the high levels of condensation. The Court of Appeal upheld the local authority's appeal holding that the landlord was not in breach of the repairing obligation because the problem was caused by a design defect not disrepair.

9.35   The question of whether a problem is caused by a design defect or by disrepair is closely related to the issue of whether the landlord's repairing obligation can extend to remedying a design defect.

Repair or improvement?

9.36   A tenant cannot bring a civil action to force a landlord to remedy a design defect. However, if the tenant can show that there is disrepair, the landlord's repairing obligation may extend to remedying the design defect that has caused the disrepair. Whether a landlord's

26   (1985) 18 HLR 66.

repairing obligation will extend to taking action to remedy a design defect will depend upon the following factors:

- Whether the works are to the whole or substantially the whole of the structure or only a subsidiary part;
- Whether the effect of the works will be to produce a building of a wholly different character than that which had been let; and
- The cost of the work in relation to the previous value of the building and the effect of the works on the value and lifespan of the building.

These criteria were set out in the case of *McDougal v Easington DC*.[27] The premises were stripped back to the original framework with new front and rear elevations, windows, doors and roof installed. The cost of the works exceeded £10,000, increased the value of the premises from £10,000 to £18,000 and extended the expected life of the premises by about 30 per cent. The works were held not to constitute works of repair.

9.37   Below are some examples of cases in which the court have found the landlord's repairing obligation to extend to remedying a design defect.

In *Ravenseft Properties Ltd v Davstone Holdings Ltd*[28] a block of flats was clad in stone on a concrete frame. Because of a design fault the construction lacked any expansion joints which caused the stone cladding to fall away from time to time. Without the inclusion of expansion joints this would continue to happen so that the only way to reinstate the cladding would be by also providing expansion joints. It was argued that this amounted to remedying an inherent defect and was outside the repairing covenant. The court rejected this, holding that it is always a question of fact and degree whether works constitute works of repair or improvement. The works fell within the repairing covenant.

27 21 HLR 310, CA.
28 [1980] QB 12, ChD.

Elmscroft Developments Ltd v Tankersly-Sawyer[29] concerned premises that suffered from rising damp caused by the fact that the slate damp-proof course was ineffective as it was below ground level. The county court judge found that the necessary remedial work included the installation of a horizontal DPC by silicone injection, the formation by silicone injection of vertical barriers where the front and external walls met the dividing walls, plus re-plastering and redecoration. The Court of Appeal rejected the landlord's appeal. Following *Ravenseft*, it was a question of fact and degree whether the remedial works fell within a repairing covenant. The works were works of repair.

In *Stent v Monmouth District Council*[30] there was a design defect in the premises: the concrete step outside was same level as the floor inside the entrance hall. This caused water ingress beneath the door which, in turn, caused the door to warp and eventually to rot. After carrying out patchwork repairs several times a new door was fitted by the council but this did not remedy the design defect. Several years later a self-sealing aluminium door was fitted in accordance with the recommendations of the tenant's surveyor. The Court of Appeal decided that the tenant was entitled to damages because of the council's failure to carry out appropriate remedial works. It was held that where there was no disrepair (as in the case of *Quick*) there was no obligation on the landlord to remedy design defects. However, where there was a defect that the landlord was obliged to repair, 'on a true construction of the covenant to repair there is required to be done, not only the making [good] of the immediate occasion of disrepair, but also, if this is what a sensible, practical man would do, the elimination of the cause of that disrepair through the making good of an inherent design defect at least where the making good of that defect does not involve a substantial rebuilding of the whole'.[31]

9.38   These cases can be contrasted with *Quick v Taff Ely*: the landlords had an obligation to repair and the issue was the extent of works

---

29 (1984) 15 HLR 63.
30 (1987) 19 HLR 269, CA.
31 The President, Sir John Arnold, at p285.

necessary to comply with that obligation. In *Quick* the tenant had not argued that the works were necessary to remedy disrepair but rather to alleviate the effects of the condensation and it was held that 'there must be disrepair before any question arises as to whether it would be reasonable to remedy a design fault when doing the repair'.[32]

Dampness

9.39 The fact that premises are damp does not necessarily mean that a landlord is in breach of the repairing obligation. It is for the tenant to identify the cause of the dampness. Unless it is obvious (eg a leaking roof or rotten windows) expert evidence will be needed. As is clear from the cases referred to above, if the cause of the dampness is a design defect this is not disrepair and the landlord has no obligation under the tenancy agreement to prevent the premises being damp. This has been held to be the case where the dampness was caused by condensation due to inadequate heating and thermal insulation (see *Quick* above at para 9.34).

> In *Post Office v Aquarius Properties*[33] the basement of the premises was ankle deep in water whenever the water table rose because of a design defect. However, this caused no damage to the structure. The Court of Appeal held that there was no obligation under the covenant to repair to remedy the defect.

9.40 If dampness caused by a design defect results in damage to the structure of the premises there will be an obligation to carry out repairs. This obligation may include remedying the design defect depending upon the nature of the design defect and the cost of remedial works (see the cases discussed at para 9.37).

9.41 Clearly, if dampness is caused by disrepair (such as defective windows or leaking roof) then the landlord will be liable if he or she has failed to carry out repairs within a reasonable period of time.

9.42 As in any civil claim it is for the claimant to prove the case 'on balance of probabilities'.

---

32 (1985) 18 HLR 66 Lawton LJ at 77.
33 [1987] 1 All ER 1055.

In *Southwark LBC v McIntosh*[34] an award of general damages of £7,500 was made to the tenant whose flat was damp and whose claim against the council alleged a breach of the repairing covenant. The council's appeal was up held: the tenant had failed to establish that the dampness was caused by a breach of the covenant or that the dampness had caused damage to the structure and exterior. All that the tenant had pleaded was the existence of dampness which was insufficient to establish that the landlords were in breach.

9.43   This does not mean that there is nothing a tenant can do about damp conditions where there is no actual disrepair. The premises may be 'prejudicial to health' so that a prosecution under the Environmental Protection Act can be brought against the landlord. Also, the dampness may constitute a 'hazard' under the Housing Health and Safety Rating System (HHSRS). This would give the local authority the right to serve an improvement notice on the landlord. These options are discussed below and in chapter 10.

Common disputes

Kitchen units

9.44   Kitchen units and work surfaces are not covered by section 11 – they are neither part of the structure and exterior nor installations. It is therefore the tenant's responsibility to repair or replace broken or worn out parts, unless the tenancy agreement provides otherwise.

9.45   It should be noted, however, that in the social rented sector works have been or are being carried out in many homes to improve properties in order to bring them up to the 'Decent Homes' standard (see para 10.82). In most cases this includes installing new kitchens and bathrooms. If a new kitchen is fitted by the landlord the work must be carried out to a reasonable standard and any problems caused by poor workmanship or defective fittings will be the landlord's responsibility. However, future repairs needed because of 'fair wear and tear' will not be the landlord's responsibility unless the tenancy agreement expressly states that the landlord will be responsible.

34 [2002] 08 EG 164.

Broken windows and other 'accidental' damage

9.46 Window panes are covered by section 11. However, many social landlords will not agree to repair windowpanes without evidence that the damage was not caused by the tenant or their family or visitors. Alternatively, the landlord may agree to replace the pane but 're-charge' the repairs to the tenant (see para 9.50 below).

9.47 A landlord is not legally responsible for repairing damage caused by the tenant: section 11 (2)(a) provides that a landlord is not required to carry out works or repairs for which the tenant is liable by virtue of the duty to use the premises in a 'tenant-like manner'. The duty to use the premises in a tenant-like manner includes a duty not to cause damage to the premises deliberately or carelessly, see below.

9.48 Some landlords have a policy that they will repair broken windowpanes provided the tenant can provide a crime reference number as evidence that the damage was caused by someone outside the premises and was reported to the police as a crime.

9.49 Sometimes there may be a dispute about the evidence available regarding the cause of the damage. If unexplained damage has been caused within the premises it is reasonable for the landlord to hold that the tenant is responsible.

9.50 A landlord may carry out repairs for which the tenant is legally responsible but then charge the cost of the repairs to the tenant. Most public sector tenancy agreements will include a term permitting the landlord to do this. It is common for a landlord to then enter the charge as arrears of rent on the rent account. If the landlord then seeks possession on the basis of rent arrears, this can be challenged. The correct way for the landlord to recover the cost of repairs is by sending to the tenant an invoice and seeking a money judgment in the county court if the invoice is not paid.

Tenant's improvements and tenant's fixtures

9.51 Tenants may carry out works of improvement or install fittings that become 'fixtures'. A fixture is something that becomes part of the premises. This would include laminate flooring, shower fittings, fitted cupboards and fitted shelving. Usually tenancy agreements require the tenant to obtain the landlord's consent to carry out such works. A tenant who fails to obtain consent is in breach of the tenancy agreement and this can provide a ground for possession. However, the ground is a discretionary one and a possession order will only be made if it is reasonable to do so. A tenant who has carried out improvements without the landlord's consent can seek consent retrospectively and consent must not be unreasonably withheld.

9.52   Installations and improvements made by the tenant without consent will not fall within the landlord's repairing obligation. Further, most public sector tenancy agreements provide expressly that the landlord is not responsible for repairs and improvements carried out by the tenant.

9.53   As a principle of landlord and tenant law, tenant's fixtures become part of the premises and should be left in the premises when the tenant leaves. However, many tenancy agreements in the social housing sector provide that a tenant should remove fixtures and fittings and ensure that the premises are in their original state before leaving.

Knowledge/notice of disrepair

Disrepair within the dwelling

9.54   A landlord is only in breach of section 11 if he or she has had notice of the disrepair and has failed to carry out effective repairs within a reasonable time.[35]

9.55   There is no requirement that the tenant gives notice in a particular way and the landlord may be placed on notice by events other than a direct complaint by the tenant. For example:

- a local authority inspection that is communicated to the landlord;[36]
- a visit by an agent or employee of the landlord such as a rent collector, environmental health officer or housing officer provided the disrepair is visible;[37]
- a report prepared by a rent officer that is sent to the landlord;
- a valuer's report prepared in respect of a Right to Buy application sent to the chief executive's office.[38]

9.56   A tenancy agreement may provide that notice of disrepair must be given in a particular form or within a particular period. However, this does not mean that the tenant cannot prove that the landlord is in breach of the tenancy agreement if notice is given in a different

---

35 *O'Brien & Anor v Robinson* [1973] 1 All ER 583; *McGreal v Wake* (1984) 13 HLR 107.
36 *McGreal v Wake* (1984) 13 HLR 107.
37 *Dinefwr BC v Jones* (1987) 19 HLR 445.
38 *Dinefwr BC v Jones* (1987) 19 HLR 445.

way.[39] Oral notice is sufficient although obviously more difficult to prove than written notice.

9.57   It is not necessary for the tenant to identify the cause of any problem or specify each defect. It is sufficient that the landlord is made aware that something may need to be investigated.[40]

Disrepair in the building in which the dwelling is situated

9.58   Where the disrepair is in the building rather than within the dwelling itself the landlord is liable as soon as the disrepair occurs regardless of notice.

In *British Telecommunications plc v Sun Life Assurance Society plc*[41] the landlords argued that any liability for damages could only start after a reasonable period had elapsed from the date the defect became apparent. The Court of Appeal rejected this holding that the general rule where a landlord had to keep premises in repair was that the landlord was liable as soon as the premises fell into disrepair. It was an exception to this general rule that in relation to disrepair inside the premises let, liability only arose after notice had been given and the landlords had had a reasonable opportunity to carry out the repairs.

So, in *Passley v Wandsworth LBC*[42] the council were held liable when pipes in the roof of a block of flats burst causing damage to the belongings of the tenant in the top flat. Neither the tenant nor the landlord had been aware that the pipes were in disrepair prior to the flood.

9.59   The reason for this distinction is that a landlord can inspect the exterior and common parts of the building at any time but, because a tenant has exclusive possession of the premises let, the landlord must be given notice of disrepair within the premises.

9.60   This does not mean that a tenant need not report defects in the building to the landlord. A tenant who knows about disrepair to the

---

39 *Dinefwr BC v Jones* (1987) 19 HLR 445. Further, such a term may contravene the Unfair Terms in Consumer Contracts Regulations 1999 and be unenforceable, see para 3.158.

40 *Griffin v Pillet* (1926) 1 KB 17.

41 [1995] 4 All ER, CA.

42 [1998] 30 HLR, CA.

building and fails to inform the landlord may have any damages reduced on the basis that he or she failed to 'mitigate' loss (see para 9.67 below).

Long leases

9.61   The situation is different if the tenant is a long leaseholder as the landlord may have a duty to consult all of the long leaseholders before carrying out works. In such a case the duty to repair will be set out in the lease and section 11 will not apply as the lease will be for more than seven years.[43]

> In *Earle v Charalambous*[44] the disrepair was in a building let to various long leaseholders. In a claim for damages for breach of the landlord's repairing obligation the parties had proceeded on the basis that the starting point for liability was the date of notice. The Court of Appeal held that, following notice by the tenant, the landlord was entitled to a further reasonable period to carry out the works and commented that the *British Telecommunications* case was about a commercial lease and was not decided in the context of the modern statutory and contractual framework concerning residential leases. A landlord's repairing obligation in respect of a residential long lease was linked to the leaseholder's obligations to pay service charges and subject to a duty to consult the leaseholders about major works and the Court of Appeal suggested that the rule set out in *British Telecommunications v Sun Life* case may have to be modified to take account of modern residential long leases.

Failure to carry out repairs within a reasonable time

9.62   What is a reasonable time will depend on the effect of the disrepair and the nature of the repairs needed. A landlord may be in breach if he or she fails to repair a leaking pipe within a number of hours but a time scale of several months may be reasonable if the works are extensive, eg fitting a new roof. Where extensive works will take a long time to complete a landlord may be expected to carry out patchwork repairs to ensure minimum inconvenience in the interim.

---

43   LTA 1987.
44   [2006] EWCA Civ 1090.

9.63   Social landlords sometimes publish expected response times for certain kinds of repairs and these may provide a good starting point in deciding what would be a reasonable time. However, these response times are set by the landlords and the court may find that a landlord is liable even when the repairs have been carried out within the target time. A surveyor will be able to comment on what is a reasonable time to repair a particular defect.

9.64   There may be a dispute about whether a landlord has carried out repairs within a reasonable time when ineffective works have been done and the problem has recurred. This is common when the defects concern central heating systems. Tenants often complain that the system keeps breaking down and that the landlord carries out works so that the system functions only for a short time before breaking down again. Whether and at what point a landlord must accept that the whole system or boiler needs to be replaced will normally be a matter for expert evidence. If this is in dispute it may be necessary to obtain expert evidence from a heating engineer rather than a general surveyor.

Tenant's inconvenience or loss

9.65   If a tenant is claiming damages for the landlord's breach, it must be established that he or she has, as a result, suffered some inconvenience or loss.

9.66   Damages are not limited to quantifiable loss, such as damage to furniture or belongings or the cost of alternative accommodation. Damages may also be awarded to compensate for the tenant's loss of the enjoyment of the accommodation and for such things as injury to health. See below for a description of the way in which such damages are assessed.

Mitigating loss

9.67   A tenant has a duty to 'mitigate' (or minimise) his or her losses. For example if water is leaking into the premises the tenant would be expected to place a bucket to catch the falling water rather than to allow it to damage carpets.

Giving access to the landlord and workmen

9.68   Landlords sometimes argue that they are not in breach of the repairing obligation because the tenant has not given access. If it is proved that access has been unreasonably refused it may be held that the landlord is not in breach or damages may be reduced on the basis that the tenant has delayed the completion of the works (and thereby failed to mitigate his or her loss). Disputes often arise in relation to access. Advisers should ensure that the tenant is aware of the obligation to give access. Where it is alleged that a tenant has failed to give access the tenant should also be advised to keep records of the dates and times access has been requested and whether the tenant has been at home when it is alleged that access has not been given. Sometimes landlords allege a failure to give access when an unscheduled attendance was made and the tenant was not at home. The duty to give access under section 11 is conditional upon the landlord giving written notice 24 hours in advance. However, once works have been agreed a tenant will be expected to act reasonably in giving access to the landlord's workmen and contractors. If a court takes the view that the tenant has failed to act reasonably damages could be reduced on the basis of the tenant's failure to mitigate his or her loss.

9.69   If reasonable access *is* being refused a landlord can seek an injunction to obtain access and any legal costs incurred will be set off against any damages subsequently awarded to the tenant.

Disturbance during works

9.70   In every tenancy agreement it is implied that a landlord will allow the tenant 'quiet enjoyment' of the premises. The covenant is breached if a landlord 'does anything which substantially interferes with the tenant's title to or possession of the ... premises or with his ordinary and lawful enjoyment of the demised premises. The interference need not be direct or physical'.[45] The carrying out of works of repair may cause some unavoidable interference with the tenant's enjoyment of his or her home but the landlord has a duty to minimise the interference: a landlord should take 'all reasonable precautions' to avoid disturbing the tenant but need not take 'all possible' precautions.[46] Where a landlord fails to take all reasonable precautions, the tenant may be awarded additional damages for breach of the covenant of quiet enjoyment. Alternatively, the damages recovered in the disrepair claim may be higher to reflect the additional distress and inconvenience.

45 Lord Millett, *Southwark LBC v Tanner* [2001] 1 AC 1 at 23.
46 *Goldmile Properties v Lechouritis* [2003] EWCA Civ 49.

Alternative accommodation during works

9.71   One issue that often arises when extensive works of repair are to be carried out is whether it is necessary for the tenant to vacate the premises and, if so, who will arrange for alternative accommodation to be provided.

9.72   Whether it is necessary for the tenant to vacate will depend on the nature and extent of the works and whether it is possible to carry out the works so as to minimise inconvenience without disproportionately increasing the cost of the work. Experts should be asked to comment on whether works can reasonably be expected to be carried out with the tenant in occupation.

9.73   If it is necessary for the tenant to give vacant possession to enable the works to be completed the court can make an order to this effect.[47] In practice it is often the tenant who maintains that it will be necessary to move into alternative accommodation while the landlord proposes to carry out extensive work with the tenant in occupation. The dispute often occurs because of the expense to the landlord of providing alternative accommodation.

9.74   In fact, there is no legal obligation on a landlord to arrange alternative accommodation for a tenant even if it is clearly necessary for the tenant to vacate to enable the works to be completed. However, if the landlord is in breach of the repairing obligation and vacant possession is necessary for the works to be completed, the tenant can include in the claim for damages the cost of the alternative accommodation. In practice, social landlords will usually arrange alternative accommodation if satisfied it is necessary. In *McGreal v Wake* the court held that, although it would have been possible to remain in occupation during the works, it was reasonable for the tenant to choose to move into temporary accommodation as this meant that the works could be carried out more quickly and more cheaply. On that basis the cost of the temporary accommodation could be recovered by the tenant as part of her damages for the landlord's breach of covenant.

9.75   If a landlord is refusing to provide alternative accommodation and the tenant cannot afford to obtain it and claim re-imbursement later from the landlord, the tenant may make an application to the court for interim payment of damages. To obtain an interim payment a claim has to be commenced in the county court and the court must

---

47 See *English Churches Housing Group v Shine* [2004] EWCA Civ 434.

be satisfied that it the claim went to trial the tenant would obtain judgment for a substantial amount of money from the landlord.[48]

9.76   Where works are being carried out by a private landlord in compliance with a local authority notice (see chapter 10), the local authority may agree to provide alternative accommodation for which the landlord must pay.

Redecorating following works

9.77   A landlord is responsible for 'making good' decorations following repair works. Disputes often arise about the extent of this duty.

> In *Vukelic v Hammersmith & Fulham LBC*[49] damage was caused to the tenant's restaurant due to the landlord's nuisance. The landlord argued that, following repair works, the obligation was to redecorate only the immediate areas in which repairs had been carried out. The court held that 'the decoration should be undertaken utilising good quality materials and a good standard of workmanship. It is not ... demonstrating a good standard of workmanship to hang a couple of strips of non-matching wallpaper on a wall where the other paper would not otherwise need replacement, or to patch a hole in wallpaper caused by removal of a light switch by sticking a random piece of non-matching wallpaper over the hole. It makes no difference ... that the non-matching wallpaper and the original wallpaper is then painted the same colour if the non-matching wallpaper remains ... obtrusive'.[50]

Other implied contractual terms

Fitness for habitation

9.78   There is no general term implied into tenancy agreements that a property let as a dwelling is 'fit for habitation'.[51] If a property is unfit for habitation the local authority has the power, or in some cases a duty, to take action against the landlord (see chapter 10). However,

---

48   CPR 25.7, see chapter 22.
49   [2003] EWHC 188.
50   HHJ Richard Seymour QC, at 102.
51   The Law Commission recommended that a fitness term should be implied into tenancy agreements in its report 'Landlord and Tenant: Responsibility for the State and Condition of a Property', report number 238, published in 1996. This is one of the Commission's reports still awaiting implementation by the government.

the fact that there is no contractual term as to fitness means that a tenant cannot bring legal proceedings against his or her landlord on the grounds that the premises let are unfit for human habitation.

9.79   There are, in fact, two situations in which a term as to fitness for habitation is implied but both are extremely limited:

Furnished dwellings

9.80   In relation to lettings of furnished houses and flats, common law implies a contractual term that they are fit for habitation at the date of letting. The term relates to initial fitness only.[52]

Premises let at low rent

9.81   Section 8 of the Landlord and Tenant Act 1985 implies into lettings at a low rent a contractual term that the premises are fit for habitation at the date of the letting and that they will be kept fit for habitation by the landlord throughout the tenancy.

9.82   The current limit was set in 1957 and has remained unchanged: for lettings starting on or after 1 April 1965, the term is implied only where the rent is less than £80 per annum (£1.54 per week!) in Greater London and £52 per annum elsewhere. It would be surprising if there were a single tenancy to which this implied term applies. Moreover, any tenancy at such a low rent would fall outside all the schemes of statutory protection and the tenant would have no long-term rights.[53]

Unfit premises and human rights

9.83   In *Lee v Leeds City Council and Ratcliffe and Others v Sandwell MBC*[54] the tenant argued that the effect of the Human Rights Act 1998 was that a local authority landlord had a duty to ensure that her home was fit for habitation. The argument was rejected by the Court of Appeal but the court did accept that there may be cases in which the state of the premises is such as to establish a breach of human rights.

Maintaining common parts and facilities

9.84   Where a landlord retains control of facilities that are essential or necessary to the tenant, the landlord is under a contractual obligation

---

52 *Smith v Marrable* (1843) 11 M&W 5; *Wilson v Finch Hatton* (1877) 2 Ex D 336.
53 See chapter 2.
54 [2002] EWCA Civ 6.

to maintain those facilities so that they remain available for the use of the tenant. This will include communal stairs, lifts and door entry systems.[55]

9.85   A repairing obligation may also be implied into the tenancy agreement if necessary to give the agreement 'business efficacy', ie to make it workable. Such a term will only be implied when 'necessary', not because it appears fair or desirable.

In *Barrett v Lounova*[56] the tenancy was granted in 1941 so section11 did not apply. The only term relating to repairs provided that the tenant was responsible for internal repairs. The exterior of the premises fell into substantial disrepair causing water penetration and damage to the internal plaster and timbers. The Court of Appeal held that the only way to make the tenancy agreement 'workable' was to imply a repairing obligation on the landlord in respect of the exterior of the premises.

Landlord's covenant of quiet enjoyment

9.86   This has been referred to above at paragraph 9.70 in relation to the way in which repair works are carried out. It is also discussed below at paragraph 9.142 in relation to inadequate sound insulation.

9.87   A landlord's breach of a repairing obligation may also constitute a breach of the covenant of quiet enjoyment. This was held to be the case in *Gordon v Selico Ltd*[57] where the failure to observe a covenant regarding the building in which the flat was situated caused water penetration and extensive dry rot in the leased flat. The covenant however cannot create an obligation to repair where none exists by virtue of the express or implied terms of the tenancy agreement.

Non-derogation from grant

9.88   It is also implied into every tenancy agreement that a landlord shall not 'derogate from the grant' of the tenancy. This is an obligation on the landlord not to do anything in relation to premises he or she

---

55   *Liverpool Corporation v Irwin* [1977] AC 239. This is in addition to section 11(1A) which applies only to tenancies commencing on or after 15 January 1989, see para 9.11 above.

56   (1988) 20 HLR 584.

57   (1986) 18 HLR 219.

retains control of that will interfere with the tenancy. This obligation is closely related to the covenant of quiet enjoyment.

9.89   As is the case with the covenant for quiet enjoyment the covenant does not create new repairing obligations.

9.90   It is more likely that a landlord will be found to be in breach of the covenant of quiet enjoyment and/or non-derogation from grant by virtue of the way in which works are carried out than by virtue of an omission to carry out works.

Using the premises in a tenant-like manner

9.91   A tenant has an obligation to use the premises in a 'tenant-like manner' which means 'taking proper care of the place'. This includes mending lights and fuses, clearing minor blockages in the sink, and doing 'the little jobs about the place which a reasonable tenant would do'. It also means that a tenant must not damage the premises wilfully or negligently. However, it does not extend to carrying out works where premises fall into disrepair through fair wear and tear or carrying out the necessary regular maintenance to ensure the premises do not fall into disrepair.[58]

9.92   See above in relation to broken windows.

The limits of contractual claims

Tolerated trespassers

9.93   As is explained in chapter 5, a tenant against whom a suspended order for possession has been made in the past is likely to have ceased to be a tenant and become a 'tolerated trespasser'. A tolerated trespasser cannot enforce any obligations set out in the tenancy agreement as the tenancy has come to an end. The Housing and Regeneration Act (H&RA) 2008 will abolish tolerated trespass and those who are tolerated trespassers when the Act comes into force will get new tenancies.

9.94   The position before the H&RA 2008 comes into force is that before any action can be taken to enforce the repairing obligations an application must be made to the county court to vary the possession order so as to revive the tenancy (see paras 5.129–5.135). Such an order has retrospective effect which means that the tenant can sue for breach of the contractual obligations even for period where, at the time, he or she was a tolerated trespasser. [59] When the

58   *Warren v Keen* [1954] 1 QB 15.
59   See *Lambeth v Rogers* (2000) 32 HLR 361.

H&RA 2008 comes into force all former tolerated trespassers will again become tenants. However, the new tenancy is not automatically treated as a continuation of the previous tenancy. An application must be made to the court for an order that the new tenancy be treated as the same tenancy continuing uninterrupted in order to be able to seek damages for the period between the loss of the tenancy and the new tenancy arising under the H&RA 2008. See paras 5.141–5.143.

Only parties to the contract can sue

9.95   The general rule is that only a party to a contract can take action to enforce the contract or claim damages for a breach of the contract. This rule is called 'privity of contract'. This means that a civil claim for breach of the repairing obligation can only be brought by the tenant or tenants. However, a tenant can include a claim for damages for the inconvenience and loss suffered by his or her family as the benefit of the contract is for the whole family.[60]

Tort

9.96   A tort is a civil wrong which does not depend on a contractual relationship. The law recognises that certain situations create a 'duty of care': one party owes the other a duty to take reasonable care to ensure that he or she does not suffer injury or damage by reason of some act or omission. A breach of the duty gives the injured party the right to seek damages in the civil courts. The relationship of landlord and tenant does not, of itself, create a duty of care. What this means is that, at common law, a landlord may let to a tenant a property that is unsafe, unfit for habitation or in a poor state of repair. The landlord does not commit a tort by doing so. The tenant's rights relating to the state of the premises are contractual: they are found in the express terms of the tenancy agreement or implied by section 11. Nevertheless, there are some situations in which a duty of care *is* placed on a landlord.

9.97   Some torts have developed through case law and are called 'common law' torts, others are set out in legislation and are called 'statutory' torts. In a disrepair claim the common law torts of nuisance and negligence may be relevant. Also, the Defective

---

60 *Jackson v Horizon Holidays* [1975] 3 All ER 92, CA.

Premises Act 1972 and the Occupiers Liability Act 1957 set out statutory duties of care that may be owed in relation to residential premises. Some of the statutory duties set out in those Acts reflect common law duties, previously recognised by the courts.

9.98   An action in tort is usually only possible *after* a person has suffered some injury or damage to belongings. In a disrepair claim it is usually the case that the tenant is relying on both breach of the contract *and* a breach of a duty of care, sometimes arising out of the same facts.

Defective Premises Act 1972

The builder's duty

9.99   Section 1 of the Defective Premises Act (DPA) 1972 places a duty on those who carry out work in connection with the provision of a dwelling. This includes building or converting premises. The duty is to do the work in a workmanlike or professional manner; to use proper materials; and to ensure that the dwelling is fit for human habitation when completed. The duty is owed to the person for whom the dwelling was provided and to anybody who later acquires an interest, including future tenants. It applies to all work commenced after 1 January 1974.

9.100   Dwellings covered by the National House Building Council (NHBC) warranty scheme are excluded from DPA 1972.[61] Most new dwellings in the private sector are covered by the NHBC scheme.

9.101   A social landlord that builds or converts a building for letting therefore owes a duty of care to the initial tenant and subsequent tenants. Any injury or damage suffered as a result of any breach of the duty under DPA 1972 s1 will create a liability.

Common law duty

9.102   In addition to DPA 1972, there is a common law duty on a person who builds or designs a dwelling to use reasonable skill and care and a landlord also has a common law duty to exercise a reasonable degree of care and skill when undertaking works of repair or improvement.[62]

---

61   DPA 1972 s2.
62   *Ball v London CC* [1949] 2 KB 159 and *Billings (AC) & Sons v Riden* [1957] 3 All ER 1.

In *Rimmer v Liverpool CC*[63] the tenant injured himself on a glass pane in an internal wall. It was held that, although landlords of unfurnished dwellings did not owe any general duty of care to tenants, a landlord who also designed and built the dwelling owed a duty of care to anyone who might reasonably be expected to be affected by faults in the design or construction of the premises. The authority was held to have been negligent and liable to pay damages.

Maintaining/repairing the dwelling

9.103   Section 4(1) of the Defective Premises Act 1972 provides that where premises are let on a tenancy under which the landlord has an obligation to repair or maintain the premises:

> 'the landlord owes to all persons who might reasonably be expected to be affected by defects in the state of the premises a duty to take such care as is reasonable in all the circumstances to see that they are reasonably safe from personal injury or from damage to their property caused by a relevant defect.'

9.104   A landlord who has a *right* to enter to carry out any kind of maintenance or repair is treated as if he or she were under an *obligation* to maintain or repair.[64]

9.105   The duty is owed 'if the landlord knows ... or if he ought in all the circumstances to have known of the relevant defect'.[65] The duty therefore exists independently of actual notice being given to the landlord.

9.106   The landlord cannot restrict or exclude liability. Any provision in the tenancy agreement attempting to do so, will be void.[66]

Relevant defects

9.107   The 'section 4 duty' depends on there being a 'relevant defect'. A relevant defect is one that arises or continues because of the landlord's failure to carry out repairs or maintenance (whether there

---

63 [1984] 1 All ER 930. The premises were built before 1974 so DPA 1972 was not relevant.
64 DPA 1972 s4(4).
65 DPA 1972 s4(2).
66 DPA 1972 s6(3).

is a duty or only a right to repair or maintain). It covers items of repair or maintenance even where notice has not been given.[67]

9.108　　The definition of 'relevant defect' is therefore tied to the definition of 'disrepair' – it does not extend to a defect that arises from something other than the landlord's obligation or right to carry out 'repairs'. It does not include design defects or defects that arise because of the tenant's failure to carry out any obligation under the tenancy.[68] However, the duty under section 4 is wider than the contractual repairing obligation in the following ways:

- the landlord may be liable for defects that affect not only the tenant but also other occupiers and visitors to the property;
- the landlord may be liable for a defect that has not been reported if the landlord 'ought' to have known of the defect; and
- the defect may arise from disrepair that the landlord is not obliged to remedy but that he or she has a right to remedy.

9.109　　The following cases illustrate the way in which liability under DPA 1972 s4 is more extensive than the landlord's contractual repairing obligation.

In *Clarke v Taff Ely BC*[69] the sister of one of the joint tenants was helping them to decorate. She suffered an injury when the leg of a table on which she was standing went through the floorboards. No complaint had been made to the council about the floorboards but it was known that the area was damp and that there was no ventilation under the floorboards. It was held that the council was liable for the injury suffered: arrangements should have been made for regular inspections and the tenant's sister was someone who 'might reasonably be expected to be affected by defects' in the premises.

In *Smith v Bradford MDC*[70] a tenant had built a patio outside the dwelling. A subsequent tenant complained to the council that it was dangerous and later suffered an injury when he fell from the patio onto a grassed area several feet below. The Court of Appeal held that the council was liable: the patio was part of the 'premises' and the council had a right to enter and repair it and were therefore liable.

67　DPA 1972 s4(3).
68　DPA 1972 s4(4).
69　(1984) 10 HLR 44.
70　(1982) 4 HLR 86.

9.110   However, DPA 1972 s4 does not extend to an obligation to make safe; the duty arises only in relation to defects, ie disrepair.

> In *Alker v Collingwood Housing Association*[71] the tenant injured her hand on a glass panel to the entrance door of her home. The panel was not constructed of safety glass but ordinary annealed glass. It was likely that, at the time of construction, the door complied with the relevant building regulations but it has been accepted since at least 1963 that the use of annealed glass in doors presents a safety hazard. The tenancy agreement set out the landlord's repairing obligations, including the term: 'We must keep your home in good condition'.
>
> The Court of Appeal held that the landlords were not liable as the unsafe glass panel was not a 'relevant defect': it was not in need of repair or maintenance. Even the duty to keep the premises in good condition did not encompass a duty to put them in safe condition.

Occupiers' Liability Act 1957

9.111   The Occupiers' Liability Act 1957 provides that the occupier of premises owes a common duty of care to visitors. A landlord who lets premises but retains control of the common parts, such as stairs, paths and other means of access, is the occupier for the purposes of the Act. The landlord therefore owes a duty to all visitors 'to take such care as in all the circumstances of the case is reasonable to see that the visitor will be reasonably safe in using the premises'.

Common law duty

9.112   There is also a common law duty of care owed by the occupier of premises to visitors. Again, this duty rests on a landlord in relation to the common parts that remain in his or her control.[72]

Common law negligence and nuisance

Negligence

9.113   In addition to the specific instances in which the law recognises a duty of care, set out above, the common law also recognises a general

---

71   [2007] EWCA Civ 343, 7 February 2007.
72   *Dunster v Hollis* [1918] 2 KB 795; *Cockburn v Smith* [1924] 2 KB 119.

duty not to cause injury or damage because of careless or negligent behaviour.

9.114   The tort of negligence is committed when a person fails to do something which a reasonable person in similar circumstances would have done, or does something which a reasonable person in similar circumstances would not have done. If, as a result of the act or omission, a person suffers damage or injury the courts can award compensation.

9.115   When letting premises a landlord does not owe to the tenant a duty of care and the premises may be unfit or dangerous when let without the landlord being liable. However, this does not mean a landlord is immune from liability for acts or omissions during the course of the letting. An example would be where the landlord fits a dangerous installation[73] or carries out repair works in a negligent way.

Nuisance

9.116   'Nuisance' is some act or state of affairs in one set of premises which amounts to unlawful interference with another person's use or enjoyment of neighbouring premises.[74] Where the condition of common parts, retained by the landlord, is affecting the tenant's enjoyment of the premises let an action may be brought in nuisance. This would cover, for example, a leaking pipe from a communal boiler which is causing dampness in the tenant's premises. If the tenancy was granted on or after 15 January 1989 the tenant could rely on the extension of section 11 to the common parts. If not, the tenant could rely on the law of nuisance.

9.117   It should be noted that the definition of 'statutory nuisance' is different. This is explained at paras 9.215–9.220 below.

Infestations

9.118   Tenants may complain of infestations of vermin. Cockroach and ant infestations frequently occur in local authority estates of a certain design. Infestation in itself is not disrepair and the landlord's repairing obligation will not usually extend to preventing or abating infestation within a dwelling. Although infested premises will usually be unfit for human habitation, as we have seen there is

---

73 See *Ball v London CC,* referred to above at para 9.101.
74 *Read v Lyons & Co Ltd* [1945] KB 216.

no implied term in most tenancy agreements that the premises are fit for habitation.

9.119 There are two situations in which the landlord may be held liable for an infestation under the repairing covenant:

- if the tenancy agreement contains an express term such as that the landlord will keep the premises 'in good or habitable state' this may be interpreted as including an obligation to prevent infestations; and
- if there is disrepair that is causing or contributing to the infestation, such as holes in the floors or skirting boards.

9.120 In some circumstances it may be possible to use the law of nuisance and/or negligence to take action to force a landlord to take action to prevent infestations and to claim damages for a failure to do so.

In *Sharpe v Manchester MDC*[75] the tenant of a local authority flat suffered from a cockroach infestation. It was likely that the cockroaches came through the service ducts which remained in the control of the authority, although other flats were unaffected. The authority carried out ineffective works to eliminate the infestation over a two year period. The Court of Appeal held that the council were liable in nuisance and were also negligent as they had failed to treat the service ducts and the other spaces in the walls and floors and had used a discredited insecticide.

However, in *Habinteg Housing Association v James*[76] there was no liability on the landlord for an infestation of cockroaches even where several tenants on the estate suffered from similar problems. There was no evidence that the infestation emanated from property occupied by the landlord. Although, following service of a statutory notice by the local authority, an effective block treatment had been carried out to abate the nuisance, there had been no negligence in failing to carry out a block treatment earlier; the association did not have the power to carry out a block treatment in the absence of the local authority notice.

9.121 Where premises are suffering from an infestation and the landlord cannot be held responsible, complaint may be made to the

75 (1977) 5 HLR 71.
76 (1994) 27 HLR 299.

local authority. Local housing authorities have powers and duties in relation to premises that are prejudicial to health or contain health hazards (see chapter 10). If the landlord is the local authority, while it may not be responsible as a landlord, most have pest control departments which will carry out treatments to eradicate infestations. Most authorities charge for such services although in some cases tenants of the authority are not charged. Alternatively, private companies offer pest control services.

In the county court case of *Dolan v Sefton MBC*[77] the tenant brought a claim in nuisance and negligence for three years of severe cockroach infestation following which she abandoned the premises. After two days of evidence the council agreed to pay £16,000 in damages and to abandon a claim for rent arrears of £2,500. Personal injury claims in respect of the claimant's two children were also settled. Each had suffered insect bites that became infected and developed a disease causing rashes, swollen joints and abdominal pains for a year. The court approved awards of £2,000 per child.

Leaks from neighbouring properties

9.122   Tenants of flats may suffer from water penetration from neighbouring flats, usually those above. Landlords often deny responsibility, maintaining that the tenant must take up the issue with the tenant above. Liability depends on whether the water penetration causes 'disrepair' to the tenant's premises and the reason for the water penetration.

Disrepair caused by flooding

9.123   Where a flood from a neighbouring property causes damage to the structure of the tenant's premises (eg, collapsed ceiling) the tenant's landlord has an obligation to repair, regardless of the cause of the water penetration.

9.124   However, unless the landlord is responsible for the flood, there will be no liability for any damage caused to the tenant's belongings or to compensate for any inconvenience caused by the flood. The landlord is only responsible for damage and inconvenience which results from the landlord's breach, ie failing to carry out repairs within a reasonable period of being notified.[78]

9.125   If the flood was caused by the neighbour's misconduct or carelessness (e.g. badly fitted washing machine, or bath left to overflow) action could be taken against the neighbour in nuisance or negligence. The landlord could claim damages from the neighbour for the cost of the repairs and the tenant could also make a claim against the neighbour for compensation for inconvenience and damage to belongings.

Sustained water penetration

9.126   Where there is a problem of less severe but enduring water penetration, liability for repairs also depends on whether the water penetration causes damage to the structure.

9.127   Where there is damage to the ceiling plaster, responsibility for repairs will depend on the terms of the tenancy agreement. Tenancy agreements in the social sector often include internal plaster as part of the landlord's responsibility. If so, the landlord will be responsible for carrying out repairs. However, the case of *Irvine v Moran* (see para 9.20 above) held that internal plaster does not form part of the structure, so unless there is an express term in the agreement the landlord will not be responsible for carrying out repairs. If the only damage is to the tenant's belongings, the landlord will not be liable unless the water penetration is caused by disrepair (eg leaking service pipes).

9.128   If sustained water penetration is caused by the neighbour's conduct, although the landlord will have an obligation to repair any consequent damage to the structure, the tenant will have to take direct action against the neighbour to prevent ongoing problems. A tenant may bring a county court action in nuisance and/or negligence to obtain an injunction against the neighbour. Alternatively, he or she may bring a criminal prosecution against the neighbour based on 'statutory nuisance', described below at para 9.214.

Neigbouring tenants with same landlord

9.129   A tenant may want the landlord to take action against another tenant where there is sustained water penetration or repeated floods. If the

---

78 See *Hyde Southbank Homes v Oronsay and Obadiara*, 18 February 2005, December 2005 *Legal Action* 28.

problem is caused by the other tenant's misconduct or carelessness the landlord can take possession proceedings against him or her under the nuisance ground. However, one tenant cannot take legal action against a landlord to compel the landlord to take action against another tenant guilty of nuisance.[79]

9.130   If the tenants share a social landlord, a complaint may be made if the landlord declines to take action against the neighbour. Social landlords must have a published policy on nuisance and anti-social behaviour, see para 9.136 below.[80]

Disrepair in the neighbour's flat

9.131   It may be that the cause of the water penetration is disrepair in the neighbour's flat. If this is the case and the landlord is notified of the need for repair, or inspection but takes no effective action, the landlord may be liable not only for the repairs to the affected flat but also for loss, inconvenience and damage to the tenant's belongings. It is no defence for the landlord to argue that access cannot be obtained to the premises above. If access is refused, the landlord can apply for an injunction to force the tenant to give access.

9.132   As disputes about access often delay matters being resolved, tenants should try to maintain an amicable relationship with the neighbour where possible. If the neighbour agrees to allow the tenant access to inspect, the cause of the water penetration should be ascertained more quickly.

Noise nuisance/sound insulation problems

9.133   The intrusion of noise from other tenants is also a common problem in flats. The cause may be particularly noisy neighbours or inadequate sound insulation between the flats. Sometimes this is difficult to determine or the problem may be a combination of both. Sensitivity to noise varies from one person to another and tenants who have suffered from noise penetration for some time may become 'hyper-aware' of the sound of their neighbours.

9.134   There are two types of sound transmission: airborne sound and impact sound. Inadequate sound insulation between properties can mean that ordinary footsteps sound like stamping and that the

---

79 *O'Leary v Islington LBC* (1983) 9 HLR 83, CA. The situation may be different if the tenancy agreement contains a term stating that the landlord will take action to prevent nuisance by other tenants.

80 HA 1996 s218A, as amended by ASBA 2003 s12.

bass notes of amplified music are heard in another property. This can lead tenants to believe, incorrectly, that the problem is excessively noisy neighbours. If other household sounds are also heard such as telephones ringing, toilets flushing, light switches etc this suggests a sound insulation problem.

9.135   It may be necessary to obtain an expert report on the cause of the problem. This will require the co-operation of the neighbour so it is important to avoid bad feeling if possible.

Noisy neighbours

9.136   If the problem is caused by the behaviour of the neighbours who are also tenants of the same landlord complaint may be made to the landlord. Local authorities and RSLs must publish their policies on 'anti-social behaviour'. This should set out the steps a landlord will take on receipt of a complaint, including the time scale for action.[81] The landlord may serve notice of seeking possession and take steps to evict the tenant. Sometimes the service of notice will be sufficient to stop the behaviour. In most cases, it is advisative for tenants to first make the neighbours aware of the way their behaviour is disturbing them to see if the problem can be resolved amicably.

9.137   Tenants who complain in the hope that their neighbours will be evicted should be aware that the landlords may decide not pursue a possession claim. The complaining tenant cannot force the landlord to do so (see para 9.129 above). If possession proceedings *are* issued, the complaining tenant will usually be required to give evidence by way of a statement and/or in person at a possession hearing.

9.138   Alternatively, or in addition, complaint can be made to the local authority's environmental health team. Some authorities operate mobile noise patrols and may visit the neighbouring property to measure the noise and to advise the occupier about reducing the noise. The authority can also serve a notice requiring the occupier to 'abate' the nuisance and can prosecute if the notice is not complied with.[82]

Action against the neighbour

9.139   An occupier may bring a civil claim against a neighbour relying on the common law tort of nuisance. The court can award damages and

---

81   Section 218A of the Housing Act 1996, as amended by section 12 of the ASBA 2003.

82   This is under the Environmental Protection Act 1990, discussed below and in chapter 10.

an injunction to restrain future nuisance. Public funding is available for such an action but the Legal Services Commission (LSC) will require that the applicant has tried alternative ways to resolve the issue (such as ADR or mediation), and the 'cost benefit' test must be satisfied before public funding will be granted.[83]

9.140   In addition, an occupier may bring a private prosecution in the magistrates' court under the Environmental Protection Act 1990, seeking an order that the neighbour 'abate' the nuisance (see para 9.225 below).

Action against the landlord for inadequate sound insulation

9.141   Current building regulations require minimum levels of sound insulation in newly built dwellings or conversions. However, the regulations do not have retrospective effect and, before 1976 for new dwelling and 1985 for conversions, there were no specific requirements for builders to meet designated standards for sound insulation.[84] Many dwellings and conversions therefore have little or no sound insulation.

9.142   As noted above, in respect of most tenancies there is no implied term that premises are fit for habitation. A landlord therefore has no contractual obligation to ensure that premises are properly insulated against sound transmission from outside.

In *Southwark LBC v Mills* and *Camden LBC v Baxter*[85] the tenants relied on the covenant of quiet enjoyment[86] and the tort of nuisance in claims brought against their respective landlords. Both tenants occupied local authority flats, one in a purpose built block and the other, a converted house. They complained that the absence of sound insulation meant that they were disturbed by the ordinary household noise made by their neighbours. Both wanted their landlords to carry out works to remedy the situation. The House of Lords held that the landlords had no obligation to

---

83 See para 22.179 below.

84 The minimum standards for the construction of buildings are set out in the Building Acts and Regulations. Local authorities are responsible for ensuring that the minimum standards are met.

85 [1999] 4 All ER 449.

86 Despite the term, the covenant is not specifically about noise but about the tenant's right to use the premises without interference by the landlord.

install sound insulation. There was no breach of the covenant of quiet enjoyment: the covenant can only be breached by the landlord doing something to substantially interfere with the tenant's quiet enjoyment *after* the grant of the lease, not by reason of the state of the premises at the commencement of the tenancy and thereafter. With regard to nuisance, it is possible for a landlord to be liable for nuisance caused by his or her tenant if the landlord authorises or permits the nuisance. However, the nuisance complained of was caused by the other tenants using their premises in the ordinary way. Such use is not capable of being an actionable nuisance.

9.143   There is therefore no way for a tenant to bring a civil action against a landlord to compel the landlord to install sound insulation.

9.144   Further, it is not possible to use the Environmental Protection Act to achieve the same aim.[87]

Remedies in county court proceedings

9.145   The above notes describe the possible 'causes of action' in a civil claim for disrepair. In practice, in most disrepair claims the same set of facts may establish several different causes of action.

9.146   The cause of action is the legal basis for the tenant's claim. The 'remedy' is what the tenant is asking the court to order.

9.147   In most disrepair claims the tenant will be seeking:

• damages (compensation); and
• an order for works.

9.148   The vast majority of claims are settled before a final hearing; the parties agree what works will be carried out and how much compensation will be paid. Since the introduction of the Disrepair Protocol, described at para 9.184 below, it is common for works to be started soon after the landlord receives the initial Protocol letter. This may mean that when the claim is issued the tenant is seeking damages only or that no proceedings are issued as damages are agreed without the need for litigation.

9.149   Even though most claims are settled without a final hearing advisers must be familiar with the powers of the court and the likely

---

87 See *R on the application of Vella v Lambeth LBC* [2005] EWHC 2473 (Admin), at para 9.224 below.

damages that a court would award. Any settlement will be agreed by the parties on the basis of what the court would be likely to order.

9.150   In disrepair claims there are usually two kinds of damages awarded:

- 'general damages': these are quantified by the court to compensate the tenant for the inconvenience and loss of enjoyment caused by the disrepair; and
- 'special damages': these are damages capable of precise quantification by the claimant.

The assessment of general damages

9.151   Where a landlord has breached the contract and/or a duty of care towards a tenant the purpose of damages is to place the tenant in the position he or she would have been in had the landlord not breached those legal obligations, as far as it is possible for a financial award to do so.

'Loss of value'

9.152   In many of the early cases a tenant's damages were assessed on the basis of 'loss of value' or 'diminution of value' to the tenant. These cases have mostly concerned tenancies that had a commercial value to the tenant: the tenant had a long lease and was entitled to sub-let or assign the lease. In such cases the assessment of damages will be straightforward: the difference between the value of the lease with the property its present condition and the value of the lease had the property been kept in repair. This may be settled by obtaining expert valuation evidence. Such an approach is not appropriate when assessing damages for a tenant who remains in occupation while the property is in disrepair. Further, for most periodic tenants, as opposed to long leaseholders, the tenancy does not have a commercial value – it cannot be sub-let or sold.

In *Calabar Properties Ltd v Stitcher*[88] the Court of Appeal considered the way in which damages should be assessed when a tenant remains in occupation of a property in disrepair. The Court held:

---

88 (1983) 11 HLR 20, CA.

1. 'The object of awarding damages against a landlord for breach of his covenant to repair is not to punish the landlord but, so far as money can, to restore the tenant to the position he would have been in had there been no breach';
2. Where a tenant remains in occupation it is 'wholly artificial' to award ... damages on the basis of the loss in market value;
3. In such a case valuation evidence is unnecessary; and
4. When a tenant remains in occupation the damages should 'include the cost of the redecoration, a sum to compensate for the discomfort, loss of enjoyment and health involved in living in the damp and deteriorating flat and any reasonable sum spent on providing alternative accommodation after the flat became uninhabitable'.[89]

'Global awards' and assessing by reference to rent

9.153   Although 'diminution of value' is not an appropriate way to assess damages for a tenant in occupation, one approach adopted by the courts has been to assess damages by reference to the rent paid by the tenant. For example, if one third of a property has been affected by disrepair it may be appropriate to assess damages on the basis of a 'rebate' of one-third of the rent for the relevant period. However, this approach sometimes leads to an award that is inadequate to compensate a particular tenant for the 'discomfort, loss of enjoyment and health' caused by the landlord's breach. Courts may therefore adopt an alternative approach of making a 'global' award of damages to cover such loss.

In *Wallace v Manchester CC*[90] the tenant argued that the court was bound to assess damages on both bases: diminution of value/rent rebate *plus* an award for discomfort and inconvenience. The Court of Appeal rejected this argument holding that 'diminution of value' and 'discomfort' were alternative ways of expressing the same concept for to a tenant who remains in occupation: damages for the 'loss of comfort and convenience which results from living in a property which was not in the state of repair it ought to have

---

89 Griffiths LJ at 34 and 36.
90 (1998) 30 HLR 1111, CA.

been if the landlord had performed his obligation.' A court may assess damages on one basis or the other, or by a combination of the two. The Court recommended that where damages are assessed on a global basis it is advisable to cross-check the assessment by reference to the rent payable for the period of disrepair. This will avoid over- or under-assessment 'through failure to give proper consideration to the period of the landlord's breach of obligation or the nature of the property'.[91] The Court also held that when assessing damages by reference to the rent payable the fact that most or all of the rent is actually paid by housing benefit is irrelevant.

In *English Churches Housing Group v Shine*[92] the Court of Appeal overturned a global award of £19,000 for a seven-year period and substituted an award of £8,000. The original award exceeded the total amount of rent payable over the relevant period. The judge had failed to cross-refer the global award with the rent payable and had failed to give reasons for the award. It was held that 'the basic rule of thumb [is] that – all other things being equal – the maximum award for damages in the case such as the present should be the rental value of the premises'.[93] The Court, however, recognised that there will be cases in which an award in excess of the rent payable will be justified but held that in such a case clear reasons need to be given.

The amount of general damages

9.154 In *Wallace* the appeal was argued on the basis that there was an 'informal tariff' for damages for discomfort and inconvenience. The Court of Appeal did not decide the issue but did consider the damages awarded on the assumption that there was such a 'tariff' ranging from £1,000 per year at the bottom of the tariff to £2,750 per year at the top. Given inflation this would translate, in 2008, as a range of between £1,300 and £3,500 per year. For information about the levels of damages awarded by county courts (or agreed between the parties to litigation) advisers should refer to the 'disrepair roundup' published in *Legal Action* on a regular basis.

---

91 Ibid, Morritt LJ at 1121.
92 [2004] EWCA Civ 434.
93 Wall at 109.

Special damages

9.155   Special damages are those that can be precisely calculated by the claimant. If possible, the parties should agree the amounts. A defendant may agree the quantification of special damages while maintaining that he or she is not liable for the loss. In a disrepair claim special damages may include eg the value of damaged belongings, the cost of alternative accommodation, the cost of extra heating to dry out damp premises or while central heating systems were not functioning and any other item of expenditure caused by the landlord's breach.

9.156   The calculation of Special Damages should be included as a schedule in the Particulars of Claim if possible. Sometimes Special Damages are ongoing and it will be necessary to serve a Schedule of Special Damages at a later date.

Damaged belongings

9.157   Where disrepair causes damp conditions damage is often caused to items of furniture, carpets and clothing. Details of the damage caused and the amount claimed must be detailed and included in the special damages schedule. Appendix 1 to this chapter gives an example of a schedule giving the relevant details. It is important that the amounts claimed are realistic and not exaggerated. Landlords will sometimes indicate that they will only offer compensation for items where there is proof of purchase such as receipts or bank statements. Tenants on low incomes often do not have such documentation as many goods are purchased with cash at markets or second hand shops. There is no reason why the courts will not award compensation on the basis of the tenant's oral evidence or witness statement provided the amounts claimed are reasonable.

9.158   If an item can be repaired or professionally cleaned then the tenant will only recover the cost of this and not replacement value.

9.159   There is often a dispute as to whether items were so badly damaged that they needed to be disposed of. Tenants should be advised to keep damaged belongings for a reasonable period to allow the landlord to inspect. Further, photographs should be taken before damaged goods are disposed of.

Valuing damaged belongings

9.160   When something has been damaged beyond repair the damages awarded should enable the tenant to replace the item. If a tenant chooses to replace the damaged item with something better the damages awarded will not be for the full amount of the replacement item but will be discounted to take account of the fact that the tenant is getting something better than that which was damaged. This is referred to as 'betterment'. However, if the tenant has no choice but to purchase something that, incidentally, is better than the original item there should be no discount. Further, if the landlord is maintaining that there should be a discount for 'betterment' the landlord must establish this.

In the case of *Lagden v O'Connor*[94] the House of Lords held:

> It is for the defendant who seeks a deduction from expenditure in mitigation on the ground of betterment to make out his case for doing so. It is not enough that an element of betterment can be identified. It has to be shown that the claimant had a choice, and that he would have been able to mitigate his loss at less cost. The wrongdoer is not entitled to demand of the injured party that he incur a loss, bear a burden or make unreasonable sacrifices in the mitigation of his damages.[95]

9.161   In terms of damages for disrepair this may mean, for example, that there would be no discount for replacing a fitted carpet with a new fitted carpet even though the existing carpet was a few years old. However, where it is possible and reasonable to purchase second-hand items, only the second-hand cost would be awarded.[96]

Order for works

Interim injunction

9.162   A tenant may apply for an injunction to compel a landlord to carry out urgent repairs before the final hearing. However, interim injunctions (unlike final orders for works) are discretionary remedies. They are to be granted only in exceptional circumstances.

---

94 [2003] UKHL 64, 4 December 2003.
95 Lord Hope at 34.
96 It may be argued that it is reasonable to purchase a second-hand table but not more personal items such as a beds, bedding or clothing.

In *Parker v Camden*[97] a number of tenants took action against the local authority because they were without heating and hot water as a result of a strike of boiler workers employed by the council. They sought a mandatory injunction on an urgent basis to compel the council to restore the heating and hot water systems. The council admitted the breach but offered to provide electric heaters and undertake to reduce heating charges at a future date. It argued that to bring in external contractors would risk escalating the industrial dispute. The Court of Appeal held that mandatory interlocutory injunctions should only be granted in 'the most exceptional circumstances' but that this was such a case in that there was 'an undoubted breach of covenant giving rise to actual and immediate major discomfort and inconvenience and to a real risk of damage to health flowing from the admitted breach'.[98]

9.163   To succeed in obtaining an interlocutory injunction, a tenant will need to have an expert report identifying those repairs that require urgent attention and the remedial works necessary. The application must be supported by evidence in the form of a witness statement from the tenant and a copy of the expert report. Three clear days notice must be given to the landlord (this does not include the date notice is given or the date of the hearing).[99] In a case of exceptional urgency an application may be heard without three clear days notice but in all cases the landlord should be notified and invited to put forward proposals to deal with the urgent issues.

Final order for works

9.164   Unless the outstanding works have been completed when the claim is heard, part of the final order will be that the landlord carries out specified works within a specified time. If they are works the landlord is contractually obliged to carry out the order is an order of 'specific performance'. Otherwise the order will be a 'mandatory injunction'. An injunction is a discretionary remedy which means that it may be

97   (1985) 17 HLR, CA.
98   Browne Willkinson LJ at 389.
99   CPR Part 23.7(1)(b).

refused because of the tenant's conduct. An order for specific performance is not discretionary: Landlord and Tenant Act 1985 s17.

9.165　The terms of the order must be sufficiently clear for the defendant to know exactly what must be done and by what time.[100]

9.166　It is usual for a schedule of works to be drawn up by the expert or experts with a deadline for completion and some mechanism for ensuring that the works are completed satisfactorily (e.g. confirmation by the tenant's surveyor). This agreed schedule will be attached to a Consent Order. Such an Order is known as a 'Tomlin Order': see appendix to chapter 22 for a precedent. A Consent Order must be signed by the parties or their representatives and sent to the court for approval. Once approved and sealed by the court it will be sent to the parties. Alternatively, at a hearing the landlord may give to the court an undertaking to carry out works set out in an agreed schedule by an agreed time.

Enforcement of orders

9.167　A court order is legally binding. However, the court does not take action to enforce the orders it makes unless the claimant makes further application. Social landlords usually comply with orders although there may be some delay before they do so. For tenants of private landlords it is more often necessary to make further application to the court after the order has been made.

Money judgments

9.168　The various methods of enforcing money judgments are set out in CPR parts 70 to 73, summarised at para 22.126 below.

9.169　It is essential *before* starting a claim for damages against a private landlord to know whether it is going to be possible to enforce the order. A land registry search may be carried out to establish who owns the premises let and/or the landlord's home address, if known.[101] Such a search will reveal whether the premises are mortgaged. The Legal Services Commission must be satisfied that a landlord has the means to pay damages before granting funding for a claim.

---

100 *Morris v Redland Bricks Ltd* [1970] AC 652.
101 See para 3.138 above.

Orders for works

9.170   An injunction or order of specific performance will require that the landlord carry out certain works within a specified time period. If the landlord does not comply with the order it may be enforced by an application to commit the landlord to prison for contempt of court.[102]

9.171   An application can only be made for committal if the order contains a 'penal notice'. This is a notice addressed to the respondent warning him or her that disobedience with the order is a contempt of court punishable by imprisonment. A penal notice can be attached when the order is made or approved. If not, a further application must be made for a penal notice to be attached to the order.

9.172   In all cases the order must have been personally served on the respondent. In the case of a local authority landlord the order will usually be served on the Director of Housing or the chief executive and in the case of an RSL on the Chief Executive or other person of sufficient seniority.

9.173   An application for committal will be listed for a hearing before a Circuit Judge. The respondent must be personally served with the application notice and notice of the hearing date. Unsurprisingly, when an application for a penal notice or committal is made the landlord will usually ensure that the works are completed. The court may make a suspended order for committal providing that if the works are not completed by a certain time the landlord, or the named officer employed by the landlord will be liable to imprisonment.

9.174   An undertaking given by a landlord may also be enforced by committal proceedings.[103]

9.175   If the works and the time scale have been agreed between the parties and set out in a schedule to a Consent Order (a 'Tomlin Order') the proceedings must be restored and the court asked to make an order against the defendant with penal notice attached.

Appointment of receivers

9.176   The court also has the power to appoint a Receiver who can receive rents and arrange for works to be completed in compliance with any order.[104]

---

102 The procedure is set out in CCR Order 29.

103 CCR Order 29 Rule 1A.

104 CPR 69, see para 22.126. In addition, under the Commonhold and Leasehold Reform Act 2002, leaseholders have a right to manage, see para 4.61.

Time limits for county court claims

9.177 The time limits for bringing civil claims are set out in the Limitation Act 1980. The general rule for claims in contract and tort is that they must be brought within six years. In a disrepair claim where the breach is ongoing this means that any damages can only be awarded for a period starting six years before the claim was issued. However, the time limit is 12 years if the agreement is a deed, which includes long leases.

9.178 In respect of a contractual claim the time limit begins at the date of the breach (not necessarily the date the premises first fell into disrepair, see para 9.54 above). In respect of a claim in tort the time limit runs from the date of the damage or injury, even though the negligence or unlawful act may have occurred years earlier.

9.179 Personal injury claims must be brought within three years. Where a disrepair claim includes a claim for personal injury (eg a claim that ill health has been caused by the housing conditions) the three-year time limit applies to the whole claim. Prior to issuing a disrepair claim that includes a claim for personal injury both the personal injury and the disrepair protocols should be followed. In practice disrepair claims often make reference to the effect of the disrepair on the claimant's health without being treated by the courts as personal injury claims. Advisers should, however, be aware that including a claim for personal injury may result in the period for which damages are awarded being limited to three years rather than the usual six years.[105]

9.180 Where a claim is for injury to the health of a child a separate action should be brought in the name of the child. A litigation friend must be appointed to represent the child (see para 6.118). As time limits do not begin to run until a child reaches adulthood, a claim can be brought up to the child's twenty-first birthday.

9.181 The 'limitation' of actions is a defence that must be pleaded by the defendant. If the defence fails to refer to the limitation period there will be no limit to the period for which damages can be awarded. However, the courts will usually be willing to allow a late amendment to permit the defendant to rely on the limitation defence.

105 For example in *Vukelic v Hammersmith & Fulham LBC* (see para 9.77 above) the claimant included a claim for injury to health, namely depression and anxiety. The conditions complained of had existed for many years. The court limited the period for which damages could be claimed to three years prior to issue even though ultimately it was decided that the claimant was not entitled to damages for personal injury. Had the claimant omitted the reference to injury to health she would have been entitled to claim for a six-year period.

9.182   There are certain situations in which claims can be brought outside the usual time limits and the court has a discretion to extend the time limits. Expert advice would need to be sought before commencing an action which is outside the relevant limitation period.

Procedural issues

9.183   Advisers must be aware of the way in which claims are dealt with under the Civil Procedure Rules in order to advise a person about the most appropriate course of action. Most importantly there is a pre-action protocol that must be followed before proceedings are issued. Further, the value of the claim will determine how the court will deal with it and whether public funding will be granted.

The disrepair protocol

9.184   The Pre-Action Protocol for Housing Disrepair applies to all civil claims arising from the condition of residential premises. The Protocol can be found on the Ministry of Justice website at www. justice.gov.uk and includes precedent letters for use by advisers or litigants in person. If a claim proceeds to litigation, the court will expect all parties to have complied with the Protocol as far as possible. The court has the power to order parties who have unreasonably failed to comply with the Protocol to pay costs or be subject to other sanctions

9.185   The protocol does not apply to EPA 1990 prosecutions (see para 9.213 below) or to disrepair claims brought as Part 20 Claims (counterclaims).

9.186   The Protocol is intended to encourage the exchange of information between parties at an early stage and to encourage the settlement of claims prior to issue.

9.187   The specific aims of the Protocol are:

- to avoid unnecessary litigation;
- to promote the speedy and appropriate carrying out of any repairs which are the landlord's responsibility;
- to ensure that tenants receive any compensation to which they are entitled as speedily as possible;
- to promote good pre-litigation practice, including the early exchange of information and to give guidance about the instruction of experts; and
- to keep the costs of resolving disputes down.

9.188   The steps set out in the Protocol include the following.

Letter to landlords

9.189   The tenant must send to the landlord a letter setting out the nature of the potential claim. If the claim needs further investigation this will be in the form of an early notification letter, if not, it will be in the form of a letter of claim. Precedents for both are included in the Protocol. Certain information must be included in the initial letter (whether an early notification letter or a letter of claim), including:

- the tenant's name, address and telephone number;
- details of the defects;
- details of previous notice given to the landlord;
- proposed single joint expert;
- proposed letter of instruction to expert;
- disclosure of relevant documents in the tenant's possession.

9.190   The letter should request disclosure from the landlord of relevant documents including the tenancy agreement and records of complaints and works carried out.

9.191   If the initial letter is a letter of claim it should also include the following information:

- the effect of the defects on the tenant; and
- details of special damages.

Landlord's response

9.192   The landlord should respond within 20 working days and should:

- give the disclosure requested; and
- respond to the tenant's proposal for an expert indicating whether the single joint expert is agreed or, if not agreed, whether the landlord agrees to a joint inspection.

9.193   If the letter is a letter of claim the landlord's response should also indicate:

- whether liability is admitted;
- any points of dispute;
- a full schedule of intended works with time scale for completion;
- any offer of compensation; and
- any offer of costs.

9.194   This may be done either 20 days after receipt of the letter of claim or 20 days after receipt of an expert report or schedule of works.

Failure to respond

9.195   If no response is received to an early notification letter, a letter of claim should be sent. If no response is received to a letter of claim, proceedings may be issued.

Cases of urgency/preserving evidence

9.196   It is specifically stated that the Protocol does not prevent a tenant from instructing an expert at an earlier stage if it is considered necessary because of urgency or to preserve evidence.

ADR

9.197   The Protocol provides that the parties should consider whether some form of alternative dispute resolution procedure would be more suitable than litigation and, if so, should endeavour to agree the form of ADR.

Experts

9.198   Expert evidence is essential in most disrepair claims. The written evidence of a surveyor,[106] in the form of an inspection report, will usually be necessary to:
- specify the outstanding works;
- express an opinion on which works are the landlord's responsibility under the tenancy agreement;
- comment on the severity of each defect;
- specify the works necessary to remedy the defect;
- give an estimate of the cost of the necessary works; and
- express an opinion on the likely timescale for the completion of the works

9.199   Before the Protocol was introduced the parties would usually instruct separate experts, with social landlords often using 'in-house' surveyors. The Protocol recommends the use of a single joint expert (SJE). If the parties can agree on which SJE to use they will jointly instruct the SJE whose duty is to the court rather than to the parties. In disrepair claims against social landlords it is common for the landlord to refuse to agree the proposed SJEs put forward by the tenant's advisers and to either maintain that it is not necessary to instruct an expert at all or put forward one of their own employed surveyors as the

---

106 Depending on the nature of the defect/s, reports may also be needed by other experts such as heating engineers or damp proof specialists.

proposed SJE. As landlords must usually prepare a schedule of works anyway they often send their own surveyors to inspect and continue to use them as their 'expert'. Despite the Protocol therefore it is common in disrepair cases for each party to instruct their own expert witness. In all cases attempts should be made to ensure that there is a joint inspection by the experts and that the experts clarify precisely what is agreed. The courts will sometimes order the experts to provide a 'Statement of Issues' specifying precisely what is agreed and what is disputed. If fundamental issues, such as the cause of dampness, cannot be agreed it will be necessary for the parties to seek the court's permission to call the experts to give oral evidence.

> In the cases of *McIntosh v Southwark LBC* and *Ball and Ball v Plymouth City Council*[107] the claimants and the defendants each relied on written expert evidence which was conflicting. In both cases the tenants failed to satisfy the court, on balance of probabilities, that the dampness was caused by the landlord's failure to carry out repairs and the claims were dismissed.

9.200 As is the general rule in county court litigation, if the tenant is successful in bringing a claim the court should order that the landlord pays the tenant's legal costs. Commonly under the protocol landlords carry out works in response to a protocol letter leaving only the amount of damages at issue. In such a case, even if the damages are less than £5,000, the landlord should pay the tenant's pre-allocation costs.[108]

Track allocation

9.201 A defended claim will be allocated to one of the three tracks which are:[109]

- the small claims track;
- the fast track; and
- the multi-track.

9.202   The main criteria in determining track allocation is the financial value of the claim. In respect of money claims the small claims track

---

107 [2004] EWHC 134 (QB) and see para 9.42 above.
108 See *Birmingham CC v Lee* [2008] EWCA Civ 891, 30 July 2008.
109 See CPR Parts 27, 28 and 29.

is for claims of less than £5,000, the fast track for claims of between £5,000 and £15,000 and the multi-track for claims of more than £15,000. For the purpose of track allocation the claimant must, when completing the claim form, estimate the amount of damages he or she expects to recover. However, factors other than the value of the claim are also taken into account and a claim will not generally be allocated to the fast track if it is likely to take more than one day to resolve and there is disputed expert evidence.

9.203   For disrepair claims where the only claim is for damages the small claims limit of £5,000 applies: claims for less than this amount will be allocated to the small claims track on receipt of the defence. However, if a claim includes an application for an order for works it will only be allocated to the small claims track if *both*:

- the estimated damages are less than £1,000; and
- the estimated cost of the works is less than £1,000.

9.204   So if either is expected to exceed £1,000 the claim should be allocated to the fast track or the multi-track.

9.205   An expert should always be asked to give an opinion on the estimated cost of the works so that the claim can be allocated appropriately.

9.206   The other factors that should be taken into account in allocating claims are:

- the complexity of fact, law or evidence;
- the number of parties or the importance of the case to people who are not parties;
- the amount of oral evidence that will be required; and
- the views and circumstances of the parties.

9.207   In practice, the allocation is usually done on the basis of the estimated damages and/or cost of works and any more subtle arguments may have to be made on an application to re-allocate to a different track.

9.208   The court can make an order for works in a claim allocated to the Small Claims track: *Joyce v Liverpool City Council*.[110]

Public funding

9.209 A public funding certificate will not be granted for claims likely to be allocated to the small claims track.

---

110 (1995) 27 HLR 548, CA.

9.210   Further, even if a claim is not within the small claims limit, public funding will only be granted if the 'cost benefit' test is met. This test compares the likely benefit to the client with the likely cost of the claim. Where a claim has an 80 per cent or more chance of success the likely damages must exceed the estimated cost. Where a claim has a 60–80 per cent chance of success likely damages must exceed estimated costs by 2:1 and if the chance of success is 50–60 per cent the likely damages must exceed estimated costs by 4:1. So, even if a claim is likely to be allocated to the fast track, public funding could be refused if, for example, costs are likely to be high because the expert evidence is disputed, and the likely damages will not sufficiently exceed the likely costs. The likelihood of success, level of costs and damages are usually estimated by the solicitor who completes the public funding application forms for the tenant.

9.211   If the principal remedy sought is not damages but an order for works, public funding may be granted on the basis that the claim is of overwhelming importance to the claimant even if any damages are unlikely to sufficiently exceed costs.[111]

Alternative funding

9.212   It is possible for claims to be funded by conditional fee agreements (CFA) but if the claim cannot attract public funding because of failing to meet the cost benefit test it is unlikely that an insurer will offer the necessary cover to fund the claim under a CFA.

Action in the magistrates' court

Environmental Protection Act 1990

9.213   The Environmental Protection Act (EPA) 1990 concerns dwellings and public nuisances that may affect health. The EPA 1990 replaced the Public Health Act 1936 which had itself replaced earlier legislation first introduced to address concern about outbreaks of cholera and typhus. The temporary Act of 1846 provided 'For the speedy removal of certain nuisances'. Prosecution could follow a certificate of two doctors 'of the filthy and unwholesome condition of any dwelling house or other building, or of the accumulation of any offensive or noxious matter, refuse, dung, or offal, or of the existence

111 The criteria are set out in the Funding Code, part of the LSC Manual provided to contracted suppliers.

of any foul or offensive drain, privy, or cesspool' and that 'the same is likely to be prejudicial to the health' of the occupiers or neighbours. The concept of dwellings that are 'prejudicial to health' remains central under EPA 1990.

9.214   Under EPA 1990 local authorities have the power to take action to ensure that nuisances are 'abated' so as to prevent the possible prejudice to health. This is done by the service of an abatement notice by the local authority which may then prosecute a person who fails to comply with a notice. However, sometimes the buildings that constitute a nuisance are owned or controlled by local authorities. To enable action to be taken against local authorities, EPA 1990 provides a procedure for a private individual to bring a prosecution in order to abate a nuisance. The procedure is set out in section 82. Although it has mainly been used against local authority landlords by their tenants a 'section 82 prosecution' may be brought against any landlord. In recent years the number of these private prosecutions has diminished mainly because legal aid is not available and alternative funding is problematic. This is explained in more detail below.

'Statutory nuisance'

9.215   Prosecutions under EPA 1990 depend upon there being a 'statutory nuisance' as defined in section 79. This includes 'any premises in such a state as to be prejudicial to health or a nuisance'.[112] Section 79 lists a number of 'matters' that may constitute a statutory nuisance. The definition is not confined to dwellings and may include such things as smoke, fumes and noise.

'Prejudicial to health'

9.216   In relation to dwellings there are two alternative limbs to the definition of a statutory nuisance: *either* prejudicial to health *or* a nuisance.

9.217   Prejudicial to health means 'injurious, or likely to cause injury, to health'.[113] Premises are prejudicial to health if they are in such a state as would cause a well person to become ill or the health of a sick person to deteriorate further. 'Health' has been interpreted broadly to include physical and mental health and well-being.[114]

---

112 EPA 1990 s79(1)(a).
113 EPA 1990 s79(7).
114 *Malton Board of Health v Malton Manure Company Ltd* (1879) 4 Ex D 302.

9.218   To succeed in a prosecution based on prejudice to health the burden is on the tenant to prove beyond reasonable doubt that the state of the premises is likely to cause ill health. It is not necessary to prove that the state of the premises has actually caused ill health, only that it is likely to do so. If possible, medical evidence of the effect of the premises on the health of the occupants should be obtained. However, it may be sufficient to rely on the expert evidence of an environmental health officer (EHO) where the conditions are such that 'prejudice to health' is well established, such as premises severely affected by dampness and mould growth. In most cases an EHO report will be essential to prove the case beyond reasonable doubt and because the court will need expert opinion on the works necessary to abate the nuisance.

'Or a nuisance'

9.219   The term 'nuisance' in section 79 has been interpreted restrictively to mean either:[115]

- a public nuisance at common law. This requires that the comfort or quality of life of the general public, or of a class of persons, is adversely affected); or
- a private nuisance at common law. This means something that causes substantial interference with the use and enjoyment of neighbouring property.

9.220   If it is conditions *within* the property that are affecting the occupiers of the property there will not be such a nuisance. In most cases therefore when an occupier is bringing action against a landlord it is the 'prejudice to health' limb of the condition that is relied upon.

When are premises prejudicial to health?

Dampness and mould growth

9.221   Many successful prosecutions have been brought in relation to buildings that are badly designed and prone to condensation and mould growth, the kind of property described in the case of *Quick v Taff Ely* (see para 9.34 above). There is considerable evidence that such conditions may cause injury to health by exacerbating asthma and other respiratory conditions.

115 *National Coal Board v Thorne* [1976] 1 WLR 543.

Likelihood of accident

9.222 In *R v Bristol ex p Everett*[116] the Court of Appeal held that an offence under EPA 1990 is not committed where the design of the premises is dangerous and likely to cause accidental injury. 'Prejudicial to health' means a risk of disease or illness and does not extend to the danger of accidental physical injury.

Unhygienic layout

Similarly, in *Oakley v Birmingham City Council*[117] the House of Lords held that the 'unhygienic layout of premises' is not a statutory nuisance. In *Oakley* the only WC was located next to the kitchen. There was no hand basin or room to install one. The Court accepted that there was a risk of cross infection because it was necessary, after using the WC, for the tenant and her family to either wash their hands in the kitchen sink or to cross the kitchen to get to the bathroom. However, by a majority of 3:2 it was decided that the implications of holding that a landlord must carry out works to re-arrange the layout were such, in terms of the expenditure of public funds, that this was a decision for Parliament and not the courts.

9.223 In fact the kind of 'hazards' that were the cause of complaint in both *Everett* and *Oakley* may now be dealt with by a local authority under the Housing Act 2004, see chapter 10.

Lack of sound insulation

9.224 Premises that lack sound insulation so that the occupant is disturbed by the noise of his or her neighbours are not in such a state as to be prejudicial to health or a nuisance.

In the case of *R on the application of Vella v London Borough of Lambeth*[118] a tenant of an RSL was disturbed by noise from the flat above and the communal stairs caused by a lack of sound insulation. He requested that the local authority serve an abatement

116 (1999) HLR 1102, CA.
117 (2000) 33 HLR 283, HL.
118 [2005] EWHC 2473 (Admin).

notice on his landlords to force them to carry out works of sound insulation. There was evidence that the tenant suffered from depression and that the 'noise pollution' he suffered was a 'significant perpetuating factor' in his depressive illness. The local authority refused to serve an abatement notice and the tenant sought judicial review of that decision. The court, following *Everett* and *Oakley*, held that EPA 1990 and the previous legislation are 'sanitary statutes' and that 'there can be no room for holding that a lack of sound insulation sufficient to comply with current standards renders premises in such a state as to be prejudicial to health'.[119] The earlier cases of *Southwark LBC v Ince*[120] and *Network HA v Westminster*,[121] were held to have been wrongly decided in light of the judgments in *Everett* and *Oakley*.

Noisy neighbours

9.225   Section 79(1)(g) of EPA 1990 specifically provides that 'noise emitted from premises so as to be prejudicial to health or a nuisance' is a statutory nuisance. This, however, is distinct from noise pollution caused by the state of the premise. Section 79(1)(g) can be used against a person who is making excessive noise. As this is a private nuisance at common law (see para 9.219 above) it is not necessary to prove prejudice to health. This is one option for a person who is suffering from disturbance by a noisy neighbour. The prosecution is brought against the neighbour and the court can make an abatement order requiring the neighbour to stop making the noise. Alternatively, the local authority can be asked to prosecute (see chapter 10).

Parties to the proceedings

The complainant

9.226   Proceedings can be brought by 'any person aggrieved by the statutory nuisance'.[122] This will usually be the occupier of the premises if the complaint is about the state of premises.

---

119 Poole J at 69.
120 (1989) 21 HLR 505.
121 (1995) 27 HLR 189.
122 EPA 1990 s82(1).

The defendant

9.227　Where the statutory nuisance arises from any defect of a structural character, proceedings must be brought against the owner of the premises.[123]

9.228　If the statutory nuisance is noise caused by a neighbour, he or she will be the defendant.

Procedure

Notice of intended prosecution

9.229　Before proceedings under section 82 can be started, the tenant must give written notice of the intended prosecution to the intended defendant.[124] There is no prescribed form for such notice but it must state the nature of the statutory nuisance and its effect on the occupants. It is not necessary to specify the works required to remedy the nuisance.[125] If an expert report has been obtained it should be attached to the notice. If the complaint is about the state of the premises, the notice must give the defendant at least 21 days to respond; if it is about excessive noise, at least three days notice must be given.

9.230　If the action is against a local authority, notice must be served on the chief clerk or chief executive and, if posted, must be sent to the registered or principal office, unless the authority have specified a different address at which notices must be served.[126] In the case of *Leeds v London Borough of Islington*[127] notice was served on the senior estate manager of the local housing office. The proceedings were dismissed on the basis that notice had not properly been given.

Starting the prosecution

9.231　The action is a criminal prosecution, initiated by 'laying a complaint or information' in the local magistrates' court. There is no prescribed form but the complainant must describe the offence in ordinary language and give the necessary particulars to provide reasonable information about the nature of the charge.[128] On the basis of

---

123 EPA 1990 s82(4)(b).
12$ EPA 1990 s82(6).
125 *East Staffs BC v Fairless* (1998) EGCS 140.
126 EPA 1990 s160(4)–(5).
127 (1998) Env LR 655; (1998) EGCS 15.
128 See section 1 of the Magistrates' Court Act 1980 and the Criminal Procedure Rules 2005, Part 7.

this a summons with a hearing date will be issued by the court and sent to the defendant. A copy should also be sent by the complainant in case of any dispute about service of the summons.

Hearings

9.232 At the first hearing the defendant will usually be asked to enter a plea of guilty or not guilty to the charge of failing to abate a statutory nuisance. Sometimes the defendant may seek an adjournment with the intention of carrying out the necessary works to abate the nuisance. If works are completed before the final hearing there will be no conviction. It is the court's decision whether to grant an adjournment but the wishes of the parties will be relevant. The complainant may be willing to adjourn if this means that the works will be carried out quickly. However, if the nuisance is abated before a guilty plea is entered or before a trial, the court will have no power to award compensation.

9.233 If a plea of not guilty is entered the court will list the case for a trial to take place at a later date. At the trial the court will hear evidence from both parties and decide whether the complainant has proved the case beyond reasonable doubt. Any expert witness must be available to give oral evidence.

9.234 If the defendant pleads guilty it will not be necessary to call evidence to prove the offence. In practice a schedule of works with timetable will usually be agreed for the court to endorse. Evidence may be given to enable the court to assess the appropriate fine or compensation.

Court's powers

Order for works

9.235 If the court is satisfied that a statutory nuisance exists at the date of the hearing it must make an order requiring the defendant to abate the nuisance. The abatement order must set out in detail the works to be carried out and the time limit. The court will usually adopt a schedule prepared by the EHO acting on the complainant's behalf or agreed between the parties. If, at the date of the hearing, the nuisance has abated but the court is satisfied that recurrence is likely it can make an order requiring works within a specified time to prevent recurrence. In either case a conviction will be entered against the defendant.

9.236 The court may order the defendant to do whatever is necessary to abate the nuisance.

In the case of *Birmingham DC v Kelly*[129] the order required the authority to install central heating. The council's appeal was dismissed: the order was made not because the absence of central heating was prejudicial to health but because mould growth was present and was likely to cause health problems and food poisoning. The installation of central heating was a way to remove the threat to health created by the mould growth. The court was entitled to make such an order even though the effect was to require the landlord to improve the premises.

Fines and compensation

9.237   The court can impose a fine and can also order the defendant to pay compensation to the complainant. The compensation is for 'any personal injury, loss or damage' resulting from the offence.[130] The action is a 'summary' prosecution which means that it must be brought within six months of the offence. A failure to abate a statutory nuisance will usually be a continuing failure so this does not prevent someone bringing a prosecution even if the problem started more than six months ago. However, the court cannot award compensation for losses occurring earlier than six months before the complaint was laid. Further, the offence is only committed if a nuisance is not abated within 21 days of notice being given. Therefore compensation can only be for the period starting 21 days after the notice was served.[131] As this is usually a period of weeks or months (to a maximum of six months before the proceedings commenced), compensation is limited. The maximum compensation the courts can award is £5,000. The maximum fine is also £5,000.

9.238   The court can only award compensation or impose a fine if there is a conviction. If the nuisance is abated, and not likely to recur, before the final hearing (or guilty plea) there will be no conviction.

Costs

9.239   Where a court is satisfied that the statutory nuisance existed when the information was laid then, even if it has been abated by the time of the hearing, the court *must* order the defendant to pay the complainant's fair and reasonable legal costs.

9.240   However, a costs order can only be made if there is a valid agreement between the complainant and his or her solicitor that he

---

129 (1985) 17 HLR 572.
130 Powers of the Criminal Court (Sentencing) Act 2000 s130(1).
131 *R v Liverpool Crown Court ex p Cooke* (1997) 29 HLR 249.

or she will be responsible for the solicitor's costs, or there is a Conditional Fee Agreement (see para 9.243 below).

Enforcement

9.241   If there is a failure, without reasonable excuse, to comply with any requirement of a nuisance order within the time limit specified, the defendant commits a further offence.[132] A further prosecution may be brought for the non-compliance. On conviction, a further fine may be imposed and, if the nuisance remains unabated, the court can impose, in addition, a daily fine continuing until such time as the order is fully complied with.

Funding an EPA 1990 action

9.242   Public funding is not available for representations in private prosecutions. The Legal Help scheme is available for advice and assistance preparatory to the issue of proceedings. This could include obtaining an expert report and drafting the complaint but will not cover representation at any hearings.

9.243   It is possible for a solicitor to represent a client in an EPA 1990 prosecution under a conditional fee agreement (CFA).[133] However, it may be difficult to find solicitors willing to do so. Also, expert evidence is almost always needed to succeed in a prosecution and the client must be able to pay the fees for any expert required to attend at court.

Costs orders against the complainant

9.244   Unlike civil proceedings when the usual order is that the unsuccessful party must pay the legal costs of the successful party, a complainant can only be ordered to pay the costs of the defendant if he or she required proceedings to be issued or continued improperly.[134]

Formal complaint/landlords' internal procedures

9.245   This section examines the ways a tenant may use a landlord's internal procedures to ensure that repairs are completed and compensation paid. This is generally only possible if the landlord is a social landlord.

132 EPA 1990 s82(8).
133 Courts and Legal Services Act 1990 s58(a), as amended by section 27(1) of the Access to Justice Act 1999.
134 See sections 16–19 of the Prosecution of Offences Act 1985.

Voluntary compensation schemes

9.246   Many local authorities and RSLs operate internal procedures for compensating their tenants for disrepair, particularly the loss of heating and hot water caused by the failure of block systems. Such a scheme will usually be for the payment of compensation on a daily or weekly basis after a minimum period during which the tenant has been without services. The levels of compensation tend to be low, some schemes only reimbursing charges actually paid by the tenant to the landlord as part of an inclusive rent.

Statutory 'right to repair' scheme

9.247   In addition, for secure tenants there is a statutory 'right to repair' scheme.[135] Assured tenants of RSLs have the benefit of a similar scheme under the Tenants' Guarantee.[136]

9.248   The scheme is convoluted and of limited application. It applies only to 'qualifying repairs' which are specified in a schedule. Each type of repair has a prescribed period before which the repair should be completed. These are essentially minor repairs that will not, in the opinion of the landlord, cost more than £250 to carry out. The process is triggered by the tenant giving notice of the necessary repair, following which the landlord must, if satisfied that the repair is a qualifying repair, issue a repair notice to a contractor.

9.249   If the work is not then carried out within the prescribed period, the tenant may require the landlord to appoint a different contractor. If still not completed within the prescribed period, the tenant is entitled to compensation of £10 plus £2 per day, up to a maximum of £50 for any one repair.

9.250   The disadvantages of the scheme are:

- the onus is on the tenant to serve the appropriate notices on the landlord;
- the scheme depends on the landlord accepting that the repair is a qualifying repair;
- the prescribed period may be suspended by the landlord if there are exceptional circumstances beyond the landlord's control;
- only relatively minor repairs are covered;
- the level of compensation is extremely low.

135 Secure Tenants of Local Housing Authorities (Right to Repair) Regulations 1994 SI No 133; also DoE Circular 2/94.

136 The Tenants Guarantee refers to guidance issued by the Housing Corporation for the management of assured tenancies by RSLs.

Formal Complaint and Ombudsman Complaint

9.251   The complaints procedure and the Local Government and Housing Ombudsman schemes are described in detail in chapter 21.

9.252   The investigation reports published by both Ombudsman schemes show that a significant proportion of complaints concern the failure by social landlords to carry out repairs. The Housing Ombudsman's report for the year 2007 indicates that disrepair was the single most common problem referred to the Ombudsman service, making up 31 per cent of all complaints.

9.253   Most complaints are resolved or abandoned prior to an investigation by the Ombudsman. In a disrepair claim resolution may mean that outstanding works are carried out but no compensation offered. If compensation is offered or recommended by the Ombudsman it will usually be much less than the amount that a court would award.

9.254   The Ombudsman can recommend that the authority or association make a contribution to any legal costs incurred by the complainant but have expressed the view that legal representation is unnecessary in pursuing complaints to the Ombudsman and such recommendations are rare.

Rent and disrepair

9.255   There are three different situations to consider regarding unpaid rent:

- a tenant may withhold rent and use the money to pay for repairs;
- a tenant may withhold rent in protest to try to force a landlord to carry out repairs; and
- a tenant whose landlord is in breach of the repairing obligation may be in arrears of rent for reasons unconnected with the disrepair.

Applying rent to pay for repairs

Common law rights

9.256   There is a common law right to use money due as rent to pay for repairs.[137] However, a tenant must follow the following steps:

137 *Lee-Parker v Izzett* [1971] 1 WLR 1688.

- give the landlord notice of the need for repair in writing;
- if, after a reasonable period has elapsed, the repairs have still not been done, write again telling the landlord of the intention to arrange the repairs and to deduct the cost from the rent;
- obtain estimates for the cost of the work from at least two reputable contractors and write again enclosing copies of the estimates, and giving the landlord a deadline to carry out the work, failing which the tenant will arrange for the works to be done and deduct the cost from the rent;
- if there is no response from the landlord, arrange for the work to be done by the contractor who submitted the lowest estimate, obtaining receipts showing the extent of the work;
- send to the landlord a copy of the receipts and explain exactly how the rent deductions will be made, or have been made, so as to cover the cost of the work.

Poor tenants and housing benefit

9.257   This remedy depends upon the tenant being able to pay the contractor at the time of carrying out the work and recouping the money from future rent payments or from rent previously withheld. It is therefore unlikely to be available to a tenant with a limited income where the repair works are extensive. Further, a tenant in receipt of housing benefit may not be in control of the payment of rent as benefit may be paid direct to the landlord. Housing benefit for local authority tenants is made by way of a rent rebate.

Withholding rent/'rent strike'

9.258   A tenant may simply withhold rent to try to force the landlord to carry out works or as a 'protest' for the landlord's breach. When landlords are receiving rent regularly they may have little incentive to carry out expensive works of repair, but this is a dangerous tactic. Tenants on a low income who withhold rent often find it difficult not to use the money for ordinary household expenses. A tenant in rent arrears risks the landlord issuing possession proceedings. If the tenant is an assured tenant the mandatory ground (Ground 8) is made out if there is at least eight weeks arrears. Although the tenant can seek to 'counterclaim' in the possession proceedings, the court could exercise its discretion not to permit this and order that the disrepair claim be heard separately (see para 6.42).

9.259   If the tenant is an assured shorthold tenant the landlord is entitled to possession as of right and any counterclaim in disrepair will be irrelevant.

'Set off' against rent

9.260   A tenant sued for arrears of rent may have a defence of 'set off': a tenant is entitled to 'set off' any damages awarded against arrears of rent. The defence exists even when the damages have yet to be assessed. See paras 6.40–6.42.

9.261   It is often the case that advisers are consulted only after rent arrears have built up, at the point when the tenant receives a notice of possession or a possession summons. Even if there appears to be a strong claim for damages for disrepair the tenant should be advised to pay current rent plus a regular payment towards the arrears, pending a final hearing. This is to guard against the possibility that the arrears exceed the damages awarded. If the ground for possession is a discretionary one a tenant who has been making regular payment towards arrears will be more likely to succeed in establishing that it is not reasonable to make a possession order even if the arrears exceed damages.

APPENDIX

Example of Schedule of Damaged Belongings

Item	Age/ Date of purchase	Purchase price/ value	Place of purchase	Nature/cause of damage	Repaired/ replaced	[Estimated] cost of repair/ replacement
Two-seater sofa	2003	£350	Argos	Damaged by damp and mould growth. Stained and foul smelling. Beyond repair and disposed of.	No	£400
Fitted carpet in living room	2001	£800	Carpet World	Stained by flood of foul water.	Professionally cleaned	£70
School uniform blazers × 2	6 months old	£40 each	Bloggins	Stained by flood of foul water.	Dry cleaned	£7 per item × 2=£14
Midi hi-fi system	Dec. 2005	£80.00	2nd hand at market	Blew up because of water penetration. Beyond repair.	No	£80
						Total: £564

Disrepair and housing conditions – action by local authorities

Key points

- Local authorities have a power and in some cases a duty to take action against landlords of premises that pose a risk to the health and safety of the occupants. However, such action cannot be taken against a local authority landlord.
- Local authorities can prosecute landlords for failing to abate a statutory nuisance, which may include the state of premises.
- Local authorities can force landlords to carry out improvements to premises that contain 'hazards' – risks to the health and safety of the occupants.
- Local authorities can also prohibit landlords from letting certain buildings for residential use and can make orders that buildings are demolished or that whole areas are cleared.
- Local authorities and other social landlords are committed to improving dwellings so that all meet the 'Decent Homes' Standard by 2010. The government's interim targets, however, have not been met.
- If a local authority fails to take action against a landlord following a tenant's complaint, the authority's internal complaints scheme may be used and complaint may be made to the Ombudsman.
- In some circumstances a person may judicially review a local authority's decision or failure to take action.

10.1   A local housing authority has a range of powers and duties with regard to the condition of dwellings in its area. They are set out in a number of different statutes:

- the Environmental Protection Act (EPA) 1990 – power to deal with 'statutory nuisances';
- the Building Act 1984 – an emergency procedure for dealing with 'statutory nuisances' in dangerous buildings; and
- the Housing Act 1985 and the Housing Act 2004 – power to deal with 'hazards' in dwellings and houses in multiple occupation (HMOs).

10.2   Although an authority may act on its own initiative most action will be prompted by a complaint to the authority. A person making a complaint need not identify the powers under which they wish the authority to act but must draw attention to the conditions about which they are concerned. As local authorities are sometimes slow to respond to complaints it is sensible to put the complaint in writing with sufficient information to enable the authority to prioritise the complaint. Alternatively, if made by telephone, a note should be kept of the date of the call and the name of the officer who recorded the complaint.

10.3   Complaint will usually be made to the authority's Environmental Health Department but some authorities have other teams such as 'Housing Standards' and specific teams dealing with HMOs.

10.4   Each Act and the powers given to local authorities is described below.

Environmental Protection Act 1990

10.5   The EPA 1990 is described at paragraph 9.213 in relation to private prosecutions. The EPA 1990 provides that it is the duty of every local authority to inspect its area from time to time to detect any statutory nuisances which ought to be dealt with. However, local authority action under EPA 1990 will usually be instigated by a complaint made by an occupier to the local authority. Where a complaint of a statutory nuisance is made to an authority by someone living within its area the authority is under a duty 'to take such steps as are reasonably practicable to investigate the complaint'.

10.6   The procedure is different from action taken by a tenant under section 82 of EPA 1990 and is set out in section 80. If the authority is satisfied that a statutory nuisance exists or is likely to recur, the authority must serve an 'abatement notice' on the person responsible for the nuisance.[1] The notice must contain the following information:[2]

- require that the nuisance be abated or prevented from recurring;
- if works are required to abate the nuisance, specify the works;[3]
- specify the time limit for compliance; and
- indicate the time limit for appealing against the order (21 days).

10.7   A person served with an abatement notice must carry out the works specified or appeal to the magistrates' court within 21 days of service of the notice.

---

1   EPA 1990 s80(1).
2   EPA 1990 s80.
3   *Kirklees MBC v Field* (1997) 30 HLR 869.

10.8   If the person does not appeal and does not comply with the notice without reasonable excuse, he or she is guilty of an offence. A landlord convicted of the offence is liable to a fine of up to £5,000, plus a further fine of £500 for each further day of non-compliance.

10.9   Whether or not the authority prosecutes the owner, the authority can itself do the work necessary to abate the nuisance and seek reimbursement from the owner or from the person served with the abatement notice. In practice, local authorities are very reluctant to carry out works as obtaining re-imbursement is difficult.

10.10   It should be noted that the authority has a *duty* to take reasonable steps to investigate and, if satisfied that a statutory nuisance exists, a *duty* to serve a notice. Where an authority fails or refuses to act on a complaint or, having inspected, declines to serve a notice, an application may be made for judicial review to obtain a mandatory order against the authority. Alternatively, a formal complaint may be made and, if not resolved satisfactorily, the complaint may be referred to the Local Government Ombudsman (see chapter 21).

Building Act 1984: emergency procedure

10.11   A speedier procedure which local authorities can use in urgent cases is found in section 76 of the Building Act (BA) 1984. This provides that, where a local authority is satisfied that a statutory nuisance exists and that following the standard procedure under the EPA 1990 would cause unnecessary delay, it may serve the landlord with a notice stating its intention to do the remedial works and specifying the defects which it proposes to remedy.

10.12   Nine days after service, the authority may carry out the work and recover its expenses from the person on whom the notice was served. However, this cannot be done if, within seven days of the notice, the landlord serves a counter-notice on the authority stating that he or she intends to remedy the defects. The authority can then take no further action unless:[4]

- the landlord fails to start remedial works within a reasonable time; or
- having started them, the landlord proceeds unreasonably slowly or makes no progress at all.

---

4 BA 1984 s76(3).

Housing Acts 1985 and 2004

10.13 Since the middle of the nineteenth century local authorities have been able to enforce improvements to dwellings and to demolish slums and build new dwellings. These powers are now contained in the Housing Act (HA) 1985 and the Housing Act (HA) 2004. Not all of HA 2004 is in force at the time of writing. Under these Acts local authorities have a range of options when dealing with dwellings in poor condition. These include serving notice on an owner to improve a dwelling, carrying out works in default, prohibiting the use of a building as a dwelling, demolishing individual buildings or providing that whole areas be cleared of dwellings.

10.14 The Housing Act 1985 was, until April 2006, the statute which set out these powers. The key concept was 'fitness for habitation'. If premises were unfit by reason of specific matters[5] the local authority could serve notice on the landlord to carry out the necessary works to make the dwelling fit for habitation. The 'fitness standard' has now been replaced by the Housing Health and Safety Rating System (HHSRS)[6] introduced by HA 2004. The new system is based on identifying 'hazards' in dwellings and is described below.

10.15 In addition to the powers relating to unfit premises, HA 1985 also gave local authorities powers in relation to houses in multiple occupation (HMOs) and overcrowded premises. The Housing Act 2004 has replaced the provisions of HA 1985 in relation to HMOs but the powers relating to overcrowding are still found in HA 1985.

10.16 Although the assessment process and enforcement action to improve dwellings is now governed by HA 2004, the local authority powers to make demolition orders and declare clearance areas are still to be found in HA 1985, as amended by HA 2004.

---

5 These matters were set out in HA 1985 s604 and concerned: structural stability, serious disrepair, damp that is prejudicial to health, adequacy of lighting, heating and ventilation, adequacy of supply of 'wholesome' water and facilities for the preparation and cooking of food (including a sink with hot and cold water), suitably located WC, baths, showers and wash hand-basins with hot and cold water, and effective drainage.

6 HA 2004 Part 1 and the Housing Health and Safety Rating System (England) Regulations 2005 (SI No 3208) and Housing Health and Safety Rating System (Wales) Regulations 2006 (SI No 1702): 'HHSRS Regulations'.

Housing Act 2004 – hazardous dwellings

10.17   The 'fitness standard', as the trigger for local authority action, has been replaced by the concept of 'hazards' in residential premises. A hazard is a risk of harm to the health or safety of an actual or potential occupier of a dwelling or HMO that arises from a deficiency in the dwelling or HMO or any building or land in the vicinity. The 'deficiency' may arise because of the construction of the building, or because of a failure to maintain or repair.[7]

10.18   A prescriptive system of assessment is set out in HA 2004, the HHSRS Regulations 2005 and Guidance. The assessment should result in a determination as to whether there are in the premises serious hazards ('Category 1' hazards) and/or less serious hazards ('Category 2' hazards). Authorities have a duty to take enforcement action in relation to Category 1 hazards and a power to do so in relation to Category 2 hazards.

Triggering an assessment

10.19   Local authorities are required to keep housing conditions in their area under review.[8] However, in practice it will usually be necessary for the occupier to request that the local authority carry out an inspection. Local authorities are sometimes slow to respond to such requests or give them low priority so that there may be a considerable delay before an inspection is arranged.

Official complaints

10.20   If an authority receive an 'official complaint' which indicates that a Category 1 or 2 hazard may exist, an inspection must be made by a 'proper officer'.[9] An official complaint means one made by a Justice of the Peace with local jurisdiction or by the parish or community council.[10] An occupier whose request for a local authority inspection is ignored should therefore arrange for an official complaint to be submitted on his or her behalf. This will place the authority under a duty to inspect.

---

7   HA 2004 s2(1).
8   HA 2004 s3.
9   HA 2004 s4.
10   Parish and community councils are the first tier of local government in England and Wales. In Wales the community councils are the equivalent of parish councils in England (although there are some DEFRA funded rural community councils in England).

10.21   If, following an official complaint, an authority refuses or fails to inspect, a claim for judicial review can be brought for a mandatory order forcing the authority to inspect and comply with its duties under the HA 2004.

10.22   Alternatively, a complaint may be made under the authority's complaints procedure. Ultimately, complaint may be made to the Ombudsman if the authority does not resolve the complaint satisfactorily (see chapter 22).

Assessing hazards

10.23   The inspection must be carried out in accordance with the HHSRS Regulations and Guidance published by the ODPM[11] and, if the officer is of the opinion that a Category 1 or 2 hazard exists, a report in writing must be made to the authority. The authority must consider any report made to them as soon as possible and take the most appropriate action in relation to the hazard. See below.

10.24   The HHSRS Regulations set out the assessment process. There are two stages: first, an assessment of the likelihood of an occupier suffering any harm as a result of the hazard; then, an assessment of the range of probable harmful outcomes. The two factors are combined using a standard method and expressed as a numerical score. There are prescribed bands applicable to the range of numerical scores: where a hazard falls within bands A, B or C the hazard is a Category 1 hazard. Where it falls within any other band it is a Category 2 hazard.

10.25   The assessment must record the presence of all hazards. Whether they are classed as Category 1 or Category 2 will determine the action the local authority must or may take. A record of the inspection must be prepared and kept either in written or electronic form.[12]

10.26   The HHSRS Regulations list the 'matters and circumstances' that may give rise to a hazard and set out the classes of harm that may occur. The classes of harm are set out in four bands: Classes I to IV.

10.27   By way of example, the first two 'matters and circumstances' listed are:

11 The 'Housing Health and Safety Ratings System – Operating Guidance' was published in February 2006, runs to 188 pages and is available on the website of the Communities and Local Government Department (formerly ODPM): www.communities.gov.uk.

12 HHSRS Regs 2005 reg 5.

- damp and mould growth – exposure to house dust mites, damp, mould or fungal growths; and
- excess cold – exposure to low temperatures.

10.28   In the list of classes of harm 'regular severe pneumonia' is included under Class I, 'cardio-respiratory disease', 'asthma' and 'non-malignant respiratory diseases' under Class II and 'occasional mild pneumonia' and 'regular serious coughs or colds' under Class IV.

10.29   The likelihood of the class of harm arising as a result of the matter described, combined with the severity of the class of harm will result in a numerical assessment of the hazard such that it can be classified as Category 1 or Category 2.

Action following the assessment

10.30   If a local authority discovers a Category 1 hazard it has a duty to take the most appropriate enforcement action. Where a Category 2 hazard exists the authority has a power to take enforcement action.

10.31   The action available to local authorities is:

- serving an improvement notice;
- making a prohibition order;
- serving a hazard awareness notice;
- making a demolition order; or
- declaring the area to be a clearance area.

10.32   In addition, in cases of imminent risk from a Category 1 hazard, an authority may:

- take emergency remedial action; or
- make an emergency prohibition order.

10.33   In deciding which course of action to take, authorities must have regard to the Enforcement Guidance issued by ODPM in February 2006.[13]

10.34   If only one course of action is possible the authority must take that action. If more than one course of action is possible they must decide which is the most appropriate. More than one form of action cannot be taken at the same time but if the chosen action does not prove satisfactory the authority may take another course of action in the list.[14]

13 The Enforcement Guidance is also available at www.communities.gov.uk.
14 HA 2004 s5(3)–(5).

10.35   Although the authority may have a duty to act it is for the authority to decide which course of action to take. If this is to serve a hazard awareness notice this merely warns the occupier of the existence of the hazard.

10.36   When the authority has decided on one of the above courses of action it must prepare a statement of the reasons for their decision and serve the statement of reasons on every person on whom the relevant notice or order is served.

Improvement notices

10.37   An improvement notice requires the person on whom it is served to take specified remedial action in respect of the hazard or hazards concerned.[15] Where a Category 1 hazard exists, the remedial action must, as a minimum, be sufficient to ensure that the hazard ceases to be a Category 1 hazard but may extend beyond such action.[16] The notice must give certain information about the hazard, specify the remedial action required and give a date when the action must start and be completed. It must also inform the recipient of the right of appeal and the time limit for bringing an appeal, which is 21 days.

10.38   As is clear from the name, the works that a landlord can be forced to carry out may be works to improve as well as works to repair the premises. An example might be the installation of central heating or the fitting of a handrail on a steep stair.

Suspension of notices

10.39   The notice may provide for its operation to be suspended until a time or event specified in the notice.[17] This could be the time when certain kinds of occupiers move in or out of the premises.

10.40   If the notice is complied with the local authority must revoke it. If the notice specifies more than one hazard the authority must revoke the part of the notice that concerns the hazard or hazards that have been remedied. The authority may vary the remainder of the notice.[18]

15 HA 2004 s11(2).
16 HA 2004 s11(5).
17 HA 2004 s14(1) and (2).
18 HA 2004 s16.

Prohibition orders

10.41   A prohibition order prohibits the use of premises for specified purposes, for example, use as a dwelling or HMO.[19]

10.42   A prohibition order must also specify the hazard concerned and the action the authority considers would result in revocation of the order.[20] The order must also inform the recipient of the time limit for appealing which is 28 days.

10.43   Prohibition orders may also be suspended until a time or event specified in the order. For example, if the order prohibits the use of the building as a dwelling its operation may be suspended until the current occupiers have vacated. The effect of such an order would be to then prohibit future use of the premises as a dwelling until works had been carried out to remove the hazard or hazards.

10.44   The prohibition order must be revoked when the hazard specified in the notice has been removed.

Tenants' loss of security

10.45   If a prohibition order is made, and its operation is not suspended, any tenants and/or licensees may be evicted by the landlord. The security of tenure enjoyed by statutory and assured tenants is effectively removed by the making of such an order.[21]

10.46   The Enforcement Guidance requires the authority to 'consider the availability of local accommodation for re-housing any displaced occupants' when considering the making of a prohibition order[22] and states that 'the authority may consider offering temporary or permanent alternative accommodation to the tenant to assist in progressing remedial works'.[23] If the tenant loses his or her home because of the order there is a limited re-housing duty on the authority, see paragraph 10.66 below.

10.47   It is likely that authorities will avoid making outright prohibition orders whenever possible and, in a case where remedial works cannot be carried out with the tenants in occupation, may opt to serve a suspended prohibition order or a hazard awareness notice.

---

19 HA 2004 s20(3).
20 HA 2004 s22(e).
21 Section 33 provides that nothing in the Rent Act 1977, Housing Act 1988 and the Rent (Agriculture) Act 1976 prevents a landlord from obtaining possession if necessary to comply with the order.
22 Paragraph 5.23 of the Enforcement Guidance.
23 Paragraph 5.21 of the Enforcement Guidance.

Access

10.48   It may be that the works can be carried out with the tenants in occupation. In such a case if access is not given the magistrates court has the power to order an occupier to permit the owner or manager of the premises to carry out any action necessary and expedient for the purpose of complying with an improvement notice or a prohibition order.[24]

Emergency cases

10.49   If a local authority is satisfied that a Category 1 hazard exists on any residential premises and that 'the hazard involves an imminent risk of serious harm to the health or safety of any of the occupiers' it can take 'emergency remedial action' or make an 'emergency prohibition order'.

Emergency remedial action

10.50   This means 'such remedial action in respect of the hazard concerned as the authority consider immediately necessary in order to remove the imminent risk of serious harm'.[25]

10.51   If emergency remedial action is decided upon as the most appropriate course of action the local authority has an immediate right of access and the notice regarding the remedial action must be served on the occupiers. Notice may be served by being fixed to a conspicuous part of the premises or building: section 40(6). Notice must also be served on the owner or manager within seven days of starting emergency remedial action. This notice must identify the hazard, the works that are to be carried out and must give information about the right of appeal.

10.52   The local authority may recoup the cost of taking emergency remedial action from the owner or manager.

Emergency prohibition orders

10.53   This is an alternative to carrying out emergency remedial action. An emergency prohibition order also has immediate effect.[26] The order must be served on the day it is made.

---

24 HA 2004 s5(2).
25 HA 2004 s40.
26 HA 2004 s43.

Appeals

10.54   The person on whom a notice of improvement or a prohibition order is served has a right to appeal. The time limit for appealing is 21 days in the case of an improvement notice and 28 days in the case of a prohibition order. Appeals against emergency remedial action or an emergency prohibition order must be brought within 28 days. Appeals are to a residential property tribunal.

Sanctions

10.55   Failure to comply with an improvement notice or prohibition order is an offence punishable by a fine of up to £5,000.[27] In respect of a prohibition order, a further fine of £20 per day can be imposed for each day following the conviction that the defendant uses or permits the premises to be used in contravention of the order.

Hazard awareness notices

10.56   A hazard awareness notice is a notice advising the person on whom it is served of the existence of a Category 1 or Category 2 hazard.[28] It must specify the nature of the hazard and give details of any remedial action the authority consider would be practicable and appropriate. However, the notice does not *require* that such action is taken.

10.57   There is no appeal against a hazard awareness notice.

Demolition orders

10.58   A demolition order may only be made if there is a Category 1 hazard and the building is not a listed building. In deciding whether to make a demolition order the authority must take into account the availability of local accommodation for re-housing the displaced occupants, the demand for and the sustainability of the accommodation if the hazard was remedied, the prospective use of the cleared site, and the impact on the local environment.[29]

10.59   A demolition order may be substituted by a prohibition order if proposals are submitted to use the premises other than for human habitation.

10.60   An appeal lies to the residential property tribunal and must be exercised by 'an aggrieved person' within 21 days.

27 HA 2004 ss30 and 33.
28 HA 2004 ss28 and 29.
29 HA 1985 s265, as amended by HA 2004, and paragraph 5.44 of the Enforcement Guidance.

Clearance areas

10.61 An authority can declare an area a clearance area if satisfied that each of the residential buildings in the area contains a Category 1 hazard or that the buildings are dangerous or harmful to the health and safety of inhabitants because of the arrangement of the buildings.[30] The declaration of a clearance area means that all of the buildings in the area will be demolished. It will be part of the authority's proposals for the wider neighbourhood of which the area forms part. Such a declaration will only be made after extensive consultation with all owners and occupiers and the authority must be satisfied that alternative accommodation can be provided for the displaced occupiers.

10.62 Such action may be taken in conjunction with the declaration of a renewal area under the Local Government and Housing Act 1989.

Compensation and re-housing

10.63 Whenever a house is demolished as a result of a demolition order or slum clearance, displaced occupiers are entitled to compensation. Displaced owner occupiers are entitled to a 'Home Loss' payment of up to £47,000 depending on the value of the property.[31]

10.64 Tenants who are permanently displaced are entitled to a 'home loss' payment of £4,700. To qualify the tenants must have occupied the property as their only or principal home for at least 12 months prior to eviction.

10.65 Although local authorities will not make prohibition orders or demolition orders in relation to their own properties, they may decide to demolish properties or redevelop areas. In such cases possession can be gained under Grounds 10 or 10A (see appendix to chapter 6) which require the landlord to make suitable alternative accommodation available for the tenant.

10.66 For tenants of other landlords who lose their homes as a result of a prohibition order, demolition order or clearance order, the local authority has duty to ensure that some form of alternative accommodation is available. The Land Compensation Act 1973

---

30 HA 1985 s289, as amended by HA 2004 and paragraph 5.48 of the Enforcement Guidance.

31 Land Compensation Act 1973 s30; Home Loss Payments (Prescribed Amounts) (England) Regulations 2008 (SI No 1598). The prescribed amounts are regularly increased.

provides that wherever 'suitable alternative residential accommodation on reasonable terms is not otherwise available to that person, then ... it shall be the duty of the relevant authority to secure that he will be provided with such other accommodation'. However, this duty has been interpreted by the courts as requiring the authority to do no more than to act reasonably and to do their best, as soon as practicable, to provide the person with other accommodation. They are not required to give the person priority over other people on the waiting list.[32] Temporary accommodation will be sufficient pending permanent accommodation becoming available.[33] Many local authorities award a certain level of priority under their allocation schemes to those forced to move because of demolition and redevelopment schemes (see chapter 6).

Houses in multiple occupation

10.67   HMOs are buildings in which more than one household lives, sharing facilities. The Housing Act 2004 has introduced a new system of regulation in relation to HMOs.

10.68   The following are now defined as HMOs:[34]

- a house or flat which is let to three or more tenants who form two or more households and who share a kitchen, bathroom or toilet;
- a house converted into bed-sits or other forms of non-self contained accommodation which is let to three or more tenants who form two or more households;
- a house converted into one or more flats which are not wholly self contained (ie, do not contain within the flat a kitchen, bathroom and toilet) and which is occupied by three or more tenants who form two or more households;
- a building converted entirely into self-contained flats if the conversion did not meet the standards of the 1991 Building Regulations and more than one-third of the flats are let on short-term tenancies.

10.69   In order to be an HMO the property must be used by the occupiers as their only or main residence[35] and must be used solely or mainly as residential accommodation.

---

32 *R v Bristol Corporation ex p Hendy* [1974] 1 All ER 1047.
33 *R v East Hertfordshire DC ex p Smith* (1990) 23 HLR 26, CA
34 HA 2004 ss254–260.
35 This includes students occupying while undertaking a full time course of education and those occupying a building as a refuge: HA 2004 s259(2).

10.70   A 'single household' means members of the same family which includes spouses, unmarried couples (including same sex couples) and blood relatives.[36]

Mandatory licensing

10.71   Larger HMOs are subject to mandatory licensing operated by the local authority. These are HMOs which:

- have five or more occupants,
- comprise of two or more households; and
- are situated in a dwelling that has three or more habitable storeys.

10.72   Application must be made to the local authority for a licence and before granting a licence the authority must be satisfied that:

- the HMO is reasonably suitable for occupation for the number of people allowed under the licence;
- the proposed licence holder is a fit and proper person and the most appropriate person to hold the licence;
- the proposed manager, if there is one, is a fit and proper person;
- the proposed management arrangements are satisfactory and the manager/s competent;
- the financial structures for the management are suitable.

10.73   An appeal against the refusal of a licence is to a residential property tribunal and should be made within 28 days.

Penalties for failing to apply

10.74   The licensing provisions came into force on 6 April 2006 and landlords were given until 6 June 2006 to apply. If a landlord fails to apply for a licence he or she commits an offence and can be fined up to £20,000. Further, a tenant living in a property that should have been licensed but wasn't can apply to a residential property tribunal to re-claim rent paid during the unlicensed period, for a maximum period of 12 months and the local authority can reclaim the total amount of housing benefit paid during the unlicensed period.[37]

---

36 HA 2004 s258.
37 HA 2004 s73.

Selective registration

10.75   In addition to the mandatory scheme HA 2004 provides for local authorities to operate local registration and licensing schemes for HMOs that do not fall within the mandatory scheme.

Overcrowding

10.76   The mandatory licensing provisions for HMOs give local authorities the power to specify the number of people permitted to live in a property. It is an offence to permit more people than the maximum specified and the offence carries a fine of up to £20,000.

10.77   Overcrowding is also relevant to the hazard rating process. One of the 'matters and circumstances' that may give rise to a potential hazard is 'a lack of adequate space for living and sleeping'. Depending upon the number of occupants and the likely consequences in relation to the health and safety of the occupants overcrowding may therefore create a Category 1 or Category 2 hazard in any dwelling.

'Statutory overcrowding'

10.78   The Housing Act 1985 still sets out the 'statutory' test for over-crowding.[38] The provision is often misunderstood. The statutory overcrowding test is the basis for local authority powers to prevent overcrowding in private sector dwellings. Overcrowding was first recognised in legislation in the Nuisance Removal Act of 1855. The concern was about the moral as well as the health consequences of overcrowding, hence a statutory definition that focuses on preventing people of opposite sex (other than couples) being required to share a sleeping room.

10.79   There are two alternative tests to determine whether a dwelling is 'statutorily overcrowded': the room standard and the space standard.[39] Under the room standard, a household is overcrowded whenever two persons of the opposite sex must share a sleeping room. However, in applying the room standard, children under the age of 10 are not considered at all. Under the space standard the number of people in the household is compared to either the number of sleeping rooms or the floor area of those rooms. In applying the space standard children under the age of 10 count as half a person and children under the age of one are not considered at all. Whichever standard is

38   HA 2004 makes provision for this test to be amended by regulations but there are no firm plans to do this at present.

39   HA 1985 ss325 and 326.

applied living rooms are considered to be rooms in which people can sleep.

10.80   An occupier or landlord may be prosecuted for causing premises to be 'statutorily overcrowded' but no offence is committed if the overcrowding is caused by children in the household reaching the age of 10. In practice, many overcrowded households are living in dwellings owned by local authorities and RSLs and have become overcrowded because of the natural growth of their families.[40]

10.81   Many occupiers who live in overcrowded accommodation believe that if they are 'statutorily overcrowded' they must be entitled to be transferred or allocated social housing. Unfortunately, this is not the case. Most allocation and transfer schemes give some priority to overcrowded households but this will not guarantee an offer of more suitable accommodation. Further, statutory overcrowding does not mean that the occupiers will qualify as homeless although it is one factor an authority must take into account when deciding whether it is reasonable for the occupier to remain in occupation. See *Harouki v Kensington & Chelsea RLBC*[41] which is referred to at paragraph 13.168.

'Decent homes'

10.82   In the Green Paper 'Quality and Choice: A Decent Home for All' published in July 2000 the Government set out targets in relation to the quality of social housing. The Green Paper defined a 'decent home' as 'one which is wind and weather tight, warm and has modern facilities'. The two targets set by the government were:

- to reduce by one-third the number of dwellings in the social rented sector which fall below the standard by 2004; and
- to have all social rented homes meet the Standard by 2010.

10.83   The Decent Homes Standard is based around four components. To comply with the Standard a dwelling should:

- be free from Category 1 hazards;
- be in a reasonable state of repair;
- have reasonably modern facilities (in particular kitchens and bathrooms); and
- offer a reasonable degree of thermal comfort, which means having efficient heating, insulation and ventilation.

40 The offence can also be committed by a local authority but the consent of the Attorney-General is needed for an authority to be prosecuted.
41 [2007] EWCA Civ 1000.

10.84   The first target has not been met: the number of non-fit homes had been reduced by only 22 per cent by April 2004.

10.85   Part of the Decent Homes programme is to encourage, or coerce, local authorities to transfer stock to RSLs or to enter into Private Finance Initiatives (PFI) with the private sector. The creation of Arms-length Management Organizations (ALMOs) to manage housing stock is also encouraged. Authorities are required to consult tenants about the options they pursue and in those areas where tenants have rejected stock transfer the funds for housing improvement and maintenance have been withheld by central government.

10.86   Many local authorities and RSLs are currently engaged, through PFI, in undertaking large scale works of repair and improvement, including the installation of new bathrooms and kitchens, in order to meet the Decent Homes standard.

Gas Safety Regulations

10.87   Under the Gas Safety (Installation and Use) Regulations 1998 landlords are legally responsible for making sure that any gas appliances, gas piping and flues are well maintained and safe.[42] The landlord must ensure that an annual gas safety check is carried out by a CORGI registered gas engineer.[43] A landlord who fails to do so commits a criminal offence.

10.88   The regulations are enforced by the Health and Safety Executive (HSE) whose website is www.hse.gov.uk. This gives information about the local HSE offices to whom complaint may be made. Alternatively, the matter can be reported to the local authority who may take action under the HA 2004, see above.

10.89   The duty is owed by any landlord of a short-term tenancy, eg a tenancy for a period of seven years or less, and to residential licences. It does not apply to long leases.

---

42   Reg 36.
43   Reg 36(3). CORGI is the national watchdog for gas safety. All CORGI registered gas engineers must carry photo id bearing their CORGI registration number. This can be checked on the CORGI website at www.trustcorgi.com.

CHAPTER 11

Relationship breakdown

Key points

- Being married or in a civil partnership with someone gives a person the right to occupy the shared home and to pay the rent or mortgage. These are known as 'home rights'.
- Additionally, where accommodation is shared the court can make orders to regulate rights of occupation. An 'occupation order' may give a person a right to occupy and/or prevent a person who is otherwise entitled to occupy accommodation from exercising a right to occupy.
- To protect a person from violence or harassment a 'non-molestation order' may be made against any 'associated person'. Associated persons are not confined to those who are or have been a 'couple'. It includes relatives and other people who share accommodation.
- It is a criminal offence to breach a non-molestation order without reasonable excuse.
- Non-molestation orders and occupation orders are for limited duration to protect a person or child until a long term housing solution is achieved.
- If the shared home is rented and the parties are married, in a civil partnership or have been co-habiting together the court can transfer the tenancy from one party to the other.
- Where property is owned by one or both parties the court may transfer ownership or order a sale only if the parties are married or in a civil partnership.
- A person who is not a legal owner may be able to establish a beneficial interest by having contributed to the purchase of a property.
- Where the parties have children the court can transfer a tenancy or ownership for the benefit of the children.

Introduction

11.1   The chapter deals with some of the housing issues that arise when a relationship breaks down. Where the parties are in dispute about finance, property and/or children it will be necessary to consult a specialist family lawyer. This chapter, therefore, provides only an overview of the following issues:

Immediate/short term issues

- protection from domestic violence
- establishing rights of occupation
- homeless applications

Long term solutions – property adjustment

- transfer of tenancies
- owner occupied accommodation

Immediate/short term issues

Protection from domestic violence

11.2   Where someone is facing violence within or around the home he or she may do one or more of the following:
- apply to the local authority as a homeless person;
- obtain emergency shelter in a refuge or with friends or family;
- apply to the court for an injunction (a non-molestation order) and/or for an order excluding the prepetrator from the home (an occupation order).

Homeless applications

11.3   A person is homeless if it is probable that continuing to occupy accommodation will lead to violence against him or her. Violence is defined as 'violence from another person; or threats of violence from another person which are likely to be carried out', see paragraph 13.158. A local authority only has a duty to house applicants who have priority need. This includes those with dependent children and those considered vulnerable as a result of having become homeless because of violence, see paragraphs 13.179–13.181.

11.4   Some applicants will want temporary accommodation only until they can take other steps, such as applying for an injunction, an occupation order and/or a property adjustment order. Some applicants, however, may wish to be permanently accommodated away from the home in which they suffered domestic violence. An authority cannot find that a person is intentionally homeless because the person does not wish to seek an injunction and return home, see paragraph 13.160.

Womens' refuges

11.5   A local authority may discharge its immediate duty to secure emergency accommodation by securing a place in a refuge. However, it is also possible to contact Womens' Aid directly to find a place in a refuge.[1]

11.6   Refuge places are generally only available to people who have the funds to pay for the accommodation or who can claim housing benefit. Victims of violence who are subject to immigration control may not be entitled to claim benefits or apply as homeless, see paragraphs 8.16 and 13.1. Their only option may be to seek help from social services if they have children or have community care needs, see chapters 17 and 18.

11.7   Womens' Aid offers refuge only to female victims of domestic violence. There is no similar organisation for men and, at time of wirting, there are just two refuges for men in the UK. Information about support available to male victims of domestic violence may be obtained by contacting 'Supportline' at www.supportline.org.uk.

Non-molestation orders

11.8   The courts' powers to make injunctions to protect the victims of domestic violence are found in Part IV of the Family Law Act (FLA) 1996. The injunction is known as a 'non-molestation order' which means an order that:[2]

- prohibits a person from molesting an 'associated' person; and/or
- prohibits a person from molesting a relevant child.[2]

What is 'molestation'?

11.9   The term is not defined in legislation. It covers actual or threatened violence but also includes behaviour that may be considered to be 'pestering'.[3] It has been held to include 'any conduct which can properly be regarded as such a degree of harassment as to call for the intervention of the court.'[4] The following are examples of behaviour that amounts to molestation:

---

1   Womens' Aid operate the National Domestic Violence Helpline: Tel 0800 2000247.
2   FLA 1996 s42.
3   *Vaughan v Vaughan* [1973] 3 All ER 449.
4   *Horner v Horner* [1982] Fam 90, Ormrod LJ at 93.

- a man, who had previously been violent, repeatedly calling on his ex-wife at her home and workplace, making a 'perfect nuisance of himself', knowing that his behaviour was frightening to his ex-wife;[5]
- a man giving his wife notes that were upsetting and intercepting her journey to the railway station;[6]
- a man rifling through a woman's handbag.[7]

11.10   It has been held that an order cannot be granted to an applicant who is living with and intends to continue living with the respondent.[8] The decision was not a decision of a higher court and is not therefore binding. However, where a couple are still living together and intend to continue to do so the courts are likely to take a different view of what behaviour amounts to molestation than where the relationship has ended and one is still 'pestering' the other.

Who may be protected by an order?

11.11   An application may be made to protect an 'associated person' or a 'relevant child'.

Associated persons

11.12   A person is associated with another person if:[9]

- they are or have been married to each other;
- they are or have been civil partners;
- they are cohabitants or former cohabitants ie a couple who live together as husband and wife or (if of the same sex) in an equivalent relationship;
- they live or have lived in the same household, otherwise than merely by reason of one of them being the other's employee, tenant, lodger or boarder;
- they are relatives;[10]
- they have agreed to marry each other;

---

5   *Vaughan v Vaughan* [1973] 3 All ER 449.
6   *Horner v Horner* [1982] Fam 90.
7   *Spencer v Camacho* (1983) 4 FLR 662.
8   *F v F* [1989] 2 FLR 451, per Nigel Fricker J, QC.
9   FLA 1996 s62(3).
10 Relatives are defined in FLA 1996 s63(1).

- they have entered into a 'civil partnership agreement', ie an agreement to become civil partners;[11]
- they 'have or have had an intimate personal relationship with each other which is or was of significant duration';
- in relation to any child, they are both parents of the child or have or have had parental responsibility for the child;
- in relation to an adopted child, one person is the natural parent or grandparent and the other is the child or any adoptive parent or prospective adoptive parent;
- they are parties to the same family proceedings (not under FLA 1996 Part 4).[12]

Relevant child

11.13   In addition the court has a general power to make an order in relation to 'any relevant child'. A 'relevant child' means:

- any child who is living with either party;
- any child in relation to whom an order is in question in the proceedings;[13] and
- any other child whose interests the courts considers relevant.[14]

11.14   A relevant child therefore includes any child the court considers needs protection.

11.15   A child may apply for an order but the leave of the court is required if the child is under the age of 16 years. The court will only grant leave if satisfied that the child has sufficient understanding to make the proposed application.[15]

When will the court make an order?

11.16   In deciding whether to make an order the court must have regard to 'all the circumstances including the need to secure the health, safety and well-being' of the applicant and any relevant child.[16]

11.17   As a general rule the courts are reluctant to grant civil injunctions against anyone who is mentally ill because the person may not be

---

11 This is defined in the Civil Partnership Act 2004 s73. Orders in relation to those who have married or agreed to be civil partners can only be made within three years of the termination of the agreement: s42(4).

12 This would include a party to adoption proceedings, such as the natural father.

13 The proceedings may be under the Adoption Act 1976, Adoption and Children Act 2002 or Children Act 1989.

14 FLA 1996 s62(2).

15 FLA 1996 s43.

16 FLA 1996 s42(5).

capable of complying with the order and the order may not be enforceable by way of committal.[17]

11.18   It is common practice where the respondent attends the hearing for the court to accept an 'undertaking' instead of making an injunction. An undertaking should not be accepted in a case where the respondent has used or threatened violence against the applicant or a child. In such a case the court should make a non-molestation order, breach of which is a criminal offence, see paragraph 11.22 below.[18]

Urgent cases – orders without notice

11.19   Under FLA 1996 s5 the court may make an order before the respondent has been given notice of the proceedings. In deciding whether to do so the court must consider all of the circumstances including:

- a risk of significant harm[19] to the applicant or a relevant child if the order is not made immediately;
- whether it is likely that the applicant will be deterred or prevented from pursuing the application if an order is not made immediately; and
- whether there is reason to believe that the respondent is aware of the proceedings but deliberately evading service and that the applicant or a relevant child will be seriously prejudiced by any delay in arranging service of the papers.

11.20   If an order is made without notice to the respondent, he or she must be given an opportunity to make representations at a full hearing. The practice of the courts when making a without notice order is to either list the application for a full hearing at a later date, or to give the respondent the right to apply for a full hearing, the order remaining in force until any further hearing.

The scope of a non-molestation order

11.21 The order may prohibit molestation in general, particular acts of molestation, or both. It may be for a specified period or until further order.[20]

17 *Wookey v Wookey* [1991] 3 WLR 135.
18 FLA 1996 s46(3A).
19 'Harm' is defined in section 63. In relation to an adult it means ill treatment or the impairment of physical or mental health and, in relation to a child it means ill treatment or the impairment of physical or mental health or development.
20 FLA 1996 s42(6)–(7).

Sanctions for breach of non-molestation order

11.22   Since 1 July 2007 it has been a criminal offence to breach a non-molestation order without reasonable excuse.[21] The offence can only be committed at a time when the respondent is aware of the existence of the order. The maximum punishment is up to five years imprisonment and/or a fine, if dealt with by a Crown Court. If the magistrates court deal with the case the maximum punishment is up to 12 months imprisonment and/or a fine not exceeding £5,000.

11.23   In consequence of the new criminal offence, the court can no longer attach a power of arrest to a non-molestation order. This is in contrast to occupation orders in respect of which the court can still attach power of arrest, see paragraph 11.67 below.

11.24   It is still possible for a person who breaches a non-molestation order to be committed to prison for contempt of court, see paragraph 22.129. However, a person cannot be convicted of the criminal offence of breaching a non-molestation order *and* punished for contempt of court.[22]

Protection from Harassment Act 1997

11.25   A victim may also apply for an injunction under the Protection from Harassment Act (HA) 1997 or make a complaint to the police who can prosecute a person guilty of harassment. See paragraph 7.10 for a summary of the provisions of PHA 1997.

Occupation orders

11.26   In addition to or instead of a non-molestation order an application may be made for an occupation order under FLA 1996. An occupation order may grant a person a right to occupy and may prevent another person from interfering with such a right. It may also suspend another person's rights of occupation or even exclude the person from the area where the home is. The purpose of an occupation order is to provide short-term protection where there has been violence or where one of the parties, or children living in the home, are likely to suffer harm without the court's intervention.

---

21   FLA 1996 s42A was inserted by the Domestic Violence, Crime and Victims Act 2004 s1.
22   FLA 1996 s42A(3) and (4).

11.27   Occupation orders are always for a temporary period pending a more long term arrangement being agreed or ordered by a court.

11.28   The courts' powers under FLA 1996 depend on the parties' existing rights of occupation. A person may have a right to occupy under the general law, eg because he or she is a tenant or owner or under FLA 1996 by virtue of marriage to or civil partnership with the tenant or owner. These rights of occupation are summarised below.

Rights to occupy under the general law

Joint tenancy/jointly owned property

11.29   Where accommodation is let to two joint tenants or is jointly owned both are entitled to occupy the whole of the accommodation, see paras 1.50–1.53. Other than by applying for an order under FLA 1996 one joint tenant or owner cannot exclude the other.

11.30   However, one joint tenant can terminate a joint tenancy without the consent of the other (see para 1.65). This may be done in order to frustrate a future application for a transfer into the sole name of one of the joint tenants (see below para 11.88). It is also sometimes encouraged by local authority landlords that have a duty to accommodate the victim of domestic violence. The notice to quit determines the tenancy and the authority can then seek a possession order. An authority must, however, consider the remaining occupier's right to respect for his or her home and whether such a course of action is necessary and proportionate.[23]

Sole tenancy/sole ownership

11.31   Where one party is the sole tenant or sole owner of a property and the parties are not married or in a civil partnership that person's co-habitant does not have a *right* to occupy. He or she has a 'licence' (permission) to occupy given by the sole tenant or owner. Because they share the accommodation the tenant or owner may give to the other reasonable notice to leave (see para 1.122). What is reasonable notice depends on the circumstances. If there has been violence or unreasonable behaviour, very short or immediate notice may be considered reasonable. The notice need not be in writing.

11.32   After the period of notice has expired the tenant or owner can exclude the co-habitant by changing the locks. However, the use of

23 See *McCann v UK*, App No 19009/04, 13 May 2008, ECtHR and para 21.41 below.

force to evict a person who is inside the home is a criminal offence under the Criminal Law Act 1977 (see para 7.41).

11.33   Where a cohabitant refuses to leave, a sole tenant or owner may apply for a possession order and use the court bailiffs to evict even though under landlord and tenant law this is not necessary. See chapter 5 for an explanation of the procedure for possession claims and chapter 22 for a general description of civil proceedings.

11.34   In theory a person who has been excluded and believes that he or she was not given reasonable notice can apply to a court for an injunction ordering the other party to allow the person to continue to occupy until reasonable notice has expired. In practice a court is unlikely to make an order that forces two people whose relationship has broken down to live together even for a short period.

Rights to occupy under FLA 1996 – 'home rights'

11.35   The right of a spouse to occupy the 'matrimonial home' is well established and such rights were prevously referred to as 'matrimonial home rights'. Since the Civil Partnership Act 2004 these rights have been renamed 'home rights': a spouse or civil partner has a legal right to occupy accommodation that is solely owned or rented by the other spouse or civil partner, provided it is or has been their shared home during the marriage or civil partnership.[24]

Extent of home rights

11.36   Home rights are set out in FLA 1996 s30. The following points should be noted:

- home rights only exist in relation to accommodation which is, has in the past been, or was intended to be, a matrimonial home or a civil partnership home;[25]
- home rights can exist in relation to a dwelling-house, which includes a building or part of a building, a caravan, house-boat or any structure occupied as a dwelling;[26]

---

24 FLA 1996 s30. The provisions are not limited to right of occupaion under tenancies. Section 30(1)(b) also refers to 'any enactment giving ... the right to remain in occupation'. This would therefore extend to occupation as a tolerated trespasser after the making of a possession order, see para 5.126.

25 FLA 1996 s30(7).

26 FLA 1996 s63(1).

- if the spouse or civil partner claiming home rights is in actual occupation, the right exists independently of the court. However, if the person is not in actual occupation he or she must apply for the permission of the court to gain the right to enter and occupy.[27]
- the right of occupation ends when the marriage or civil partnership ends, unless extended by court order.[28]

11.37   In relation to tenancies, the occupation of a spouse or civil partner satisfies any residence condition necessary for the tenant to have long-term security.[29]

11.38   A spouse or civil partner exercising a home right is entitled to pay rent or mortgage payments and any payment or offer of payment is 'as good' as if made by the tenant or borrower.[30] Housing benefit can be awarded if necessary to enable the person to continue living in the home (see para 8.15).

11.39   Where accommodation is owner-occupied, home rights can be registered as a charge with the Land Registry.[31] This would protect the right in the event that the sole owner tried to sell the property.

Applying for an occupation order

11.40   Different provisions apply depending on the status of the applicant and whether he or she has a right to occupy.

FLA 1996 s33: applicant entitled to occupy

11.41   Most applications are made under FLA 1996 s33 which applies when the applicant has a right to occupy, whether under the general law or by virtue of a home right under FLA 1996, see para 11.35 above.

The court's powers

11.42   The court may make an order to:[32]

---

27 FLA 1996 s30(2).
28 FLA 1996 s30(8)(a).
29 FLA 1996 s30(4). See paras 3.2–3.4 for an explanation of the issues arising in relation to tenants' residence conditions.
30 FLA 1996 s30(3). This means, for example, that if a landlord refuses a payment from the spouse or civil partner, the landlord cannot then bring a claim for possession on the grounds that the tenant has failed to pay the rent.
31 FLA 1996 s31.
32 PCA 1996 s33(3).

- enforce the right of occupation against the other person ('the respondent');
- require the respondent to permit the applicant to enter and remain in the home;
- regulate the occupation of the home by either or both parties;
- prohibit, suspend or restrict the rights of a respondent who is ordinarily entitled to occupy under landlord and tenant law;
- restrict or terminate a right of occupation the respondent has under section 30 of FLA 1996 (home rights)
- require the respondent to leave the home or part of it;
- exclude the respondent from a defined area where the home is.
- in practice the courts will usually make orders to restrict a right of occupation where there has been violence.

11.43   The court may also make orders declaring that a person has a right of occupation by virtue of the general law or under FLA 1996 s30, where this is in dispute. Such orders simply state the entitlement and do not restrict the exercise of any right of occupation.

Criteria for making orders

11.44   When deciding whether to make an order and in what terms the court must have regard to all of the circumstances, including:[33]

- the housing needs and housing resources of each of the parties and any relevant child;
- the financial resources of each of the parties;
- the likely effect of any order, or refusal to make an order, on the health, safety or well-being of the parties and any relevant child; and
- the conduct of the parties in relation to each other and otherwise.

11.45   See paragraph 11.13 above for the definition of 'relevant child'.

The balance of harm test

11.46   The court must make an order if it appears that the applicant or any relevant child is likely to suffer significant harm if an order is not made which is greater than the harm the respondent or any child is

---

33   FLA 1996 s30(6).

likely to suffer if an order *is* made.[34] There is a presumption therefore in favour of making an order.[35]

11.47   When considering an occupation order and applying the balance of harm test the court will take account of whether an applicant or respondent is likely to be owed a homeless duty.

> In *B v B*[36] a woman left her husband because of his violence. She took their two-year-old daughter leaving him and his six-year-old son from a previous relationship in occupation of their home. She was placed in temporary accommodation by the local authority and applied for an occupation order. An order was made ordering him to vacate with his son. The Court of Appeal allowed his appeal. The authority was likely to find that he was intentionally homeless and that no housing duty was owed. The likely harm to the son would therefore be greater to that caused to the wife and daughter who would be housed by the local authority.

11.48   When considering an occupation order a central factor will be who is likely to have primary responsibility for any children in the future and an application for an occupation order can be made at the same time as application for a residence order under the Children Act 1989.[37]

11.49   Where the court is making a declaratory order relating to entitlement rather than restricting the exercise of a right of occupation the balance of harm test need not be applied.

How long does the order last?

11.50   Occupation orders are for limited duration. An order must be for a specified period, until a specified event or until further order.[38]

11.51   The court may make an order that home rights extend beyond the death of the spouse or civil partner or the end of the marriage or civil partnership.[39]

---

34   FLA 1996 s33(7).
35   See paragraph 11.19, note 19 for definition of harm.
36   (1999) 1 FLR 715, CA.
37   FLA 1996 s39(2).
38   FLA 1996 s33(10).
39   FLA 1996 s30(5).

FLA 1996 s35: applicant (former spouse or civil partner) not entitled to occupy

11.52   An application for an occupation order may be made by a former spouse or former civil partner who has no existing right of occupation.[40] This would be the case when a marriage or civil partnership has ended, thereby terminating any home rights previously enjoyed by virtue of FLA 1996 s30. An order may only be made in respect of a dwelling which was or was intended to be the matrimonial or civil partnership home. The application will be against the former spouse or civil partner.

11.53   If an order is made it must:

- if the applicant is in occupation, give the applicant the right not to be evicted or excluded from the home and prohibit the respondent from doing so;
- if the applicant is not in occupation, give the applicant the right to enter into and occupy the home and require the respondent to permit the exercise of the right.

11.54   An order may also restrict the respondent's rights of occupation, as under section 33 (see para 11.42 above).

11.55   When considering an application relating to the applicant's occupation the court must apply the criteria set out at paragraph 11.44 above but in addition the court must consider the following:

- the length of time that has elapsed since the parties ceased to live together;
- the length of time that has elapsed since the marriage or civil partnership ended;[41] and
- the existence of any pending proceedings for property transfer or relating to the legal or beneficial ownership of the home, see paragraph 11.96 below.[42]

11.56   If the court is considering an order that restricts the respondent's occupation rights, the court need not take account of the additional considerations set out above, save for the time since the parties lived together. However, the balance of harm test must be applied, see paragraph 11.46 above.

---

40   FLA 1996 s35.
41   FLA 1996 s35(6)(f).
42   FLA 1996 s35(6)(g). Such applications may be pending under the Matrimonial Causes Act 1973, Civil Partnership Act 2004 or Children Act 1989.

11.57   If the court is also considering an order that restricts the respondent's occupation rights, the balance of harm test must also be applied, see paragraph 11.46 above.

An order under section 35 may not be made for a period longer than six months, but one application to extend the period for a further six months may be made.

FLA 1996 s36: applicant (co-habitant or former co-habitant) not entitled to occupy

11.58   A co-habitant who has no right of occupation may apply under section 36 for an occupation order. An order may only be made in respect of a dwelling in which the parties cohabit or at any time cohabited or intended to cohabit. The application will be against the other cohabitant or former cohabitant.

11.59   If an order is made it must:

- if the applicant is in occupation, give the applicant the right not to be evicted or excluded from the home and prohibit the respondent from doing so;
- if the applicant is not in occupation, give the applicant the right to enter into and occupy the home and require the respondent to permit the exercise of the right.

11.60   An order may also restrict the respondent's rights of occupation.

11.61   When considering an application relating to the applicant's occupation the court must apply the criteria set out at paragraph 11.44 above but in addition the court must consider the following:

- the nature of the parties' relationship and in particular the level of commitment involved in it;
- the length of time during which they cohabited;
- whether there are or have been any children of the relationship, or children for whom both parties have or have had parental responsibility;
- the length of time that has elapsed since the parties ceased to live together; and
- the existence of any pending proceedings for financial provision under the Children Act 1989 or relating to the legal or beneficial ownership of the property, see paragraph 11.96 below.

11.62   If the court is considering an order that restricts the respondent's occupation rights, the court need not take account of the additional considerations set out above but the balance of harm test must be applied (see para 11.46 above). However, under section 36 there is no presumption that an order should be made, as there is when the court is considering making an order under sections 33 or 35.

11.63   An order under section 36 may not be made for a period longer than six months, but one application to extend the period for a further six months may be made.

Occupation orders: other circumstances

11.64   Under FLA 1996 s34 an occupation order can be made in relation to premises where the respondent's interest has passed to someone else. Under section 37 an order may be made where neither party is entitled to occupy the premises where the parties have been married or civil partners. Under section 38 an order may be made in respect of co-habitants where neither has a right to occupy.

Occupation orders: ancillary provisions

11.65   When making an occupation order the court may also make orders:[43]

- that either party is responsible for repairs and maintenance, the payment of rent, mortgage payments or other outgoings;
- that a party occupying the home makes payments to the other;
- that either party has possession or use of furniture or other contents; and
- that either party takes reasonable steps to keep the home and any furniture or contents safe.

Occupation orders: cases of urgency

11.66   An occupation order may also be made at a hearing of which the respondent has not been given notice if the court considers it just and convenient to do so. The same criteria apply when considering making such an order as when considering a non-molestation order, see paragraph 11.19. However, the court should only make an occupation order without notice in an exceptional case. In the case of *Moat Housing Group-South Ltd v Harris and Hartless*,[44] which concerned anti-social behaviour injunctions, the Court of Appeal commented that 'as a matter of principle no order should be made in civil or family proceedings without notice to the other side unless

---

43   FLA 1996 s40(1).
44   [2005] EWCA Civ 287, 16 March 2005. See para 6.72 above.

there is a very good reason for departing from the general rule that notice must be given.'

Occupation orders: enforcement

11.67 The court can attach a power of arrest to an occupation order and must do so unless satisfied that the applicant or any child will be adequately protected without one. However, if the order is made without notice the court may only attach a power of arrest if it appears that the respondent has used or threatened violence against the applicant or a relevant child and there is a risk of significant harm to the applicant or child attributable to the respondent if a power of arrest is not attached immediately.

11.68 Where a power of arrest is attached this means that the police can arrest the perpetrator and bring him or her before the civil courts to be punished for contempt of court. Otherwise, the applicant must make an application for committal, see paragraphs 9.170 and 22.129. Breach of an occupation order, unlike breach of a non-molestation order, is not a criminal offence.

Long term solutions

Property adjustment

The courts' powers to transfer ownership/tenancies

11.69 Under FLA 1996 when a marriage, civil partnership or cohabiting relationship breaks down the court can make an order transferring a tenancy from one party to another, or from joint names into sole names.

11.70 In addition, under the Matrimonial Causes Act (MCA) 1973[45] and under the Civil Partnership Act (CPA) 2004[46] a court can transfer ownership of property from one party to the other on divorce or termination of a civil partnership.[47] Alternatively the court can order that a property is sold and the proceeds of sale divided between the parties.

---

45 MCA 1973 s24.

46 CPA 2004 Sch 5.

47 Such orders can also be made on judicial separation (married partners) or when a separation order is made (civil partners). This means that the partners are formally separated but the marriage or civil partnership has not ended.

11.71   Under the Children Act (CA) 1989 the court can order one party to transfer property to a child or to another adult for the benefit of the child.[48]

11.72   In addition, where a property is legally owned by one person, a party who made a contribution to the purchase may have a 'beneficial interest'. If this cannot be agreed between the parties an application may be made to a court. This is not the same as property adjustment; it is asking the court to make a declaration about the ownership of the property in accordance with the principles of the law of trusts. In the same proceedings the court can be asked to make an order for the sale of the property and the division of the proceeds of sale. A brief summary of the relevant principles is set out at paragraphs 11.96–11.104 below.

Transfer of tenancies

11.73   Under FLA 1996 on divorce, the termination of a civil partnership[49] or if cohabitants cease to cohabit, the following tenancies may be transferred from one party to the other or from joint names into sole names:

- a secure tenancy;
- an introductory tenancy;
- an assured tenancy;
- an assured agricultural occupancy;
- a protected tenancy;
- a statutory tenancy;
- a statutory tenancy under the Rent (Agriculture) Act 1976.

11.74   The following are not capable of being transferred:

- any licence;
- a right of occupation as a 'tolerated trespasser';[50]
- a demoted tenancy.

11.75   See chapter 2 for an explanation of the types of tenancy listed above.

11.76   The court can only make an order in relation to dwelling-house which was a home shared by the parties.[51]

---

48 CA 1989 Sch 1 para 1.
49 Again, such orders may also be made when a decree of judicial separation or a separation order is made.
50 See para 5.126. It should be noted that tolerated trespass will be abolished by the Housing and Regeneration Act 2008.
51 FLA 1996 Sch 7 para 4.

11.77   A landlord must be notified of a pending application.[52]

How does the transfer happen?

11.78   Under FLA 1996 the court order has the effect of transferring the interest. The tenancy vests in the party at the date specified in the order.

11.79   Under MCA 1973, CA 1989 and CPA 2004 the court can order one party to assign the tenancy to the other. If such an order is made, the tenancy is only transferred when the actual assignment takes effect. This must be done by a properly executed deed entered into by both parties, see paragraphs 3.56–3.57.[53]

11.80   If the tenancy agreement prohibits assignment, the fact that the court has ordered the assignment does not mean that it is not in breach of the tenancy agreement. An assignment in breach of the tenancy agreement will give the landlord a ground for possession but the ground is discretionary and the circumstances in which the transfer took place will be relevant.

When will the court transfer a tenancy?

11.81 The court must apply certain criteria when deciding whether to transfer a tenancy. These are set out in the relevant Acts.

11.82   Under FLA 1996 where the transfer is on the termination of a marriage or civil partnership the criteria are:[54]

- the circumstances in which the tenancy was granted;
- the housing needs and housing resources of each of the parties and of any relevant child;
- the financial resources of each of the parties;
- the likely effect of any order, or refusal to make an order, on the health, safety or well-being of the parties and any relevant child;
- the suitability of the parties as tenants.

11.83 If parties are cohabitants the court must also have regard to:

- the nature of the parties' relationship and in particular the level of commitment involved in it;
- the length of time during which they cohabited;
- whether there are or have been any children of the relationship, or children for whom both parties have or have had parental responsibility;

---

52 FLA 1996 Sch 7 para 14(1).
53 FLA 1996 Sch 7 para 5.
54 FLA 1996 Sch 7 paras 7(2)–(4), 8 and 9. See para 3.31 for a description of the different rights of succession.

- the length of time that has elapsed since the parties ceased to live together.

The effect of a transfer

11.84　When a tenancy is transferred, whether by a court order or by assignment, the new tenant takes the tenancy subject to any limits or restrictions on the tenancy. If the tenancy was a tenancy by succession, the new tenant will be treated as if he or she is a tenant by succession.[55]

11.85　The court can order that one party pays compensation to the other for the loss of the tenancy[56] and can also make orders setting out the respective liabilities of the parties, eg ordering one party to pay rent arrears pre-dating the transfer.[57]

Protecting home rights and/or safeguarding future transfer

Tenants' residence conditions

11.86　Where the tenant is out of occupation but his or her spouse or civil partner remains in occupation this fulfils any residence condition under the tenancy agreement, see above at paragraph 11.37. However, this applies only as long as the marriage or civil partnership subsists. It is essential therefore that the tenancy is transferred before the divorce is made absolute or the civil partnership terminated. Otherwise the landlord may terminate the tenancy and evict the occupier on the basis that the tenancy has ceased to be statutorily protected.

Preventing dispositions that would frustrate a transfer

11.87　As indicated above, a spouse or civil partner can protect home rights in relation to owner occupied accommodation by registering a charge at the Land Registry. Further, the court can prevent a party from making a 'disposition' intended to defeat an application for a property adjustment order. If the disposition has already been made it can be set aside.[58]

55　FLA 1996 Sch 7 para 10.
56　FLA 1996 Sch 7 para 11.
57　MCA 1973 s37(2); CPA 2004 Sch 5 para 74.
58　*Sanctuary Housing Association v Campbell* (2000) 32 HLR 100, CA.

11.88   A home right in relation to a tenancy cannot be registered. In most cases it will not be possible to 'sell' or transfer the tenancy to another person to avoid an application for a transfer to an ex-partner. However, the tenant can terminate the tenancy in order to defeat such an application. A sole tenant can do this by either surrendering the tenancy or by serving notice to quit.[59] A joint tenant can serve notice to quit to end a periodic joint tenancy, regardless of the wishes of the other joint tenant, see paragraph 1.65.

11.89   A surrender is a disposition of property and could be prevented by the court or set aside where the parties are or have been married or in a civil partnership. However, a notice to quit is not a disposition and where a joint tenant serves notice to quit in order to prevent a future application for a transfer of the tenancy into the other tenant's sole name the court does not have the power to set the notice aside.[60]

11.90   A joint tenant can apply for an injunction to prevent the other party from serving notice to quit. This was suggested by the Court of Appeal in *Bater v Greenwich LBC*.[61] However, it is unclear whether an order prohibiting service of a notice to quit would render a notice served in breach of the order ineffective. The point is undecided but it may be that while serving notice would be contempt of court the notice would nevertheless determine the joint tenancy.[62]

Assignment by agreement

11.91   Where the parties are in agreement that the tenancy should be transferred into the sole name of one person the tenancy may be assigned. However, in most cases assignment will be prohibited and an assignment in breach of the tenancy agreement will give the landlord a ground for possession. The landlord's consent should always be sought. If the landlord does not object to the proposed transfer, the landlord may, instead of consenting to an assignment, grant a new tenancy to the party remaining in the home. Some social landlords have policies under which an offer of alternative accommodation will be made to the departing tenant on relationship breakdown. However, such policies are increasingly rare; more commonly a tenant who voluntarily leaves the home following the breakdown of a relationship will be left with the possibility of a

---

59

60   *Newlon Housing Association v Al-Sulaimain* (1998) 30 HLR 1132, HL.

61   [1999] 4 All ER 944.

62   *Harrow LBC v Johnstone* (1997) 29 HLR 475, HL.

homeless application and/or an application for an allocation. See paragraphs 13.187–13.197 below for a discussion on the homeless duty when the care of children is to be shared by two parents living in different places.

11.92   If the landlord will not agree to an assignment an application may be made for an order under FLA 1996 transferring the tenancy. The landlord will have an opportunity to make representations as to why the tenancy should not be transferred.

11.93   Under HA 1985 a secure tenant can assign to a person qualified to succeed to the tenancy which would include a spouse or civil partner or a cohabitant who has lived with the tenant for at least one year. However, such an assignment would prevent a future succession so a transfer under FLA 1996 may be preferred.

Owner occupied accommodation

11.94   Under MCA 1973 and CPA 2004 the court may transfer the ownership of property from one party to the other or may order the sale of property and the division of the proceeds of sale. An order for sale may be postponed until a future date, for example when children reach a certain age. Such orders will usually be made as part of a package of financial provision and the assistance of a specialist family lawyer should be sought to negotiate and make the necessary applications.

11.95   The court has no power to make such orders in relation to cohabitants unless there are children of the family, in which case an application can be made under CA 1989 for the benefit of the children.

Beneficial ownership

11.96   Where property is held in the sole name of one party, another party may nevertheless have a 'beneficial' interest. This arises under the law of trust, see paragraph 1.39.

11.97   An express trust may be created by deed setting out the terms of the trust.

11.98   In addition, a person who has contributed to the purchase of a property may be able to establish that an implied trust has arisen even though the parties did not expressly agree that the property was to be held on trust.

11.99   Where the parties intended that the interest would be shared this is known as a 'constructive trust' and indirect as well as direct contributions may be taken into account, such as payment of household expenses.

11.100   Where there is no shared intention that the interest would be shared this is known as a 'resulting trust'. In such a case only direct contributions to the purchase will be taken into account. This would include paying part of the deposit or the mortgage payments.

11.101   The extent of the beneficial interest will correspond to the contributions made. If the parties made equal contributions to the deposit and the mortgage payments the property will usually be held in equal shares.

11.102   If the parties are in dispute about whether there is a trust or the extent of the respective shares it will be necessary to apply to the court for a declaration. The court can also order that the property be sold and the proceeds of sale (the 'equity') divided between the parties in the proportions determined by the court. See paragraph 1.142.

11.103   Where a party is seeking to establish a beneficial interest, specialist advice should be sought. If the parties are able to reach agreement about the existence of a trust and their respective interests the costs of legal proceedings will be avoided. If not, the costs incurred will reduce the value of one or both parties' interests. This is the case even if one party is legally aided as the statutory charge will usually apply, see paragraph 22.183.

11.104   It should be noted that a spouse or civil partner who is a beneficial owner but not a legal owner is treated as having a right of occupation by virtue of FLA 1996 (as opposed to the beneficial interest). Such a home right can be registered as a charge to prevent sale until resolution of any dispute about the beneficial ownership.[63]

---

63   FLA 1996 s30(9).

CHAPTER 12

Homelessness applications, inquiries and miscellaneous duties

continued

Key points

- A local authority should accept a homeless application and make formal inquiries if it has *reason to believe* a person *may be* homeless and eligible (an immigration test).
- If the authority also has *reason to believe* the person *may be* in priority need, interim accommodation must be provided until inquiries are complete and a decision made.
- 'Homeless Prevention' strategies often result in people being discouraged from making homeless applications and encouraged to find privately rented accommodation. A homeless person is entitled to pursue a homeless application and to insist on a formal written decision from the authority as to what housing duty, if any, is owed to him or her.
- The interim accommodation provided pending inquiry must be suitable but, because it is for a very temporary period, what is deemed suitable may be of a low standard.
- A failure or refusal to accept a homeless application or to provide suitable interim accommodation pending a decision can be challenged by an application for judicial review.
- An applicant who has had a negative decision may apply again to the same authority but if the application is on the same facts the authority need not investigate. It is for the applicant to demonstrate that the application is not on the same facts.

12.1   This chapter provides an overview of the law on homelessness, and examines the following issues:

- applications;
- interim accommodation pending decision;
- the local authority duty to make inquiries;
- repeat applications;
- miscellaneous duties.

Introduction

12.2   Some homeless people are entitled to be provided with accommodation by a local housing authority. The duties of local authorities in relation to the homeless are set out in statute, with some of the detail being found in statutory instruments. Additionally, when dealing with homeless applications, local authorities must have regard to the 'Homelessness Code of Guidance for Local Authorities'. Since 1997 there has been a clear distinction between a local authority's duty to accommodate homeless applicants and the way permanent accommodation is allocated by authorities. Part VII of the Housing Act (HA) 1996 sets out the homeless duties and Part VI deals with the way permanent accommodation is allocated.

Reference materials

12.3　The main reference materials when dealing with homeless applications are:

Housing Act 1996 Part VII	Sets out: the legal tests applied to decide whether a housing duty is owed; the nature of the housing duties; and the way decisions are challenged.
Homelessness Act 2002	Amended the 1996 Act and added some general duties to prepare and review homelessness strategies.
Homelessness Code of Guidance	A summary of the law and good practice. Local authorities must 'have regard' to the Code. It is regularly updated. The current version is dated 6 July 2006 and came into force on 4 September 2006.[1]
The Homelessness (Priority Need) Order 2002[2]	Sets out some additional categories of people with priority need.
The Allocation of Housing and Homelessness (Eligibility) (England) Regulations 2006	Sets out the classes of people from abroad who are and are not eligible for homeless assistance.[3]
Case-law	The courts are frequently asked to decide disputes between applicants and local authorities. The decisions of the Court of Appeal and above are binding. County courts generally follow the decisions of the Administrative Court.

1　The Code can be downloaded from the website of the Department of Communities and Local Government at: www.communities.gov.uk.
2　This applies in England. A similar order applies in Wales, see para 13.178.
3　For issues of eligibility other regulations relating to European nationals are also relevant: see para 13.37.

Case-law *continued*	Previous decisions will be reflected in the Code of Guidance. Many challenges succeed because of a failure in the process of decision making rather than on the merits of the decision itself.

12.4   A duty to provide accommodation specifically for homeless people was first introduced by the Housing (Homeless Persons) Act 1977. Previously, local authorities had various powers and duties to provide temporary accommodation only in emergencies.

12.5   The way a duty to accommodate homeless persons is established has changed little since 1977: the authority must investigate an application to 'satisfy' itself of certain matters relating to the applicant's circumstances and the way in which he or she became homeless. The outcome of the authority's investigations will determine what duty is owed. This may range from simply providing advice and assistance to securing suitable accommodation for the applicant and his or her family. In some cases the authority's duty will be limited to providing a written decision giving reasons why no substantive duty is owed.

The 'full housing duty'

12.6   What has changed most significantly since the Housing (Homeless Persons) Act 1977 is the nature of the 'full housing duty'. Before HA 1996, if an authority determined the relevant issues in favour of the applicant and accepted the 'full housing duty' this usually resulted in an offer of a long-term tenancy by the authority or other social landlord. HA 1996 was introduced because of concern that most permanent tenancies of social housing were being allocated to homeless applicants who had priority over those on local authority housing waiting lists. HA 1996 provides that the 'full housing duty' to homeless applicants is a duty to provide temporary accommodation only; the person's need for permanent accommodation is assessed in the same way as waiting list applicants. Everyone in need of housing, including those housed temporarily as homeless people, are allocated permanent accommodation through the particular authority's allocation scheme. All such schemes must comply with the provisions of Part VI of HA 1996 which specifies the groups to whom 'reasonable preference' must be given. Homeless people are a group that must be given reasonable preference, but local authorities have considerable discretion regarding how much priority to give each group. Given the shortage of social housing, this means that many successful homeless applicants may reside in 'temporary' accommodation under Part VII for many years before they obtain permanent accommodation under Part VI. The way permanent accommodation is allocated is dealt with in chapter 16.

'Homelessness prevention'

12.7   The number of people applying and being accepted as homeless and owed a housing duty ('acceptances') increased year on year between 1997 and 2001. At the same time, families accommodated by authorities were spending longer periods in temporary accommodation before securing a permanent home. The government began to promote 'homelessness prevention' strategies following the publication of its report: 'More than a roof – a report into tackling homelessness' in March 2003. Some local authorities have adopted measures to encourage homeless or potentially homeless applicants to find accommodation in the private sector by offering rent guarantee schemes and by liaising with private landlords to encourage lettings. However, many local authorities have also adopted procedures to discourage or even prevent people pursuing homeless applications – such practices are commonly known as 'gatekeeping'. The recent homelessness statistics[4] show that the numbers of both homeless applications and homeless acceptances have fallen to the lowest levels since the early 1980s. Further, the number of households in temporary accommodation has started to decline since it reached 100,000 in 2005. These figures, however, are based on local authority returns, which indicate only those applications recorded by the authority. What is not recorded are the numbers of homeless people who approach an authority, but whose approaches are not recorded as formal applications. Ways of assisting those faced with 'gatekeeping' are discussed below.

A summary of the homelessness tests and duties

12.8   A housing authority must be satisfied of certain matters (referred to here as the 'homelessness tests') before deciding whether a

---

4   Available from the website of the Department for Communities and Local Government: www.communities.gov.uk.

housing duty is owed. Each test is dealt with in chapter 13. They are summarised here as they are essential to an understanding of the process of homeless applications and the nature of the duty that may be owed.

12.9   The full housing duty will be owed if, after inquiry, the authority is satisfied of the following matters:

- the applicant is *homeless*;
- the applicant is *'eligible for assistance'* – an immigration test;
- the applicant has a *priority need*;
- the applicant is not *intentionally homeless*.

12.10   Although the full housing duty will be owed, it may be that the duty is not owed by the authority that investigated the application. At this point the authority *may* consider:

- Whether the applicant can be referred to another authority to be housed by the other authority.

12.11   It is important that the homeless tests are applied in the correct order because the duties of the authority depend on the outcome of each test. If an applicant 'fails' one test, it may be unnecessary to go on to determine other matters. A summary of the tests and the duties owed is as follows:

The test	The duty
Is the applicant eligible?[5] Yes: apply the next test	No. Decision letter only.
Is the applicant homeless? Yes: apply the next test	No. Decision letter only.[6]
Is the applicant in priority need? Yes: apply the next test	No. Decision letter and housing advice and assistance addressing the applicant's needs.[7]

5   An authority may inquire first into homelessness or eligibility. In either case, if the answer is no, the authority's duty is limited to issuing a decision letter giving reasons.

6   An applicant who is found not eligible or not homeless is entitled to use the advice and information services that authorities are bound to provide or fund locally but there is no specific duty to advise and assist the particular applicant.

7   An authority has the power to accommodate non-priority need applicants, but only if they are found not intentionally homeless.

Is the applicant intentionally homeless? No: apply the next test	Yes. Decision letter and housing advice and assistance addressing the applicant's needs plus accommodation for a 'reasonable' period.
Can the applicant be referred elsewhere?	No. Full housing duty owed. Yes. Full housing duty owed by the other authority. Duty to accommodate temporarily continues until referral is accepted or any dispute resolved.

Making an application

12.12   It should be easy to apply as homeless to a local authority: no particular form of application is prescribed and an authority has a duty to make formal inquiries under Part VII if they 'have reason to believe' a person 'may be' homeless and eligible. Often, however, the opposite is true and the most difficult part of the process is persuading the authority to accept an application in the first place. Those who approach an authority for help may be told:

- 'you can't apply here as you have no local connection';
- 'you aren't homeless if you had somewhere to sleep last night';
- 'you have no priority need, so we can't help you';
- 'you were previously evicted for rent arrears or anti-social behaviour, so you will be found intentionally homeless';
- 'here is an application form for the housing waiting list';
- 'we can't see you until next week';
- 'we will make an appointment with the private sector team who can help you to find somewhere to live'.

12.13   In many cases the approach is not recorded or is recorded as a simple housing inquiry. It is unlawful and amounts to maladministration for an authority to refuse to accept a homeless application for such reasons.[8] However, it is often difficult to prove that the authority had evidence sufficient to trigger the duty to commence inquiries under Part VII. Advisers may therefore find

8   See the Ombudsman report into a complaint against Thurrock Council: 05/A/09461. Three approaches had been made by a woman who was clearly homeless and in priority need. However, none resulted in a proper inquiry or any decision letter being issued. The Ombudsman found that there had been injustice caused by maladministration and recommended compensation of £2,250.

it useful to ensure that a letter is sent or taken by the applicant summarising the situation and making clear that the person wishes to make an application under Part VII. See appendix for an example of such a letter.

The law on applications and the duty to make inquiries

12.14   Sections 183 and 184 of HA 1996 provide that:

> ... where a person applies to a local housing authority for accommodation, or for assistance in obtaining accommodation, and the authority have reason to believe that he is or may be homeless or threatened with homelessness ... they shall make such enquiries as are necessary to satisfy themselves – whether he is eligible for assistance, and if so, whether any duty, and if so, what duty, is owed to him under [Part VII].

12.15   The duty to make inquiries under Part VII should therefore be triggered not only when a person specifically indicates a wish to make a homeless application, but whenever a person seeks help with housing, provided the authority have *reason to believe* that the applicant *may be* homeless or threatened with homelessness.[9]

12.16   Authorities must also ensure that emergency assistance is available to applicants out of office hours. This may be by arrangement with social services or sometimes the local police, who may arrange emergency accommodation until a formal application can be taken.[10]

12.17   A refusal to accept an application may be challenged by judicial review. See chapter 21.

Restrictions on who can apply

12.18   Part VII imposes no restriction on who can make an application. However, the courts have considered arguments by local authorities that they are not bound to accept applications from the following:

- people in the UK unlawfully;
- dependent children; and
- people lacking mental capacity.

---

9   See Code of Guidance, paras 6.2 and 6.6.
10   Code of Guidance, para 6.8.

12.19   In *R on the application of Westminster v Castelli and Tristan-Garcia*[11] the Court of Appeal held that an authority was not bound to accept an application from a person who was present in the UK unlawfully. Since 1997 the eligibility test has excluded such people from assistance, along with those whose leave to remain in the UK is limited. An authority would now determine that an applicant was not eligible rather than refuse to accept an application. However, an applicant found to be ineligible has the right to a decision letter giving reasons and can challenge the decision by seeking a review and, if appropriate, by county court appeal.

12.20   Applications by children aged one year and five years were considered by the House of Lords in *R v Oldham ex p Garlick* and *R v Bexley LBC ex p Bentum* respectively.[12] The applications had been submitted on behalf of the children because the parents had been found intentionally homeless. The House of Lords held that the authorities owed no duty. This was not because an applicant must be an adult but because dependent children had no priority need: it was presumed that they were cared for by adults and it was the adults with whom they lived who had priority need.

12.21   There is clearly no requirement that an applicant be an adult as 16- and 17-year-olds are an identified class who have priority need. For those under 16 who live with adults, they will be deemed to have no priority need. For those with no adult to care for them or provide them with accommodation social services will owe a duty. See chapter 18.

12.22   In *R v Tower Hamlets ex p Begum*[13] an application was submitted on behalf of a profoundly disabled adult whose parents had been found intentionally homeless. The House of Lords held that an authority was entitled to refuse an application from someone who lacked the capacity to make an application herself, to instruct an agent to do so or to respond to an offer and understand the responsibilities of being a tenant. Again, if such a person was in need of accommodation, social services would owe a duty, but this may not extend to the whole family.[14]

11 (1996) 28 HLR 607, CA.
12 [1993] AC 509; 25 HLR 319, HL.
13 [1993] AC 509; 25 HLR 319, HL.
14 National Assistance Act 1948 s21. See para 17.13.

Multiple applications

12.23   It is possible for a person to apply to more than one authority at the same time. The Code of Guidance, at para 6.7, suggests that where this happens the authorities should agree which authority will take responsibility for making inquiries. In reality, many authorities will instead indicate that only one application can be pursued and that an application will be closed unless the other is withdrawn. This approach may be challenged, although it is difficult to see any benefit to pursuing more than one application simultaneously.

12.24   The issues that arise when a person makes a further application, having previously received a negative decision, or where an authority has discharged its duty are dealt with below at paragraphs 12.57–12.75.

Accommodation pending inquiries

12.25   An authority should accept an application if it has 'reason to believe' that a person may be 'homeless'. However, it must still go on to make full inquiries to 'satisfy' itself of the necessary matters to decide what duty, if any, is owed. In most cases the necessary inquiries will take several days at least, more often weeks or months. The Code of Guidance recommends that inquiries be completed within 33 working days,[15] but where the authority is seeking information from third parties they may take longer. In most cases the authority will have a duty to provide 'interim accommodation' until they have completed their inquiries. This duty is referred to as the 'section 188 duty'.

The nature of the accommodation duty: HA 1996 s188

12.26   Section 188(1) provides:

> If the local housing authority have reason to believe that an applicant may be homeless, eligible for assistance and have a priority need, they shall secure that accommodation is available for his occupation pending a decision on the duty (if any) owed to him under [Part VII].

12.27   The key features of the duty under section 188 are:
- the duty to provide interim accommodation arises on the basis of a low level of 'evidence': whenever the authority have reason to

15 Para 6.16 of The Code of Guidance.

believe the applicant may be homeless, eligible and in priority need: section 188(1);

- the duty arises immediately and there is no 'reasonable period' for a local authority to find accommodation;
- the duty arises irrespective of any possible referral to another local authority: section 188(2);
- the duty ends when the applicant is notified of a decision: section 188(3);
- the authority have a discretion to provide interim accommodation after a negative decision, pending a review: section 188(3);
- the accommodation must be provided for the applicant and the family members he or she normally lives with, and for anyone who might reasonably be expected to live with the applicant: section 176;
- the accommodation must be suitable: section 206.

Common issues in relation to interim accommodation

Avoiding the section 188 duty

12.28   The Act is clear – applicants with apparent priority need who present as homeless to local authorities should not remain without accommodation until a final decision is made. However, the cost of providing interim accommodation is such that many authorities seek to avoid doing so. This is usually done in one of two ways:

Refusing to admit that a homeless application was made

12.29   This can be challenged by ensuring that the local authority has sufficient evidence such that the duty to inquire and to provide interim accommodation arises, eg reason to believe that the person may be homeless, eligible and in priority need. A letter summarising the person's situation should be sufficient (see appendix to this chapter).

Arguing that there is no evidence that the person is homeless or in priority need

12.30   If the authority is saying that it has satisfied itself of these issues, a decision letter should be requested. If the authority is unable to provide a decision letter, or indicate that their inquiries are not complete, this itself indicates that the interim duty to accommodate is owed.

12.31   An example of a letter to a local authority regarding the section 188 duty is in the appendix to this chapter.

12.32   In both cases, if the authority maintains its refusal to provide interim accommodation, a claim for judicial review can be made.

Suitability of interim accommodation

12.33   The accommodation provided on an interim basis must be suitable. It is expressly provided that to be suitable, accommodation must be affordable.[16] Further, in deciding what is suitable, the authority must have regard to the law on slum clearance, overcrowding and houses in multiple occupation: HA 1996 s210. The accommodation must be suitable for the particular needs of the applicant.[17]

12.34   It is for the local authority to decide what is suitable and the temporary nature of the accommodation will be relevant: accommodation that is suitable for short-term occupation may not be suitable in the longer term. The limited resources of an authority may mean that accommodation secured for short-term occupation may not be of a high standard. However, there is a 'bottom line' for the standard, below which the accommodation could not be said to be suitable, however constrained resources are: see *R on the application of Sacupima v Newham LBC* below.

12.35   Any challenge to the suitability of interim accommodation must be brought by way of judicial review.

12.36   Because of the very temporary nature of the accommodation and the pressure on authorities' resources, the courts are reluctant to interfere with local authority decisions as to the suitability of section 188 accommodation. Set out below are a number of cases in which the issue has been considered.

Location

In *R on the application of Sacupima v Newham LBC*[18] a decision to provide section 188 accommodation in the Great Yarmouth area to a family settled in Newham was quashed. The authority had failed to have regard to the effect on the children's schooling and the employment of other family members.

---

16 Homelessness (Suitability of Accommodation) Order 1996 (SI No 3204).

17 *R v Brent LBC ex p Omar* (1991) 23 HLR 446, QBD.

18 (2000), 33 HLR 1, CA.

In *R on the application of Yumsak v Enfield LBC*[19] the court upheld the challenge to an offer of accommodation under section 188. The applicant was a single parent who had lived as an asylum-seeker in Enfield for seven years with her three children. The accommodation had been provided by social services. After being granted leave to remain in the UK, she applied as homeless and was provided with bed and breakfast accommodation in Birmingham. She contended that the accommodation was unsuitable as she suffered from epilepsy, she had no friends or family in Birmingham and her children's schooling would be disrupted. Further, the children's father was based in London and was keen to maintain contact with the children. The court held that there was an interference with the applicant's rights under ECHR article 8 and that the authority had not provided any evidence to demonstrate that no other accommodation had been available or to justify the interference.

Split accommodation

In *R v Ealing LBC ex p Surdonja*[20] the authority made an offer of section 188 accommodation to a family comprising a couple and their three young children. The accommodation was at two separate addresses less than a mile apart. The court held that the accommodation was not suitable: section 176 requires that accommodation must be available for the applicant and those family members who normally live with the applicant.

Size

In *R on the application of Flash v Southwark LBC*[21] the applicant challenged the suitability of a one-bedroom flat provided for her and her grandson on the grounds that it was too small. The court held that the offer was suitable: the grandson could sleep in the living room.

---

19 [2002] EWHC 280 (Admin).
20 (1998) 31 HLR 686.
21 [2004] EWHC 717 (Admin).

Bed & breakfast accommodation

12.37 Bed & breakfast (B&B) accommodation is commonly used as interim accommodation. The Code, however, provides that authorities should avoid using B&B accommodation wherever possible and where it is used in an emergency situation applicants should be moved to more suitable accommodation as soon as possible (see para 7.6).

12.38 There may, however, be specific reasons why B&B may not be suitable for particular applicants, such as those with disabilities or mental health problems.

Families

12.39 In relation to families and pregnant women, B&B accommodation is not to be regarded as suitable unless there is no other accommodation available and then only for a period of up to six weeks.[22]

Young people

12.40 The Code provides that B&B accommodation is unlikely to be suitable for 16- and 17-year-olds who are in need of support and that where it is used for this group it ought to be as a last resort for the shortest time possible. Further, housing authorities should ensure that appropriate support is provided where necessary (see para 12.14).

Refusal of offers made under section 188

12.41 The nature of the interim duty means that an applicant rarely has the opportunity to view accommodation or take advice if he or she believes it to be unsuitable. An applicant may be sent to the accommodation late in the evening, it may be a considerable distance away and may be in a hostel or B&B establishment. An applicant may fail to go to the accommodation or may decline to accept the offer. Alternatively, an applicant may move into the accommodation but be evicted because of his or her conduct.

12.42 In such a situation two issues arise:

- whether the authority has any further duty to make interim accommodation available; and

---

22 Homelessness (Suitability of Accommodation)(England) Order 2003 (SI No 3204). In Wales, the Homelessness (Suitability of Accommodation)(Wales) Order 2006 (SI No 3204) is more prescriptive in relation to the matters to be taken into account in relation to suitability, and more restrictive in relation to the use of B&B accommodation, for any applicant.

- the authority's duty to continue with its inquiries into the homeless application.

Continuation of the section 188 duty

12.43   If an applicant has refused an offer of interim accommodation, a decision must be made as to whether the authority's decision as to suitability can be challenged. As indicated, accommodation may be deemed suitable for very short-term occupation that would not be suitable in the longer term. Because of this, successful challenges to the suitability of interim accommodation are rare. Applicants may be well advised to indicate to the authority that, having taken advice, they now wish to accept the accommodation. The section 188 duty is not like the full housing duty: there is no express provision that the duty is ended because of a failure to accept an offer of interim accommodation. It may be argued that the applicant misunderstood the nature of the offer or did not intend to refuse it. An authority that adopts a rigid approach, maintaining that the duty has ended because of the failure to take up the offer may be challenged by way of judicial review.

12.44   Where an applicant is evicted from interim accommodation because of his or her behaviour, an authority may indicate that it has no further section 188 duty. There is no authoritative case law on this issue but the Court of Appeal have considered it in relation to accommodation offered under section 21 of the National Assistance Act (NAA) 1948.[23]

In *R v Kensington and Chelsea RLBC ex p Kujtim*[24] an asylum-seeker was provided with hotel accommodation by the authority under NAA 1948. He was evicted from two hotels because of his behaviour.

The Court of Appeal held that the duty under section 21 was a continuing duty: once a person had been assessed as needing accommodation, the authority was under a duty to provide it. However,

> if an applicant assessed as in need of ... accommodation [under section 21] either unreasonably refuses to accept the accommodation provided, or if, following its provision, by his conduct he manifests

---

23   See para 17.12 for an explanation of the duties under NAA 1948.
24   (1999) 32 HLR 579.

> a persistent and unequivocal refusal to observe the reasonable requirements of the local authority in relation to the occupation of such accommodation then the local authority is entitled to treat its duty as discharged and to refuse to provide further accommodation. That will remain the position unless or until, upon some subsequent application, the applicant can satisfy the local authority that his needs remain such as to justify provision of ... accommodation and that there is no longer reason to think that he will persist in his refusal to observe the reasonable requirements of the local authority in respect of the provision of such accommodation.[25]

12.45   It should be noted that the court held that the section 21 duty was discharged by a 'persistent and unequivocal refusal to observe reasonable requirements' but that the duty may be revived if the applicant is able to satisfy the authority that he or she will no longer persist in the behaviour complained of.

Continuation of the duty to inquire into homeless application

12.46   Even if an applicant refuses section 188 accommodation unequivocally, this does not mean that the authority can treat the homeless application as withdrawn or closed. The authority is still under a duty to complete its inquiries and issue a decision. However, a refusal of section 188 accommodation may have an adverse effect on the outcome of the inquiries. This may be the case if an applicant chooses to remain in accommodation he or she was previously told to leave or which it is argued is unreasonable for continued occupation.

12.47   Some authorities, however, encourage applicants to remain in their current accommodation by accepting a 'homeless at home' application. In such cases advisers must ensure that the authority proceeds to make a decision on the housing duty and, if a duty is owed, makes an offer of suitable accommodation without delay.[26]

Homeless inquiries

12.48   The triggering of the duty to inquire is dealt with above. To decide what, if any, housing duty is owed, the authority must satisfy itself that

---

25 Potter LJ at 593.
26 See *R on the application of Aweys v Birmingham CC* [2008] EWCA Civ 48.

the relevant 'tests' are met: homelessness, eligibility, priority need and unintentional homelessness. As a general rule, it is the local authority that must make the decision and it cannot be delegated to another person or body. An authority can, however, ask for assistance from another body in the discharge of its functions.[27] Further, it is now possible for an authority to contract out almost all of its functions under Part VI and VII.[28]

Extent of the inquiries

12.49   The burden is on the authority to make appropriate inquiries to obtain the relevant information. An applicant is not required to 'prove' his or her case, but must co-operate with the authority's inquiries.[29] This will mean agreeing to the authority contacting third parties for information and providing information when required.

12.50   The inquiries should be rigorous, but an authority need not conduct 'CID type' inquiries.[30]

12.51   An authority is not under an obligation to make all necessary inquiries to determine the truth, but can be challenged if they fail to make an inquiry that no reasonable authority could fail to regard as necessary:

> In *R v Nottingham CC ex p Costello*[31] the applicants had left accommodation that was adapted for their disabled son, alleging that it was unsuitable because they were dissatisfied with the modifications. Also, Mr Costello alleged that the property was troubled by a poltergeist. Social services had indicated that Mr Costello blamed his wife for the visitations and believed that they would occur wherever she was present. The authority made inquiries into the adaptations and decided they were suitable. In the decision letter stating that the applicants were intentionally

---

27   See HA 1996 s213; *R v West Dorset HA ex p Gerrard* (1994) 27 HLR 150, QBD; *R v Hertsmere BC ex p Woolgar* (1995) 27 HLR 703, QBD.

28   Local Authorities (Contracting Out of Allocation of Housing and Homelessness Functions) Order 1996 (SI No 3205).

29   See Code of Guidance, para 6.15, and *R v Woodspring DC ex p Walters* (1984) 16 HLR 73, QBD.

30   *Lally v Kensington and Chelsea RLBC* (1980) *Times*, 27 March, QBD.

31   (1989) 21 HLR 301, QBD.

homeless no reference was made to the poltergeist. A claim for judicial review was brought on the grounds that the authority had failed to make inquiries from witnesses about the occurrences at the premises. The authority subsequently considered the matter further and decided that in light of Mr Costello's belief that the visitations were likely to recur wherever the family lived, it was impractical for them to be moved to another location. Mr Costello denied that he had ever expressed such belief. It was submitted that the authority ought to have inquired directly of Mr Costello. This was rejected, the court holding that:

> The duty to make necessary enquiries is not a duty to make all enquiries in fact necessary before the truth is ascertained. A council which makes numerous enquiries can, in my judgment, only be attacked for failing to make one more, if it fails to make an enquiry which no reasonable council could have failed to regard as necessary.[32]

12.52 Nevertheless, if it is found that an authority has carried out inadequate inquiries, its decision will be unlawful (see para 21.68).

12.53 An alleged failure to inquire into relevant matters may now be corrected during the review process. Any complaint about inadequacy of inquiries must be raised at the review stage. An applicant may be prevented from arguing at an appeal matters not put to the authority on review.

The Court of Appeal considered challenges in relation to priority need decisions in the cases of *Cramp v Hastings BC* and *Phillips v Camden LBC*.[33] At the county court appeal it was argued that the decisions were flawed because of failures to make sufficient inquiries. However, this point had not been made in the representations submitted as part of the reviews and the Court of Appeal held that it was not appropriate to interfere with the local authorities' decisions that the applicants were not in priority need:

---

32 Schiemann, J at 309.
33 [2005] EWCA Civ 1005, 29 July 2005.

> Given the full-scale nature of the review, a court whose powers are limited to considering points of law should now be even more hesitant than [before the right of review was introduced] if the applicant's ground of appeal relates to a matter which the reviewing officer was never invited to consider, and which was not an obvious matter he should have considered.[34]

Fairness

12.54   The inquiries should be conducted fairly and interviews conducted in a sympathetic way, but this does not preclude asking searching questions in appropriate cases.[35]

12.55   Where an authority intends to take account of information adverse to the applicant, it should give the applicant the opportunity to comment on the information.[36] An authority cannot take account of information obtained in confidence if it is not able to disclose it to the applicant and obtain the applicant's comments.[37]

12.56   If, following inquiries, the authority is undecided, the issue should be resolved in favour of the applicant.[38]

Repeat applications

12.57   Many of those who receive a negative decision, or to whom a housing duty has ended, remain homeless. Several issues arise: the circumstances in which an applicant can apply again to the same authority; whether another member of the household can make an application; and whether an application can be made to a different authority.

Same applicant applying to same authority

12.58   If the reason an applicant was refused assistance is because the person was found to be not homeless, not eligible or not in priority need, it may be that there is a change of circumstances which means

---

34 Brooke LJ at [14].

35 *R v Tower Hamlets LBC ex p Khatun* (1994) 27 HLR 465, CA.

36 *R v Tower Hamlets LBC ex p Rouf* (1989) 21 HLR 294.

37 *R v Poole BC ex p Cooper* (1994) 27 HLR 605, QBD.

38 *R v North Devon DC ex p Lewis* [1981] 1 WLR 328, QBD; *R v Thurrock BC ex p Williams* (1981) 1 HLR 129, QBD.

that a fresh application may be made. For example, a person may be evicted from accommodation, having previously argued that it was not reasonable to occupy the accommodation; a woman found not to be in priority need on health grounds may become pregnant; a previously ineligible person may be granted leave to remain in the UK.

12.59   The issue will be less clear where the basis of the claim is the same, but the issue is one of degree: a person found not to be in priority need may claim that a medical condition has worsened or that they have obtained a new medical report. A person found not to be homeless on the basis of the condition of accommodation may claim that the conditions have deteriorated.

12.60   The issue also arises when the authority has found that an applicant is intentionally homeless or decided that the section 193 duty has come to an end because an offer of suitable accommodation has been refused.

12.61   The combined effect of sections 183 and 184 and section 193(9) suggest that there is nothing to prevent such a person from making a further application to the authority, which will be bound to carry out full inquiries and offer interim accommodation pending a decision. Not surprisingly, the issue has been considered by the courts on a number of occasions.

12.62   The question is whether the authority is required, in every case, to go through the whole statutory inquiry process. Alternatively, is there a 'threshold test' the authority can apply before deciding whether it is under a duty to undertake the full inquiry process? If so, what is the 'threshold test'?

In *R v Harrow ex p Fahia*[39] the court considered a second application made by a woman previously found to be intentionally homeless by the same authority. Since the first decision, she had remained in the accommodation previously provided as interim accommodation, successfully applying for housing benefit to be paid. After 12 months she was evicted and made a fresh application to the authority. The authority declined to accept the application on the basis that she had not had settled accommodation since the decision. Following a number of previously decided cases, it maintained that a fresh application would only be considered if there had been a 'material change of circumstances' or some new relevant fact had come to light.

39 [1998] 1 WLR 1396; 30 HLR 1124, HL.

The House of Lords held that this was the wrong approach. Where a person has been found intentionally homeless, he or she cannot make a further application 'based on exactly the same facts as [the] earlier application' but such cases are 'very special cases' where it can be said that there is no application before the authority.[40] Harrow had argued that they were entitled to make 'non-statutory inquires' before deciding whether they were under a duty to take a fresh application. This was rejected: there was no such short-cut available to the authority. Unless the application was based on exactly the same facts, the authority was bound to make inquiries under section 184 and to provide interim accommodation under section 188.

12.63   *Fahia* suggested that there *was* a threshold test: whether the application was based on exactly the same facts as the previous application. Having specifically excluded the possibility of 'non-statutory' inquiries, however, this left open the question of how an authority could decide whether the application was based on the same facts without making some inquiry.

12.64   This issue was considered by the Court of Appeal in the case of *Rikha Begum v Tower Hamlets LBC*.[41]

In *Rikha Begum* the applicant had rejected a suitable offer of accommodation made under Part VII. She returned to live with her parents. Subsequently, two of her brothers, one a heroin addict, also moved in. After almost two years she applied to the authority again. The authority declined to accept her application on the basis that there was no material change in her circumstances since the authority had discharged its duty on the previous application. Following *Fahia*, the court held that the authority had applied the wrong test: there was no requirement that the applicant demonstrate a material change of circumstances. Rather, an authority may only treat a fresh application as 'no application at all' if it is based on exactly the same facts as the previous application. The court went on to consider how an authority should determine the issue, setting out the following principles:

40 Brown Wilkinson at 1402D–E,
41 [2005] EWCA Civ 340.

- in deciding whether an application is based on the same facts, the authority must compare the facts at the date of the subsequent application with the facts known at the date of the previous determination (ie the section 184 decision or decision on review, not at the date of application);
- it is the applicant's responsibility to identify which facts make the application different from those at the date of the previous determination;
- if no new facts are revealed or if the facts are, to the authority's knowledge, not new or are fanciful or trivial, the authority should reject the application;
- if the new facts are not within the authority's knowledge and are not, in light of the information known to them, fanciful or trivial, the authority must accept a new application;
- it is not open to the authority to investigate the accuracy of the new facts before deciding whether to accept a new application.

12.65   It should be noted that whether an application is accepted is an issue distinct from the question of whether any duty will be owed. In *Rikha Begum* it was specifically suggested that the likely outcome of the application would be a decision that no housing duty was owed.

Applications by other household members

12.66 Where a decision has been made that no duty is owed to an applicant can another member of the household make an application in his or her name? This will depend on the reason for the decision that no duty is owed.

Intentional homelessness

12.67 If the issue is intentional homelessness another member of the household may apply to the authority. The authority cannot refuse to accept the application on the basis of the previous decision: each individual is entitled to individual consideration. The authority may, however, decide that the applicant is also intentionally homeless, having acquiesced in the decision or behaviour that caused the homelessness, see paragraph 13.270.

Discharge of duty

12.68   The Court of Appeal held in *R v Camden LBC ex p Hersi*[42] that an adult daughter who had been unaware of her mother's refusal of an offer could not re-apply on behalf of the household. At best she could apply for housing as a single person.

12.69   In *Hersi* the daughter had no priority need because the children in the household were not dependent on her.[43] It should be noted, however, that since July 2002 homeless children aged 16 and 17 have priority need (see para 13.181). Although this provision was clearly intended for children estranged from their families this is not specified. If a housing duty is owed to a homeless person, the duty is to provide accommodation for the applicant and the family members with whom he or she normally lives (see para 13.139). It would seem therefore that where a duty to the parents has been discharged, or they have been found intentionally homeless, a 16- or 17-year-old child in the household could apply and if a housing duty is owed it will be to accommodate the whole family.

Applying to another authority

12.70   There is nothing to prevent a person refused assistance by one authority from applying to a different authority. The outcome will depend on two things:

- whether the applicant can be referred, under the local connection provisions, back to the first authority; and
- the reason no duty is owed by the first authority.

No local connection referral possible

12.71   If the applicant has been refused because the applicant failed one of the substantive tests, the second authority cannot simply adopt the findings of the first authority.[44] It must make its own decision. Usually, however, the authority will obtain information from the first authority and is likely to make the same decision. While carrying out the inquiries, interim accommodation must be provided if there is reason to believe the applicant has priority need.

---

42 (2001) 33 HLR 52, QBD.

43 Note that dependent children do not have priority need in their own right. It is the adults on whom they depend who have priority need, see para 12.20 above.

44 *R v Basingstoke and Deane DC ex p Webb*, December 1989 *Legal Action* 15, QBD.

12.72   If the applicant is homeless because the section 193 duty owed by the first authority ended, the second authority must consider the application, but is likely to conclude that the person is intentionally homeless (eg because of refusing an offer or being evicted from the section 193 accommodation because of rent arrears). Alternatively, the second authority may find that no duty is owed (eg because the person has become ineligible).

12.73   If the authority makes a different decision from the first authority on a substantive issue (eg, priority need or intentional homelessness), the second authority may owe the full housing duty.

Local connection referral possible

12.74   Again, if the applicant was refused assistance by the first authority because of failing one of the substantive tests, the second authority must consider the application and make its own decision. An authority that knows that the full housing duty will be owed by another authority may be less rigorous in its inquiries. The authority may find that the person is in priority need or not intentionally homeless when the first authority had decided those issues negatively. Unless the first authority can challenge the decision by way of judicial review, it will be under a duty to accept a referral and will owe the full housing duty.[45]

12.75   However, if a section 193 duty owed by the first authority has ended (eg, because of the refusal of an offer) the first authority can refuse to accept the full housing duty following a local connection referral on the basis that it has already discharged its duty to the applicant. In that instance, a duty will be owed by neither authority.

Miscellaneous duties

Duties to particular applicants

Threatened homelessness

12.76   Local authorities also have duties to those who are 'threatened with homelessness'. A person is threatened with homelessness if he or she is likely to become homeless within 28 days.[46]

---

45 See *R v Newham LBC ex p Tower Hamlets LBC* [1992] 2 All ER 767.
46 Section 175(4).

12.77   If the authority is satisfied that a person is eligible, has a priority need and is not threatened with homelessness intentionally, the duty is to 'take reasonable steps to secure that accommodation does not cease to be available for [the applicant's] occupation'.[47]

12.78   If the authority is not satisfied that the applicant has a priority need, or is satisfied that the applicant is threatened with homelessness intentionally, the duty is to provide the applicant with advice and assistance in any attempts he or she makes to secure that the accommodation does not cease to be available. Alternatively, it may refer the applicant to another agency for such advice and assistance.[48]

12.79   In practice local authorities rarely make full inquiries or issue decision letters at the stage when a person is threatened with homelessness. Assistance will usually be given by the authority's housing advisory services or by voluntary agencies acting in co-operation with the authority. Strictly, the duty does not arise unless homelessness is likely within 28 days. However, where there is a chance of avoiding homelessness, for example by negotiating with a landlord or helping to resolve housing benefit problems, few authorities will restrict the help they give.

12.80   The duty is most relevant when a person is certain to become homeless, but the date of actual eviction is not imminent. In such cases most authorities' homeless persons departments will advise a person to return nearer or on the date of eviction. The specific duty to begin the inquiry process in relation to a particular applicant does not arise until the date of expected homelessness is within 28 days. However, within the 28 day period steps should be taken by the authority to identify suitable accommodation.[49]

12.81   Local authorities also have general duties regarding the provision of advice and assistance and in relation to the prevention of homelessness and those services will be available to an applicant even if a specific duty has not yet arisen.

Protection of property

12.82   A local authority has a duty in relation to the property of a homeless applicant, where the authority:

---

47 Section 195(2).
48 Section 195(5).
49 *R v Newham LBC ex p Khan and Hussain* (2000) 33 HLR 29, QBD.

have reason to believe that –

(a) there is a danger of loss of, or damage to, any personal property of an applicant by reason of his inability to protect it or deal with it, and

(b) no other suitable arrangements have been or are being made.[50]

12.83 The duty is to 'take reasonable steps to prevent the loss of the property or mitigate damage to it'.[51] The authority may make 'reasonable charges' and may specify conditions regarding the disposal of the property, for example if charges are not paid or the belongings not collected.[52] In most cases when an applicant is in receipt of means tested benefit there will be no or minimal charges made. However, the full cost of the storage of belongings may be charged to an applicant with sufficient means to pay.

Liaison with social services – children

12.84 Where a local authority has reason to believe that an eligible applicant whose household includes a dependent child may be intentionally homeless, or threatened with homelessness intentionally, it must ask the applicant for consent to refer his or her case to the relevant social services department. If consent is given, the case must be referred to the social services department to consider exercising its powers and duties under the Children Act (CA) 1989.[53]

12.85 Local authorities may give financial assistance to such a family under CA 1989 s17 to assist them to secure private sector accommodation. However, such assistance is discretionary and many authorities will instead offer assistance by way of taking the children into care. See chapter 18 for an explanation of social services' duties under CA 1989.

Advice and assistance

12.86 Local authorities have a duty to provide advice and assistance to applicants who are found not to be in priority need and to those found intentionally homeless. In both cases the advice and assistance must be tailored to the needs of the applicant:[54]

---

50 Section 211(1).
51 Section 211(2).
52 Section 211(4).
53 Section 213A.
54 See sections 190 and 192.

- the authority must provide the applicant with advice and assistance in any attempts he or she makes to find accommodation (or must ensure that others do so);
- the applicant's housing needs must be addressed before advice and assistance is given; and
- the advice and assistance must include information about the likely availability of types of accommodation appropriate to the person's housing needs (including in particular, the location and sources of such types of accommodation).

12.87   It should be noted that under section 192(3) an authority has a power to secure accommodation for a person found not to have a priority need. For someone found to be intentionally homeless there is a duty to provide temporary accommodation for a reasonable period (see para 15.14).

General duties

Advice and information

12.88   Every local authority must ensure that advice and information about homelessness and the prevention of homelessness is available free of charge in their district.[55] An authority may also fund voluntary organisations to provide services to prevent or alleviate homelessness.

Homelessness strategies

12.89   Under the Homelessness Act 2002 all local housing authorities have a duty to formulate and publish a 'homelessness strategy'. Further, a new homelessness strategy must be published every five years.[56] The deadline for the publication of the first homelessness strategies was July 2003, so that new strategies should have been published no later than July 2008.

12.90   The published document must set out the authority's strategy for:[57]

- preventing homelessness;
- ensuring that sufficient accommodation is available for the homeless in the district; and

---

55 Section 179(1).
56 Homelessness Act 2002 s1. The duty is disapplied in relation to local housing authorities Categorised as 'excellent' under the Local Government Act 2003.
57 Homelessness Act 2002 s3.

- securing the satisfactory provision of support for the homeless in the district.

12.91   In exercising its functions (including those under Part VII) the authority must take its homelessness strategy into account.[58]

12.92   Often, an authority's strategy may be expressed in expansive terms, in contrast to the restrictive application of Part VII by the authority's homeless persons' department. Being familiar with the authority's strategy may assist in challenging a decision made in relation to an individual application.

In *R on the application of Omatoyo v City of Westminster*[59] the applicant was a man with a history of homelessness, drug and substance abuse, offending and prison. He was found not to be in priority need and refused interim accommodation pending review. The council's homelessness strategy indicated that it aimed to reduce the numbers of rough sleepers in the district and that it had a target of ensuring that all offenders released on licence were assisted to access appropriate accommodation. Mr Omatoyo applied for permission to bring judicial review proceedings to challenge the decision not to provide interim accommodation. At the hearing the court was required to consider the merits of the decision subject to review. One of the factors the judge considered relevant to the lawfulness of the decision was that the authority had failed to take account of its own homelessness strategy. Permission to bring the claim was granted.

---

58   Homelessness Act 2002 s1(5).
59   [2006] EWHC 2572 (Admin), 21 September 2006.

Homeless applications

Letter to local authority – homeless applications and interim accommodation

Dear Sir/Madam,

Re: Mrs A

We are advising the above named who has made a homeless application to your authority.

[Set out some details about application/dealings with the council]

Mrs A is a British national who has lived in the UK all her life. She is therefore eligible for assistance.

Mrs A is homeless, having been told to leave her sister's accommodation.

Mrs A is pregnant and has a dependant child, aged two years. She is clearly in priority need.

Mrs A first approached your authority on [date] and informed you that she had been asked to leave her sister's accommodation as it is overcrowded. She was advised by an officer at reception that her sister was required to give her written notice. Her sister then gave her seven days written notice and she returned to your offices on expiry of the notice. She was then advised that she could not be seen until the following week. She was forced to return to her sister's home and her sister reluctantly agreed that she could stay until her appointment with the homeless person's unit.

At the appointment a homeless application form was completed but Mrs A was told that she must remain at her sister's home until a decision had been made. Our client's sister indicated that our client could stay for only two further days.

When our client returned to your offices two days later she was told that the authority did not accept that she was homeless. When we telephoned your office we were told that your authority were of the view that our client could continue to reside with her sister but that any decision must be approved by the manager who was currently on leave.

[Set out the law]

As your authority is aware, under section 188 of the Housing Act 1996 if you have *reason to believe* that an applicant *may be* homeless you have a duty to carry our inquiries under Part VII of the Act. Further, if you have *reason to believe* that an applicant *may be* eligible and in priority need you have a duty to provide interim accommodation until a decision is notified to our client.

If you are still carrying out inquiries then the duty is to provide interim accommodation until our client is notified of your decision.

If you have concluded your inquiries then our client is entitled to be notified in writing of the decision.

[What you want them to do and by when]

Can you please confirm by close of business today that interim accommodation will be provided to Mrs A until you notify her of your decision on her application. Alternatively, please can you forward to us the decision letter made pursuant to section 184. We enclose our client's signed authority for you to send this to us.

If we do not hear from you by [time and date] we can only assume that you are refusing to either provide interim accommodation or to issue a decision letter.

We will then advise our client to commence judicial review proceedings/refer our client to our legal team/a solicitor with a view to a claim for judicial review.

Yours faithfully

Adviser
Advice Agency

[If this letter is being sent by solicitors or an agency with an LSC contract to provide legal representation the letter should be in the form of a judicial review protocol letter – see chapter 17, appendix 2 for an example. This means that proceedings can be issued immediately if the issue is not resolved within the deadline]

CHAPTER 13

The homelessness tests

continued

continued

Key points

- A local authority has to provide accommodation for homeless people only if it is satisfied of the matters set out below.

The person is homeless

- A person can be homeless if s/he has accommodation but it isn't reasonable to continue to live in it.
- It is not reasonable to live in accommodation if violence is probable.

The person is eligible

- Certain people from abroad are 'ineligible'. This includes people who do not have leave to be in the UK or who have leave that is limited. It also includes European nationals who do not have a 'right to reside' in the UK and some people, including British nationals, who are not habitually resident in the UK. If a person is ineligible no housing duty will be owed.

The person has priority need

- There are several categories of priority need. If a homeless person does not have priority need the only duty an authority has is to give advice and assistance to find accommodation. Some categories of priority need depend on the local authority finding that a person is 'vulnerable'. Such decisions usually depend on the strength of expert evidence about a person's physical or mental health.

The person is not intentionally homeless

- If a person has caused his or her homelessness by something done or not done deliberately he or she will usually be intentionally homeless. There are several elements to the test and each element must be addressed. An authority must identify the deliberate act or omission that caused the homelessness.

The person may be referred to another authority

- If a person applies to a local authority where he or she has no local connection, that authority may refer the person to another

> authority to be housed. This should only be done after all the inquiries have been completed and it has been decided that a housing duty is owed.

Eligibility

13.1   In homelessness law 'eligibility' has a specific meaning: it is a test that excludes certain people from abroad from homeless assistance.[1]

13.2   The test of eligibility is relevant to three classes of people:

- people from outside Europe who need leave to enter or remain in the UK;
- European nationals and their families;
- people who are not 'habitually resident'.

13.3   The basic provisions are set out in section 185 of the Housing Act 1996 with the detail set out in regulations. The most important regulations are:

- the Allocation of Housing and Homelessness (Eligibility) (England) Regulations 2006 (Eligibility Regulations 2006), as amended;[2]
- the Immigration (European Economic Area) Regulations 2006 (EEA Regulations 2006).[3]

13.4   A person who is not eligible cannot be provided with homeless assistance: section 185(1). Further, an authority must disregard anyone in the applicant's household who is ineligible when deciding whether the applicant is homeless or in priority need: section 185(4).

---

1   Similar tests are applied to exclude access to social security benefits and community care services.
2   SI No 1294. These regulations apply to all applications made on or after 1 June 2006. For applications made before that date the regulations in force at the time apply. Between 1996 and 2006 the regulations were amended and replaced several times. The 2006 Regulations were amended by the Allocation of Housing and Homelessness (Miscellaneous Provisions) (England) Regulations 2006 (SI No 2527).
3   SI No 1003.

Persons subject to immigration control

13.5   Anyone 'subject to immigration control' is not eligible unless they are in one of the classes of exceptions set out in the Eligibility Regulations 2006: section 185(2).

13.6   To apply the test therefore the first question is whether the person is subject to immigration control. If so, the next question is whether they are on the list of exceptions.

Who is subject to immigration control?

13.7   Anyone who needs leave (permission) to enter or remain in the UK, whether or not such leave has been granted, is a person subject to immigration control.[4] It is simplest to list those persons who do not need leave to enter or remain. They are:[5]

- British citizens;
- Commonwealth Citizens with 'right of abode';[6]
- nationals of certain European countries who have a right to reside (see below);
- Irish nationals.[7]

13.8   Anyone not listed above will be subject to immigration control. To be eligible such a person must be in a class listed in regulation 5 of the Eligibility Regulations 2006. These are set out below.

People subject to immigration control and eligible

Class A: refugees

13.9   This means someone recognised as a refugee in the UK who has been granted leave on that basis.

---

4   See HA 1996 s185(2); IAA 1996 s13(2); IA 1971 s1, and IA 1988 s7(1).

5   In addition, certain diplomatic and military personnel do not require leave to enter or remain in the UK.

6   Right of abode is enjoyed by Commonwealth citizens born before 1 January 1983 who had a parent born in the UK, and women who were Commonwealth citizens before 1 January 1983 and who were married before that date to a man who was born, registered or naturalised in the UK, or who is a Commonwealth citizen with a parent born in the UK. Whether or not a person has a right of abode may be endorsed in the passport. It is also possible to obtain a 'certificate of entitlement' from the Home Office. In the absence of such evidence of right of abode or if there is any uncertainty, a person who believes they may have a right of abode should be referred to a specialist in immigration and nationality law. In immigration law a person claiming a right of abode has the burden of proving the right.

7   See section 1(3) of the Immigration Act 1971.

13.10   The current Home Office practice is to grant five years 'limited' leave to refugees. Prior to 30 August 2005 the practice was to grant Indefinite Leave to Remain (ILR).

Class B: exceptional leave – no condition as to public funds

13.11   A person with exceptional leave to remain[8] (ELR) is eligible provided the leave is not subject to a condition that he or she cannot have 'recourse to public funds'.

13.12   ELR means any leave granted outside the Immigration Rules. ELR used to be given to asylum-seekers who were not granted full refugee status but who nevertheless needed protection. Since April 2003 this type of ELR has been replaced by humanitarian protection and discretionary leave. Humanitarian protection is granted under the immigration rules and is dealt with below. Discretionary leave remains a form of exceptional leave granted outside the immigration rules. It is granted to child asylum-seekers whose asylum claims have been refused and is now granted until the child is 17.5 years old. It is also used when a person is disqualified from a grant of humanitarian protection but nevertheless cannot be removed. Where discretionary leave is granted to an asylum-seeker it will not be subject to the 'no recourse to public funds' rule.

13.13   Leave may also be granted outside the immigration rules for 'compassionate' reasons, for example to allow an elderly relative to join family members in the UK. In such cases the leave will usually be subject to the 'no recourse to public funds' condition which should be stamped on the passport. Such people are not eligible for homeless assistance.

Class C: leave to enter or remain without limit or condition

13.14   The grant of leave to enter or remain in the UK that is not subject to any limitation or condition is often referred to as Indefinite Leave to Remain (ILR). It is also referred to as 'settlement' or 'settled status'. ILR used to be granted to refugees prior to 30 August 2005. ILR is granted to certain people who have previously enjoyed more limited leave, eg spouses of British nationals. Since April 2007 most applicants for ILR must pass a test in English and demonstrate knowledge of life in the UK.

---

8   In April 2003 the Home Office announced that the term Exceptional Leave to Remain would not be used in future and that the term 'Leave Outside the Rules' (LOTR) would be used. However, the term ELR is still more commonly used.

Sponsored immigrants

13.15　An exception to the general rule that a person with ILR is eligible applies to some sponsored immigrants. Sponsorship exists when a person is given leave to enter the UK on the basis of an undertaking given by someone else in the UK that he or she will be responsible for that person's accommodation and maintenance. A sponsored immigrant is not eligible unless more than five years have passed (since entry or the undertaking was given, whichever is later) or the sponsor has died.

13.16　In all cases a person who is eligible because of having ILR must also be habitually resident in the UK, the Channel Islands, the Isle of Man or the Republic of Ireland (see below).

Class D: humanitarian protection

13.17　A person who has been granted humanitarian protection ('HP') under the immigration rules is eligible. HP is granted to people who are not recognised as refugees but who would, if returned, face a real risk of suffering serious harm. 'Serious harm' consists of: the death penalty or execution; unlawful killing; torture or inhuman or degrading treatment or punishment; or, serious and individual threat to life by reason of indiscriminate violence in situations of international or internal armed conflict.[9] In some cases a person may be excluded from humanitarian protection, for example, because of war crimes or other serious crimes, or being deemed a threat to national security. Such people will usually be granted discretionary leave.

Class E: pre April 2000 asylum-seekers

13.18　Before 1996 all asylum-seekers were entitled to homeless assistance. Between 1996 and 2000 only asylum-seekers who claimed asylum at the point of entry to the UK were entitled to homeless assistance. However, eligible asylum-seekers became ineligible if the asylum claim was refused, despite having the right to appeal against the decision. There remains some transitional protection for those who claimed asylum before the law changed in 1996 and 2000. The following asylum-seekers are still eligible for homeless assistance:

- an asylum-seeker who claimed asylum before 3 April 2000 on arrival in the UK;

9　Immigration Rules paras 339C–D.

- an asylum-seeker who was in Great Britain when a 'declaration of upheaval' was made and who claimed asylum within three months – this applies only to nationals of Sierra Leone or Democratic Republic of Congo (DRC, formerly Zaire) who made their claims in 1997;[10] and
- an asylum-seeker who claimed asylum on or before 4 February 1996 and who was, on that date, entitled to housing benefit.

13.19   Note that in all of the above cases the Home Office must have recorded the claim for asylum at the relevant date. The provisions only apply to those whose claim for asylum is still outstanding. In a small number of cases in which the claim for asylum was made many years ago, no decision has yet been made by the Home Office. If the claim is refused the person immediately becomes ineligible. If some kind of leave is granted, the person will be eligible under Class A, B or D above.

13.20   Advisers should take care when assisting someone whose claim for asylum was made several years ago. Some asylum-seekers may be unaware that a negative decision has been made. For those whose claims were made before 2000 it is advisable to contact the Home Office general enquiry number to find out what their records indicate. The Home Office reference number will be needed.

13.21   All other asylum-seekers are ineligible: they need leave to enter the UK and do not have it. The 'temporary admission' granted to asylum-seekers is not leave.

Common problems for persons subject to immigration control

Spouses and domestic violence

13.22   A person who marries a British national or someone settled in the UK will be granted leave to remain for an initial period of two years and this will be subject to the 'no recourse to public funds' condition. This is because, before granting leave, the Home Office must be satisfied that the couple will have adequate accommodation and resources without relying on state benefits. If, during this two-year period, the foreign spouse is the victim of domestic violence and leaves the matrimonial home, he or she will be ineligible for homeless assistance or any social security benefits. The only possible

---

10   The only relevant declarations were made on the following dates: DRC – 16 May 1997, Sierra Leone – 1 July 1997. The person must also have been in Great Britain on the day the declaration was made.

assistance will be from social services under the Children Act 1989, or, if the person has community care needs, under the National Assistance Act 1948: see chapters 17 and 18 below.

13.23   The Home Office has a policy to grant Indefinite Leave to Remain to such victims of domestic violence provided the necessary evidence of the domestic violence exists.[11] However, until a decision is made by the Home Office the person remains ineligible for homeless assistance.

Long-standing residents without documentation

13.24   Some people, particularly from Commonwealth countries, have been in the UK since childhood but have never been granted any form of leave to enter or remain in the UK. Often such people will have a National Insurance number and may have been living and working in the UK for many years. However, unless they have a right of abode (see para 13.7 above) they are subject to immigration control and are therefore ineligible for homeless assistance (and social security benefits).

13.25   Such a person may apply for ILR and, depending on the circumstances, this may be granted under the Immigration Rules, under certain policy concessions, or because the refusal of leave would involve a breach of human rights. However, there may be a delay before a decision is made on an application and in the meantime the person will be ineligible for homeless assistance.

Leave that expires

13.26   A person with leave to enter or remain in the UK may apply to extend the period of leave, or to vary the conditions of leave. Provided an application is made before the leave expires the person is treated as continuing to have the same leave subject to the same conditions until the Home Office make a decision.[12] If refused, an appeal can be made from within the UK and the person continues to be treated as having the same leave until the appeal is determined.

13.27   However, if leave expires before an application is submitted to the Home Office the person becomes an 'over-stayer' and does not have any form of leave pending a Home Office decision. Such a person is

---

11 Immigration Rules, para 289A.
12 Immigration Act 1971 s3C.

ineligible for homeless assistance until the Home Office grants further leave.

Home Office delays

13.28   In all of the above examples, great hardship may be caused by the long delays that are common when the Home Office are considering applications.[13] Until the Home Office grant leave to remain the applicant may face destitution: rules similar to those applied in relation to homelessness will prevent the person from receiving social security benefits such as income support and housing benefit and, in most cases, the person will be prohibited from working.

13.29   It may be appropriate in such a case for an application to be made for judicial review of the Home Office failure to make a decision. The person's immigration solicitor or adviser should be asked to advise on this course of action: sometimes a person's right to remain in the UK will be stronger if a decision is made after a longer period of residence.

European nationals

Introduction

13.30   The European Union (EU)[14] is a group of countries that have entered into treaties whereby certain rights are enjoyed by nationals of each member state in other member states. The most significant of these rights is the right to work and to seek work in another member state. Member nationals who are exercising EU rights in another European country generally enjoy the same rights as nationals of that country.[15] The UK therefore has an obligation under the EU treaties to allow EU nationals, exercising treaty rights, access to the UK's social welfare provisions.

13.31   One confusing factor in relation to EU nationals is that law and practice diverge. In theory, an EU national who is not exercising rights under the EU treaties is a person subject to immigration

---

13 The Home Office claim to be addressing a 'backlog' of between 400,000 and 450,000 outstanding asylum applications and aim to complete the task by 2011.

14 The European Community was established in 1957 and renamed the European Union in 1993 by the Maastricht Treaty. The terms 'EC' and 'EU' are generally used interchangeably.

15 Discrimination on the grounds of nationality is unlawful provided the person is exercising an EU right.

control.[16] However, under EU law the UK has an obligation to admit all European nationals to the UK on production of a national identity card or passport.[17] Local authorities must therefore make decisions not on documentary evidence of immigration status but on an assessment of a person's current or past activity and residence in the UK.

13.32   In 1996, as part of a raft of legislation restricting the access of persons from abroad to various kinds of social assistance, the 'habitual residence test' (HRT) was introduced in housing and benefit law. The test was directed at so called 'benefit tourism' and provided that certain European and British nationals who were not habitually resident in the UK were ineligible for homeless assistance. However, the test could not exclude from assistance EU national exercising European community rights in the UK: such people were exempt from the test.

13.33   In 2004 the EU was enlarged when ten new countries became members. In response to concern that nationals from the poorer of the new member states would become eligible for homeless assistance and social security benefits a further condition was introduced: only those with a right to reside were eligible. The right to reside is enjoyed by a person exercising certain European treaty rights, principally the right to work in another member state. However, for nationals of eight of the new member states it was necessary not only to be working but, for an initial period, to be registered to work in order to be eligible.

13.34   The relevant law is found in the regulations introduced under the European Communities Act 1972 which bring into domestic law the rights granted by virtue of EU directives. They are summarised below.

The European Economic Area

13.35   The European Economic Area (EEA) comprises the countries that are members of the EU plus four countries that are members of the European Free Trade Association (EFTA), which have free trade agreements with the EU. All the EEA countries are listed below, with a distinction made between some of the more recent member states whose nationals' rights are currently limited (known as the 'Accession States' or the 'A10' states) and 'full member' states.

16   Immigration Act 1988 s7(1).
17   Directive 2004/38/EC and Reg 11 of the of the EEA Regulations 2006.

Full Member States	'A8' States – joined 1 May 2004	'A2' States – joined 1 January 2007
EU Members	EU Members – limited rights	EU Members – limited rights
Austria		
Belgium	Czech Republic	Bulgaria
Cyprus	Estonia	Romania
Denmark	Latvia	
Finland	Lithuania	
France	Hungary	
Germany	Poland	
Greece	Slovakia	
Ireland	Slovenia	
Italy		
Luxembourg		
Malta		
Netherlands		
Portugal		
Spain		
Sweden		
Plus		
Iceland		
Liechtenstein		
Norway		
Switzerland		
Workers' rights	**Workers' rights**	**Workers' rights**
Right to reside if working	Right to reside if working but must be registered for the first 12 months	Right to reside if working but must be registered for the first 12 months Must obtain registration before taking up employment in UK

Europeans and eligibility

13.36 Only European nationals with a 'right to reside' in the UK can be eligible for homeless assistance. However, two types of right to reside do not confer eligibility: a 'jobseeker's' right to reside and an initial right to reside for three months. If a person's only right to reside is one or both of these rights, he or she is not eligible for homeless assistance.[18]

18 Eligibility Regulations 2006 reg 6(b).

13.37   The relevant regulations in relation to European nationals and eligibility are:

Regulations	Provisions	Short Name
The Immigration (European Economic Area) Regulations 2006 (SI No 1003)	Sets out the way in which rights of residence are established	EEA Regulations 2006
The Accession (Immigration and Worker Registration) Regulations 2004 (SI No 1219)	Sets out the registration requirements for Accession State nationals	Accession Regulations 2004
The Accession (Immigration and Worker Authorisation) Regulations 2006 (SI No 3317)	Sets out the particular registration requirements for A2 nationals. Makes some amendments to the Accession Regulations 2004, to include reference to A2 nationals.	Accession Regulations 2006

The right to reside

13.38   The EEA Regulations 2006 set out which EEA nationals have a right to reside in the UK. They are intended to bring into UK law the rights and obligations contained in the EC Directive: 2004/38/EC.[19] This is a directive 'on the right of citizens of the Union and their family members to move and reside freely within the territory of the Member States'.

13.39   Under the EEA Regulations 2006 'qualified persons' and their family members are entitled to reside in the UK while the relevant person remains a qualified person.[20] In addition, some provision is made for family members to enjoy extended rights of residence in certain circumstances. Further, permanent rights of residence may be acquired after certain periods of residence and/or activity.

---

19 This Directive amended and repealed certain previous directives that concerned the rights of free movement and residence throughout the EU. The repealed directives are: 64/221/EEC, 68/360/EEC, 72/194/EEC, 73/148/EEC, 75/34/EEC, 75/35/EEC, 90/364/EEC, 90/365/EEC and 93/96/EEC. The Regulation No 1612/68 is amended and partly repealed.
20 Regulation 14(1) and (2) of the EEA Regs 2006.

Qualified persons and family members

13.40 A qualified person is an EEA national who is in the UK as one of the following:[21]

- a job-seeker;
- a worker;
- a self-employed person;
- a self-sufficient person;
- a student.

13.41 Workers and the self-employed may retain their status during temporary periods of incapacity in certain circumstances.

13.42 In addition, close family members of qualified persons also have a right to reside. Extended family members may have a right to reside if they satisfy certain conditions. This is dealt with below.

Job-seekers

13.43 Job-seekers from full member states have a right to reside but neither they nor their family members are eligible for homeless assistance if this is their only right to reside.

13.44 A 'job-seeker' means a person who entered the UK to seek employment and who can provide evidence that he or she is seeking employment *and* has a genuine chance of being engaged.[22]

13.45 Accession state nationals do not gain rights of residence by virtue of being job-seekers.[23]

Unemployed former workers who are job-seekers

13.46 A former worker who is unemployed and registered as a job-seeker may continue to be classed as a worker and therefore continue to have a right to reside and to be eligible for homeless assistance. See below at para 13.55.

Workers

13.47 Qualified persons include:

- full member nationals who are working;
- A10 nationals who are registered as workers; and

---

21 EEA Regs 2006 reg 6.
22 EEA Regs 2006 reg 6(4).
23 The Accession Regulations 2004 reg 4(2).

- A10 nationals who have been registered workers for 12 continuous months and are now working unregistered.

Rights of residence by working – full member nationals

13.48 For full member state nationals simply working in the UK gives a right to reside. Such a person becomes eligible as soon as he or she commences employment.

13.49 Further, the status of 'worker' may be retained during even extended periods of unemployment, provided certain conditions are met, see below.

Rights of residence by registered working – A10 nationals

13.50 A10 nationals have a right to reside initially only if they are registered as workers. After a continuous period of 12 months as a registered worker the same rules apply as for full member state nationals – simply working is sufficient and the status of worker may be retained during periods of unemployment. In calculating the continuous 12 month period, a period of up to 30 days (over the whole period) unemployment is disregarded (see para 13.62).

13.51 The rules are different for A8 nationals and A2 nationals. A8 nationals are free to come to the UK, find work and then to register. A2 nationals must obtain registration documentation before taking up employment in the UK and authorisation to work will only be granted for certain occupations.

13.52 The registration requirements are explained in more detail below.

Meaning of 'worker'

13.53 The European Court's decisions on the question of what it is to be a worker indicate the following:

- being a worker means being employed, in the sense of being obliged to provide services for another person in return for money and being subject to the control of the other person as regards the way the work is done;
- there is no minimum period for which the person must have been employed and the employment need not be permanent or full time;
- the employment must be 'effective and genuine economic activity' and not activity that could be regarded as 'purely marginal and ancillary';

- the fact that the remuneration may be below the minimum wage or insufficient to support the person without the person claiming benefits in addition is irrelevant.[24]

Sickness and unemployment

13.54 Full member nationals and A10 nationals who have completed 12 continuous months of registered employment may still be considered a worker during periods of sickness and unemployment.

13.55 Such a person is still treated as a worker if he or she:[25]

- is temporarily unable to work as a result of an illness or accident; or
- having been employed in the UK, is unemployed involuntarily, provided he or she has registered as a jobseeker; and
  - was previously employed for at least one year before becoming unemployed; or
  - has been unemployed for no more than six months; or
  - can provide evidence that he or she is seeking employment in the UK and has a genuine chance of being engaged; or
- is unemployed involuntarily and has embarked on vocational training; or
- has voluntarily stopped working and has embarked on vocational training related to the previous employment.

Accession State nationals – the worker registration scheme

The first 12 months

A8 Nationals[26]

13.56 All Accession State nationals must register with the Home Office as an Accession State worker for the first 12 months of being employed in the UK. A8 nationals may commence employment and apply for registration within the first month. The employer is known as an 'authorised employer' and the registration is specific to that employer. An A8 national is eligible for homeless assistance if he or she is:

- within the first month of employment;[27] or

---

24 See Homelessness Code of Guidance, particularly Annex 12.

25 EEA Regs 2006 reg 6(2).

26 The registration requirements for A8 nationals are set out in the Accession Regulations 2004, as amended by the Accession Regulations 2006.

27 Accession Regulations 2004 reg 7(3).

- has applied for registration within the first month but the application has not yet been processed by the Home Office;[28] or
- has been given an Accession Worker Registration Card and an Accession Worker Registration Certificate (and is still working for the authorised employer).[29]

13.57   If an A8 national stops working for the authorised employer but finds employment with another employer, a new application for registration must be made, again within the first month of the new employment.

A2 nationals[30]

13.58   A2 nationals must obtain registration documents from the Home Office before commencing employment. Registration documents will only be issued if the proposed employment falls within an authorised category of employment.[31] These include 'Sector Based Schemes' (mainly temporary contracts in agriculture and food processing), au pair placements, domestic workers in private households, postgraduate doctors, dentists and trainee GPs. The aim of the scheme is to limit the number of unskilled workers entering the UK.

13.59   In addition, registration documents will be issued to A2 nationals who qualify for work permits under the Home Office work permit scheme and to 'highly skilled' persons seeking employment in the UK. A highly skilled person means someone with a degree with 2nd class honours or above, a masters degree or doctorate awarded by an institution in England, Wales or Northern Ireland or a Higher National Diploma or degree awarded by an institution in Scotland.

13.60   In all cases, to have a right to reside in the UK and to be eligible for homeless assistance the worker must have the necessary documentation from the Home Office authorising them to work for a particular employer, unless authorised to *seek* work as a highly skilled person.

---

28 Accession Regulations 2004 reg 7(2)(b).
29 Accession Regulations 2004 reg 5(2).
30 The relevant regulations for A2 nationals are the Accession Regulations 2006. However, these regulations also amended the Accession Regulations 2004 so as to include Bulgarian and Romanian nationals in the general definition of 'Accession State national'. For A2 nationals therefore reference must be made to both the 2004 and the 2006 regulations.
31 These are set out in Schedule 1 of the Accession Regulations 2006.

13.61   All A10 nationals are eligible for homeless assistance while they are registered workers. However, such a person ceases to be eligible if he or she becomes unemployed for longer than the 30-day period permitted. Any duty to accommodate will cease. If the person is subsequently able to find alternative employment and obtain registration again, he or she will again become eligible.

After 12 months continuous employment

13.62   After 12 months continuous employment the worker will become entitled to the same rights as a full member national. A cumulative period of up to 30 days unemployment in the first 12 months is permitted and will not break the required 12-month period. However, if the period of unemployment exceeds 30 days in the first 12 months, this means that the worker will have to build up a further 12 months of continuous employment.

13.63   For an A2 national, the same rules apply. However, it will be more difficult for an A2 national to satisfy the condition if not employed continuously by the same employer. An A2 worker cannot legally commence employment without registration in advance. To ensure continuity an A2 national would have to find new employment and obtain the necessary documents from the Home Office before commencing that employment, all within 30 days.

Self-employed people

13.64   Article 43 of the EU Treaty[32] specifically provides that European nationals have a right to 'establish' themselves in another member state for the purpose of being self-employed or running a business. The EEA Regulations 2006 do not define 'self-employment' but simply state that a self-employed person means a person who establishes him or herself to pursue activity as a self-employed person in accordance with article 43.[33]

13.65   To establish eligibility a person will have to provide evidence of their economic activity as a self-employed person, such as invoices, bank statements and tax returns.

13.66   It is not necessary for a self-employed person also to be 'self-sufficient'. Those who are self-employed but whose income is limited may be eligible for Working Tax Credit and Child Tax Credit as well as Housing Benefit and Council Tax Benefit.

32 The Treaty of Nice.
33 Regulation 4(1)(b) of the EEA Regs 2006.

13.67   Arguably, self-employment must, like employment, be 'genuine and effective' and more than a 'marginal and ancillary' activity.

13.68   Accession state nationals are not required to register in order to be self-employed in the UK. Conversely, being self-employed for 12 months does not give accession state nationals the rights enjoyed by full member nationals.

13.69   A person temporarily unable to pursue activity as a self employed person as the result of an illness or accident is still treated as self-employed.[34]

Self-sufficient people

13.70   A self-sufficient person is someone who has:

- sufficient resources not to become a burden on the social assistance system of the UK during the period of residence; and
- comprehensive sickness insurance in the UK.[35]

13.71   Self-sufficient people have a right to reside and are therefore eligible but the very fact of applying for homeless assistance may be evidence that the conditions are not met and that the person is therefore not, or is no longer, a qualified person. However, the circumstances of the person's homelessness will be relevant. If the difficulty is temporary or caused by an emergency such as a flood or fire, it may be argued that the emergency assistance required does not necessarily mean that the person has become a burden on the social assistance system.

13.72   It should be noted, however, that, in contrast to workers and the self-employed, there is no specific provision that a person in temporary difficulty should continue to be regarded as self-sufficient.

13.73   The Homelessness Code of Guidance[36] suggests that where an applicant was previously self-sufficient, guidance should be sought from the Home Office.

13.74   Accession state nationals are not required to register as self-sufficient persons. However, being self-sufficient for 12 months does not qualify accession state nationals for the rights enjoyed by full member nationals.

---

34 EEA Regs 2006 reg 6(3).

35 EEA Regs 2006 reg 4(1)(c).

36 Annex 12, para 34.

Students

13.75 An EEA national who is a student in the UK has a right to reside. However, the term 'student' is strictly defined. A student is someone who:[37]

- is enrolled to follow a course of study at a private or public establishment listed on the Department of Education and Science Register, or an establishment financed from public funds. This may include vocational training; and
- has comprehensive sickness insurance; and
- assures the Home Office, by means of a declaration or something similar, that he or she has sufficient resources not to become a burden on the social assistance system of the UK during the period of residence.

13.76 Accession State nationals who are students have the same rights of residence as full member nationals.

13.77 If the student has family members who will live with him or her in the UK, the assurance given to the Home Office must cover the whole family who must also be covered by comprehensive sickness insurance.[38] The family members of students who enjoy rights of residence are more restricted than for other qualifying persons (see para 13.98).

13.78 In contrast to those who are self-sufficient, a student does not cease to be a qualified person by virtue of making an application for social assistance, eg making a homeless application. However, such an application would suggest that the assurance given to the Home Office initially has not been honoured.

Working while studying

13.79 There is no limit on the number of hours a student who is a national of a full member state may work while studying. An EEA student who is working as well as studying will also have a right of residence as a worker provided the work is not marginal and ancillary.

13.80 Students from the Accession States are permitted to work for up to 20 hours a week and as part of vocational training and during vacations. A2 nationals must have registration certificates confirming this. However, an Accession State national who satisfies the criteria to live in the UK as a student is not required to obtain worker

37 EEA Regs 2006 reg 4(1)(d).
38 EEA Regs 2006 reg 4(3).

authorisation under the worker registration scheme, but unregistered working will not lead to 'full member' rights after 12 months.

Permanent rights of residence

13.81   Those who have a right of residence by virtue of working, being self-employed, self-sufficient or a student retain the right of residence while they are pursuing the relevant activity and may continue to be qualified persons during temporary periods of inactivity. The Regulations also make provision for an EEA national, and his or her family members, to gain a right of permanent residence after certain periods of activity and residence in the UK.

13.82   The following people may gain a right of permanent residence:[39]

- those who have lived in the UK continuously for five years 'in accordance with the regulations';
- those who have previously worked in the UK but are now retired or permanently incapacitated;
- the family members of the above;
- the family members of a deceased worker who was a qualifying person.

Five years' continuous residence

13.83   The regulations provide that an EEA national who has resided in the UK 'in accordance with these Regulations for a continuous period of five years' acquires the right to reside in the UK permanently.[40] Also, a non-EEA national who has resided in the UK as a family member of an EEA national for the same period 'in accordance with these Regulations' also acquires the right to reside in the UK permanently.[41]

13.84   The meaning of residing 'in accordance with these Regulations' is unclear. The Regulations are intended to implement the Directive 2004/38/EC and article 16 of the Directive provides:

> Union citizens who have resided legally for a continuous period of five years in the host Member State shall have the right of permanent residence there.

---

39   EEA Regs 2006 reg 15(1).
40   EEA Regs 2006 reg 15(1)(a).
41   The condition specifically includes any period during which a person carried out an activity or was resident in accordance with the EEA Regulations 2000 which preceded the EEA Regs 2006: Sch 4 para 2.

13.85   It may be argued that the right described in the Directive is not as circumscribed as the EEA Regulations 2006 suggest. However, in an Immigration Appeal Tribunal case it was held that article 16 was to be construed as a reference to legal residence under European rather than domestic law: an A8 national who only became an EEA national on the accession in 2004 could not rely on lawful residence prior to that date to establish a right of permanent residence on the basis of five years lawful residence in the UK.[42]

13.86   In addition to qualifying persons and their family members, those family members who have 'retained' rights of residence (see para 13.107) also gain a permanent right to reside after five years continuous residence.[43]

Retirement or permanent incapacity

13.87 A worker or self-employed person who has ceased activity, because of retirement or permanent incapacity, will gain a permanent right to reside if the conditions set out below are met.

Retirement

13.88 If retired, the person must have been employed or self-employed for at least 12 months and have lived in the UK continuously for more than three years. If previously employed, the person must either have reached the age to qualify for a state pension or have taken early retirement. If previously self-employed, the person must have reached the age to qualify for a state pension.[44]

Incapacity

13.89 If permanently incapacitated, either:

- the person must have lived in the UK continuously for more than two years before the termination; or
- the incapacity must have been caused by an accident at work or an occupational disease that entitles him or her to an occupational pension paid in full or part by a UK institution.[45]

---

42 *GN (EEA Regulations: five years' residence) Hungary* [2007] UKIAT 00073, 26 June 2007.

43 EEA Regs 2006 reg 15(f).

44 EEA Regs 2006 reg 5(2).

45 EEA Regs 2006 reg 5(3).

The minimum periods of residence and employment or self-employment

13.90   In both cases the necessary period of residence or activity must have been immediately before termination of employment or self-employment.[46]

13.91   The requirement for a minimum period of residence or activity does not apply to an EEA national who is married to or in a civil partnership with a UK national.[47]

13.92   During periods of inactivity a person may still be treated as being employed or self-employed provided if it is for reasons not of the person's own making, or due to illness or accident, see above. Similarly, a worker who is registered as a job-seeker during a period of involuntary unemployment is classed as continuously working for these purposes.[48]

Family members on death of worker or self-employed person

13.93   Where the worker or self-employed person has died, a family member gains a right to reside in the UK permanently if the following conditions are met:

- the family member resided with the person immediately before the death; and, either
  - the deceased had resided continuously in the UK for at least the two years immediately before the death; or
  - the death was the result of an accident at work or an occupational disease.[49]

Meaning of 'continuous residence'

13.94   In calculating any period of 'continuous residence' referred to in the regulations, the following are disregarded:[50]

- any periods of absence from the UK that do not exceed 6 months in total in any year;
- periods of absence for military service; and

---

46 See paras 13.55 and 13.69.
47 EEA Regs 2006 reg 5(6).
48 EEA Regs 2006 reg 5(7).
49 EEA Regs 2006 reg 15(1)(e).
50 EEA Regs 2006 reg 3.

- any one absence from the UK not exceeding 12 months for an important reason such as pregnancy and childbirth, serious illness, study or vocational training or an overseas posting.

Losing the permanent right of residence

13.95   Once acquired, the right of permanent residence is only lost through absence from the UK for a period exceeding two consecutive years.[51]

13.96   However, all of the permanent rights of residence are subject to the Home Office powers to remove or exclude EEA nationals in limited circumstances.

Family members of qualifying persons

Close family members

13.97   The close family members of qualified EEA nationals (other than students) and EEA nationals with a permanent right of residence also enjoy a right to reside. Close family members are defined as:[52]

- a spouse or civil partner;
- children and grandchildren, including those of the spouse or civil partner, provided they are under 21 or dependent on the qualified person or his or her spouse or civil partner; and
- dependent parents and grandparents, including those of the spouse or civil partner.

Students

13.98   In the case of those who are qualified as students, the only family members who have a right to reside for longer than for an initial three months are:

- a spouse or civil partner;
- dependent children under the age of 18.[53]

Family resources – self-sufficient persons and students

13.99   If the EEA national is a qualified person by virtue of being self-sufficient, the resources of the whole family must be sufficient to

---

51   EEA Regs 2006 reg 15(2).
52   EEA Regs 2006 reg 7.
53   In all cases the children and grandchildren must be the direct descendents of the qualified person or his or her spouse or civil partner. This, however, includes adopted and step children.

ensure that none become a burden on the social assistance scheme and the necessary comprehensive sickness insurance must cover all of the family members.[54]

13.100   If the qualified person is a student the assurance given by the student to the Home Office regarding sufficient resources is satisfied only if the resources are sufficient to avoid the student and his or her family members becoming a burden on the social assistance system.[55]

13.101   When calculating whether a family has sufficient resources the resources will be deemed sufficient if they are more than the maximum level to qualify for social assistance (ie above the income limit for eligibility for receipt of income support).[56]

Extended family members

13.102   The following relatives and members of the household may gain a right to reside as 'extended family members' if they satisfy certain conditions.:[57]

Dependent member of household

13.103   This means a relative of an EEA national, his or her spouse or civil partner who is dependent on him or her and is a member of the household.

Relatives requiring personal care

13.104   This means a relative of an EEA national, his or her spouse or civil partner who 'on serious health grounds' strictly requires the personal care of the EEA national, his or her spouse or civil partner.

Relatives who would qualify for ILR

13.105   This means a person who is a relative of an EEA national and who, if he or she were applying to join a non-EEA national who was present and settled in the UK, would qualify for indefinite leave to remain on that basis.

---

54 EEA Regs 2006 reg 4(2). However, if the family members are themselves EEA nationals they may be qualified persons in their own right.
55 EEA Regs 2006 reg 4(3).
56 EEA Regs 2006 reg 4(4).
57 EEA Regs 2006 regs 7(1)(d) and 8(2)–(5).

Co-habitees

13.106 This means the same or opposite sex partner of an EEA national who is not a civil partner or spouse and who can prove he or she is in a durable relationship with the EEA national.

Family members – retaining the right of residence

13.107 The general rule is that family members enjoy a right of residence in the UK only so long as the EEA national remains a qualified person and they remain family members.[58] However, the EEA Regulations 2006 make provision for the family members' rights of residence to continue in some situations. They are:

- on the death of the qualified person;
- on divorce or termination of a civil partnership;
- where children are in education.

Death of qualified person[59]

13.108 If the qualified person dies, a non-EEA family member retains the right of residence provided he or she had lived in the UK for at least the year immediately before the death and is a worker, self-employed or self-sufficient person or the family member of such a person.

13.109 Note that, in addition, in certain circumstances a family member of a qualified person who dies may gain a permanent right of residence, see para 13.93 above.

Termination of marriage or civil partnership[60]

13.110 Where a non-EEA national ceases to be a family member of a qualified person because of the termination of the marriage or civil partnership the right of residence will be retained provided the following conditions are satisfied:

- the person must have been residing in the UK at the date of termination; and
- he or she must be a worker, self-employed or self-sufficient person or the family member of such a person; and
- one of the following conditions is satisfied:
  - the marriage or civil partnership had lasted for at least three years and the parties had resided in the UK for at least one year of its duration,

---

58 EEA Regs 2006 reg 14(2).
59 EEA Regs 2006 reg 10(2).
60 EEA Regs 2006 reg 10(5).

- the former spouse or civil partner has custody of a child of the qualified person,
- the former spouse or civil partner has the right of access to a child (under the age of 18) of the qualified person and a court has ordered that it must take place in the UK, or
- the continued right of residence in the UK is warranted by particularly difficult circumstances, such as the person or another family member having been a victim of domestic violence during the marriage or civil partnership.

13.111   In all the above cases the right to reside is only retained if the family members are themselves working, self-employed or self-sufficient. Family members who are EEA nationals already have such rights by virtue of their nationality. This provision therefore only benefits non-EEA family members.

Children in education

13.112   Where a qualifying member dies or ceases to be a qualified person on ceasing to reside in the UK, any children or grandchildren attending educational courses in the UK retain a right of residence as long as they continue to attend such a course.[61] The person must have been attending an educational course immediately before the qualified person died or ceased to be a qualified person.

13.113   In addition, if the person is a child, any parent with actual custody also retains a right of residence in the same circumstances.[62]

13.114   The conditions set out in the EEA Regulations 2006 are described above, but the Regulations do not necessarily set out exhaustively the rights of EU nationals and their family members (see para 13.120 below).

Exclusion and removal

13.115   All of the rights of residence referred to, including permanent rights, are subject to the right of the government to exclude or remove a person if it is justified on grounds of public policy, public security or public health. Regulations 19 and 20 set out the criteria on which such decisions are made. The criteria for exercising these powers are stricter when considering excluding or removing a person with a permanent right to reside than otherwise.

---

61 Regulation 10(3) of the EEA Regs 2006.
62 Regulation 10(4) of the EEA Regs 2006.

Documents and evidence of status

13.116 EEA nationals must be admitted freely to the UK[63] and they are not required to have any form of documentation, such as a residence permit or passport stamp confirming a right to enter or to reside in the UK.

13.117 The only people with a right to reside that derives from EU law who are required to have documentation to confirm their status are as follows:

Person	Documents issued by Home Office
Accession State workers and their family members in first 12 months of working	Workers Registration Certificate and Workers Registration Card
Non-EEA nationals with a right to reside by virtue of being the family member of an EEA national	Family Permit, residence card or permanent residence card

13.118 Any other EEA national or family member who has a right to reside *may* apply for registration or a residence card from the Home Office but need not do so in order to establish a right to reside. Such documents will be issued free of charge. A local authority is not entitled to insist that a person obtain such documentation.

13.119 In all cases the local authority must assess for itself whether the person has a right to reside in the UK. Clearly, a local authority will usually need to seek documentary evidence of status in the form of, for example, contracts of employment, wage slips, tax returns, bank statements, marriage or civil partnership certificates etc. However, as in all cases, obtaining documentary evidence is part of the inquiry process and not a pre-requisite before the inquiry process can begin or before interim accommodation can be provided.

Rights of residence outside the regulations

13.120 With regard to the right to reside under EU law there remains an unresolved issue: whether the Directive 2004/38/EC and the EEA Regulations 2006 exclusively govern the right to reside. It has been argued in two cases before the Court of Appeal that a right to reside may be established outside of the EEA Regulations 2006.

---

63 EEA Regs 2006 reg 11(1).

In *Abdirahman v Leicester City Council & Secretary of State for Work and Pensions, Ullusow v Secretary of State for Work and Pensions*[64] the Court of Appeal considered the cases of two EEA nationals who had been refused benefits. Both appellants were in the UK to be near to family members but did not have a right to reside by virtue of either their own economic activity or being the family member of a qualified person. They argued that they had each entered the UK lawfully; they had remained in the UK without any breach of immigration law; and, they were entitled to remain unless and until action was taken to remove them. They submitted that they must be regarded as having a right to do what they were doing lawfully, that is, residing in the UK and relied on article 18 of the EU Treaty which provides that:

> Every citizen of the Union shall have the right to move and reside freely within the territory of the Member States, subject to the limitations and conditions laid down in this Treaty and by the measures adopted to give it effect.

The Court of Appeal dismissed the appeals holding that article 18 did not establish a right of residence so as to entitle the appellants to benefits because the relevant directive provided that:

> ... beneficiaries of the right of residence must not become an unreasonable burden on the public finances of the host Member State.

Any rights of residence were subject to the limitations imposed by the directive which were proportionate to the legitimate objective of protecting the public finances of the host Member State.

In *Ibrahim v Harrow LBC*[65] the applicant was a Somali national married to a Danish citizen. He was working in the UK and she came to the UK to live with him. Two of the couple's four children were at school in the UK. Having worked for less than a year her husband stopped working and received incapacity benefit for a few months. He was then declared fit for work but did not resume work and after a short period he left the UK and lived in Eastern

---

64 [2007] EWCA Civ 657, 5 July 2007.
65 [2008] EWCA Civ 386, 21 April 2008.

Europe for a period. Under the EEA Regs 2006 he ceased to be a qualified person shortly before he left the UK.

The housing authority decided that the applicant was not eligible for homeless assistance because neither she nor her husband were exercising community law rights to reside in the UK. At her appeal she argued that although her husband had ceased to be a qualified person before leaving the UK she could rely on a provision of the EC Regulation 1612 of 1968 which provides:

> The children of the national of a Member State who is or has been employed in the territory of another Member State shall be admitted to that State's general educational, apprenticeship and vocational training courses under the same conditions as the nationals of that State, if such children are residing in its territory.

> Member States shall encourage all efforts to enable such children to attend these courses under the best possible conditions.

The county court found that the appellant had a directly enforceable right to reside by reason of being the parent and primary carer of children who had acquired directly effective rights of residence under this provision. Although the authority had correctly applied regulation 10 of the EEA Regs 2006, that regulation was deficient in that it did not give proper effect to the rights arising under article 12 of the 1968 Regulations. The respondent therefore erred in law in failing to give effect to those rights and the decision was quashed.

The local authority appealed to the Court of Appeal which has referred the issue to the ECJ for determination. The case is unlikely to be decided before 2009 or 2010.

13.121   When dealing with issues of eligibility advisers may wish to consult the Directive as well as the EEA Regulations. The Directive is binding on the UK and in some respects suggests that rights of residence may be established in circumstances less prescriptive than those set out in the Regulations. The directive can be downloaded from the website of 'EUR-Lex': http://eur-lex.europa.eu.

The habitual residence test

13.122 When first introduced in 1996 the test was designed to exclude European nationals who were not ordinarily resident in the UK and who would otherwise have been eligible for homeless assistance immediately on arrival in the UK. The test had to be applied equally to British and European nationals otherwise it would have breached EU law. Between 1996 and 2004 any EEA national who was habitually resident in the UK was eligible for homeless assistance. Further, any European exercising a treaty right, such as working, did not have to satisfy the test at all. The test is less important now since only those EEA nationals with a right to reside can be eligible and most of those with a right to reside are exempt from the habitual residence test.

Who must satisfy the habitual residence test?

13.123   The following homeless applicants must be habitually resident in order to be eligible:

- persons who are subject to immigration control but who have indefinite leave to remain in the UK;
- British nationals;
- EEA nationals whose right to reside is by virtue of being self-sufficient;
- EEA nationals, and their family members, who have a permanent right to reside by virtue of five years residence.

Who is exempt from the habitual residence test?

13.124   None of those persons who are subject to immigration control but eligible, except those with ILR, are required to be habitually resident.[66]

13.125   Further, the Eligibility Regulations 2006 provide that the following people shall not be treated as ineligible by virtue of not being habitually resident:[67]

- EEA nationals who are workers, self-employed or registered accession state workers, and their family members;
- EEA nationals who have a right to reside permanently in the UK under regulation 15(c), (d) or (e) of the EEA Regs 2006 (workers and self-employed people who are retired or permanently incapacitated and their family members, plus the family members of a deceased worker or self-employed person: see paras

---

66   These classes of eligible persons are those who may not have been in the UK for a long period and may not necessarily wish to settle in the UK: refugees, those with unconditional ELR or HP and asylum-seekers.

67   EEA Regs 2006 reg 6(2).

13.87–13.93 for the conditions as to gaining a permanent right of residence under these provisions); and

- a person who is in the UK as a result of deportation, expulsion or other removal by compulsion of law from another country to the UK.

What is the habitual residence test?

13.126 To satisfy the test a person must be habitually resident in the UK, the Channel Islands, the Isle of Man or the Republic of Ireland: the Common Travel Area (CTA).

13.127 Legislation provides no definition of the term 'habitual residence' but it has been considered by the courts in a number of cases. Usually, a person must show that he or she has taken up residence and lived for a period in the CTA.[68] However, the situation is different for a person who has previously been habitually resident and is returning to resume an habitual residence previously established. He or she should not fail the habitual residence test solely on the ground that he or she has not lived in the CTA long enough.[69]

13.128 There is no minimum period that will establish habitual residence. The central question is where a person's 'centre of interest' is. This will involve considering the person's home, family ties, social connections and employment. Someone who has lived in the UK for only a few months may nevertheless be found to have established his or her centre of interest in the UK. Another person may have been in the UK for longer but his or her centre of interest may be elsewhere, for example someone who retains a home elsewhere and whose family is in another country. The test is not simply about how long a person has been present in the UK but about whether he or she is resident for a settled purpose.

13.129 Annex 10 of the Code of Guidance sets out a useful summary of the application of the test.

Ineligible members of the household

13.130 Section 185(4) provides that a person who is not eligible must be disregarded for the purpose of deciding whether another person is homeless or in priority need. This will be relevant where a couple has no accommodation they can occupy together. If one partner is

---

68 *Nessa v The Chief Adjudication Officer* [1999] 1 WLR 1937, HL.
69 *Swaddling v Adjudication Officer* (ECJ) [1999] ECR I-1090, EC.

ineligible, he or she is ignored and the eligible person will be found not to be homeless if he or she has accommodation that can be occupied as a single person. Similarly, if the female partner is pregnant, ordinarily both individuals would have a priority need but if the pregnant woman is ineligible she would be ignored and her partner would have no priority need. It may be the case that the applicant is eligible but has a dependent child who is ineligible.[70] Again, the child is ignored and the applicant will not have a priority need by virtue of the child.

13.131   This only applies in relation to homelessness and priority need: if the applicant is homeless and in priority need for other reasons, and the full housing duty is owed, account must be taken of the ineligible members of the household when deciding what accommodation is suitable for the household.

> In *R on the application of Morris v Westminster City Council*[71] the applicant was a British citizen but her young daughter was subject to immigration control. She applied for homeless assistance but the authority decided, applying HA 1996 s185(4), that they could take no account of her daughter and therefore Ms Morris had no priority need. By the time of the final hearing her daughter had become a British national and was therefore eligible. However, the Court of Appeal made a declaration under the Human Rights Act 1998 that section 185(4) was incompatible with the European Convention on Human Rights. The provision discriminated on the grounds of nationality and could not be justified. However, to date, section 185(4) remains in force.
>
> The Court also considered whether, in such a situation, an authority was bound to exercise its discretion to provide accommodation under other powers to avoid a breach of human rights. The Court held that an authority was not bound to do so; indeed, it would be an illegitimate use of discretion to exercise it in order to circumvent the legislation, even though the legislation was incompatible with the Convention.

---

70   It is unusual but possible for the nationality or immigration status of the child to be different from that of the parent.

71   [2005] EWCA Civ 1184.

13.132   Until the government takes action to deal with the incompatability authorities are bound to apply section 184(4). At the time of writing, the government has announced an intention to amend the law so as to create a temporary, limited housing duty to those in Ms Morris' position.

Homelessness

13.133 The homelessness test, like the eligibility test, can be described as a 'threshold' test: if the authority is not satisfied that a person is homeless, no duty is owed under Part VII of The Housing Act 1996.

13.134   To be homeless does not necessarily mean to be without any form of accommodation. A person is also homeless under Part VII if he or she has accommodation but living in it puts person at risk of violence, or if the nature of the accommodation is such that it is not reasonable to continue to live there.

Definition of homelessness

13.135 HA 1996 s175, defines homelessness as follows:

> (1) A person is homeless if he has no accommodation available for his occupation, in the United Kingdom or elsewhere, which:
>   (a) he is entitled to occupy by virtue of an interest in it or by virtue of an order of a court,
>   (b) he has an express or implied licence to occupy, or
>   (c) he occupies as a residence by virtue of any enactment or rule of law giving him the right to remain in occupation or restricting the right of another person to recover possession.
> (2) A person is also homeless if he has accommodation but:
>   (a) he cannot secure entry to it, or
>   (b) it consists of a moveable structure, vehicle or vessel designed or adapted for human habitation and there is no place where he is entitled or permitted both to place it and to reside in it.
> (3) A person shall not be treated as having accommodation unless it is accommodation which it would be reasonable for him to continue to occupy.

13.136 HA 1996 s177 refers to the risk of violence. It provides:

> (1) It is not reasonable for a person to continue to occupy accommodation if it is probable that this will lead to domestic violence or other violence against him, or against:

(a) a person who normally resides with him as a member of his family, or

(b) any other person who might reasonably be expected to reside with him.

For this purpose 'violence', means violence from another person; or threats of violence from another person which are likely to be carried out; and violence is 'domestic violence' if it is from a person who is associated with the victim.

13.137 Broadly therefore there are three possible ways in which a person may be homeless:

1. *No accommodation*: the person has no accommodation in which he or she is permitted or has a legal right to reside;

2. *Accommodation but not reasonable to occupy*: the person may have accommodation but it is not reasonable to occupy it.[72] This may be because of the risk of violence or for other reasons;

3. *Accommodation but excluded from occupation*: the person may have a legal right to occupy accommodation but be physically excluded from it; or the accommodation may be a mobile home and the person has no pitch or mooring for it.

13.138 The legislation and case law in respect of each of these categories is examined below.

Meaning of 'available' accommodation

13.139 In every case, accommodation must be available for a person to occupy together with his or her family or 'household'. A central aim of the homelessness legislation has always been to keep families together. HA 1996 s176 applies in relation to any reference in Part VII to 'accommodation' and provides:

Accommodation shall be regarded as available for a person's occupation only if it is available for occupation by him together with:

(a) any other person who normally resides with him as a member of his family, or

(b) any other person who might reasonably be expected to reside with him.

---

72 Although the term used is 'continue to occupy', it is not necessary that the person has previously occupied: *Waltham Forest LBC v Maloba* [2007] EWCA Civ 1281, 4 December 2007. See para 13.154 below.

13.140 Section 176 applies not only to the definition of homelessness but also to the definition of intentional homelessness and to the accommodation provided by an authority when discharging its housing duties.

13.141   Family members are not defined, but the Homelessness Code of Guidance provides that 'the phrase "member of the family" will include those with close blood or marital relationships and cohabiting partners (including same sex partners)'.[73]

Who might reasonably be expected to live with the applicant?

13.142 Family members who normally live with a person must be regarded as part of that person's household. However, it is for the authority to decide in respect of other people whether it is reasonable to expect them to reside with the person. This could include partners who have not previously lived together or other family members who do not normally live together but wish to do so. In addition it may include people who are not family members and the Code suggests that this group 'might include a companion for an elderly or disabled person, or children who are being fostered by the applicant or a member of his or her family'.[74]

13.143   The family members who normally live with a person and anyone else who might reasonably be expected to live with a person are referred to in this chapter as 'the household'.

1. Having no accommodation

What constitutes 'accommodation'?

13.144 The mere fact that a person's right to occupy accommodation is only temporary does not mean that the person is homeless. However, he or she must occupy 'a place which can fairly be described as accommodation'.[75] The following has been held not to be 'accommodation':

- a night shelter where a bed was provided on a nightly basis and the occupant was not allowed to remain indoors during the day;[76]
- a prison cell occupied by someone eligible for release on licence.[77]

---

73 Paragraph 8.5.
74 Paragraph 8.6.
75 *R v Brent LBC ex p Awua* [1996] 27 HLR 453 at 459.
76 *R v Waveney DC ex p Bowers* [1983] 4 HLR 118, CA.
77 *R on the application of B v Southwark LBC* [2004] HLR 3, QBD.

13.145 This issue overlaps with the question of whether it is reasonable to occupy accommodation which is dealt with below.

What is a right or permission to occupy accommodation?

13.146 Section 175 of the Housing Act 1996 srefers to entitlement to occupy by virtue of an interest or by virtue of a court order. A tenant or owner-occupier has an 'interest' in a property. A person may occupy by virtue of a court order where a family court has made an order that he or she may occupy a former matrimonial home despite not being the tenant or owner. Section 175 also refers to having an express or implied licence to occupy. This would include a person granted permission to share premises as a lodger or family members who live in the family home. A person may also occupy a home because of 'any enactment or rule of law' that gives the person the right to remain in occupation or that restricts 'the right of another person to take possession'. This would include a statutory tenant who no longer has a contractual tenancy (see para 2.86) and also a person against whom a possession order has been made but who has not yet been evicted.

Practical issues

Possession proceedings – when does the occupier become homeless?

13.147 As is described in chapter 5 the court can make possession orders that allow occupiers to remain in occupation provided they comply with certain conditions. Some orders end the tenancy and others give the landlord the right to apply to end the tenancy if the conditions are breached. Even where the order ends the tenancy, a person who remains in occupation (as a 'tolerated trespasser') is not homeless as there is a restriction on the right of the landlord to take possession. Further, even where the court has no power to suspend or postpone possession, the occupier does not actually lose the right to occupy until the date of the eviction.

> In the case of *R v Newham LBC ex p Sacupima*[78] the Court of Appeal considered the issue of exactly when someone subject to a possession order becomes homeless. The applicant had an assured shorthold tenancy and occupied the accommodation with

78 (2001) 33 HLR 1, CA.

her five children. Her landlord obtained a possession order and she approached the local authority for help. She was advised to await the bailiff's warrant and to return on the day of the eviction with her children and belongings. Ms Sacupima brought the claim to challenge the suitability of the interim accommodation. She also argued that the authority's duty to provide interim accommodation under section 188 had arisen as soon as the possession order was made, as this ended her legal right to occupy the accommodation. The Court of Appeal held that this was not the case: she became homeless only when evicted by the bailiffs. Until that date there was a restriction on the landlord's right to take possession.

13.148   It is the practice of many local authorities to advise people against whom a possession order has been made to return on the day of the eviction or shortly before. However, an authority should always consider whether it is reasonable for an occupier to remain in occupation until the eviction. Indeed this issue may need to be addressed at an earlier point – when the occupier receives notice of intended possession proceedings, particularly where the occupier has no defence to a possession claim.

13.149   The Code of Guidance sets out the approach an authority should take to applicants who have received notice of possession proceedings:

> Para 8.32: Each case must be decided on its facts, so *housing authorities should not adopt a general policy of accepting – or refusing to accept – applicants as homeless or threatened with homelessness when they are threatened with eviction but a court has not yet made an order for possession or issued a warrant of execution.* In any case where a housing authority decides that it would be reasonable for an applicant to continue to occupy their accommodation after a valid notice has expired – and therefore decides that he or she is not yet homeless or threatened with homelessness – that decision will need to be based on sound reasons which should be made clear to the applicant in writing ...
>
> *The Secretary of State considers that where a person applies for accommodation or assistance in obtaining accommodation, and:*
>
> (a) *the person is an assured shorthold tenant who has received proper notice in accordance with section 21 of the Housing Act 1988;*
> (b) *the housing authority is satisfied that the landlord intends to seek possession;*

and

> (c) *there would be no defence to an application for a possession order; then it is unlikely to be reasonable for the applicant to continue to occupy the accommodation beyond the date given in the section 21 notice, unless the housing authority is taking steps to persuade the landlord to withdraw the notice or allow the tenant to continue to occupy the accommodation for a reasonable period to provide an opportunity for alternative accommodation to be found.*

[the italic emphasis appears in bold in the Code]

13.150   In practice authorities rarely issue a formal decision at this stage, but the Code is clear: authorities should consider whether it is reasonable for such a person to remain in occupation pending eviction and, if they decide that it is, a reasoned decision should be given in writing. The decision will be a decision that the person is not homeless and carries a right of review.

13.151   An authority may lawfully depart from the Code if there is reason to do so. Many authorities will justify their decision on the grounds of the expense of interim accommodation and the fact that the time people spend in interim accommodation can be reduced by remaining in their own home as long as possible. However, this will only be a valid justification if the authority is actively dealing with the application prior to eviction rather than just advising people not to approach until the day of eviction. Advisers may wish to press an authority for a written determination at an early stage, addressing the issue of whether it is reasonable for the occupier to remain in occupation. When forced to explain the decision in writing, the authority may concede the issue and offer interim accommodation prior to the actual eviction.

The cost of possession proceedings

13.152   When a possession order is made by the county court the usual rule is that the occupier will be ordered to pay the landlord's legal costs. It is possible for any party to civil proceedings to make an application to join another party (a third party) to the proceedings and to seek an order that the third party pays the costs of the claimant, the defendant or both (see para 22.167). It is possible therefore, in possession proceedings, to ask the court to join the local authority and order it to pay the costs of the landlord. However, if such an application is made and is unsuccessful, this will increase the total costs of the proceedings and the occupier will usually be ordered to pay both the costs of the landlord and the local authority.

13.153   An alternative course of action is to make a formal complaint to the authority and seek reimbursement of the costs of the possession claim. If not resolved satisfactorily, further complaint may be made to the Local Government Ombudsman. However, the Ombudsman would have to find that there was maladministration in order to uphold the complaint and recommend compensation.[79]

Accommodation available anywhere in the world

13.154 If an applicant has accommodation anywhere in the world, he or she may not be homeless. The accommodation must, however, be available to the applicant and his or her household, and it must be reasonable to live in the accommodation.

In *Nipa Begum v Tower Hamlets LBC*[80] the Court of Appeal considered a decision that the applicant was not homeless because accommodation was available to her in Bangladesh. Ms Begum was a 21-year-old British national, born in Bangladesh. She had lived in the UK from the age of 13 or 14, but at the age of 17 had married in Bangladesh before returning to the UK. Later she stayed in Bangladesh with her husband at his father's home for 12 months. Shortly after returning to the UK, she gave birth to a son and then travelled to Bangladesh with her son, again staying in her husband's father's house. After a short while her son became ill and she returned to the UK. Her husband remained in Bangladesh awaiting entry clearance to join her in the UK. After a short stay with relatives she was asked to leave and applied to the authority as homeless. The authority decided that she was not homeless because her father-in-law's accommodation in Bangladesh was available to her and was reasonable to occupy. She requested a review, arguing that she could not afford to live in Bangladesh permanently, but acknowledging that it was Bengali tradition for a married couple to live with the husband's family, that she could continue to live in the house and that her husband's family were supporting him financially. The review decision confirmed the original decision. A county court appeal was lodged and the court quashed the decision holding, amongst other things, that the authority had failed to consider the issue of whether Ms Begum could afford to travel to the accommodation. The authority appealed.

79 See para 21.106.
80 (1999) 32 HLR 445, CA.

The Court of Appeal upheld the authority's appeal, holding that:

> Financial inability to travel is only one of many possible reasons why it may not be reasonable for an applicant to return to occupy overseas accommodation. In addition to factors concerning the legal availability, suitability and affordability of the accommodation, others may be, for example, connected with family or other personal problems, ill health, immigration restrictions, physical security and many others. In the absence of an indication of a particular difficulty or difficulties of that sort it is not, in my view, an authority's duty to take an applicant through a check list to negative all possible obstacles to his or her return to the overseas property.[81]

In *Waltham Forest LBC v Maloba* the applicant was from Uganda but had lived in the UK for many years and become a British citizen. He met his wife on a visit to Uganda and they married and lived for two years in an annex to the family home. After his father's death other family members moved into the house and Mr Maloba and his wife and child returned to the UK and applied as homeless. The local authority found that he was not homeless, arguing that they were not required to consider whether it was reasonable for Mr Maloba and his family to live in the accommodation in Uganda; it was sufficient that it was available. The court quashed the decision and the authority appealed. The Court of Appeal held that 'continue to occupy' did not mean that reasonableness was only relevant if the person was still in occupation. To find that a person was not homeless an authority must be satisfied not only that accommodation was available, but also that it was reasonable for the person to reside in it. The authority's alternative argument was that, when considering reasonableness, it was required only to consider the size, structural quality and amenities of the accommodation. The Court of Appeal rejected this: the authority had erred in failing to consider whether it was reasonable for Mr Maloba to relocate to Uganda, having lived in the UK for many years and becoming a British citizen.

13.155   As is clear from the judgment in *Nipa Begum*, it is essential to put forward to the authority any reasons why it would not be reasonable

81 Auld LJ at 458.

to occupy accommodation. However, the authority must consider, in all cases, the affordability of the accommodation (see para 13.167 below).

Matrimonial/civil partnership home

13.156 A person who is married or in a civil partnership has a right to occupy accommodation owned by or rented by the spouse or civil partner, provided that it has been the matrimonial or civil partnership home. This right lasts until the marriage or civil partnership comes to an end. Where the relationship has broken down, the authority will consider whether it is reasonable for the person to continue to occupy the shared accommodation. An authority may decide that it is, in spite of the fact that the couple no longer wish to be in partnership. Relevant factors will be the size of the accommodation and the nature of the relationship. However, if continued occupation means that a person would be at risk of domestic violence, he or she should be accepted as homeless (see below).

2. Not reasonable to continue to occupy

13.157 There are two distinct parts to this category: (1) where it is not reasonable to occupy because of the risk of violence; and (2) where it is not reasonable to occupy for other reasons. If violence is probable, an authority must find the applicant to be homeless. If considering reasons other than the risk of violence, the authority has a wide discretion and can take account of housing needs in its own area.

Probability of violence

13.158 HA 1996 s177 provides that 'it is not reasonable for a person to continue to occupy accommodation if it is probable that this will lead to violence against him or her, or a member of the household'. Violence is defined as 'violence from another person; or threats of violence from another person which are likely to be carried out'.

What is violence?

13.159 The Code provides at para 8.21: 'the term "violence" should not be given a restrictive meaning, and "domestic violence" should be understood to include threatening behaviour, violence or abuse (psychological, physical, sexual, financial or emotional) between persons who are, or have been, intimate partners, family members or members of the same household, regardless of gender or sexuality'.

13.160   A local authority must make a finding of fact: whether violence is probable if the person remains in occupation. The authority cannot refuse assistance or find a person not homeless because there are other remedies available for his or her protection. If the authority concludes that violence is probable, they must find the person to be homeless.

In *Bond v Leicester City Council*[82] the applicant had fled two properties because of domestic violence from the father of her two young children. She was re-housed by a housing association, but again suffered violence from the same man. He began to visit her at the premises and would refuse to leave when asked. On one occasion he assaulted her and she began to refuse to allow him into the property, but he continued to visit, shouting and throwing stones at the windows. Ms Bond left and fled to London. After staying in a refuge, she returned to Leicester and alternated between her mother's address and a friend's. She then applied to the council. At that stage the housing association property was still available and the authority decided that it was reasonable for her to return there and that she was not homeless. The authority noted that although she had a long history of fleeing harassment from the perpetrator, she had 'never taken any preventative measures to address this matter', referring to the possibilities of contacting the police or other bodies in relation to the 'alleged harassment'. She was advised to 'take action to address the alleged harassment'. A request for a review was made. The housing association property was then repossessed and the review decision found that Ms Bond was, by then, homeless, but homeless intentionally. The reason was that she had deliberately ceased to occupy accommodation that was available for her occupation and reasonable for her to continue to occupy. The review letter accepted that Ms Bond had been the subject of domestic violence for some considerable time, but stated that in the opinion of the reviewing officer she 'should have taken action under the criminal/civil law to prevent [the perpetrator] from coming near her' or her property. The letter went on to detail the various actions Ms Bond could or should have taken and stated that 'she became homeless intentionally as she failed to take these measures and as a consequence of her failure, she ceased to occupy accommodation which was available for her occupation and would have been reasonable for her to continue to occupy'.

82 [2002] HLR 6 CA.

The Court of Appeal held that when considering whether a person is homeless or intentionally homeless: 'The only test is what is probable. This ... is a pure question of fact, devoid of value judgments about what an applicant should or should not do'.[83]

The decision was varied to the effect that Ms Bond was not intentionally homeless.

13.161   The Code reflects the decision in *Bond v Leicester City Council*: 'An assessment must be based on the facts of the case and devoid of any value judgments about what an applicant should or should not do, or should or should not have done, to mitigate the risk of any violence (eg seek police help or apply for an injunction against the perpetrator)'.[84]

13.162   Nevertheless, an authority may legitimately advise the applicant of the measures that may be taken to provide protection or increase security in the home. The Code recommends that authorities should consider the option of improving the security of the applicant's home, which may enable him or her to continue to live there safely and thereby prevent homelessness. However, it is a matter for the applicant whether to accept such assistance or to pursue the application for homeless assistance.

Evidence of violence

13.163   It is not necessary to show a history of violence. The question is whether it is probable that continued occupation would lead to violence, which includes the threat of violence from someone likely to carry out the threat. Local authorities sometimes suggest that certain kinds of evidence are necessary before they can accept a homeless application from someone alleging violence: police reports, doctor's letters or court orders are often requested. While it is lawful for the authority to request supporting evidence to complete its enquiries, it is unlawful to refuse assistance on the basis that an applicant cannot provide the evidence requested. The availability of evidence is relevant to the determination of whether violence is probable. An authority is entitled to conclude that, on the available evidence, violence is not probable, but if they are rejecting the applicant's account this must be made clear to the applicant and reasons given.

83 Hale LJ at 25–26.
84 Para 8.22.

Unreasonable to occupy for other reasons

13.164 If the issue is whether someone is homeless because it is not reasonable to occupy accommodation for reasons other than the risk of violence, an authority has a wide discretion. There is no restriction on the nature of the factors that may make it unreasonable to occupy accommodation, but paragraphs 8.29–8.34 of the Code of Guidance draw attention to the following factors:

- affordability;
- physical characteristics;
- type of accommodation;
- people fleeing harassment;
- the fact that a person has been given notice to leave (see para 13.149 above).

13.165   When considering the issue an authority may take account of the general housing circumstances in its area. HA 1996 s177(2) provides:

> In determining whether it would be, or would have been, reasonable for a person to continue to occupy accommodation, regard may be had to the general circumstances prevailing in relation to housing in the district of the local housing authority to whom he has applied for accommodation or for assistance in obtaining accommodation.

13.166 This means that in an area of great need, where many people are living in dwellings that are overcrowded and/or in substantial disrepair, it will be difficult to satisfy the authority that it is not reasonable to continue to occupy on the basis of the condition of the accommodation.

Affordability

13.167 Affordability must be considered in all cases. The Homelessness (Suitability of Accommodation) Order 1996[85] specifies that an authority must take into account the financial resources available to the applicant, the cost of the accommodation, any maintenance payments made in respect of a former spouse or children, and the applicant's reasonable living expenses. If a property is not affordable, an authority must find the applicant to be homeless. However, it is for the authority to decide what are reasonable living expenses.[86] Most authorities will consider a property to be affordable if, after

---

85 SI No 3204.
86 See *R v Brent ex p Baruwa* (1997) 29 HLR 915, CA.

discharging all necessary outgoings, including rent or mortgage payments, a person is left with a disposable income equivalent to the level of Income Support. If arguing that a property is unaffordable, it will usually be necessary to prepare a detailed financial statement.

Overcrowding

13.168 Overcrowding is a factor that may mean that it is not reasonable to remain in occupation of accommodation. Paragraph 10.78 above explains 'statutory overcrowding' – a legal measure of overcrowding that can lead to prosecution of owners or occupiers. The threshold for statutory overcrowding is very high, but even a household that is statutorily overcrowded is not necessarily homeless.

> In *Harouki v Kensington and Chelsea RLBC*[87] the Court of Appeal upheld a decision by the authority that the applicant was not homeless. The family of six occupied a small three bedroom flat in contravention of the 'space standard' set out in HA 1985. Despite the fact that this meant that the occupation constituted a criminal offence, the authority were entitled to find that it was reasonable for the family to remain in occupation and await an allocation under Part VI.[88]

Challenging decisions

13.169 It is very difficult to successfully challenge decisions under this provision. If it is argued that conditions are such that it is unreasonable for the person to remain in occupation, strong evidence will be needed, such as medical reports, environmental health reports and recommendations from social services. Even then, the final decision is one for the housing authority. If an authority has considered all the relevant issues and decided that it is reasonable to continue to occupy, the only possible challenge will be that the decision is irrational or perverse, ie a decision no reasonable authority could reach (see para 21.72).

13.170 However, local authorities have certain powers and duties in relation to the condition of private sector accommodation. These are

---

87 [2007] EWCA Civ 1000, 4 July 2007.

88 However, in *Elrify v Westminster CC*, [2007] EWCA Civ 632, the local authority's decision that the family were not homeless was held to be flawed as it had applied the overcrowding standard incorrectly. The authority was ordered to reconsider its decision.

described in chapter 10. Even where a person wants to pursue a homeless application rather than remain in occupation, it may assist to report the premises to the appropriate department of the authority. This may result in enforcement action that compels a private landlord to carry out works. Alternatively, it may result in the landlord terminating the tenancy and claiming possession.

13.171   Whether there is any advantage in pursuing a homeless application rather than awaiting an allocation or bidding under a choice based lettings scheme depends on the level of priority given to those in unsatisfactory housing conditions in the particular authority's allocations scheme. A successful homeless application may result in more suitable accommodation being provided temporarily, but may also mean that the applicant will wait longer for suitable permanent accommodation.

3. Excluded from occupation

Illegal eviction

13.172 A person who has been unlawfully evicted retains a legal right to occupy, but is homeless under HA 1996 s175(2)(a). Such a person will usually be entitled to a court order to gain re-entry. In such a case, if the person is in priority need, a local authority should provide temporary accommodation for as long as it takes to obtain and enforce an injunction. However, there may be reasons why a person does not wish to seek re-entry, for example, fear of the landlord, having limited rights of occupation, being unable to obtain legal aid or find a solicitor to assist. Authorities often indicate that a person who does not enforce his or her rights through the courts will be found intentionally homeless. In making such a decision an authority must consider whether it would have been reasonable for the person to take the necessary steps to be able to resume occupation, taking account of the reasons for not doing so.

Mobile homes

13.173 A caravan or houseboat is capable of being 'accommodation' so that an occupant may not be homeless. However, this is only the case if there is somewhere the person can keep the mobile home and live in it. The fact that a site or mooring is only temporary will not of itself mean that the person is homeless.[89]

---

89 Code of Guidence, para 8.17.

Being threatened with homelessness

13.174 A person is threatened with homelessness if it is likely that he or she will become homeless within 28 days: HA 1996 s175(4). A specific duty may arise under section 195 in relation to a person threatened with homelessness. The duty is described at paras 12.76–12.81.

Priority need

13.175 An authority owes no housing duty under HA 1996 Part VII to a person who does not have a 'priority need' for accommodation. Such a person is entitled to advice and assistance only. Authorities do, however, have a power to provide accommodation to those who do not have a priority need (see below).

The categories of priority need

13.176 There are several categories of priority need. Some are easily established on the facts, others depend on a judgment by an authority as to whether something is 'reasonable' or whether a person is 'vulnerable'.

Priority need categories under section 189(1)

13.177 HA 1996 s189(1) provides:

> The following have a priority need for accommodation
>
> (a) a pregnant woman or a person with whom she resides or might reasonably be expected to reside;
> (b) a person with whom dependent children reside or might reasonably be expected to reside;
> (c) a person who is vulnerable as a result of old age, mental illness or handicap or physical disability or other special reason, or with whom such a person resides or might reasonably be expected to reside;
> (d) a person who is homeless or threatened with homelessness as a result of an emergency such as flood, fire or other disaster.

13.178 Section 189(2) provides that further categories may be added by the Secretary of State and by the Welsh National Assembly. In both cases regulations have been made, adding further classes of priority need: young people, care leavers, those leaving institutions and those fleeing violence. The substance of the English and Welsh regulations is different.

The Welsh regulations

13.179 The Welsh regulations came into force on 1 March 2001[90] and added the following further categories of priority need:

- 18- to 20-year-olds who are 'care leavers' or who are at 'particular risk of sexual or financial exploitation';
- children aged 16 or 17;
- a person without dependent children who has been subject to domestic violence, is at risk of such violence or, if he or she returns home, is at risk of domestic violence;
- former armed service personnel who have been homeless since leaving the armed forces;
- former prisoners who have been homeless since leaving custody and who have a local connection with the area of the local housing authority.

13.180 None of the Welsh categories of additional priority need require that the person is vulnerable. However, 18- to 20-year-olds who are not care leavers are only in priority need if judged to be at 'particular risk of sexual or financial exploitation'.

The English regulations

13.181 In England the following further categories were added by regulations as from 31 July 2002:[91]

- children aged 16 or 17 (provided they are not owed certain accommodation duties by social services under the Children Act 1989)
- 18- to 21-year-old 'care leavers' (provided they are not students to whom social services owe a duty to provide out of term accommodation).
- a person who is vulnerable as a result of:
  – being a care leaver who is 21 or older,
  – having been in the armed forces,
  – having been in custody, or
  – having become homeless because of violence.

13.182 Each category of priority need is examined below.

---

90 The Homeless Persons (Priority Need) (Wales) Order 2001 (SI No 607).
91 The Homeless Persons (Priority Need for Accommodation) (England) Order 2002 (SI No 2051).

Pregnancy

13.183 This should be a relatively straightforward category. There is no minimum period of pregnancy required. However, disputes often arise at the point of application about the evidence of pregnancy.

The interim duty to accommodate

13.184 This arises if the authority *has reason to believe* that a woman *may* be pregnant (as well as homeless and eligible). If a woman approaches an authority in an emergency late in the day or out of hours, she may have no 'evidence' of her pregnancy. In such a situation her explanation of why she believes she is pregnant should be sufficient until she can obtain a doctor's letter. However, it is common for authorities to refuse interim accommodation until supporting evidence is produced. This is unlawful, but in practice it is easier to obtain a doctor's letter than to challenge the authority by way of judicial review.

Inquiries/full decision

13.185 As in all cases, the burden is on an authority to satisfy itself of the relevant matters. An applicant will usually be requested to provide documentary evidence in the form of doctors' letters, pre-natal appointment cards, copies of scans or letters stating the expected date of delivery. If an applicant fails to provide any such evidence, an authority may decide decide that it is 'not satisfied' that she is pregnant.

13.186 It is unlawful for an authority to delay making a decision in case the pregnancy does not go to full term.[92] Further, once a decision has been made that a housing duty is owed, the duty does not end if the applicant is no longer in priority need (see para 15.46).

Dependant children

13.187 There are three possible issues the authority must decide:

- is the child dependent on the applicant?
- does the child reside with the applicant? Or, if not,
- is the applicant someone with whom the children 'might reasonably be expected to reside'?

---

92 *R v Ealing LBC ex p Sidhu* (1982) 2HR 45, QBD: it is unlawful for an authority to defer a decision in case there is a change of circumstance in the future. This is discussed below in relation to priority need based on age.

Dependence

13.188 The term 'dependent children' is not defined. The courts have held that a 16 year old who was in receipt of a training allowance was not dependent on his father, but indicated that the concept of dependence was not confined to financial dependence: *R v Kensington and Chelsea RLBC ex p Amarfio*.[93]

13.189 The Code states that authorities 'may wish to treat as dependent all children under 16, and all children aged 16–18 who are in, or are about to begin, full-time education or training or who for other reasons are unable to support themselves and who live at home': para 10.7.

13.190 The children need not be the natural children of the applicant, but there must be 'some form of parent/child relationship'.[94] Where an application was made by a man married to a person under the age of 18 on the basis that she was a dependent child, the court upheld the authority's decision that he was not in priority need: *Hackney LBC v Ekinci*.[95]

13.191 The child must be dependent in some way on the applicant, but need not be 'wholly and exclusively' dependent on the applicant.[96]

In *R v Westminster CC ex p Bishop*[97] the applicant had two children. When he and their mother separated it was agreed that the children would live with him for part of each week and that during holidays they would divide their time equally. The mother received child benefit for both children. He applied for homeless assistance from the council. The authority decided that he was not in priority need, as it was not satisfied that the children were dependent children who resided with him. The reasons were that the children were adequately housed with their mother and they were not dependent on him because the mother received child benefit for them and the applicant did not have the financial means to support them. His application for judicial review was dismissed: it was necessary that a child should be dependent at least in part on an applicant, and it was for the authority to decide the issue. The authority had taken account of relevant facts and was entitled to reach that conclusion.

93 (1995) 27 HLR 543, CA.
94 Para 10.8.
95 [2001] EWCA Civ 776, 24 May 2001.
96 *R v Lambeth LBC ex p Vagliviello* (1990) 22 HLR 392, CA.
97 (1997) 29 HLR 546, QBD.

Residing with the applicant

13.192 There must be some degree of permanence or regularity in the residence, as opposed to a temporary or limited arrangement.

13.193   Where parents are separated, it is possible for children to reside with both parents, but an authority may find, as a matter of fact, that children do not reside with the parent with whom they spend less time.

> In *R v Port Talbot BC ex p McCarthy*[98] the parents were separating. They agreed that their child would stay with Mrs McCarthy for four nights each week and with Mr McCarthy for three. The authority decided that he was not in priority need and that the arrangement was one of 'staying access' rather than residence. The court upheld the decision.

13.194   In the following case, the decision was quashed because the authority had failed to apply the correct test.

> In *R v Leeds ex p Collier*[99] the parents had separated and the father applied for housing, indicating that the children stayed with him for part of each week. The authority found that he had no priority need on the basis that the children's mother had 'greater residency responsibility for the children'. The court held that the council's decision was 'fatally flawed' as it had applied an incorrect test.

Reasonable to reside with the applicant

13.195 Where a separated parent does not have accommodation and is therefore unable to have the children residing with him or her, the authority must be satisfied of two things: first, that the children are dependent in some way on the non-resident parent and, second, that the person is someone with whom they might reasonably be expected to reside. The courts have considered this in the following cases.

> In *R v Kingswood BC ex p Smith-Morse*[100] the applicant's son lived with him for part of the week following his divorce. The authority

---

98 (1990) 23 HLR 207, CA.
99 June 1998 *Legal Action* 14, QBD.
100 (1994) *Times*, 8 December.

found that he had no priority need as the child's 'main residence' was with the mother. The decision was quashed: the authority should have gone on to consider whether the child might reasonably be expected to reside with the applicant in the future.

13.196   In *R v Westminster CC ex p Bishop* (para 13.191 above), however, the fact that the children were adequately housed with the mother and that the father could not support them financially was held to justify a decision that they were not dependent on him.

13.197   In the following cases the courts had made joint residence orders following the separation of the parents:

The applicant in *R v Oxford CC ex p Doyle*[101] was the father of four children and was separated from the mother. A joint residence order provided that, during term time, they would stay with the mother in the former shared home from Monday afternoon until Thursday afternoon. The applicant was to have the children from Thursdays after school until Monday mornings. He had two jobs which enabled him to support the children financially. The authority found that he was not in priority need because it was not reasonable to expect the children to reside with him. The authority took into account the difficulties the applicant would face in getting the children to and from school because of his work, the fact that the children were adequately housed with the mother, and the fact that he received no benefits for them. The claim for judicial review failed: it was open to the authority to find that the children could not reasonably be expected to reside with him.

In *Holmes-Moorhouse v London Borough of Richmond-upon-Thames*[102] the family court had made a joint residence order by consent in respect of three children. In such a case the family court is not required to consider the parents' capability to meet the children's needs, including the ability to provide appropriate accommodation. The Court of Appeal held that where an order was made by consent, it was not determinative of the issue of

101 (1997) 30 HLR 506, QBD.
102 [2007] EWCA Civ 970, 11 July 2007.

whether it was reasonable to expect a child to live with a separated parent. However, if the order was contested, so that the decision was made by the family court, having considered such issues, the housing authority would have to accept that it was reasonable to expect the children to live with both parents. A housing authority should be given the opportunity to make representations in the family proceedings. The court also held that the limited resources of an authority was not a matter that could be taken into account when deciding whether it was reasonable to expect the children to live with more than one parent.

The authority has been granted permission to appeal to the House of Lords.

Children in the care of the local authority

13.198 The local authority's duty to consider whether it is reasonable to expect children to reside with an applicant is to avoid a 'Catch 22 situation': applicants who cannot live with their children for lack of accommodation being refused housing because they do not live with their children. Although the decision about reasonableness is a judgment for the housing authority, where social services wish the children to return to their parents, this should determine the issue. The Code states that in such a case 'liaison with the social services authority will be essential'.[103]

Vulnerability

13.199 Several categories of priority need depend on the local authority being satisfied that a person is 'vulnerable' because of some personal characteristic or circumstance. The term 'vulnerable' is not defined in HA 1996, but it has been considered by the courts on many occasions.

13.200   In the case of *R v Waveney DC ex p Bowers*[104] it was held that the term means 'less able to fend for oneself so that injury or detriment will result when a less vulnerable man will be able to cope without harmful effects'. Subsequent cases suggested that a person would be vulnerable only if two tests were satisfied: first, being less able to obtain suitable accommodation than the ordinary person and,

103 Para 10.11.
104 (1983) 4 HLR 118, CA, Waller LJ at 122.

second, if suitable accommodation is not found, that he or she will suffer more than most. However, the Court of Appeal in the case of *R v Camden LBC ex p Pereira*[105] held that this approach was wrong.

> In *Pereira* the applicant was a former drug addict. He was accommodated on an interim basis while the authority investigated his application. There was psychiatric evidence that if he became homeless he would be under immense psychological stress that would adversely affect his efforts at rehabilitation. The authority applied the two part test suggested by previous case law and found Mr Pereira not to be vulnerable; the council's medical officer found that he had an ability to find accommodation and was therefore no less able to fend for himself than other people. The Court of Appeal held that this was the wrong approach. The authority should have asked whether the applicant was, when homeless, less able to fend for himself than an ordinary homeless person so that injury or detriment to him would have resulted when a less vulnerable man would be able to cope without harmful effect. There is a single composite test that is about the applicant's ability to cope with being homeless. A particular inability of a person to obtain housing for himself may be an aspect of his inability as a homeless person to fend for himself.

13.201   The Code of Guidance reflects the *Pereira* test in setting out the approach an authority should take in deciding whether a person is vulnerable:[106]

> 10.13 It is a matter of judgement whether the applicant's circumstances make him or her vulnerable. When determining whether an applicant in any of the [relevant] categories ... is vulnerable, the local authority should consider whether, when homeless, the applicant would be less able to fend for him/herself than an ordinary homeless person so that he or she would suffer injury or detriment, in circumstances where a less vulnerable person would be able to cope without harmful effects.
>
> 10.14 ... The assessment of an applicant's ability to cope is a composite one taking into account all of the circumstances. The applicant's vulnerability must be assessed on the basis that he or she is or will become homeless, and not on his or her ability to fend for him or herself while still housed.

105 (1999) 31 HLR 317.
106 Paragraphs 10.13–10.14.

13.202   It is for the authority to weigh up all of the relevant factors in deciding whether a person is vulnerable and, if all relevant issues have been taken into account, the decision can only be challenged on the grounds that it is irrational or perverse (see chapter 21). Some common errors in decisions on vulnerability are:

- Considering the person's physical or mental health at a time when interim accommodation is being provided. What the authority must do is to assess whether the person would suffer injury or detriment *when homeless*.
- Considering several potential categories of vulnerability, including 'other special reason', in isolation. An authority must consider whether, as a result of a combination of all of the relevant factors, the person is vulnerable.
- Delegating decision making to a medical expert. The decision as to whether a person is vulnerable must be taken by the housing authority, not by a medical adviser. An authority should take account of the opinion of a medical adviser, but it is not for the medical adviser to decide whether an applicant is in priority need.[107]

The non-vulnerable homeless person

13.203   The applicant's ability to cope with homelessness is compared with that of the non-vulnerable homeless person. It was recently observed that this is 'a legal test which itself makes the dubious assumption that homelessness is something fit people can always cope with'.[108] However, any person is likely to suffer injury or detriment if homeless. The issue is whether, because of one of the specified reasons, the applicant would suffer more than the non-vulnerable homeless person. In relation to depression, it has been held that any homeless person is likely to suffer depression and that continued homelessness is likely to exacerbate the depression.[109] To establish vulnerability, evidence will be needed that, in the applicant's case, homelessness will cause or exacerbate his or her depression to a significant extent.

---

107 *R v London Borough of Lambeth ex p Carroll* (1987) 20 HLR 142, QBD.

108 *Shala v Birmingham City Council* [2007] EWCA Civ 624, 27 June 2007, Sedley LJ at 24.

109 See *R on the application of Yeter v London Borough of Enfield* [2002] EWHC 2185 at [16].

Extent of necessary inquiries

13.204 In cases of vulnerability it is often argued that the authority have made insufficient inquiry. In such a case it is not enough to show that the authority could have made more inquiries; it must be established that the inquiries the authority failed to make are those that no reasonable authority could have failed to regard as necessary.

13.205   In *Cramp v Hastings BC* and *Phillips v Camden LBC*[110] (see para 12.53) the Court of Appeal held that the county court had been wrong to quash decisions on the basis of insufficient inquiry into potential vulnerability. At the review stage no representations had been made that further inquiry was necessary: and 'The duty to decide what inquiries are necessary rests on [the review officer], and her decision will be a lawful decision unless no reasonable council could have reached the same decision on the available material'.[111]

13.206   However, it has also been observed by the courts that in certain cases, what is at stake for the applicant is such that the authority's duty to inquire may be set at a high level.

In *Khelassi v London Borough of Brent*[112] the authority was considering an application by a man suffering from depression. A psychiatrist had expressed concern about the risk of suicide. The authority, without offering reasons, preferred the opinion of a general practitioner whose opinion was that he was not vulnerable. At the applicant's appeal the county court judge stated:

> I agree ... that the local authority's duty is to make such enquiries as are necessary ... I further agree ... that the decision as to what inquiries are necessary is primarily a question for the decision maker, not for the court. What is necessary will depend on what is at stake. Where a significant risk of suicide is in issue a great deal is at stake.

The decision was quashed and the Court of Appeal endorsed the county court decision and refused the authority permission to appeal.

---

110 [2005] EWCA Civ 1005, 29 July 2005.
111 Brooke LJ at [68].
112 [2006] EWCA Civ 1825.

Decisions to be made by local authority not court

13.207 In all cases involving local authority decision-making, the starting point is that local authorities, not the courts, have the decision-making responsibility. This has been emphasised in relation to decisions about priority need.

> In *Osmani v Camden LBC*[113] the applicant's doctor confirmed that he was suffering from depression and post traumatic stress disorder, that this made it difficult for him to find secure accommodation and that leaving him without secure accommodation would put his mental health at risk. However, the authority found that he was not vulnerable. The Court of Appeal dismissed his appeal: the council had applied the correct test and reached a decision that was not perverse; the issue of vulnerability is not exclusively or even necessarily a medical question.
>
> 'Given that each authority is charged with local application of a national scheme of priorities but against its own burden of homeless persons and finite resources, such decisions are often likely to be highly judgmental. In the context of balancing the priorities of such persons a local housing authority is likely to be better placed in most instances for making such a judgment'.[114]

13.208 So, the courts have held that the authority must deal with the competing needs for accommodation which locally is best placed to make the decision. However, the authority is not entitled to take into account the shortage of suitable accommodation when deciding whether a particular person has priority need.

> The case of *Holmes-Moorhouse v London Borough Richmond-upon-Thames*[115] was about whether dependent children could reasonably be expected to reside with the applicant. However, the Court of Appeal considered the role of resources in decision making, and commented:

113 [2004] EWCA Civ 1706, 16 December 2004.
114 Auld LJ at 38.
115 [2007] EWCA Civ 970, 10 October 2007, see para 13.197 above.

[Parliament] has, in the context of the scarcity of [public housing], decided that priority shall be afforded to those with whom dependent children might reasonably be expected to reside. It seems to me therefore that there is no room for permitting the scarcity of resources to play a part in considering the reasonableness of the expectation.[116]

13.209   In such cases, local authorities are required to make a value judgment as to the reasonableness of the expectation, whereas in the field of vulnerability the judgment is restricted to the person's coping ability when homeless. It must surely be the case therefore that the scarcity of resources can play no part in decisions about vulnerability.

The role of medical evidence

13.210 The long-established categories of priority need include those who are vulnerable as a result of mental illness, disability and 'other special reason'. Medical evidence of the extent of a person's mental illness or disability will usually be needed. If it is of the opinion of the authority that medical evidence is necessary it is the authority's responsibility to obtain it. Initially most authorities will require an applicant to complete a medical questionnaire which may then be referred to a medical adviser employed by the authority. Alternatively, the authority may send a questionnaire to the applicant's GP. The decision on vulnerability will be taken on the basis of the contents of the questionnaire indicating the nature of any illness or disability and the treatment received.

13.211   The Code provides that where there is doubt as to the extent of vulnerability authorities 'may' consider seeking a clinical opinion, but stresses that the final decision is for the authority to make: para 10.16.

13.212   In practice authorities are reluctant to seek an independent clinical opinion because of the cost. Those representing applicants under the Legal Help scheme will be able to obtain an independent report paid for by the Legal Services Commission provided the 'sufficient benefit test' is met (see para 22.179).

116 Moses LJ at [43].

13.213   If an expert is asked to offer an opinion it is essential that he or she is asked to give relevant information, namely:

- a description of the person's health problems/disability;
- an opinion as to how the person would be able to cope if homeless, in light of the health problems/disability; and
- an opinion as to the likely effect on the person of being homeless; in particular, whether the person would suffer greater 'injury or detriment' when homeless, than the average person, by reason of his or her health problems/disability.

Contested medical reports

13.214   Several recently reported cases have concerned applicants who have obtained medical reports suggesting vulnerability, while the authority's medical adviser offers the opinion that the person's condition is not severe enough to establish vulnerability.[117] Some of the principles established in those cases are as follows:

- where the potential vulnerability arises from a mental health problem, it may be necessary to obtain an opinion that is more expert than that of a GP;
- an authority should bear in mind that the opinion of a medical adviser who merely considers another expert's report and advises the authority on its content does not have the same 'weight' as the opinion of an expert who has actually examined the patient. It is a valid role, but must be distinguished from the role of an expert who has examined the patient or who has personal knowledge of the patient;
- where the authority relies on the advice of a medical adviser on the content of a report, it should make this clear in the decision letter. Where the opinion of the medical adviser differs from that of the other expert, the authority should indicate why it prefers the view of one over the other;
- where the authority obtains an opinion that raises new issues or contentious points, the applicant should normally be given a chance to comment on the opinion, in the interests of fairness. However, if the advice is merely directed to helping the authority assess the weight of evidence on matters already fully in play, there is no automatic obligation to disclose it. There is no 'absolute

---

117 See: *Hall v LB Wandsworth; Carter v LB Wandsworth* [2004] EWCA Civ 1740, 17 December 2002; *Bellouti v LB Wandsworth* [2005] EWCA Civ 602, 20 May 2005; *Khelassi v LB Brent* [2006] EWCA Civ 1825; *Shala v Birmingham CC* [2007] EWCA Civ 624, 27 June 2007.

rule of natural justice that an applicant must have the last word in every case'.[118]

- if there is a difference of opinion between the medical adviser and the applicant's expert, the medical adviser could be asked to examine the patient or to contact the applicant's expert to resolve the difference of opinion.

Vulnerability because of old age

13.215 Authorities must not apply a rigid age criteria, either by accepting all applicants over a certain age or by rejecting those below a certain age; an applicant is only in priority need if vulnerable.[119]

Other special reason

13.216 There is no restriction on the nature of the 'other reasons' that may make a person vulnerable.

13.217   The Code provides:[120]

> The legislation envisages that vulnerability can arise because of factors that are not expressly provided for in statute. It does not permit housing authorities to predetermine that some groups can never be considered vulnerable for an 'other special reason'. Moreover, other special reasons giving rise to vulnerability are not restricted to the physical or mental characteristics of a person. Other special reasons may include a combination of factors and circumstances that render a person less able than others to fend for him or herself when homeless. Where applicants have a need for support but have no family or friends on whom they can depend they may be vulnerable as a result of an other special reason.

The new categories: institutional history and fleeing violence

13.218 The Welsh regulations provide that those fleeing violence and those who have been homeless since leaving the armed forces or custody are automatically in priority need. There is no requirement that they are also vulnerable. The English regulations require that those with an institutional background are also vulnerable. In the English regulations care leavers aged 21 or over who are vulnerable are in priority need. There is no equivalent in the Welsh regulations.

---

118 *Bellouti v Wandsworth LBC* [2005] EWCA Civ 602, Jonathon Parker at [62].
119 Para 10.15.
120 Para 10.30.

Institutional background

13.219 The following notes on vulnerability refer only to the English regulations. The Code of Guidance sets out the relevant factors in assessing potential vulnerability amongst these groups. Common to all those with an institutional background are the following relevant factors:

- the length of time a person was in care, in prison or in the armed forces;
- the length of time since the person was in care, in prison or in the armed forces and whether the applicant has been able to obtain and/or maintain accommodation during that period; and
- whether the person has existing support networks, particularly by way of family, friends or mentor.

Fleeing violence

13.220 In relation to those who have left accommodation because of violence, the Code also provides that the authority may wish to take account of:[121]

(i) the nature of the violence or threats of violence (there may have been a single but significant incident or a number of incidents over an extended period of time which have had a cumulative effect);

(ii) the impact and likely effects of the violence or threats of violence on the applicant's current and future well being;

(iii) whether the applicant has any existing support networks, particularly by way of family or friends.

13.221 The Code also provides:[122]

> In cases involving violence, the safety of the applicant and ensuring confidentiality must be of paramount concern. It is not only domestic violence that is relevant, but all forms of violence, including racially motivated violence or threats of violence likely to be carried out. Inquiries of the perpetrators of violence should not be made. In assessing whether it is likely that threats of violence are likely to be carried out, a housing authority should only take into account the probability of violence, and not actions which the applicant could take (such as injunctions against the perpetrators).

121 Para 10.29.
122 Para 10.28.

Children and care leavers

13.222 In addition to the new classes of vulnerability, two other categories of priority need were added in both England and Wales by regulation: children aged 16 or 17 and young people aged 18 to 20 who are 'care leavers'. In both cases there is some overlap between the duties that a local housing authority may owe under HA 1996 and the duties a local social services authority may owe under the Children Act (CA) 1989.

13.223 See chapter 18 for an explanation of CA 1989, in particular the accommodation duties arising under sections 17 and 20 and the duties under the 'leaving care' provisions.

Children aged 16 and 17

13.224 Under the English regulations any child aged 16 or 17 is in priority need unless a duty to accommodate is owed by social services. In Wales there is no such exception: all homeless 16 and 17-year-olds have priority need.

13.225 In the following circumstances in England, the young person will not be in priority need:

- where social services owe a duty to accommodate him or her as a 'child in need' under section 20 of CA 1989; or
- where he or she is a 'relevant child' under the Children (Leaving Care) Act 2000. This will be the case if the child has previously been in the care of the authority for at least 13 weeks, ending after the age of 16 (see para 18.29).

13.226 It should be noted that these exceptions will apply only if the child is already known to social services, either as a child who has been assessed as a child in need or as a child who has previously been in their care. The fact that there may be a social services duty that overlaps with that of the housing department does not mean that the child is not in priority need. The Code of Guidance makes clear that where a child presents to the housing department and it believes the child may be a child in need or an eligible child they should contact the appropriate social services department but 'where necessary should provide interim accommodation under section 188 pending clarification': para 12.6. It is unlawful for the housing department to refuse assistance on the basis that the child should instead seek assistance from social services.

13.227   The situation will be different if a homeless child instead presents to the social services department. In such a case the authority will have a duty to carry out an assessment as to whether the child is a child in need. Under section 20 of CA 1989 an accommodation duty may arise to a child in need where there is no one with parental responsibility for the child, if the child has been lost or abandoned or if the person who was caring for the child is prevented from providing suitable accommodation or care. In relation to a child aged 16 or older a duty to accommodate will arise if the child's welfare is likely to be seriously prejudiced if accommodation is not provided.[123] These duties, however, depend upon social services carrying out a child in need assessment. Chapter 18 describes the assessment process and the steps that may be taken to compel an authority to commence an assessment.

In *R on the application of M v Hammersmith & Fulham LBC*[124] a 17-year-old had presented to the local authority following the breakdown of her relationship with her mother. It was alleged that she had first presented to social services and been referred to the housing department. The housing department arranged interim accommodation under section 188. There was some dispute about where she was actually living for the next few months but eight months after she had presented she was sentenced to four months in a Young Offenders Institution. She turned 18 while in custody. On her release it was argued that she should have been treated as a child in need and accommodated under section 20 of the CA 1989 by social services. On that basis she would have been entitled to ongoing support as a child leaving care. The House of Lords considered the relationship between local authorities' housing duties and social services duties to homeless teenagers:

... the statutory guidance given to both housing and social services departments stresses the need for joint protocols for assessing the needs of homeless 16- and 17-year-olds. This is needed, not only to avoid a young person being passed from pillar to post, but also to ensure that the most appropriate agency takes responsibility for her. The 2002 Priority Need Order clearly contemplates that, if the criteria in section 20 of the 1989 Act are met, social services rather than housing should take the long

123 CA 1989 s20(3).
124 [2008] UKHL 14, 27 February 2008.

term responsibility. Such a young person has needs over and above the simple need for a roof over her head and these can better be met by the social services.[125]

Where a local authority's social services department had provided accommodation in circumstances where it should have taken action under section 20 it could not side step the further obligations that arose under CA 1989. However, this did not mean that the actions of an authority's housing department should be categorised according to what its social services department should have done if the case had been drawn to its attention.

M's appeal was dismissed.

13.228   The situation in *M* was distinguished from the situation in *R on the application of S v Sutton LBC*[126] in which the child had been assisted by social services to obtain a place in a hostel. The case is summarised at para 18.19.

13.229   These cases demonstrate the difficult relationship between the duties of a housing authority under HA 1996 and a social services authority under CA 1989. Sadly, a common problem is that applicants are refused assistance by one department or authority on the basis that the duty to accommodate lies with the other department or authority. The House of Lords decision makes clear that the immediate duty to provide emergency accommodation to a homeless 16- or 17-year-old lies with the housing authority. If the housing authority believes that the social services authority may owe a long term duty under CA 1989 a referral should be made and the social services authority should conduct a child in need assessment (see paras 18.22–18.23). However, the fact that the housing authority has made a referral does not mean that it is no longer under a duty to provide interim accommodation. If the two authorities, or departments, are in dispute and neither are willing to accommodate the child, a claim for judicial review may be necessary against one or both authorities.

---

125 [2008] UKHL 14, Baroness Hale at [31].
126 [2007] EWCA Civ 790, 26 July 2007.

13.230   Whether a young person will benefit more from being assisted by
housing or social services will depend on the circumstances. Advisers
should bear in mind the following considerations:

- not all homeless 16- and 17-year-olds will be assessed as needing
accommodation under CA 1989 s20. Social services may assist
such a person by helping to find accommodation under section
17. However, an authority cannot avoid its duties simply by stating
that they are assisting under section 17 rather than accommodating
under section 20;[127]
- a young person who is intentionally homeless will not be provided
with long-term accommodation under HA 1996 Part VII.
Intentional homelessness plays no part in the assessment process
under CA 1989;
- if a housing authority accept an accommodation duty, the duty
does not end because the child reaches the age of 18;
- some authorities give very high priority to children who are or
have been in care when allocating permanent accommodation. In
some cases this means that a young person may obtain permanent
accommodation as soon as he or she leaves care;
- an 18 to 20-year-old who has previously been in care has a priority
need if he or she becomes homeless (see para 13.233 below);
- a child who has previously been in care for at least 13 weeks,
ending after the age of 16, is entitled to ongoing support from
social services as a care leaver, even after the age of 18.

Delays in decision making

13.231 Clearly, as automatic priority need depends upon the child's age, it is
essential to apply in sufficient time so that a decision is made before
the child reaches the age of 18. In most homeless applications a
final decision is not made immediately on presentation. The general
rule is that a decision under Part VII is made on the basis of the
circumstances at the date of the decision, whether this is an initial
decision or a decision following a review.[128] However, a local authority
cannot take advantage of this general rule to refuse assistance to an
applicant who was in priority need by virtue of age when he or she
applied to the authority.

127 *R on the application of H v Wandsworth LBC, R on the application of Barhanu
v Hackney LBC* and *R on the application of B v Islington LBC* [2007] EWHC
1082, 23 April 2007. However, see *R on the application of G v Southwark LBC*,
summarised at para 18.18 below.
128 *Mohamed v Hammersmith & Fullham LBC* [2001] UKHL 57.

In the case of *Akilah Robinson v Hammersmith and Fulham LBC*[129] the court held that an authority had acted unlawfully in postponing a decision on priority need with the effect that the young person had turned 18 when the decision was taken.

The applicant applied to the authority having been asked to leave the family home by her mother. Initially she was told that it would take 28 days for her case to be investigated and that, as she would be 18 within 28 days, there was no point in continuing with the application. However, having taken advice, she approached the authority again the following day. She was placed in interim accommodation and the authority referred her case for mediation, in accordance with the Code. It postponed making a decision until after mediation. The mediation failed and the authority then made its decision that, having become 18, the applicant was not in priority need. The decision was upheld on review on the basis that the decision maker had been correct to refer the case to mediation.

The Court of Appeal held that the authority had acted unlawfully in postponing a decision. It was clear when Ms Robinson first applied that she was homeless unintentionally and, as she was under the age of 18, was in priority need. The fact that inquiries normally take a certain time does not mean that a person who will become 18 within that time is not priority need.

Further, if, on review, the decision had been found to be unlawful, the review officer should have ensured that she had the rights she would have had if the decision had been lawful.

Nevertheless, there are cases in which it may take a reasonable period of time for the necessary inquiries to be made and the applicant may reach the age of 18 before the inquiries are complete. In such a case the authority is entitled to take the decision by reference to the facts as they exist at the date of the decision.

13.232   It may be difficult to distinguish between a case in which an authority is carrying out legitimate inquiries and one in which the authority is deliberately delaying a decision until after the young person reaches the age of 18. If possible, advisers should ensure that

129 [2006] EWCA Civ 1122.

the authority has sufficient evidence to be satisfied of the necessary issues prior to the child's 18th birthday, to avoid any delay in a decision being taken.

Care leavers aged 18–20

13.233 A care leaver under the age of 21 is in priority need, regardless of vulnerability. The English and Welsh regulations differ slightly. In England the person must have been in care after reaching the age of 16 but while under the age of 18. In Wales the period in care is 'at any time while still a child'. In both cases this means having been 'looked after, accommodated or fostered'.[130] In England 'relevant students' are excluded. These are students to whom social services owe a duty under the Children (Leaving Care) Act 2000, which includes a duty to provide out of term accommodation.

13.234 A child provided with accommodation under section 20 is a 'looked after' child but a child assisted under section 17 is not.[131] There have been a number of cases examining the difference between section 17 assistance and section 20 accommodation provided to children in need (see paras 18.15–18.21). In a number of cases the courts have held that where the conditions set out in section 20 are met and accommodation is provided or arranged by the authority, it is not open to the authority to simply designate the assistance they are giving 'section 17' assistance, in order to avoid ongoing duties when the child reaches the age of 18. There may, however, be circumstances in which an authority may decide that the provision of accommodation under section 20 is not required and instead assist the young person to obtain his or her own accommodation.

13.235 Where an authority simply asserts that a child was assisted under section 17 and not section 20, advisers should seek further information. The young person may request a copy of his or her social services file under the Data Protection Act 1998 (see para 21.111). Even if the assistance has been referred to as 'section 17' it may be possible to establish that, in reality, the authority were acting under a section 20 duty.

13.236 Most care leavers will also be entitled to ongoing support from the social services department as children leaving care. This may include assistance to pursue a homeless application.

---

130 This is defined in section 24 of the Children Act 1989.
131 CA 1989 s22.

Emergency or disaster

13.237 Someone made homeless because of an emergency such as a flood, fire or other disaster is treated as having a priority need regardless of personal circumstances.[132]

13.238   The event that makes the person homeless must be both an emergency and a disaster. Homelessness resulting from an unlawful eviction does not come within this category.[133] The sudden disappearance of a mobile home, however, was accepted as an emergency akin to flood or fire as: 'It involved the sudden and wholly unexpected loss of [his] home in circumstances wholly outside his control by the loss of the structure in which he made his home'.[134]

Household members

13.239 It should be noted that most of the 'old' priority need categories provide that anyone with whom such a person resides or might reasonably be expected to reside also has a priority need. The exception is a person made homeless as a result of flood, fire or other disaster. However, none of the new categories of priority need extend to household members.

13.240   It should also be noted that any ineligible person, such as a dependent child or a spouse or partner with health problems, must be ignored for the purpose of deciding priority need (see para 13.130 above).

13.241   However, if a duty is accepted accommodation must be made available for the person to whom the duty is owed:

> together with:
> (a) any other person who normally resides with him as a member of his family, or
> (b) any other person who might reasonably be expected to reside with him.[135]

Intentional homelessness

13.242 Being 'intentionally homeless' does not mean intending to become homeless. Rather, it means that a person's homelessness was caused

132 This is a category of priority need that reflects the original provisions of the National Assistance Act 1948 – local authorities owed a duty to provide emergency accommodation to people made homeless in such circumstances.
133 *R v Bristol CC ex p Bradic* (1995) 27 HLR 584, CA.
134 *Higgs v Brighton & Hove CC* (2004) HLR 2, Kay LJ at [20].
135 HA 1996 s176.

by something he or she did (or did not do) deliberately. Where a person is found to be intentionally homeless the local authority's duty will be limited; it must provide advice and assistance and accommodation for a 'reasonable period' to give the person an opportunity to find his or her own accommodation.

13.243   The definition of intentional homelessness is set out in section 191:

> (1) a person becomes homeless intentionally if he deliberately does or fails to do anything in consequence of which he ceases to occupy accommodation which is available for his occupation and which it would have been reasonable for him to continue to occupy and
>
> (2) ... an act or omission in good faith on the part of a person who was unaware of any relevant fact shall not be treated as deliberate.

13.244   In addition, since 1996 there has been an additional limb to the test of intentional homelessness: 'contrived homelessness'. This is dealt with below.

13.245   There are several elements to the definition. In all cases, the following questions must be asked:

- Which accommodation did the person cease to occupy, thereby causing the homelessness?
- Was that accommodation available to the applicant, ie available for the occupation of the applicant *and* his or her household?
- Would it have been reasonable for the applicant to continue to occupy the accommodation?
- What was the act or omission in consequence of which he or she ceased to occupy?
- Was the act or omission deliberate?
- If apparently deliberate, was it an act or omission made in good faith in ignorance of a relevant fact?

13.246   It is useful to examine each of these questions separately.

Which accommodation did the person cease to occupy, thereby becoming homeless?

Ceasing to occupy

13.247   First, it must be noted that to be intentionally homeless a person must cease to occupy accommodation.[136] A failure to take up

---

136 *R v Westminster CC ex p De Souza* (1997) 29 HLR 649, QBD.

accommodation does not, in most cases, make a person intentionally homeless. An apparent exception to this is when an offer of suitable accommodation is refused (whether under Part VI or Part VII of HA 1996). In such a case, the person can be said to have ceased to occupy interim or temporary accommodation provided by the authority in consequence of refusing the offer.[137]

13.248   This situation must be distinguished from that of a person who, when homeless, declines to take up accommodation that is made available to him or her.

13.249   Under 'homeless prevention' strategies (see para 12.7 above) many authorities offer to those who present as homeless help to obtain private sector accommodation. Applicants may prefer to take a tenancy in the private sector rather than pursue a homeless application. However, an authority should not advise the person that to refuse an offer of accommodation from a private landlord will render them intentionally homeless. A person can only be intentionally homeless if he or she ceases to occupy accommodation *as a result of* his or her act or omission. A person who is already homeless or threatened with homelessness cannot be found intentionally homeless for refusing to accept assistance to take up a private sector tenancy.

13.250   However, this must be distinguished from a situation in which an authority accepts a homeless duty and discharges its housing duty by arranging a private sector tenancy. In such a case the housing duty *will* end if a suitable offer is refused. If the offer is being made pursuant to a housing duty the authority must write to the applicant clearly stating the effect of a refusal and informing the applicant of the right to seek a review of the suitability of the accommodation. See below at paras 15.64–15.73 for an explanation of the different situations in which private sector accommodation is used in discharging the homeless duty.

Which accommodation?

13.251   It may be that the loss of the most recent accommodation cannot be said to be the cause of the person's homelessness.

In *Dyson v Kerrier*[138] the applicant voluntarily gave up a council tenancy and took an unprotected 'out of season' holiday let. When

---

137 *R v East Hertfordshire DC ex p Hunt* (1986) 28 HLR 51, QBD.
138 [1980] 3 All ER 313, CA.

she was required to leave the unprotected tenancy she applied to the local authority as homeless. The authority found that she was intentionally homeless; her homelessness had been caused by the deliberate act of giving up her council tenancy. The court upheld the council's decision. The cause of the applicant's homelessness was not the loss of the unprotected tenancy but the previous deliberate act of giving up the council tenancy.

13.252 *Dyson v Kerrier* was decided in 1980 and subsequently the courts developed the notion of 'settled accommodation'[139] and applied it in the following ways:

- when considering intentional homelessness an authority was to ignore any non-settled accommodation;
- a person who did not have settled accommodation was by definition homeless; and
- it was necessary that the accommodation provided by an authority under the homeless duty was settled.

13.253 In 1995 the House of Lords held that this was the wrong approach. In the case of *R v London Borough of Brent ex p Awua*[140] it was held that the concept of settled accommodation was only applicable in relation to intentional homelessness. Moreover, it was only relevant to the *Dyson v Kerrier* type of situation: to ensure that a person who is intentionally homeless, following the loss of permanent accommodation, does not cease to be intentionally homeless by obtaining non-settled accommodation which later ceases to be available. What this means is:

- a person who has non-settled accommodation is not homeless provided it is reasonable to continue to occupy the accommodation;
- the duty to secure accommodation does not necessarily mean securing accommodation that is settled;
- in relation to intentional homelessness, non-settled accommodation is only ignored if the person has lost that accommodation unintentionally. Then the authority can look back to the

---

139 *Din v Wandsworth LBC* [1982] 1 HLR 73, HL.
140 (1995) 27 HLR 453, HL.

accommodation previously occupied. However, a person may be intentionally homeless from non-settled accommodation.[141]

13.254   Given the development of the case law regarding settled accommodation advisers must be cautious of cases to settled accommodation decided before the decision of *Awua* in 1995.

What is 'settled' accommodation?

13.255 The term 'settled' means something more than merely temporary. 'What amounts to a "settled residence", is a question of fact and degree depending upon the circumstances of each individual case'.[142] An assured shorthold tenancy is capable of being settled accommodation but is not necessarily so, depending on the circumstances.

In *Knight v Vale Royal BC*[143] the applicant had been found intentionally homeless by the authority. She then obtained an assured shorthold tenancy for a six-month term. She was informed by the landlord from the outset that he would require the property back after six months. After she was evicted the authority again found her to be intentionally homeless on the basis that there was still a causal link between her previous loss of accommodation and her homelessness. She argued that she had had settled accommodation which had broken the 'chain of causation'. In the Court of Appeal it was submitted that because the assured shorthold tenancy was the most commonly available form of tenure in the private sector such a tenancy must necessarily be settled accommodation. The court rejected this, holding:

> In our judgment the occupation by a tenant of accommodation let on a six months' assured shorthold tenancy is capable of constituting settled accommodation for the purposes of breaking a chain of causation from past intentional homelessness ... What we cannot

141 In *Manchester CC v Moran* and *Richards v Ipswich BC* [2008] EWCA 378, 17 April 2008 the applicants argued that they could not be found intentionally homeless from a womens' refuge. The Court of Appeal rejected the argument: a refuge could be described as 'accommodation' and it could be reasonable, depending on the circumstances, for a woman to continue to occupy such accommodation.

142 Ackner LJ, *Din v Wandsworth BC*, CA (23 June 1981, unreported).

143 [2003] EWCA Civ 1258, 31 July 2003.

> accept is that the occupation by a tenant of accommodation let on a six months' assured shorthold tenancy is, as a matter of law, always sufficient to constitute settled accommodation. The question remains one of fact and degree to be determined by the local authority in the circumstances of a particular case.[144]
>
> Ms Knight's appeal was dismissed.

13.256   While the parties' intentions are relevant in deciding whether accommodation is settled, the test is not entirely subjective; an authority may find that accommodation was not settled even if the applicant states that the intention was to remain in the accommodation permanently.[145] Other factors, such as the level of security and the suitability of the accommodation, will also be taken into account.

Examining the 'accommodation history'

13.257   What all this means is that, in deciding the cause of homelessness, a local authority can look back through an applicant's history of previous accommodation until it finds either settled accommodation which was not lost intentionally or accommodation, settled or not, from which the applicant was intentionally homeless. The finding in the first case would be that the person is not intentionally homeless and in the second case that he or she is intentionally homeless.

13.258   This is also referred to as 'breaking the chain of causation': in most cases a person who is intentionally homeless will only cease to be intentionally homeless ('break the chain of causation') by obtaining settled accommodation. If this is later lost unintentionally, the person's present homelessness will no longer be 'intentional'. However, there may be other events which can break the chain or be the true cause of present homelessness, such as suffering domestic violence or relationship breakdown. See para 13.280.

Was the accommodation available for the applicant and his or her household?

13.259   The authority must be satisfied that the accommodation was available for the applicant to occupy together with any other person

---

144 Sir Martin Nourse at [24]–[25].
145 *R v Purbeck DC ex p Cadney* (1985) 17 HLR 534, QBD.

who normally resides with the applicant as a member of his or her family, or any other person who might reasonably be expected to reside with him or her.[146]

13.260   Which family members normally live with the applicant is a question of fact. However, in relation to other people, it is for the authority to decide whether it is reasonable to expect a person to live with the applicant.[147] It is not necessary that the person has previously lived with the applicant.

Would it have been reasonable for the applicant to continue to occupy that accommodation?

13.261   The test is the same as when considering whether a person is homeless. If the authority is satisfied that violence would have been probable if the person had remained it cannot find the person to be intentionally homeless. The fact that the person could have taken other steps to protect him or herself is irrelevant: *Bond v Leicester City Council*, para 13.160 above.

13.262   If the applicant contends that it would not have been reasonable to remain for some other reason, the issue is one for the authority to decide. In making the decision, it may take account of housing conditions in the local area.[148]

13.263   The question is not whether it was reasonable to leave but whether it would have been reasonable to remain.[149] This is judged on the basis of the facts at the time the accommodation ceased to be available, not at the date of the application. So, the fact that accommodation would inevitably have been lost does not prevent a person from being found intentionally homeless if he or she decided to leave at a time when it would have been reasonable to remain.[150] Further, it will not assist an applicant who left accommodation when it would have been reasonable to remain that a subsequent change in circumstances (eg having children) would have made it unreasonable for continued occupation.[151]

---

146 Section 176. See *R v Hillingdon LBC ex p Islam* (1981) 1 HLR 107, HL.
147 See *R v Barking & Dagenham LBC ex p Okuneye* (1995) 22 HLR 174, QBD.
148 Section 177(2).
149 *R v Hammersmith and Fulham LBC ex p Duro-Rama* (1983) 9 HLR 71.
150 *R on the application of Wandsworth LBC ex p Din* (1981) 1 HLR 73, HL.
151 See *R v Hackney LBC ex p Ajayi*, June 1997 *Legal Action* 23, CA, and *R v Brent LBC ex p Yusuf* (1997) 29 HLR 48, QBD.

13.264   It may be that a person was acting reasonably in giving up accommodation but if it would also have been reasonable to remain in occupation, he or she may be intentionally homeless. The reasons why a person left accommodation will, however, be relevant if considering whether a person was acting in good faith, in ignorance of a relevant fact (see para 13.284).

What was the act or omission in consequence of which he or she ceased to occupy

13.265   The authority must identify what the applicant is alleged to have done or failed to do and be satisfied that this act or omission caused the homelessness. Where the act or omission was not that of the applicant, he or she may nevertheless be intentionally homeless if there was 'acquiescence' in the act or omission.

Causation/foreseeability

13.266   Where the law provides that one act must cause another, or that an outcome must be a consequence of an act, this is referred to as 'causation'. Related to this is the notion of 'foreseeability': for a person to be deemed to have caused a certain event by his or her action, the consequence of the action must be, to a certain degree, foreseeable.

13.267   For an act or omission to be the cause of a person's homelessness this must be a reasonably foreseeable consequence of the act or omission. The courts have considered this issue in the following cases.

Tenant's imprisonment

In *R v Hounslow LBC ex p R*[152] the applicant was convicted of several offences of indecent assault and sentenced to seven years' imprisonment. He surrendered his tenancy while in prison as he could not maintain the rent payments. On his release he applied as homeless, but was found to be intentionally homeless on the basis that the commission of the offences were deliberate acts and that the surrender of the tenancy was the 'direct and reasonable' result of the acts. His judicial review of the decision was dismissed. The court held that:

152 [1997] 29 HLR 939.

the question to be asked is whether his ceasing to occupy the accommodation would reasonably have been regarded at the time as the likely consequence of the deliberate conduct. It is an objective, not a subjective test'.[153]

The same test was approved and applied by the Court of Appeal in *Stewart v Lambeth LBC*.[154] Mr Stewart was a tenant of the authority, but a suspended possession order had been made on the basis of rent arrears. He was sentenced to five years' imprisonment for drugs offences and made an arrangement that, while he was in prison, his sister would maintain his tenancy and pay the rent. No rent was received and a warrant was executed. He found out after the event. When he applied as homeless following his release on licence, he was found to be intentionally homeless. It was argued that the cause of his homelessness was not his imprisonment, but the failure by the sister to make rent payments. The Court of Appeal held that 'the chain of events that ultimately led to Mr Stewart's eviction began with the supply of heroin in respect of which he was duly convicted'.[155] The fact that arrangements could have been, or were, made to avoid the eviction were irrelevant, especially as the arrangements made were ineffectual. The authority's decision that he was intentionally homeless was upheld.

Rent/mortgage arrears

13.268   Where rent or mortgage payments are unaffordable, the failure to pay will not be deliberate. However, a person may be intentionally homeless because of a decision to enter into an unaffordable arrangement.

In *R v Barnet ex p Rughooputh*[156] an applicant was evicted following mortgage possession proceedings, having entered into a mortgage she could not afford. She had represented that she earned £18,000 a year, but was in fact unemployed. The council decided that she

153 Stephen Richards at 947.
154 [2002] EWCA Civ 753, 26 April 2002.
155 Longmore LJ at [20].
156 (1993) 25 HLR 607.

was intentionally homeless. The deliberate act causing the homelessness was not the failure to make the mortgage payments, but the taking out of the mortgage. The Court of Appeal upheld the council's decision.

13.269 The same principles may apply where a person agrees to a tenancy at a clearly unaffordable rent although where an applicant moves from one rented property to another, other issues may arise: eg whether the subsequent accommodation was settled and whether the applicant was acting in good faith, in ignorance of something relevant. See para 13.284 below.

'Acquiescence'

13.270 The act or omission must be that of the applicant. Although authorities often treat applications by couples or families as 'joint' applications, there is no provision under the Act for doing so. An authority may be required to consider each applicant individually where it is the act or omission of one person that is alleged to have caused the homelessness. However, a party who acquiesced in (i.e. passively accepted) the act or omission of another may also be found homeless intentionally.

13.271 An authority is entitled to assume that members of a family were party to the conduct of one, unless there is evidence to the contrary.[157]

In *R v North Devon DC ex p Lewis*[158] a man who gave up his employment and lost his tied accommodation was found to be intentionally homeless. His wife then applied and the authority found her also to be intentionally homeless on the basis that she had acquiesced in her husband's decision to give up his job. Her application for judicial review was dismissed, Woolf J holding:

... the fact that the Act requires consideration of the family unit as a whole indicates that it would be perfectly proper in the ordinary case for the housing authority to look at the family as a whole and assume, in the absence of material which indicates to the contrary, where the conduct of one member of the family was such that he should be regarded as having become homeless intentionally, that was conduct to which the other members of the family were a party.

157 *R v LB Tower Hamlets ex p Khatun* (1993) 27 HLR 344, CA.
158 [1981] 1 WLR 328, QBD.

So, for example, where the husband is a tenant and gives notice in circumstances where he is properly to be regarded as having become homeless intentionally, the wife, even though she was not the tenant and she did not give the notice, can be regarded in the same way. In normal circumstances this would be treated as a joint decision. If, however, at the end of the day because of material put before the housing authority by the wife, the housing authority are not satisfied that she was a party to the decision, they would have to regard her as not having become homeless intentionally.

13.272   The reasoning in *Lewis* has been approved in a number of subsequent cases.

13.273   The correct approach therefore is that:

- each family member is entitled to individual consideration;
- an authority may assume that the members of a family agree to the decision of one family member;
- however, there may be evidence that this is not the case.

13.274   Effectively, this means that where a person says that they did not acquiesce in another's decision, the burden of proof is reversed and the person must provide evidence of this.

13.275   The courts have upheld decisions that a family member has acquiesced in the act or omission causing the homelessness in the following cases:

In *R v Swansea CC ex p John*[159] the applicant was the sole tenant of a council property. A possession order was made because of nuisance and annoyance caused by the tenant's long term partner, who was her lodger. The court found that the tenant had acquiesced, in as much as she could have terminated his right to occupy, but failed to do so.

R v East Hertfordshire DC ex p Bannon[160] concerned an application made by the ex-partner of a man whose anti-social behaviour had led to both being evicted. The decision that she was intentionally homeless, having either been a party to his behaviour or done nothing to prevent it, was upheld.

159 (1982) 9 HLR, 58, QBD.
160 (1986) 18 HLR 515.

13.276   The same approach is appropriate when a family is evicted because of a failure to pay rent:

> In *R v LB Ealing ex p Salmons*[161] a couple were evicted for rent arrears of some £12,000. Both maintained that the husband had been unaware of the arrears and that he had provided his wife with the money to pay the rent but she had not done so. The authority held that it was inconceivable that he was unaware of the arrears or the threat of eviction and that he had acquiesced in the non-payment of the rent. The court dismissed the claim for judicial review of the decision: the authority had made sufficient enquiries and were entitled to conclude that the applicant had known about, or at least turned a blind eye to, the arrears.

13.277   However, simply being aware of arrears may not be sufficient to establish that there was acquiescence.

> In *R v East Northamptonshire DC ex p Spruce*[162] a couple were evicted because of substantial rent arrears. The evidence was that Mrs Spruce had become aware of the arrears only at a late stage. The court quashed the decision that she was intentionally homeless: it was not sufficient that she was aware of the arrears; the authority had failed to make sufficient inquiries into whether or not she had acquiesced in the failure to pay the rent.

13.278   Even where an applicant has had no part in a decision leading to the loss of accommodation, if he or she is content to leave such decisions to someone else, an authority may find there has been acquiescence.

> In *R v LB Tower Hamlets ex p Khatun*[163] a man gave up accommodation with his brother when his wife was about to give birth to their third child. They subsequently applied as homeless and his wife argued that her husband had not consulted her about the decision and that she had not wanted to leave, but that

161 (1990) 23 HLR 272, QBD.
162 (1988) 20 HLR 508, QBD.
163 (1993) 27 HLR 344, CA.

her husband had told her that if she wanted them to remain together she must follow him. She was nevertheless found to be intentionally homeless. Her claim for judicial review was refused and her appeal dismissed by the Court of Appeal: if a wife is content to leave decisions about where the family lives to her husband, then a decision in which she co-operates may be regarded as a decision in which she had joined, unless there is some reason for holding that she did not do so.

Breaking the chain of causation

13.279   If found to be intentionally homeless, when, in the future, might a person no longer be homeless intentionally? In other words, when might the chain of causation be broken?

13.280   It will usually be necessary for a person who is intentionally homeless to obtain settled accommodation in order to break the chain. However, it is possible that some other event may break the chain: for example, a person who subsequently becomes homeless as the result of domestic violence or a relationship breakdown.[164]

13.281   This issue is discussed at para 12.57.

Was the act or omission deliberate?

13.282   It is not the case that the person must have deliberately become homeless: only that the act or omission was deliberate in the ordinary sense of the word.

13.283   A person who is suffering from a mental health problem may act in a way that cannot be said to be deliberate. This will depend upon the nature of the mental illness and an opinion of a psychiatrist will usually be needed. However, a person may be found to be in priority need by reason of mental illness but be capable of deliberate acts or omissions.[165]

Was the act or omission made in good faith in ignorance of a relevant fact?

13.284   This provision is to ensure that a person who gives up accommodation, honestly but mistakenly believing that circumstances are such that

---

164 See for example: *R v Camden LBC ex p Aranda* (1998) 30 HLR 76, CA; and *R v Basingstoke and Deane BC ex p Bassett* (1983) 10 HLR 125, QBD.
165 See *R v Wirral MBC ex p Bell* (1995) 27 HLR 234.

they will have accommodation elsewhere, is not found intentionally homeless. The fact of which the person is ignorant must, of course, be relevant to the person's housing.

13.285 A person may give up accommodation to move to another area or country in order to work there. In such a case the courts have distinguished between 'mere aspiration' and belief in specific employment or housing opportunities.

In *Aw-Aden v Birmingham CC*[166] the applicant, a well qualified scientist, came from Belgium to the UK to seek work. He was unable to find work and when his family joined him in Birmingham the accommodation he was staying in became overcrowded and he applied as homeless to the authority. He was found intentionally homeless for giving up his accommodation in Belgium. He submitted that he had not acted deliberately, having been ignorant of his true prospects of finding employment and therefore his ability to afford to pay for accommodation privately. The Court of Appeal dismissed his appeal, approving the approach of the court in the case of *Obeid*[167] in which it was said:

... an applicant's appreciation of the prospects of future housing or future employment can be treated as 'awareness of a relevant fact' for the purposes of this subsection, provided it is sufficiently specific (that is related to specific employment or specific housing opportunities) and provided it is based on some genuine investigation and not mere 'aspiration'.

13.286 In all cases, to benefit from the provision the person must have acted in good faith. The question is not whether the person acted reasonably, although this may be relevant to whether or not the person was acting in good faith. It is possible to be guilty of 'honest blundering and carelessness' but still be acting in good faith.[168]

13.287 Ignorance of the law or the legal consequences of an act or omission should be disregarded when considering whether an act or omission is deliberate.[169] So, for example, the provision will not

---

166 [2005] EWCA Civ 1834, 7 December 2005.

167 *R v Westminster City Council ex p Obeid* [1996] 29 HLR 389, Carnwath J at 398.

168 *R v LB Hammersmith & Fulham ex p Lusi* (1991) 23 HLR 260, QBD.

169 See *R v Eastleigh BC, ex p Beattie (No 2)* (1984) 17 HLR 168, QBD; *R v LB Croydon, ex p Toth* (1988) 20 HLR 576, CA.

assist a person who claims that he or she did not know that abandoning premises would lead to the loss of a tenancy. However, a belief that premises were still available, despite having been out of the UK for a long period, has been held to constitute ignorance of a relevant fact.[170]

13.288   It is not always easy to draw a distinction between ignorance of the law and ignorance of fact: ignorance about a person's entitlement to housing benefit has been held to constitute ignorance of a fact.[171]

Contrived homelessness

13.289   An additional definition of intentional homeless was introduced by the Housing Act 1996. Section 191(3) provides that:

> A person shall be treated as becoming homeless intentionally if:
> (a) he enters into an arrangement under which he is required to cease to occupy accommodation which it would have been reasonable for him to continue to occupy, and
> (b) the purpose of the arrangement is to enable him to become entitled to assistance under this Part,
> and there is no other good reason why he is homeless.

13.290   The provision is to prevent collusion in order to take advantage of the homeless duty. The Code refers to the possibility of parents and children taking advantage of the automatic priority need given to homeless 16 and 17-year-olds: a situation in which a parent and child agreed that the child would be given notice to leave to enable the child to make a homeless application may make the child intentionally homeless. However, it is likely that authorities will find it difficult to obtain evidence of such an agreement and the Code stresses that the authority must 'be satisfied that collusion exists, and must not rely on hearsay or unfounded suspicions'. Further, for a person to be intentionally homeless 'there should be no other good reason for the person's homelessness'. Examples of good reasons are identified as overcrowding or an obvious relationship breakdown.

Decision letters

13.291   If a decision is made that a person is intentionally homeless, the authority must ensure that all of the elements of the test are

---

170 *R v LB Tower Hamlets ex p Rouf* (1991) 23 HLR 460, QBD.
171 *R v Westminster ex p Moozary-Oraky* (1994) 26 HLR 213, QBD.

addressed. In cases where a complex accommodation history is at issue this is particularly important.

13.292   In the case of *City of Gloucester v Miles*[172] the Court of Appeal held that the decision letter must state:

- that the authority is satisfied that the applicant became homeless intentionally;
- when the applicant is considered to have become homeless;
- what the deliberate act or omission was that caused the homelessness; and
- that it would have been reasonable for the applicant to have continued to occupy the accommodation.

13.293   Further, if an issue is raised that suggests the act or omission should not be treated as deliberate, the authority must explain why it has found otherwise.

> In *O'Connor v Kensington and Chelsea RLBC*[173] a couple were assured tenants of a housing trust. They went to Ireland to attend to an ailing relative who subsequently died. They had intended to be absent for a short period only and left a friend looking after the property who was expected to pay rent. The rent was not paid and a suspended possession order was made in their absence. After 16 months they returned to the UK and discovered the arrears and possession order and the fact that the friend had allowed others into occupation of their home. They were able to pay off most of the arrears, but the trust nevertheless executed a warrant of possession. The authority found that they were intentionally homeless, but failed to state the date at which the authority considered them to have become homeless. The authority had therefore failed to consider whether the act or omission at that time had been in good faith. The Court of Appeal quashed the authority's decision.

Referral to another authority

13.294   A homeless person may apply for assistance to any local authority, regardless of whether he or she has ever lived in that authority's area. The duty to make inquiries falls on the authority to which the

172 (1985) 17 HLR 292, CA.
173 [2004] EWCA Civ 394, 30 March 2004.

application is made. However, after this authority has decided whether a housing duty is owed, it may consider whether the person can be referred to another authority for the actual provision of housing. HA 1996 is clear that referral should only be considered if and when the authority is satisfied that the applicant is eligible, homeless, in priority need and not intentionally homelessness.[174] Unfortunately, it is common for authorities to consider the issue on first presentation. While an authority may legitimately advise a person that the duty to provide housing will probably rest with a different authority, it is unlawful to refuse to accept an application while informing the person that they must apply to a different authority. Such an approach can be challenged by way of judicial review.

The local referral conditions

13.295 The conditions for a referral are set out in section 198 of the Act. There are three circumstances in which a referral can be made:

- where the person has no local connection with the authority making the referral;
- where the person was accommodated in the area within the last five years by another authority, acting under a homeless duty;
- in respect of asylum-seekers only, where the two authorities agree. This provision was part of an agreed programme of dispersal of asylum-seekers from authorities in London and the South East to other parts of the UK. Given that all asylum-seekers arriving after April 2000 have been ineligible, this provision is no longer relevant.

13.296 The most common reason for a referral is under the 'local connection' provisions.

Local connection referral

13.297 An authority can refer a case to another authority if it considers that the relevant conditions are satisfied. The conditions are:

- neither the applicant nor any person who might reasonably be expected to live with the applicant has a local connection with the district of the authority to which the application was made; and

174 HA 1996 ss184(1)-(2) and 198(1).

- the applicant or any person who might reasonably be expected to live with the applicant has a local connection with the other district; and
- neither the applicant nor any person who might reasonably be expected to live with the applicant would run the risk of domestic violence in the other district, or he or she has suffered violence (other than domestic violence) in the other district and it is probable that the return to that district will lead to further violence of a similar kind.[175]

13.298 A referral cannot be made because an applicant has a stronger connection with another authority. Only if there is *no* local connection with the referring authority can a referral be made.

What is a local connection?

13.299 HA 1996 s199(1) provides that:

> A person has a local connection with the district of a local housing authority if he has a connection with it:
>
> (a) because he is, or in the past was, normally resident there, and that residence is or was of his own choice,
> (b) because he is employed there,
> (c) because of family associations, or
> (d) because of special circumstances.

Residence of choice

13.300 Residence must be residence of choice. This is not the case if the residence is because of service in the armed forces or while in prison or some other form of detention.[176] Similarly, service in the regular armed forces does not count as employment in the district.[177]

Former asylum-seekers

13.301 Former asylum-seekers who have previously been provided with accommodation by NASS in a dispersal area do gain a local connection in the dispersal area despite this not being residence of choice: section 199(6). If a person was accommodated in more than one dispersal area, the local connection is with the area in which he or she was most recently accommodated: section 199(7)(a). However,

---

175 Violence is defined in the same way as under section 177 above.
176 HA 1996 s199(3).
177 HA 1996 s199(2).

being accommodated in an 'accommodation centre'[178] does not create a local connection: section 199(7)(b).

13.302   The situation is different for asylum-seekers who were dispersed in Scotland (where the HA 1996 does not apply). Where a former asylum-seeker who was previously accommodated in dispersal accommodation in Scotland has no local connection with any authority in Scotland, England or Wales, no duty under section 193 arises.' An authority does have power to provide accommodation for a reasonable period to enable the applicant to find accommodation in the private sector and to provide advice and assistance.[179] The intention is that the person should either find accommodation privately or return to apply as homeless to the Scottish authority in whose area he or she was dispersed.

13.303   It should be noted however that an asylum-seeker or family member may gain a local connection by obtaining employment in the relevant area or may have a local connection by virtue of family association. In such a case referral to the dispersal area will not be possible. Similarly, after a period of residence in the area a local connection will be established. As in all cases, no referral can be made unless there is no local connection with the authority to which the application is made.

The local authority agreement

13.304   To avoid disputes between authorities about local connection, an agreement between local authorities operates. This is the Local Authority Association Joint Local Connection Agreement. It sets out a working definition of the way in which local connection is established. The Agreement provides:[180]

- 'normal residence' should be accepted if the person has lived in the area for six months during the previous 12 months or no less than three of the previous five years;
- 'family associations' normally arise where an applicant or a member of the household has parents, adult children or brothers or sisters currently living in the area who have been resident for at least five years, and the applicant indicates a wish to be near them;

---

178 Section 22 of the Nationality, Immigration and Asylum Act 2002 provides for accommodation centres to be set up for asylum-seekers but none have yet been established.

179 Asylum and Immigration (Treatment of Claimants) Act 2004 s11(2)–(3).

180 Paragraph 2.5.

- a referral should not be made on the basis of family association if the person objects;
- employment should not be of a casual nature.

13.305   The Agreement is not law, and where an applicant challenges a referral it may be possible to establish a local connection even if the Local Authority Agreement tests are not met.

> In *R v Southwark ex p Hughes*[181] a woman moved to Southwark to set up a permanent home with a man by whom she became pregnant. The relationship ended because of domestic violence and she applied as homeless. The authority's decision to refer her to another authority on the basis that she had resided in Southwark for less than six months was quashed: the authority had failed to make proper enquiry into whether she had gained a local connection by virtue of ordinary residence or other special reason.

13.306   However, the question is whether the local authority is entitled, on the evidence, to decide that a person has no local connection. While the Agreement must not be applied rigidly, an authority is entitled to take it into account as a guideline.

> In *Betts v Eastleigh BC*[182] an applicant and his family had moved to the district of Eastleigh to take up employment. The employment ended and he was forced to leave his private sector accommodation. The family had lived in the area for less than six months but it was their intention to settle in the area. Eastleigh found that the full housing duty was owed, but referred him to the local authority where the family had previously resided. Both authorities agreed that the referral was properly made, but the applicant sought judicial review, arguing that the family were normally resident in the area of Eastleigh and that the authority had erred in applying the criteria contained in the Local Connection Agreement too rigidly. Although the challenge was successful in the Court of Appeal, the House of Lords upheld the local authority's appeal.

181 (1998) 30 HLR 1082, QBD.
182 *Re Betts* [1983] 2 AC 613, HL.

It is for the local authority to decide whether an applicant has a local connection because of normal residence. The decision must be made by reference to the facts of each individual case, but an authority may operate a policy or establish guidelines, provided they do not close their mind to the particular facts of the individual case. On the facts of the case the authority had made a lawful decision.

Relevant date for establishing local connection

13.307   The general rule in relation to homeless decisions is that the person's circumstances are assessed as at the date of the decision, not the date of the application. In relation to local connection, this means that an applicant may not have local connection by way of normal residence when the application is made, but may have established such a connection by the time of the decision.

In *Mohammed v Hammersmith and Fulham LBC*[183] the applicant applied to the authority after living in the borough for about three months. He and his family were placed in interim accommodation and a decision was made that they would be referred to another authority. He argued that he had acquired a local connection because of the time the family had spent in interim accommodation awaiting a decision. The House of Lords held that the relevant time for deciding on local connection was the date of the decision, whether the original decision or the decision on review. Further, time spent in interim accommodation could, in appropriate circumstances, amount to 'normal residence' for the purpose of establishing a local connection.

Disputes between authorities

13.308   The authority proposing to refer the applicant must notify the applicant and the other authority at the same time, giving reasons why it is considered that the local referral conditions are met.[184] The applicant may challenge the decision by requesting a review and, if

183 [2001] UKHL 57, 1 November 2001.
184 Section 184(4).

unsuccessful, appealing to the county court. As between the two authorities, any issue as to whether the local referral conditions are met should be decided by agreement or, in the absence of agreement, by arbitration.

13.309   The procedure is set out in the Homelessness (Decisions on Referrals) Order 1998.[185] The Local Government Association operates an independent panel to resolve such disputes.

13.310   If the authorities are in dispute about the referral, the applicant should be kept in temporary accommodation by the referring authority until the dispute is resolved. It is unlawful for the referring authority to simply terminate interim accommodation on the basis that they believe the referral conditions are met. The applicant must continue to be accommodated until either the referral is accepted or the dispute resolved. If the referral is ultimately accepted, the referring authority may claim reimbursement from the receiving authority for the cost of interim accommodation pending the resolution of the dispute.

Challenging the decision that a housing duty is owed

13.311   A referral can only be considered after it has been decided that a housing duty is owed. A local authority, aware it will be referring an applicant to another authority, may be tempted to apply the relevant tests less rigorously than usual. In such a case, the authority to whom the referral is made may challenge the decision by way of judicial review if the decision is flawed on recognised public law grounds.

> In *R v Newham ex p Tower Hamlets LBC*[186] Newham found that a housing duty was owed to the applicant. It then referred the case to Tower Hamlets, where the applicant had a local connection. He had previously been found to be intentionally homeless by Tower Hamlets while Newham had found him not intentionally homeless. In reaching that decision, Newham had taken account of housing conditions in the area of Newham. Tower Hamlets challenged the decision, arguing that Newham had erred in law in considering housing conditions in its own area rather than in the area of Tower Hamlets. The Court of Appeal agreed and quashed Newham's decision that a housing duty was owed.

185 SI No 1578.
186 (1990) 23 HLR 62, CA.

13.312   It should be noted that in such a case the receiving authority must have the decision quashed by a court on public law grounds. A dispute about whether the housing duty is owed cannot be resolved through the arbitration procedure.[187] Unless the decision is quashed by a court, the receiving authority is bound to accept the referral provided the referral conditions are met.

Challenging a decision not to refer

13.313   The decision to refer an applicant to another authority is discretionary: there is no right to be referred or to review a decision not to refer.

> In *Hackney v Sareen*[188] a homeless application was made to Hackney with an indication that the family would like to be housed in another part of London because of family and friends who lived there. Hackney made inquiries and decided that a housing duty was owed. The decision letter made no reference to referral, but stated that the applicant had a right to a review of the decision. The applicant requested a review of the decision not to refer the case to the area where he wished to be housed, stating that he had no local connection with Hackney, but did have connections with the other local authority. Hackney responded that he had no right to a statutory review of the decision, but agreed to reconsider the issue. It then confirmed the decision not to refer. A county court appeal was lodged and was successful. However, the Court of Appeal upheld Hackney's appeal, holding that the decision to refer was discretionary and that: (1) there was no duty to investigate local connection, only a power to do so; (2) there was no right to a statutory review of a decision not to refer; (3) there was therefore no county court appeal in relation to such a decision; and (4) although an 'extra statutory' reconsideration could be challenged if there were grounds, this would not be by way of county court appeal, but by judicial review.
>
> Put simply: 'If an applicant wants to be housed in another local authority housing area, he should apply there'.[189]

---

187 *R v Slough ex p Ealing LBC* [1981] 1 All ER 601.
188 [2003] EWCA 351, 19 March 2003.
189 Auld LJ at [28].

Out of borough placements

13.314 This provision is to ensure that authorities cannot avoid future responsibility by placing homeless applicants outside its own area. It operates regardless of any local connection and also takes no account of any risk of violence in the area to which the referral is made. As the HA 1996 s193 duty now lasts indefinitely unless one of the events specified in section 193 occurs, this provision is rarely relevant. If the section 193 accommodation ceases to be available, the placing authority will be bound to provide alternative accommodation under its continuing section 193 duty.

Homeless decisions, reviews and appeals

Key points

- A local authority must give written notification of its decision to a homeless applicant.
- The notification must give reasons for any adverse finding.
- An applicant can request a review of the decision but must do so within 21 days of notification.
- An authority may agree to conduct a review outside the 21-day time limit.
- The review should be completed by the authority within eight weeks of the request.
- The review must be conducted by someone who was not involved in the original decision and, if an officer, must be someone senior to the decision maker.
- The parties can agree in writing to extend the time limit for completion of the review.
- An authority has a power but not a duty to provide interim accommodation pending a review.
- The review decision must be notified in writing, with reasons, to the applicant.
- An applicant may appeal to a county court against a negative review decision on a point of law. This covers all of the matters that can be challenged by judicial review.
- The appeal must be lodged within 21 days of notification of the review decision.
- The court may allow an out of time appeal in certain circumstances.
- An authority has a power but not a duty to provide interim accommodation pending the appeal.
- If interim accommodation pending review is refused the applicant may judicially review the decision.
- If interim accommodation pending appeal is refused the applicant may appeal to the county court.

Notification of the decision

14.1   When inquiries are complete, the authority must notify the applicant of its decision.[1] The decision letter is often referred to as a 'section 184 decision'. The section 184 decision must:

1   HA 1996 s184(3).

- be given in writing;
- inform the applicant of the decision and give reasons for any issue decided against the applicant's interests;
- inform the applicant of the right to request a review of the decision; and
- inform the applicant of the time within which the request must be made, which is 21 days from the date of notification.

Reasons

14.2   The reasons given by the authority must explain why the decision has been reached. It is not sufficient simply to recite the relevant legal test, list all of the matters taken into consideration and state the conclusion. The Court of Appeal has held that:[2]

> where ... an authority is required to give reasons for its decision, it is required to give reasons which are proper, adequate and intelligible and enable the person affected to know why they have won or lost. That said, the law gives decision-makers a certain latitude in how they express themselves and will recognise that not all those taking decisions will find it easy to express themselves with judicial exactitude.

14.3   A decision may be found to be flawed solely because of a failure to give reasons or sufficient reasons for the decision. However, the review process enables local authorities to correct such a deficiency. In such a case the applicant must be given the opportunity to make further representations before the final review decision. See below.

Matters arising after the decision

14.4   After the decision has been made, in the absence of fraud or a mistake of fact, an authority has no power to make further enquiries or re-open the decision unless the applicant seeks a review or makes a fresh application.

In *R v Lambeth ex p Miah*[3] following acceptance of a housing duty the applicant was granted a non-secure tenancy. The authority, having evidence that the applicant was not living in the

---

2   *R v Brent LBC ex p Baruwa* [1987] HLR 915, Schiemann LJ at 920.
3   (1994) 27 HLR 21, QBD.

accommodation but was sub-letting it, issued a second decision letter stating that the applicant was not homeless. The court held that the authority had no power to make further inquiries following the decision: there was no application to be investigated. In such a situation, however, a local authority may consider itself discharged from its obligation to continue to provide accommodation and if the authority believed the applicant was abusing the temporary accommodation the correct course of action would have been to determine the licence to occupy.

14.5   This decision pre-dates the HA 1996 and the position is now clearer: section 193 sets out the specific circumstances in which the duty to accommodate ends. This includes becoming homeless intentionally from the accommodation provided or ceasing to occupy it.

Fraud/false information

14.6   The situation is different where there has been fraud or the information given to the authority is untrue.

In *R v Dacorum BC ex p Walsh*[4] an applicant was found to be homeless and not intentionally homeless, having reported a threat of an eviction by her landlord. Subsequently the authority conducted further inquiries and concluded that she had pretended to be locked out of her home and her claim to be threatened with eviction was false. A second decision was made stating that she was intentionally homeless. The applicant's claim for judicial review was dismissed: it was absurd to suggest that the Act made it impossible to do what the authority had done.

Re-opening an application wrongly decided

14.7   Where an application was decided against the applicant, an authority may re-open the application after receiving new information.[5] However, where the applicant wishes the authority to consider new information, the proper course of action is to seek a review and to submit the new information in support of the review.[6]

---

4   (1991) 24 HLR 401.
5   *R v Hambleton DC ex p Geoghan* [1985] JPL 394, QBD.
6   *Demetri v Westminster CC* (2000) 32 HLR 470, CA.

14.8   An authority is also entitled to re-open an application where its decision was based on a fundamental mistake of fact.

> In *Porteous v West Dorset DC*[7] the applicant had a secure tenancy of a local authority property in London. She moved to Germany in 2002, believing that the tenancy had been transferred into her sister's name. In fact the tenancy had not been transferred and remained in the applicant's sole name. On her return from Germany she applied to the authority as homeless. The authority's inquiries did not reveal that the tenancy remained in her sole name and a decision was made that she was eligible, homeless, in priority need and not intentionally homeless and was therefore owed a housing duty. A few weeks after the decision was made, the London authority contacted West Dorset DC and informed them that Ms Porteous was still the tenant of the property and that it remained available for her occupation. A second decision was then made stating that she was not homeless as she had a right to reside in the London property and it was reasonable for her to do so. Ms Porteous applied for a review. Although a notice to quit was served in respect of the London property, the landlord authority indicated that is would await the outcome of the review before commencing possession proceedings. The review decision confirmed the later decision that Ms Porteous was not homeless. She appealed to the county court. At the hearing of the appeal, evidence was submitted that the London property remained available for her occupation. Her appeal was dismissed, the judge holding that the authority had been entitled to re-consider their original decision and that the London property was available to Ms Porteous.
>
> The Court of Appeal dismissed her appeal, holding that an authority was entitled to revisit and change a decision if the decision results from a fundamental mistake of fact, even where there was no bad faith on the part of either party.

The statutory review

14.9   Before 1997 the only way to challenge a homeless decision was by way of judicial review. The Housing Act 1996 introduced a statutory

7   [2004] HLR 30, 4 March 2004.

right to an internal review and a county court appeal on a point of law in respect of most substantive homeless decisions. Judicial review remains available in respect of decisions that do not carry the right of review.

14.10   The way in which reviews are conducted is set out in regulations, currently the Allocation of Housing and Homelessness (Review Procedures) Regulations 1999 ('the Review Regulations').[8]

Decisions with a right of review

14.11   Under section 202 of HA 1996 an applicant has a right to a review of a decision that he or she:[9]

- is not eligible;
- is not homeless or threatened with homelessness;
- is not in priority need;
- is intentionally homelessness;
- is to be referred to another authority.

14.12   There is also a right to a review of any decision on:

- the suitability of accommodation offered following the acceptance of a housing duty;
- the suitability of accommodation offered under Part VI in discharge of the homeless duty (the refusal of which may end the duty to provide temporary accommodation);
- whether the duty to accommodate has come to an end.

Decisions with no right of review

14.13   There is no right of review in relation to:

- a refusal to accept a homeless application;
- a refusal to provide interim accommodation pending a decision;
- the suitability of interim accommodation pending decision;
- a decision not to provide interim accommodation pending a statutory review and/or appeal to the county court;
- decisions about the protection of an applicant's belongings;
- a refusal to review a decision which has already been reviewed;

---

8   SI No 71.

9   HA 1996 s202 refers specifically to decisions about eligibility, local referral and suitability. In relation to the other matters it refers to any decision as to what duty (if any) is owed under sections 190–193, 195 and 196. The duties owed under these sections depend upon the decisions regarding the substantive issues of homelessness, priority need, and intentional homelessness.

- a refusal to extend the time limits within which a review should have been requested.

14.14 Decisions about these issues may be challenged by judicial review, with the exception of decisions about interim accommodation pending a county court appeal: such decisions are challenged by way of a second county court appeal (see para 14.59 below).

Time limits

Requesting the review

14.15 The request for the review must be made within 21 days of the 'day on which [the applicant] is notified'.[10] The time limit runs from the receipt of the letter, not the date of the letter. If the letter is not received by the applicant, or there is no address where it can be sent, it can be treated as having been given to him or her if it is made available at the authority's office for a reasonable period for collection.[11]

14.16 It is only the request for the review that must be made within 21 days. Representations and any new evidence can be submitted later. In most cases, the way the decision was made will be relevant and advisers should always request a copy of the homeless file at the same time as requesting a review, indicating that further representations may follow. A standard letter requesting a review is included in the appendix to this chapter. At the same time it may be necessary to request an extension of interim accommodation pending review. This is dealt with in chapter 15 and a model letter is included in the appendix to chapter 15.

Completing the review

14.17 Following a request for a review, the authority should complete the review in accordance with the procedure set out in regulations and within a specified time, currently eight weeks from the day the request is made. This time limit may be extended by written agreement between the parties.[12]

---

10 HA 1996 s202(3).
11 HA 1996 s184(6).
12 Reg 9(1)–(2) of the Review Regulations 1999. The time limits are different if the review concerns a disputed local referral. In such a case the time limit may be 10 or 12 weeks, depending on the nature of the decision: reg 9(1)(b)–(c).

Out of time reviews

14.18   An authority has a discretion to extend the time for requesting a review and must exercise its discretion in a lawful way. This means that the decision must not be made in bad faith or capriciously for improper motives. Further, it must not be limited to rigidly defined situations as that would involve an unlawful fetter on the discretionary power given by the Act[13] (see para 21.68).

14.19   In most cases the authority will consider both the reasons for the delay in requesting a review and the potential merits of the review when exercising its discretion. However, the discretion is very wide and it is not necessary in all cases to consider the merits of the review.[14] Notwithstanding this, there may be some cases where a failure to consider the merits of a review would be 'obvious perversity' if, on the face of it, the review was bound to succeed.[15]

Conduct of the review

14.20   The following rules are laid down in the Review Regulations:

- after receiving a review request the authority must notify the applicant:
    - of the right to make written representations, and
    - what the authority's review procedure is;
- the authority must then carry out the review, considering any representations made;
- if the person conducting the review is an officer (as opposed to a member or person independent of the authority) he or she must be someone who was not involved in the original decision and who is senior to the officer who made the original decision;
- if the reviewer considers that there is a deficiency or irregularity in the decision or the way it was made, but is still minded to make an adverse decision, the reviewer must notify the applicant:
    - that the reviewer is so minded and the reasons why, and
    - that the applicant has the right to make oral and/or written representations (in person or by a representative).

---

13 *R on the application of C v Lewisham LBC* [2003] EWCA Civ 927, 4 July 2003.
14 *R on the application of C v Lewisham LBC* [2003] EWCA Civ 927, 4 July 2003.
15 *R on the application of Radhia Slaiman v London Borough of Richmond upon Thames* [2006] EWHC 329 (Admin), 9 February 2006.

Scope of the review

14.21   The review is not limited to a consideration of whether the original decision was correct. The reviewer must take account of any representations made in support of the review and must make a decision based on all of the information and evidence available at the date of the review.[16]

Submissions

14.22   When making submissions in support of a review, it is important that the alleged flaws in the original decision are identified. If not, it may not be possible to rely on these flaws in any subsequent county court appeal.

14.23   In *Nipa Begum* (see para 13.154 above) the court refused to quash a decision even though the authority had failed to consider whether the applicant could afford to travel to Bangladesh to occupy accommodation there, because the issue had not been raised during the review process.

14.24   Similarly, in *Cramp v Hastings* (see para 12.53 above) the court upheld the council's appeal against the quashing of a decision for failure to make adequate inquiries. The inquiries the applicants alleged should have been made had not been mentioned in the review submissions.

14.25   There are, however, certain issues that an authority must address, regardless of the review submissions. An example is the affordability of accommodation when the issue is whether it is reasonable to occupy.[17]

New information/evidence

14.26   Where vulnerability is the issue, it is common for advisers to seek further medical evidence to submit as part of the review. While this is often the most effective way to challenge a decision, the agency advising the applicant may not be in a position to pay for expert evidence.[18] In such a case, the submission should nevertheless be

---

16   The previous regulations (the Allocation of Housing and Homelessness (Review Procedures and Amendment) Regulations 1996) stated: 'The authority shall – ... carry out the review on the basis of the facts known to them at the date of the review.' The 1999 Review Regulations do not state this, only that the reviewer should consider any representations made.

17   Homelessness (Suitability of Accommodation) Order 1996 (SI No 3204).

18   The fee for further expert evidence may be covered by the Legal Help scheme.

made that further medical evidence is necessary. If the authority declines to obtain such evidence the county court may uphold a challenge based on inadequate inquiry.

14.27   Where a local authority does obtain new medical evidence or advice it will usually be necessary, in the interests of fairness, to disclose it to the applicant and invite his or her comments. However, if the advice relates to issues of which the applicant is fully aware this may not be necessary.[19]

Relevant date for decision

14.28   The requirement to consider the information and evidence at the date of the review means that the review decision must take account of any change of circumstances since the original decision.

14.29   This was held to be the case even where an applicant had no local connection when he applied as homeless, but had established one by the time of the final decision: *Mohamed v Hammersmith and Fulham LBC* (see para 13.307).

> The same principle was applied in the case of *Sahardid v Camden LBC*.[20] The review was about the suitability of an offer of accommodation. The offer had been made in accordance with the council's policy to offer a single parent with a child under the age of five years a one-bedroom dwelling. The review decision was taken three days after the child's fifth birthday and the Court of Appeal held that the decision was flawed as it had failed to take account of the fact that the applicant was entitled, under the council's policy, to accommodation with two bedrooms.

14.30   An exception to this rule is a decision in respect of priority need by virtue of being aged 16 or 17. Priority need is automatically lost when the young person reaches the age of 18. An authority cannot take advantage of an unlawful decision made at a time when the applicant was under 18 by finding, on review, that the young person, having turned 18, no longer has priority need: *Akilah Robinson v Hammersmith & Fulham LBC* (see para 13.231).

---

19 See *Hall v Wandsworth LBC* and *Carter v Wandsworth LBC* and *Bellouti v Wandsworth LBC*. See paras 13.210–13.214.
20 [2004] EWCA Civ 1485, 26 October 2004.

Independence of reviewing officer

14.31 The review may be conducted by a panel of members or may be contracted out to an independent person.[21] If the review is carried out by an officer, he or she must be senior to the original decision maker and must not have been involved in the original decision. However, a reviewing officer may be assisted in making inquiries by the junior officer who made the original decision.[22]

14.32 In some cases there will be more than one review. An authority may accept that a review decision was flawed and agree to carry out a further review. Also, in most successful county court appeals the review decision will be quashed, with the result that the authority must carry out a further review. It is not unlawful for a subsequent review to be carried out by the same officer who carried out the first review.[23] However, as in all local authority decision-making, actual bias would make the decision unlawful (see paras 21.77–21.78).

Irregular decision – further representations

14.33 Regulation 8(2) of the Review Regulations 1999 provides that an applicant must be given the opportunity to make further representations where the reviewer has decided that there was a 'deficiency or irregularity' in the original decision or the manner in which it was made, but is nevertheless minded to make an adverse decision on review.

In *Hall v Wandsworth LBC*[24] the original decision that the applicant had no priority need made no reference to any medical evidence. On review, medical evidence was submitted on behalf of the applicant and the authority took advice from a medical adviser which they did not disclose to the applicant. The review decision made no reference to a deficiency or irregularity, but stated that because the decision was adverse full reasons would be given. The Court of Appeal held that to comply with regulation

---

21 Local Authorities (Contracting Out of Allocation of Housing and Homelessness Functions) Order 1996 (SI No 1996).
22 *Butler v Fareham BC*, May 2001 *Legal Action* 24, CA.
23 *Feld v London Borough of Barnet; Ali Pour v Westminster City Council* [2004] EWCA Civ 1307, 18 October 2004.
24 [2004] EWCA Civ 1740, 17 December 2004.

> 8(2) the authority should have disclosed the substance of the
> medical advice they had relied on and given the applicant the
> opportunity to make further representations. The decision was
> quashed.

14.34   The requirement of regulation 8(2) is often overlooked by local
authorities and may mean that the decision can be challenged on
that ground alone. If, however, the court takes the view that the
procedural error made no difference to the outcome an appeal may
be dismissed.

Notification and reasons

14.35   Notification of the review decision must be given in writing. If it is
not received, it is treated as having been given if it is made available
at the authority's office for a reasonable period for collection.[25]

14.36   If the original decision is confirmed, reasons must be given.[26]
Further, the applicant must be informed of the right to appeal to the
county court on a point of law and of the time limit for bringing such
an appeal, which is 21 days from the date of notification.[27] If reasons
are not given or if the applicant is not informed of the right to appeal
to the county court, the notice of the decision is treated as not having
been given.[28] This means that any deadline for appealing to the
county court does not apply until proper notice is given.

Outcome of review

14.37   The best outcome for the applicant will be an acceptance of the full
housing duty. Often, however, the review decision is that the section
184 decision should be withdrawn and further inquiry carried out.
If this is the outcome, then the authority will automatically have
a duty to provide interim accommodation pending further decision
(provided there is reason to believe the applicant is in priority
need).

14.38   If the review decision confirms the adverse conclusion of the
section 184 decision, the applicant may bring an appeal in the county
court.

---

25 Section 203(8).
26 Section 203(4).
27 Section 203(5).
28 Section 203(6).

Appeals to the county court

14.39   Section 204 of the HA 1996 provides that:

> if an applicant who has requested a review under section 202:
> (1) is dissatisfied with the decision on the review, or
> (2) is not notified of the decision on the review within the time prescribed ...
> he may appeal to the county court on any point of law arising from the decision or, as the case may be, the original decision.

Time limits

14.40   An appeal must be brought within 21 days of the applicant being notified of the review decision. If the appeal is being brought to challenge the original decision, following a failure to carry out a review within the statutory period, it must be brought within 21 days of the date he or she should have received notification (in most cases this means 11 weeks from the original notification).[29]

14.41   Where the 21 days ends on a day on which the court is closed, an appeal is brought in time if lodged on the next working day.[30]

Out of time appeals

14.42   The court may give permission for an appeal to be brought out of time only if satisfied that there was a good reason for the failure to bring the appeal in time and for any delay in applying for permission.[31] It is also possible to apply, *within* the 21-day period, for permission to lodge the appeal out of time. If a person is in a position to make such an application, it is probably better to simply draft and lodge the appeal notice itself, as the detailed grounds can be lodged by way of a skeleton argument later.

14.43   When considering permission for a late appeal, the court must be satisfied that there is a good reason for the delay. If not, permission must be refused and the court should not consider the merits of the appeal.[32]

---

29   Section 204(2).
30   *Adan v Brent LBC* (1999) 32 HLR 848, CA.
31   Section 204(2A).
32   *Short v Birmingham CC* [2004] EWHC 2112, 10 September 2004.

Procedure on appeals

14.44   Although there is no requirement to be legally represented, in most cases the applicant will need to instruct solicitors to advise whether there is a 'point of law' arising from the decision and to draft the notice of appeal, or to instruct a barrister to do so. Legal aid is available, depending on the applicant's means and the likelihood of success. It is important that someone seeking to challenge a review decision is referred to solicitors without delay; it will usually be necessary for the solicitor to send a letter before claim to the authority and consider the response before legal aid will be granted. Most solicitors will then instruct a barrister to draft the appeal notice.

14.45   The procedure is set out in Part 52 of the Civil Procedure Rules and the appeal notice is form N161. Part 52 and form N161 are available online, along with guidance notes. Chapter 22 contains a general explanation of county court procedure. In most cases the form N161 will be drafted by a solicitor or barrister, as it is necessary to set out the legal grounds on which it is argued the decision is unlawful. A 'skeleton argument' setting out the legal principles and case law relied on should either be included in the appeal notice or filed within 14 days. The forms and procedure are confusing as they are designed primarily for appeals against court decisions rather than local authority decisions.

14.46   The hearing of an appeal will usually consist of purely legal argument about the lawfulness of the decision. Oral evidence is not given and it is unusual even for witness statements to be used. If the appellant (the homeless applicant) is legally represented, he or she is not strictly required to attend the hearing. However, it is good practice to do so as proposals may be put forward to resolve the appeal on which his or her instructions will be needed.

Reconsidering a review decision

14.47   There is nothing to prevent an authority re-considering a decision made on review.[33] Indeed it is common for an authority to respond to a letter indicating an intention to appeal by offering to reconsider the decision. However, if this is agreed between the parties, the authority must be asked to confirm that it is withdrawing its previous review decision and that the reconsidered decision will be the review decision for the purposes of any appeal. If the authority does not agree, any appeal must be lodged within 21 days of the notification of the review decision.

33 *R v Westminster CC ex p Ellioua*, 31 HLR 440, CA.

In *Demetri v City of Westminster*[34] the authority's decision on review was notified in the correct form to the applicant, including information about the right to appeal to the county court within 21 days. The applicant's advisers discovered that certain documents had not been sent to the review officer and the council agreed to consider its review decision further in light of these documents. Two months later the council indicated that it had considered the documents, but would not change its review decision. An appeal was lodged in the county court but was struck out on the grounds that it had been lodged out of time. The applicant's appeal to the Court of Appeal was dismissed.

14.48   It should be noted that *Demetri* was decided at a time when the county court had no power to extend the time for an appeal. However, advisers should always ensure that the authority confirms that the first review decision is withdrawn pending reconsideration. In *Demetri* the court indicated that where an applicant is unrepresented the authority must make clear if the time for a county court appeal is not being extended.

Appealing the original section 184 decision

14.49   Where a review is requested but the authority fails to carry out the review, the applicant has two choices: a county court appeal against the original decision or judicial review to force the authority to carry out the review. Often it will be sufficient to invite the authority to agree an extension of time to complete the review. This must be confirmed in writing. If agreed, the deadline for any county court appeal will be 21 days after the agreed deadline. Where the applicant wishes to submit new information or make submissions to the authority, it will be better for a review to be conducted than to appeal against the original decision. Any such appeal will be limited to a consideration of the lawfulness of the decision at the time it was made. If the appeal is successful the likely outcome is the quashing of the decision so that the authority must make a fresh section 184 decision. Further, there is nothing to prevent an authority from notifying the applicant of the decision on review after a county court appeal has been commenced. The appellant would then need to

34 (2000) 32 HLR 470, CA.

amend the appeal grounds or (if the review decision is positive, or unchallengeable) to withdraw the appeal. In such a case the local authority should be ordered to pay the costs of the appeal.

What is a 'point of law'?

14.50   A 'point of law' is not limited to matters of legal interpretation, but embraces all of the matters usually challenged by way of judicial review, including irrationality and inadequacy of reasons.[35]

14.51   Broadly, the main types of judicial review challenge have been categorised under the following heads:[36]

- illegality;
- irrationality; and
- procedural impropriety.

14.52   In addition, a failure to give reasons, or adequate reasons, may in itself make a decision unlawful.

14.53   The grounds for judicial review are examined in more detail in chapter 21. All of the grounds that may be used in judicial review proceedings may be argued as a 'point of law' in a homeless appeal.

The powers of the county court

14.54   It is not for the court to reach its own decision on the facts. The court is exercising a 'supervisory' function, as in judicial review, and is limited to considering the lawfulness of the authority's decision. The court may:[37]

- confirm a decision;
- quash a decision; or
- vary a decision.

14.55   If an appeal is successful, the most common order is the quashing of the review decision. This means that the authority must conduct a fresh review. This may of course mean that even after a successful appeal the authority then make another negative review decision. Indeed, it is sometimes the case that an authority makes several review decisions in relation to the same applicant.

---

35 *Nipa Begum v Tower Hamlets LBC* (1999) 32 HLR 445, CA.
36 *CCSU v Minister for Civil Service* [1985] AC 374, HL.
37 Section 204(3).

14.56   When a court is asked to vary a decision, the question is whether there is any real prospect that the authority, acting rationally and with the benefit of further enquiry, might be satisfied that the issue could be decided in an adverse way.[38] If so, the decision should be quashed, rather than varied.

> In *Ekwuru v Westminster*[39] the Court of Appeal considered an appeal against a county court decision not to vary a decision that the appellant was intentionally homeless. In this case the authority had already agreed on two occasions to its decision being quashed, following successful appeals by Mr Ekwuru. On the third occasion they again indicated that they would submit to the decision being quashed and carry out what would be a fourth review. Mr Ekwuru argued that the court should vary the decision. The county court declined to do so on the basis that such a decision would involve a hearing of the original facts. Mr Ekwuru appealed to the Court of Appeal, who considered his appeal almost four years after he had applied as homeless. It was held that there was no realistic possibility that the further inquiries the authority proposed would produce more information than was available at the date of the third review. On the basis of the material before the authority at that time, it could not lawfully have come to the conclusion that Mr Ekwuru was intentionally homeless and the court varied the decision to one that he was not intentionally homeless.

Time limit for further review

14.57   There is no specific provision for a time limit for a further review, following the quashing or withdrawal of a previous review decision. If the review is to be carried out following a county court appeal, the court may be asked to stipulate a time limit for the further review decision. If the review is withdrawn by agreement, a time limit should also be agreed.

14.58   In all cases advisers will wish to stipulate that the applicant is provided with interim accommodation pending any further review decision.

---

38 *R on the application of Deugi v Tower Hamlets LBC* [2006] EWCA Civ 159, 7 March 2006.

39 [2003] EWCA Civ 1293, 31 July 2003.

Accommodation pending appeal

14.59   An authority has a discretion to provide interim accommodation pending an appeal. If this is refused an applicant may bring a second appeal in the county court, under section 204A, to challenge the refusal. Interim accommodation pending review or appeal is discussed in chapter 15.

Request for review

Dear Sir/Madam,

Re: Mrs A – section 184 decision dated

We are advising Mrs A with regard to her homeless application.

Mrs A requests a review of the above decision.

Please provide to us a copy of the complete homelessness file under the Data Protection Act 1998. We enclose a cheque in the sum of £10 together with our client's signed authority.

We intend to make representations in support of the review following receipt of the file. We would therefore be grateful if this could be provided as a matter of urgency.

Yours faithfully,

Adviser

Advice Agency

Homelessness: accommodation duties

Key points

- Whenever an authority is under a duty to provide accommodation it must be available to the applicant and the family members he or she normally lives with and any other person who might reasonably be expected to live with the applicant.
- An authority must provide interim accommodation pending a decision if it has reason to believe the applicant may be in priority need.
- An authority may provide interim accommodation pending review or appeal.
- Interim accommodation must be suitable but the temporary nature of the accommodation means the standard may be low.
- If the 'full housing duty' is owed the authority must make available suitable accommodation. The applicant can challenge the suitability of accommodation offered by way of review and county court appeal.
- If an applicant refuses the accommodation and fails, through a review or appeal, to change the decision about suitability the authority will owe no housing duty.
- An applicant can accept the accommodation and still challenge the suitability by way of review and county court appeal.
- The duty to provide suitable accommodation under the full housing duty is indefinite: it only ends in specified circumstances set out in s193.
- The accommodation provided under the full housing duty will not give long term security to the applicant.
- Accommodation with long term security will only be made available through the authority's allocations scheme.

Introduction

15.1   At various stages throughout the homeless application process an authority may have a duty or a power to provide accommodation for the applicant. The different stages at which an accommodation duty may arise are as follows:

Temporary accommodation

- interim accommodation pending decision;
- interim accommodation pending review;
- interim accommodation pending appeal;

- temporary accommodation to a person found intentionally homeless.

The 'full housing duty'

- indefinite accommodation under HA 1996 s193.

Permanent accommodation

- the allocation of permanent social housing.

15.2   The principles involved at each stage vary, as do the ways of challenging decisions. Chapter 12 deals with the interim accommodation duty pending decision. This chapter deals with the power to provide interim accommodation pending review and appeal, the accommodation duty owed to those found intentionally homeless and the 'full housing duty' under section 193. The allocation of permanent accommodation is dealt with in chapter 16.

Temporary accommodation duties

Accommodation pending decision

15.3   This is dealt with in detail in chapter 12. The principal features of the duty to provide interim accommodation pending a decision are:

- the duty is triggered when the authority have reason to believe the applicant may be eligible, homeless and in priority need;
- the accommodation must be suitable and it must be made available for the applicant and his or her household;
- the duty ends when a decision is made on the homeless application;
- challenging a failure to provide accommodation or to the suitability of the accommodation is by way of judicial review.

Accommodation pending review

15.4   The duty to provide interim accommodation ends if a negative decision is made. If the applicant seeks a review, the authority has a power to continue to provide interim accommodation pending the review decision.

15.5   The authority is not bound to consider whether to provide or extend interim accommodation pending review unless requested to do so.[1]

1   *R v Newham LBC ex p Lumley* (2003) 33 HLR 111, 28 January 2000.

15.6   A refusal to provide interim accommodation pending review is challenged by way of judicial review.

15.7   The principles to be applied by an authority in deciding whether or not to provide interim accommodation were set out by the Court of Appeal in *R v Camden LBC ex p Mohammed*.[2]

> In *Mohammed* the authority operated a policy of exercising its discretion to provide interim accommodation only in exceptional circumstances. The evidence was that the proportion of successful reviews was small. The Court of Appeal held that it is not unlawful to operate such a policy and that an authority must balance the objective of maintaining fairness between homeless persons to whom they have decided no duty is owed, with proper consideration of the possibility that the applicant may be right and may therefore be deprived of an entitlement. In carrying out the balancing exercise certain matters will always require consideration:
>
> • the merits of the case – that is, the merits of the case that the decision is flawed, not the merits of the case on the facts, once all necessary inquiries have been made;[3]
> • whether there is new material, information or argument which should be considered and could have a real effect on the decision under review; and
> • the personal circumstances of the applicant and the consequences of a refusal to provide interim accommodation.
>
> In *Mohammed* the applicant claimed to have left her home because of domestic violence from her husband. The authority had taken account of inconsistencies in her account of his conduct. The authority did not give her the opportunity to explain the inconsistencies, but decided that accommodation was available to her and she was not therefore homeless. The court decided that the merits of the challenge to the initial decision were such that the original decision was tainted with unfairness; the authority had been wrong to refuse to provide interim accommodation pending review.

2   (1997) 30 HLR 315, CA.
3   See the comments of Brooke LJ at paras 52 and 54 in *Lumley* (see para 15.9 below). This is an important distinction, as in many cases the quality of the initial decision making is poor, with cursory inquiries being made and letters issued in a pro forma manner. The conclusion may be the same following full inquiries, but the applicant is entitled to a lawful decision made in accordance with the Act and properly explained.

15.8   These criteria should be addressed when requesting interim accommodation. Because such requests usually have to be made on an urgent basis, it is useful to use a template when submitting such a request. An example of such a letter is contained in the appendix to this chapter.

15.9   Local authorities often cite the case of *R v Brighton and Hove Council ex p Nacion*[4] in arguing that, where an authority has considered all material factors, successful judicial review applications will be exceptional. *Nacion* concerned a refusal to provide interim accommodation *after* a review decision and pending a county court appeal.[5] In *Nacion* the court did refer to the fact that the provision of accommodation pending appeal *and review* was entirely within the discretion of the local authority. However, it is more likely that there will be merit in the argument that the original decision is flawed rather than that the review decision is flawed. On the other hand, a local authority that has extended acommodation pending review will usually agree a further extension until appeal.

In *R v Newham LBC ex p Lumley*, the applicant was a man suffering from depression who had been homeless for some time. The authority was provided with a medical report referring to the risk of suicide if he remained homeless. The authority's medical officer considered the doctor's report and indicated, without giving reasons, that he did not consider the applicant to be vulnerable. The decision letter, it was conceded, simply recited the terms of section 189 (the priority need categories) 'parrot-fashion' and gave no substantive explanation for its decision that the applicant was not in priority need. It was held that the authority had failed in its duty to carry out proper inquiries into his psychiatric history.

In relation to the provision of interim accommodation pending review, the court held that the authority 'had clearly not yet made a lawful decision, because of the shortcomings which [were conceded]. Justice therefore demanded that it should continue to provide him with temporary accommodation until it did.'[6]

4   (1999) 31 HLR 1095.
5   This was at a time when judicial review was the only way to challenge such decisions.
6   Brooke LJ at 55.

Accommodation pending appeal

15.10   An authority also has a power to provide interim accommodation pending a county court appeal: section 204(4). Prior to the Homelessness Act 2002 the only way to challenge a refusal to do so was by way of judicial review (as in the case of *Nacion*), see para 15.9 above. Now such challenges are brought by way of a county court appeal.

15.11   The HA 1996 s204A(2) provides that, where an applicant has a right to a county court appeal against a homeless decision, the applicant may also appeal against a decision not to provide accommodation up to the date of appeal.

15.12   If the appeal succeeds, the court may order the authority to secure that accommodation is available until the determination of the main appeal, or an earlier time, as specified, and shall confirm or quash the decision appealed against. The court cannot order the authority to provide interim accommodation beyond the final determination of the homeless appeal.[7]

15.13   An order by the court that an authority should provide interim accommodation may only be made if the court is satisfied that a failure to exercise the power would 'substantially prejudice the applicant's ability to pursue the main appeal'.[8] The most compelling argument will be where, without interim accommodation, the appellant will be 'street homeless' pending the appeal, so that his or her solicitors may find it impossible to obtain instructions to pursue the appeal.

Temporary accommodation to the intentionally homeless

15.14   If an applicant is found to be eligible, homeless and in priority need, but intentionally homeless, section 190(2) provides that an authority must:

   (a) secure that accommodation is made available for his occupation for such period as they consider will give him a reasonable opportunity of securing accommodation for his occupation; and

   (b) provide him with advice and such assistance as they consider appropriate in the circumstances in any attempts he may make to secure that accommodation becomes available for his occupation.

7   Section 204A(6)(b).
8   Section 204A(6)(a).

15.15   In determining what is a reasonable period the authority must consider an applicant's individual circumstances and should not operate a blanket policy as to the period of temporary accommodation offered in all cases.[9]

> The Court of Appeal considered the nature of the section 190 duty in *R on the application of Conville v London Borough of Richmond upon Thames*.[10] The decision that the applicant was intentionally homeless was made in February 2005 and she was told she could remain in the interim accommodation for a further 28 days. She was subsequently granted a number of extensions until 8 June 2005. She made genuine but unsuccessful attempts to find her own accommodation. Her efforts were hampered by the fact that she could not afford the deposit and advance rent required by most private landlords. She could not borrow the money and was ineligible for the council's rent deposit scheme. In deciding on the period that was reasonable, the authority had taken into account the applicant's circumstances and the authority's limited resources and the needs of other homeless applicants.
>
> The Court of Appeal held that the authority should not have taken account of its resources, but should have assessed what was a reasonable period
>
>> by reference to the particular needs and circumstances of the applicant. It should have regard to the possibilities open to the applicant ... If the applicant is not making reasonable efforts to pursue the possibilities open to him, that will be a strong indication that he should not be given more time.[11]
>
> However, giving a person a reasonable opportunity to find accommodation does not mean a period sufficient to ensure that the person will necessarily succeed.
>
>> What amounts to a reasonable opportunity will depend on the particular circumstances but it is an assessment the authority are capable of making without converting it into a duty to meet the appellant's needs. In this statutory context, a distinction is maintainable between giving a reasonable opportunity and giving such opportunity as will succeed in obtaining accommodation.[12]

9   *Lally v RLBC Kensington and Chelsea* (1980) *Times*, 27 March.
10   [2006] EWCA Civ 718, 8 June 2006.
11   Pill LJ at [38].
12   Pill LJ at [40].

Advice and assistance

15.16   In addition to providing accommodation for a reasonable period, the authority must also provide, or ensure the applicant is provided with, advice and assistance in any attempt made to secure accommodation: section 190(2)(b). Before providing the advice and assistance the applicant's housing needs must be assessed: section 190(4). Further, the advice and assistance provided must include information about the likely availability in the district of the types of accommodation appropriate to his or her housing needs (including, in particular, the location and sources of such types of accommodation): s190(5).

The 'full' housing duty – section 193

15.17   If, following inquiry, the authority is satisfied that the applicant is eligible, homeless, in priority need and not intentionally homeless, the 'full' housing duty is owed. The duty will be owed by the authority to which the application was made, unless the local referral conditions are met, in which case it will be owed by the authority to which the case is referred.

How the section 193 duty can be discharged

15.18   HA 1996 s193(2) provides that the 'full housing duty' is to 'secure that accommodation is available for occupation by the applicant'. Section 206 provides that this can be done in the following ways:

(a) by securing that suitable accommodation provided by them is available;

(b) by securing that he obtains suitable accommodation from some other person; or

(c) by giving him such advice and assistance as will secure that he obtains suitable accommodation from some other person.

15.19   Most commonly, an authority will provide the accommodation itself, or arrange for some other person or agency to provide it. However, in some circumstances it could simply be to give advice and assistance such that it will be obtained from someone else. This could cover, for example, advising and assisting a person with sufficient means to purchase accommodation. It could also include mediation to ensure that accommodation provided by family members was made available.[13]

15.20 If the authority offers a tenancy, it will be a non-secure tenancy. If an arrangement is made with a private landlord or an RSL, any tenancy will be an assured shorthold tenancy. Tenancies with social landlords can only become secure or fully assured if the person subsequently qualifies for an allocation under Part VI. The accommodation does not have to be under a tenancy and could, for example, be a licence in a hostel, provided the accommodation was suitable.

15.21 Although the tenancy or licence will not give the occupier long term rights in the particular property, the duty of the authority to provide accommodation under section 193 is indefinite. It ends only in the circumstances set out in section 193, listed at para 15.46 below. This means that a person who is provided with an assured shorthold tenancy under section 193 must be provided with alternative accommodation if the landlord subsequently seeks possession. The section 193 duty is a continuing one and the person need not make a fresh homeless application. This should be made clear to the applicant when the offer of accommodation is made.[14]

When does the duty arise?

15.22 Usually, when a decision is made that the full housing duty is accepted, the applicant will be residing in interim accommodation. It is possible for the authority to propose that the applicant remain in the same accommodation pursuant to the section 193 duty. If so, it must make clear that the accommodation currently occupied is considered suitable, that the applicant has the right to seek a review of its suitability and state the time limit for requesting a review. This information may be included in the section 184 letter stating that a duty is accepted. If the applicant does not agree that the accommodation is suitable for occupation for the immediate future, he or she must request a review within 21 days.

15.23 More commonly, the interim accommodation will be unsuitable for long-term occupation. Clearly, in all cases, some time will elapse before the authority can identify and make available accommodation suitable for longer-term occupation. However, disputes may arise where there is significant delay in providing suitable accommodation.

---

13 See *Akilah Robinson v Hammersmith & Fulham LBC* (para 13.23 above).
14 *Griffiths v St Helens Council* [2006] EWCA Civ 160, 7 March 2006.

In some cases an authority may acknowledge that the accommodation being provided is not suitable, but maintain that no suitable accommodation is currently available.

Delays in providing suitable accommodation

15.24   The following cases illustrate the courts' approach to the issue of delay.

> In *R v Southwark ex p Anderson*[15] the section 193 duty was accepted in May 1997. The authority agreed to discharge its duty by providing four-bed accommodation. However, to speed the process the applicants agreed to take three-bed accommodation, in or out of the borough. Three offers were made, but withdrawn because they were unsuitable. A fourth offer was the subject of an internal review. The applicants sought judicial review of the council's failure to secure accommodation between May 1997 and February 1999. The application was dismissed. It was held that 'there is no time limit within which the housing authority is obliged under the statute to comply with a duty to secure available accommodation for those who fall within section 193'. On the evidence the council was trying to secure suitable accommodation but was hampered by the lack of available stock; it was in the process of complying with its duty and was not in breach of its obligations.
>
> In *R v Merton LBC ex p Sembi*[16] the council accepted a section 193 duty towards a disabled applicant. It decided that her needs would be best met by specially adapted long-term accommodation.
>
> In the meantime, she was provided with a place in a home for the elderly and terminally ill. The applicant sought judicial review of the delay in securing more appropriate accommodation. Her application was dismissed. The suitability of the current accommodation could be challenged by way of a review and county court appeal. With regard to the delay, the reasoning of *Anderson* was followed. The authority was not in breach of the duty, but were in the process of complying.

15   (1998) 32 HLR 96, QBD.
16   (1999) 32 HLR 439, QBD.

In *R v Newham LBC ex p Begum and Ali*[17] it was decided that any suggestion in *Anderson* and *Sembi* that an authority had a 'reasonable period' to comply with the section 193 duty was incorrect.

The applicants comprised a family including six children, another young relative and an elderly disabled relative who was a wheelchair-user. On their application they were provided with bed and breakfast accommodation outside the borough. This was conceded to be unsuitable. Following acceptance of the full duty, the family was placed in a four-bedroom privately leased house which was also unsuitable as it was not adapted for wheelchair use. The applicants sought judicial review to require the council to discharge its duty by providing suitable accommodation. The council argued that, following *Anderson* and *Sembi*, there was no time limit for the provision of section 193 accommodation and that provided it was using its best endeavours it could not be criticised. Alternatively, the HA 1996 was to be read as giving a reasonable period for a council to find suitable accommodation, and the authority could not be required to achieve the impossible – the provision of suitable accommodation if none was available.

The application for judicial review was allowed. It was held that section 193 (and sections 188, 190 and 200) required that the council secure suitable accommodation as soon as the duty to accommodate arose. The performance of those duties could not be deferred and any suggestion in *Anderson* and *Sembi* that that was the case was based on an erroneous approach to Part VII.

The 'safeguards' for a council faced with a housing duty under Part VII were threefold: (1) the test of suitability was flexible – what could be provided might not be ideal, but might be suitable if intended for the very short-term; (2) a premature application to the court would be refused; and (3) if the court was satisfied that performance was really impossible, relief might be refused.

However, in this case the council had not considered using its own stock, but had confined itself to considering 'temporary' accommodation such as privately leased premises and bed and breakfast hotels. An order was made, compelling the council to provide suitable accommodation within 28 days.

17 (1999) 32 HLR 808, QBD.

In *R on the application of Aweys v Birmingham CC*[18] the Court of Appeal considered the position of applicants who had been found to be homeless because it was not reasonable for them to continue to occupy grossly overcrowded accommodation. Having accepted the applicants as homeless, the authority then indicated that they should remain in that accommodation until suitable permanent accommodation became available. The authority's allocations policy, however, gave less priority to the applicants, classed as 'homeless at home', than to homeless applicants occupying temporary accommodation provided by the authority. The Court of Appeal determined that it was unlawful for the authority to seek to discharge the section 193 duty by leaving a homeless family in their accommodation when the authority had decided that it was not reasonable for them to continue to occupy that accommodation. Further, the allocations policy was unlawful in giving the applicants less priority than those in temporary accommodation provided by the authority.

The Court of Appeal however, referring to the fact that a court would not make an order to force a local authority to do the impossible, declined to determine the more difficult question: whether a local authority is in breach of its statutory duty until such time as it finds suitable accommodation for a person following the acceptance of a duty.

15.25   So, although the authority does not have a 'reasonable period' to find suitable accommodation, the courts may decline to intervene if satisfied that the authority is doing its best to find something. If an applicant contends that the accommodation being provided is not suitable, he or she should seek a review. In assessing suitability, the relevant standards will be lower if accommodation is intended for only short-term occupation, pending more suitable accommodation being found.

15.26   If it seems that an authority is not using its best endeavours to find suitable accommodation, or is limiting the type of accommodation that may be used (for example only considering private sector accommodation), a claim for judicial review may be appropriate. A request should be made for the authority to disclose the steps it is taking to find suitable accommodation. Often, such pressure results in more suitable accommodation being located. If, however, the authority is making all reasonable endeavours but is hampered by

18   [2008] EWCA Civ 48, 7 February 2008.

the lack of suitable accommodation, a court may refuse to make an order. This is more likely to be the case where only accommodation of an unusual size or type will be suitable.

15.27   Most authorities use private landlords to discharge their section 193 duties. Complaints about the standard of accommodation and disrepair are common. If a tenancy has been granted, the occupier will have the right to have certain repairs carried out by the landlord: see chapter 9. However, in many cases the occupier communicates not with the landlord directly, but with a local authority's temporary accommodation section or with an RSL who has management responsibilities. He or she may be more concerned to be allocated alternative accommodation than to have repairs carried out. In such a case the making of a formal complaint and, ultimately, an Ombudsman complaint may be effective.

> An Ombudsman Complaint was made against Hackney LBC[19] about a seven-year delay in making accommodation available to a homeless applicant. A duty to house under the 1985 Act was accepted in 1992 and a succession of private sector leased properties were made available until 1999, when the applicant was nominated to a housing trust for permanent accommodation. A complaint was made of maladministration for (1) the delay in securing permanent accommodation, and (2) the poor quality of the temporary accommodation. The Ombudsman found that in 1993 an offer of permanent accommodation had been made, but had been sent to an old address and had not come to the applicant's attention. This had resulted in the applicant remaining in temporary accommodation for six years longer than necessary. Further, because of mistakes by the council's agents (a housing association), the quality of the temporary accommodation had been unsatisfactory and for three years the family had lived in accommodation deemed 'prejudicial to health' by the council's Environmental Health Department. The ombudsman recommended compensation of £6,000.

Suitability

15.28   It is for the authority to decide what is suitable. In doing so they must have regard to:

19 98/A/1857, reported in November 1999 *Legal Action* 17.

- the legislation on slum clearance, overcrowding and houses in multiple occupation (HMOs);[20]
- the particular circumstances of the applicant and his or her family, including any medical and physical needs or social considerations such as the risk of racial harassment or domestic violence, access to and stability in schools, and access to other facilities;[21]
- the affordability of the accommodation, in particular, the financial resources available to that person, the cost of the accommodation and that person's other reasonable living expenses.[22]

Housing standards

15.29　It should be noted that section 210 requires that an authority 'have regard to' the legislation on slum clearance, overcrowding and HMOs. The legislation is found in the Housing Acts 1985 and 2004 (see chapter 9) and gives enforcement powers to local authorities where properties in the private sector fall below certain standards. The 'fitness standards' previously set out in the HA 1985 have been replaced by a system of hazard assessment, which is described at paras 10.23–10.29. The Code of Guidance provides:

> *The Secretary of State recommends that when determining the suitability of accommodation secured under the homelessness legislation, local authorities should, as a minimum, ensure that all accommodation is free of Category 1 hazards. In the case of an out-of-district placement it is the responsibility of the placing authority to ensure that accommodation is free of Category 1 hazards.*[23]

The particular circumstances of the applicant

15.30　Generally, a homeless applicant has little choice over the type or location of accommodation offered under section 193. While an authority must take account of the needs of the applicant's household, it is difficult to challenge decisions as to suitability unless the applicant has particular needs that have been ignored.

20　Section 210.
21　Code of Guidance: paras 17.5–6.
22　Homelessness (Suitability of Accommodation) Order 1996 (SI No 3204).
23　Paragraph 17.5.

In *R v Brent ex p Omar*[24] the applicant was offered accommodation in a basement flat on an estate. She had been granted refugee status, having been imprisoned and abused in Somalia. She rejected the offer, indicating that the premises were reminiscent of the conditions of her imprisonment and that she would rather commit suicide than live there. The authority maintained that the offer was suitable because there were no pure medical grounds or other social grounds why it should not be accepted. The applicant's judicial review claim was upheld. In addition to the matters the Act referred to, an authority must also have regard to the particular circumstances of the applicant and her family. This was an exceptional case in which no reasonable housing authority, properly directing itself, could conclude that the property was suitable for the applicant.

Location

15.31   The location of accommodation is relevant to suitability, and the Code refers to the need to take account of family members in paid employment and to minimise disruption to the education of young people, particularly at critical points, such as when they are close to taking GCSE examinations: para 7.41. Many applicants wish to be accommodated in the locality where they are settled, and where their family and friends live. However, given the shortage of available accommodation, very strong reasons will be needed to challenge the suitability on the grounds of location.

In *Abdullah v City of Westminster*[25] an applicant rejected accommodation on the grounds that it was too far from her family and friends who provided her with support to care for her children. The county court upheld her first appeal: the review officer had failed to take sufficient account of her need to be near family and friends. A reconsideration was undertaken, but the review officer again found that the property was suitable. On a second county court appeal the decision was upheld. The Court of Appeal dismissed her appeal. The review officer had relied on advice and information received from social services to the effect that the property was suitable. The medical officer had indicated that it would be advantageous for the applicant to be near family and

24   (1991) 23 HLR 446, QBD.
25   Lawtel: LTL 21/6/2007, November 2007 *Legal Action* 38.

friends, but not that she would be unable to cope without it. There was sufficient material for the review officer to reach the decision and no grounds to appeal against the county court's refusal to interfere.

Out of area placements

15.32   Section 208 of HA 1996 provides that:

> So far as reasonably practicable a local housing authority shall in discharging their housing functions under this Part secure that accommodation is available for the occupation of the applicant in their district.

15.33   An authority's starting point must be to locate accommodation within its own area. However, it is not unlawful to operate a policy under which some out-of-borough accommodation is used, providing it is suitable for the particular applicant. In deciding whether it is reasonably practicable to secure accommodation within the borough, the authority may take into account the cost of providing the accommodation.

In *R on the application of Calgin v LB Enfield*[26] the court held that the authority's policy of using accommodation in Birmingham and Luton to house a small proportion of homeless applicants was lawful. Further, when deciding what was 'reasonably practicable' the issue of the authority's resources and the comparative cost of providing accommodation within and outside the borough were relevant. In the circumstances the offer of accommodation in Birmingham was suitable, having regard to the needs of the family and their links in the borough of Enfield.

15.34   However, as in all cases, the accommodation must be suitable for the particular applicant. A challenge to the same authority was successful in the case of *R on the application of Yumsak v Enfield LBC*[27], see para 12.36. The applicant had a number of good reasons to remain in the area she had lived for seven years and the authority had failed to justify the breach of her rights under Article 8 of the European Convention on Human Rights that would be involved in her being accommodated in Birmingham.

26 [2005] EWHC 1716 (Admin), 29 July 2005.
27 [2002] EWHC 280 (Admin), 5 February 2002.

Affordability

15.35 An authority must in all cases consider whether accommodation is affordable for the applicant. The Homelessness (Suitability of Accommodation) Order 1996[28] requires a local authority to take account of the income and necessary outgoings as well as the reasonable living expenses of a household when deciding if it is affordable to the particular applicant.[29] The Code of Guidance suggests that if, after taking these into account, the 'residual income' would be less than that of a household reliant on income support, a property is unaffordable (see para 17.40 below).

15.36 It is common in the private sector for the amount of housing benefit awarded to a tenant to be less than the full amount of the rent. Where an authority discharges its duty by arranging for the offer of a private tenancy, it may use its powers to 'top up' payments of housing benefit so that the landlord receives the full rent.[30] It may be argued that where an applicant is in receipt of income support, any shortfall that he or she is expected to meet makes the property unaffordable and therefore unsuitable. On the other hand, where the shortfall is small, an authority may argue that other tenants in the same situation must make such payments in order to maintain private tenancies.

Reviews of suitability

Accepting or refusing the offer

15.37 An applicant can accept an offer and still seek a review of its suitability.[31]

15.38 Conversely, where an applicant refuses accommodation and seeks a review of its suitability, the authority are not obliged to keep the accommodation available pending the outcome of the review.[32]

15.39 Challenges to the suitability of accommodation offered under section 193 rarely succeed. It is therefore always safer for an applicant to accept an offer while challenging the suitability. A person who refuses an offer and is unsuccessful in challenging the suitability will be entitled to no further housing assistance. The section 193

---

28 SI No 3204.
29 The Order prescribes the income and outgoings that must be taken into account.
30 See Code of Guidance, para 16.20.
31 Section 202(1A).
32 *Osseily v Westminster CC* [2007] EWCA 1108, 5 October 2007.

duty will have ended and the person will also lose any priority given under the allocations policy to those who are owed a homeless duty by the authority.

15.40   When advising on the merits of a challenge to suitability, it must be remembered that it is for the local authority to decide whether the offer is suitable. If it has taken account of all relevant information, an authority will only be acting unlawfully if no reasonable authority could have decided the particular accommodation was suitable for the particular applicant.

15.41   The Code of Guidance on Allocations provides that, in relation to Part VI offers, an applicant should be given a reasonable time to consider the offer. However, the Homelessness Code makes no similar provision. In practice, most authorities will allow an applicant a short time to decide whether to accept an offer. Nevertheless, the Court of Appeal has held[33] that an authority is not obliged to allow an applicant to view accommodation offered under section 193 before being required to sign a tenancy agreement. It is for the authority to decide whether the accommodation is suitable and, if the applicant disagrees, he or she may request a review of its suitability.

15.42   It may happen that an applicant indicates to the authority, before having taken advice, that he or she will not accept the accommodation. If, following advice, the person agrees to accept the offer while seeking a review of its suitability, urgent steps need to be taken to contact the authority to see if the property is still available. Provided the property has not been let to someone else, an authority will usually allow the person to accept the offer. An authority that rigidly applies an arbitrary deadline for acceptance may be subject to challenge by way of judicial review. However, if the applicant was properly advised of his or her rights by the authority and nevertheless refused the accommodation, the authority need not keep the accommodation vacant until the dispute about suitability is resolved.[34]

15.43   Section 193 prescribes the information that must be given to an applicant in relation to offers made under section 193 or under Part VI, and is detailed below.

Change of circumstances

15.44   Section 193 accommodation may be occupied for many years. During that time the composition of the applicant's household may

---

33   *LB Newham v Khatun, Zeb, Iqbal & the OFT* [2004] EWCA Civ 55, 24 February 2004.
34   See *Osseily* above.

change or the applicant's health may deteriorate. If the applicant argues that, because of a change of circumstance, the accommodation has become unsuitable, a request for a review of the suitability should be made. The duty to provide suitable accommodation is an ongoing duty and, provided there has been a change in circumstance, a local authority has a duty to conduct a statutory review on request.[35] If the review decision is unfavourable, a county court appeal may be brought. If the authority fails to respond to the request for a review, a county court appeal may be brought to challenge the decision that the accommodation is suitable. The deadline for such an appeal is 21 days from the date the review should have been completed (ie 11 weeks from the date of the request).

When does the section 193 duty come to an end?

15.45 The accommodation provided under section 193 is not permanent accommodation and the occupier will not have long-term security of tenure. However, although an applicant may be evicted from particular accommodation, the section 193 duty will continue until ended by a specific event.

15.46 Section 193 sets out the only circumstances in which the duty to accommodate ends. The duty ends if the applicant:

- refuses an offer of suitable accommodation, made under section 193, provided he or she was informed of the possible consequences of refusal and the right to request a review of suitability: section 193(5);
- ceases to be eligible for assistance: section 193(6)(a);
- becomes homeless intentionally from the accommodation made available by the authority ('the section 193 accommodation'): section 193(6)(b);
- accepts an offer of accommodation under Part VI: section 193(6)(c);
- accepts an offer of an assured tenancy (other than an assured shorthold tenancy) from a private landlord: section 193(6)(cc);
- voluntarily ceases to occupy the section 193 accommodation as his or her only or principal home: section 193(6)(d);
- refuses a final offer made under Part VI, having been informed of the possible consequences of refusal and of the right to a review of suitability: section 193(7); or

---

35 *R on the application of Zaher v Westminster* [2003] EWHC 101 Admin, 28 January 2003.

- accepts a 'qualifying offer' of an assured shorthold tenancy from a private landlord: section 193(7B).

Decision that section 193 duty has ended

15.47   An applicant has a right to seek a review of the decision that the section 193 duty has ended.[36] Despite this, there is no express duty under section 193 to inform the applicant of the decision or to give reasons. This is discussed below.

15.48   The way an applicant is informed that the section 193 duty has ended will depend on the reason for the duty ending. Broadly, the reasons fall into three categories:

- refusing an offer of accommodation (under Part VII or Part VI);
- accepting an offer of accommodation (under Part VI or from a private landlord);
- a change of circumstance, such as ceasing to be eligible, becoming homeless intentionally from the section 193 accommodation or ceasing to occupy it.

Refusing an offer

15.49   The duty ends if an applicant refuses an offer of temporary accommodation under section 193 or an offer of permanent accommodation under the allocations scheme (Part VI). In both cases certain conditions must be met and certain information given to the applicant.

Refusal of part VII offer

15.50   For the section 193 duty to end following an offer of temporary accommodation, the following conditions must be met:

- the authority must be satisfied that the accommodation is suitable;
- the applicant must be informed of the possible consequences of refusing the offer and of the right to request a review of the suitability of the accommodation;
- the applicant must refuse the offer;
- the authority must notify the applicant that they regard themselves as having discharged their section 193 duty.

---

36 See section 202(1)(b) and *Warsame v Hounslow LBC* (1999) 32 HLR 335, CA.

15.51   As indicated above, an applicant may accept the offer and request a review of suitability. There is no express duty to inform the applicant of this, but it would be unreasonable not to do so. If an authority was seeking to pressurise an applicant to accept the accommodation by indicating a deadline, it may be argued that, where an applicant indicates that he or she wishes to take advice, the accommodation was not refused.

Refusal of final part VI offer

15.52   For the section 193 duty to end because of the refusal of a final offer made under the allocation scheme, the following conditions must be met:

- the authority must be satisfied that the accommodation is suitable;
- the authority must be satisfied that it is reasonable for the applicant to accept the offer;
- the offer must be made in writing and must state that it is a final offer;
- the applicant must be informed of the possible consequences of refusing the offer and of the right to request a review of the suitability of the accommodation;
- the applicant must refuse the offer;
- the authority must notify the applicant that they regard themselves as having discharged their section 193 duty.

15.53   For these purposes it is provided that an applicant may reasonably be expected to accept the offer, even though he or she has obligations in respect of existing accommodation, provided it is possible to bring those obligations to an end before being required to take up the offer.[37] This should prevent an authority indicating that an offer must be accepted and the new tenancy commence before an applicant can terminate an existing tenancy.[38]

15.54   As is the case for offers of Part VII accommodation, the applicant may accept the offer and request a review of its suitability. If the offer is not accepted an authority has no obligation to keep the offer open until the review process is complete.

---

37 Section 193(8).
38 Usually a tenant will be required to serve a minimum of four weeks or one month's notice on a landlord to terminate a tenancy. However if the tenancy is within an initial fixed period this may not be possible. See para 1.79.

Accepting an offer

15.55   Unsurprisingly, the duty ends if a person *accepts* an offer under Part VI. The duty also ends if a person accepts an offer of an assured tenancy by a private landlord. Since it is rare for private landlords to offer assured, as opposed to assured shorthold, tenancies, this is unlikely.

'Qualifying offers'

15.56   One further way in which the section 193 duty ends is if an applicant accepts a 'qualifying offer'.[39] This is the offer of an assured shorthold tenancy by a private landlord arranged and approved by the local authority. The authority must be satisfied that the accommodation is suitable, it must be offered for a fixed period and the offer must be accompanied by a written statement. The written statement must explain that there is no obligation to accept the offer but that if it is accepted the authority will no longer be under a duty under section 193. The applicant must sign a statement indicating that he or she has read and understood the statement.

15.57   Most importantly, the refusal of a qualifying offer does not end the section 193 duty. It is only the acceptance of the offer that brings the section 193 duty to an end. Where a person accepts a qualifying offer, and the landlord seeks possession in the future, the applicant may again apply as homeless. However, the application will be assessed at that date. If the person no longer has a priority need, no housing duty will be owed. This is in contrast to an assured shorthold tenancy offered by way of temporary accommodation in discharge of the section 193 duty. In that case, the section 193 duty continues, and if possession is sought by the private landlord in the future, alternative section 193 accommodation must be provided.

Change of circumstances

Ceasing to be eligible

15.58   A person whose immigration status changes may cease to be eligible after a duty has been accepted. If this happens, the section 193 duty will end.

15.59   Examples of when this may happen are:

---

39 Section 193(7A–E).

- where a person's leave to remain in the UK expires without an application having been made to extend or vary the leave;
- in rare cases the Home Office may revoke a person's leave;
- the eligibility of a European national depends on the person having a right to reside and this right may end, for example, if a person who was working is no longer working. The law relating to the gaining or loss of a right or residence is complex and is explained in chapter 13.

Becoming homeless intentionally

15.60 If a person is evicted from the section 193 accommodation because of a failure to pay rent or anti-social behaviour, he or she is likely to be found to be 'intentionally homeless'. If so, the duty ends. The definition of intentional homelessness is found in section 191 (see para 13.243). For the section 193 duty to end, all of the elements of the intentional homelessness test must be met; a policy that the duty will end in relation to any person evicted because of rent arrears or complaints of nuisance will be unlawful.

Ceasing to occupy as only or principal home

15.61 Again, this has a specific meaning and it will not be sufficient for an authority to conclude that the duty has ended simply because a person has been absent from accommodation for a period. Where a person is occupying hostel accommodation, the accommodation provider may simply terminate the licence on the basis of a short absence, or a failure to sign a register. This is not sufficient to end the section 193 duty unless the test for intentional homelessness is met or there is evidence that the person no longer occupies as his or her only or principal home. See para 3.5 for an explanation of the law on 'only or principal home'.

Notifying the applicant of the decision

15.62 Where the duty ends because of a refusal of an offer, the applicant will usually be informed that the section 193 duty has ended and of the right to seek a review following the refusal. Where the duty ends because an applicant accepts an offer, it is common that no notification is given and rare that there will be any dispute about the ending of the section 193 duty. However, disputes will commonly arise where it is alleged that the duty has ended because of a person being evicted from the section 193 accommodation or ceasing to occupy it.

15.63   Although there is no express duty to give a written explanation of a decision that the section 193 duty has ended, the applicant has a right to request a review of the decision and to bring a county court appeal. Arguably, the authority must give written notice, indicating the grounds on which the duty has ended, and giving sufficient reasons to enable the applicant to know if the decision can be challenged.

Use of the private sector under Parts VI and VII – a summary

15.64   Most local authorities use private landlords to assist in the discharge of their various housing duties under Part VII. The standard form of occupation agreement in the private sector is the assured shorthold tenancy and there are many different situations in which a homeless applicant may be offered an assured shorthold tenancy by a private landlord. Below is a summary of the different ways in which such tenancies may be used and the implications for the applicant.

Homeless prevention/gate-keeping

15.65   Some authorities offer to those approaching them as homeless or threatened with homelessness assistance to obtain an assured shorthold tenancy from a private landlord. If an assured shorthold tenancy is accepted, no homeless application is recorded and no ongoing duty is owed by the authority. If the offer is refused, the applicant may pursue the homeless application.

Discharge of section 193 duty

15.66   Where an authority accepts the full housing duty, it may discharge this duty by making an arrangement with another person to secure that accommodation becomes available. This may be done by arranging that a private landlord enters into an assured shorthold tenancy with the applicant. The accommodation must be suitable for the applicant.

15.67   An authority must inform the applicant:

- that the accommodation is offered in discharge of the section 193 duty;
- that the applicant has a right to seek a review of its suitability; and
- that the applicant can accept the offer and seek a review.

15.68 In addition the Court of Appeal has indicated that the authority should make clear to the applicant that if, in the future, the accommodation ceases to be available, the section 193 duty will nevertheless continue.[40]

15.69 Accepting the offer means that the applicant continues to be owed the section 193 duty and retains priority under the allocations scheme.

15.70 Refusing the offer means that the authority's duty under section 193 ends. Further, any priority under the allocations scheme given to those to whom a homeless duty is owed will be lost.

Qualifying offers

15.71 A qualifying offer is an offer of an assured tenancy that is approved by the local authority. The conditions for a qualifying offer are set out above.

15.72 If an applicant refuses a qualifying offer this has no effect on the continuation of the section 193 duty.

15.73 If an applicant accepts a qualifying offer, the section 193 duty comes to an end. If the accommodation made available ceases to be available in the future, the applicant must make a fresh homeless application.

Fresh applications

15.74 Section 193(9) provides:

> A person who ceases to be owed the [s193] duty ... may make a fresh application to the authority for accommodation or assistance in obtaining accommodation.

15.75 An authority may decide that no duty is owed, but cannot simply refuse to accept an application on the basis that the section 193 duty has ended following a previous application. See para 12.57.

---

40 *Griffiths v St Helens Council*, above.

Request for review and interim accommodation

Dear Sir/Madam,

Re: Mrs A – section 184 Decision dated _____

We are advising Mrs A with regard to her homeless application.

[Request for review]

Mrs A requests a review of the above decision.

[Request for Interim Accommodation to be Extended]

We ask you to confirm that our client will continue to be provided with interim accommodation pending the outcome of the review. It is our view that our client satisfies the test set out in the case of *R v Camden LBC ex p Mohammed* (30 HLR 315, CA):

The merits of the case

[what is wrong with the decision]

New information or argument

[anything likely to change the decision, including medical evidence not yet obtained]

The applicant's personal circumstances

[whether any alternative accommodation, likely effect of being homeless on applicant children etc]

[Deadline for reply]

Our client has been informed that she must leave the accommodation currently provided on ... In order that we may advise our client about possible judicial review proceedings we would ask you to communicate your decision regarding interim accommodation no later than 4 pm on ... If the decision is that interim accommodation will not be provided pending review please given reasons.

[Data Protection Request]

Please provide to us a copy of the complete homelessness file under the Data Protection Act 1998. We enclose a cheque in the sum of £10 together with our client's signed authority.

We intend to make further representations in support of the review following receipt of the file. We would therefore be grateful if this could be provided as a matter of urgency.

Yours faithfully,

Adviser
Advice Agency

CHAPTER 16

Allocation of social housing

continued

Key points

- All new allocations of social housing must be made through the local housing authority's 'allocations scheme'.
- Authorities must publish their allocations scheme and a summary must be available free of charge.
- Certain assistance must be given free of charge to people in the district who wish to apply and may have difficulties, eg language and literacy.
- Certain people from abroad cannot be allocated social housing – they are 'ineligible'.
- An authority can also treat as 'ineligible' a person guilty of unacceptable behaviour, eg behaviour that makes him or her unsuitable to be a tenant.
- Although an authority may decide that a person is ineligible for an allocation or that little or no priority will be given, all applications must be considered.
- Authorities have a wide discretion as to the kind of allocation scheme they operate but must give 'reasonable preference' to certain people and must ensure that the scheme gives priority to those in greatest need.
- 'Reasonable preference' does not mean absolute preference.
- There is a right of review for decisions about eligibility and unsuitability to be a tenant. There is also a right of review about the facts taken into consideration in making an allocation decision. There is no county court appeal but decisions may be challenged by judicial review.
- A scheme itself may be unlawful if it is not in accordance with the principles set out in the Housing Act 1996 Part VI. This can only be established by judicial review.
- Authorities are encouraged to operate choice based lettings schemes but must ensure that certain people are given reasonable preference within the system and that those in the greatest need are given priority.
- The government has set a target that all local authorities should operate choice based lettings schemes by 2010.

Introduction

16.1   In most areas of the UK there is a severe shortage of affordable rented accommodation. Since 1989 tenancies available in the private sector are at market rents and usually offer no more than six months' security. This means that for many households the only way to obtain a secure home at an affordable rent is to be allocated social housing, eg accommodation let by local authorities and other social landlords, known generally as 'registered social landlords' (RSLs).[1] However, the supply of social housing has decreased significantly in recent years. The Barker report, published in March 2004, estimated that the supply of social and affordable houses would need to increase by 17,000 units per year for the next 10 years to meet the anticipated need for social housing.[2]

16.2   In a recent case heard by the Court of Appeal,[3] the local authority presented evidence that in its area, for the relevant year, the number of people on the waiting list for social housing was 14,107 and the number of new local authority lettings was 1,607. It is clear that, in some areas only a small proportion of those who apply for social housing have a realistic chance of ever being offered a tenancy.

16.3   Not surprisingly, therefore, many people will seek advice about the fact that they are in housing need and have been on the council's waiting list for a considerable time without receiving any offers of accommodation. In most cases there is little that can be done: there is no right to an allocation of social housing. Part VI of the Housing Act (HA) 1996 requires all local housing authorities to have an allocations scheme and sets out the principles upon which such schemes must operate. A person who wishes to obtain social housing has a right, with some exceptions, to make an application, to have the application recorded and to be given the appropriate level of priority, in accordance with the particular authority's allocation scheme. However, there is no guarantee that the person will ever be offered social housing.

16.4   The common issues that arise are:

• whether an authority is entitled to decide that a person is not eligible for an allocation, or to defer or suspend an application;

• whether an authority is entitled to give a person no priority on the basis of being unsuitable to be a tenant (see para 16.44 below);

1   Under the Housing and Regeneration Act 2008, registered social landlords will become the 'registered providers of social housing'.

2   Kate Barker, 'Review of housing supply, delivering stability: securing our future housing needs', March 2004. The report can be downloaded from: www.hm-treasury.gov.uk.

3   *Lambeth LBC v A* and *Lambeth LBC v Lindsay* [2002] EWCA Civ 108, 23 July 2002.

- whether an applicant has been given the correct level of priority, in accordance with the authority's policy;
- whether the authority's allocations policy is lawful, ie whether it complies with Part VI and is in accordance with recognised principles of good administrative decision making.

16.5 Before examining these issues, this chapter sets out the way in which Part VI governs allocation schemes.

Allocation of housing: Housing Act 1996 Part VI

16.6 Since 1980 the stock of social housing has decreased, primarily because of the introduction of the right to buy for secure tenants. At the same time, the number of homeless applicants, to whom authorities have a statutory housing duty, has increased. This resulted in a situation where, in some areas, almost all social housing was allocated to those owed a homeless duty. This was seen as unfair to those in housing need who were not statutorily homeless. To address this problem, the aim of Part VI is to create 'a single route into social housing'.[4] Part VII sets out the homeless duty: instead of granting long term social tenancies to homeless applicants, the duty is to provide only temporary accommodation. Homeless applicants temporarily accommodated by authorities have the right to be considered for an allocation in the same way as others in housing need. The fact that a homeless duty is owed will give the person some priority on the allocation scheme.

16.7 Whenever a local housing authority is allocating accommodation it must comply with Part VI.[5] Local authorities are given a broad discretion as to the way in which they frame their allocation policies; subject to the provisions of Part VI 'a local housing authority may allocate housing accommodation in such manner as they consider appropriate'.[6] However, once it has devised an allocation scheme an authority can only allocate in accordance with the scheme. Part VI sets out the principles that must be followed when framing the policy.

16.8 Authorities must have regard to the relevant Code of Guidance.[7] The current version of the Code of Guidance on the Allocation of

---

4 Hansard (HC), Standing Committee G, 16th Sitting, 12 March 1996, Minister for Local Government, Housing and Urban Regeneration, col 614.
5 HA 1996 s159(1)
6 HA 1996 s159(7).
7 HA 1996 s169.

Accommodation in England was published in November 2002 and is available on the website of the Department for Communities and Local Govenment: www.communities.gov.uk. The Welsh Code is dated April 2003 and is available from the website of the Welsh Assembly at: www.wales.gov.uk. A further Code was published 28 August 2008: 'Allocation of Accommodation: Choice Based Lettings – Code of Guidance for Local Housing Authorities'. The Code can also be downloaded at www.communities.gov.uk.

Allocations governed by Part VI

16.9   An allocation is defined as:[8]

- selecting someone to be a secure or introductory tenant of accommodation held by the local authority. This includes notifying an existing tenant or licensee that he or she is to become a secure tenant of the same premises. It also includes a new tenancy offered by way of a 'transfer', at the tenant's request;[9]
- nominating someone to be a secure or introductory tenant of accommodation held by a different authority;
- nominating someone to be an assured tenant of accommodation held by an RSL.

Allocations not governed by Part VI

16.10   Part VI does not apply to:

- the provision of alternative accommodation to an existing secure or introductory tenant where this is instigated by the authority (usually as a decant for major works).

16.11   In addition, the following are not 'allocations' for the purpose of Part VI:[10]

- a succession to a secure or introductory tenancy;[11]
- an assignment of a secure or introductory tenancy by mutual exchange;

---

8   HA 1996 s159(2).
9   Prior to the Homelessness Act 2002 all transfers were excluded from the requirements of Part VI. Part VI now governs transfers instigated by the tenant: s159(5).
10   HA 1996 s160.
11   See para 3.28 above.

- an assignment of a secure or introductory tenancy to someone who would have been entitled to succeed to the tenancy;
- a transfer of a secure or introductory tenancy pursuant to a court order made in matrimonial proceedings or on relationship breakdown;[12]
- an introductory tenancy becoming secure.

Dealing with applications

16.12 A housing authority must ensure that:[13]

- advice and information is available free of charge to people in the district who wish to apply for an allocation;
- any necessary assistance in making such an application is available free of charge to those people in the district likely to have difficulty making an application without assistance;
- the fact that a person is an applicant is not divulged to any other member of the public without his or her consent; and
- any applicant is informed of his or her right to request information about the application, how it is likely to be treated, whether appropriate housing is likely to be made available and when that is likely to happen.

Most importantly, every application for an allocation must be considered by the authority.[14]

16.13 An authority cannot refuse to make a decision on an application or simply advise a person that he or she cannot make an application. A formal decision must be made, informing the applicant of the outcome of the application (ie whether the person is eligible and what priority has been given) and of the right to seek a review of certain decisions made in relation to the application (see para 16.53 below).

An applicant's duty

16.14 An applicant for an allocation must give correct information to the authority in support of the application and may commit an offence if false information is given or if information is withheld.

---

12 This includes orders made under section 24 of the Matrimonial Causes Act 1973, section 17(1) of the Matrimonial and Family Proceedings Act 1984, Schedule 1 of the Children Act 1989 and Schedules 5 and 7 of the Civil Partnership Act 2004. See chapter 11 (Relationship breakdown).
13 HA 1996 s166.
14 HA 1996 s166(3).

16.15   HA 1996 s171 provides that an offence is committed if, in connection with an application under Part VI, a person:

- knowingly or recklessly makes a statement which is false in a material particular; or
- knowingly withholds information which the authority has reasonably required.

16.16   The offence can be committed by any person, not just the applicant, and is punishable by a fine of up to £5,000.

16.17   In addition, if an assured or secure tenancy is granted because of a false statement made by the tenant or someone acting on his or her behalf, the landlord has a ground for possession and may seek possession of the tenancy if this comes to light after the tenancy has been granted, see appendix to chapter 6.

Eligibility for allocations

16.18   A local authority cannot allocate housing accommodation to a person who is not 'eligible'.[15] This includes certain people from abroad, together with people who the authority has decided will be treated as ineligible because of 'unacceptable behaviour'.

People from abroad

16.19   As is the case under Part VII, certain people from abroad are not eligible for an allocation of accommodation. The rules regarding eligibility are applied in the same way as for homeless assistance. The provisions are set out briefly below. More detail is found in chapter 13.

Persons subject to immigration control

16.20   A person who is subject to immigration control[16] is not eligible for an allocation unless he or she is prescribed by the regulations as being eligible. The classes of eligible people are the same as for homelessness, save for asylum-seekers (see para 16.21 below) and are set out in the same regulations: Allocation of Housing and Homelessness (Eligibility) (England) Regulations 2006 (Eligibility Regs 2006).[17] Those who are eligible are set out in regulation 3:

15 HA 1996 s160A.
16 As defined in the Asylum and Immigration Act 1996.
17 SI No 1294.

- Class A – a refugee;
- Class B – a person with exceptional leave to remain in the UK that is not subject to the condition that he or she cannot have recourse to public funds;
- Class C – a person who has leave that is not subject to any limitation or control and who is habitually resident in the UK, Channel Islands, the Isle of Man or the Republic of Ireland (this is generally known as 'indefinite leave to remain' or 'settled status'). This does not include 'sponsored' immigrants unless more than five years has passed (since entry or the undertaking was given, whichever is later) or the sponsor has died.
- Class D – a person who has been granted humanitarian protection under the Immigration Rules.

16.21 It should be noted that no asylum-seekers are eligible for an allocation, whereas a small number of asylum-seekers who applied for asylum before April 2000 are eligible for homeless assistance. Former asylum-seekers granted some form of leave to remain in the UK will usually be eligible for an allocation under one of the categories listed above.

Persons not subject to immigration control

16.22 As is the case in relation to homeless assistance, a person may be treated as ineligible because of not being habitually resident or having no 'right to reside' in the UK.

16.23 The following are treated as ineligible:[18]

- people who are not habitually resident in the UK, Channel Islands, Isle of Man or Republic of Ireland (unless they are exempt from this requirement: see para 16.24 below);
- people whose only right to reside in the UK is derived from being a job-seeker, or is an initial three months' right of residence under the EEA Regs 2006;[19]
- people whose only right to reside in the Channel Islands, the Isle of Man or the Republic of Ireland is equivalent to one that is derived from being a job-seeker, or is an initial three months' right of residence under the EEA Regs 2006.

---

18 Eligibility Regs 2006, reg 4(1).
19 The 'EEA Regs 2006' are the Immigration (European Economic Area) Regulations 2006 (SI No 1003). The Regulations are summarised in chapter 13.

16.24   The following are not to be treated as being ineligible by virtue of not being habitually resident:[20]

- a worker;
- a self-employed person;
- an accession state worker[21] who is registered as a worker for an initial period;
- a family member of any of the above;
- certain people with a permanent right of residence in the UK under the EEA Regs 2006 which is derived from: (1) being former workers or self employed people who are now retired or permanently incapacitated; (2) being the family members of such people; and (3) being the family members of deceased workers or self-employed EEA nationals;[22]
- a person who left Montserrat after 1 November 1995 because of the volcanic eruptions; and
- a person in the UK as a result of deportation, expulsion or other compulsory removal from another country to the UK.

Summary: main categories of ineligible people from abroad

16.25   The main categories of people who are ineligible for an allocation will be the following:

- a person whose leave to enter or remain in the UK is subject to a condition that they can have no recourse to public funds;
- a person who requires leave to enter or remain and does not have it. This will include 'overstayers', asylum-seekers and failed asylum-seekers. This is the case even if the person has an application for leave outstanding with the Home Office. However, a person who previously had leave to enter or remain in the UK and has made an 'in-time'[23] application to extend or vary that leave is treated as continuing to have the same leave until a decision is made by the Home Office;

---

20 Eligibility Regs 2006 reg 4(2).
21 The term 'accession states' refers to ten states that joined the EU in 2004 and 2007 for which special rules apply.
22 A person who has a permanent right of residence for another reason, such as by virtue of five years previous residence, must be habitually resident to qualify for an allocation.
23 This means an application submitted before the leave expires. A person whose leave expires before submitting an application is an 'overstayer'.

- European nationals who are not working, self-employed or self-sufficient (with some exceptions for those who have established a right to reside in the UK under the EEA Regs 2006);
- anyone subject to the habitual residence test who has recently come to the UK, or returned to the UK and not yet established habitual residence. Note, however, that most Europeans with a right to reside are exempt from the habitual residence test: including workers, self employed and self sufficient people and members of their families.

16.26   The rules regarding the right to reside under European law are complex and are described in more detail in chapter 13.

Existing tenants

16.27   These provisions do not affect the eligibility of anyone who is already a secure or introductory tenant or an assured tenant of an RSL.[24] Unlike the provision of temporary accommodation to a homeless applicant, such a tenancy cannot be terminated because of a change in the tenant's immigration status which means that he or she ceases to be eligible. Further, there is no restriction on an existing tenant applying for and being granted a transfer regardless of his or her immigration status.

Unacceptable behaviour

16.28   In addition, an authority may decide to treat a person as ineligible because of 'unacceptable behaviour'.[25] Unacceptable behaviour is behaviour serious enough to make the applicant unsuitable to be a tenant of the authority[26] and is limited to behaviour by the applicant or a member of his or her household that would entitle the authority to a possession order if the applicant were a secure tenant.[27]

16.29   This provision is described in more detail below at para 16.44.

Future applications

16.30   A person treated as ineligible for this reason may make a fresh application on the basis that he or she should no longer be treated as

---

24 HA 1996 s160A(6).
25 HA 1996 s160A(1)(b).
26 HA 1996 s160A(7)(a).
27 HA 1996 s160A(8).

ineligible.[28] An example would be where a person previously evicted for rent arrears has established a good record of payment in a subsequent tenancy or where people in the household have been guilty of anti-social behaviour and the tenant has established a period of untroubled occupation of accommodation, or the perpetrators have left the household.

16.31   Clearly a person who was ineligible because of being a person from abroad can also re-apply if his or her status changes, eg leave to remain is granted or a European national obtains employment.

Decisions about eligibility

16.32   If an authority decides that an applicant is ineligible for an allocation, it must notify the applicant in writing of the decision and the grounds for the decision.[29] The applicant has the right to request a review of the decision.[30]

Allocation schemes

16.33   HA 1996 s167(1) provides that:

> Every local authority shall have a scheme (their 'allocation scheme') for determining priorities, and as to the procedure to be followed, in allocating housing accommodation.
>
>   For this purpose 'procedure' includes all aspects of the allocation process, including the persons or descriptions of persons by whom decisions are to be taken.

16.34   The authority can only allocate accommodation in accordance with its allocation scheme.[31]

16.35   The scheme must include a statement of the authority's policy on offering applicants a choice of accommodation, or an opportunity to express preferences.[32] Note that this does not mean that the scheme must offer choice or the opportunity to express a preference: only that the scheme must state what the authority's policy is.

---

28   HA 1996 s160A(11).
29   HA 1996 s160A(9).
30   HA 1996 s167(4A)(d).
31   HA 1996 s167(8).
32   HA 1996 s167(1A).

The reasonable preference categories

16.36 The scheme must be framed so as to secure that reasonable preference is given to the following classes:[33]

(a) people who are homeless within the meaning of Part VII – this includes non-priority need applicants to whom no duty is owed;

(b) people who are owed a duty by an authority under section 190(2) (intentionally homeless but in priority need), section 193(2) (the full housing duty) or section 195(2) (duty to those threatened with homelessness) or those accommodated under section 192(3) (discretion to accommodate non-priority need homeless applicants);[34]

(c) people occupying insanitary or overcrowded housing or otherwise living in unsatisfactory housing conditions;

(d) people who need to move on medical or welfare grounds, including grounds relating to a disability; and

(e) people who need to move to a particular locality in the district where a failure to meet that need would cause hardship to themselves or others.

16.37 In addition, the scheme may be framed so as to give additional preference to people with urgent housing needs.[35] This group may include those in urgent need as a result of domestic or other violence or harassment, and witnesses in criminal cases who may be at risk of intimidation.[36]

16.38 In deciding on the relative priority of people to whom reasonable preference must be given (groups (a) to (e) above), the scheme may allow the following factors to be taken into account:

- the financial resources available to the applicant to meet his or her housing costs;
- any behaviour affecting the suitability of the applicant or a member of his or her household to be a tenant (see para 16.44 below);
- any local connection (as defined under Part VII) existing between the applicant and the authority.

---

33 HA 1996 s167(2).

34 This provision covers those actually accommodated by an authority as homeless applicants. Also included are those who applied as homeless prior to the coming into force of the HA 1996 and who are owed a duty under sections 65(2) or 68(2) of the HA 1985.

35 HA 1996 s167(2A).

36 See para 5.18 of the English Code and para 4.20 of the Welsh Code.

What is 'reasonable preference'?

16.39   In a number of cases the courts have considered challenges brought on the grounds that an allocation scheme fails to give reasonable preference to the groups set out in HA 1996 s167(2). The Code of Guidance summarises some of the principles elaborated in these cases as follows:

> 5.9. It is important that the priority for housing accommodation goes to those with greater housing need. In framing their allocation scheme to give effect to section 167(2), housing authorities must have regard to the following considerations:
>
> (1) the scheme must include mechanisms for:
>   (a) ensuring that the authority assess an applicant's housing need, and for
>   (b) identifying applicants in the greatest housing need.
> (2) the scheme must be framed so as to give reasonable preference to applicants who fall within the categories set out in section 167(2), over those who do not;
> (3) the reasonable preference categories must not be treated in isolation from one another. Since the categories can be cumulative, schemes must provide a clear mechanism for identifying applicants who qualify under more than one category, and for taking this into account in assessing their housing need;
> (4) there is no requirement to give equal weight to each of the reasonable preference categories. However, housing authorities will need to be able to demonstrate that, overall, reasonable preference for allocations has been given to applicants in all the reasonable preference categories. Accordingly it is recommended that housing authorities put in place appropriate mechanisms to monitor the outcome of allocations; and
> (5) a scheme may provide for other factors than those set out in section 167(2) to be taken into account in determining which applicants are to be given preference under a scheme, provided they do not dominate the scheme at the expense of those in section 167(2) ...
>
> Otherwise, it is for housing authorities to decide how they give effect to the provisions of section 167(2) of the 1996 Act in their allocation scheme.

16.40   Reasonable preference does not mean absolute preference; it has been defined as meaning giving an applicant a 'reasonable head start'.[37] Authorities do not have to give equal priority to each category

---

37 *R v Wolverhampton MBC ex p Watters* (1997) 29 HLR 931, Leggatt LJ at 936.

but must give reasonable preference and ensure that the scheme does not result in a situation where one of the categories is effectively given no priority at all.

16.41   However, 'preference' should not be confused with the prospect of being successful in obtaining accommodation: it is possible that a person with reasonable preference may never be allocated accommodation under Part VI: *R on the application ofMei Ling Lin v Barnet LBC* (see para 16.43 below).

16.42   Most schemes will accord priority in groups that mirror the reasonable preference categories but it is not unlawful for a scheme not to do this provided the scheme as a whole does reflect those categories.

16.43   In the following cases the courts have considered whether allocation schemes give reasonable preference as required by Part VI.

In *R v Westminster CC ex p Al-Khorsan*[38] the council introduced a scheme whereby half of all the available allocations in a year would be allocated to homeless applicants. Within that quota, allocation was by date order based on the date that the homelessness application under Part VII had been accepted.

The scheme was held to be unlawful: this was not because of the quota itself but because the allocation within the quota was based solely on date of application, which unlawfully excluded the other factors required to be given reasonable preference.

In *Lambeth LBC v A* and *Lambeth LBC v Lindsay*[39] the Court of Appeal considered an allocation scheme introduced in anticipation of the 2002 Homelessness Act which encouraged 'choice-based lettings'. The scheme divided applicants into seven allocation groups. Offers of housing were made within the groups in order of placement on the list, subject to a minimum percentage for mainstream allocations. Anybody on the list could shorten their waiting time by being prepared to accept less desirable accommodation.

38   (1999) 33 HLR 77, QBD, 14 December 1999.
39   [2002] EWCA Civ 1084, 23 July 2002.

624   Housing Law: an adviser's handbook / chapter 16

The policy was challenged on two principal grounds: first, that it did not provide for the reasonable preference required by section 167(2) since it covered not only those who were entitled to such preferences but also those who were not; and second, that it did not enable those who fell within more than one of the reasonable preference categories to achieve a greater priority. The court held that the scheme was unlawful: it failed to give a 'head start' to those in the reasonable preference groups. It was held that:

> The Council's scheme is based on date order and includes those ... who are not entitled to any preference ... Unless it is clear that no applicants who are not entitled to preference are able to compete on equal terms with those who are, the scheme cannot secure that the necessary head start is given. The self-assessment of need cannot in my judgment provide the preference since all within the Group have an equal entitlement to widen their options and the individual's personal assessment of his or her need cannot secure that only those who are within section 167(2) are accorded the preference.[40]

The court also held that the scheme failed to ensure that those with greatest need were identified and given priority. Lambeth claimed that the self-assessment process was a rational means of solving this problem: those in greatest need would be willing to accept less desirable accommodation. The court rejected this argument, holding that permitting an applicant to assess his or her need so highly that inferior accommodation was accepted does not amount to conferring a preference.[41]

In *R on the application of Mei Ling Lin v Barnet LBC*[42] the authority's scheme gave extra points to homeless applicants in temporary accommodation, but these were insufficient to enable them to bid successfully for an allocation. It was only when the temporary accommodation was coming to an end (often as long as 10 years after the applicant was given the accommodation) that

---

40 Collins J at [16].
41 Pill LJ at [38].
42 [2007] EWCA Civ 132, 22 February 2007.

sufficient points were given to enable an applicant to bid success-fully. One of the grounds of challenge was that the policy failed adequate priority to homeless applicants.

The Court of Appeal rejected the argument, stating that:

> Preference should not be confused with prospects of success. Prospects of success depend on many factors, of which the most material is the fact that the demand for accommodation greatly exceeds the supply. It is quite possible for a lawful scheme to give reasonable preference to a person within section 167(2) and for that person never to be allocated Part VI housing. Such a person is entitled to no more than a reasonable preference.[43]

Unacceptable behaviour – suitability to be a tenant

16.44   An authority may decide that a person is guilty of 'unacceptable behaviour' such that he or she should be given no priority despite being a person who ordinarily would have priority under the authority's scheme.[44] The definition of unacceptable behaviour is the same as when determining eligibility (see para 16.28 above). An authority therefore has a choice: it may have a policy that those guilty of unacceptable behaviour are not eligible or that they are eligible but will be given no or limited priority.

16.45   In either case, an authority must be satisfied that, at the time of the application, the person is unsuitable to be a tenant by reason of the behaviour. The behaviour must be such that it would, if the person were a secure tenant, entitle the authority to a possession order on one of the tenant's fault grounds.[45] In respect of all these grounds the court must be satisfied not only that the ground is made out but also that it is reasonable to make a possession order. In all cases the court has the power to postpone a possession order or suspend its execution.

---

43   Dyson LJ at [25].

44   HA 1996 s167(2B).

45   The relevant grounds are those in Part 1, Schedule 2 of the HA 1985: (1) rent arrears or other breach of the tenancy agreement; (2) nuisance and annoyance; (2A) domestic violence; (3) neglect causing deterioration of premises; (4) neglect causing deterioration of furniture; (5) obtaining the tenancy by deception; (6) mutual exchange with illegal payment; and (7) inappropriate conduct in non-housing accommodation. For further details about the statutory grounds for possession, see appendix to chapter 6.

16.46   Whether it is likely that an order would be postponed or suspended is relevant when deciding if the behaviour is sufficient to make the person unsuitable to be a tenant. The English Code of Guidance provides:

> Having concluded that there would be entitlement to an order, the housing authority will need to satisfy itself that the behaviour is serious enough to make the person unsuitable to be a tenant of the housing authority. For example, the housing authority would need to be satisfied that, if a possession order were granted, it would not be suspended by the court.[46]

> In *Dixon v Wandsworth LBC*[47] the claimant sought to challenge a decision that he was ineligible on the grounds of unsuitability to be a tenant. He had previously been a tenant of the authority, and following the determination of that tenancy by his joint tenant, it was agreed that he would receive a discretionary offer of alternative accommodation under the authority's allocation policy. A few months before the decision was made, he had pleaded guilty to a charge of possession of cocaine at his home. Shortly afterwards he had also been cautioned for possession of a small quantity of cannabis at the premises. His precise criminal history was disputed, but he had received a caution for the possession of cannabis ten years previously and admitted that he had also used cocaine at that time. The authority decided that he was unsuitable to be a tenant, finding that his behaviour was unacceptable and behaviour against which the county court would be able and willing to grant an outright possession order. The authority also referred to his problems with substance misuse being 'very long standing and therefore ... likely to be more difficult to overcome'. The court held that where an authority has reason to believe that a person may be ineligible for this reason, the following approach should be adopted:
>
> (1) The authority must satisfy itself that there has been unacceptable behaviour such as to found a claim for possession.

---

46 Paragraph 4.22(ii). The Welsh Code at para 3.17(ii) makes similar provision.
47 [2007] EWHC 3075 (Admin), 20 December 2007.

(2) Having concluded that there would be entitlement to an order, it must satisfy itself that the behaviour is serious enough that an outright order should be made.

(3) It must satisfy itself that the behaviour is serious enough, at the time the application is made, that an outright order should be made; and

(4) Only if satisfied on all those matters, can the authority consider exercising its discretion to treat the applicant as ineligible for an allocation. In reaching such a decision, the authority must act reasonably and consider all relevant matters before it.

In this case the court held that the authority had adopted this approach and was entitled to make the decision to treat the applicant as ineligible.

Right to information and reviews

General information

16.47   Authorities must publish a summary of their allocation scheme and provide a copy free of charge to any member of the public on request.[48]

16.48   The scheme itself must be available for inspection at the principal office of the authority and a copy provided on request to any member of the public, on payment of a reasonable fee.[49]

16.49   In fact, many authorities now publish a summary and/or the full allocation policy on their websites.

16.50   Any alterations to the scheme reflecting major changes of policy should be brought to the attention of those likely to be affected within a reasonable time.[50]

Particular information

16.51   An authority's allocation scheme must also ensure that an applicant has the right to the following information, on request:[51]

- general information so as to be able to assess how his or her application is likely to be treated;

---

48   HA 1996 s168(1).
49   HA 1996 s168(2).
50   HA 1996 s168(3).
51   HA 1996 s167(4A)

- whether he or she is likely to be given preference under the scheme;
- whether it is likely that accommodation will be made available; and,
- if so, the time scale; and
- the facts that have been taken into account (or are likely to be taken into account) in considering whether to allocate accommodation to him or her.

16.52   Further, an applicant has the right to be notified in writing of a decision that he or she is to be given no priority by virtue of being guilty of unacceptable behaviour, and of the grounds for the decision.

Reviews

16.53   There is a right to request a review of any of the following:[52]

- a decision that, because of unacceptable behaviour, an applicant is ineligible or is to be given no priority;
- a decision that an applicant is ineligible by virtue of being a person from abroad;
- a decision about the facts of an applicant's case which have been taken into account in considering the application for an allocation.

16.54   It should be noted that these are the only decisions which carry the right of review. If an applicant believes that he or she has been given insufficient priority, unless this concerns a decision about the facts taken into consideration, there is no right of review. Further, there is no right of review where the applicant is seeking to challenge the lawfulness of the policy itself.

16.55   Unlike homeless decisions, there is no right of appeal to the county court following the internal review. Judicial review will therefore be the only way to challenge a decision confirmed on review, as well as any decision that does not carry the right of review. However, as with all public decision making, an authority may reconsider a decision and advisers will usually invite an authority to do so before beginning a claim for judicial review.[53]

---

52 HA 1996 s167(4A)(d).
53 Initially regulations provided for the procedure to be followed in conducting both homeless and allocation reviews. However, the power to make such regulations was contained in section 165, which was repealed in 2003, and no similar provision is contained in section 167(4A). An authority should nevertheless follow a fair procedure and this should be described in the published scheme.

Choice-based lettings schemes

16.56   The Housing Green Paper, 'Quality and Choice: A Decent Home For All', published in April 2000, proposed that authorities adopt choice-based lettings schemes. It was suggested that such a scheme could operate at its simplest level on the basis of three 'bands' of applicants:

- those with an urgent need for social housing;
- those in non-urgent need of social housing; and
- those with no particular need for social housing.

16.57   Within the bands, priority could be determined on the basis of waiting time. However, it was recognised that 'in areas of high demand the number of households within the urgent category will be significant. Authorities in such areas may decide to introduce additional bands to differentiate between demand priorities. However, the principle of giving priority according to the time spent in housing need remains valid.'[54]

16.58   It is the government's target that all local authorities will have adopted a choice-based lettings scheme by 2010 and their statistics show that by 2005, 27 per cent of authorities had done so. As the cases below illustrate, however, many authorities have failed to devise lawful schemes that offer choice whilst ensuring that those in greatest need are given sufficient priority.

16.59   One of the amendments introduced by the Homelessness Act 2002 to facilitate choice-based lettings schemes was the addition of section 167(2E), which provides that, subject to the requirement to give reasonable preference to the certain categories of people, 'the scheme may contain provision about the allocation of particular housing accommodation ... to a person who makes a specific application for that accommodation'.[55]

16.60   Prior to the promotion of choice-based lettings, most housing authorities operated 'points based' systems. These generally operate on the basis that a certain number of points are awarded to an applicant based on an assessment of the level of need, and which reflect the reasonable preference categories: a person with a serious

---

54 Paragraph 9.3.

55 Further, section 167(2E) also permits an authority to determine that particular accommodation may be allocated to persons 'of a particular description' whether or not they are in the reasonable preference categories. This enables authorities to allocate accommodation to essential workers or in order to effect a change in the ratio of adults to children on a particular estate. See para 5.26 of the English Code.

medical condition affected by his or her housing will be awarded more points than a person with a less serious condition. Further, to reflect cumulative need, a household with more than one member with particular needs should be awarded more points than a household with only one member in need, and applicants who qualify under several reasonable preference categories should be awarded more points than those who qualify under only one category. Those with the highest number of points when a suitable property becomes available will be offered that property. One of the problems with such a scheme is that new applicants coming onto the scheme may be awarded more points, so that a person who was 'top of the list' is then pushed down the list. Also, although such schemes usually allow an applicant to express some preference as to area and type of accommodation, the decision as to whether to offer particular accommodation is made by the authority. This sometimes leads to a significant proportion of offers being refused, often with the consequence that further offers will not be made for a period of time, if at all.

16.61   Choice-based lettings systems also begin with an assessment of need. However, in a simple 'three band' scheme, this will usually mean a decision as to whether a person in need of social housing falls into the 'general' band of need or the 'urgent' and 'exceptional' band. Instead of vacant properties being identified by the authority and offered to the applicant with the highest points, vacant properties are advertised locally with an indication of which 'bands' may bid for a property. Usually the applicant who has been on the 'waiting list' for longest will secure the property. Some choice-based lettings schemes will instead operate more complex banding systems so that those with the greatest needs are given greater priority in the bidding system. As several of the cases below illustrate, a broad banding system in which priority is accorded based on waiting time will usually, in areas of high demand, fail to give sufficient priority to those with the greatest housing need.

16.62   On 28 August 2008 the Department of Communities and Local Government issued the 'Allocation of Accommodation: Choice-Based Lettings – Code of Guidance for Local Authorities'. Local authorities must have regard to the Code when making decisions.

16.63   The main advantage of choice-based lettings systems is that there is more transparency regarding the way in which properties are allocated: authorities often publish the outcomes of the bidding process so that applicants know the level of priority of the successful applicant. For an applicant with an urgent need to move or with a limited number of points, it may be necessary to bid for less attractive properties in unpopular areas to have any chance of success. However, the fundamental problem for local authorities in operating any allocation system is that demand greatly exceeds supply, so most applicants will be disappointed, whether they are awaiting an offer that never materialises or bidding unsuccessfully under a choice-based system. As was pointed out in the case of *Lambeth LBC v A &* *Lindsay* (para 16.43 above) in respect of a scheme in which 'choice' was the main criteria: 'What has helped [as a result of introducing choice-based lettings] is not necessarily choice but a greater knowledge of what an applicant was prepared to accept. Furthermore, in many ways the policy provides the antithesis of choice. A realisation that what would otherwise be regarded as substandard accommodation in an unwanted area can be the only way of avoiding an unacceptably long wait, is hardly what most would regard as a real choice.'[56]

Common issues for advisers

16.64   In practice, the most common complaint is simply that an applicant has been waiting for a long time but no offers have been made. Under the choice-based lettings schemes the complaint is likely to be that numerous unsuccessful bids have been made. In most cases this will be because the number of applicants greatly exceeds the number of available properties and only a small minority of applicants will obtain accommodation. In some cases, however, it may be possible to challenge the way in which the applicant's priority has been assessed or the lawfulness of the decision making or the policy itself.

Has the applicant been given the correct number of points or placed in the correct band?

16.65   To advise a person as to whether their needs have been properly assessed, it may be necessary to obtain further information from the authority. Note that in addition to the right to information under the Data Protection Act 1998 an applicant has a right to specific information pursuant to section 167(4A) (see para 16.51 above).

16.66   An example of a pro forma letter requesting relevant information is contained in the appendix to this chapter.

---

56 [2002] EWCA Civ 1084, 23 July 2002, Collins J at [14].

16.67   If the facts taken into account are correct and the level of priority awarded is in accordance with the policy, there will be no action that can be taken on a client's behalf unless the policy itself is unlawful. Advisers must also make clients aware that, even if a policy is declared to be unlawful or a re-assessment ordered, this will not necessarily result in an offer of accommodation to a particular applicant. The court cannot order an authority to make an offer, only to operate a lawful scheme and to allocate in accordance with such a scheme.

16.68   Where medical assessment is at issue, an applicant may find it useful to obtain his or her own medical report and to request a re-assessment of any medical priority. As is the case for priority need, any request for a medical report should set out clearly the relevant criteria under the allocation scheme and ask the expert to express an opinion directed to the relevant issues.

Challenging the lawfulness of the policy itself

16.69   Judicial review is available to challenge not only a specific decision, but also the authority's adoption of a particular scheme. Chapter 21 explains the general principles of administrative decision making. This chapter highlights some of the principles established by case law regarding the lawfulness of allocation policies.

Allocations must be in accordance with the policy

16.70   Section 167(8) provides that an authority can only allocate accommodation in accordance with its published policy. There are two aspects to this:

- an authority cannot make decisions in accordance with policies or practices that are not clearly indicated in the allocation scheme; and
- an authority cannot 'ear mark' a vacant property for a particular applicant prior to allocation through the scheme.

16.71   The following case illustrates the first point:

> In *Gallacher v Stirling Council*[57] the authority operated a policy of only considering homeless applicants for low-demand, high-turnover housing, but this policy did not appear in the published

---

57   May 2001 *Legal Action* 22. See also *R on the application of Faraah v Southwark LBC* [2008] EWCA Civ 807, 11 July 2008.

housing allocations scheme. An application for judicial review by a person offered accommodation following a homeless application was successful. It was held that the policy was invalid is so far as it rendered inapplicable to homeless applicants the provisions of its allocations policy and applied special rules to such applicants. Further, any decision made in accordance with a policy that was unpublished would be invalid. To treat as valid an unpublished rule or a decision made on the basis of such a rule would destroy the value of requiring the publication of allocations schemes.

16.72   With regard to the second point, it is very common for applicants to become aware of a vacant property which they believe would be suitable and wish to be allocated to them. Authorities will rarely accede to such a request and, under Part VI, such an allocation may be unlawful.

In *Amirun Begum and Nashima Begum v Tower Hamlets LBC*[58] the claimants had applied as homeless and were placed in temporary accommodation, consisting of two neighbouring houses sub-let by the authority to an RSL. The household comprised 14 individuals, several of whom had special needs. Wheelchair-adapted accommodation was required. The authority conceded that the accommodation provided was unsuitable. There was a proposal that the two houses should be adapted to comprise a single home. A judicial review claim was commenced, seeking, amongst other things, an order that the authority nominate the family for the allocation of specific accommodation, ie the same two houses, following refurbishment and adaptation. It was conceded at the hearing that the court could not make such an order, the judge stating:

I am satisfied that only in exceptional circumstances, if at all, may a local authority lawfully earmark a property for a particular applicant on its waiting list before that property is allocated. It must apply its policy, and exercise any residual discretion, when it allocates the accommodation in question, not before. There is otherwise a risk that when the accommodation is allocated, there will be someone who has priority according to the allocation scheme over the person for whom the property has been earmarked.[59]

58   [2002] EWHC 633 (Admin), 30 April 2002.
59   Stanley Burnton at [29].

16.73   Similarly, those in unlawful occupation of council accommodation may argue that the authority would owe a homeless duty if they were evicted and that they should therefore be allowed to remain in occupation and be granted a secure tenancy. This may arise, for example, where a tenant dies and a family member is not entitled to succeed to the tenancy. Unless the authority has a policy to grant 'non-statutory succession' (see para 3.47) an authority would be acting unlawfully if it sought to grant a secure tenancy to such a person outside of its allocation scheme.

The scheme must sufficiently explain the way accommodation is allocated

16.74   This is closely related to the above principle. Allocations must be in accordance with the published policy and the published policy must describe, in sufficient detail, how the policy operates. This includes the criteria upon which priority is assessed.

> In *R on the application of Mei Ling Lin v Barnet LBC* (see para 16.43), although the applicant failed to establish that the policy did not give reasonable preference to homeless applicants, it was nevertheless held to be unlawful in failing to make sufficiently clear the way in which extra points were awarded to homeless applicants when their temporary accommodation was coming to an end.

16.75   However, provided a decision is properly explained, it is not necessary, in the allocation scheme, to set out in prescriptive detail how priority is awarded.

> In *R on the application of Ahmad v Newham LBC*[60] although the scheme was held to be unlawful (see para 16.80 below), the court rejected the argument that the scheme gave insufficient detail of the criteria

---

60 [2008] EWCA Civ 140, 29 February 2008.

applied in assessing medical or social need. It was held that: '... it is unnecessary to gloss or expand upon the statutory criterion as to reasonable preference on medical or welfare grounds. There are many factors of potential relevance ... I do not think that this level of detail needs to be included in the scheme. It is sufficient that the factors taken into account in reaching a decision on an individual assessment are spelled out in the decision.'[61]

Deferrals and suspensions

16.76 Long before Part VI came into force, the courts had considered the lawfulness of the deferring or suspending of applications by local authorities. Many authorities operate a policy of suspending active consideration of applications because of such factors as rent arrears owed to the authority or a previous refusal of an offer of accommodation. The courts have held that such policies are not unlawful, provided they are not so rigidly applied as to 'fetter' the discretion of the authority.

R on the application of Wolverhampton MBC ex p Watters[62] concerned an authority's policy regarding applications by those in rent arrears to go on the council's waiting list. The applicant had been a council tenant, but had been evicted because of rent arrears in excess of £2,300. The council's policy was that applicants with more than two weeks' rent arrears would not be eligible for council accommodation unless (a) they had a social or medical need award of 60 points in one single category; (b) they had made substantial efforts to reduce the arrears; or (c) there were other exceptional circumstances. The applicant brought judicial review proceedings to challenge the policy. The applicant fell into three of the statutory groups to whom reasonable preference was to be given. She argued that the council's policy was unlawful because its effect was that she was accorded no preference at all. The court dismissed her application: the policy was not so inflexible as to be a fetter on the council's discretion. Further, the council were required only to give reasonable and not

---

61 Richards LJ at [82].
62 (1997) 29 HLR 931, QBD.

absolute preference to certain groups and this meant that the authority was entitled 'to consider any other relevant fact including the extent to and circumstances in which the applicants have failed to pay due rent or have otherwise been in breach of the obligations of their existing or earlier tenancies. Such considerations are not excluded from the selection process.'[63]

16.77   The issue has also been considered in relation to allocations governed by Part VI.

In *R v Westminster CC ex p Nadhum Hussain*[64] the authority's policy was to suspend applicants from the waiting list for two years if they unreasonably refused an offer. The authority's social services department had carried out an assessment and referred to the need for an additional room to enable a carer to stay from time to time. The assessment also stated that 'Mr Hussain needs separate sleeping and living rooms to be able to store specialist equipment for that room'. An offer was made of a ground floor bed-sit and the authority made no reference to the social services assessment. When the applicant refused the offer, he was suspended from the waiting list.

The court held that, as the policy to suspend applicants did not, in most cases, allow for exceptions, it was therefore an unreasonable fetter on the discretion of the authority. The decision was also flawed as no mention had been made of the social services assessment (see para 16.93 below).

Identifying those in greatest need/giving priority to 'cumulative need'

16.78   It is a fundamental principle that an allocation scheme must give applicants with the greater housing need higher priority. The Code of Guidance provides that 'the scheme must include mechanisms for:

(1) ensuring that the authority assess an applicant's housing need;
(2) identifying applicants in the greatest housing need.'[65]

---

63 Judge LJ at 938.
64 (1998) 31 HLR 645.
65 Paragraph 5.9(a).

16.79   This does not mean simply giving those in the most extreme need the highest priority, but also making a 'fair and reasonable assessment of the relative needs of applicants'.[66] Many cases have concerned an authority's failure to award sufficient priority to those households with 'cumulative needs'. More recent cases have considered the issue in relation to the broad banding approach adopted in many choice-based lettings schemes.

R v Islington BC ex p Reilly and Mannix[67] concerned the council's transfer scheme under which fixed points were awarded for different categories of housing need (e.g. medical, overcrowding etc.). The authority had an overriding discretion to award more points in 'exceptionally serious cases'. There was limited provision for accumulating points under more than one category of need and no allowance was made for the number of people in each household affected by a particular need. The court held that the scheme was incapable of producing a fair assessment of each applicant's housing need as there was no facility to produce a composite assessment of all relevant housing needs. The scheme was not saved by the overriding discretion, which was too vague and uncertain. The scheme was therefore irrational and unlawful.

Similarly, in *R v Tower Hamlets ex p Uddin*[68] the council's transfer policy gave additional preference for medical needs, but only one medical category could be accorded per household. Three transfer applicants brought judicial review proceedings. It was held that a rational transfer policy must observe the principle of greater preference being given to more severe cases of need. The policy was unlawful because it was irrational not to give extra priority to households with more than one member in medical need. Alternatively, it failed to take account of a relevant consideration – eg the medical needs of the whole family.

16.80   *Reilly and Mannix* and *Uddin* both concerned transfer schemes which, at the time, were not governed by Part VI. More recently the

66 Lloyd Jones J in *Cali* at [34].
67 (1998) 31 HLR, 651.
68 (1999) 32 HLR, 391.

courts have considered choice-based lettings schemes which placed applicants in bands, priority within the band being accorded solely by waiting time.

In the case of *R on the application of Cali, Abdi and Hassan v Waltham Forest LBC*[69] the authority had replaced a points-based system with a system based on three bands. The three bands were those with 'additional preference', those with 'reasonable preference' and those with no preference. Those in the additional preference band had priority over all others. The additional preference band was deliberately narrow, so that the great majority of applicants with a need for accommodation were placed in the reasonable preference band. The three applicants all lived in overcrowded accommodation and had family members with medical needs. However, none had been awarded 'additional preference' which was granted only if a member of the household had an exceptional medical or social need. The court held that the scheme was unlawful in failing to award priority to families with 'cumulative' or 'composite' needs over others in the reasonable preference band. Lloyd Jones J held:

> ... The overall effect of this [failure to give preference to those with cumulative needs] is intensified by the fact that the reasonable preference band is, under the Defendant's scheme, a very wide band so that the failure to recognise the additional qualifying needs is that much more serious. A large number of needs of widely varying severity are banded together and thereafter priority is determined solely on the basis of waiting time.[70]

The Court of Appeal made a similar finding in the case of *R on the application of Ahmad v Newham LBC*,[71] which also concerned a system of banding. In this case 'priority home seekers' and ordinary transfer applicants were placed in the same band, although only 5 per cent of allocations went to transfer applicants. Within this band, priority was given according to waiting time. The authority also operated a scheme whereby those assessed as having 'multiple needs' were not part of the choice-based lettings

---

69   [2006] EWHC 302 (Admin), 24 February 2006
70   Llloyd Jones J at [31].
71   [2008] EWCA Civ 140, 29 February 2008.

having 'multiple needs' were not part of the choice-based lettings scheme, but received direct offers. The award of 'multiple needs' status, however, depended on three family members having a certain level of need. The family of six, who lived in very overcrowded accommodation, had one daughter who was very severely disabled. The father also suffered from depression and one of the other children had behavioural problems. According to the scheme, unless both could pass the 'multiple needs' threshold, no additional priority would be given. The court held that the scheme was unlawful for the same reasons as in *Cali*: the scheme failed to give preference to those with cumulative need over others in the same band. Further, in including ordinary transfer applicants in the same band, the scheme failed to give reasonable preference to those in housing need, as required under section 167. The court, however, rejected the argument that where a scheme operated choice-based lettings all applicants should have choice (instead of the most needy receiving direct offers).

16.81   What these cases make clear is that to distinguish between applicants on the basis of waiting time will only be lawful if the applicants have a similar level of need. In areas of severe housing shortage where there will be large numbers of applicants in need it will be necessary to operate some system of prioritisation within a band (or a system with many more bands than three) to ensure that the relative need of those applicants is properly assessed.

Failing to reflect the reasonable preference categories

16.82   Similarly, systems in which those with reasonable preference and those without are placed in the same band, distinguished only by waiting time, will be unlawful for failing to give reasonable preference as required by section 167. This issue was considered in the cases of *R v Westminster CC ex p Al-Khorsan*,[72] *Lambeth LBC v A*; *Lambeth LBC v Lindsay*[73] and *R on the application of Mei Ling Lin v Barnet LBC*[74] (all of which are summarised at para 16.43 above).

---

72 (1999) 33 HLR 77, QBD.
73 [2002] EWCA Civ 1084, 23 July 2002.
74 [2007] EWCA Civ 132, 22 February 2007.

Exercising Discretion

16.83   Where a local authority is by statute given a discretion to make certain decisions, a policy that is rigidly applied may be unlawful on the basis that it 'fetters' the discretion of the authority. This aspect of decision making is discussed in detail in chapter 21.

16.84   As is illustrated in the case of *Nadhum Hussain* (see para 16.77 above), a policy that suspends or defers applications in certain circumstances may be unlawful if it fails to provide for exceptions to be made.

16.85   Similarly, if an authority adopted a policy that any tenant who had previously been evicted because of rent arrears would be ineligible for an allocation, this would be unlawful. A decision about eligibility based on unsuitability to be a tenant must be made in accordance with Part VI (see *Dixon v Wandsworth LBC*, para 16.46 above) and must be the lawful exercise of the authority's discretion, not a 'foregone conclusion'.

16.86   Not only might authorities act unlawfully in fettering their discretion, but a broad and unspecified discretion will not cure flaws in the allocation system and may itself be unlawful.

> In *R v Islington BC ex p Reilly and Mannix* (see para 16.79 above) the authority's transfer policy was found to be unlawful for failing to award sufficient priority for the 'cumulative' needs of a family. The authority argued that it had an overriding discretion to award extra priority in such cases, but the court held that:
>
> > ... the residual discretion is not a satisfactory way of bridging the gap between the outcome of the category-based points calculation and the true assessment of need. It is too vague and uncertain and results in a disproportionately large element of need being subject to assessment on an undefined and unguided discretionary basis.[75]

Fairness

16.87   As in all administrative decision-making, the process of decision making must be 'fair' and comply with the rules of 'natural justice'. As is explained in chapter 21 the rules of natural justice are embodied in a duty to act fairly and the extent of that duty varies according to the circumstances.

75 (1998) 31 HLR, 651, Richards J at 666.

16.88   It is a fundamental principle of fair decision making that a person should be given notice of adverse information and the opportunity to comment on any such information.

16.89   In many allocation cases an applicant will submit medical reports and the authority may take its own medical advice on reports sent by the applicant or obtain medical information directly from those treating the applicant. In such cases, where significant information is obtained by the authority, there will be a duty to disclose this to the applicant and invite him or her to comment on the information. However, there is no duty to give the applicant the 'last word' in every case.[76]

In the case of *Amirun Begum and Nashima Begum v Tower Hamlets LBC*[77] (see para 16.72 above) information sent to the authority by the applicant's GP was inconsistent with that provided by the applicant. It had been taken into account by the authority without offering the applicant the opportunity to comment. It was held that: 'The information provided by the claimants' general practitioner is significant, and has materially affected [the defendant's] conclusions. It follows that the defendant may not lawfully finally decide whether any particular accommodation is suitable for the claimants without taking into account their responses, now in evidence, to their general practitioner's letters'.[78]

16.90   Part of the duty of fairness also requires that a decision is taken by a person who is impartial. Most allocations decisions will be taken by officers who are employed to do so and whose impartiality will not be questioned.[79] However, some authorities may use elected members as part of an appeal or review process. Regulations provide that no elected member may take part in any decision making in relation to

---

76 *Bellouti v London Borough of Wandsworth* [2005] EWCA Civ 602, 20 May 2005, Jonathan Parker LJ at [62]. This case concerned the assessment of priority need under Part VII but similar principles apply when medical evidence is at issue in relation to an assessment of an application for an allocation.

77 [2002] EWHC 633 (Admin), 30 April 2002.

78 Stanley Burnton at [35].

79 Applicants may complain that an officer they have dealt with is 'biased'. However, it is extremely difficult to establish bias in such cases, see chapter 21 (challenging local authorities).

allocations if either the accommodation is in his or her ward or the person concerned lives in that ward.[80]

Giving reasons

16.91   There is no general duty on local authorities to give reasons for all decisions made. However, Part VI requires that reasons are given when a decision is made:

- that a person is ineligible (on the grounds of being a person from abroad or because of unacceptable behaviour); or
- that a person will be given no priority because of unacceptable behaviour.

16.92   Where an authority is required to give reasons for a decision, the reasons must be 'proper, adequate and intelligible and enable the person affected to know why they have won or lost'.[81]

16.93   In addition to these statutory requirements a in respect of specific decisions, there may be situations in which the circumstances demand that reasons be given, even when there is no express duty to give reasons.

In the case of *R v Westminster CC ex p Nadhum Hussain* (see para 16.77 above) it was held that the authority could lawfully have decided not to follow the recommendation of the social services department had they identified reasons for declining to do so. However, the decision letters had ignored the assessment altogether and the authority had therefore failed to provide adequate reasons for the offer of a bed-sitting room rather than a flat with a bedroom and separate living room. This was a further reason for holding the decision unlawful.

---

80 Allocation of Housing (Procedure) Regulations 1997 (SI No 483) reg 3. However, those regulations were made under HA 1996 s165 which has since been repealed.
81 *R v Brent ex p Baruwa* (1997) 29 HLR 915 at 929.

Letter requesting information about allocation decision

Dear Sir/Madam,

Re: *[name of client/DOB/current address]*

We are advising [client] who has applied to your authority for an allocation of accommodation.

In order that we may advise him/her as to the way in which the application is being dealt with can you please provide the following information:

- A copy of our client's application form, any relevant documents submitted in support and a summary of the relevant facts that have been taken into account in considering his/her application.
- A breakdown of the number of points/the priority category into which our client has been placed.
- Whether any medical priority has been awarded to our client and, if so, a breakdown of the way in which the points have been awarded/explanation of the way in which the priority has been assessed.
- How likely it is that accommodation will be made available to our client, and when this is likely to happen.

This request is made pursuant to our client's right to information under section 167(4A) of the Housing Act 1996. Our client's signed authority is enclosed and we look forward to receiving the information requested.

[Please treat this request as also being made pursuant to the Data Protection Act 1998. A cheque in the sum of £10 is enclosed.]

Yours faithfully,

[Adviser]

Notes:

(1) Advisers may prefer to give to clients a draft letter addressed to the authority from the client.

(2) The letter may need adaptation depending upon whether the authority has a system of points or banding and how medical priority is assessed.

(3) The advantage of also making reference to the Data Protection Act is that there is a statutory time limit for the provision of the information and an applicant is entitled to all relevant data held, not just the information specified in section 167. An authority may decline to provide copy documents under section 167 as the section refers only to information about the facts that have been taken into account. If the request is made under the DPA a fee of £10 is usually required by the authority before they will comply with such requests – see chapter 21.

Community care: accommodation duties to adults

Key points

- The main community care accommodation duty for adults is the duty to provide residential accommodation to adults in need of care and attention (section 21 of the National Assistance Act 1948). It is a social services duty.

- For section 21 to apply there must be a need for care and attention because of age, illness, disability or any other circumstance.

- Ordinary accommodation and financial support may be provided under section 21 if this is necessary to ensure that the need for care and attention is met.

- If, following an assessment, an authority decides a person needs accommodation then this may become an enforceable duty.

- For some patients discharged from detention under the Mental Health Act 1983 there is a duty to provide after care services which may include accommodation and financial support. This is a joint social services and health authority duty.

- The first step is for the local authority to carry out an assessment. A refusal or failure to assess may be challenged by an application for judicial review.

- In cases of urgent need an authority may be required to provide emergency services, including accommodation, until the assessment is completed. A refusal to provide emergency services may also be challenged by judicial review.

- Local authorities must operate a formal complaints procedure for both adults and children in relation to social services.

Introduction

17.1   The main ways of obtaining accommodation from a local authority are by applying for an 'allocation' of accommodation under the authority's allocation scheme or by making a homeless application. The allocation of accommodation and homelessness are governed by Parts VI and VII of the Housing Act (HA) 1996 are described in detail in chapters 12 to 16. In addition, a local authority may have a duty to provide accommodation to a person in need of 'community care' services. In practice, it is usually those who are unable to obtain suitable accommodation under HA 1996 who seek accommodation under community care law.

17.2   This chapter deals with the main accommodation duties under community care law in relation to adults. Chapter 18 deals with the possible accommodation duties to children and chapter 19 with the immigration restrictions on access to community care services. Chapter 20 deals with other kinds of community care services that may be provided to improve or adapt existing accommodation.

17.3   This chapter covers the following:

- the definition of community care services;
- possible accommodation duties to adults;
- the duty to assess adults' needs;
- judicial review and complaints.

Sources of community care law

Legislation

17.4   There are a number of statutes that set out the powers and duties of local authorities to provide what are referred to as 'community care services'. The NHS and Community Care Act (NHSCCA) 1990 places the responsibility for arranging community care services on local authorities. The NHSCCA 1990 defines community care services and provides the legal framework for the assessment of the need for community care services and for the provision of such services.

17.5   The primary legislation listed below sets out the kinds of services that a local authority social services department *may*, or, in some cases, *must* provide. Social services departments were created by statute and the Local Authority Social Services Act (LASSA) 1970 provides that they must act in accordance with statutory guidance and directions issued by the Secretary of State for Health.[1]

Directions

17.6   Directions are mandatory and authorities must act in accordance with them. An example is the Secretary of State's Approvals and Directions under section 21(1) of the National Assistance Act 1948, (LAC(93)10) referred to below. Directions and Guidance are usually referred by the year of issue and the number. 'LAC' stands for 'Local Authority Circular' and this was the tenth circular issued in 1993.

1   LASSA 1970 s7.

Guidance

17.7   Formal guidance issued under LASSA 1970 s7 is usually referred to as 'policy guidance' and will state that it is issued under section 7. Such guidance should be followed by local authorities but an authority has 'liberty to deviate from it where the local authority judges on admissible grounds that there is good reason to do so, but without freedom to take a substantially different course'.[2]

17.8   Additionally, general or 'practice' guidance is issued by the Department of Health. Local authorities should have regard to such guidance but are not bound to follow it. A decision could be challenged on the basis that an authority had failed to have regard to relevant guidance. However, an authority would be acting unlawfully if it could show that it had taken the guidance into consideration but decided, for a legitimate reason, not to follow it.

What are community care services?

17.9   NHSCCA 1990 defines 'community care services' as services that a local authority may provide or arrange to be provided under any of the following provisions:

(1) **Part III of the National Assistance Act (NAA) 1948.**
NAA 1948 places on local authorities a duty to provide residential accommodation to adults in need of care and attention not otherwise available. This is the Act most often relied on to obtain accommodation for adults excluded from the provision of housing under HA 1996.

(2) **Section 45 of the Health Services and Public Health Act (HSPHA) 1968.**
Under section 45 local authorities may make arrangements 'for promoting the welfare of old people'. This may include assisting a person to find lodgings but there is no direct duty on an authority to provide accommodation under this Act.

(3) **Section 21 and Schedule 8 of the National Health Service Act (NHSA) 1977.**
This Act sets out the government's general duty to provide a comprehensive health service designed to secure improvement in the population's physical and mental health and to prevent,

2   *R v Islington LBC ex p Rixon* (1998) 1 CCLR 119, 15 March 1996, Sedley J at 123.

diagnose and treat illness. Section 21 and Schedule 8 empowers local authorities to provide services in the home, day centres and training facilities but there is no power or duty to provide accommodation.

(4) Section 117 of the Mental Health Act (MHA) 1983.
Section 117 provides that when certain patients are released from detention under MHA 1983 the local social services authority and the health authority jointly owe a duty to provide after-care services which may include accommodation. This is dealt with below.

17.10   The main community care provisions that may be used to obtain accommodation are therefore NAA 1948 s21 and MHA 1983 s117.

17.11   In addition to the Acts specifically referred to, a local authority may provide community care services under section 2 of the Chronically Sick and Disabled Persons Act (CSDPA) 1970. This Act mainly concerns the provision of adaptations and services in the home and is dealt with in chapter 20.

National Assistance Act 1948

17.12   NAA 1948 was part of the post-war package of social welfare legislation. When introduced, it made provision for both adults and children in need of care and attention and included a system for the payment of social security benefits (national assistance). Part III of the Act, dealing with accommodation, included a duty to provide temporary accommodation for those made homeless in unforeseen circumstances. The provisions for children are now contained in the Children Act 1989. Social security benefits are governed by different statutes and regulations. The duty to provide accommodation to the homeless was removed from Part III when the Housing (Homeless Persons) Act 1977 came into force. Part III, however, still contains the main accommodation duty to adults in need of care and attention and remains the 'safety net' for those unable to gain access to mainstream accommodation. It has been described as 'the last refuge for the destitute'.[3]

Section 21 accommodation duty

17.13   Local authorities have a duty to provide:

---

3   See *R v London Borough of Wandsworth ex p O* and *R v Leicester City Council ex p Bhikha*, (2000) 3 CCLR 237, CA, 26 February 2000. See also para 19.12.

'residential accommodation for persons who are aged 18 or over who by reason of age, illness, disability or any other circumstances are in need of care and attention which is not otherwise available to them.'[4]

17.14   Also, local authorities *may* 'make arrangements to provide residential accommodation for expectant and nursing mothers who are in need of care and attention which is not otherwise available to them'.[5]

17.15   It should be noted that in relation to nursing mothers local authorities have a power but no duty to provide accommodation and that the power is not limited to those who are over the age of 18 years.

The nature of the section 21 duty

17.16   Since 1996 the courts have considered the duty under section 21 in a number of cases. This has been the consequence of legislation restricting the rights of people from abroad to work, claim benefits or gain access to mainstream housing. This legislation has created a large group of destitute adults who are prevented from providing for themselves and have therefore sought the help of local authorities. In addition, other people unable to obtain appropriate housing under HA 1996, have sought to use NAA 1948 to obtain accommodation. This has created a significant volume of case law about the nature of the section 21 duty which is summarised below.

Local authorities may provide ordinary housing

17.17   There is no requirement that the 'residential accommodation' provided by the authority be institutional accommodation where other services are also provided. The duty may be discharged by providing ordinary accommodation with food or vouchers being provided in addition.

> In *R v Newham LBC ex p Medical Foundation for the Care of Victims of Torture*[6] the local authority accepted a duty under section 21 to provide accommodation to the applicants but argued that the duty

---

4   NAA 1948 s21(1)(a) and Secretary of State's Approvals and Directions under section 21(1) of the National Assistance Act 1948 (LAC(93)10).

5   NAA 1948 Section 21(1)(aa).

6   (1998) 30 HLR 955. The case concerned destitute asylum seekers before NAA 1998 was amended to exclude those need arose solely because of destitution, see para 19.11.

was to provide residential accommodation together with board and other services as part of a package. They offered accommodation in a hotel in Eastbourne on the grounds that this would enable them to provide the package of services required under NAA 1948. The court rejected the authority's argument, holding that the services additional to accommodation need not be provided 'in' the accommodation. Further, statutory guidance required an authority, as far as possible, to preserve or restore normal living. It is therefore lawful for an authority to provide ordinary accommodation, which is suitable to the needs of the applicants. Other services may be provided from outside the accommodation.

There must be a need for care and attention

17.18 While the need may be met by providing ordinary accommodation rather than a package of care, a section 21 duty will only arise if there is an un-met need for care and attention as opposed to a need for housing or for more appropriate housing.

In the case of *R on the application of Wahid v Tower Hamlets LBC*[7] the applicant suffered from schizophrenia. He and his wife lived with their eight children, aged between 28 and 9, in a two-bedroom flat. The applicant's wife was his carer and wished to continue to be his carer but the family contended that his mental health was likely to deteriorate because of the stress of the overcrowded home. Social services decided that he was not in need of care and attention that was 'not otherwise available'; his needs were being met. The Court of Appeal confirmed that this was a decision for the local authority not the court. Tower Hamlets were entitled to conclude that the overcrowding did not create the need for care and attention within section 21. The need for care and attention is a pre-condition to the duty to accommodate under section 21. The fact that a person is in need of ordinary accommodation does not make him in need of care and attention. The provision of ordinary accommodation is merely one way in which a need for care and attention can be met.

7   (2001) 4 CCLR 455, 7 March 2002.

17.19   The situation will be different, however, where the person is excluded from mainstream housing and benefits because of immigration status. In such a case the provision of accommodation may be essential even if family members are able to provide the care and attention. See for example the case of *R on the application of Mani v Lambeth LBC*[8] at para 19.16 below.

The duty is enforceable

17.20   If an authority has assessed a person's needs and found that appropriate accommodation is a need that should be met, this may create an enforceable duty.

17.21   In the case of *R v Kensington and Chelsea, ex p Kujtim*[9] the Court of Appeal described the section 21 duty as follows:

> Once a local authority has assessed an applicant's needs as satisfying the criteria laid down in section 21(1)(a), the local authority is under a duty to provide accommodation on a continuing basis so long as the need of the applicant remains as originally assessed.[10]

In *R on the application of Batantu v London Borough of Islington*[11] the local authority's social services department carried out an assessment of a man with mental health and mobility problems. He lived with his wife and four children in a two bedroom flat on the twelfth floor of a high rise block. The authority's assessment was that he needed a ground floor property with enough space to house the rest of the family. Proceedings were issued to force the authority to provide the accommodation and, nine months after the assessment, the court made an order that the authority provide accommodation in accordance with its statement of need. The authority was given three months to identify suitable accommodation, in consultation with the family, and a further three months to make the accommodation available to the family.

17.22   It should be noted that in *Batantu* the social services department prepared a care plan stating that the applicant needed a safe, secure,

8   [2003] EWCA Civ 836, 9 July 2003.
9   [1999] 2 CCLR 340, 9 July 1999.
10   Potter LJ at 354C.
11   (2001) 4 CCLR 445, QBD.

easily accessible and spacious environment. Having assessed this as a need, the social services department could not just leave the issue to be resolved by the housing department. In contrast, in *Wahid*, the authority determined that the applicant did not have any un-met need for care and attention.

17.23   Whether an enforceable duty to accommodate arises will depend on the precise terms of the needs assessment. Where a person is seeking *more appropriate* accommodation, following cases such as *Bantatu*, local authorities generally take care to address housing need in terms of providing assistance to ensure high priority within the housing department's allocation scheme.

In *R on the application of Mooney v Southwark LBC*[12] the claimant was a disabled single parent with three children, including twins, both of whom had special needs. A community care assessment was carried out, as were Children Act 1989 assessments and a carer's assessment on the claimant's eldest child. A number of recommendations were made including that the twins should have separate bedrooms and that the family should have new accommodation in which the claimant could gain access to all rooms. Following this, and in accordance with the council's allocations scheme, the social services department made a nomination to the housing department. The nomination was accepted and she was placed in the highest priority band for re-housing under the authority's choice based lettings scheme. After 11 months the claimant had not obtained a suitable property. This was because of a combination of factors: others in the same band took precedence having being registered before the applicant; not every four-bedroom property was capable of being fitted with a lift; and, the claimant wasn't willing to accept any area in the borough because she wanted to be near her extended family who provided support and assistance. It was also held that, even within those constraints, she had been 'overly selective' in the properties she had bid for.

A claim for judicial review was made, alleging a continuing failure to make provision for the family's need. A mandatory order was sought requiring the authority to identify and make available an appropriate property.

12 [2006] EWHC Admin 1912, 6 July 2007.

The claim was dismissed. Although the assessments undoubtedly identified a need for more suitable accommodation, this did not trigger a duty under section 21. As in *Wahid*, the court held that the assessments did not identify any need for care and attention that was not available other than by the provision of accommodation under section 21. Rather, the assessment concluded that the proper course was for social services to provide additional support and to make a priority nomination under the allocations policy. Further, section 21(8) of NAA 1948 provided that section 21 did not authorise or require a local authority to make any provision that was authorised or required to be made by another statute. The fact that suitable accommodation can be provided under HA 1996 prevented an obligation arising under section 21.

17.24   Nevertheless, where social services have assessed a person as having an un-met need for care and attention which requires the provision of accommodation, judicial review proceedings can be brought to enforce the duty. In addition, where there is a delay in providing for the assessed need, damages may be awarded on the grounds that the authority's failure has lead to a breach of the person's human rights.

In the case of *R on the application of Bernard v London Borough of Enfield*[13] the applicant was a wheelchair-user, living in un-adapted accommodation, having previously been found intentionally homeless by the housing department. An assessment prepared by the authority concluded that the family needed assistance to move to suitably adapted property but no steps were taken to make such accommodation available for 20 months. In judicial review proceedings damages were claimed on the grounds that the applicant's rights under article 3 (inhuman and degrading treatment) and article 8 (the right to respect for private and family life) of the European Convention on Human Rights had been breached. For the period in question Mrs Barnard had been unable to access the toilet or keep herself clean without great difficulty. She soiled herself several times each day, was unable to

13 [2002] EWHC Admin 2282, 25 October 2002.

go out of the house or upstairs and relied on her husband to assist her to move about downstairs. She had no privacy as she shared a room with her husband and two youngest children, and the older children had to pass through the room to go upstairs. Her husband's back problem was exacerbated by having to carry her to the bathroom. The court did not uphold the claim under article 3 on the basis that the authority had failed to deliver a service rather than subjecting the family to 'treatment'. However, it found that there had been a breach of the claimant's rights under article 8. Damages of £10,000 were agreed.

Immigration status

17.25 Where the person in need of community care services is a 'person subject to immigration control' the duty under section 21 only arises if the person's need for care and attention is not caused solely by destitution. The people to whom this applies includes asylum-seekers and those who have leave to enter or remain in the UK that is subject to the condition that they can have no recourse to public funds. This is explained in detail at para 19.6 below.

Mental Health Act 1983

17.26 MHA 1983 s117(2) provides that:

> It shall be the duty of the Primary Care Trust or Health Authority and of the local social services authority to provide, in co-operation with relevant voluntary agencies, after-care services for any person to whom this section applies until such time as the Primary Care Trust or Health Authority and the local social services authority are satisfied that the person concerned is no longer in need of such services ...

17.27 The duty applies to patients who have been detained in hospital under one of the following sections of MHA 1983:
- section 3: detention for treatment (as opposed to detention for assessment under section 2);
- section 37: a 'hospital order' made by order of a criminal court after conviction of an offence committed when the offender was suffering from a 'mental disorder';[14]

14 Mental disorder means mental illness, psychopathic disorder, severe mental impairment or mental impairment.

- section 45A: detention following a direction by the Crown Court that a person suffering from a psychopathic disorder should be detained in a specified hospital. This power is available, when sentencing such a person to a term of imprisonment;
- section 47: detention of a prisoner serving a sentence who is suffering from a mental disorder;
- section 48: detention of a prisoner, imprisoned on remand, a civil prisoner or someone detained under the Immigration Act 1971, who is suffering from a mental disorder.

17.28   Section 117 does not define 'after-care services' and there is limited guidance on the nature of the duty. However, the Code of Practice to the MHA 1983[15] refers to the identification of needs, including 'daytime activities or employment, appropriate accommodation, out-patient treatment, counselling and personal support and assistance in welfare rights and managing finances'. The Guidance on the Mental Health (Patients in the Community) Act 1995 also refers to section 117 services including 'appropriate daytime activities, accommodation, treatment, personal and practical support, 24-hour emergency cover and assistance in welfare rights and financial advice'.

17.29   The duty arises on discharge and continues until the authorities 'are satisfied that the person concerned is no longer in need of such services'. A person who has been discharged from one of the relevant sections some time ago should receive after care services until he or she is assessed as no longer needing such services.

17.30   The section 117 duty applies to only a small proportion of patients who receive in-patient psychiatric care. However, other people with mental health problems are entitled to receive services under NAA 1948 providing they have an un-met need for care and attention.

17.31   Local authorities can make charges for the provision of most community care services, including under NAA 1948, subject to an assessment of means. However, no charge can be made in respect of services provided under section 117.[16]

Immigration status

17.32   There is no restriction on the section 117 duty by reason of a person's immigration status.

---

15 The Code of Practice was issued in 1990 and amended in April 1999.
16 *R v Mancester CC ex p Stennett and others* (2002) 5 CCLR 500.

How to obtain community care services

17.33   The two main community care duties that may result in accommodation being provided to an adult therefore are section 21 of the NAA 1948 and MHA 1983 s117. However, the duty to provide accommodation will only arise when a person has been assessed as needing accommodation. In practice it is often very difficult to persuade an authority to carry out an assessment of an adult in need of care and attention. The situation is different in relation to the accommodation duty under MHA 1983 s117. The duty arises when the person ceases to be detained. The Code of Practice to MHA 1983 provides that before a decision is taken to discharge or grant leave to any in-patient it is the duty of the responsible medical officer (RMO) to ensure that the patient's needs for health and social care are fully assessed and are addressed in the care plan. 'Appropriate accommodation' is specifically identified as one of the possible needs that should be addressed in the care plan. The professionals working with the patient will be involved in the planning of the discharge and must decide what services are to be provided under section 117 prior to discharge. Disputes about the failure to accept a duty to provide accommodation under section 117 are therefore likely to arise in relation to any consequential delay in discharging the patient.

17.34   The duty to assess therefore is mainly of relevance when seeking to persuade an authority of a duty under NAA 1948.

Community care assessments

17.35   Section 47 of the NHSCCA 1990 sets out the circumstances in which local authorities have a duty to carry out an assessment of a person's need for community care services. Section 47(1) provides:

> ... where it appears to a local authority that any person for whom they may provide or arrange for the provision of community care services may be in need of such services, the authority –
>
> (a) shall carry out an assessment of his needs for those services; and
> (b) having regard to the results of that assessment, shall then decide whether his needs call for the provision by them of any such services.

17.36   The duty to assess a person's needs should therefore be easily triggered. The authority should not refuse to assess because they anticipate that the person may not actually be eligible to *receive* a service. The duty arises if it *appears* that a person for whom the authority *may* provide a service *may* be in need of services. This is a 'very low threshold test'.[17] In practice authorities are reluctant to carry out assessments and only do so on threat of legal action.

17.37   It is often necessary to make a request for an assessment in writing and a precedent letter for such a request is contained in appendix 1 to this chapter.

The assessment procedure

17.38   Section 47 requires an authority to carry out a two stage procedure:

(1) to assess the apparent needs of the person ('presenting needs'), and

(2) to decide which of them call for the provision of services ('eligible needs').

17.39   The authority must 'have regard to' the results of the assessment of need in deciding what services to provide. There is no obligation to meet all presenting needs.

The relevance of resources

In the case of *R v Gloucestershire CC ex p Barry*[18] the House of Lords considered services provided under NAA 1948 s29 and the Chronically Sick and Disabled Persons Act 1970 (CSDPA 1970). The court held that an authority could not assess a person as needing a service but decline to provide it because resources were limited. However, in determining which needs called for the provision of a service an authority was entitled to take account of the availability of resources.

17.40   Since 2003 local authorities have been obliged to set 'eligibility criteria' in accordance with the Fair Access to Care Services (FACS) 2002 Policy Guidance in England.[19] The criteria are set with a view to preserving or facilitating independence and are contained in bands based on risk factors. The four bands are graded on the basis of the likely consequences of failing to provide a service as follows:

---

17 See *R v Bristol CC ex p Penfold* (1998) 1 CCLR 315 and the Fair Access to Care Services 2002 Policy Guidance, para 30.

18 [1997] 2 All ER 1, 20 March 1997.

19 LAC(2002)13, and for Wales see the Unified and Fair System for Managing Care (UFSAMC) 2002.

- critical;
- substantial;
- moderate; and
- low.

17.41   The FACS guidance means that authorities must estimate the likely need for services and determine the costs of meeting needs falling into each band. If the authority's resources are sufficient only to meet critical need then its eligibility criteria would mean that only critical needs would be met. If the resources were sufficient to meet critical and substantial, then needs assessed as falling into those bands would be met. So, although each authority is obliged to follow the same process in setting its eligibility criteria, different authorities will operate different criteria and some will provide services that others will not.

17.42   Local authorities frame their community care assessments in accordance with the FACS guidance. Increasingly, authorities assess a person's need as moderate or low and conclude that the person does not 'meet the authority's eligibility criteria' and is therefore not eligible for a service such as accommodation under NAA 1948 s21.

17.43   There is some doubt as to whether the decision in *Barry* covers all possible community care services, including accommodation under section 21 of the NAA 1948. The subsequent cases of *R v Sefton MBC ex p Help the Aged and others*[20] and *R v East Sussex County Council ex p Tandy*[21] suggested that the decision in *Barry* was confined to services provided under CSDPA 1970.

17.44   It should also be noted that the FACS criteria do not apply when a duty to accommodate destitute asylum-seekers and failed asylum-seekers is at issue. See paras 19.17–19.18 below.

Form of assessment

17.45   There is no statutory requirement that the assessment is in writing. However, local authorities usually complete pro forma documentation and practice guidance recommends that a 'copy of the assessment of needs should normally be shared with the potential service user ... Except where no intervention is deemed necessary, this record will normally be combined with a written care plan.'[22] The FACS policy

---

20 (1997) 1 CCLR 57, CA, 26 March 1997.
21 (1998) 1 CCLR 352, HL, 20 May 1998.
22 Care Management and Assessment: A Practitioner's Guide (1991), para 3.54.

guidance states that the person should receive a copy of the care plan.[23]

Cases of emergency

17.46   Section 47(5) provides that a local authority may temporarily provide a service without carrying out a prior assessment of needs 'if, in the opinion of the authority, the condition of that person is such that he requires those services as a matter of urgency'. Where services are provided in an emergency, the duty to assess still remains and an assessment should be done as soon as reasonably practicable. Although this is a power rather than a duty an authority must consider whether or not to exercise the power and in clear cases of urgent need the courts will order an authority to make provision pending an assessment.

NAA 1948: which authority?

Ordinary residence

17.47   Under NAA 1948 the responsibility for providing accommodation under section 21 is that of the authority in whose area the person is 'ordinarily resident'. Ordinary residence means 'abode in a particular place or country which [a person] has adopted voluntarily and for settled purposes as part of the regular order of his life for the time being, whether of short or long duration'.[24] Any dispute between authorities as to which owes the accommodation duty can be determined by reference to the Secretary of State. However, pending the determination of such a dispute, one or other of the authorities must provide accommodation. Unless it is clear which authority owes the accommodation duty, where two authorities are in dispute and both are refusing to provide accommodation proceedings may be issued against both, seeking an order that either one provide emergency accommodation pending resolution of the dispute. See *S v Lewisham LBC, Lambeth LBC and Hackney LBC* at para 17.48 below.

Urgent cases and people with no settled residence

17.48   When a person has no settled residence or is of no fixed abode, the authority to which they present should accept responsibility. Asylum seekers who have lived in different areas for short periods may have no ordinary residence.

---

23   Fair Access to Care Services (FACS) 2002 Policy Guidance, para 49.
24   *Shah v Barnet LBC* [1983] 1 All ER 226, 16 December 1982.

> In the case of *R on the application of S v Lewisham LBC, Lambeth LBC and Hackney LBC*[25] the claimant had come to the UK from Jamaica in 1999. Between 2000 and 2003 she lived in Lambeth but was imprisoned in May 2003, being released in May 2004. From 12 May she stayed with a friend in Hackney, presenting to the social services office in Lewisham on 26 May. It was accepted that as at 26 May 2004 the she had no settled residence. The court held that the applicant's physical presence in Lewisham was sufficient to entitle her to seek assistance under NAA 1948 s21.

17.49   Further, whenever there is urgent need, the authority to which the person presents should assist on an emergency basis. The case may then be transferred to the authority where the person is ordinarily resident.[26]

Remedies: judicial review or complaint?

17.50   Social services authorities must operate complaints procedures in accordance with specific regulations. However, social services decision-making is also amenable to challenge by way of judicial review. Judicial review is described in more detail in chapter 21. This section highlights some of the issues that arise in relation to social services decision making and explains when decisions should be challenged by judicial review and when the complaints procedure will be appropriate.

17.51   The issues arising in relation to decision making for adult and children services are similar and the complaints procedures share the same fundamental features. This section therefore applies in relation to services for both adults and children.

17.52   The sources of community care law are complex. Several different statutes provide for community care powers and duties, and must be read in conjunction with a plethora of directions and guidance. Nevertheless, local authorities are subject to the following clear duties:

---

25   [2008] EWHC 1290 (Admin), 15 May 2008.
26   NAA 1948 s24 and LAC(93) 7 and 10.

- a duty to assess a child or adult who is potentially in need of services;
- a duty to produce a written assessment setting out the person's needs and stating what services are to be provided, by whom and by when;
- a duty to provide accommodation to adults assessed to be in need of care and attention not otherwise available;
- a duty to provide accommodation to children with no parent or carer;
- a duty to provide support and, in some cases, accommodation to children leaving the care of the authority.

17.53 It is the *enforcement* of these duties that has generated a large volume of litigation. In most cases the reason for this is, as Lord Nicholls pointed out in *G, W and A* (see para 18.9 below), 'the seemingly intractable problem of local authorities' lack of resources'.[27]

17.54 There are two possible ways of challenging a local authority's action or inaction in relation to the provision of community care services:

- judicial review; and
- social services complaints procedure.

Judicial review

17.55 Most decisions made in relation to the provision of community care services can be challenged by judicial review proceedings. For a fuller explanation of judicial review proceedings see chapter 21.

17.56 In judicial review, the role of the court is 'supervisory'; a claim for judicial review is not an appeal against a decision. Judicial review is a review of the lawfulness of a decision, action or failure to act in relation to the exercise of a public function.[28]

17.57 The most common reasons for judicial review claims in community care cases are:

- failure or refusal to carry out an assessment;
- delay in carrying out an assessment;
- failure or refusal to provide interim services, including accommodation, pending full assessment;
- unlawful assessment.

27 [2003] UKHL 57, 23 October 2003, At [10].
28 Civil Procedure Rules, rule 54.1(2)(a).

17.58   A challenge may be that an assessment is unlawful for the following reasons:

- failing to take account of relevant information/failing to make sufficient inquiries;
- unfair procedure (eg failing to consult the applicant);
- error of law: given the requirement to determine a person's immigration status and to carry out 'human rights assessments' there is an increased possibility that an authority may make an error of law (see chapter 19).

17.59   The main advantage of using judicial review is that an application to the court can be made on an urgent basis. An interim order can be obtained at short notice to force an authority to commence an assessment and to provide services on an urgent basis.

Alternative dispute resolution

17.60   Before a claim for judicial review is issued parties should consider alternative ways of resolving the dispute.[29]

In *Cowl v Plymouth City Council*[30] the applicant issued a claim for judicial review to challenge the authority's decision to close a residential care home. The authority responded proposing that the issue be dealt with as a complaint and the proceedings adjourned. The applicants rejected this proposal. The Court of Appeal held that the courts should not permit, except for good reason, proceedings for judicial review to go ahead if a significant part of the issues between the parties could be resolved outside the litigation process.

17.61   In a case of urgent need, however, the complaints procedure would not be appropriate unless the authority were prepared to offer assistance pending the resolution of the complaint.

Limits of judicial review

17.62   The disadvantage of judicial review is that the court's role is limited. It is not generally possible to challenge the merits of a decision by way of judicial review.

29 See Judicial Review Protocol, para 3.1 (CPR).
30 [2001] EWCA Civ 1935, 14 December 2001.

In *P, W, F and G*[31] (see para 18.16 below) Munby J was considering challenges to a local authority decision to offer accommodation under section 17 and not section 20 of CA 1989 and stated:

> I am here concerned with an area of decision-making where Parliament has chosen to confer the relevant power on the County Council; not on the court or anyone else. It follows that we are here within the realm of public law, not private law. It likewise follows that the primary decision maker is the County Council and not the court. The court's function in this type of dispute is essentially one of review – review of the County Council's decision, whatever it may be – rather than of primary decision making. It is not the function of the court itself to come to a decision on the merits. The court is not concerned to come to its own assessment of what is in these children's best interests. The court is concerned only to review the County Council's decisions, and that is not a review of the merits of the County Council's decisions but a review by reference to public law criteria ... Although I am, in a sense, concerned with the future welfare of very vulnerable children, I am not exercising a 'best interests' or 'welfare' jurisdiction, nor is it any part of my functions to monitor, regulate or police the performance by the County Council of its statutory functions on a continuing basis.[32]

Judicial review to obtain an assessment

17.63   Judicial review or the threat of judicial review is commonly used to force a local authority to carry out an assessment and to provide interim accommodation pending assessment. A precedent letter requesting an assessment is contained in Appendix 1 to this chapter.

17.64   If the authority refuses to assess or fails to respond within the deadline indicated, the next step may be a judicial review protocol letter. A precedent pre-action protocol letter is contained in Appendix 2 to this chapter.

17.65   In urgent cases, especially where a person has already approached the authority for help, it may be appropriate to send a judicial review protocol letter immediately.

Social services complaints

17.66   The limited scope of judicial review means that in the following circumstances a complaint will be the most appropriate way of challenging a decision:

31   [2004] EWHC 2027 (Admin), 19 August 2004.
32   At [32]–[33].

- where a person wishes to challenge a particular aspect of service provision, eg the way services are delivered or the standard of accommodation provided;
- where services are being provided but there was delay in setting up the services (if services are still not being provided judicial review may be more appropriate);
- where the complaint is about the way a person has been treated, eg rudeness or failure to keep a person informed.

17.67 An authority may decline to deal with a complaint if legal action is pending or is threatened (see para 17.69 below). However, where legal action or the threat of legal action results in an assessment and/or provision of services this would not preclude a complaint being submitted about any delay or the initial refusal to assist.

The statutory complaints procedure

17.68 Local authorities must operate complaints procedures in relation to services to adults and children.[33] In 2006 new complaints procedures were introduced following a public consultation exercise. Although the regulations and guidance are different, the procedures and time scales for complaints in respect of adult services and children's services are the same and are summarised below.[34]

17.69 The regulations and guidance provide that:

- local authorities must appoint a complaints manager;
- as soon as it becomes clear that a person wishes to make a complaint the authority must inform the complainant of the procedure;
- a complaint must be made within 12 months of being aware of the matter complained of. The local authority has power to accept a complaint outside this time limit;
- the authority may refuse to accept a complaint if the complainant has indicated in writing that he or she is or is intending to take

---

33 LASSA 1970 s7B.
34 For Adults see Local Authority Social Services Complaints (England) Regulations 2006 (SI 2006 No 1681) and Guidance issued by the DoH: 'Learning from Complaints, Social Services Complaints Procedure for Adults'. For Children, see Children Act 1989 Representations (Procedure) (England) Regulations 2006 (SI 2006 No 1738) and Guidance issued by the Department for Education and Skills: Getting the Best from Complaints, Social Care Complaints and Representations for Children, Young People and Others. In both cases the Guidance is issued under LASSA 1970 s7 and therefore should be followed unless there are exceptional circumstances which justify a variation.

legal proceedings about the matter, or if disciplinary proceedings or criminal proceedings are pending or contemplated. If the complaint is not accepted because of other proceedings, the authority must notify the complainant of the outcome of those proceedings and the complainant then has 12 months to re-submit the complaint.

17.70   The complaints procedure has three stages:

Stage of complaint	Timescale
Stage 1: Informal resolution by the authority.	Within 10 working days of receiving the complaint, extendable by 10 working days in exceptional circumstances.
If the complainant is not satisfied, he/she can refer to stage 2.	Within 20 working days.
Stage 2: Formal investigation. Investigation by an Independent Officer who submits a report to an Adjudication Officer. The Adjudication Officer is employed by the authority and he or she responds to the report, indicating which findings are accepted, which rejected and setting out what action the authority will take.	Deadline: within 25 working days, extendable, in complex cases to a maximum of 65 working days.
If the complainant is not satisfied, he/she can request a stage 3 review panel.	Within 20 working days
Stage 3: Review panel. Consists of three people, of whom two must be independent. The role of the review panel is to consider whether the authority adequately investigated the complaint at Stage 2, not to re-investigate the complaint. The complainant has a right to attend the panel hearing and be accompanied by a representative who should not ordinarily be a lawyer.	The panel should be held within 30 working days. It should notify the complainant of its findings within 5 working days. The authority should notify the complainant of its response within 15 working days of receiving the panel's report.
If the complainant is not satisfied, complaint to Ombudsman.	Within 12 months of awareness of subject of complaint.

17.71   It should be noted that the complaint to the Ombudsman must also be made within 12 months of knowledge of the matters complained of. However, the Ombudsman will not consider a complaint unless the authority have been given the opportunity to resolve the complaint. Even if everything is done within the deadlines it may take up to 35 weeks for a complaint to be resolved at Stage 3. The complaint may be referred to the Ombudsman before the authority have resolved the issue if the authority is not complying with the relevant deadlines. Further, the Ombudsman has a discretion to accept a complaint outside the 12 month deadline and is likely to exercise the discretion if the delay was caused by the local authority's failure to comply with statutory deadlines.

17.72   See chapter 21 for further information about Ombudsman complaints.

Letter requesting community care assessment (adult)

To:
Duty Manager
Assessment Team
X Local Authority

Dear Sir/Madam,

Re: Mrs A
DOB: 01.01.1968

We are assisting Mrs A who is a failed asylum seeker from [country]. We are referring her to your authority for an assessment under section 47 of the NHS & Community Care Act 1990.

[Reasons for possible community care services]

Mrs A suffers from depression which her GP describes as 'sometimes severe' (letter attached). She is receiving treatment for post traumatic stress disorder from the ... clinic. The claimant also has mobility problems caused by an historic hip fracture. This injury causes her pain and means that she cannot carry heavy bags and cannot walk far without additional pain and discomfort.

[Detail where she has been staying, why she can no longer stay there, how managing re food/support etc.]

Mrs A's claim for asylum was refused on [date] and her appeal refused on [date]. Mrs A was being supported and accommodated by NASS until [date]. Since then she has been homeless and destitute. For a period of two weeks she was street homeless but on ... a friend, Mrs D of [address], permitted her to stay in her home for a maximum of two weeks. Mrs A has no financial support but has been provided with food by Mrs D for the past week. Mrs D has informed Mrs A that she must leave her home on [date].

Mrs A attended your offices on [date] seeking help but was advised that no help could be given as she was a failed asylum-seeker.

[Authority's possible duty to provide community care services]

We believe that your authority may be under a duty to provide support and accommodation to Mrs A under section 21 of the National Assistance Act 1948. Section 21 places a duty on a local authority to provide residential accommodation to an adult in need of care and attention because of age, illness, disability or other circumstance. Mrs A is in need of care and attention and her need does not arise solely from destitution.

[What local authority is being asked to do]

Please can you contact us so that the appropriate arrangements can be made for our client to be assessed. [Or, our client is delivering this letter to you. Please inform him/her of when and where s/he should attend for the assessment to be commenced].

[Deadline]

Please notify us/Mrs A no later than 4 pm on [date] of your agreement to carry out an assessment under section 47.

[In cases of urgent need]

Please also confirm that you will make arrangements to provide accommodation and financial support to Mrs A until the assessment has been completed.

[Consequences of failure to reply]

If we do not hear from you by 4 pm on [date] we will assume that your authority is refusing to carry out an assessment and will take appropriate action/refer our client to solicitors with a view to taking legal action against your authority.

Yours faithfully,

Pre-action protocol letter (failure to assess)

Proposed claim for judicial review

To:
Director of Social Services
X Local Authority
Address

The claimant
Mrs A
Of No Fixed Abode

Reference details
The claimant's advisers have spoken by telephone to Mr B, the Duty
Manager of the assessment team.

The details of the matter being challenged

(1) The failure/refusal of the defendants to carry out an assessment
    of the claimant's needs under section 47 of the National Health
    Service and Community Care Act (NHSCCA) 1990;
(2) The failure/refusal of the defendants to provide interim accom-
    modation and support to the claimant pending an assessment
    under section 47 of NHSCCA 1990.

The issue
The claimant is a failed asylum-seeker who has been homeless
and destitute since ... She has for the past two weeks been staying
with a friend at ... but was told she must leave no later than ... as the
premises are overcrowded. The claimant has no other friends with
whom she can stay when she has to leave this accommodation. The
claimant has no means of support.

The claimant suffers from depression which her GP describes as
'sometimes severe' (letter attached). She is receiving treatment for
post traumatic stress disorder from the ... clinic. The claimant also

has mobility problems caused by an historic hip fracture. This injury causes her pain and means that she cannot carry heavy bags or cannot walk far without additional pain and discomfort.

The claimant has attended the offices of the defendant's social services assessment team on two occasions. The first time was approximately two weeks ago when she was advised that the defendants could not assist her because of her immigration status. The second time was approximately one week ago when the claimant delivered a letter requesting a community care assessment (copy attached). The claimant was advised that she should apply to NASS for assistance.

The claimant's advisers spoke to the defendant's duty manager, Mr B, by telephone yesterday. He stated that the defendants could not assist the claimant as she was a failed asylum-seeker and that she should apply to NASS for section 4 support.

The defendants are acting unlawfully in refusing to conduct an assessment under section 47 of NHSCCA 1990. The claimant is clearly a person who may be in need of community care services that the defendants may provide. In particular, the claimant is in need of accommodation and support under section 21 of the National Assistance Act 1948 as she is destitute and in need of care and attention not otherwise available. Her need does not arise solely from destitution.

The details of the action that the defendant is expected to take:

(1) Confirm that it will immediately commence an assessment of the claimant's needs;

(2) Confirm that it will arrange for the claimant to be provided with accommodation and support under section 21 of the National Assistance Act 1948 on an interim basis until the assessment is completed.

The details of the legal advisers, if any, dealing with this claim

CC and Company

[address]

The details of any interested parties

There are no interested parties at present

The details of any information sought

If the defendants maintain that it has no duty to assess the claimant a full explanation is required.

The details of any documents that are considered relevant and necessary.

The claimant requests a complete copy of her social services file under the Data Protection Act 1998. The claimant's signed authority is enclosed and a cheque in the sum of £10 is enclosed with the hard copy of this letter.

[If an assessment has been conducted request a copy of the assessment]

The address for reply and service of court documents

CC and Company

[address]

Proposed reply date

By 4 pm on ... [two days before the claimant is due to be evicted from her current accommodation]

Yours faithfully,

Community care: accommodation duties to children

Key points

'Children in need'

There are two possible provisions regarding accommodation for children in need under sections 17 and 20 of the Children Act (CA) 1989:

- The section 17 duty is a 'target duty' towards children and families generally. It includes a power to provide accommodation, or financial help to obtain accommodation. Section 17 does not create an enforceable duty, unlike NAA 1948 s21.
- The section 20 duty is a duty to provide accommodation to children in need who have no parent or guardian or whose parent or guardian is unable to provide accommodation and care. In addition, for a child aged 16 or 17 the duty applies if the child's welfare would be seriously prejudiced if no accommodation is provided.
- Unless the child is known to the local authority the first step will be to request a 'child in need' assessment. There is no requirement that the child be permanently resident or have a local connection: the duty to assess is on the local authority for the area where the child is present.
- The duty to accommodate children in need is owed by the social services authority. In addition homeless 16 and 17-year-olds may be owed a housing duty by the housing authority.
- In an emergency the housing authority should provide accommodation pending a referral to social services unless an assessment has already carried out a child in need assessment.

Children leaving care

- A local authority may also have a duty to accommodate a person aged 18 to 20 (or, in some cases, up to age 23) who has previously been in the care of the authority or accommodated under section 20 for at least 13 weeks.

18.1   This chapter examines:

- the accommodation duties to children in need;
- the duty to assess children's needs;
- the duties to children leaving care.

Local authority duties to children: Children Act 1989

18.2 The Children Act (CA) 1989 consolidated previously fragmented legislation about children. It reformed and simplified child care law, particularly in relation to child protection. One of its central tenets was that children should, as far as possible, be looked after by their families. Part III of the Act deals with 'Local Authority Support for Children and Families' and contains two provisions that may result in a local authority providing accommodation for the benefit of a child. These are sections 17 and 20.

The 'child in need'

18.3 Part III of CA 1989 sets out the responsibilities of local authorities for children 'in need.' The concept of a 'child in need' is central to the local authority duties set out in Part III.

18.4 Section 17(10) defines a 'child in need' in the following terms:

a child shall be taken to be in need if:

(a) he is unlikely to achieve or maintain, or to have the opportunity of achieving or maintaining, a reasonable standard of health or development without the provision for him of services by a local authority under this Part;

(b) his health or development is likely to be significantly impaired, or further impaired, without the provision for him of such services; or

(c) he is disabled.

18.5 Section 17(11) provides further definition: a child is 'disabled' if he or she is 'blind, deaf or dumb or suffers from mental disorder of any kind or is substantially and permanently handicapped by illness, injury or congenital deformity or such other disability as may be prescribed.' 'Development' is defined as 'physical, intellectual, emotional, social or behavioural development' and 'health' means 'physical or mental health.'

Duty under CA 1989 s17

18.6 Section 17(1) provides that every local authority has a 'general duty':

(a) to safeguard and promote the welfare of children within their area who are in need; and

(b) so far as is consistent with that duty, to promote the upbringing of such children by their families, by providing a range and level of services appropriate to those children's needs.

18.7   The services may be provided for the family of the child or any members of the child's family, so long as they provided with a view to safeguarding or promoting the child's welfare.[1]

18.8   The services may include providing accommodation and giving assistance in kind, or, in exceptional circumstances, in cash.[2]

Accommodating children and parents under section 17

18.9   Previously, many local authorities have used section 17 to provide accommodation, or financial help to obtain accommodation, to families who were homeless but unable to gain access to accommodation by way of a homeless application or through the allocations scheme. However, since the House of Lords considered the nature of the section 17 duty in 2003, authorities are less likely to do so.

R on the application of G v Barnet LBC, R on the application of W v Lambeth LBC and R on the application of A v Lambeth LBC (G, W and A)[3] concerned three single parents seeking to compel the local authorities to provide accommodation under section 17 of CA 1989 for themselves and their children. *G* was excluded from housing and benefits because she was from Holland and was not 'habitually resident' (see para 13.22 above). *W* had been found intentionally homeless and was therefore owed no long term housing duty under Part VII of HA 1996. *A* had two disabled children and social services had carried out an assessment concluding that 'the family needs re-housing to an appropriate accommodation.'

The House of Lords held, by a majority of 3:2, that section 17(1) does not impose a duty on social services in respect of the needs of a particular child. The duty is a general duty to safeguard and promote the welfare of 'children within their area who are in need' and to promote the upbringing of such children by their families:

1   CA 1989 s17(3).
2   Section 17(6) as amended by the Adoption and Children Act 2002.
3   [2003] UKHL 57, 23 October 2003.

A social services authority which provides a range and level of services appropriate to meet the various needs of children in its area has discharged its duty under section 17(1). This cannot be read as a duty to meet the needs of any particular child. It is sufficient that the authority maintains services for which his particular needs make him eligible.[4]

In contrast to the duty under section 21 of NAA 1948, in relation to adults, the general duty under section 17 is not enforceable by an individual 'child in need':

it is difficult to see how [s21] can be read otherwise than as imposing a concrete duty on the authority to see to it that accommodation is provided for persons assessed as falling within one or other of the classes specified. But the contrast between the wide and general language of section 17(1) of the 1989 Act and the way in which the various other duties in Part III and the specific duties set out in Part I of Schedule 2 which I have discussed above are qualified so as to leave matters to the discretion of the local authority is very marked.[5]

18.10   The local authority in *A* and *W* had a general policy of offering to accommodate the children of a family faced with homelessness (ie take the children into voluntary care under section 20 of CA 1989, see below) but not accommodating parents and children together under section 17. The House of Lords held that operating a general policy in those terms was not unlawful although each case would have to be considered on its merits. An authority would always have to have regard to the right to respect for private and family life under article 8 of the ECHR when making a decision on a particular case, see chapter 21.

Accommodating 16 and 17-year-olds

18.11   Where a 16- or 17-year-old is not being provided with accommodation by a parent or guardian and is therefore homeless he or she may make a homeless application (see para 13.224 above) or may be accommodated by social services under CA 1989. If accommodated by social services, this will usually be under section 20. However, it is also possible for an authority to provide assistance, including

4   Lord Millett at [109].
5   Lord Hope at [90].

assistance with accommodation, under section 17. When an authority is deciding how to assist, the child's wishes and feeling should be taken into account as far as practicable (see para 18.15 below).

18.12　The following features of the section 20 duty should be noted:

- a child to whom a duty is owed under section 20 of CA 1989 does not have priority need for the purpose of a homeless application;
- a child accommodated under section 20 must be provided with financial support by the authority and cannot apply for social security benefits;[6]
- a child who is accommodated under section 20 for at least 13 weeks in total, ending after the age of 16, will be entitled to ongoing support under the Children (Leaving Care) Act 2000 after the age of 18, see below;
- a 'care leaver' (defined as someone who was accommodated under section 20 between the ages of 16 and 18), who is under the age of 21 has automatic priority need if homeless (see para 13.233).

Accommodation duty under CA 1989 s20

18.13　CA 1989 s20 sets out the duty of a local authority to provide accommodation to a child who has no parent or guardian or whose parent or guardian is unable to provide suitable accommodation or care. Section 20(1) provides that:

> ... every local authority shall provide accommodation for any child in need within their area who appears to them to require accommodation as a result of:
>
> (a) there being no person who has parental responsibility for him;
> (b) his being lost or having been abandoned; or
> (c) the person who has been caring for him being prevented (whether or not permanently, and for whatever reason) from providing him with suitable accommodation or care.

Children aged 16 or older

18.14　In relation to children who are 16 years or older a duty to accommodate a child in need arises if the authority consider that the

6　CA 1989 s23(1).

child's welfare is likely to be seriously prejudiced if they do not provide him or her with accommodation.[7]

Accommodation under section 17 or section 20: duty to consult the child

18.15 Before providing accommodation under section 20 a local authority must:

> ... so far as is reasonably practicable and consistent with the child's welfare
>
> (a) ascertain the child's wishes regarding the provision of accommodation, and
>
> (b) give due consideration (having regard to his age and understanding) to such wishes of the child as they have been able to ascertain.[8]

18.16 In a number of cases an authority has claimed that, following consultation with the child, it has been decided that it is more appropriate to provide accommodation under section 17 rather than section 20. Usually the issue arises when a young person who has previously been accommodated by an authority seeks ongoing services under the leaving care provisions, see below.

In *R on the application of P, W, F and G v Essex County Council and others*[9] two of the applicants challenged the local authority's decision to provide accommodation under section 17 rather than section 20. Although the issue was not fully argued the judge commented that:

> ... it is not open to a local authority to choose between providing accommodation under section 17 and section 20. Nor can a local authority decide to provide accommodation under section 17, rather than under section 20, merely because it believes that a section 17 package would be better or would offer more flexibility. If the conditions in either section 20(1) or section 20(3) are satisfied then, subject only to sections 20(6) [the duty to consult the child] and 20(7) [parental consent, if necessary], it is the duty of the local authority to provide accommodation under section 20, with all the consequences that flow from that.

7   CA 1989 s20(3).
8   CA 1986 s20(6).
9   [2004] EWHC 2027 (Admin), 19 August 2004.

And in relation to the duty to consult the child under section 20(6) the judge stated:

> In particular, a local authority has to have regard to the reality that young people faced with proffered support packages which are perceived as being unacceptable may well reject the support being offered and simply vote with their feet. A young person may, for example, prefer the financial independence of managing their own benefits rather than living on local authority pocket-money, and for that reason prefer to be accommodated under section 17 rather than under section 20. Similarly, a young person may not wish to be subjected to the more intrusive role which a local authority is likely to need to adopt if the young person is, by reason of being accommodated under section 20, to be treated as a looked after child. There is therefore nothing objectionable in principle to a local authority deciding to accommodate under section 17 rather than under section 20 a young person who would otherwise qualify for accommodation under either section 20(1) or section 20(3), provided always, that is, that the young person has been given a genuine choice and has made a fully informed decision. I emphasise these important qualifications because in the nature of thing the young people seeking local authority support will often, like W, P, F and G, be vulnerable. Nor, in the nature of things, can one blind oneself to the financial and other incentives that a local authority may have for persuading a young person to accept support under section 17 rather than under section 20.[10]

18.17   Asylum-seeking children are the responsibility of local authorities under the CA 1989 and not NASS (see para 19.5 below). Because of this the issue has frequently arisen in relation to those accommodated by local authorities pending a decision on the asylum claim.

> In *R on the application of H v Wandsworth LBC, R on the application of Barhanu v Hackney LBC* and *R on the application of B v Islington LBC*[11] all three applicants arrived in the UK as unaccompanied asylum seeking children. Each were provided with accommodation by the defendant authorities which maintained that the

---

10 Munby J at [9] and [10].
11 [2007] EWHC 1082 (Admin), 23 April 2007.

accommodation had been provided under section 17 so that no ongoing duties were owed when the applicants reached the age of 18. The applicants sought judicial review of the decisions.

In the *Wandsworth* case the authority claimed to have consulted the child and that he had opted not to become a 'looked after' child but instead accepted help with accommodation under section 17.

In the *Hackney* case the authority did not claim to have consulted the child but argued that the section 20(1) duty is only triggered if the child appears to the authority to 'require accommodation' as opposed to 'help with accommodation.'

In the *Islington* case the authority did at one point provide accommodation under section 20 but not for the minimum 13 week period which creates the 'leaving care' duty. They had, after providing accommodation for a short period, assisted the applicant to obtain a tenancy from a private landlord and to claim housing benefit.

The court held that, although in certain circumstances a local authority could decide to provide assistance with accommodation under section 17, 'if a local authority do provide accommodation for a child in need, and if on the facts a duty to do so did arise under section 20, then the local authority must be regarded as providing that accommodation under section 20 and not under section 17.' In relation to the *Wandsworth* case it was commented that to confront a recently arrived 17 year old asylum seeker with the need to make a choice between two statutory provisions as 'little short of bizarre.'[12]

It was held that both Wandsworth and Hackney had in fact provided accommodation under section 20 and owed a duty to the young people under the leaving care provisions. In the Islington case, on the facts, when the child had been assisted with a deposit and had signed a tenancy agreement, the authority had not been providing accommodation under section 20. The total period for which accommodation was provided under section 20 did not amount to 13 weeks so no leaving care duty arose.

18.18   So, the fact that an authority states that assistance was given under section 17 and not section 20, does not determine the issue: an authority may claim or believe that it is acting under section 17

12 Holman J at [160] P18.

but nevertheless be held to have been providing accommodation under section 20. However, more recently, the Court of Appeal has confirmed that an authority may lawfully decide that it will provide assistance under section 17 by referring a child to the housing department, even where the child wishes to be provided with accommodation under section 20.

R on the application of G v Southwark LBC[13] concerned a 17-year-old who was homeless as he could no longer live with his mother. Through his solicitors he requested that accommodation be provided under section 20. A child in need assessment was carried out which concluded that he did not require accommodation under section 20 as his housing needs could be met by the provision of housing by the housing department; what he required was 'help with accommodation.' The Court of Appeal, by a majority of 2:1 decided that the authority were acting lawfully in deciding that the applicant did not require accommodation to be provided under section 20. Rix LJ dissented and in his judgment reviewed the relevant case law on the section 20 duty. He concluded that for homeless children the CA 1989 takes precedence over the HA 1996; while it was legitimate to provide help under section 17 to a child who, following consultation, does not wish to be accommodated under section 20, it 'ought to be illegitimate for a local authority who is dealing with a child in need who requires accommodation for a section 20 reason to pass that child over to its housing department on the basis that the housing department will be able (and required) to provide accommodation on the very ground that the local authority has declined to deal with the case under section 20.'[14]

Nevertheless the majority decision is that such a course of action is not unlawful and it is expected that many local authorities will adopt this approach. It is likely that the decision will be appealed to the House of Lords for a definitive decision on the relationship between the housing and social services duties to homeless 16- and 17-year-olds.

13 [2008] EWCA Civ 877, 29 July 2008.
14 At [46].

18.19　Moreover, where a section 20 duty arises and social services assist the child to obtain accommodation that is actually arranged by the housing department, this may itself constitute an ongoing duty under section 20.

In the case of *R on the application of S v Sutton LBC*[15] a 17-year-old who was in a Youth Offenders Institution (YOI) was assisted by social services to make the necessary application to be placed in a hostel on release. The authority accepted that a section 20 duty arose immediately before the child was released from the YOI. However, it claimed that the fact that a hostel placement was secured meant that she no longer required accommodation so that they were no longer under a section 20 duty. In correspondence with her solicitors the authority claimed (wrongly) that if it were to accommodate her under section 20 it would have to be by way of a foster placement or residential care. The Court of Appeal held that Sutton 'was seeking to "side step" its duties under section 20(1) by having [the applicant] declare herself homeless ...'[16] There was no evidence that Sutton had offered her the choices of accommodation that she should have been offered, nor was there any evidence that they could not have placed her in the hostel in under its CA 1989 duties. It was held that the applicant was placed by Sutton at the hostel under the section 20 duty and that this obligation continued from the time of her release.

18.20　However, this is not the case if the child is accommodated by the housing department as a homeless applicant and does not come to the attention of social services in such circumstances if it cannot be argued that the child has been accommodated under section 20 even if the social services department would have been under such a duty. Homeless persons' units should always refer a potential child in need for an assessment by social services.[17]

18.21　Where a dispute arises whether an authority has acted, or is acting, under section 17 or section 20, a request should be made for

---

15　[2007] EWCA Civ 790, 26 July 2007.

16　Hooper LJ at [50].

17　See *R on the application of M v Hammersmith and Fulham LBC* [2008] UKHL 917, 15 January 2008 which is summarised at para 13.227 above.

disclosure of the young person's social services file. The documents disclosed may assist in establishing that, although an authority claim to have acted under section 17, in reality the authority were acting under a section 20 duty.

Assessment of children in need

18.22   There is no specific duty to assess potential children in need equivalent to the duty in relation to adults, set out in section 47 of NHSCCA 1990. However, CA 1989 places on a local authority a duty to take reasonable steps to identify the extent to which there are children in need in their area[18] and makes clear that this will involve assessing the needs of each child found to be in need. More often it will be an approach by the family of a child in need or a referral from an adviser or other agency that brings the potential 'child in need' to the notice of the authority.

Timescale

18.23   In 2000 the government published The Framework for the Assessment of Children in Need and their Families (FACNF). FACNF is policy guidance issued under the Local Authority Social Services Act 1970 s7 and should be complied with unless there are exceptional reasons which justify a departure.[19] FACNF describes the response to an initial contact or referral as 'critically important' and lays down a timetable for the assessment process:

- *Decision about response.* Within one working day of a referral being received a decision should be made about what response is required. This may include a decision that no action is to be taken but the decision should be made promptly and recorded.[20]
- *Initial assessment.* A decision to gather more information constitutes an initial assessment, which should be undertaken within a maximum of seven working days. This could be very brief depending upon the child's circumstances. It should determine whether the child is in need, the nature of the services required, from where and within what timescales, and whether a further, more detailed, core assessment should be undertaken.[21]

---

18   Schedule 2, paras 1 and 3.
19   *R v Islington ex p Rixon* (1997) 1 CCLR 119, see para 17.7.
20   FACNF para 3.8.
21   FACNF para 3.9.

- *Core Assessment.* A core assessment is an in-depth assessment which addresses the central or most important aspects of the needs of a child. The timescale for completion of the core assessment is a maximum of 35 working days. A core assessment is deemed to have commenced at the point the initial assessment ended. Where specialist assessments have been commissioned by other agencies or independent professionals it is recognised that they will not necessarily be completed within the 35 working day period.

Cases of emergency

18.24   FACNF provides that 'Appropriate services should be provided whilst awaiting the completion of the specialist assessment.'[22] As with services to adults, in cases of obvious need the courts will readily order an authority to provide services on an interim basis pending full assessment.

Which authority?

18.25   A dispute may arise about which local authority is responsible for assessing the child in need and for providing the necessary services.

18.26   Unlike NAA 1948, there is no requirement under CA 1989 for a child to be 'ordinarily resident' in the area of a local authority. The authority's duty is to children 'within their area.'

In the case of *R on the application of Stewart v Wandsworth LBC, Hammersmith and Fulham LBC and Lambeth LBC*[23] a dispute arose between three authorities as to which should carry out a child in need assessment. Hammersmith and Fulham had temporarily accommodated a woman and her two children in the area of Lambeth, following a homeless application. The children attended school in the area of Wandsworth LBC. She was found to be intentionally homeless and then sought a child in need assessment with a view to obtaining accommodation under section 17. Each of the three authorities denied that it had a duty to carry out the assessment. The court held that Hammersmith and Fulham did not have a duty, as the children were not 'within

---

22 Para 3.11.
23 [2001] EWHC 709 (Admin), 17 September 2001.

their area.' The fact that they had investigated a homeless application did not place them under a duty to carry out a child in need assessment. To establish a duty it was both necessary and sufficient for the children to be 'physically present' in an area. Both Wandsworth and Lambeth were under a duty to carry out assessments and were ordered to do so.

Children leaving care

18.27　The Children (Leaving Care) Act (C(LC)A) 2000 provides that local authorities retain some responsibility for children previously in their care, after the age of 18.[24]

'Looked after children'

18.28　The 'leaving care' duties apply only to young people who have been 'looked after' children. This means having been provided with accommodation by social services for a minimum of 13 weeks in total. The period in care must end after the child reaches the age of 16 years. The period need not be continuous but the child must have been in the care of the authority for at least 13 weeks in total after the age of 14 years.[25] Accommodation provided under section 17 or under the leaving care duties does not count towards the total.[26] The duties therefore apply to children accommodated under section 20 of CA 1989 and to children taken into the care of the authority under the child protection provisions of CA 1989.

18.29　　The powers and duties under C(LC)A 2000 apply to 'eligible' children, 'relevant' children and 'former relevant' children. These are defined as follows:

24　The Act amended the CA 1989 by introducing duties to children who are leaving or have left the care of the authority. Reference should also be made to Children (Leaving Care)(England) Regulations 2001 (SI No 2874) and the Guidance issued under section 7 of LASSA 1970 (LAC(2003)13). For Wales: the Children (Leaving Care)(Wales) Regulations 2001 (SI No 2189).

25　See CA 1989 s22 and reg 3 of the Leaving Care Regs. Periods of care in pre-planned placements of less than four weeks (ie, respite care) do not count towards the 13-week total.

26　CA 1989 s22(1), as amended by the Adoption and Children Act 2002.

- *Eligible child*: a child aged 16 or 17, who has been looked after for the minimum period, and is still being looked after.[27]
- *Relevant child*: a child aged 16 or 17, not presently being looked after by any local authority, but who has previously been a 'looked after child' for the minimum period.[28]
- *Former relevant child*: someone aged between 18 and 20 who was previously a 'looked after child' for the minimum period. Further, a young person who, at the age of 21, is being supported by the responsible authority with education or training remains a 'former relevant child' until the end of the agreed programme of education or training even if that takes him or her past the age of 21. This 'extension' of duties can last only until the age of 24.[29] The duty to a former relevant child falls on the authority that was the last 'responsible authority.' This means the authority that most recently owed a duty under the leaving care provisions, or, if there is no such authority, the authority in whose care the child was under CA 1989.[30]

Duties to 'eligible' children

18.30 The local authority must appoint a 'personal adviser' and to carry out an assessment of the child's needs with a view to deciding what advice, assistance and support should be provided while the child is still looked after, and after the authority stops looking after him or her. Following the assessment of need, a 'pathway plan' must be drawn up.[31] The pathway plan must set out the way in which the authority propose to meet the needs and must be recorded in writing, see below.[32]

Duties to 'relevant' children

18.31 The authority must take reasonable steps to keep in touch with the child, whether or not he or she is still within their area. The authority must also appoint a personal adviser, carry out an assessment of need and prepare a pathway plan (if not already done). The pathway plan must be kept under regular review.

27 CA 1989 Schedule 2, para 19B.
28 CA 1989 s23A.
29 CA 1989 s24B(3).
30 CA 1989 s23C.
31 CA 1989 Sch 2 para 19B.
32 Children (Leaving Care) Regs 2001 reg 8.

18.32   In relation to support and accommodation the authority has a duty to safeguard and promote the child's welfare and (unless satisfied that his or her welfare does not require it) support the child by:

- maintaining the child; and
- providing the child with or maintaining the child in suitable accommodation.[33]

18.33   The presumption therefore is that a local authority should provide accommodation and financial support to a 16- or 17-year-old who has previously been a looked after child. The authority must be satisfied that the child's welfare does not require such assistance to avoid the duty.

18.34   If a local authority has lost touch with a relevant child it must consider how to re-establish contact and take reasonable steps to do so. This duty continues until contact is made or the child reaches the age of 18.

Duties to 'former relevant' children

18.35   The authority must take reasonable steps to keep in touch with the young person, whether within their area or not and, if they lose touch, must take reasonable steps to re-establish contact. It must continue the appointment of a personal adviser and continue to keep the pathway plan under regular review.

18.36   In relation to support and accommodation, the authority must give assistance to the young person to the extent that his or her welfare, educational or training needs requires it. This may include contributing to living expenses to enable the child to be near employment, training or education. The authority must also give other assistance to the extent that his or her welfare requires it.[34]

18.37   Any duty to provide assistance with accommodation and living expenses therefore depends upon the authority having assessed that the young person's welfare requires such assistance. This question should be addressed in the assessment of need and the pathway plan. A failure to prepare the needs assessment and/or the pathway plan may be challenged by way of an application for judicial review. Further, a failure to address the issue of accommodation in those documents may be challenged (see para 17.50 below).

33   CA 1989 s23A.
34   CA 1989 s23C.

Accommodation in student vacations

18.38   Where the local authority is satisfied that a person in full time further or higher education needs accommodation during a vacation, because the term-time accommodation is not available, there is a duty to provide suitable accommodation during the vacation or to pay the person enough to enable him or her to secure accommodation.[35]

The assessment and pathway plan

18.39   The Department of Health Guidance, LAC (2003) 13, sets out in detail the role of the personal adviser and the way the assessment of need and pathway plan should be prepared. The Guidance states that 'The Pathway Plan should be explicit in setting out the objectives and action needed to achieve [the child's needs]; this should include who is responsible for achieving each action and timescale for achieving it.'[36]

In *R on the application of J v Caerphilly County Council*[37] the court considered a pathway plan prepared in respect of a child who was in the care of the local authority and ready for release from a Young Offenders Institution. The pathway plan was criticised for containing little more than vague aspirations. In relation to the boy's accommodation on release the pathway plan recorded that the local authority would 'continue to explore accommodation options in preparation for [his] release.' The judge held that the pathway plan was 'hopelessly inadequate': 'A pathway plan must clearly identify the child's needs, and what is to be done about them by whom and by when. Or, if another aphorism would help, a pathway plan must spell out who does what, where and when.'[38]

Remedies: judicial review or complaint?

18.40   Decisions made by local authorities about services to children may be challenged by judicial review. Also, local authorities must operate

---

35   CA 1989 s24B(5).
36   Paragraph 7.7.
37   [2005] EWHC 586 (Admin), 12 April 2005.
38   Munby J at [45].

a complaints procedure in accordance with the Children Act 1989 Representations Procedure (England) Regulations 2006. The alternative ways of challenging social services decision-making is discussed at para 17.50 and judicial review is explained in chapter 21.

Community care: accommodation duties to migrants

Key points

- Access to most adult community care services is restricted for certain migrants.
- The Immigration and Asylum Act 1999 amended the National Assistance Act 1948 to exclude certain classes of immigrant, including asylum-seekers, if their need for care and attention arose solely because of destitution.
- The Home Office provides support and accommodation for most asylum-seekers. However asylum-seekers who have a need for care and attention are the responsibility of local authorities. This responsibility is not limited to the provision of community care services but includes the provision of accommodation and subsistence.
- The Nationality Immigration and Asylum Act 2002 provides that for certain other classes of immigrants no community care services can be provided except to the extent necessary to avoid a breach of human rights or rights under the European Community treaty. This mainly affects European nationals and people in the UK in breach of immigration law.
- There is no restriction on services provided directly to children.

Introduction

19.1   Restrictions on access to housing and benefits and the prohibition on employment[1] means that many migrants, including former asylum-seekers whose claims have been refused, face destitution in the UK. Many destitute migrants have been forced to seek help from local authorities under the 'safety net' provisions of community care law described in chapters 17 and 18. This has lead to significant developments in the scope of community care law. However, it has also led to two major pieces of legislation which restrict community care duties to certain migrants:

---

1   Until 23 July 2002 asylum-seekers whose claims were outstanding for more than six months could be granted permission to work. This right was removed by the NIAA 2002 but, in accordance with the EU Directive 2003/9/EC, a right to seek permission to work where a claim was outstanding for at least 12 months was re-introduced as from January 2005. The right ends when the asylum claim is determined.

- the Immigration and Asylum Act (IAA) 1999; and
- the Nationality, Immigration and Asylum Act (NIAA) 2002.

19.2   This chapter examines these restrictions and the legal tests that must be applied when a migrant seeks help from a social services authority. A flow chart is included in the Appendix to illustrate how the tests should be applied.

Asylum-seekers: history of support arrangements

19.3   Before 1996 asylum-seekers were entitled to homeless assistance and social security benefits while awaiting a decision on their asylum claims. In 1996 access to benefits and housing was restricted for large numbers of asylum-seekers. This led to destitute asylum-seekers requesting support from local authorities. It was clear that a duty was owed to families with children under the Children Act (CA) 1989. It was also established through the courts that an authority could owe a duty to destitute asylum-seekers without children under the National Assistance Act (NAA) 1948.

R v Hammersmith and Fulham LBC ex p M, R v Lambeth LBC ex p P, R v Westminster CC ex p A and R v Lambeth LBC ex p X ('*M, P, A and X*')[2] concerned four single, healthy asylum-seekers who applied for assistance under section 21 of the NAA 1948. As a result of the Asylum and Immigration Act 1996 they were not entitled to benefits or homeless assistance because they had applied for asylum after entering the UK. They argued that because of their destitution they were in need of care and attention not otherwise available to them. The Court of Appeal held that destitute asylum-seekers were 'in need of care and attention' and were therefore eligible for residential accommodation, under section 21(1)(a). Further, even if they were not yet in need of care and attention their destitution would lead to an almost certain future need, and it was not necessary for social services to wait for that point before providing assistance.

19.4   Between 1996 and 1999 local authorities were providing support and accommodation for large numbers of destitute asylum-seekers. Others (who claimed asylum at the port of entry) were able to claim

2   (1997) 1 CCLR 85, CA, 17 February 1997.

homeless assistance and social security benefits until their asylum claims were decided.

NASS

19.5   One of the central aims of the Immigration and Asylum Act (IAA) 1999 was to transfer responsibility for the support and accommodation of asylum-seekers to the Home Office. IAA 1999 created a system of support administered by a branch of the Home Office: the National Asylum Support Service (NASS).[3] under which accommodation and support is provided to asylum-seekers and their households, usually in areas other than London and the South East. If the asylum claim is refused NASS support terminates unless there are dependent children in the household in which case it continues until the family leaves the UK or any children reach the age of 18.[4] Under the IAA 1999 local authorities are prevented from providing housing and financial assistance under CA 1989 s17 to anyone who is entitled to NASS support. NASS, however, provide accommodation only for adults and families. Unaccompanied asylum seeking children are not accommodated by NASS but by local authorities under CA 1989. For adults, NAA 1948 was amended to exclude those who are 'subject to immigration control' and whose need arises solely from destitution. IAA 1999 came into force on 6 December 1999.

Immigration and Asylum Act 1999

Persons subject to immigration control

19.6   IAA 1999 s115(9) defines a 'person subject to immigration control' (PSIC) as a person who is not a national of an EEA State[5] and who:

---

3   NASS was officially 'disbanded' in 2006 and asylum support is now administered by the UK Border Agency (which replaced the Immigration and Nationality Department – IND). However, the system of asylum support is still commonly referred to as 'NASS support'.

4   This is subject to a provision contained in the Asylum and Immigration (Treatment of Claimants etc) Act 2004 under which a family can be 'certified' as failing to make sufficient effort to leave the UK. If this happens NASS support will terminate. As with most decisions regarding asylum support an appeal lies to the Asylum Support Tribunal.

5   The EEA refers to the European Economic Area. For a complete list of EEA countries, see para 13.35 above.

- requires leave to enter or remain in the United Kingdom but does not have it;
- has leave to enter or remain in the United Kingdom which is subject to a condition that he or she does not have recourse to public funds;
- has leave to enter or remain in the United Kingdom given as a result of a maintenance undertaking; or
- continues to have leave to enter or remain in the United Kingdom only as a result of an appeal against a decision to vary, or to refuse to vary any limited leave.

Asylum-seekers

19.7   Asylum-seekers are PSIC: they require leave to enter or remain in the UK. 'Temporary admission' is often granted to asylum-seekers pending a decision. Temporary admission is not leave to enter but is an alternative to detention. Until a decision is made on the asylum claim an asylum-seeker is in the UK lawfully but is nevertheless a PSIC.[6]

19.8   If the claim for asylum is refused and no leave granted, the legality of the person's presence in the UK will depend on whether the application for asylum was made 'on entry' or 'in country' (after entry) into the UK. An asylum-seeker who claimed asylum after entering the UK unlawfully will be in the UK in breach of immigration law after the claim has been refused and all appeal rights exhausted. This is relevant if the person seeks social services assistance after the asylum claim has been refused (see para 19.29 below).

No recourse to public funds

19.9   Under the immigration rules people can be granted leave to stay in the UK for limited periods under various categories, such as 'visitor', 'student' or 'spouse'.[7] For most of these categories leave is only granted on the basis that the person will be supported and

---

6   PSIC as defined under IAA 1999 s115 are also excluded from social security benefits including housing benefit.

7   A spouse will initially be granted leave for a limited period of time and, at the end of that period, indefinite leave to remain should be granted provided the marriage still subsists.

accommodated without 'recourse to public funds'.[8] The condition is therefore applied to most forms of leave. It is not applied to refugees, asylum-seekers or their dependants.

Maintenance undertakings

19.10   These are generally required when an application is made for a dependent relative (other than spouses and children) to join family members in the UK. Such people are normally granted indefinite leave to remain and it is not possible for such leave to be conditional upon having no recourse to public funds. Therefore the Home Office usually require that a nominated 'sponsor' offer an undertaking to be responsible for supporting the applicant in the UK. This must be a formal written undertaking.

National Assistance Act 1948 s21 and PSIC

19.11   In relation to PSIC, as defined above, the duty under NAA 1948 is restricted so that such a person may not be provided with residential accommodation under section 21(1)(a) if his or her need for care and attention has arisen solely:

(a) because he or she is destitute, or
(b) because of the physical effects, or anticipated physical effects, of being destitute.[9]

19.12   The National Health Services Act 1977 and the Health Services and Public Health Act 1968 have also been amended in the same way. However, these Acts concern duties to those who are elderly or ill and whose need is less likely to be caused *solely* by destitution.

When does need arise solely from destitution?

19.13   The courts have considered this question in a number of cases.

In the cases of *R v London Borough of Wandsworth ex p 'O'* and *R v Leicester City Council ex p Bhikha*[10] the claimants were persons

---

8   'Public funds' do not include assistance under community care duties, such as NAA 1948 and CA 1989. It does include homeless assistance and social security benefits. A leaflet issued by the Home Office: 'No recourse to public funds' lists all of the prescribed funds and can be down loaded from the website on: www.bia.homeoffice.gov.uk.

9   NAA 1948 s21(1A).

10   (2000) 3 CCLR 237, CA.

subject to immigration control, as defined in section 115 of IAA 1999. Mrs O had serious mental health problems and Mr B was suffering from cancer. The local authorities argued that they could not provide services under section 21 because the applicants' need arose solely from destitution. The court rejected this, holding that if an applicant has a need for care and attention made more acute by something other than destitution then a duty arises which is not excluded because of a person's immigration status.

19.14   The test set out in *O* and *Bhika* was subsequently confirmed by the House of Lords in *Westminster City Council v NASS*.[11]

19.15   A person who is destitute and who has a need for care and attention may be entitled to accommodation under NAA 1948 even though the level of need is not high.

In *R on the application of Mani v Lambeth LBC*[12] the applicant was also an asylum-seeker. He had a leg abnormality and required some help with housework and heavy shopping. He also had a history of mental health difficulties. The Court of Appeal confirmed the test set out in *O and Bhika*, and found that he came within section 21. The fact that he would probably not have a need for care and attention were he not an asylum-seeker, because he would be housed, did not disentitle him. On the contrary the fact that he is an asylum-seeker means that care and attention 'is not otherwise available' to him. As in *Westminster v NASS* this meant that the local authority and not NASS were responsible for providing support and accommodation, under section 21.

19.16   Moreover, if a person seeking accommodation under section 21 is a destitute asylum-seeker or failed asylum seeker, the authorities' usual 'eligibility criteria' set under the Fair Access to Care Services (FACS) guidance do not apply.[13] The *Department of Health (DoH) Practice Guidance on FACS, 'Implementation Questions And Answers* published on the DoH website in March 2003 states that the FACS criteria are not applicable in such cases. The Guidance states that:

11   [2002] 1 WLR 2956, HL, 17 October 2002.
12   [2003] EWCA Civ 836, 9 July 2003.
13   See para 17.40.

where destitute asylum-seekers have assessed care needs for which councils may provide community care services, no matter whether these care need fall within or outside council's eligibility criteria, councils should accommodate such asylum-seekers under section 21 of the 1948 Act. The services provided must be sufficient to address their needs, as they are cut off from all other means of support. This position was confirmed by the Law Lords judgment in the case of *Westminster City Council v NASS* in 2002.

In *R on the application of N v LB Lambeth*[14] the applicant had been provided with accommodation and support by the local authority for several years, initially under interim arrangements for asylum support which came to an end in 2006. She was HIV positive and had a young daughter. Although her appeals against the refusal of leave to remain in the UK had been exhausted in the UK courts, she was awaiting the outcome of an application to the European Court of Human Rights.

The authority re-assessed the applicant's needs under their eligibility criteria and decided that her needs fell into the moderate and low bands. As the authority only provided for substantial or critical needs, it proposed to withdraw the services. N sought judicial review of the decision.

The court held that the decision was unlawful as the authority had applied the wrong test. Walker J held:

> There is ... nothing in the authorities to suggest that it is appropriate for the defendant to treat eligibility criteria formulated in accordance with [FACS] as eligibility criteria which answer the statutory question posed by section 21 of the 1948 Act.[15]

Further, with reference to the DoH practice guidance, it was stated: 'I do not consider that there is any material difference as between actual asylum-seekers and failed asylum-seekers for the present purposes. The question is simply whether the general approach to eligibility ... is one that can be adopted or whether, as is concluded in the [guidance], where destitute asylum-seekers have assessed care needs, even though they may fall outside the council's eligibility criteria, councils should accommodate such asylum seekers under section 21 of the 1948 Act.'[16]

---

14 [2006] EWHC 3427 (Admin), 20 December 2006.
15 At [60].
16 At [66].

The guidance correctly set out the law in accordance with the case of *Westminster CC v NASS* and the authority's decision was quashed (see para 19.14 above).

19.17 In all cases however there must be a need for care and attention. A person who has no such need but who has a health problem for which NHS treatment is available is not entitled to accommodation and support under NAA 1948.

In *R on the application of M v Slough BC*[17] the applicant was a person subject to immigration control. He was HIV positive but was taking medication and was physically well. He was staying with a cousin but could not do so on a long-term basis so applied to the authority for accommodation and support under section 21. He needed continuing medical treatment and a fridge to store his medication. The authority decided that he had no current need for care and attention within the meaning of section 21 and therefore they had no responsibility. Further, they argued that if a need arose in the future this would arise solely from destitution so that he would be excluded from section 21.

Initially, the authority's assessment was quashed, the judge holding that the applicant's medical condition made him more vulnerable than most people so that if he lost his accommodation he would have a need for care and attention made more acute by something other than destitution, namely his medical condition. The Court of Appeal rejected the authority's appeal. However, the authority successfully appealed to the House of Lords.

It was held that M's needs did not amount to a need for care and attention. The need for care and attention was more than a need for accommodation. It meant a need to be 'looked after' which meant doing something for the person that the person could not do for him or herself. It did not matter that if the person was housed the care and attention could be provided in his or her home. But there had to be a need for care and attention (ie looking after) as opposed to a need for medical care. Provided that there was such a need the local authority should intervene before the need became worse but the duty under section 21 did not arise if there was no present need for care and attention.

17 [2008] UKHL 52, 30 July 2008.

19.18   The House of Lords decision in *Slough v M* casts doubt on the decision in *M, P, A and X*, at para 19.3 above, that a duty under section 21 may arise where there was no present need for care and attention but where a need would arise imminently. Rather, the Law Lords held that for a duty to arise there must be a present need for care and attention. Nevertheless, the need may not be substantial for a duty to arise and the decision in *Mani*, at para 19.15 above, was confirmed as correct.

Disabled asylum-seekers with children

19.19   The duty to provide accommodation and support to a disabled asylum-seeker does not extend to the whole family.

> In *R on the application of O v Haringey LBC & Secretary of State for the Home Department*[18] the applicant, who had two dependent children, was HIV positive. She and the Home Office argued that the responsibility for the whole family fell on the local authority. The authority accepted that it was responsible for the applicant and that she should be accommodated with her children but argued that NASS should be responsible for paying for the children. The court held that the authority were not responsible for providing accommodation and support for the whole family. However, its responsibility to the applicant must be taken into account by NASS in determining what level of support must be provided to the family.

19.20   In such a case, accommodation for the whole family should be provided by the local authority together with financial support for the disabled adult. NASS should contribute financial support and a proportion of the cost of the accommodation for the children.[19]

19.21   However, where it is the children of an asylum-seeker who are disabled, the responsibility for providing adequate accommodation and financial support falls on NASS.[20]

18   [2004] EWCA Civ 5351, 4 May 2004.
19   This is set out in the NASS Policy Bulletin No 82.
20   *R on the application of A v NASS & Waltham Forest LBC* [2003] EWCA Civ 1473.

Failed asylum-seekers: section 4 support

19.22　In relation to failed asylum-seekers IAA 1999 also introduced a power to provide accommodation and support pending voluntary return or removal. This is referred to as 'section 4' support (previously 'hard cases' support) and is administered by the Home Office. To qualify for section 4 support the applicant must in all cases be destitute, or likely to become destitute within 14 days. Most section 4 support is provided outside London. It is available only if the failed asylum-seeker satisfies one of five criteria. These are:[21]

- the person is taking all reasonable steps to leave the UK;
- the person is unable to leave the UK by reason of a physical impediment to travel or for some other medical reason;
- the person is unable to leave the UK because, in the opinion of the Secretary of State, there is currently no viable route of return available;
- the person has an outstanding application for judicial review of a decision in relation to his or her asylum claim; or
- the provision of accommodation is necessary to avoid a breach of the person's human rights. (This is normally accepted where a person has an outstanding application with the Home Office, such as a possible fresh asylum claim or a claim under articles 3 or 8 of ECHR, or an application for permission to bring an asylum appeal out of time.)

19.23　In relation to failed asylum-seekers issues often arise as to whether accommodation should be provided by a local authority under community care duties or by the Home Office under section 4. This is discussed below at para 19.29.

Nationality Immigration and Asylum Act 2002

19.24　In January 2003 NIAA 2002 came into force and introduced further restrictions on the access to community care services by persons from abroad.

19.25　NIAA 2002 goes further than IAA 1999: for certain people from abroad a local authority is prohibited from offering a service, except to the extent necessary to avoid a breach of a person's human rights or a person's rights under the European treaties.[22]

---

21 See IAA 1999 s4 and Asylum and Immigration (Provision of Accommodation to Failed Asylum-seekers) Regulations 2005.
22 Schedule 54 and Schedule 3.

Who is excluded from services: 'Schedule 3'

19.26   The list of people is set out in Schedule 3 of NIAA 2002. They are therefore often referred to as 'Schedule 3' people. They comprise:

- a person who has refugee status in an EEA state (see para 13.35 above) and the dependants of such a person (para 4);
- a national of an EEA state and the dependants of such a person (para 5);
- a person who was, but is no longer, an asylum-seeker and who has failed to co-operate with removal directions issued against him or her and the dependants of such a person (para 6);
- a person who is in the UK in breach of the immigration laws and who is not an asylum-seeker and the dependants of such a person (para 7); and
- a person who is treated as an asylum-seeker only because of having a dependent child in the household, whom the Secretary of State has certified as having failed, without reasonable excuse, to take reasonable steps to leave the UK voluntarily (para 7A).[23]

EEA nationals

19.27   EEA nationals may seek accommodation and support under community care law because they are excluded from mainstream benefits, social housing and homeless assistance. EEA nationals are only eligible for benefits and housing if they have a 'right to reside' in the UK. This is mainly established by being economically active. This is explained in more detail in chapter 13.

Failed asylum-seekers

19.28   Paragraph 6 refers to failed asylum-seekers who have failed to co-operate with removal directions. When removal directions are issued a formal notice is served informing the person of the date and time of travel. The notice gives a right of appeal. This should not be confused with Home Office letters that state that the person is 'subject to removal'.

19.29   Paragraph 7 deals with people in the UK in breach of immigration law. This includes some failed asylum-seekers.

---

23   This category was introduced by section 9 of the Immigration and Asylum (Treatment of Claimants etc) Act 2004. Such a person must have received a copy of the certificate and becomes a 'Schedule 3' person 14 days after receipt. There is an appeal to the Asylum Support Tribunal against a decision to certify. The making of such certificates was piloted in certain areas of the country in 2005 but was not widely implemented thereafter.

In *R on the application of AW v Croydon LBC and R (A, D & Y) v Hackney LBC*[24] the court considered the position of failed asylum-seekers who had made their claims for asylum after entering the UK ('in country'). No removal directions had been set. The court held that the applicants fell within para 7 of Schedule 3. Prior to making their claims for asylum they were in the UK in breach of immigration law. This was also the position after their claims for asylum were exhausted. The position is different for a person who claimed asylum 'at port'. A 'port applicant' may be detained or granted 'temporary admission' at port. A person who is either detained or granted temporary admission is not deemed to have entered the UK and is not in the UK in breach of immigration laws. A failed asylum-seeker who claimed asylum at port only falls within Schedule 3 if removal directions are set and he or she fails to comply with them, or if he or she fails to comply with reporting or other conditions.[25]

The Court of Appeal also decided that failed asylum-seekers awaiting a Home Office decision on a potential fresh claim should be accommodated and supported by the local authority under section 21 of NAA 1948 if they had a need for care and attention. The court rejected the authority's arguments that they should be accommodated and supported by the Home Office under section 4.

19.30   In relation to a failed asylum-seeker it is therefore crucial to know whether the claim for asylum was made 'at port' or 'in country'.

What services are excluded

19.31   Schedule 3, para 1 provides that 'Schedule 3' persons shall not be eligible for support or assistance under the following provisions:

Provision	What kind of services
Sections 21 and 29 of the National Assistance Act 1948	Local authority provision of accommodation and welfare to those in need of care and attention
Section 45 of the Health Services and Public Health Act 1968	Local authority provision for the welfare of the elderly

24 [2007] EWCA Civ 266, 4 April 2007.

25 Temporary admission is usually given subject to a condition that the person regularly reports to a police station.

Section 21 and Schedule 8 of the National Health Services Act 1977	Local authority provision of services at home to avoid hospital admission
Sections 17, 23C, 24A and 24B of the Children Act 1989	Local authority provision (including accommodation) to adults, including care leavers
Sections 188(3) and 204(4) of the Housing Act 1996	Local authority interim accommodation pending review or appeal in homelessness cases
Section 2 of the Local Government Act 2000	Local authority power to spend funds promoting well being in the local area
Any provision of the Immigration and Asylum Act 1999 or the Nationality Immigration and Asylum Act 2002	Asylum support. This includes mainstream NASS support and support under section 4 of IAA 1999 (hard cases support)

19.32   The equivalent duties contained in Acts specific to Scotland and Northern Ireland are similarly excluded.

Retrospective effect of Schedule 3

19.33   A power or duty under one of the excluded provisions may not be exercised in relation to a Schedule 3 person whether or not they have previously been in receipt of support or assistance under that provision.[26] However, services may continue be provided if necessary to avoid a breach of rights under ECHR or the European treaties.

British citizens and children

19.34   Schedule 3 does not prevent the provision of support or assistance to:

- a British citizen; or
- a child.

19.35   The duties and powers in the CA 1989 that are excluded are those that may be exercised in relation to adults. A child may still be assisted directly under either CA 1989 ss17 or 20.

26 Schedule 3, para (1).

The test: possible breach of human rights or European treaty rights?

19.36 Paragraph 3 of Schedule 3 provides that the exercise of a power or duty is not prevented 'if, and to the extent that' it is necessary to avoid a breach of a person's Convention rights or a person's rights under the Community Treaties.

19.37 The most likely human rights that may be breached by a refusal of assistance are:

- article 3: the right not to be subject to torture, inhuman and/or degrading treatment or punishment;
- article 8: the right to respect for private and family life;
- article 6: the right to a fair and public hearing.

19.38 See chapter 21 for an explanation of these rights.

19.39 The European treaties confer the right of free movement to European nationals in order to exercise such rights as working, studying and setting up in business in another member state.

19.40 In examining whether there will be such a breach if a service is refused, it is necessary to consider what powers and duties the authority does have in relation to Schedule 3 people, apart from the excluded provisions.

The Travel Regulations 2002

19.41 Schedule 3 gives the Secretary of State the power to make regulations to provide for travel and accommodation for some Schedule 3 people.[27] The relevant regulations are the Withholding and Withdrawal of Support (Travel Assistance and Temporary Accommodation) Regulations (the Travel Regulations) 2002.[28] Under Schedule 3 and the Travel Regulations local authorities have the following powers:

- travel arrangements can be made in relation to EEA nationals and their dependants and EEA refugees and their dependants (ie, to return to the member state from which they came);
- accommodation may be provided pending travel to such people only if they have dependent children;

---

27 Paragraphs 8, 9 and 10.
28 SI No 3078.

- accommodation may also be provided to a person who is in the UK in breach of immigration law, provided that he or she has not failed to comply with removal directions. Again this is only possible for those who have dependent children.

19.42   There is no power to provide accommodation for any person who has failed to comply with removal directions, whether a failed asylum-seeker or some other person in the UK in breach of immigration law.

19.43   Schedule 3 requires a local authority to inform the Home Office of any person 'in the authority's area' who is or may be a Schedule 3 person.[29]

19.44   Local authorities must act in accordance with guidance issued by the Secretary of State.[30] The Guidance refers to the provision of 'temporary short-term accommodation' arranged 'pending departure from the UK'.[31] In relation to those returning to EEA countries, the Guidance states that 'it is preferable if accommodation does not continue for more than five days from the date the family first presented for support' and 'For those returning to other countries, it is preferable if accommodation does not continue for a period of more than a further 10 days from the date the family first presented for support or assistance from the local authority'.[32]

19.45   Where an individual fails to travel without an acceptable reason further accommodation should not be provided but offers of care may be made to any children under section 20 of CA 1989.[33]

19.46   Local authorities are therefore permitted to provide 'temporary short-term accommodation' to those in the UK in breach of immigration law (if they have dependent children). However, the authorities have no power *under the regulations* to arrange for those people to travel back to their country of origin.

The Court of Appeal considered this issue in the case of *R on the application of Grant v Lambeth LBC*.[34] The applicant was a Jamaican

---

29 Paragraph 14.
30 Schedule 3, reg 2(5).
31 Guidance, para 28.
32 Guidance, para 32.
33 Guidance, para 34.
34 [2004] EWCA Civ 1711, 17 June 2004.

national in the UK unlawfully. She was awaiting the outcome of an application for leave to remain in the UK. Having become homeless with her three children she sought help from the local authority under CA 1989. The local authority concluded that they were prohibited from providing support under section 17 and that a return to Jamaica was in the family's best interests. Ms Grant argued that the local authority were obliged to provide accommodation until her most recent application for leave to remain was determined, and, if refused, until removal directions were set. Only at the point when she failed to comply with removal directions would the authority be entitled to terminate the accommodation. The local authority argued that the outer limit of any obligation to provide accommodation was the time it would take her voluntarily and with lawful financial assistance, if provided, to depart with the children to Jamaica. It was proposed that the financial assistance could be provided under section 2 of the Local Government Act (LGA) 2000.

Initially, it was decided that the authority was prevented from providing travel assistance under the LGA 2000 as this is one of the powers excluded by Schedule 3. The court held that the authority was therefore bound, under Schedule 3 and the Travel Regulations, to provide accommodation and support until Ms Grant's Home Office application had been determined.

The Court of Appeal upheld the local authority's appeal, holding that the authority *was* entitled to use the powers under LGA 2000 s2. The Travel Regulations provided a *power* to provide temporary accommodation but there was no *duty* to exercise the power, except to the extent necessary to avoid a breach of Convention rights. The authority was therefore entitled to use the powers under section 2 to assist with travel so as to avoid a breach of Convention rights.

19.47   A local authority therefore may offer to pay for a person to travel to their country of origin outside the EEA using its powers under LGA 2000. If the person has dependent children temporary accommodation may be arranged pending travel. An authority must, however, be satisfied that such a course of action would not mean that a person's human rights were breached.

In *R on the application of M v Islington LBC and SSHD*[35] heard before the case of *Grant*, the applicant's daughter was British and had a British father who lived apart from the applicant. The local authority proposed to assist M and her daughter to return to her country of origin, Guyana. The Court of Appeal held that the local authority had failed to adequately investigate the actual prospects for the child's welfare in Guyana or to properly consider the potential breach of article 8, given that the child was British and her father lived in the UK.

19.48   Where a person has an outstanding application with the Home Office in which it is claimed that removal from the UK would breach the person's human rights it will usually be impossible for the authority to argue that it can lawfully refuse long-term support and accommodation by offering travel assistance.

In the case *R on the application of Binomugishu v Southwark LBC*[36] the applicant had been in the care of the local authority as an asylum-seeking child. As an adult he suffered from mental health problems and the authority therefore had potential duties to provide accommodation both under the Children (Leaving Care) Act 2000 and NAA 1948. The applicant's asylum claim had been refused but he had a pending application for leave to remain relying on article 8. The authority carried out a 'human rights assessment' to determine whether services should be provided despite him being a 'Schedule 3 person'. The assessment rejected the opinion of two psychiatrists and decided that there would be no breach of article 8 if the applicant were to return to Uganda. The court held that it is a task for the immigration authorities and not local authorities to make such decisions and that 'a local authority ... should only make its decisions on the basis that a person such as the claimant is free to go back to his own country if an outstanding human rights claim to remain in the UK is manifestly unfounded'.[37] The decision was quashed.

---

35 [2004] EWCA Civ 235, 2 April 2004.
36 [2006] EWCH 2254 (Admin), 18 September 2006.
37 Andrew Nicol QC at [13]. See also *R on the application of PB v Haringey LBC and otherrs* [2006] EWHC 2255, 18 September 2006.

Summary of local authority powers under Schedule 3

19.49   The following chart summarises the powers of a local authority in relation to a Schedule 3 person.

Class of person	Travel arrangements	Accommodation pending travel
EEA national and dependants	Yes, under the Travel Regulations	Yes, if dependant children
EEA refugee and dependants	Yes, under the Travel Regulations	Yes, if dependant children
Failed asylum-seeker who has failed to comply with removal directions	No (if the authority report the person to the Home Office he or she may be detained pending removal)	No
Person who is in UK in breach of immigration law	Not under Travel Regulations but possible under LGA 2000 provided it is necessary to avoid breach of human rights	Yes, if dependant children but not if failed to comply with removal directions

19.50   The appendix to this chapter contains a flow chart for assessing the relevant tests for a person whose immigration status means that a community care duties may be limited.

Adults seeking support and accommodation from social services

Applying tests under Immigration and Asylum Act 1999 (1999 Act) and Nationality Immigration and Asylum Act 2002 (2002 Act).

Question 1: does person fall under Schedule 3? (2002 Act)

Schedule 3

If yes:
- EEA national or family
- EEA refugee or family
- Failed asylum seeker who didn't comply with removal directions
- Person in UK in breach of immigration law
- Person certified under IATCIA 2004

If no: Support can only be provided to extent necessary to avoid a breach or human rights or EU community rights

Relevant questions:
- can person return home?
- any outstanding application to Home Office?
- Is person exercising rights under EU treaty? e.g. working.

Question 2: Is person a PSIC? (1999 Act)

PSIC

If yes:
- needs leave and doesn't have
- has leave but 'no recourse to public funds'
- leave dependent on maintenance undertaking
- leave only granted to appeal refusal

If no: No accommodation under s21 if need arises solely from destitution. If not, support and accommodation must be provided. No restriction on duties to care leavers.

Section 21 duty will arise provided unmet need for care and attention.

N.B Asylum seekers and failed asylum seekers
Asylum seekers do not have leave so are PSIC
Failed asylum seekers may be Schedule 3 or PSIC:
- If claimed asylum in-country will be Schedule 3
- If claimed on entry will be PSIC (unless failed to comply with removal directions, in which case will be Schedule 3)

Housing improvement and adaptation

Key points

- Mandatory grants for home improvements are no longer available. Instead local authorities have a wide discretion as to how assistance will be given to improve private sector accommodation. This may include giving grants and loans. Authorities must publish their policies.
- Disabled facilities grants (DFGs) remain mandatory for works costing up to £30,000. Discretionary grants may be awarded for costs above this limit.
- There are clear statutory provisions, including time limits, regarding local authority decision making in relation to DFGs. Despite this many applicants face delays and other difficulties in obtaining grants.
- To qualify for a mandatory grant the works must be for a specified purpose to make the premises more suitable for the disabled person.
- The works must also be necessary and appropriate to achieve the specified purpose and it must be reasonable and practicable to carry out the works in the particular dwelling.
- DFGs are means tested for adults. No means test is applied where the disabled occupant is under the age of 19 years.
- DFGs are administered by local housing authorities.
- Adaptations may also be carried out by social services under the Chronically Sick and Disabled Persons Act 1970.

Housing improvement: grants and assistance

20.1   Until 2002 discretionary and mandatory grants administered by local authorities were available for the improvement of private dwellings. The Regulatory Reform (Housing Assistance) (England & Wales) Order 2002[1] replaced the system of discretionary and mandatory grants with a new scheme which gives to local authorities a general power to improve housing.

20.2   Under the 2002 Order local authorities may, for the purpose of improving living conditions in their area, give financial assistance to enable a person to:[2]

---

1   SI No 1860.
2   2002 Order para 3(1).

- acquire living accommodation, in or out of the area;
- adapt or improve living accommodation;
- repair living accommodation;
- demolish buildings comprising or including living accommodation; and
- where buildings have been demolished, constructing replacement living accommodation.

20.3   The 2002 Order requires every authority to adopt and publish its policy as to how it intends to use these powers for the renewal of the private sector. Most authorities publish their policies on their websites and they are commonly referred to as Private Sector [Housing] Renewal Strategies.

Home improvement grants

20.4   A local authority must have a policy about home improvement grants. The policy may be available on the authority's website. If not, a copy should be requested from the authority.

20.5   Under the 2002 Order authorities have a wide discretion as to how to exercise their powers to improve standards in private sector accommodation. It is common for authorities to limit the availability of assistance by providing that grants are available only:

- to vulnerable groups, such as the elderly or disabled;
- for specific works, such as works to improve heating systems and thermal insulation;
- to those on means tested benefits; and
- to owner occupiers and not to tenants.

20.6   In addition to grants, some local authorities operate schemes whereby loans are made available through equity release schemes run by not-for-profit companies, such as the Home Improvement Trust.

20.7   While local authorities have a wide discretion as to how much assistance they give to improve and repair private sector homes, they must act lawfully in devising and operating their policies, see para 21.68.

Disabled facilities grants

20.8   The system of grants for disabled adaptations, known as disabled facilities grants (DFGs), is set out in sections 19 to 24 of the Housing

Grants, Construction and Regeneration Act (HGCRA) 1996.[3] The DFG scheme provides that:

- grants up to a certain level are mandatory provided the necessary conditions are met; and
- decisions and payments must be made within a prescribed time period.

20.9   Despite the clear terms of HGCRA 1996 the administration of DFGs is problematic which is reflected in the high proportion of Ombudsman complaints about DFGs. This section describes the criteria for DFGs and examines some common problems and how decisions may be challenged.

The legal provisions

Who can apply for a grant

20.10   An application may be made by:[4]

- an owner (or a person about to become an owner);[5]
- a tenant;[6]
- a licensee;
- an occupier of a houseboat or park home.

The conditions

20.11   To qualify for a mandatory grant the following conditions must be met.

Disabled occupant

20.12   There must be a disabled occupant. This means:[7]

- a person whose sight, hearing or speech is substantially impaired;
- a person who has a mental disorder or impairment of any kind; and
- a person who is physically substantially disabled by illness, injury, impairment present since birth or otherwise.

---

3   The Act previously also set out the provisions for home improvement and regeneration grants but those provisions were repealed by the 2002 Order.
4   HGCRA 1996 s19.
5   This includes a landlord applying for the benefit of a disabled tenant.
6   This includes introductory tenants, agricultural occupiers and employees occupying tied accommodation: section 9(5).
7   HGCRA 1996 s100.

20.13 The following are taken as being disabled for the purpose of a DFG:

- any adult for whom social services have made welfare arrangements under section 29(1) of the National Assistance Act (NAA) 1948 or who is registered by the authority as such;[8]
- any child who is, in the opinion of social services, a disabled child as defined in CA 1989, or who is registered as such.[9]

Only or main home

20.14 The disabled occupant must live in the premises as his or her only or main residence and it must be intended that he or she should do so for at least five years.[10]

Purpose of the works

20.15 The purpose of the works must one or more of the following:[11]

- to facilitate access by the disabled occupant to and from the dwelling or building;
- to make the dwelling or building safe for the disabled occupant and other persons residing with him or her;
- to facilitate access by the disabled occupant to the main family room, or to a bedroom, or to provide such a room;
- to facilitate access by the disabled occupant to a lavatory, a room with a bath or shower or wash hand basin, or to provide such a room or facilities;
- to facilitate the preparation and cooking of food by the disabled occupant;
- to improve or install a heating system to meet the needs of the disabled occupant;
- to facilitate the use by the disabled occupant of power, light or heat by altering the position of the controls; or
- to facilitate access and movement by the disabled occupant around the dwelling to enable him or her to care for another person who is normally resident and in need of such care.

20.16 For an applicant to qualify for a mandatory grant the proposed works must be for one of the above purposes. However, a discretionary

8 See para 17.12.
9 See para 18.5.
10 HGCRA 1996 s22(2).
11 HGCRA 1996 s23(1).

grant may be awarded to make the dwelling more suitable generally for the disabled occupant.[12]

Need and practicality of works

20.17   The authority must also be satisfied that the proposed works are:[13]
- 'necessary and appropriate' to meet the needs of the disabled occupant; and
- that 'it is reasonable and practicable' to carry out the works having regard to the age and condition of the dwelling or building.

20.18   In deciding whether the works are necessary and appropriate the authority must consult social services.[14] Most local authorities will obtain an occupational therapist's report to advise on whether the proposed adaptations will meet the disabled person's needs, increase independence and reduce the requirement for care or support.

20.19   The authority's resources cannot be taken into account in deciding whether the proposed works are necessary or appropriate.[15]

20.20   To decide whether the works are 'reasonable and practicable' the authority will usually rely on an assessment by its own building experts.

20.21   The question of whether the purpose of the works fall into one of the specified categories is separate from the question of whether they are necessary and appropriate to meet the disabled occupant's need.

In *R on the application of B v Calderdale MBC*[16] the claimant was the father of four children, the eldest of whom (D) was autistic. The family lived in a three-bedroom house owned by a housing association. D shared a bedroom with his younger brother and was uncontrollably aggressive towards him, frightening him while he slept and attacking him when they were in the bedroom together. The claimant applied for a DFG to convert the loft into a separate bedroom for D. The occupational therapy reports obtained suggested that an extra bedroom would be helpful and would enable D to feel safe and to enable his condition to be managed

---

12   HGCRA 1996 s23(2).
13   HGCRA 1996 s24(3)(a) and (b).
14   HGCRA 1996 s24(3).
15   *R v Birmingham CC ex p Mohammed* [1999] 1 WLR 33.
16   [2004] EWCA Civ 134, 4 February 2004.

more effectively. The authority refused the application holding that the evidence related to D's behaviour generally rather than the physical layout of the premises or the number of bedrooms. They decided the works proposed did not fall within the criteria for a mandatory grant and the application was refused.

The claimant sought judicial review of the decision. Initially the application was dismissed: it was held that in deciding whether the purpose of the works was to make 'the dwelling ... safe for the disabled occupant and other persons residing with him' under section 23(1)(b) the authority were entitled to take account of the evidence that D's behavioural problems went beyond the issue of the shared bedroom and that his behaviour outside the home had improved. The decision was within the council's discretion on the basis of the material before it. The claimant appealed.

The Court of Appeal held that the correct approach was to separate the two questions: (1) whether the purpose of the proposed works fell within the criteria for a mandatory grant; and (2) whether the proposed works were necessary and appropriate to meet the needs of the disabled occupant.

The council had erred in considering both questions at the same time. On the basis of the facts known to the council the case clearly fell within section 23(1): the purpose of providing a separate bedroom for D was to make the dwelling as safe as was reasonably practicable for D, and, more particularly, for his younger brother. The decision was quashed and it was directed that the council must go on to decide whether a loft conversion was necessary and appropriate to meet D's needs, including the need not to harm his brother. This was a matter for the council's judgment.

The means test

20.22   For disabled adults a financial assessment is carried out to determine eligibility.[17] However, if the disabled occupant is under the age of 19 years there is no means test. Certain benefits such as Disability Living Allowance and Income Support are generally ignored. Savings

---

17 HGCRA 1996 s30. The assessment process and applicable amounts are set out in the Housing Renewal Grants Regulations 1996 (SI No 2890) as amended by the Housing Renewal Grants (Amendment) (England) Regulations 2005 (SI No 3323).

are taken into account but the first £6,000 is disregarded. The assessment does not take account of *actual* outgoings but makes standard deductions for items of expenditure, including rent or mortgage payments. The assessment may result in a decision that a contribution is payable. Above a certain level the contribution is 100 per cent.

20.23   Changes to the means test are proposed which will mean that more applicants will qualify for a grant without being subject to a contribution (see para 20.40 below).

The maximum grant

20.24   The current maximum mandatory award is £30,000.[18] If a person qualifies for a mandatory grant the authority *must* award a sum up to this amount and has a discretion to award a grant in excess of these limits where the works will cost more than the maximum. The grant may be paid in full on completion or by instalments.[19]

20.25   Where an authority does not exercise its discretion to pay a grant in excess of the statutory limit a person may be able to obtain a loan from the Home Improvement Trust to fund the excess, see para 20.6 above.

How to apply

20.26   There is a prescribed application form which can be obtained from the relevant local authority.[20]

20.27   Applications must be accompanied by the relevant certificates.[21] An owner occupier who applies must provide an owner's certificate and a tenant who applies must provide a 'tenant's certificate' confirming that it is intended that the disabled occupant will live in the dwelling as his or her only or main residence for at least five years. Unless the authority consider it unreasonable, where a tenant applies, an 'owner's certificate' must also be provided from the landlord confirming his or her interest.

---

18 The Disabled Facilities Grants (Maximum Amounts and Additional Purposes) (England) Order 2008 (SI No 1189); The Disabled Facilities Grants and Home Repair Assistance (Maximum Amounts) (Amendment) (Wales) Order 2002 (SI No 837).

19 HGCRA 1996 s35.

20 The Housing Renewal Grants (Prescribed Form and Particulars) Regulations 1996 (SI No 2891) as amended by Housing Renewal Grants (Prescribed Form and Particulars) (Amendments) (England) Regulations 2005 (SI No 3326).

21 HGCRA 1996 ss19 and 22.

Help available

20.28 Home Improvement Agencies (HIAs) assist homeowners and private sector tenants who are older or disabled to remain in their own home, living independently. HIAs advise on improvements and adaptations and help people to apply for grants or loans to carry out works. They also help identify reputable local contractors, oversee works and arrange payments. Many agencies also run schemes to provide handypersons to carry out small repairs or specific schemes to improve safety and security in the home, to improve energy efficiency or make homes suitable for people to return to after a stay in hospital.

20.29 HIAs are usually small, locally based not-for-profit organisations. Some are local authority agencies. Others are independent organisations and are often managed by a housing association or charity. They are often called 'Care and Repair' or 'Staying Put' agencies.

20.30 'Foundations' is the national co-ordinating body for HIAs in England and is appointment by the Department of Communities and Local Government (DCLG) to provide advice, training and support to HIA staff and managing organisations. A full list of all HIAs in England is contained on the Foundations website: www. foundations.uk.com.

Decisions and time limits

20.31 A local authority must notify an applicant in writing whether the application has been approved or refused as soon as reasonably practicable and, in any event, not later than six months after the date of the application.[22] If the application is approved the decision letter must specify the works that are eligible for a grant and the amount of grant to be paid. If the application is refused reasons must be given.[23]

20.32 Delays in dealing with applications are common. If action is to be taken to challenge delay advisers must ensure that the application has been properly made and supported by the relevant certificates, see para 20.27 above. Authorities 'shall not entertain' an application that is not accompanied by the relevant 'certificates'.[24]

---

22 HGCRA 1996 s34(1).
23 HGCRA 1996 s34(4).
24 HGCRA 1996 ss19 and 22.

20.33   Payment of the grant should be made no later than 12 months from the date of the application.[25]

Common problems

Delays

20.34   Despite the fact that grants are mandatory and that there is a statutory time limit for decision-making, obtaining a DFG is often difficult and delays are common. In practice it is often the case that the delay occurs before a completed application is submitted. The first step in obtaining a DPG will usually to be to request an assessment from social services (see para 17.35). The fact that authorities must carry out a means assessment and must take advice from social services and building experts about the proposed works means that decisions are rarely made within the six-month time limit.

20.35   The average delay before an occupational therapist assessment is completed in relation to a DFG is almost 20 weeks.[26] Further delays in the drawing up of plans, the obtaining of planning permission and building regulation approval are also common. The fact that applicants may have to fund part of the cost may also add to the delay if funds must be raised by the household.

Funding

20.36   Central government funding for DFGs does not meet the full cost to local authorities which means that many local authorities struggle to find the funding to meet their part of the costs.[27] Further, funding for adaptations for those occupying local authority owned accommodation is not available from the central government grant but must be paid for from the authority's housing budget. Most local authorities therefore do not actively encourage applications.

Limits on maximum grant

20.37   The maximum mandatory grant of £30,000 may be insufficient to pay for substantial adaptations, such as an extension to a dwelling, which may be required for those with the most severe disabilities.[28]

---

25 HGCRA 1996 s36.
26 See *Reviewing the Disabled Facilities Grant Programme*, Bristol University, 2005.
27 In 2003–4, 47 per cent of all housing authorities had insufficient capital to meet valid DFG applications.
28 It is proposed that the maximum may be increased to £50,000 in the future but this would required more funding to be made available to local authorities.

Private sector tenants – lack of security

20.38 Given that most private sector tenants have security of tenure for only the first six months of a tenancy, it will be difficult to establish that the disabled occupier intends to remain in the accommodation for at least five years. Moreover, a private landlord may be unwilling to consent to adaptations.

DFGs – future proposals

20.39 In February 2008 the DCLG published 'Disabled Facilities Grant – The Package of Changes to Modernise the Programme'.

20.40 In addition to the increase of the maximum grant in England to £30,000 and changes to the means test, the government announced the following changes to the DFG system:

- changes to the funding arrangements so that local authorities will no longer have to match funding provided by DCLG for each grant approved and increased flexibility about the way DFG funding can be used by local authorities. Further changes are proposed as from 2010–2011, removing the 'ring-fencing' of the DFG grant paid by central government. This will enable DFG funds to be used for the adaptation of local authorities properties.
- joint guidance is to be issued by DCLG and the Housing Corporation to RSLs on how adaptations are both funded and delivered.
- further changes to the means test are proposed to bring it in line with the tests applied for related services.
- further funding is to be made available as from 2009 to enable more older people to get help with minor adaptations and repairs.
- the role of the HIAs in delivering adaptations is to be enhanced.

Chronically Sick and Disabled Persons Act 1970

20.41 The Chronically Sick and Disabled Persons Act (CSDPA) 1970 lists a range of services that a local social services authority may be under a duty to provide in relation to a disabled person. The duty applies to both disabled adults and children. For the duty to arise the following conditions must be satisfied:

- the person must be disabled;[29]
- the person must be ordinarily resident in the area of the local authority; and
- the authority must be satisfied that it is necessary to make the arrangements to meet the person's needs.

20.42   Included in the list of services that may be provided under CSDPA 1970 to meet a disabled persons needs is:

> the provision of assistance for that person in arranging for the carrying out of any works of adaptation in his home or the provision of any additional facilities designed to secure his greater safety, comfort or convenience.[30]

20.43   Where an assessment of the needs of a disabled adult or child reveals a need for services under CSDPA 1970, the authority is under a duty to provide those services. An authority's duty to carry out an assessment is described at paras 17.35 and 18.22.

20.44   A social service authority may discharge the duty to 'assist' a disabled person in arranging for the carrying out works of adaptation by assisting the person to apply for a DFG. However, there may be a delay in the application process, the application may be refused, or the DFG may not cover all of the necessary works. If this is the case, provided the social services authority are satisfied that the works are necessary to meet the disabled person's needs, it is under a duty to provide the services. See the Ombudsman complaint summarised at para 20.54 below.

20.45   In England minor adaptations that cost less than £1,000 should be provided free of charge.[31] In practice many local authority social services departments provide adaptations themselves if they cost less than £1,000 and provide assistance to apply for a DFG if the cost is likely to exceed this amount.

20.46   If services described in the CSDPA 1970 are provided by an authority for a disabled child, it is not open to the authority to maintain that the services are provided instead under the CA 1989.[32] The distinction is important since the courts have held that the duty

---

29 This means: persons who are blind, deaf or dumb or who suffer from mental disorder of any description or who are substantially and permanently handicapped by illness, injury or congenital deformity. See NAA 1948 s29 and CA 1989 s17(1).
30 DSCPA 1970 s2(1)(e).
31 See the Community Care (Delayed Discharges etc) Act 2003, ss15 and 16.
32 *R v Bexley LBC ex p B* (2000) 3 CCLR 15, QBD.

to provide services under CSDPA 1970 is a specific enforceable duty but that the duty under section 17 of the Children Act 1989 is a 'target duty': see para 18.6.

Means testing

20.47 There is no provision for local authorities to charge people for services provided under CSDPA 1970. However, it is not possible to avoid the means testing scheme under the DFG system by requesting that adaptations are carried out instead under the CSDPA 1970.

In *R on the application of Spink v Wandsworth LBC*[33] it was held by the Court of Appeal that a local authority could decide that it was not satisfied that it was necessary to provide services for a disabled child under the CSDPA 1970 until it had been shown that, having regard to the parent's means, it was not reasonable for the parents to provide them.

20.48 Means testing does not now apply to adaptations for disabled children but the same principle will apply in relation to adaptations for adults.

Provision of equipment

20.49 In addition to adaptations, CSDPA 1970 s2 also provides for the provision of 'additional facilities' designed to secure the disabled person's 'greater safety, comfort or convenience'. Such facilities may include handrails, alarm systems and moveable baths.

Challenging decisions

20.50 Local authority decision-making is challenged principally by:

- judicial review proceedings; and
- formal complaints.

20.51 Both courses of action are described in more detail in chapter 21. The merits of judicial review and complaints in relation to social services are discussed at para 17.50.

33 [2005] EWCA Civ 302, 18 March 2005.

20.52   One of the main causes of complaint in the administration of DFGs is delay. Some delay may be caused by the need for housing authorities to consult with social services, usually occupational therapists, and building experts. Further delays may be caused by the need to obtain planning consent and building regulation approval for major works. However, the lack of funding for DFGs means that many authorities are reluctant to approve applications and several published Ombudsman investigations concern local authority procedures for dealing with DFGs. However, because the complaints procedure is itself very slow, advisers should consider an application for judicial review where an application has been made and the authority are delaying making a decision. Authorities should be reminded of the statutory time limits for decisions and payment and the duty to give reasons if an application is refused.

20.53   A claim for judicial review may be brought against an authority to:

- compel the authority to make a decision;
- to give reasons for a negative decision; or
- to challenge a refusal to award a grant, where it appears that the authority has applied the law wrongly.[34]

20.54   The following are examples of successful Ombudsman complaints concerning adaptations.

Ombudsman Complaint: 03/A/08718

The complaint was about the authority delaying making a decision, referring to possible start dates for works without informing the applicant that the authority might not fund the cost of works above £25,000 and deciding not to exercise its discretion to fund works above the mandatory limit without giving reasons. Following an appeal the authority decided to offer a final grant of £35,000 but this was three years after the applicant first applied for help and by then he had decided he could not afford to pay the extra and that he would move instead.

The Ombudsman found that there had been maladministration because of the council's failure to advise the applicant about the policy on grants for extensions; to ensure adequate liaison between officers in processing the application; and, to record reasons for the decision or to inform the applicant of the reasons.

---

34 As in the case of *R on the application of B v Calderdale*, see para 20.21 above.

The Ombudsman recommended that the council should pay compensation of £2,000 because the applicant had spent two years longer than necessary in unsuitable accommodation; a £500 contribution to moving costs; and £150 for the applicant's time and trouble pursuing the complaint.

Ombudsman Complaint: 05/C/13157

A complaint was made by the husband of a woman who was seriously ill and profoundly disabled about the handling of a DFG application. The Ombudsman found that the council had delayed in completing a financial assessment; had failed to review the Grant Section's position that a DFG could not be used to provide or retain a family room (which was wrong in law) and had failed to deal with the conflict between what was thought necessary by the Occupational Therapist and the woman's husband, and what the Grants Section would fund. The council also failed to recognise its duties under section 2 of the CSDPA 1970. As a result for two years longer than necessary the woman was confined to bed in the front living room and was unable to use a special wheelchair provided to relieve her pain and discomfort. She was unable to use a toilet, bath or shower and had to be strip washed by her carers. She was also unable to sit outside or with her family.

To remedy the injustice, the council agreed to pay £6,605 to the complainant; to establish a mechanism to resolve disputes about the adaptations required to meet a disabled person's needs; to ensure that all relevant officers were aware of the duty under section 2 of the CSDPA 1970; and, to produce a report about the lessons to be learnt from the complainant's experience and the changes it would make to its practice and procedures.

Alternative accommodation was also identified which would be adapted to meet the woman's needs.

Challenging decisions by public bodies

continued

Key points

- The Human Rights Act 1998 means that rights under the European Convention on Human Rights can be enforced in UK courts.
- There is a difference between 'public law' and 'private law'. Public law concerns decision-making by public bodies. Private law concerns disputes between individual legal persons.
- A public body, such as a local authority, is governed by public law when acting in its capacity as a public body (eg in relation to homeless applications) and by private law when acting in a private capacity (eg in relation to carrying out repairs as a landlord).
- Most arguments about 'public law' duties will be brought by way of judicial review.
- It is, however, possible to raise some public law arguments, including under the Human Rights Act, by way of a defence to a claim for possession.
- Registered social landlords may be susceptible to judicial review and bound by the Human Rights Act depending on whether they can be classed as a 'public authority'. This depends on the nature of the RSL.
- An alternative way of resolving 'public law' decisions by local authorities and RSLs is by making a formal complaint to the body and, if not resolved, to the appropriate Ombudsman.
- Important information about a public body's decision making may be obtained under the Data Protection Act 1998 and the Freedom of Information Act 2000.

Public law and private law

21.1 Housing law involves both private law and public law. Private law determines the legal relationship between private individuals, including landlord and tenant. Although a person's landlord may be a public body, such as a local authority, the general rule is that, when acting as a landlord, the authority is not acting as a public body but as a private legal 'person' and is subject to the usual private law obligations. For example, a local authority landlord has an obligation to carry out repairs and to allow a tenant 'quiet enjoyment' of the tenancy, see chapters 7 and 9. Similarly, when a landlord wishes to evict a tenant the rules regarding notices and the obtaining of court orders apply in the same way whether the landlord is a public body or a private individual.

21.2   However, in recent years the role of the social landlord has become more distinct from that of the private landlord. Not only are social landlords effectively the sole providers of affordable long-term rented accommodation but they have additional powers to deal with anti-social behaviour by tenants and others.

21.3   Further, the introduction of the Human Rights Act (HRA) 1998 has affected the way local authority landlords (and some other social landlords) operate, as all 'public authorities' must act in accordance with HRA 1998. This chapter seeks to explain how the decisions of local authorities and other social landlords may be challenged.

21.4   Private legal rights arising in the sphere of housing law are dealt with in chapters 1–11. Chapters 12–20 deal with the public law duties of local housing and social services authorities. This chapter examines the ways of challenging decision making in the public law sphere. Chapter 22 examines civil court proceedings dealing principally with the enforcement of private legal rights.

21.5   This chapter examines with the following:

- the effect of the HRA 1998 on housing law;
- judicial review as a way of challenging decisions;
- complaints and non-legal regulation of social landlords;
- obtaining information held by public bodies and landlords.

Human Rights Act 1998 and housing law

21.6   The Human Rights Act (HRA) 1998 came into force on 2 October 2000. It incorporated into UK law most of the rights contained in the European Convention on Human Rights (ECHR or 'the Convention'). The Convention is an international treaty of the Council of Europe, ratified by the UK in 1951. The 'human rights' protected by the ECHR are referred to as Convention rights. HRA 1998 means that those rights can now be enforced in UK courts. Previously, Convention rights could only be enforced by application to the European Court of Human Rights (ECtHR) in Strasbourg.

Effect of the Human Rights Act 1998

Enforcement of Convention rights in UK courts

21.7 HRA 1998:

- lists the Convention rights which are made part of UK law;
- makes it unlawful for any 'public authority' to act in a way that is incompatible with Convention rights;
- enables a person alleging a breach of a Convention right to bring a claim in the UK courts against the relevant public authority; and
- allows such a person to claim compensation for a breach of Convention rights.

UK law must be compatible with the Convention

21.8 HRA 1998 provides that:

- the courts are 'public authorities' and must not act in a way that is incompatible with Convention rights;
- UK courts and tribunals must *take account* of decisions made by the European Court of Human Rights when making decisions about Convention rights;
- legislation must be interpreted in a way that is compatible with Conventions rights 'so far as it is possible to do so';[1] and
- if this is not possible higher courts can make 'declarations of incompatibility', stating that legislation is not compatible with Convention rights.[2]

Convention rights that are part of UK law

21.9 The following Convention rights are now part of UK law:[3]

article 2: the right to life
article 3: the prohibition on torture and inhuman or degrading treatment or punishment
article 4: the prohibition on slavery and forced labour
article 5: the right to liberty and security

---

1 HRA 1998 s3(1).
2 HRA 1998 s4(2).
3 Articles 1 and 13 of the Convention have not been incorporated. Article 1 is an obligation on the state to ensure that everyone within its jurisdiction has their rights safeguarded and article 13 is an obligation to ensure that there is a way of enforcing Convention rights in the state's own courts or institutions. The reason these articles have not been incorporated is that the very purpose of HRA 1998 is to secure those rights.

article 6: the right to a fair trial

article 7: protection from punishment for acts that were not offences at the time they were committed

article 8   the right to respect for private and family life, home and correspondence

article 9: freedom of thought, conscience and religion

article 10: freedom of expression

article 11: freedom of assembly and association

article 12: the right to marry and found a family

article 14: the prohibition of discrimination in relation to the enforcement of Convention rights.

Under Protocol 1 to the Convention:

article 1: the right to property

article 2: the right to education

article 3: the right to free and fair elections.

Under Protocol 13 to the Convention

article 1: the abolition of the death penalty and prohibition on condemnation to death.

How Convention rights work

Absolute and qualified rights

21.10   Some Convention rights are 'absolute' and others 'qualified'. What this means is that in relation to qualified rights, individual rights are balanced against collective rights. The state may be justified in restricting the exercise of qualified rights in the interests of other people. Article 3 is an absolute right: there can be no justification for subjecting a person to torture, inhuman or degrading treatment. Article 8 is a qualified right: it is the right to 'respect' for private and family life, home and correspondence. The state may interfere with article 8 rights if necessary in certain circumstances.

Derogation and reservation

21.11   The state may enter a 'reservation' about particular Convention rights and may, in times of war or public emergency 'derogate' from the Convention. It may only do this if the situation 'strictly requires' the suspension of the rights. Reservation and derogation are not possible in relation to absolute rights.

Convention rights and housing

21.12   The Convention rights most relevant to housing law are articles 6, 8, 14 and article 1 of the 1st Protocol. In addition, article 3 has been used to challenge the government's policy of refusing housing and subsistence to asylum-seekers and failed asylum-seekers thereby causing destitution, see chapter 19 and para 21.18 below.

21.13   These Convention rights are examined below with reference to case law.

Article 3

21.14   Article 3 provides: 'No-one shall be subjected to torture or to inhuman or degrading treatment or punishment.'

21.15   Torture is deliberate inhuman treatment which causes very serious suffering.[4]

21.16   Inhuman treatment or punishment is less severe than torture and need not be deliberately inflicted. The threat of torture and very poor conditions of detention may amount to inhuman treatment.

21.17   Degrading treatment is that which 'grossly humiliates' or 'debases' the victim. To establish a breach of article 3 the treatment must reach a minimum level of severity.[5]

In the case of *Pretty v UK*[6] the ECtHR considered the types of 'treatment' that fell within the scope of article 3 of the Convention. It is

'ill-treatment' that attains a minimum level of severity and involves actual bodily injury or intense physical or mental suffering. Where treatment humiliates or debases an individual showing a lack of respect for, or diminishing, his or her human dignity or arouses feelings of fear, anguish or inferiority capable of breaking an individual's moral and physical resistance, it may be characterised as degrading and also fall within the prohibition of article 3.[7]

Treatment

21.18   As a general rule the withholding of a service, such as benefits or housing, does not amount to 'treatment'. However, if it is part of a system under which people are prevented from fending for themselves it may amount to treatment that constitutes a breach of article 3.

---

4   *Selmouni v France*, ECtHR AG0000970, 28 July 1999.
5   *Ireland v UK* (1979–80) 2 EHRR 25 at para 162, 18 January 1978.
6   ECtHR (2346/02), 26 April 2002.
7   At [52].

R on the application of Limbuela and Others v Secretary of State for the Home Department[8] concerned section 55 of the Nationality Immigration and Asylum Act (NIAA) 2002. This applies to asylum seekers who, in the opinion of the Home Office, did not make their claim for asylum as soon as reasonably practical; they may not be provided with any accommodation or support pending consideration of the asylum claim. This is subject to the proviso that support should be provided if necessary to avoid a breach of Convention rights. Asylum seekers cannot work and are ineligible for benefits or homeless assistance.

The House of Lords determined that although the withdrawal of support does not of itself amount to treatment that is a breach of article 3, it will do so 'once the margin is crossed between destitution [as defined in the asylum support legislation] and the condition that results from inhuman or degrading treatment'.[9] The fact that the asylum support system prohibited asylum-seekers from working and claiming mainstream benefits meant that the provisions did not just amount to the refusal of a service but was 'treatment' under article 3.

The question was whether the degree of suffering endured or imminently to be endured reached the severity prohibited by article 3. The threshold is high but the court held that to place asylum-seekers in a situation of having to endure the indefinite prospect of being without shelter or money for food and clothing was both inhuman and degrading.

21.19   In contrast, in the case of *Bernard v Enfield LBC*[10] the claimant failed to establish a breach of article 3 while succeeding in establishing a breach of article 8 where a local authority had failed to provide suitable disabled adapted accommodation after accepting a duty to do so.

Article 6

21.20   Article 6(1) provides: 'In the determination of his civil rights and obligations or of any criminal charge against him, everyone is entitled to a fair and public hearing within a reasonable time by an independent and impartial tribunal established by law.'

8 [2005] UKHL 66, 3 November 2005.
9 Hope LJ at [57].
10 See para 17.24.

Internal reviews

21.21 There are many cases in which 'civil rights' are determined by tribunals other than courts. Indeed, since 1996 the role of the courts in challenging decision making by local authorities has been reduced. Instead, many decisions are subject to a right to request an internal review by the authority. This applies to most decisions about the homelessness duty and the allocation of social housing. Similarly, introductory and demoted tenants may challenge a decision to seek possession by requesting an internal review. It is established that at such reviews there is a determination of civil rights. It has also been held that the reviewing officer is not 'an independent and impartial tribunal'. However, the House of Lords has determined that the availability of judicial review to challenge the lawfulness and/or fairness of the review means that the process, looked at as a whole, complies with article 6. This has been held in relation to: a review of an allocation decision which led to an authority discharging its housing duty;[11] a review of a decision to seek possession against an introductory tenant;[12] and a review of a decision to see possession against a demoted tenant.[13]

21.22 Whether judicial review provides an adequate safeguard *'for the resolution of sensitive factual questions'*, however, was doubted by the ECtHR in *McCann v UK* (see para 21.40 below).

21.23 In *Doherty* (see para 21.41 below) it was suggested that the judicial review procedure may have to be adapted to enable factual disputes to be resolved.

21.24 In housing cases article 6 is closely connected with article 8: an interference with rights under article 8 may be justified but if there is no forum for an occupier to challenge whether the interference is justified, the rights under both articles 6 and 8 may be breached.

21.25 So, there remains an issue as to whether judicial review is an appropriate forum for the resolution of certain types of dispute. Further, whether public law arguments can give a tenant a defence in county court proceedings or must be raised by way of judicial review is also a contentious issue and has received much judicial consideration recently, see below and paras 6.129–6.133.

---

11 *Runa Begum (FC) v Tower Hamlets LBC* [2003] UKHL 5, 13 February 2003.
12 *McLellan v Bracknell Forest BC* [2001] EWCA Civ 1510, 16 October 2001.
13 *R (Gilboy) v Liverpool City Council & Secretary of State for Communities and Local Government* [2008] EWCA Civ 751, 2 July 2008.

21.26   A good example of tribunals held not to be compliant with the requirements of article 6 were the local authority Housing Benefit Review Boards (HBRB).

> In the case of *Tsfayo v UK*[14] the ECtHR considered a decision by a Housing Benefit Review Board that an applicant had failed to establish good cause for a late claim. The Court decided that the Review Board was not independent and impartial. This was because the issue was a simple question of fact and the Board not only lacked independence but was directly connected to one of the parties to the dispute. Further, the availability of judicial review did not correct the deficiency as the issue went to the credibility of the applicant and the Administrative Court had no jurisdiction to rehear evidence or substitute its own finding as to the applicant's credibility.

Housing benefit appeals are now heard by the independent Social Security and Child Support Appeal Tribunals.

Article 8

21.27   Article 8 is the Convention right of most direct relevance to housing law. It provides:

> (1) Everyone has the right to respect for his private and family life, his home and his correspondence.
> (2) There shall be no interference by a public authority with the exercise of this right except such as is in accordance with the law and is necessary in a democratic society in the interests of national security, public safety or the economic well-being of the country, for the prevention of disorder or crime, for the protection of health or morals, or for the protection of the rights and freedoms of others.

21.28   A particular decision made by a public authority may constitute an unlawful interference with a person's article 8 rights. Alternatively, a person may claim that the law under which an authority (or private individual) acts constitutes a breach of article 8. Further, if the matter is before a court, the court is under a duty, where possible, to interpret a particular law in a way that is compatible with article 8 even if this is contrary to previous case law.

14   ECtHR (60860/00), 14 November 2006.

21.29   Leaving aside for the moment the issue of whether the particular body is a 'public authority' (see para 21.50 below), the way article 8 operates is that first the person relying on article 8 must establish:

- that what is at stake is his or her 'home'; and
- that the decision being challenged 'interferes' with the 'right to respect for' his or her home.

21.30   If this is established, the burden is on the public authority to show that the decision:

- 'is in accordance with the law';
- is made in order to further one of the legitimate interests of the state, in housing cases, this will usually be 'the economic well-being of the country' and/or the 'protection of the rights and freedoms of others'; and
- that the extent of the interference is necessary to further one of those legitimate interests. This is also referred to as the 'proportionality' test.

21.31   It is now settled that in relation to possession claims:

- whether a place is a person's 'home' is a question of fact; a person may occupy as a home a place in which he or she has no legal right to occupy;[15] and
- an eviction is an interference with the right to respect for the home.

21.32   Assuming that the body seeking to evict is acting in accordance with the substantive and procedural law relating to the right to possession, the issue will be whether the decision to evict is necessary to further one of the legitimate interests of the state. Or, to put it another way, whether the interference is proportionate to the legitimate aim pursued'.[16]

Necessity/proportionality

21.33   The Convention aims to set a fair balance between the demands of the general interest of the community and the need to protect individual rights.[17]

21.34   It is a matter for each state to pursue economic policies and devise laws that it determines are 'in the interests of national security, public safety or the economic well-being of the country, for

---

15 *Harrow LBC v Qazi*, below.
16 *Silver v UK* [1983] 5 EHRR 344, 24 October 1983.
17 *Soering v UK* [1989] 11 EHRR 439, 7 July 1989.

the prevention of disorder or crime, for the protection of health or morals, or for the protection of the rights and freedoms of others'.

The margin of appreciation

21.35   The 'margin of appreciation' refers to the extent to which an issue is one which individual states should determine, being best placed to evaluate local needs and conditions.

21.36   The ECtHR has held that the margin will vary according to the nature of the Convention rights in issue. It will tend to be narrower where the right at stake is crucial to the individual's effective enjoyment of intimate or key rights. In spheres involving the application of social or economic policies, such as in the planning context, the ECtHR cases suggest that the margin of appreciation is wide.[18]

21.37   The application of article 8 to claims for possession against occupiers with no rights of occupation has been considered by the House of Lords and the ECtHR in a number of cases.

> The case of *Harrow LBC v Qazi*[19] concerned the rights of an occupier whose joint tenancy had been ended by the service of a notice to quit by his ex-partner. Under domestic law Mr Qazi had no right to remain in occupation and the local authority sought a possession order. The House of Lords held that article 8 could not operate so as to give a person rights of occupation where none existed in domestic law: provided the possession claim was brought in accordance with domestic law the interference with article 8 rights would be justified and the making of a possession order lawful.

21.38   Subsequent to the *Qazi* decision the issue came before the ECtHR in *Connors v UK*.

> Mr Connors and his family had been evicted after 16 years occupation on a local authority gypsy site. The authority alleged anti-social behaviour but used a summary procedure such that he had no opportunity to challenge the allegations or the eviction. The ECtHR found that there was a violation of article 8 as:

18   See *Connors v UK* (2004) HLR 53, 27 May 2004, at para 21.39.
19   [2003] UKHL 43, 31 July 2003.

the eviction of the applicant and his family from the local authority site was not attended by the requisite procedural safeguards, namely the requirement to establish proper justification for the serious interference with his rights and consequently cannot be regarded as justified by a 'pressing social need' or proportionate to the legitimate aim being pursued.[20]

21.39 In light of the ECtHR judgment in *Connors* the issue was revisited by the House of Lords in the case of *Kay and Others v Lambeth and Leeds CC v Price and Others*.[21]

In *Kay and Price* seven Law Lords considered article 8 in two cases: in one the eviction was of a family from a gypsy site after a short period in occupation (Price) and in the other the eviction was of a number of occupiers of 'short-life' accommodation who had actually been in occupation for many years. In both cases the domestic law provided no defence to the occupiers. It was agreed that an eviction constituted a breach of the occupier's rights under article 8. The questions were whether the interference was justified and how an occupier could challenge the decision. All of the Law Lords agreed that in the vast majority of cases the domestic law would provide sufficient justification for an eviction and that the public authority seeking to evict is not obliged to plead or prove that the eviction is justified under the HRA 1998; and it will be enough to establish that the eviction is in accordance with domestic law. It is for the occupier to raise any defence based on article 8. However, the House was split on the issue of what may constitute a defence under article 8. The majority (4:3) held that it was not open to an occupier to argue that article 8 was breached because of his or her personal circumstances. Rather, the only two possible ways of establishing a breach of article 8 were:

(a) A seriously arguable point that the domestic law that enabled the possession order to be made was incompatible with article 8. Unless the court could give effect to the law so as to be compatible the court should adjourn the proceedings to enable the issue of incompatibility to be dealt with by the High Court: or

20 At [95].
21 [2006] UKHL 10, 8 March 2006.

(b) A challenge to the decision to bring the claim for possession on established public law grounds, such as irrationality or bias.

The dissenting minority were of the view that the occupier's personal circumstances could be relevant to the issue but only in wholly exceptional circumstances.

21.40   The issue was again before the ECtHR in May 2008 in the case of *McCann v UK*.[22]

In *McCann v UK*, like *Qazi*, the former tenant was evicted by a local authority following the service of notice to quit by his joint tenant. Mrs McCann had signed the notice at the instigation of the local authority without advice as to its meaning and had sought to withdraw it a week later. The county court hearing had taken place before the House of Lords decision in *Qazi*. The county court judge found that although Mr McCann had no defence under the common law or under the HA 1985 the circumstances were such that the authority had not acted as required by article 8(2) and the claim was dismissed.

The authority appealed and the Court of Appeal made its decision after the House of Lords judgment in *Qazi*. It was held that article 8 was not available as a defence to the possession proceedings. The council had acted lawfully and within its powers in obtaining the notice to quit which had the effect of terminating the tenancy.

Mr McCann also applied for judicial review of the authority's decision to procure a notice to quit from his wife and seek possession. The application was refused on the grounds that the council's decision to apply its domestic violence policy was neither unlawful nor outside the range of decisions open to the council.

Mr McCann was evicted on 22 March 2005. His application to the ECtHR was decided in May 2008. In the ECtHR the parties agreed that article 8 was engaged but disagreed about whether the eviction had been 'necessary' under article 8(2).

22   Application 19009/04, 13 May 2008.

The UK government argued that the interference was justified and that the case could be distinguished from *Connors v UK* which concerned gypsies who were a vulnerable minority, where there was an absence of procedural protection and where the domestic law discriminated between gypsies on private sites and those on local authority sites. Here it was not argued that the domestic law was incompatible with article 8 and judicial review was an adequate remedy to challenge the authority's decision.

The ECtHR held the interference with article 8 was in accordance with the law and pursued the legitimate aim of protecting the rights and freedoms of others in two respects: firstly, it protected the authority' right to regain possession against an individual who had no right to be there; and secondly it ensured the statutory scheme for housing provision was property applied for the benefit of others.

The central question therefore was whether the interference was proportionate to the aim pursued and therefore 'necessary in a democratic society'. Article 8(2) raises a question of procedure as well as one of substance.

The procedural safeguards available to the individual will be especially relevant in deciding whether the respondent state has, when fixing the regulatory framework, remained within its margin of appreciation. In particular, the ECtHR must examine whether the decision-making process leading to measures of interference was fair and such as to afford due respect to the interests safeguarded to the individual by article 8.

The ECtHR rejected the argument that the reasoning in *Connors* was confined only to cases involving the eviction of gypsies or cases where the applicant sought to challenge the law itself rather than its application in his particular case.

> The loss of one's home is a most extreme form of interference with the right to respect for the home. Any person at risk of an interference of this magnitude should in principle be able to have the proportionality of the measure determined by an independent tribunal in the light of the relevant principles under article 8 of the Convention, notwithstanding that, under domestic law his right of occupation has come to an end.[23]

23 At [50].

It did not appear that the authority had given any consideration to the applicant's right to respect for his home. Moreover, it was suggested that under domestic law it wasn't open to the county court to consider any issue concerning the proportionality of the possession order unless something had happened since the service of the notice to quit to fundamentally alter the rights and wrongs of the proposed eviction. The procedural safeguards required by article 8 for the assessment of the proportionality of the interference were not met by the possibility of judicial review.

Judicial review procedure is not well-adapted for the resolution of sensitive factual questions which are better left to the county court responsible for ordering possession.'[24]

The court did not accept that allowing an occupier to raise an issue under article 8 in the possession proceedings would have serious consequences for the functioning of the system or for the domestic law of landlord and tenant. As the minority of the House of Lords in *Kay and Price* observed it would only be in very exceptional cases that an applicant would succeed in raising an arguable case which would require a court to examine the issue; in the great majority of cases, an order for possession could continue to be made in summary proceedings.

The ECtHR held that the lack of an adequate procedural safeguard meant the there had been a violation of article 8 and damages were awarded.

21.41 Following the ECtHR decision in *McCann* the House of Lords gave judgment in the case of *Doherty and others v Birmingham City Council*[25], another case concerning an eviction from a local authority gypsy site. The case is referred to at para 6.132. In *Doherty* the House of Lords confirmed that the earlier decision in *Kay and Price* correctly summarised the two 'gateways' to challenging a claim for possession under article 8: (a) a challenge to the law itself, or (b) a challenge to the decision to seek possession, on 'traditional judicial review grounds'. However, at the same time when remitting the case to the county court it was suggested that the court should not confine itself

24 At [53].
25 [2008] UKHL 57, 30 July 2008.

to *Wednesbury* grounds but should consider the proportionality of the decision.[26]

Article 14

21.42 Article 14 provides:

> The enjoyment of the rights and freedoms set forth in this Convention shall be secured without discrimination on any ground such as sex, race, colour, language, religion, political or other opinion, national or social origin, association with a national minority, property, birth or other status.

21.43 The right not to be discriminated against is not 'free-standing'. Article 14 is engaged only if there is discrimination in relation to Convention rights and freedoms.

21.44 The case of *Mendoza v Ghaidan*[27] provides a good example of the operation of article 14 and of the courts' duty to interpret domestic law in accordance with the Convention. It also illustrates the way in which articles 8 and 14 may be engaged in a dispute between individuals, as opposed to one between an individual and a public authority.

Mendoza v Ghaidan concerned a claim by a same sex partner to succeed to a Rent Act 1977 tenancy. RA 1977, at the time, provided that the right of succession was enjoyed by a spouse or a person living with the deceased tenant as husband or wife. Cases determined prior to HRA 1998 had held that a same sex partnership could not fall within this definition. The House of Lords held that although the dispute was between two private individuals once the state has chosen to intervene in a factual area involving those rights protected by article 8, article 14 is engaged if there is relevant discrimination in the mode of that intervention. The question was whether the discrimination could be justified. The landlord argued that the discrimination fell within the legitimate ambit of the state's discretion to arrange its housing schemes and the disposition of its housing stock. Alternatively it was argued that the policy of distinguishing between heterosexual and homosexual couples was legitimate and reasonable.

26 See Hope LJ at [55].
27 [2004] UKHL 30, 21 June 2004.

The court held that once discrimination has been demonstrated it is for the discriminator to establish an objective and reasonable justification for that discrimination. It is not enough to claim that what has been done falls within the permissible ambit of Parliament's discretion.

The House of Lords rejected the argument that the policy of the Rent Act was the protection of the family or that the exclusion of homosexuals from succession to a statutory tenancy would, in any event, be necessary to pursue such a policy.

To remedy this breach of the Convention the court must, if it can, interpret the Rent Act so that its provisions are rendered compatible with the Convention rights of the survivors of same-sex partnerships. That duty can be properly discharged by reading the words 'as his or her wife or husband' to mean 'as if they were his or her wife or husband'.[28] This included a same sex partner of a relationship that had the characteristics of a marriage.

Article 1 of the 1st Protocol

21.45   Article 1 of the 1st Protocol provides:

> Every natural or legal person is entitled to the peaceful enjoyment of his possessions. No one shall be deprived of his possessions except in the public interest and subject to the conditions provided for by law and by the general principles of international law.
>
> The preceding provision shall not, however, in any way impair the right of a state to enforce such laws as it deems necessary to control the use of property in accordance with the general interest or to secure the payment of taxes or other contributions or penalties.

21.46   The term 'possessions' includes a landlord's interest in premises let to tenants. It also includees the interests of tenants.

In *Chapman and others v UK*[29] the applicants wanted to live in caravans on their own land but were refused planning permission by the local authorities. Their complaints included that there had been a violation of their rights under article 8 and Protocol 1

---

28 In fact the RA 1977 has now been amended by the CPA 2004 to provide specifically that partners living together as if they were civil partners are entitled to succeed, see para 3.31.

29 (2001) 33 EHRR 18, 18 January 2001, ECtHR.

article 1. Their claims were dismissed. The ECtHR held that the decisions to refuse planning permission were in accordance with the law and pursued the legitimate aim of protecting the rights of others through the preservation of the environment. Domestic authorities must be given a wide margin of appreciation in the case of planning decisions. The interference with the claimant's right to respect for the home under article 8 and the right to peaceful enjoyment of their property under Protocol 1 article 1 was proportionate and struck a fair balance between individual rights and the public interest.

Public authorities

21.47 HRA 1998 applies to the decisions and actions of public authorities. Under HRA 1998 s6(6) a public authority includes:[30]

- a court or tribunal; and
- any person certain of whose functions are functions of a public nature.

21.48 But, in relation to a particular act, a person is not a public authority by virtue only of this provision if the nature of the act is private.[31]

RSLs

21.49 Local authorities, when making decisions about homelessness and the allocation of accommodation, or about community care duties, are clearly public authorities. However, whether a Registered Social Landlord is a public authority for the purpose of HRA 1998 is a more complex issue. This will depend on the nature of the RSL and the particular function being performed.

In *Poplar Housing and Regeneration Community Association Limited v Donaghue*[32] the Court of Appeal considered a claim for possession against an assured shorthold tenant. The claimants had become the defendant's landlords following a stock transfer of accommodation previously owned and managed by the local authority. The defendant had been provided with her tenancy by the authority, originally as interim accommodation pending a

30 HRA 1998 s6(6)(3).
31 HRA 1998 s6(5).
32 [2001] EWCA Civ 595, 27 April 2001.

homeless decision. On the stock transfer her tenancy became an assured shorthold tenancy. Following a finding by the authority that the defendant was intentionally homeless the claimants served notice under section 21 of the HA 1988 and sought possession. The defendant argued that the provisions of section 21(4) were incompatible with articles 6 and 8 of the ECHR, that the association was a public authority for the purpose of the HRA 1998 and therefore under a duty to act in a way compatible with Convention rights.

The Court of Appeal held:

(1) The HRA 1998 section 6 requires a generous interpretation of who is a public authority and is inspired by the approach previously developed by the courts in relation to those bodies that are susceptible to judicial review. The emphasis on public functions reflects the approach adopted in judicial review cases.

(2) When the authority transferred their housing stock to the association it did not transfer its primary public duties. The association was no more than the means by which the authority sought to perform those duties.

(3) The act of providing accommodation for rent, without more, is not a public function for the purpose of HRA 1998 s6.

(4) The fact that a body is a charity or not-for-profit organisation means it is likely to be motivated by what it perceives to be the public interest but that does not point to the body being a public authority. Even if such a body performs functions that would be considered to be of a public nature if performed by a public body, such acts may nevertheless remain of a private nature.

(5) It is a feature or combination of features that imposes a public character on the act that can make an act public that would otherwise be private. Statutory authority for what is done can help to mark the act as being public, as can the extent of control over the function exercised by another body which is itself a public authority. The more closely the acts are enmeshed in the activities of a public body, the more likely they are to be public. But the fact that the acts are supervised by a public regulatory body does not necessarily indicate that they are of a public nature.

(6) In this case, the closeness of the relationship between the authority and the association was relevant: the association was

created by the authority to take a stock transfer; five of its board members were also members of the authority; and it was subject to the guidance of the authority in the way it acted towards the defendant.

(7) The fact that the defendant was a sitting tenant of the authority before the transfer and was advised that she would be treated no better or worse as a result of the stock transfer was also relevant. While she remained a tenant the association stood, in relation to the defendant, in much the same position as that previously occupied by the authority.

The Court of Appeal held that in the circumstances the association was a public authority. However, the operation of HA 1988 s21 did not conflict with the defendant's rights under articles 6 or 8. The court was satisfied that, notwithstanding its mandatory terms, section 21(4) of the 1988 Act did not conflict with the defendant's right to family life. Section 21(4) is necessary in a democratic society in so far as there must be a procedure for recovering possession of property at the end of a tenancy. The question is whether the restricted power of the court is legitimate and proportionate. This is the area of policy where the court should defer to the decision of Parliament.

In *R on the application of Weaver v London and Quadrant Housing Trust*[33] the applicant was an assured tenant of the Trust (LQHT) which sought to evict her using Ground 8 (the mandatory grounds). She argued that LQHT were acting unlawfully in that she had a 'legitimate expectation' that, in accordance with Housing Corporation Guidance referred to in the in tenancy terms and conditions, they would pursue all reasonable alternatives before resorting to a Ground 8 claim for possession. Further, she argued that the decision was in breach of her rights under article 8 and Protocol 1 article 1 (see para 21.46 above). As a preliminary issue it was necessary for the court to decide whether LQHT was amenable to judicial review and whether it was a public authority for the purposes of HRA 1998.

It was held that the management and allocation of housing stock by LQHT is a function of a public nature and that it should be regarded as a public authority under section (3)(b) of the HRA 1998.

33 [2008] EWHC 1377 (Admin), 24 June 2008.

While the management and allocation of housing stock is not in itself an inherently governmental activity the nature of the activities of LQHT and the context in which it operates places it in a different situation from an ordinary commercial business.

LQHT is a non profit making charity acting for the benefit of the community in providing housing for the poor and disadvantaged. That does not necessarily mean it is a public authority but it means that it lacks the private and commercial features of the company in *YL*. The Trust operates within the social rented housing sector which is not simply subject to detailed regulation but 'is permeated by state control and influence with a view to meeting the Government's aims for affordable housing, and in which RSLs work side by side with, and can in a very real sense be said to take the place of, local authorities'.[34] The extent of public subsidy in the activities of LQHT, in common with other RSLs, was particularly important as was the voluntary transfer of housing stock from the public sector to RSLs. Although LQHT was not in the same position as Poplar HARCA (see para 21.50 above), which was formed specifically for the purpose of a stock transfer, 10 per cent of its stock had been transferred from the public sector. Also relevant was the duty of co-operation with local authorities regarding the allocation of social housing. In this LQHT did not have a purely commercial relationship with the local authority but was operating under arrangements made within the framework of that statutory duty; over half of all new lettings were the result of local authority nominations.

As to the nature of the decision to seek possession the court held that if the allocation of housing stock by LQHT is a public function, then it would be wrong to separate out the 'management' decisions, including the termination of a tenancy, as acts of a purely private nature.

> The allocation and management of the housing stock are to be regarded as part and parcel of a single function or as closely related functions. It would be artificial to separate out the act of terminating the tenancy, or indeed other acts in the course of management of a property, from the act of granting a tenancy.[35]

---

34 Richards LJ at [55].
35 Richards LJ at [62].

However, the court went on to dismiss the application on the basis that the claimant could not establish that she had a legitimate expectation regarding the Trust's approach to rent arrears. Further, even if she had, the Trust had not been in breach of any obligation to use all reasonable alternatives to recover the debt before using Ground 8.

21.50 So, while it cannot be said that all RSLs are public authorities for the purposes of HRA 1998, it seems likely that large RSLs which receive Housing Corporation grants and which offer a significant proportion of its stock to local authority nominations will be treated as public authorities.

Contracting out social services functions

21.51 The Court of Appeal reached a different conclusion in considering whether a RSL providing long-term residential accommodation for disabled residents was a public authority for the purpose of HRA 1998.

R on the application of Heather v Leonard Cheshire Foundation and another[36] a decision was made to close a residential home so that it could be operated as a high dependency unit and to move the long-term residents into community homes. The appellants had been placed in the LCF home by local authorities acting under section 21 of the National Assistance Act (NAA) 1948. The residents challenged the decision claiming that they had been promised a 'home for life' and that the decision breached their rights under article 8. The Court of Appeal upheld the decision that the defendants were not a public authority:

If the authority itself provides accommodation, it is performing a public function. It is also performing a public function if it makes arrangements for the accommodation to be provided by the LCF. However, if a body which is a charity, like LCF provides accommodation to those to whom the authority owes a duty under section 21 ... it does not follow that the charity is performing a public function.[37]

36 [2002] EWCA Civ 366, 21 March 2002.
37 Lord Woolf CJ at [15].

> The appellants continue to enjoy article 8 rights in relation to the local authority. The local authority cannot divest itself of its article 8 obligations by contracting out to a voluntary sector provider its obligations under section 21.
>
> In our judgment the role that LCF was performing manifestly did not involve the performance of public functions. The fact that LCF is a large and flourishing organisation does not change the nature of its activities from private to public.[38]

21.52   A similar approach was adopted by the House of Lords in relation to the rights of a resident placed in a private care home by a local authority under NAA 1948.

> In *YL v Birmingham City Council*[39] the House of Lords held that HRA 1998 did not apply to a private care home, Southern Cross Healthcare, even though they were providing accommodation under arrangements made under NAA 1948. The company carried on a socially useful business for profit but was not a charity; it entered into private law contracts with the residents in its care homes and with local authorities with whom it does business. It does not receive public funding and had no statutory powers and, subject to discrimination laws, could choose to accept or reject residents and to charge whatever fees it thought appropriate. Residents placed in the home retained their rights under the Convention in regard to the provision of care and accommodation against the local authority but could not assert those rights against the company.

Declarations of incompatibility

21.53   Where an action is brought against a public authority for breach of a Convention right, it is a defence if the public authority can show that it was bound to act the way that it did because of primary legislation.[40]

---

38 Lord Woolf CJ at [35].
39 [2007] UKHL 27, 20 June 2007.
40 HRA 1998 s2.

21.54   In such a claim the issue then becomes whether the legislation is incompatible with the Convention and the government would be joined as defendant. In *R on the application of Morris v Westminster City Council*[41] the Court of Appeal declared that section 185(4) of the Housing Act 1996 was incompatible with article 14 of the Convention to the extent that it required that a dependent child subject to immigration control be disregarded when deciding whether a British citizen had a priority need for accommodation.

21.55   At the time of writing the government has announced its intention to resolve the incompatibility by providing for a very limited housing duty to those in the position of Ms Morris.

Remedies

21.56   The HRA 1998 provides that 'in relation to any act (or proposed act) of a public authority which the court finds is (or would be) unlawful, it may grant such relief or remedy, or make such order, within its powers as it considers just and appropriate'. In other words the court may grant any remedy it considers appropriate provided the court already has the power to grant such a remedy.

21.57   Most of the housing cases in which HRA 1998 has been used have been possession cases in which the occupier argued an eviction would involve an unjustified breach of article 8. In such a case the 'remedy' sought will be the refusal of a possession order.

21.58   In judicial review proceedings the court can 'quash' (cancel) any decision deemed to be in breach of the Act and, to avoid a breach, can order a public authority to do something or to refrain from doing something.

21.59   It is also possible to claim damages from a court that has the power to award damages.[42] A court can only award damages if satisfied that such an award is necessary

> ... to afford just satisfaction to the person in whose favour it is made. In arriving at its decision the court must take into account all the circumstances of the case including:
>
> (a) any other relief or remedy granted, or order made, in relation to the act in question (by that or any other court) and
>
> (b) the consequences of any decision (of that or any other court) in respect of that act.[43]

41   [2005] EWCA Civ 1184, 14 October 2005, and see para 13.131.
42   HRA 1998 s8(3).
43   HRA 1998 s8(3).

Judicial review

21.60   Judicial Review means a claim to review the lawfulness of:

- an enactment; or
- a decision, action or failure to act in relation to the exercise of a public function.[44]

21.61   It is the means by which judicial control is exercised over 'administrative action' and claims are brought in the 'Administrative Court', a branch of the High Court. Claims may only be brought against bodies exercising public functions, including the government and local authorities. Many decisions relating to housing made by local authorities can only be challenged by judicial review.[45] Further, when hearing homeless appeals the county court is exercising a power akin to that of judicial review.[46]

21.62   In judicial review the courts are exercising a 'supervisory' function. A claim for judicial review is not an appeal or a challenge to the merits of a decision. The fundamental principle is that Parliament has given to certain bodies the power to make decisions and the court will only intervene if that body acts unlawfully.

21.63   Judicial review is only available to challenge 'public law' decisions. As indicated above, the distinction between public law and private law decision-making is becoming blurred at the edges. The availability of judicial review depends on the extent to which the ordinary civil courts are able to consider claims and defences that based on 'public law' arguments. The decisions of the ECtHR in *McCann v UK* and of the House of Lords in *Doherty* at paras 21.41–21.42 suggest that issues which have previously been seen as the preserve of the Administrative Court may now be resolved in the county court.

Grounds for judicial review

21.64   Judicial review is about good administrative decision-making. It mostly concerns the process rather than the substance of decision-making but the degree of scrutiny will vary according to the subject matter.

21.65   Below is a summary of the 'grounds' for judicial review, ie the reasons a decision, action or failure to act may be unlawful.

---

44   CPR 54(2)(a).
45   See chapter 14 and 16.
46   *Nipa Begum v Tower Hamlets LBC* (1999) 32 HLR 445, CA.

21.66   The House of Lords[47] has suggested that the various grounds can be classified under three heads:

- illegality;
- irrationality; and
- procedural impropriety.

Illegality

21.67 This includes the following:

- a decision based on an incorrect interpretation of the law;
- a decision made when relevant matters have been ignored, or irrelevant matters taken into account;
- a decision taken by a body not authorised to make the decision. This would include a body exceeding its powers and a decision unlawfully delegated to another person or body;
- 'fettering discretion', ie a decision taken in accordance with a rigid policy rather than being a true exercise of a discretion.

Examples

21.68 Cases regarding a local authority's duties under homelessness legislation abound with examples of decisions based on an incorrect understanding of the law or taken without regard to relevant matters (see paras 13.194 and 13.277).

21.69   In relation to unlawful delegation, a number of priority need decisions have been found to be flawed on the basis that the decision was effectively taken by a medical adviser rather than the housing authority. The authority may take advice from a medical adviser but may not delegate the ultimate decision to the medical adviser (see para 13.207).

21.70   The question of fettering discretion has often arisen in cases concerning the allocation of accommodation. In *R v Westminster CC ex p Nadhum Hussain*[48] a policy to suspend applicants from the waiting list for two years for unreasonably refusing an offer was challenged. The policy did not, in most cases, allow for exceptions, and was held to be an unreasonable fetter on the discretion of the authority.

---

47 *Council of Civil Service Unions v Minister for the Civil Service* [1985] 1 AC 374, HL (the 'CCSU' case)
48 (1998) 31 HLR 645, see para 16.77.

Irrationality

21.71   This is often referred to as '*Wednesbury* unreasonableness' after the case in which the concept was elaborated.[49] It is also referred to as 'perversity' and has been said to apply to 'a decision which is so outrageous in its defiance of logic or of accepted moral standards that no sensible person who had applied his mind to the question to be decided could have arrived at it'.[50]

21.72   More recently it has been suggested that the scope of *Wednesbury* unreasonableness is too narrow and that the court's power to intervene should not be limited to such extreme degrees of 'unreasonable' decision making. When applying HRA 1998 the courts are required to apply the test of proportionality, see para 21.34 above. The proportionality test requires flexibility in the court's approach depending on the nature of the rights that are at issue. Similarly, the House of Lords has held that 'The depth of judicial review and the deference due to administrative discretion vary with the subject matter'.[51] So, in cases where 'fundamental rights' are at issue the courts will be more willing to intervene in administrative decision-making.

21.73   It is, however, rare that a challenge to an administrative decision succeeds on the ground of irrationality alone. More commonly where a decision appears to be 'unreasonable' it may also be found to be unlawful for another reason, eg for failure to take account of relevant matters or to give adequate reasons for the decision.

Procedural impropriety

21.74   This includes a failure to act in accordance with specific procedural rules as well as a failure to observe the basic rules of 'natural justice'.

21.75   An example of the former would be an authority that fails to follow the statutory procedure when carrying out a homeless review (see para 14.33).

21.76   The term 'rules of natural justice' refers to the general duty to act fairly. The extent of this duty varies according to the nature of the

---

49   *Associated Provincial Picture Houses Ltd v Wednesbury Corporation* [1948] 1 KB 223, CA.

50   Lord Diplock in the CCSU case (see para 21.66 above).

51   *R (Daly) v Secretary of State for the Home Department* [2001] UKHL 26.

decision-making. It is generally held that two matters are fundamental to a fair process:

- the right to an unbiased decision maker; and
- the right to be informed of and to comment on adverse information.

21.77   A decision taken in 'bad faith' would clearly be unlawful as would a decision taken by an officer who was 'biased'. Such challenges, however, are rare and 'bias' usually refers to the existence of a personal interest in the decision rather than the general perception, sometimes alleged by clients, that the particular officer is 'biased' or had approached the decision with a closed mind. In *Feld v London Borough of Barnet, Ali Pour v Westminster City Council*[52] the Court of Appeal rejected allegations of bias or lack of impartiality where the same reviewing officer conducted a second review following the quashing of the first review decision. Similarly, the court rejected alleged bias where the officer who made a negative homeless decision was also responsible for making the decision as to whether interim accommodation should be provided pending a review of that decision.[53]

21.78   The duty to disclose adverse information often arises in the context of homelessness decision-making. Before making a decision an authority must offer an applicant the opportunity to comment on adverse information[54] and if the authority is unable to disclose the information it must be disregarded.[55]

Legitimate Expectation

21.79   Legitimate expectation is part of the duty of fairness or part of good administration. 'Where a public authority has issued a promise or adopted a practice which represents how it proposes to act in a given area, the law will require the promise or practice to be honoured unless there is good reason not to do so.'[56] This is known as 'legitimate expectation'. The concept is said to be grounded in fairness.

---

52 [2004] EWCA Civ 1307, 18 October 2004.
53 *Abdi v Lambeth LBC* [2007] EWHC 1565, 26 June 2007.
54 *R v Tower Hamlets LBC ex p Rouf* (1989) 21 HLR 294.
55 *R v Poole BC ex Cooper* (1994) 27 HLR 605, QBD.
56 See *R (Nardarajah and Abdi) v SSHD* [2005] EWCA Civ 1363, 22 November 2005, Laws LJ at [68].

21.80   See *R on the application of Weaver v LQHT* at para 21.50 above for an example of an unsuccessful attempt to rely on legitimate expectation in challenging the decisions to evict a tenant using the mandatory rent arrears ground.

Reasons

21.81   In addition, a decision may be challenged on the ground that the decision maker has failed to adequately explain the reasons for the decision. In homelessness decision-making there is a statutory duty to give reasons for any adverse decision.[57] Such reasons must be 'proper, adequate and intelligible and enable the person to know why they have won or lost'.[58]

21.82   There is no general duty to give reasons for administrative decisions. However, even where there is no express duty to give reasons, in certain circumstances a particular decision may call for an explanation, eg where a decision maker is rejecting an expert opinion or an account of events given by the person concerned. In the case of *R v Westminster CC ex p Nadhum Hussain*, referred to above, a further reason for quashing the decision was the authority's failure to offer any reasons for not following the recommendation of its social services department (see para 16.93). While it was open to the authority not to follow the recommendation the authority's decision was unlawful as the assessment appeared to have been ignored completely.

Judicial review remedies

21.83   The court can make one of the following orders:

- a mandatory order – requiring a body to carry out some act;
- a prohibiting order – prohibiting a body from carrying out some act;
- a quashing order – an order 'cancelling' a decision.

21.84   In addition, the court may grant an injunction to restrain a person from acting in any office in which s/he is not entitled to act.

21.85   Damages can also be awarded but a claim for judicial review cannot be based on a claim for damages alone.

---

57 HA 1996 s184(3). There are also specific decisions made in relation to allocations which require reasons to be given. See chapter 16.

58 *R v Brent LBC ex p Buruwa* (1997) 29 HLR 915, CA at 920.

21.86   The most common order is a quashing order. This means that the body must make a new decision, since the original decision no longer stands. This reflects the court's role: not to substitute its own finding but to scrutinise the lawfulness of the decision.

What bodies may be challenged by judicial review?

21.87   Local authorities are clearly public bodies and may be challenged by a claim for judicial review when making public law decisions.

21.88   RSLs may be held to be public bodies for the purposes of judicial review depending on the nature of the RSL and the particular decision under challenge, see *R on the application of Weaver v LQHT*, at para 21.49 above.

Who may bring a claim for judicial review?

21.89   The claimant must have 'sufficient interest' in the matter to which the application relates. Usually this will mean the person directly affected by the decision. However, it is possible for campaigning organisations to bring claims or to be joined as 'interested parties' particularly where they have access to information useful to the court or represent a particular interest group.

Procedure

21.90   In all but the most urgent cases a pre-action protocol letter must be sent before the claim is issued, see appendix 2 to chapter 17.

21.91   Unless urgent relief is sought, the first step will be to apply for permission to bring the claim. After issuing the application for permission, the papers must be served on the respondent who should file an Acknowledgement of Service within 21 days indicating whether the claim is to be contested and attaching summary grounds of defence.

21.92   The permission application is considered by a single judge, without a hearing (a 'paper application'). If permission is refused, an application may be made for reconsideration at a hearing. If permission is again refused the applicant may appeal to the Court of Appeal.

21.93   In urgent cases the claimant may be seeking an injunction. If so, a 'certificate of urgency' must be completed and the papers will be referred to a judge for urgent consideration within a specified period. If necessary a judge can consider an application for an injunction by telephone before the claim has been issued.

Time limits

21.94   A claim must be brought promptly, and, *in any event*, within three months from the date when grounds first arose.[59] This is usually the date of the decision that is being challenged.

21.95   The court has the power to extend the time limit where there is 'good reason' to do so. The parties have no power to extend the time limit by agreement.

Legal aid

21.96   Subject the means and the merits of the claim public funding is available for judicial review proceedings.

Complaints

Local authorities

21.97   The statutory complaints procedures operating in relation to social services duties to adults and children are described at para 17.68 above.

21.98   There is no statutory complaints procedure in relation to housing decisions by local authorities but all local authorities operate general complaints policies and some may have procedures specific to the particular department. Most local authority complaints procedures follow a similar pattern to those described at para 17.68, beginning with informal resolution, formal investigation and a final appeal or panel hearing.

RSLs and the Housing Corporation

21.99   RSLs are regulated by the Housing Corporation (HC), a government agency set up under HA 1996. The HC maintains a register of all social landlords: 'registered social landlords.' Only not-for-profit providers of housing may be registered.

21.100   HA 1988 s36 provides for the Housing Corporation to issue guidance with respect to the management of housing accommodation by RSLs. Guidance may be issued with respect to:

- provision for housing demand;
- allocation of accommodation between individuals;

59 CPR 54.5(1).

- the terms of tenancies and setting of rents;
- standards of maintenance and repair;
- services to be provided to tenants;
- complaints procedures for tenants;
- consultation and communication with tenants;
- devolution of management decisions to tenants.

21.101   In considering whether action needs to be taken to secure proper management or whether there has been mismanagement, the HC may have regard to the extent to which its guidance is being or has been followed.

21.102   The HC 'Regulatory Code and Guidance' sets out the fundamental obligations of housing associations and can be downloaded from the Corporation's website: www.housingcorp.gov.uk

21.103   RSLs are required by the HC to operate a complaints procedure for tenants and long-leaseholders. Each RSL will have its own procedure but must belong to an approved complaints scheme,[60] eg the Housing Ombudsman Service, to deal with individual tenants' complaints.

21.104   The Housing and Regeneration Act 2008 will dissolve the Housing Corporation and replace it with a new regulator of social housing: the Office for Tenants and Social Landlords. It is proposed that the Housing Ombudsman will still deal with individual tenant's complaints.

Ombudsman complaints

21.105   The Local Government Ombudsman (LGO) deals with complaints about local authorities and the Housing Ombudsman Service (HOS) with complaints about RSLs. The Ombudsmen investigate complaints about mal-administration.

21.106   Information about the Ombudsman service can be downloaded from the respective websites as can the complaints forms. The website of the HOS is: www.ihos.org.uk and the website of the LGO is: www.lgo.org.uk.

21.107   The following are common to both Ombudsman schemes:

- complaint can only be made after the authority or RSL's own complaints procedure has been exhausted;
- complaints must be made within 12 months from the date the complainant first had notice of the relevant matters.

---

60 See HA 1996, Schedule 2 para 1.

The Ombudsman can extend this time limit if s/he considers it reasonable to do so;

- the service is free;
- the Ombudsman may decline to deal with a complaint if there is a legal remedy available to the complainant or the issue is one of legal interpretation. However, there is some overlap and complaints are frequently made to the Ombudsman about such issues as disrepair or a failure to accept a homeless duty when the complainant has a clear right to issue legal proceedings;
- the Ombudsman can recommend compensation but this will usually be much less than a court would award where there is a legal remedy;
- the Ombudsman may make other recommendations, eg that the particular body changes a policy or ensures that staff are properly trained.

21.108   The main disadvantage of the complaints and Ombudsman procedure is that there is usually considerable delay before the complaint is resolved and effective action taken. Also, the Ombudsman accepts only a very small proportion of complaints for full investigation. The advantage is that it is free and legal representation is not necessary.

Obtaining information

21.109   There are two statutes under which information can be requested from a public body:

- the Data Protection Act 1998 concerns information held about an individual;
- the Freedom of Information Act 2000 concerns other information held by a public authority.

Data Protection Act 1998

21.110   For tenants of public bodies useful information may be obtained under the Data Protection Act (DPA) 1998.

21.111   DPA 1998 governs the holding and processing of personal data (information) by businesses and organisations in the public and private sector. Under DPA 1998 an individual has the right to be informed whether data is being held on him or her and to have communicated 'in an intelligible form' the information held and the source of the information.[61] Such information must be given provided the following conditions are satisfied:[62]

- the request is made in writing;
- sufficient information is provided as to the identity of the individual concerned; and
- the fee (currently a maximum of £10) is paid.[63]

21.112   If the request is made on behalf of another individual that person's consent must also be provided. A model letter requesting information under DPA 1998 is contained in the appendix to this chapter.

21.113   Provided those conditions are satisfied, the information (usually in the form of photocopies) must be provided no later than 40 calendar days after the request is received.[64] This does not mean that organisations should routinely take 40 days to provide the information: DPA 1998 s7(8) provides that: '… a data controller shall comply with a request under this section promptly and in any event before the end of [the 40 day period].'

21.114   Complaints about breaches of DPA 1998 may be made to the Information Commissioner's Office whose website is: www.ico.gov. uk. An application may also be made in the county court for an order compelling the organisation to comply with its obligations under DPA 1998.

Freedom of Information Act 2000

21.115 The Freedom of Information Act (FIA) 2000 gives a person the right to request information from a public authority.

21.116   Public authorities include:

- central and local government;
- the health service;

---

61 Certain information is exempt, for example information that may cause distress to the recipient or that may disclose the identity of a third party who does not consent.

62 DPA 1998 s7(1)–(3).

63 Data Protection (Subject Access) (Fees & Miscellaneous Provisions) Regulations 2000 (SI No 191) reg 3. Different fees apply in relation to credit agencies and health records.

64 DPA 1998 s7(8) and (10).

- schools, colleges and universities;
- the police; and
- many other non-governmental organisations, committees and advisory bodies.

21.117   Most requests are free but a person may be asked a fee for photocopies or postage. However, if the public authority thinks it will cost more than £450 (or £600 if the request is made to a central government department) the request can be refused.

Request under Data Protection Act 1998

Dear Sir or Madam,

Re: Mr/Ms Client (DOB: ....)
Request Under Data Protection Act 1998

We are advising the above named with regard to [.........].

On his/her behalf we request that you provide to us a complete copy of [his/her housing/social services file].

We enclose our client's signed authority for the release of this information together with a cheque in the sum of £10.

We look forward to receiving the information as soon as possible [include any reason for needing the information urgently, eg required for homeless submissions] and in any event within the statutory period of 40 days.

Yours faithfully,

A.N. Adviser

CHAPTER 22

Civil proceedings

continued

continued

Key points

- The civil courts consist of the county courts and the High Court together with the appeal courts which hear civil appeals against the decisions of those courts.
- Most civil claims are dealt with by the county courts which have a local jurisdiction.
- The civil courts deal mainly with disputes between individuals, eg between a landlord and tenant. This includes disrepair and claims for possession.
- In some cases the civil courts deal with challenges to the decisions of public bodies, including local authorities and government departments. In the county court homeless appeals concern the lawfulness of local authority decisions about homeless applications. In the High Court a claim for judicial review can be made to challenge a range of decisions made by public bodies.
- There is one set of procedural rules for both the county courts and the High Court: the Civil Procedure Rules (CPR).
- Fees are payable to the court for starting a claim and at certain stages in the proceedings after the claim has been started.
- Legal aid is available for most types of civil claim provided the applicant's income and savings are below a certain level and that the claim has sufficient merit or is of sufficient value.
- The general rule in the civil courts is that the unsuccessful party will be ordered to pay the legal costs of the successful party. However, a party who is legally aided has 'costs protection' which means that such an order will not be enforceable without the permission of the court.
- The amount of the legal costs that must be paid is controlled by the court. In complex cases the court may be asked to assess the amount of costs claimed. In some cases the costs are fixed in advance.
- Claims below a certain value will be allocated to the 'small claims track'. The preparatory steps will be simple and the hearing informal. The amount of costs that can be claimed is limited as the procedure is designed so that legal representation is unnecessary.
- If the court makes an order, the party in whose favour the order is made may have to take further action to enforce the order. It can be difficult to enforce an order against a person about whom little is known or who has no resources.

> • Some landlord and tenant cases are heard by tribunals and legal aid is not available for representation at tribunals.

22.1 Most housing disputes are resolved in the civil courts, principally the county court. Housing advisers therefore need an understanding of the way the civil courts operate and this chapter gives an overview of the way civil claims are dealt with by the courts.

The civil courts

22.2 The civil courts are distinct from the criminal courts in that they resolve disputes between individual legal persons (which may include a company or a public body such as a local authority). The criminal courts deal mostly with the prosecution by the state of individuals accused of committing criminal offences.

22.3 The civil courts comprise the county courts and the High Court. In addition the civil division of the Court of Appeal hears appeals from the county court and the High Court. The appendix to this chapter contains a diagram of the relationship between the various civil courts.

22.4 Housing litigation forms a substantial part of the business of the county court. It includes:

- possession proceedings;
- claims based on a landlord's failure to repair premises;
- claims based on unlawful eviction and harassment;
- homeless appeals;
- other disputes between landlords and tenants, eg disputes about the rights of secure tenants and the recovery of deposits. The county court can make a declaration to determine an occupier's status, which may confirm, for example that a tenant has the right to apply for a fair rent to be registered;
- applications for injunctions brought by local authorities and RSLs to restrain anti-social behaviour.

22.5 The jurisdiction of the county courts is local and possession claims must be brought in the court which covers the area where the premises are situated. Claims for money or other remedies may be started in any county court but it is advisable to bring such a claim in the court for the area in which the defendant lives or has its principal office.[1] The area covered by each county court is distinct from local authority boundaries. The court service website has a 'court finder' facility which indicates which court is responsible for a particular postcode. This can be accessed on www.hmcourts-service. gov.uk.

22.6   High value claims or claims that are complex may be brought in the High Court. Also, the High Court has exclusive jurisdiction for certain kinds of proceedings, including judicial review.

The organisation of the county courts

Judges

22.7   The county courts have two types of judges: district judges and circuit judges. Some practising lawyers sit as part time district judges and are known as deputy district judges. District judges deal with most of the housing litigation in the county court, including claims for possession. However, there are certain kinds of housing cases that only a circuit judge can deal with. These include homeless appeals and most applications for committal for breach of injunctions.[2] Most long trials (more than one day) are heard by circuit judges. Circuit judges also deal with most appeals from decisions made by district judges.

Court staff

22.8   Much of the work of the county court is done not by the judges but by the court office staff. This includes the issuing of claims and bailiff's warrants, the listing of hearings and the drawing up of orders. Most courts have different sections dealing with different stages of litigation, eg issuing, listing and enforcement. When a claim is issued it is given a court reference number (the 'claim number') that is endorsed on all court documents, usually in the top right hand corner. This must be quoted in all communications with the court.

---

1   A defendant may apply for the transfer of proceedings to his or her home court when filing a defence. If the claim is for a fixed amount this will automatically be done. Also, action to enforce court orders must usually be taken in the defendant's home court.
2   See CPR Part 2, PD.

The basis of a civil claim

22.9 To bring a claim in a civil court a claimant must have a recognised legal claim, known as a *cause of action*. Further the claimant must be seeking some 'remedy' that the court is capable of granting.

Causes of action

22.10 Strictly speaking the term *cause of action* means the facts out of which the right to bring a legal action arises. However, the term is generally used to refer to a claim which is recognised in law as giving a person a right to sue.

22.11 In relation to housing litigation the relevant causes of action can be summarised as follows.

Breach of contract

22.12 A party to a contract has a legal right to compel the other party to comply with the contract and/or to be compensated if the contract is breached. The cause of action in such a claim is 'breach of contract'. In housing cases this would include:

- tenants seeking compensation for disrepair and/or an order that a landlord carries out repairs;
- tenants seeking compensation for unlawful eviction and harassment and/or an order that the landlord allows them back into occupation and refrains from further harassment

22.13 A landlord who claims that a tenant is in breach of the tenancy agreement could also seek compensation and/or an order restraining further breach. However, most landlords will instead claim possession, as one of the grounds for obtaining a possession order is that the tenant is in breach of the terms of the tenancy agreement.

Tort

22.14 'Tort' means a civil wrong that is independent of a contract. Tort is based on the premise that in certain situations a person has a duty to ensure that another person does not suffer harm or loss as a result of his or her actions. Some torts are 'common law' torts, recognised by the courts in previously decided cases. Other torts are 'statutory' torts set out in legislation. The torts which will commonly be alleged in housing cases are:

Common law torts

22.15   Nuisance and negligence are common law torts that may be alleged in cases involving harassment, unlawful eviction and disrepair.

Statutory torts

22.16   The HA 1988 sets out the statutory tort of 'unlawful eviction' for which damages are payable, calculated according to a statutory formula.

22.17   The Protection from Harassment Act 1997 created the statutory tort of 'harassment' where a person is guilty of a course of conduct that causes another person alarm or distress.

22.18   In disrepair claims, the statutory torts set out in the Defective Premises Act 1972 and the Occupiers Liability Acts 1957 and 1984 may be relied upon.

22.19   All of these torts are discussed in more detail in chapters 7 and 9.

Claims for possession

22.20   Claims for possession make up a large part of the work of the county courts. The 'cause of action' is the right to possession which may be established on the basis that the tenant's right to occupy has ended or because one of the statutory grounds for possession is made out. Claims for possession are dealt with in detail in chapter 5 and 6.

Homeless appeals

22.21   The jurisdiction of the county court to hear appeals against negative homelessness decisions is entirely statutory and is set out in HA 1996. The provisions are described in chapter 8 (homelessness).

22.22   The court's role in such cases is not the same as in most county court litigation because homeless decisions are administrative decisions made by a public body. Traditionally such decisions are scrutinised by the High Court in judicial review proceedings. The volume of judicial reviews concerning homelessness decision-making during the 1980s and 1990s, however, lead to the transfer of such cases to the county court. Homelessness appeals can only be heard by circuit judges who, when hearing appeals, are applying judicial review principles ie the court is examining the lawfulness of the decision rather than considering the merits of the decision.

The principles of judicial review are explained in more detail in chapter 21.

Remedies

22.23   The cause of action is the legal basis for the claim or the facts which give rise to the claim. The remedy is what the claimant is asking the court to order.

22.24   In a claim based on tort or breach of contract the claimant will be seeking:

- damages (compensation); and/or
- an injunction (an order that a person does or refrains from doing something) or an order of specific performance (an order that a person must perform the obligations under a contract).

22.25   It is also possible to ask the court to make a declaration of a person's rights, eg whether or not they are a tenant or the nature of the tenancy.

22.26   In a claim for possession the applicant will asking the court to make a possession order. This authorises the claimant to take possession but, unless the defendant gives up possession voluntarily, must be enforced by court bailiffs. A social landlord may now also ask the court to make a demotion order in relation to a tenancy. The effect of this is to reduce the tenant's security of tenure, see chapters 4 and 5. If there are arrears of rent a landlord will usually also seek a money judgment.

22.27   In a homelessness appeal the claimant will be asking the court to make an order quashing (cancelling) the local authority's decision or varying the decision to a positive one.

The parties

22.28   In a civil claim the person who brings the claim is usually called the claimant and the person against whom the claim is brought is the defendant. A defendant may, at the same time as defending a claim, bring a counterclaim against a claimant.

22.29   In some kinds of cases the parties are instead known as the applicant and the respondent, eg in applications for injunctions and committals.

22.30   In homelessness appeals the parties are referred to as the appellant and the respondent. The same terms are used in any appeal against an order made by a court.

Civil Procedure Rules

22.31   The Civil Procedure Rules 1999 (CPR) set out a complete code for the conduct of all civil claims and apply in the county courts and in the High Court.[3] CPR can be accessed on-line at the Department of Justice website on: www.justice.gov.uk. Most of the commonly used forms can also be downloaded from the same site.

22.32   CPR are set out in different parts, each of which deals with a specific aspect of procedure or type of claim. Each part contains the relevant rules with a practice direction (PD) setting out the more practical requirements. The parts of the CPR of most relevance to housing advisers are as follows.

Part 55

22.33   This part sets out the procedural rules for most claims for possession. These are dealt with in detail in chapter 5.

Pre-action protocols

22.34   The protocol section sets out the steps the parties should take before proceedings are commenced in particular kinds of cases. The following pre-action protocols are relevant to housing cases:

- the Pre-Action Protocol for Possession Claims based on Rent Arrears;
- the Pre-Action Protocol for Housing Disrepair Claims;
- the Pre-Action Protocol for Judicial Review Claims.

22.35   The pre-action protocols for rent arrears, disrepair and judicial review are described in chapters 5, 9 and 21 respectively.

General

22.36   In addition the following parts are of general relevance in contested claims:

The Courts Power to Manage Cases	Part 3
Forms and Court Documents	Parts 4–6
How to Start and Respond to Proceedings	Parts 7–15

---

3   Previously, different rules applied in the county courts and in the High Court. Some of these rules are still in force, mainly in relation to enforcement, and are set out in a schedule to CPR. They are known as the Rules of the Supreme Court (RSC) and the County Court Rules (CCR).

Drafting Documents for Court (Statements of Case)	Parts 16–17, 22
Applying for Court Orders	Parts 23–25
Case Management and Track Allocation	Parts 26–30
Documents and Evidence	Parts 31–35
Offers to Settle Claims	Parts 36–37
Costs	Parts 43–48
Enforcement	Parts 69–73

The overriding objective

22.37 CPR came into being following a comprehensive review of civil procedure conducted by Lord Woolf. The aims of the review were: [4]

- to improve access to justice and reduce the cost of litigation;
- to reduce the complexity of the rules and modernise terminology; and
- to remove unnecessary distinctions of practice and procedure.

22.38 This is reflected in Rule 1.1 which is headed 'the overriding objective':

(1) These rules are a new procedural code with the overrriding objective of enabling the court to deal with cases justly.
(2) Dealing with a case justly includes, so far as is practicable:
   (a) ensuring that the parties are on an equal footing;
   (b) saving expense;
   (c) dealing with the case in ways which are proportionate:
       (i)   to the amount of money involved;
       (ii) to the importance of the case;
       (iii) to the complexity of the issues; and
       (iv) to the financial position of each party;
   (d) ensuring that it is dealt with expeditiously and fairly; and
   (e) allotting to it an appropriate share of the court's resources, whilst taking into account the need to allot resources to other cases.

22.39 The rule goes on to provide that the court must seek to give effect to the overriding objective when exercising its powers and interpreting rules and that the parties must help the court to further the overriding objective.

---

4   The Interim Report. This and the Final Report can be downloaded from the old DCA website on www.dca.gov.uk.

Active case management

22.40   The court has a duty to further the overriding objective by actively managing cases which includes:[5]

- encouraging the parties to co-operate;
- identifying issues at an early stage;
- encouraging the parties to use an alternative dispute resolution procedure;
- helping the parties to settle the whole or part of the case;
- dealing with the case without the parties attending court;
- making use of technology; and
- giving directions to ensure that the case proceeds to trial quickly.

22.41   The ability of the judges to manage cases actively is somewhat limited by the fact that judges rarely have the time to scrutinise cases other than when considering applications made by the parties. However, one feature of the duty is that judges are less willing to agree adjournments and extensions of time even if the parties or their lawyers are in agreement. Judges will also often take a much more active part in case management conferences in order to clarify issues and to expedite resolution.

The usual steps in a civil claim

Claims other than possession claims

22.42   Most claims are brought under Part 7 of CPR and, if defended, may involve the following stages:

- pre-action correspondence;
- issuing the claim;
- filing a reply/defence;
- track allocation and case management directions;
- parties comply with case management directions;
- off record negotiations to settle the claim;
- hearing/final order;
- enforcement – if defendant fails to comply with order.

22.43   Part 8 of CPR provides an alternative procedure and is described below at para 22.116.

---

5   CPR 1(4).

Pre-action correspondence

22.44 CPR encourages early settlement and the aim of the pre-action protocols, which apply to certain types of proceedings, is to promote settlement so as to avoid proceedings. Even if no protocol applies the parties are expected to act reasonably in exchanging information and documents relevant to the claim and generally in trying to avoid the necessity for the start of proceedings.[6]

22.45 Even before the introduction of CPR a party was expected to send a 'letter before claim/action' to the proposed defendant setting out the basis of the claim and inviting the defendant to meet the claim.

22.46 A claimant who issues proceedings without following the relevant protocol, or, if no protocol applies, without first sending a letter before claim may not be able to recover his or her costs even if the claim is successful.

22.47 If there is a protocol, the defendant will be obliged to respond to the claimant's pre-action protocol letter, disclosing relevant documents, indicating whether the claim is admitted and, if so, making an offer to settle. The sanction for failure to comply with a pre-action protocol will usually be an unfavourable costs order: costs may be disallowed or awarded to the other party on a basis more generous than usual. Further, where a defendant fails to comply with the relevant protocol, a higher than usual rate of interest may be added to an award of damages.

Issuing the claim

22.48 The claim is issued by the claimant sending the relevant forms to the court with the court fee.[7] In most cases this means a Claim Form and Particulars of Claim. The Claim Form is a court form (which can be downloaded) and is completed by the claimant.[8] In a simple case, the Particulars of Claim may be entered onto the Claim Form. In more complicated cases the Particulars of Claim will be a separate document. The Particulars of Claim should be a concise statement

---

6 CPR PD to Protocols, para 4.1.
7 When issuing a claim the amount of the fee will depend on the amount being claimed. The fees payable for each kind of claim or application are increased regularly. The current fees (as from 1 October 2007) are set out in the leaflet EX50 which can be downloaded from the court service website on: www. hmcourts-service.gov.uk.
8 Under Part 7 this is form N1.
9 CPR Part 16 deals with the content of Claims Forms and Particulars of Claim.

of the facts on which the claimant relies.[9] Both documents must be endorsed with a 'statement of truth' confirming that the contents are true to the best of the claimant's knowledge.[10] The form of the statement of truth signed by a party is:[11]

> *'I believe that the facts stated in this [Claim Form/Particulars of Claim] are true.'*

22.49   A statement of truth may be signed by a legal representative in which case the representative must ensure that the party believes the contents to be true and advise him or her of the consequences if this is not the case. The possible sanction for signing a statement of truth without an honest belief that the contents of the document are true is that contempt of court proceedings may be brought by the Attorney General or with the permission of the court.[12]

22.50   If the statement of truth is signed by a legal representative the form is:

> *'The Claimant believes that the facts stated in this [Claim Form/ Particulars of Claim] are true.'*

22.51   If the Particulars of Claim is not verified by a statement of truth, it will stand as a summary of the claim but cannot be used as evidence. Further, the court has the power to strike it out.[13] The court could, however, adjourn proceedings to permit a party to endorse the document with a statement of truth. If this means that the other party incurs unnecessary costs, the party in default will usually be ordered to pay those costs, regardless of the outcome of the claim, see para 22.168 below.

22.52   The court sends the papers to the defendant with a 'response pack' and notes as to how the defendant should respond.

Fee exemption

22.53   Claimants on a low income can apply to the court for fee exemption. This will always be granted if the claimant is in receipt of certain benefits. Otherwise a court officer will assess the claimant's means before deciding whether the fee must be paid. Claimants must take to the court original documents to establish income (eg letters from the Benefits Agency or Inland Revenue or bank statements showing

---

10 CPR Part 22 deals with statements of truth.
11 CPR 22, PD para 2.1.
12 CPR 32.14.
13 CPR 22.2.

receipt of benefit, wage slips etc.). The fee exemption form can be downloaded from the court service website on www.courts-service. gov.uk. It is currently form EX160. The same form can be used to apply for a refund of fees already paid.

22.54   Fee exemption does not apply if a party is formally represented by solicitors, ie the solicitors are on the court record as acting for the party. The solicitors must pay any court fees.

Filing a reply/defence

22.55   The usual rule is that the defendant has 14 days from the date of service to file a defence.[14] However, if the defendant files an acknowledgement of service the period is extended to 28 days from the date of service. In most cases the documents will be posted by the court to the defendant and the date of service is deemed to be the second day after posting. If the documents are delivered to the defendant's address the date of service is deemed to be the following day.[15]

22.56   The response pack sent to the defendant includes forms on which the defendant may admit the claim, admit part of the claim or dispute the claim. If the claim is defended it is sufficient to complete the defence form indicating the reasons. However, a defendant may instead file a separate document entitled: 'Defence'. In either case, the defence should deal with each allegation, stating whether it is admitted or denied. If an allegation is denied and the defendant intends to put forward a different version of events, this should be set out in the defence.[16] If the defence fails to deal with a particular allegation, that allegation will be treated as admitted, unless the defendant has set out the nature of his or her case relevant to the allegation. The form of defence must also be endorsed with a 'statement of truth' and signed by the defendant or the defendant's representative.

22.57   There is no fee for the filing of a defence. However, if the defendant wishes to make a counterclaim a Part 20 claim form must be completed[17] and a fee will be payable on the same basis as for a claim.

---

14 Generally when documents are sent or taken to the court they are referred to as being 'filed' and when they are sent or delivered to the other party they are referred to as being 'served'.

15 CPR 6.7.

16 See CPR 16.5.

17 Form N211.

Track allocation and case management directions

Track allocation

22.58   If a defence is filed the case will be allocated to one of three tracks. Allocation questionnaires sent to the parties by the court must be completed and filed so that the court has sufficient information to allocate to the appropriate track. If a claim is clearly within the small claims limit the court will usually allocate without requiring the parties to file questionnaires. This will depend on the nature of the case and the value of the claim (see below para 22.107). Defended claims are allocated to one of three tracks:

- the small claims track;
- the fast track; or
- the multi track.

22.59   This decision depends mainly on the value of the claim but other factors such as complexity and the nature of the evidence are also taken into consideration. The small claims track is described in more detail below.

Case management directions

22.60   Case management directions are the steps that each party must take before the claim can be listed for a final hearing. Standard case management directions are made in respect of small claims and fast track cases. Usually multi-track cases will require more detailed and specific case management directions and these may be agreed by the parties or made at a case management hearing.

22.61   The usual case management directions require disclosure by the parties of the documents in their possession and the evidence on which they intend to rely. This is to encourage the settlement of claims by ensuring that the parties are able to assess the relative merits of each side's case prior to the final hearing.

Disclosure of documents

22.62   Unless the claim is allocated to the small claims track the parties must disclose *all* relevant documents, including those that are unhelpful to the party's case. Certain documents are excluded from disclosure because they are 'privileged'. This includes documents and correspondence relating to the legal advice given to the party. It also includes documents created for the purpose of the proceedings, for example draft statements and expert reports that the party does not wish to rely on.

Disclosure of evidence relied on

Factual witnesses

22.63   In most cases the parties must exchange written statements of all of the witnesses they intend to call to court to give evidence. The statements are a summary of what the witness will say in court. At a final hearing the evidence will usually be given orally by witnesses. However, the parties may agree that certain uncontentious statements can be submitted as evidence so that the witness need not attend. Also, one party can serve notice on the other party that he or she intends to rely on hearsay evidence.[18] The other party can apply to the court for permission to call the relevant witness so that he or she can be cross examined. However, if the party on whom the notice is served does not object, the hearsay evidence can be used at the hearing. Hearsay evidence, however, will not have as much weight as direct evidence.

Expert witnesses

22.64   In some cases the parties rely on the opinion of experts such as doctors or surveyors. The nature of this evidence is different from that of witnesses of fact; expert witnesses may express a professional opinion. For example, a surveyor may express an opinion about the cause of dampness in a dwelling and a doctor may express an opinion about the effect of dampness on a person's health. CPR strongly encourages the use of Single Joint Experts (SJEs). This means a single expert instructed by both parties whose duty is to the court. In cases where each party instructs a different expert written reports must be disclosed in advance of the final hearing. The case management directions may order the experts to prepare a joint statement setting out what is agreed and what is at issue. It is unusual, except in multi track cases, for the experts to attend court to give evidence. The use of expert witnesses is discussed in more detail in para 9.198 on disrepair. Expert evidence may only be used if the court gives permission.

18 'Hearsay' means second hand evidence. It includes a written statement if the maker of the statement is not present in court. It also includes one person giving evidence about what another person has told him or her, if the evidence is given to prove that what the other person said was true: see, the Civil Evidence Act 1995 s1(2)(a). See also CPR Part 33.

'Interlocutory' applications and hearings

22.65   As the proceedings progress, the parties may be in dispute about procedural issues or may wish to apply to the court for remedies available prior to the final hearing (eg injunctions). Examples of issues that may arise in relation to procedure would be where one party claims that another party has documents that should be disclosed or where one party wants to use a type of expert evidence and the other party does not agree that it is necessary. An interim remedy would include an application for an 'interlocutory' (as opposed to a final) injunction or an application for an interim payment of damages.

22.66   Unless the parties reach agreement, such issues will be resolved by one party making an application to the court and the issue will be listed for a short hearing before a district judge (simple hearings can be arranged as telephone conferences). Applications for interim injunctions, however, are usually heard by circuit judges. Evidence is required in support of any interlocutory application and this will be in the form of written statements or affidavits.

22.67   The person who succeeds in making or resisting an interlocutory application will usually be awarded his or her costs of the application regardless of the final outcome of the claim (see below).

Settlement

22.68   One of the central aims of CPR is to encourage settlement by ensuring that issues are clarified and evidence disclosed at an early stage. CPR Part 36 sets out a procedure to be followed when attempting to settle claims. If this procedure is followed, certain consequences regarding the costs of the proceedings will usually follow automatically.

Part 36 offers

22.69   Either the claimant or the defendant can make an offer to settle under Part 36. In a money claim, a claimant's Part 36 offer will state the sum the claimant will accept (being less than the full amount claimed). A defendant's offer will state the sum he or she is willing to pay to the claimant. If the claim includes a claim for a non-monetary remedy, the offer will set out the other relevant terms that are proposed. For example, in a disrepair claim, the offer would also set out a list of repairs to be carried out and the time scale for completion. Again, either party may make such an offer.

Requirements of a Part 36 offer

22.70 A Part 36 offer must:[19]

- be in writing;
- state that it is intended to have the consequences of Part 36;
- specify a period of not less than 21 days for acceptance, within which period, if accepted, the defendant will be liable for the claimant's costs;
- state whether it relates to the whole or part of the claim and whether it takes into account any counterclaim.

22.71 The court form 'N242A' may be used but it is not compulsory.

22.72 If the offer is made less than 21 days before the trial the period for acceptance may be less, ie the period up to the date of the trial.[20]

22.73 During the specified period the offer may not be withdrawn or changed without the permission of the court.[21] After the period has expired the offer may be withdrawn or the terms changed. This is done by serving a written notice of withdrawal or change of terms.[22]

Acceptance of a Part 36 offer

22.74 A Part 36 offer is accepted by serving written notice on the person making the offer.[23] A copy should also be filed at court.[24] In most cases the offer may be accepted outside the specified time limit without the court's permission, provided it has not since been withdrawn or changed.[25] If a Part 36 offer is accepted, the claim is 'stayed'. This does not mean that the claim is 'put on hold' rather that the claim is at an end, other than in relation to costs and enforcement.[26] If the terms of settlement are not complied with, an application can be made to the court to enforce the agreed terms. This means that if the claimant accepts, under Part 36, a sum of

---

19 CPR 36.2(2). There are additional requirements for particular kinds of claim, eg personal injury claims for future financial loss and claims for provisional damages: see CPR 36(5–6).
20 CPR 36.2(3).
21 CPR 36.3(5).
22 CPR 36.3(6–7).
23 CPR 36.9(1).
24 CPR 36 PD para 3.1.
25 CPR 36.9(2). There are some exceptions to this, including where there are multiple defendants and where the trial has commenced. See CPR 36.9(3).
26 CPR 36.11(5).

money less than originally claimed, but the defendant does not pay, the claimant cannot re-instate the proceedings to claim the full amount but can use the court's enforcement procedures to force the defendant to pay the lesser amount agreed under Part 36.[27]

22.75   If the agreement is for the payment of money, the payment must be made within 14 days, unless the parties agree otherwise. If payment is not made, judgment can be entered for the agreed sum plus the costs to the date of notice of acceptance. See para 22.121 below for a summary of the methods of enforcement of money judgments.

22.76   An application can also be made to enforce an agreement for a non-monetary remedy. If the terms of the agreement are complex the parties will usually file a Consent Order setting out the detail of the agreement (see below at para 22.9 and appendix 2 to this chapter).

Costs consequences

22.77   Where a Part 36 offer is accepted within the relevant time period, the claimant will be entitled to his or her costs up to the date on which notice of acceptance was served.[28] The amount of the costs must be agreed or assessed by the court (see para 22.156 below). If the offer was made less than 21 days before the trial or is accepted outside the relevant time period, the parties must agree who is liable for the costs: if they cannot agree, the court will make an order as to costs.[29] If this is necessary, an application must be made to the court, which will mean additional costs being incurred.

Refusal of a Part 36 offer

Before trial

22.78   Part 36 offers are treated as 'without prejudice save as to costs' (see para 22.84 below) and must not be communicated to the trial judge until the case has been decided, unless the parties agree otherwise.[30]

27 It is possible instead to include a term that the agreement is only enforceable if performed so that a breach would give the claimant the right to continue with the claim and seek the full amount. However, this would most likely be deemed to take the agreement outside the scope of Part 36 and the automatic costs consequences of Part 36 would not apply.

28 CPR 36.10.

29 CPR 36.10(4).

30 CPR 36.13. If the permission of the court is required in relation to an aspect of a Part 36 offer the application must be dealt with by a judge other than the one dealing with the trial: paras 2 and 3.

After trial – costs

22.79 The consequences depend on whether the Part 36 offer is made by the claimant or the defendant:[31]

Defendant's Part 36 offer

22.80 If the claimant is successful but fails to obtain a judgment 'more advantageous than a defendant's Part 36 offer' the court will, unless it considers it unjust, order that the claimant pays the defendant's costs from the date when the period for acceptance of the offer expired ('the relevant date'), plus interest on those costs. At the same time, the court will usually order that the defendant pays the claimant's cost up to the relevant date. So, if the costs from the relevant date to the end of the trial exceed the costs incurred before the relevant date, the claimant will have to pay the balance, despite having succeeded in the claim.

Claimant's Part 36 offer

22.81 If the claimant is successful and obtains a judgment against the defendant that 'is at least as advantageous to the claimant' as the proposals contained in his or her Part 36 offer, the court will usually order the defendant to pay additional interest on the damages and/or costs and that the claimant's costs are assessed on a more generous basis. Again, the court may refuse such an order only if it considers it unjust.[32]

Part 36 and small claims

22.82 The usual rules on costs do not apply to cases allocated to the small claims track. The automatic costs consequences of Part 36 therefore do not apply after a case has been allocated to that track. If an offer is made and accepted before allocation, however, Part 36 will apply. The amount for which the claim is settled will always be relevant when the court assesses the amount of costs to be paid by the defendant to the claimant.

---

31 See CPR 36.14.
32 When considering whether the usual orders would be unjust the court must take account of certain matters including: the information available to the parties at the time of the offer and the conduct of the parties with regard to the giving or refusing to give information to enable an offer to be made or evaluated. So, non-disclosure by a party may justify the court departing from the usual rule (*Mamidoil-Jetoil Greek Petroleum Co SA v Okta Crude Oil Refinery* AD [2002] EWHC 2462 (Comm), 26 November 2002).

Settlement outside Part 36

22.83   Offers to settle proceedings may be made outside the Part 36 procedure. A party can make an offer in whatever way he or she chooses but if it is not in accordance with Part 36 the costs consequences referred to above will not automatically apply.[33] The court will nevertheless always take account of the parties' attempts to settle when exercising its discretion in relation to costs.

'Without Prejudice' communications

22.84   Whenever a party wishes to communicate an offer to settle a claim, any correspondence containing the proposals should be marked 'Without Prejudice Save as to Costs'. This means that the correspondence will not be disclosed to the court until after the claim has been determined; settlement proposals are relevant to the issue of costs only. The most important points in relation to Without Prejudice communication are:

- only genuine offers to compromise a claim should be marked 'without prejudice'.
- offers to compromise may be treated as without prejudice even if not marked as such. However, this would require the agreement of the other party or a decision by the court.
- if a party refers to without prejudice communications at trial the judge may decide that the hearing must be abandoned and heard by a different judge. The party who has revealed the without prejudice communication may be ordered to pay the costs that have been wasted as a result (see para 22.168 below).
- without prejudice discussions may take place by telephone (or sometimes at court). Both parties must agree that such a discussion is being conducted on a without prejudice basis.
- once an agreement has been concluded, the confirmation of the terms of that agreement should be confirmed in 'open' correspondence (ie not marked Without Prejudice). Often the terms of the agreement will be incorporated into a 'Consent Order' (see appendix 2 below).

The Hearing/final order

22.85   Unless the parties reach an agreement, the claim will be listed for a hearing. The claimant will usually be responsible for preparing a

33   Part 36.1(2).

'trial bundle' which comprises copies of all the relevant documents. The trial bundle will include: the statements of case (ie Claim, Defence and any Reply or Counter-claim); the statements of the witnesses who will give evidence; and all relevant documents. Copies of the bundle will be provided for the court and the other party or parties. Further copies should be available for the witnesses to refer to when giving evidence. The bundle should be organised chronologically and 'paginated' for ease of reference.

The final hearing

22.86 Despite a trend towards the use of written evidence at a final hearing, most of the evidence will be given orally, ie by witnesses who attend court and answer questions put by the parties' lawyers (or the parties, if unrepresented) and the judge. The format of a formal trial is as follows:

Claimant opens

22.87 This will be a brief summary of the issues and reference to the evidence to be used, including the documents in the trial bundle.

Claimant calls evidence

22.88 All the witnesses (usually starting with the claimant) will be questioned first by the claimant's lawyer and then by the defendant's lawyer (cross-examination). To save time it is usual for the witness to be asked to confirm that the witness statement in the trial bundle is true and then questioned only on certain issues. The defendant's lawyer is under a duty to challenge any evidence that is at issue. The claimant's lawyer has the chance to 're-examine' only to clarify anything raised in cross examination. The judge may also ask questions of the witnesses.

Defendant calls evidence

22.89 The defendant's witnesses will be questioned in the same way, starting with questions from the defendant's lawyer.

Defendant closes

22.90 The defendant's lawyer makes a 'closing speech'. This is a summary of the defendant's case and submissions as to why the court should find for the defendant.

Claimant closes

22.91   The claimant's lawyer also makes a closing speech.

22.92   In all but the more lengthy and complicated cases these speeches will be relatively short.

22.93   In civil cases the claimant must prove the case 'on balance of probabilities' which means that the claimant is more likely to be right than the defendant. The 'burden of proof' is on the claimant which means that if the judge cannot decide between the parties the claim will fail: the claimant will have failed to satisfy the judge on balance of probabilities.

Decision/Order

22.94   In most county court cases the judge will give his or her judgment immediately indicating whether the claimant has proved the case and, if so, assessing the amount of damages or determining the terms of the order, and dealing with the issue of costs. The judge will also give reasons for his or her decision. This enables the parties to know whether there are grounds to appeal the decision.

Rights of audience

22.95   The term 'rights of audience' refers to the right to represent a party at a hearing. The following people have a *right* to represent a party in county court proceedings:

- qualified solicitors and barristers;
- in local authority possession proceedings before a district judge: any person authorised by the local authority;[34]
- solicitor's employees only at a hearing 'in chambers' (the judge's room). In practice this means small claims hearings and interlocutory procedural hearings. It does not include possession proceedings even though these are usually now heard in private.[35]

---

34 County Courts Act 1984 s60. The Courts and Legal Services Act 2007 will extend rights of audience to authorised employees of housing management organisations. Where local authority housing is managed by organisations such as 'Arms Length Management Organisations (ALMOs) the ALMO staff will be able to conduct possession and demotion claims. At the time of writing this part of the 2007 Act is not in force.

35 Prior to CPR there was a distinction between hearings in chambers and hearings in open court. Under CPR the distinction is between hearings in private and hearings in public. However, the rules regarding rights of audience still refer to hearings in chambers: Courts and Legal Services Act 1990 s27(1)(e).

- legal executives[36] have the same rights of audience as any person employed by a solicitor but, in addition, may also appear in open court on unopposed applications for adjournments and applications for consent orders;
- an authorised employee of a company that is party to the proceedings;[37]
- 'lay representatives' in small claims proceedings (see para 22.107 below).

22.96   If a party wants any other person to represent him or her at a hearing, the court must give permission.[38] This will usually be granted on a case-by-case basis. However, in possession proceedings some courts will effectively grant permission on a general basis to those assisting in duty advice schemes or employed by certain local housing associations.

22.97   The Courts and Legal Services Act 2007 makes provision for much wider rights of audience to be granted. At the time of writing the relevant provisions are not in force but are expected to come into force during 2008.

'MacKenzie Friends'

22.98   A party who is representing him or herself is entitled to have a person assisting in court. This means taking notes and (quietly) making suggestions and giving advice but not actually speaking for the party.[39] If the court refuses permission for a non-legally qualified person to represent a party he or she could assist in this role instead. A court may refuse to permit a party to use a McKenzie Friend. However, this will be rare and will usually be because of the conduct of the particular McKenzie Friend. If permission is refused reasons should be given.

36 Legal Executives are regulated by the Institute of Legal Executives which is a body authorised to grant limited rights of audience to its members.
37 CPR 39.6. A company employee needs the court's permission to represent the company but permission should be given by the court unless there is some 'particular and sufficient reason why it should be withheld': CPR 39 PD para 5.3.
38 The court has a broad discretion to do so under section 27(2)(c) of the Courts and Legal Services Act 1990.
39 The term 'MacKenzie Friend' does not denote any particular legal status. The term was coined following the case of *McKenzie v McKenzie* [1970] 3 WLR 472 when the Court of Appeal ruled that it was in the interests of justice to allow an un-represented party assistance from another person during a hearing. See also *R v Leicester City Justices ex p Barrow* [1991] 3 WLR 368.

Consent orders

22.99   The majority of defended claims are settled by the parties before a final hearing.[40] If settlement is achieved after the claim has been issued the terms of the settlement will usually be incorporated into a 'Consent Order' which is then submitted to the court for approval. When the court approves the order it will be stamped with the court seal and is enforceable in the same way as if the order had been made by a judge following a hearing. Where the terms of agreement are complex the Consent Order will be in the form of a 'stay' of proceedings, on the terms set out in a schedule. Either party has the right to apply to the court if the other party does not comply with the agreed terms. This is known as a 'Tomlin Order', an example of which is at appendix 2 to this chapter.

Undefended claims

22.100   If a defendant fails to respond to the claim by filing a defence, the claimant can ask the court to enter 'judgment in default'. A default judgment can be enforced against a defendant in the same way as an order made by a judge. CPR Part 12 sets out the rules for default judgments.

22.101   The procedure differs according to whether the claim is for a fixed amount of money, an amount of money to be decided by the court or includes some other remedy such as an injunction or order for works.

Claim for fixed amount

22.102   After the time for filing a defence has expired the claimant can apply for judgment by completing form N225[41] and sending it to the court with a fee. A court officer will draw up the judgment and will send it to the parties.

Claim for amount to be assessed by the court

22.103   This will be the case where the claim is for damages, eg for disrepair or unlawful eviction and harassment. The amount of damages

---

40   In 2005 the total number of defended claims in England and Wales was 237,876 of which 17,318 (just over 7%) were determined at a final hearing. See Judicial Statistic (Revised) England & Wales for the Year 2005 – CM 6903, available on the Ministry of Justice website: www.justice.gov.uk.

41   Form N205A can also be completed but is not available on-line.

must be quantified by the court. In such a case the claimant applies for judgment to be entered against the defendant with damages to be assessed by the court at a later hearing. This can be done by completing Form N227.[42] If judgment is entered this means that the defendant is liable to pay some damages but can attend the hearing to make representations about the amount (known as 'quantum'). He or she cannot argue about liability unless the default judgment is set aside.

Claim for non-money remedy

22.104 A hearing is also necessary where a claimant is asking the court to grant an injunction or an order for specific performance of a contract. Such claims are usually in addition to claims for damages. In this case, an application for judgment in default must be made under Part 23 of CPR.[43] The procedure under Part 23 requires the applicant to complete an Application Notice (form N244). The application will be for judgment on liability to be entered without notice to the defendant and for a hearing to be listed to consider both the amount of damages and the application for a non-monetary remedy. The defendant must be notified of the hearing and may attend and make representations.

Possession claims

22.105 The procedure described above applies to most claims for money and other remedies such as for injunctions but not to claims for possession. Most claims for possession are dealt with as follows:

- *ordinary possession claims*: a hearing is listed when the claim is issued and there is no procedure for obtaining judgment by default. A defendant can attend the hearing and argue against the making of a possession order.

- *accelerated possession claims*: the accelerated procedure is available to a landlord seeking a possession order against an assured shorthold tenant where there is a written tenancy agreement. A possession order can be made without a hearing if the judge decides that the claim is made out after looking at the papers.

22.106 Both procedures are described in detail in chapter 5.

---

42 Again, there is an alternative form: N205B, but this is not available on-line.
43 CPR 12.4(2). Part 23 concerns any sort of application made within proceedings.

Small claims

22.107 There is no separate 'small claims court' within the civil system; rather, defended claims below a certain value are allocated to the 'small claims track'. This determines the type of case management directions that will be given and the way the final hearing will be conducted. Part 27 sets out the rules relating to the conduct of small claims.

22.108   It should be noted that if no defence is filed the claim is not allocated to track and the rules regarding default judgments described above apply.

Allocation to the small claims track[44]

22.109 The criteria for allocation are not limited to financial value but this is the main factor and the following claims will usually be allocated to the small claims track:

- money claims limited to £5,000;
- personal injury claims limited to £1,000;
- housing disrepair claims in which an order for works is sought, provided the expected damages are not more than £1,000 *and* the estimated cost of works is not more than £1,000.

22.110 Claims above these values may be allocated to the small claims track only if both parties agree.[45]

22.111   However, the following provisions apply to housing cases:

- claims in respect of harassment or unlawful eviction brought by a tenant against a landlord will not be allocated to the small claims track;[46]
- disputed claims for possession and demotion of tenancies are not generally considered suitable for the small track.[47]

Features of small claims cases

22.112 The main features of cases allocated to the small claims track are as follows:

---

44 CPR 26 sets out the criteria for allocation.
45 CPR 26.7(3).
46 CPR 26.7(4).
47 Part 26 PD, para 8.1(c).

- only very limited legal costs can be recovered by the successful party;
- public funding will not usually be granted for representation;
- simple case management directions will be made – these are usually limited to an exchange of copies of the documents each party relies on;
- the hearing will usually be held in the judge's private room and will be informal;
- lay representatives have a right of audience provided the party is present at the hearing.[48]

Costs in small claims

22.113 The general rule is that any legal costs incurred by a party in taking or defending a small claim cannot be recovered from the other party. The following costs can however be recovered:[49]

- the court fee;
- any expenses incurred by a witness (including the successful party) in attending the hearing, including travel expenses and loss of earnings (up to a maximum of £50 per person per day);
- if a claim for an injunction or specific performance is made, legal costs of up to £260;
- expert witness fees, up to a maximum of £200.

22.114 Further, if the claim exceeds the usual small claims limit but the parties have agreed to it being allocated to the small claims track the usual rules apply.

22.115 Also, in all cases further costs may be awarded if a party behaves unreasonably.[50]

CPR Part 8 procedure

22.116 Most civil claims are brought under Part 7 of CPR, which is the procedure described above. However, Part 8 provides an alternative procedure which should be used either:[51]

---

48 The Lay Representatives (Rights of Audience) Order 1992, para 2.
49 CPR 27.14(2) and the PD para 7.
50 CPR 27.14(2)(g).
51 CPR 8.1(2) and (5).

- where the court's decision is sought on a question which is unlikely to involve a substantial dispute of fact; or
- where CPR requires or permits the use of Part 8 for a specific type of claim.

22.117 The claims that *must* be brought under Part 8 are listed in the PD to Part 8, para 9.4. They do not include any of the common types of housing case.

22.118   PD, para 3 lists the claims that *may* be brought under Part 8. These include an application for the court's approval of a claim settled on behalf of a child or a protected person.[52]

22.119   The Part 8 procedure may be an appropriate procedure for a tenant applying for a remedy in relation to a tenancy deposit that has not been dealt with by a landlord in accordance with a tenancy deposit scheme (see para 3.141).

22.120   The main features of the Part 8 procedure are:

- the claim is commenced by completing a claim form[53] with written evidence attached: it is not necessary to file Particulars of Claim;
- the defendant is not required to file a defence but must file an acknowledgment of service[54] also attaching written evidence. If the defendant does not do so he or she may attend any hearing but needs the court's permission to take part in the hearing;
- there is no default procedure – the matter is usually listed for a hearing but may be dealt with by a judge without a hearing;
- a party may not use written evidence at the hearing unless it was served on the other party with the claim form or acknowledgement of service;
- the evidence at any hearing will mainly be written evidence but the court may order that oral evidence be given;
- at the hearing the court may dispose of the matter or give case management directions;
- the court may, at any stage, direct that the case proceed as if it had not been issued under Part 8, and give directions for future conduct.

---

52 See CPR Part 21. A protected party is a person who lacks capacity, see para 6.118. Children and protected parties must have another person acting on their behalf: a litigation friend. A settlement reached before issue must be approved by a court.

53 Form N208.

54 Form N210.

Enforcement

22.121 This section deals with the enforcement of money judgments and injunctions. The enforcement of possession orders is dealt with in chapter 5.

Money judgments

22.122 A successful claim for damages or the repayment of a debt will result in the court making an order that the defendant ('the judgment debtor') pays to the claimant (the 'judgment creditor') a sum of money ('the judgment debt') within a specified period. Unless the order states otherwise payment should be made within 14 days.[55] The money is paid directly to the judgment creditor and not to the court.

22.123 'Judgment debts' are normally recorded in the Register of county court judgments. If the debt is paid within one month of the order the registration can be cancelled. If the debt is paid after one month the judgment can be recorded as 'satisfied'. Applications for either cancellation or satisfaction are made by the judgment debtor to the court where the order was made and a fee is payable. The Register itself is administered by a not for profit company: The Registry Trust. Searches of the Register can be carried out on-line at their website: www.registry-trust.org.uk.

22.124 Apart from entering a money judgment on the Register the court takes no further action following judgment. If the judgment debtor fails to pay, further action to 'enforce' the judgment must be taken by the judgment creditor. The different types of enforcement action are described below.

22.125 In all cases a further court fee must be paid. Fee exemption is available for those on a limited income (see para 22.53). If a fee is paid and the enforcement action is successful the fee will be added to the judgment debt and must be paid by the judgment debtor.

Main methods of enforcing money judgments

22.126 The main methods of enforcing money judgments are as follows:[56]

---

55 CPR 40.11.
56 Reference to 'CCR' are to the County Court Rules and 'RSC' to the Rules of the Supreme Court. These are rules retained from the old procedural codes which relate to proceedings in the county court and the High Court respectively. Those still in force are set out in a schedule to CPR.

Enforcement Action	CPR/ Authority	Effect/Procedure
Warrant of execution (In the High Court called a 'writ of fi fa'.)	CPR Part 70 and CCR, Order 26 (RSC Orders 46 and 47)	A warrant of execution authorises the court bailiffs to seize property belonging to the judgment debtor. A request is filed certifying the amount outstanding under the judgment. A warrant is issued by the court which authorises court bailiffs to 'levy execution' (remove belongings) to be sold in order to satisfy the judgment debt. A warning notice is sent to the judgment debtor seven days before the proposed levy. Certain belongings are exempt. One limitation of this method of enforcement is that the bailiffs do not have the power to force entry onto premises in order to seize goods. The application must be made to the court for the area in which the debtor resides.
Attachment of earnings	CPR Part 70 and CCR Order 27 Attachment of Earnings Act 1971	An attachment of earnings order compels the employer of a judgment debtor to deduct an amount from his or her earnings until the debt is paid. Application should be made to the court for the area in which the debtor resides unless this is not known in which case it will be made to the court that made the order. The debtor is given notice of the application by the court with a form of reply. On receiving the reply a court officer may make an attachment of earnings order. A hearing may be listed if there is insufficient information for an order to be made. If an order is made without a hearing both parties have the right to apply for a hearing within 14 days. Where a debtor fails to file a reply or attend a hearing an application may be made for the debtor to be committed to prison provided service can be proved.
Third Party Debt Order	CPR Part 72	A third party debt order is an order that a person who owes money to the judgment debtor pays the amount of the judgment debt to the judgment creditor. It is

Enforcement Action	CPR/ Authority	Effect/Procedure
		generally used to obtain money directly from a person's bank or building society. The bank or building society is the 'third party'. The court first makes an interim order without a hearing and without notice to the debtor. This order is served on the third party and specifies the amount of money that must be retained pending a final order. The interim order is served on the debtor after being served on the third party. The judgment creditor may apply for a 'hardship payment' and, if he or she objects to the making of a final order, written evidence must be filed stating the objections. If no objections are made, or if the objections are not upheld, the order will be made final at a hearing and the third party must then pay the outstanding amount, plus the costs of the application, to the judgment creditor.
Charging Order	CPR Part 73	A charging order may be appropriate when a judgment debtor owns property, including his or her own home or premises let to a tenant.[57] An interim order is requested without a hearing and without notice to the judgment debtor. This can be registered at the land registry to prevent the judgment debtor transferring ownership of the property. The interim order is served on the judgment debtor who must file and serve written evidence if he or she objects to the making of a final order. If no objections are made, or if the objections are not upheld, the order will be made final at a hearing. A charging order is a form of mortgage and, if the judgment debtor does not pay, an application may be made for an order that the property be sold and the judgment satisfied from the proceeds of sale, see below.

57 This can be discovered by carrying out a Land Registry Search. See para 3.138.

Enforcement Action	CPR/ Authority	Effect/Procedure
Order for sale	CPR Parts 73 and 8	If a final charging order has been obtained and the judgment debt still not paid, an application may be made under Part 8 for an order that the property be sold.
Appointment of Receivers	CPR Part 69	A receiver may be appointed by the court to preserve or manage property pending the resolution of a dispute. Generally, other methods of enforcement will be more effective. However, in a disrepair action a receiver could be appointed to receive rents from a number of tenants to pay for essential repairs.

Oral examination

22.127 If the judgment creditor has insufficient information about the debtor's assets to decide on an appropriate method of enforcement an application may be made for an oral examination of the judgment debtor. This is summarised below.

Action	CPR	Effect/Procedure
Order that judgment debtor attend court	CPR Part 71	Application is made by request to a court officer. An order will be made without a hearing by a court officer. The order requires the judgment debtor to attend court to answer questions about his or her assets and income to enable the judgment creditor to choose best way to enforce. The order should be endorsed with a notice warning the debtor that he or she may be sent to prison for contempt if it is not obeyed. The order should be served personally on the debtor by the creditor and travel expenses must be offered. At the hearing the debtor will be questioned by a court officer or a judge. If the hearing is before a court officer, the creditor *may* attend and ask questions. If the hearing is before a judge, the creditor *must* attend and conduct the questioning. If the debtor fails to attend the hearing the matter should be referred to a judge. The judge may make a committal order provided the order was served personally and an affidavit has been filed confirming service.

22.128   Each method of enforcement requires the creditor to make an application and pay a fee. If the application is successful, the creditor will usually recover the fee paid and a fixed amount towards any legal costs. Clearly, if the judgment debtor has no assets or cannot be traced, the creditor may be unable to obtain satisfaction of the judgment and it will be pointless to incur further court fees that are unlikely to be recovered from the debtor.

Enforcing injunctions and orders for specific performance

22.129   If a party does not obey an order that he or she must do or refrain from doing something, an application can be made for the person to be committed to prison for contempt of court. Committal proceedings are described in more detail at paras 9.170–9.175.

Judicial review proceedings

22.130   The above procedural rules relate to private disputes. The High Court also deals with challenges to administrative decisions made by public bodies. The procedure to challenge such decisions is judicial review.[58]

22.131   Judicial Review means a claim to review the lawfulness of:

- an enactment; or
- a decision, action or failure to act in relation to the exercise of a public function.[59]

22.132   Claims for judicial review must be brought in the Administrative Court, which is a branch of the High Court. Such claims may only be brought against bodies exercising public functions, including the government and local authorities. Many decisions relating to housing made by local authorities are challenged by judicial review. Further, when hearing homelessness appeals the county court is exercising a power akin to that of judicial review.[60]

22.133   In judicial review the courts are exercising a 'supervisory' function. A claim for judicial review is not an appeal or a challenge to the merits of a decision. This is also the role of the county court when hearing homelessness appeals.

---

58 CPR Part 54 sets out the procedure for judicial review claims.
59 CPR 54(2)(a).
60 *Nipa Begum v Tower Hamlets LBC* (1999) 32 HLR 445, CA.

22.134　The procedure for homeless appeals is described in chapter 14. Judicial review is dealt with in chapter 21.

Costs

22.135　When one party is successful in bringing or defending a legal action against another person the usual rule is that the unsuccessful party is ordered to pay the costs of the successful party. The rules in relation to criminal prosecutions (which may be brought by individuals) are different and are outside the scope of this book. The detailed rules about costs are contained in CPR Parts 43 to 48. This section examines the main issues regarding costs that advisers are likely to encounter. These are:

- the circumstances in which a successful party may not recover costs;
- the nature of the 'costs' that can be recovered;
- what happens when one party is legally aided;
- how the amount of costs claimed is controlled;
- when costs can be ordered against someone who isn't a party;
- when costs be ordered against a party's representatives.

The circumstances in which a successful party may not recover costs

The general rule

22.136　Under CPR the court has a general discretion as to whether to make an order for costs at all.[61] If the court decides to make an order about costs, 'the general rule is that the unsuccessful party will be ordered to pay the costs of the successful party; but ... the court may make a different order'.[62] In deciding what order to make, the court must have regard to all the circumstances, including:

- the conduct of all the parties;
- whether a party has succeeded on part of his case, even if he or she has not been wholly successful; and
- any payment into court or offer to settle the case.

61　CPR 44.3(1).
62　CPR 44.(2). However, the general rule does not apply in Court of Appeal cases in relation to probate of family proceedings (CPR 44.3(3)).

22.137 The court may make an order that one party pays a proportion of another party's costs; pays costs from or until a certain date; pays costs incurred before proceedings have begun; pays costs relating to particular steps taken in the proceedings; or, pays costs relating to a distinct part of the proceedings.[63]

Conduct of the parties

22.138 This relates to conduct in relation to the proceedings, not generally. It would include such conduct as refusing to consider mediation as an alternative to litigation. However, there may be good reasons to refuse mediation and it is for the unsuccessful party to prove that it was unreasonable to refuse to mediate.[64]

Partial success

22.139 In some cases a party may be successful on one issue but not on another. In such a case the court will usually order that a proportion of the costs be paid by one party to the other. Alternatively the court may order that each party pays their own costs or make no order for costs (which has exactly the same effect).

Offers to settle

22.140 Offers made under CPR Part 36 will usually carry automatic consequences in relation to costs. These are described at [xx] above. However, when deciding what costs order to make, the court will consider attempts to settle made by the parties, even if not made in accordance with Part 36. A party who has refused a reasonable offer to settle may be unable to recover all of the costs incurred even if successful.

Costs orders made before final hearing

22.141 Hearings may take place in relation to procedural issues before the final hearing. This may happen if the parties do not agree about the steps to be taken to prepare for the hearing. Also, in some cases, an urgent injunction may be sought. An application for an order, made during the course of proceedings, requires a further court fee to be paid. Also, each party may incur legal costs in making or opposing an application. In such a case the court will usually make some kind

---

63 CPR 44.3(6).
64 *Halsey v Milton Keynes General NHS Trust* [2004] EWCA Civ 576, 11 May 2004.

costs order relating to the application and hearing. The following is a list of the kinds of orders that may be made:

- *Costs in the cause (or case)*: this means that the costs will be paid by the party who succeeds at the end of the case.
- *Costs of the Defendant/Claimant to be paid by the Claimant/ Defendant (sometimes expressed to be 'in any event')*: this means that the party who has been unsuccessful must pay the other party's costs of that particular application/hearing regardless of who is successful at the end of the case.
- *Costs reserved*: this means that the costs of the particular application/ hearing will be decided at the end of the case. This leaves open the possibility of arguing that the party who is ultimately successful should nevertheless have to pay the other party's costs of the particular application/hearing.
- *No order for costs*: this means that each party pays their own costs for the particular application/hearing. An order may also state expressly that each party should pay their own costs.

What costs can be recovered?

22.142 The costs that one party may be ordered to pay to another include:

- *Legal fees*: the legal fees paid by a party (or by the Legal Services Commission) to legal representatives (solicitors and barristers).
- *Disbursements*: fees paid to other professionals or agencies, including court fees and expert's fees.
- *Expenses*: the travel expenses and loss of earnings for the party and any witnesses attending court.

22.143 It also includes the amount allowed to a litigant in person, a 'success fee' charged under a conditional fee arrangement and a 'reward' charged by a lay representative for acting in a small claims case.[65] All of these are explained below.

Barristers' and solicitors' charges

22.144 Solicitors' costs are calculated on the basis of the amount of time spent and the number of routine letters and telephone calls made. Barristers usually charge a fee for each piece of work (eg drafting a defence, attending a hearing) but this is also calculated on the basis

---

65 CPR 43.2(1)(a).

of how much time the work takes. The court may reduce the amount recoverable because the rate is considered too high or the time claimed excessive (see para 22.161 below – assessment of costs).

Litigants in person

22.145 A person who conducts his or her own litigation is entitled to recover:

- the necessary disbursements and witness expenses; and
- an amount to compensate him or her for the time spent preparing the case.

22.146   There are two possible ways for a litigant in person to calculate the amount to be claimed for his or her time. A person who can show actual financial loss (eg a self-employed person who lost income as a result of time spent on litigation, or an employed person who had to take time off work) may recover costs on the basis of the lost income.[66] In the absence of actual loss, there is a prescribed rate of £9.25 per hour.[67] A litigant in person can claim this amount for each hour of his or her spare time spent preparing the case, subject to the courts' overall discretion to disallow claims for excessive amounts of time.

22.147   Additionally, there is an overall limit to the amount of costs recoverable by a litigant in person: the costs allowed cannot exceed two thirds of the amount that would have been allowed had a legal representative been instructed.[68]

Success fees

22.148 It is lawful for a legal representative to act on the basis of a conditional fee arrangement. This will include a 'success fee' of a certain percentage of the overall costs in the event of a successful outcome. The unsuccessful party will be responsible for paying the 'success fee' provided the costs agreement has been disclosed at the start of the litigation. The court may reduce the amount claimed if it is considered excessive.

Rewards charged by lay representatives

22.149 Lay representatives may make a charge for representing a person at the hearing of a small claim. This charge is known as a 'reward'.

---

66 CPR 48.6(4)(a).
67 CPR 48.6(4)(b).
68 CPR 48.6(2).

What happens when one party is legally aided

22.150   A person on a low income and with limited savings may be granted a 'Public Funding Certificate' to bring or defend proceedings. The granting of a certificate means that instead of the party being responsible for paying his or her own solicitor's costs, the Legal Services Commission (LSC) is responsible. However, this should not affect the court's decision when considering a costs order. The usual rule, with some exceptions, still applies: if the party who is publicly funded (known as the 'assisted person') is successful the other party should be ordered to pay his or her costs. However, the existence of the certificate does have implications for the way in which the costs are assessed. The possible outcomes are described below.

The assisted person is successful and the other party is ordered to pay costs

22.151   Even in such a case the unsuccessful party may not be responsible for paying *all* of the successful party's costs. This may be because some of the costs are considered to relate solely to obtaining public funding or because the court has previously made an order that both parties pay their own costs of a particular application or hearing. In such a case the solicitor can claim these costs from the LSC, while claiming the majority of the costs from the other party.

22.152   In all cases where the LSC pay costs to the assisted person's solicitor this sum will be deducted from any damages or money awarded to the assisted person. This is known as the 'statutory charge'. See below at para 22.183.

The assisted person is unsuccessful

22.153   Where the legally aided party loses the case, the court will usually make an order that he or she pays the costs of the successful party but the order will state that 'the order may not be enforced without the permission of the court'. This is often referred to as 'costs protection'. Costs protection is given in recognition that the assisted person has limited means. However, it leaves open the possibility of a party seeking to recover costs in the future if the unsuccessful party is in a position to pay.

22.154   In certain circumstances the successful party may claim costs from the LSC.[69]

---

69 The criteria for orders to be made against the LSC are complex and depend on when the certificate was issued. They are set out in the document 'Costs Against the Commission Manual' which is available on the LSC website at: www. legalservices.gov.uk.

Partial success or case settled and court makes 'no order for costs'

22.155 No order for costs means that each party is responsible for his or her own costs. In relation to an assisted person this means that his or her solicitors claim the whole of the costs from the LSC. If the assisted person has been awarded money or property by the court the 'statutory charge' will apply.

Controlling the amount of the costs

22.156 There are three ways in which the amount of costs may be determined:

Fixed costs

22.157 Some sorts of applications and claims are subject to 'fixed costs'. This means that a set amount can be claimed for solicitor's costs. This can only be claimed if a solicitor is actually instructed and is distinct from the fee paid by the party to the court. For example, there are fixed costs for an 'accelerated' claim for possession brought against an assured shorthold tenant: the court fee is £150 and, provided the landlord instructs a solicitor to complete the claim form, an additional fixed amount can be claimed for the solicitors costs.[70] It should be noted that these fixed costs apply only if the matter is decided without a hearing. A defendant who raises an argument that results in a hearing being held risks being ordered to pay additional costs if unsuccessful.

22.158 The proceedings that are subject to fixed costs are listed in CPR Part 45.

Summary assessment of costs

22.159 In relatively straightforward cases a court may 'summarily assess' the costs of the successful party at the end of the final hearing (or in some cases at the end of an interim hearing).[71] A party who wishes the court to do this must serve a summary of the costs he or she is claiming on the other party at least 24 hours before the hearing.[72]

---

70 The amount varies depending upon who serves the claim form.
71 CPR 44.7.
72 CPR PD to Part 45, para 13.5. The summary should be in a certain format – see Form N260.

22.160   Costs being claimed by an assisted person cannot be summarily assessed as the court must carry out a full, or 'detailed', assessment of the amount to be paid by the LSC.[73]

Detailed assessment of costs

22.161 In more complex cases the amount of costs to be paid by one party to another will be subject to 'detailed assessment' by the court. In all cases when a person has a public funding certificate the court must subject the solicitor's claim for costs against the LSC to detailed assessment.

22.162   As between the two parties there is a procedure to be followed to determine the amount of the costs. This involves the following steps:

Serving the bill

22.163 A bill is prepared setting out in detail the amounts claimed. This is served on the paying party with a notice informing them of the total amount that will be payable if they fail to respond or if the costs have to be assessed by the court.

Responding to the bill

22.164 The paying party's solicitors should respond within 21 days with 'Points of Dispute' setting out any objections to the costs, such as to the rate being charged, the time spent or particular items claimed. If they fail to do so, the receiving party's solicitors can apply to the court for a 'Default costs certificate'. This entitles the receiving party to be paid the full amount of the costs claimed.

Assessment hearing

22.165 If Points of Dispute are served and no agreement about costs reached, the receiving party's solicitors will apply to the court for an assessment hearing at which a judge will decide the amount to be paid in costs.

22.166   In practice, the parties usually negotiate 'without prejudice' to agree the amount of the costs. If an assessment hearing is necessary, additional costs will be incurred: the further court fee and the parties' costs of attending the assessment hearing. If the amount of the bill

---

73 CPR PD to Part 45, para 13.9.

is reduced at the hearing by more than a certain proportion these costs will be paid by the receiving party, if not, by the paying party.

Costs against someone who isn't a party

22.167 It is possible for the court to order a person who is not a party to the proceedings to pay the costs incurred by one or all of the parties.[74] The person against whom costs are sought must be added as a party to the proceedings, for the purpose of costs only, and must be given a reasonable opportunity to attend a hearing at which the court will consider the matter. An order may be made where it is alleged that the proceedings would not have been necessary but for the actions or default of that party. An example is the county court case of *ASRA v Coke*[75] in which the London Borough of Newham were ordered to pay the costs of both parties in a claim for possession; the claim had been brought because of the authority's failure to deal with the tenant's claim for housing benefit.

Costs ordered against a representative/'wasted costs' orders

22.168 'Wasted costs' means any costs incurred by a party 'as a result of any improper, unreasonable or negligent act or omission on the part of any legal or other representative or any employee of such a representative'.[76]

22.169 The court may order that wasted costs are disallowed or that the legal or other representative must pay the whole or part of the wasted costs.[77] 'Legal or other representatives' are defined as those exercising a right of audience or right to conduct litigation. This would include solicitors, barristers and lay representatives exercising rights under the Lay Representatives (Rights of Audience) Order 1999. However, the court clearly has the power under CPR 48.2 (costs orders against someone who isn't a party, see para 22.167 above) to make an order against others who are informally representing a party. Many advice

---

74 CPR 48.2. The rule does not apply when the court is considering an order against the LSC or a wasted costs order: CPR 42.2(2).

75 Reported in June 2001 *Legal Action* 31.

76 Supreme Court Act 1981 s 51(7). It also includes costs 'which, in the light of any such act or omission occurring after they were incurred, the court considers it is unreasonable to expect that party to pay'.

77 SCA 1981 s51(6).

agencies assist people with litigation although they are not on the court record and do not have rights of audience or representation. Such agencies should ensure that they are not inadvertently placed on the court record as formally acting for the party and should generally not agree to receive notices and correspondence from the court on behalf of a client. If notice of a hearing were sent to the agency direct and the client not notified the agency might be at risk of being ordered to pay any costs wasted as a result.

22.170   If the court is considering making a wasted costs order, the person against whom it may be made must be given a reasonable opportunity to attend a hearing to give reasons why such an order should not be made.[78]

22.171   It is not necessarily 'improper, unreasonable or negligent' to act for a party whose claim is bound to fail. However, a representative who acts in a claim which is an abuse of process, or is dishonest may be at risk of a wasted costs order.[79]

Legal aid/public funding

22.172   The legal aid scheme was introduced to ensure that people with limited means could be represented in legal proceedings. The current system is administered by the Legal Services Commission (LSC). The term 'legal aid' has largely been replaced by the term 'public funding' and the term 'legally aided person' by the term 'assisted person'.

22.173   In general only firms and organisations that have a contract with the LSC can act for clients with public funding. Contracts are awarded only to those who comply with certain quality standards monitored by the LSC.

22.174   A person may be assisted in one of two ways: under the Legal Help scheme or under a public funding certificate.

The Legal Help scheme

22.175   Under the Legal Help scheme advice and assistance can be given in relation to most legal issues.[80] It covers advising orally and in writing,

---

78   CPR 48.7(2).
79   *Tolstoy-Milosalvsky v Lord Aldington* [1996] 2 All ER 556.
80   Certain types of legal issues, such as the making of wills and disputes about land boundaries are excluded from the Legal Help scheme but advice and assistance about most aspects of housing law may be given under the scheme.

corresponding on the person's behalf and obtaining expert evidence. Since October 2007 the fees a solicitor or adviser can claim from the LSC are fixed depending on the category of law. Expenses such as interpreter's fees and expert's fees can be claimed in addition to the fixed fee.

22.176 In most cases an adviser cannot represent a person in court under the scheme. However, the scheme does cover attending court to provide 'help at court' in possession proceedings for a tenant where the only issue is the amount of any arrears, the rate of repayment of arrears and whether a warrant of possession should be suspended or not.

22.177 All those on means tested social security benefits qualify for Legal Help. For others their disposable income and savings must be below a certain amount.[81] The means assessment is conducted by the adviser who must obtain proof of income or receipt of benefit.

Public funding certificates

22.178 A public funding certificate may be granted by the LSC to cover representation in specific court proceedings. An application can be made on behalf of a prospective claimant to cover a civil claim against another person (eg a claim for damages for disrepair) or by a person who is a defendant in a claim brought by another (eg a claim for possession). The certificate is issued to a specific firm or organisation to represent the assisted person. To be eligible for a public funding certificate, the applicant must satisfy both a means and a merits test. The means test is similar to that applied in respect of Legal Help but people whose income is above a certain limit may be granted a certificate subject to payment of a financial contribution. The contribution is paid by the assisted person to the LSC every month for as long as the certificate is in force.

The merits test

22.179 In addition to qualifying on the basis of income and capital the LSC must be satisfied that the case has sufficient merit. The LSC apply a 'cost benefit' test that balances the prospect of success and the likely benefit to the assisted person against the anticipated costs of the

---

81 For the year 2008/2009 the limit on disposable income is £698 per month and the limit for savings is £8,000 (£3,000 for immigration cases). The income cap is increased each year and the LSC website includes a calculator to assess eligibility: www.legalservices.gov.uk.

proceedings. The relevant test differs according to what is at stake for the assisted person. For example, where a person's home is at stake the prospects of success need not be as high as where a person is claiming damages from a landlord. In certain cases the LSC may grant a certificate even though the benefit to the assisted person will be limited, if satisfied that the case may result in wider public benefit. An example would be a challenge by way of judicial review to a policy that may be declared to be unlawful.

22.180   The merits test must be applied continually as long as the certificate is in force. Any offers to settle a claim must be reported by the representative to the LSC and if an assisted person is considered to be acting unreasonably in his or her instructions the certificate may be terminated.

Emergency funding

22.181 In urgent cases an emergency certificate may be granted to cover such things as an application for an injunction or to represent a person at an imminent hearing. Firms and organisations that have 'devolved powers' (most contract holders) can grant emergency funding as soon as the application forms are signed. The forms must then be submitted to the LSC for the issue of a certificate within five days.

Limits of certificates

22.182 Public funding certificates are limited to taking certain steps within proceedings and it may be necessary for the representative to apply for extensions of the scope at various stages as the litigation progresses. Similarly, there is a limit to the costs that can be incurred under a certificate and for complex cases that are not resolved quickly it may be necessary to make several applications for the costs limit to be extended. At all stages the LSC must be satisfied that the cost benefit test is met.

The statutory change

22.183 The statutory charge refers to the right of the LSC to recover the costs it has incurred funding litigation that has resulted in an award of property or money to the assisted person. If an assisted person is successful in litigation the court should order the other party to pay the assisted person's legal costs. If all of the costs are recovered from the other party there should be no claim for costs made to the LSC.

The statutory charge will not therefore apply although it does mean that a solicitor cannot release monies recovered until all of the costs have actually been paid by the other side. It may be that not all of the costs can be recovered from the other party (see para 22.151 above). If this happens and some of the costs are claimed by the solicitor from the LSC the amount claimed will be deducted from the money recovered by the assisted person. Where it is property that is recovered or preserved (eg following a dispute about beneficial ownership or property transfer) the LSC may register the amount owed as a charge on the property and payment must be made when the property is sold.

Tribunals

22.184 Some housing disputes are heard not by the county court but by a tribunal. Tribunals are decision making bodies set up by statute to resolve particular kinds of dispute. Public funding is not available for legal representation at most tribunal hearings. The following are the main tribunals dealing with housing issues.

Tribunal	Issue
Rent Assessment Committees	Disputes about the level of rent between a landlord and tenant under a Rent Act or assured tenancy.
Residential Property Tribunals	Disputes about some Right to Buy issues. Disputes about local authority notices served under the Housing Act 2004 (eg Improvement Notices, Prohibition Notices, Demolition and Closing Orders).
Leasehold Valuation Tribunals	Disputes about long leaseholder's rights, including the level of service charges.
Lands Tribunal	Disputes about the levels of compensation following compulsory purchase
Social Security and Child Support Appeals Tribunal	Disputes about entitlement to housing benefit.

Structure of The Courts Service

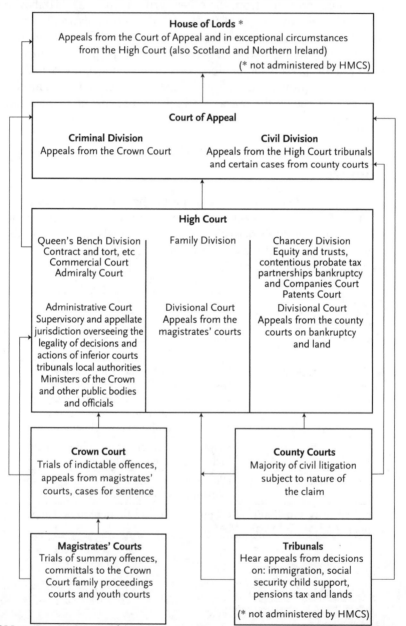

House of Lords *
Appeals from the Court of Appeal and in exceptional circumstances
from the High Court (also Scotland and Northern Ireland)
(* not administered by HMCS)

Court of Appeal

Criminal Division
Appeals from the Crown Court

Civil Division
Appeals from the High Court tribunals
and certain cases from county courts

High Court

Queen's Bench Division
Contract and tort, etc
Commercial Court
Admiralty Court

Administrative Court
Supervisory and appellate
jurisdiction overseeing the
legality of decisions and
actions of inferior courts
tribunals local authorities
Ministers of the Crown
and other public bodies
and officials

Family Division

Divisional Court
Appeals from the
magistrates' courts

Chancery Division
Equity and trusts,
contentious probate tax
partnerships bankruptcy
and Companies Court
Patents Court

Divisional Court
Appeals from the county
courts on bankruptcy
and land

Crown Court
Trials of indictable offences,
appeals from magistrates'
courts, cases for sentence

County Courts
Majority of civil litigation
subject to nature of
the claim

Magistrates' Courts
Trials of summary offences,
committals to the Crown
Court family proceedings
courts and youth courts

Tribunals
Hear appeals from decisions
on: immigration, social
security child support,
pensions tax and lands

(* not administered by HMCS)

Tomlin Order

TOMLIN ORDER

IN THE .... COUNTY COURT

CLAIM No.: ....

BETWEEN:

....

Claimant

and

....

Defendant

CONSENT ORDER

UPON the parties having agreed terms of settlement

BY CONSENT

IT IS ORDERED that all further proceedings herein be stayed upon the terms set out in Schedule 1 hereto save for the purpose of enforcing or carrying into effect the said terms, with liberty to apply for that purpose.

IT IS FURTHER ORDERED that there be no order for costs save for the detailed assessment of the Defendant's public funding costs pursuant to the Community Legal Services (Costs) Regulations 2000.

SCHEDULE 1

1...................................
2...................................
3...................................

We hereby consent to an order in the above terms:

....

Claimant   Defendant

or Claimant's solicitors   or Defendant's solicitors

Index

815